Connect

Preparing Students for the World That Awaits

Learn

Succeed

connect™ READING

Connect Reading prepares students for success in college and beyond. This online learning environment identifies and addresses individual needs, offers the visual component today's students expect, and provides progressive learning as students advance.

→ **Individualized.** When it comes to mastering reading comprehension, each student has different skills and needs. This research-based program provides individualized learning plans to target each student's specific needs.

→ **Systematic.** Connect Reading examines all aspects of reading, from the author's purpose and tone to making inferences and drawing conclusions. Within each section, a consistent step-by-step approach is employed at three levels for student advancement.

→ **Visual.** Video vignettes help students visualize reading concepts by relating them to everyday activities.

→ **Flexible.** Connect Reading can be used over one, two, or three semesters, making it flexible to meet the needs of any program.

→ **Supported.** Connect Reading offers instructors the ability to monitor and foster individual student progress in less time and with fewer distractions. With self-assessments and automatic grading provided throughout, instructors have more time to focus on teaching!

http://mhconnectreading.com

THE READER'S EDGE BOOK TWO

VICE PRESIDENT, EDITORIAL: **Mike Ryan**

DIRECTOR, EDITORIAL: **Beth Mejia**

PUBLISHER: **David Patterson**

SPONSORING EDITOR: **John Kindler**

DIRECTOR OF DEVELOPMENT: **Nancy Crochiere**

DEVELOPMENT EDITORS: **Nomi Sofer & Laura Wilk**

MARKETING MANAGER: **Jaclyn Elkins**

EDITORIAL COORDINATOR: **Jesse Hassenger**

TEXT PERMISSIONS EDITOR: **Judy Brody**

MEDIA PROJECT MANAGER: **Thomas Brierly**

PRODUCTION EDITOR: **Leslie LaDow**

MANUSCRIPT EDITOR: **Patricia Ohlenroth**

DESIGN MANAGER: **Andrei Pasternak**

INTERIOR DESIGNER: **Maureen McCutcheon**

PHOTO RESEARCH COORDINATOR: **Nora Agbayani**

PHOTO RESEARCHER: **Emily Tietz**

PRODUCTION SUPERVISOR: **Tandra Jorgensen**

1 2 3 4 5 6 7 8 9 0 WVR/WVR 0

ISBN: 978-0-07-7340725-8 (student edition)

ISBN: 978-0-07-730135-4 (instructor's edition)

MHID: 0-07-7340725-9 (student edition)

MHID: 0-07-730135-8 (instructor's edition)

This text was set in 11/13 Sabon by Thompson Type, and printed on acid-free 45# Influence Gloss by World Color Press Inc.

Because this page cannot legibly accommodate all acknowledgments for copyrighted material, credits appear at the end of the book and constitute an extension of this copyright page.

Library of Congress PCN: 2009942114

Contents

Vital Vocabulary

Operation Overview

Interesting Inquiries

Find and Mark Main Ideas

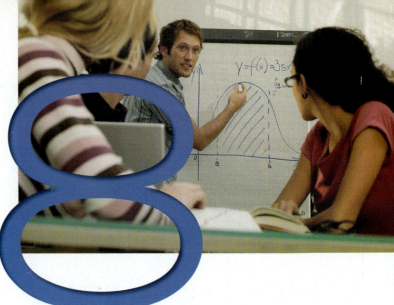

7

Patterns of Thought

8

Map Main Ideas

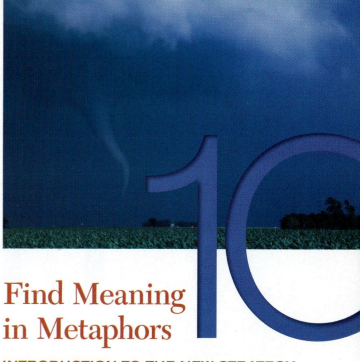

Make Inferences

Find Meaning in Metaphors

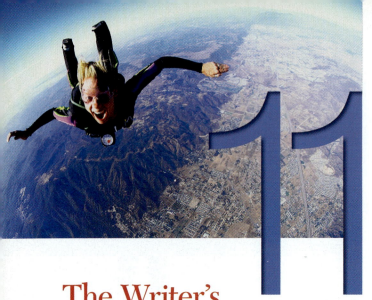

The Writer's Perspective

Write a Summary

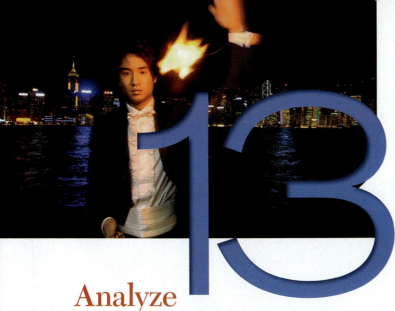
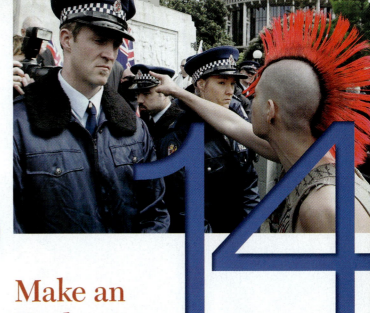

13

14

Analyze the Information

Make an Evaluation

1

Connect Now

CONNECT NOW

1 | Get a quick first impression of the topic.

2 | Relate your experience and feelings to the topic.

3 | Understand your purpose for reading and the author's purpose for writing.

Instructor Tip
Encourage students to write strategies on an index card so that they can keep the card handy while they are reading.

imagine this

One of the best ways to relax is to read. When you find a place to read that is cozy, quiet, and comfortable, whether you are outside in the sunshine or inside on your bed, you may find that reading can be very relaxing *and* entertaining. However, there is a catch.

The catch is simple—you must find a way to make the reading your own. You must find a way to understand what an author is telling *you*, specifically about you, your life, and your experiences. You must recognize that every author might have something to teach you whether or not you think you want to learn. This means you have to start with something extremely important: You must connect with the reading somehow.

Think FIRST

Instructor Tip
Think First: This is an opportunity for you to help students connect strategies to their personal lives. Discuss these as class questions.

- How do you engage yourself so that you feel connected to what you are doing?

- How do your past experiences and feelings affect how well you perform certain activities?

- How do you identify your purpose for doing a certain activity, like getting ready for school or buying a specific product?

INTRODUCTION TO THE NEW STRATEGY

Connect Now

What kinds of connections are important to you?

Instructor Tip
Have students bring in magazines and newspapers. Create a list of article titles from the magazines and newspapers and write these on the chalkboard. Read each title out loud and have students raise their hands if they would read the article due to the title alone. This will show them that a title all by itself can create a connection to a reading.

When you begin reading, you instantly become as important in the reading process as the writer and the writer's words. As you read, the writer's message will be filtered through your mind, and no one else's. So, as you read, your mind, with all its unique experiences, not only takes in the writer's words but also shapes their meaning.

Because you bring all of your experiences with you as you read, the reading process begins as soon as you know something about the reading. That often starts with the title or some other clue about the subject. Strategy 1—*Connect Now*—reminds you to see what ideas and experiences you already have that will help you connect to the reading.

This strategy doesn't take much time—with practice only a few seconds. However, those few seconds can give you a stronger **purpose** for reading—an intention, for example, to compare the writer's ideas to your own or to add new information to what you already know.

Getting an Impression of the Topic

The **topic,** or subject, is what the reading is about. It is the focus for all of the ideas in a particular piece of reading. Often you can get an idea of the subject from the title. Consider the title of the first reading selection, "The Voice

You Hear When You Read Silently" (p. 9), and ask yourself what this poem is about. If you decided "reading silently" is the topic of this poem, you are correct.

> [A]s you read, your mind, with all its unique experiences, not only takes in the writer's words, but also shapes their meaning.

If the title of a reading doesn't give you enough information about the topic, look at the first lines of the reading to get a sense of what the reading is about. The first few lines of the poem have the words "spoken," "voice," "writer's words," "in your head," and "read," which give you a clue that this poem is about reading silently.

MATTHEW McCONAUGHEY

The Case for Christ

by Lee Strobel

Books on theology seem popular with celebrities these days. Perhaps they are spending their free time between films pondering the mysteries of the universe. Not long ago, Matthew McConaughey was reading *The Case for Christ*, which investigates all the questions about Jesus Christ.

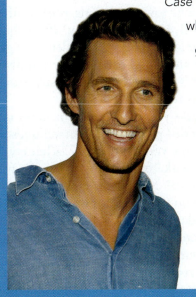

If you liked *The Case for Christ*, you might also like:

Life of Pi, Yann Martel

Stolen Lives, Malika Oufkir

The Prophet, Khalil Gibran

WHAT ARE THEY READING?

Your Experiences and Feelings

Consider how your personal experiences relate to the topic. You don't need to understand every part of the topic; you just need to make a connection. For example, maybe you didn't understand every poem you had to read in high school, and now you don't really like poetry, but you do remember some poems that you thought were all right. Will this be a poem you will like?

Use what you do remember or understand to think of ideas and questions you have for the writer. Perhaps you remind yourself that not only are poems short, sometimes they have wonderful phrases. In addition, you might focus on whether the poem offers advice on how to be a better reader. This will keep you engaged and searching for answers in the reading.

Your feelings can influence how you react to a reading. Do you have positive, negative, or neutral feelings about reading? What about

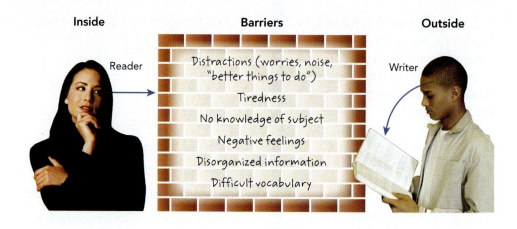

Inside	Barriers	Outside

Reader → Distractions (worries, noise, "better things to do")
Tiredness
No knowledge of subject
Negative feelings
Disorganized information
Difficult vocabulary
← Writer

your feelings toward reading poetry? If you disliked reading poetry in high school, will you dislike it now? If you have any negative feelings about either reading or about poetry, don't let them get in your way. Try to put them aside for the moment. Otherwise, they can distract you and cause you to miss what the writer is saying. (For other distractions that may create barriers to reading, see the figure above.)

How do you use your own ideas and experiences to connect with the subject of this poem? Ask yourself questions such as: "What could the writer mean by 'the voice you hear'? What could be heard as you read silently?" In addition, make predictions about the poem; for example, you might think: "What voice? Maybe he means the voice I hear in my own head." Also, comment on the topic, for example, "Hearing a voice when reading silently? Strange idea!" Finally, remember your own experiences, such as the sound of your mother's or a teacher's voice reading to you.

Involving your mind before starting to read prepares you to connect with the reading. Even if the writer explores the subject in a different way from what you were expecting, you've awakened your curiosity, and staying curious is the best way to open up to new ideas.

Your Purpose and the Author's Purpose

You may think your only purpose for reading is to complete a reading assignment, but you need to reconsider this idea. You may be reading because someone told you to, but you should read with a deeper purpose. You should read to be informed, persuaded, or entertained.

Even when you read for pleasure, you read for a purpose. You read because you need to have more information on how to change the oil in your car since you don't have time to go to a mechanic. You may read because you would like to go on a vacation, but you don't know whether to take an airplane, a

Folklorist Jan Brunvand knows that the purpose of telling urban legends is for entertainment, but every once in awhile someone mistakes a legend for actual information, as writer Jerome Beatty did.

Jerome Beatty, who wrote "Trade Winds" in the *Saturday Review* for many years, published in his July 4, 1964, column a version of "The Nude Housewife" urban legend without realizing that it was a widespread story. He confessed his error and described how he became enlightened as to the nature of folklore in an article titled "Funny Stories" in the November 1970 issue of *Esquire*:

. . . someone I know in Homewood, Illinois, told me about something that had happened to her friend, a housewife. The girl had gone into the basement to do some laundry, and while the wash was going, she threw in the clothes she was wearing. While waiting, she decided to brush a cobweb off the cellar window, and picked up a broom for that purpose. Then to protect her hair, she put on a football helmet that was nearby. Just then there was a knock and a call, "Meter man!" She grabbed a raccoon coat that was stored there and quickly put it on. The meter man came down the stairs without waiting for an answer, shined his flashlight at the meter, and wrote down the reading, all without saying a word. As he left, he glanced at the housewife, trying to hide in a corner and said, "Hope your team wins, lady."

When I repeated this tale on one occasion, authenticating it by saying it had happened to "the friend of a friend of mine in Illinois," I was told that it had been in a national magazine. I couldn't believe it, but my informant eventually sent me a clipping dated March, 1961, locating the event in East Hampton, Connecticut. When I had a chance, I queried the Homewood, Illinois, source who said that the girl was a good friend and she had *said* it had happened to her, and no one was going to call her a liar. The question with this incident, as it is with the others, is: Did it ever happen at all? But this is a question that few people ask."

In a letter to me dated October 26, 1983, Beatty added the information that the clipping came from *Reader's Digest* . . . , and he also admitted, "I was glad to see Ann Landers fall for it years later."

Brunvand, Jan Harold. *Encyclopedia of Urban Legends.* New York: Norton and Company, 2001.

car, or a train, nor which transportation method will be the cheapest on your travel budget. You read so that you can see if the murderer will get away, or if the sisters will make amends after their father's funeral, or if aliens are going to annihilate the world by the end of next week.

When you read in college, you need to read with similar purposes in mind. In your first-aid class, you read about snake bites to get enough information to help someone bitten by a snake. In your environmental studies course, you read to be persuaded that saving the rain forests will decrease global warming. When you get home from work, you might read the television guide or the comic section of the newspaper for entertainment. In college, you will often read pieces where the author's purpose for writing is the same as your purpose for reading.

Understanding a writer's purpose helps you know what kind of ideas and language to expect in a reading. It also helps you to connect with what the writer is telling you. Generally, a writer picks one of three main purposes for a piece. Those purposes are the same as your purposes for reading: to inform, to persuade, or to entertain.

When writers inform, they offer "who, what, when, where, and why" information about something. Some writers may wish to inform you about a new business or a new amusement park. Others may illustrate a point by giving reasons to exercise or offering important tips on buying a home. You find this kind of writing in newspapers, textbooks, subject-specific magazines, and so on.

Instructor Tip

Ask students to bring in a favorite (short) article. Put students in small groups and have them share their articles. Each student in a group needs to read all articles for that group. Have them identify the author's purpose for each article after everyone has read them. Have them share their results with the class.

When writers persuade, they attempt to sway your opinion and make you agree with their ideas. Writers may convince you that you should quit smoking cigarettes, vote for a certain amendment, or buy a new washing machine. This is the purpose of advertisements, credit-card offers, and sales brochures.

Finally, when writers entertain, they strike an emotional chord with you, making you chuckle, sob, or sing. They may do this by telling stories and jokes or by writing screenplays or songs. Books, poems, songs, and plays are written to entertain.

As you connect with a piece, you should consider an author's purpose. Developing this reading skill early will help you with later skills and remind you that you are reading for a reason.

EXERCISES

PRACTICE

For practice finding an author's purpose, complete the following exercises.

EXERCISE 1

Each of the following selections is written to inform, to persuade, or to entertain. Read the selection and circle the answer that states the author's purpose.

1. If you want to learn a language easily, take German. German is simpler to learn than other languages for two major reasons. First, once you learn the German alphabet, you can pronounce any German word without fear of phonetic changes or silent letters. Because you can pronounce German words, you can also spell them easily. In addition, the rules of grammar are basic and constant. The rules are very logical, which means that writing and reading in German is clearer because German's grammar is concise. Furthermore, German does not have exceptions to rules as many other languages do. Due to its alphabet and grammar rules, German is an easy language to learn.

   What is the author's purpose?

   a. to inform

   (b.) to persuade

   c. to entertain

Instructor Tip

Practice Exercises are throughout chapters. In addition, at the end of each chapter in the Practice Pages, you will find another set of similar exercises. Practice Exercises in chapters can be completed as class work while exercises at the end of the chapter can be used for homework. This fits with a teach-model-practice-apply approach.

2. Artist Doug Rhodehamel created a piece of art for a one-man, and one-worm, show at Will's Pub, a popular venue for artists and musicians. The piece of art was aptly named Larva but fondly called Bernice. Obviously female, Bernice was about sixteen feet long and as wide as four feet in some sections. Made of clear plastic drop-cloth and seamed together with green painter's tape, she was created as two separate tubes, one inside the other, and both inflated by a small fan attached to one end of the outer tube. For her setae, the hairs that propel a worm, Rhodehamel used several long, slender, half-filled purple balloons that he attached to the other end of the larva. Suspended from the ceiling with twine and detailed with evenly-spaced, green and orange circular stickers, Bernice glowed under black lights and swayed gently as people passed her. Although she will only live for a few days (she is easily punctured by wayward pool cues and stumbling patrons), Bernice is the weirdest worm squirming around Will's right now.

   What is the author's purpose?

   (a.) to inform

   b. to persuade

   c. to entertain

3. A: Knock, knock.
    B: Who's there?
    A: Dwayne.
    B: Dwayne who?
    A: Dwayne the bathtub—I'm dwowning!

    What is the author's purpose?

    a. to inform

    b. to persuade

    (c.) to entertain

Each of the following selections is written to inform, to persuade, or to entertain. Read the selection and circle the answer that states the author's purpose.

1. Jury duty should be considered an honor. People who are summoned to jury duty and who are called to serve as jurors are doing their civic duty. These people are given an opportunity to help uphold constitutional rights, not only the rights of others but theirs as well. Finally, although called a right, jury duty is really a privilege that can be taken away. So, those who are summoned should go willingly, and those who serve should feel honored.

    What is the author's purpose?

    a. to inform

    (b.) to persuade

    c. to entertain

2. A man walks into a flooring store and finds a salesman. The salesman looks at the man and sees great grey bags under his eyes and wonders if the man is okay.

    "Can I help you?" asks the salesman.

    "I'm looking for something with low shag."

    The salesman takes him to a section of rugs. They are stacked in great rolls from floor to ceiling and come in a variety of colors. "This is what we sell."

    The man nods his head, but he isn't pleased. "I need something smaller, a size which could fit the back of a pick-up truck. Or maybe the passenger seat."

A bit befuddled by the request, the salesman takes him to a scraps section where the man has many pieces and sizes from which to choose.

"This is better," says the man. "I need something quiet."

The salesman digs through the scraps and finally produces a four-foot by three-foot section of Berber. "Best I can do, sir. Strange request. Low shag, small, quiet."

"Yeah, well, I work the night shift and sleep during the day. Or used to sleep during the day until my neighbor bought a Bassett hound. Now, he takes the damn dog for rides up and down my street all day long, and the dog hangs its head out the window and bays at everything."

"I don't think I understand," replies the salesman, and he points at the Berber scrap.

"Well," says the man, "I figured I'd throw this in the passenger seat of my truck, hang it out the window and drive up and down my neighbor's street. That'll show him a good carpet!"

What is the author's purpose?

a. to inform

b. to persuade

c. to entertain

Hot or Not?

Why does acting, writing, or reading with purpose save time?

3. To make a chocolate frosting, you will need the following ingredients: one stick of butter, two-thirds of a cup of unsweetened powdered cocoa, three cups of powdered sugar, one-third of a cup of milk, and one teaspoon of vanilla extract. First, melt the butter. Then, stir in the cocoa. Carefully, add a little powdered sugar, and using a beater, beat at medium speed until the mixture is smooth. Add a little milk, and beat; then, add a little sugar, and beat. Continue until all of the sugar is gone. If the frosting is too thick, carefully add a very small amount of milk. Finally, stir in the vanilla extract. This will make about two cups of icing, which can frost a two-layer cake.

What is the author's purpose?

a. to inform

b. to persuade

c. to entertain

Instructor Tip

Apply the Strategy: Use these readings to practice and apply the strategy. Encourage students to take notes as they read to help them remember details. In addition, discuss as a class the results of applying the strategy to help the students connect to the reading.

APPLY THE NEW STRATEGY

Connect Now

Considering your feelings and experiences helped you make a connection to the poem "The Voice You Hear When You Read Silently." Now, see how the strategy adds to your understanding of the entire poem. As you make connections, use your own ideas, memories, and questions to get you involved in the reading.

As you read the poem, stop where it feels natural to do so. Keep in mind the layout of the poem—the end of a line doesn't necessarily signal the end of a sentence. These brief stops give you a chance to see how the poem answers your questions or relates to your experience.

At each stopping point think about what catches your attention:

1. Is there an idea to consider? Do you agree or disagree? Or do you need to read more to figure out what the poet is saying?

2. Is there an image—a picture that the words create in your head?

3. Do you feel impatient or frustrated at any point in the poem?

Instructor Tip
Ask students to answer the three questions that precede the reading after they have read the poem. Encourage them to keep a sheet of paper handy to take notes on readings as necessary.

The Voice You Hear When You Read Silently

THOMAS LUX

Thomas Lux is an award-winning poet and author of several books of poetry. He currently teaches at Sarah Lawrence College in New York. "The Voice You Hear When You Read Silently" first appeared in a 1997 issue of *The New Yorker* magazine.

Instructor Tip
Unfamiliar vocabulary words are placed in the margins of the readings.

The Voice You Hear When You Read Silently

1   is not silent, it is a speaking
    out-loud voice in your head: it is *spoken,*
    a voice is *saying* it
    as you read. It's the writer's words,
5   of course, in a literary sense
    his or her "voice" but the sound
    of that voice is the sound of *your* voice.
    Not the sound your friends know
    or the sound of a tape played back
10 but your voice
    caught in the dark cathedral
    of your skull, your voice heard
    by an internal ear informed by internal abstracts
    and what you know by feeling,
15 having felt. It is your voice
    saying, for example, the word "barn"
    that the writer wrote
    but the "barn" you say
    is a barn you know or knew.
        The voice
20 in your head, speaking as
        you read,
    never says anything neu-
        trally—some people
    hated the barn they know,
    some people love the barn
        they know

a sensory constellation/is lit: a collection (*constellation*) of associations with a word due to what we have *sensed*—seen, smelled, heard—in relation to it.

chirrr: the sound the oats make as they spill from the sack

so you hear the word loaded
and a sensory constellation   25
is lit: horse-gnawed stalls,
hayloft, black heat tape wrapping
a water pipe, a slippery
spilled *chirrr* of oats from a split sack,
the bony, filthy haunches of cows.   30
And "barn" is only a noun—no verb
or subject has entered into the sentence yet!
the voice you hear when you read to yourself
is the clearest voice: you speak it
speaking to you.   35

Active Readers Respond: Each reading has this section. As skills are developed, so is this section. By the end of the book, there are four parts: Vital Vocabulary (helping students build vocabulary and use context clues); Objective Operations (providing multiple-choice questions that mimic most common exit exams); Readers Write (making reading meaningful by writing about it); and Readers Discuss (getting students working together and questioning each other's opinions).

ACTIVE READERS RESPOND

After you've finished reading, use these questions to respond to "The Voice You Hear When You Read Silently." You may write your answers in the spaces provided or on a separate sheet of paper.

OBJECTIVE OPERATIONS

1. What is the author's purpose?
   a. to inform
   b. to persuade
   c. to entertain *(circled)*

2. The word "cathedral" in line 11 most nearly means
   a. a sacred place. *(circled)*
   b. a person.
   c. a medical procedure.
   d. a feeling.

3. The "voice" in the poem refers to
   a. the remembered voice of the person who first read to you.
   b. your own voice as you whisper the words to yourself.
   c. the voice in your own mind. *(circled)*
   d. someone reading the poem aloud to you.

4. According to the poem, the writer's words
   a. are not important.
   b. help to create the "voice." *(circled)*
   c. are not part of the "voice."
   d. are ignored by the "voice."

5. Lux says that this voice is "not the sound your friends know/ or the sound of a tape played back"; this means that
   a. you don't use your vocal chords to produce this voice. *(circled)*
   b. you don't sound the same to your friends or yourself when you're reading instead of just talking.
   c. people think their tape recorded voice sounds different from the voice they hear when they talk.
   d. this voice is not really yours but a voice you remember from childhood.

6. The word "abstracts" in line 13 most nearly means
   a. pictures.
   b. ideas different from other people's. *(circled)*
   c. concrete.
   d. ideas similar to other people's.

7. "The dark cathedral of your skull" in lines 11–12 refers to
   a. a library with a large, quiet space that allows your mind to concentrate on what you're reading.

b. the unique, almost sacred space inside your mind.

c. a spirit of gothic darkness that can take over your mind.

d. your imagination, brightly colored like the stained glass of a cathedral.

8. Lux uses the example of the word "barn" in the poem in order to

a. show us a vivid picture of a barn he grew up near.

b. indicate the importance of getting background so that you can picture things as you read.

c. demonstrate that a barn can be as good a place to read as a library or cathedral.

d. demonstrate that each of us has our own special associations with a word as we read it.

9. This poem demonstrates the importance of the *reader* in the reading process by

a. describing the reader as a viewer of word pictures.

b. encouraging the reader to read the writer's words aloud.

c. showing that as a reader, you need to put aside any previous ideas you've had in order to acquire new ideas.

d. showing that as a reader, you bring a unique experience to each piece of writing you read.

10. The voice you hear in your head is the

a. loudest.

b. clearest.

c. quietest.

d. smartest.

READERS WRITE

1. What does the "voice" in the poem mean to you?

(Answers will vary.)

_____

_____

2. Which part of the poem means the most to you? Why?

(Answers will vary.)

_____

_____

3. The poem shows how each of us has different associations with a word by using the example of "barn." What associations do you have for the word "barn"? What images come to mind?

(Answers will vary.)

_____

_____

4. What are different associations you have with another word for a place, such as "kitchen" or "yard" or "beach"?

(Answers will vary.)

_____

_____

5. How does this poem demonstrate the importance of the reader in the reading process?

(Answers will vary.)

_____

_____

CONNECT NOW

1 | Get a quick first impression of the topic.

2 | Relate your experience and feelings to the topic.

3 | Understand your purpose for reading and the author's purpose for writing.

Summary

CHAPTER 1

HOW DOES STRATEGY 1 HELP YOU BECOME AN ENGAGED READER?

You continually look at your own experiences to connect what you think and feel to the writer's ideas. *Connect now* reminds you to find your own associations with a subject before you start to read.

HOW DOES THE CONNECT NOW STRATEGY WORK?

To connect you use the title and first lines or paragraph to identify the subject of the reading. Then you see what feelings and experiences you have in connection with the subject.

Strategy 1 teaches you to get an impression of the topic first. You do this by using the title and other clues to identify the topic. To be an engaged reader, you must *ask questions* about what you are reading and offer your own ideas. You also look for writers to supply answers to your questions and to clarify your ideas.

Strategy 1 helps you learn to relate what you are reading to your own experiences and feelings. When you make a connection to what you are reading, you are more likely to engage with the material.

Strategy 1 shows you that you have a purpose when you read just as authors have a purpose when they write. You hope to be informed, persuaded, or entertained, and writers hope to inform, to persuade, or to entertain.

Instructor Tip
Each chapter has a summary that breaks down the strategies and their major points. Key terms from the chapter are also included. (Have students buy index cards in multiple colors. Encourage students to keep one set of index cards with the strategies, one set for key terms, and one set for vocabulary words, using a different color for each category. This will help them study for exams.)

Key Terms

purpose: the reason an author writes, that is to inform, to persuade, or to entertain

topic: what the reading is about; the focus for all the ideas

Think AGAIN >

Instructor Tip
Think Again: This is an opportunity to introduce the strategies into the students' lives and allow them a chance to develop a deeper connection to what they are learning in reading class to how they live outside of class. Use this for group discussion or class discussion or for a writing activity.

You can apply this strategy to other situations. For example, when you come to class, you connect with your surroundings by getting a quick impression (Why is everyone so quiet today? Has the professor put notes on the whiteboard?), relating your experience and feelings to your class environment (Do I feel prepared for class? Did I bring all of my supplies?), and having a purpose for coming to class (to get an education, to work on a group project, etc.).

You can also apply this strategy to other courses, such as a science course. For example, when you look over a lab experiment, you connect by getting a quick impression, relating your experience and feelings to the problems (Have you performed a similar experiment before? Are you confident about the experiment? Do you know the material required to perform the experiment?), and understanding your purpose (to get a physical or chemical reaction).

In what other ways *do* you apply this strategy? In what other ways *can* you apply this strategy?

MASTERY TEST

Now make a connection to "I Do Not Like to Read— Sam-I-Am." As you read, pause wherever you feel that the author is saying something that relates to your own early reading. Keep noticing the similarities and the differences between her experience and yours.

I Do Not Like to Read—Sam-I-Am!

READING 2

REBECCA GRABINER

Rebecca Grabiner is an alumna of the University of Chicago. She wrote about learning to read for the *University of Chicago Magazine* in 1997 toward the end of her senior year. In this reading, she talks about a very popular book for young children, *Green Eggs and Ham*, by Theodor Geisel, known throughout the world as Dr. Seuss. "Sam" is a character in the book.

1 I never knew how to read until I was forced to learn in school, in the first grade. It wasn't that I didn't like books. On the contrary, I looked forward eagerly to the time every night when I sat in my father's lap, and he read me stories and rhymes. . . . I just didn't feel any pressing need to see for myself that the words actually said what my parents told me they did. I was a very trusting child.

2 The summer before I turned 6, when I had completed kindergarten at my small, friendly, neighborhood elementary school, my father's sabbatical took us halfway across the country to Indiana. Now, my kindergarten education was by no means bad, but my school had certain revolutionary ideas: It thought children should enjoy learning. The early grades moved slowly. Lessons always seemed more like games than work, and we were never graded. At almost 6, I was a proficient finger-painter; I could draw a turkey by tracing either my right or left hand; I could count to a hundred; and I knew the alphabet, but only in capital letters.

3 At Child's School in Bloomington, Indiana, I quickly discovered that, in spite of my two-handed turkey-drawing ability, I was very much behind the

other children. My classmates laughed when they saw me carefully printing my name all in uppercase, when I thought that the more Elmer's glue you used the better it stuck, and when I didn't know the Pledge of Allegiance, even though it was printed on the inside of my pencil-box lid.

4   I was put in the lowest reading group, which had only two other members: a girl who had been left back the year before and a boy everyone feared because he had a chipped front tooth. Every day, I had to stay in at recess because I couldn't finish my phonics assignments in time.

5   When my father read to me at home and tried to help me by pointing out the letters as he read, I squeezed my eyes shut until he stopped, refusing to look at anything but the pictures. I couldn't bear to think that the books I enjoyed so much at home could have anything in common with that dreadful Dick and Jane and their horrid dog, Spot.

6   I liked listening to stories and looking at the pictures, but that wasn't what I thought of when someone mentioned reading. Reading was getting bad grades and being laughed at. It was sitting next to the boy with the chipped tooth and spending 30 minutes of hard work only to find out that Dick and Jane had gone to the market and bought apples, pears, and bananas, but that they could not buy cucumbers because the shop-keeper was out of cucumbers.

7   When I got home that day, I was almost surprised to see a cucumber in our refrigerator and thought how stupid Dick and Jane were to go to that dumb shopkeeper when they should have gone to the supermarket like my mother did. That night, my mother was going to read to me because my father was out of town for a math conference, so I went to the shelf to pick out a book while she did homework for her computer-programming class. I chose *Green Eggs and Ham*, recognizing it by the color of its binding, and squinting so my vision blurred and I couldn't see the letters on the spine.

8   My mother was taking forever to finish her work, so I began to flip through the pages, looking for my favorite picture, the one with the goat in it. What happened next was really an accident. . . . Almost without realizing it, I found myself reading the entire page, and liking it.

9   "I would not, could not, on a boat. I would not, could not, with a goat." And I found out that the words on the page were the same as the ones that my parents said, and I could read them.

10   I was reading and I wasn't bored. I was reading to myself and I could do it as quickly or as slowly as I wanted, without my name being written on the board, without check marks, and without staying in at recess. I could even read the same sentence more than once if I wanted to.

11   "I DO NOT LIKE GREEN EGGS AND HAM. I DO NOT LIKE THEM. SAM-I-AM!" I read, shouting now. I read it twice, then three times, at the top of my voice. My mother looked up from her work.

12   "I'll read it to you in just a second," she said.

13   "No! I'll read it to you!" I yelled. And I did.

When my father read to me at home and tried to help me by pointing out the letters as he read, I squeezed my eyes shut until he stopped, refusing to look at anything but the pictures.

ACTIVE READERS RESPOND

After you've finished reading, use these questions to respond to "I Do Not Like to Read—Sam-I-Am." You may write your answers in the spaces provided or on a separate sheet of paper.

OBJECTIVE OPERATIONS

1. What is the author's purpose?
   a. to inform
   b. to persuade
   c. to entertain

2. The word "sabbatical" in paragraph 2, line 2, most nearly means
   a. a period of leave from work.
   b. a religious holiday.
   c. an upset professor.
   d. a feeling.

3. When she began the first grade, Grabiner was behind the other children in reading because she
   a. had been laughed at by the children in her previous school.
   b. did not like books.
   c. had gone to a school that emphasized learning about revolutions.
   d. had gone to a school that emphasized enjoying learning.

4. According to the author, she was an excellent
   a. finger-painter.
   b. reader.
   c. writer.
   d. turkey farmer.

5. How many other students besides Grabiner were placed in the lower reading group?
   a. four
   b. three
   c. two
   d. one

6. The word "dreadful" in paragraph 5, line 5, most nearly means
   a. pleasant.
   b. wonderful.
   c. unpleasant.
   d. mediocre.

7. Even though Grabiner enjoyed having her father read to her at night, she didn't like reading partly because she
   a. didn't like sitting still long enough to read.
   b. preferred doing things such as shopping at the supermarket with her mother instead of just reading about them.
   c. didn't like the books she had to read at school.
   d. had to look at books by herself when her father was out of town.

8. Grabiner finally realized that she could enjoy reading when she
   a. recognized words on the page of *Green Eggs and Ham* by accident.
   b. read a book during recess one day at school.
   c. found *Green Eggs and Ham* by reading the title.
   d. found that the words she was reading were different from the ones her parents said.

9. According to the reading, the main reason Grabiner got over her dislike of reading before leaving the first grade was that
   a. being in the lowest reading group gave her the reading skills she needed.
   b. she'd had good experiences with books every night when her parents read to her.
   c. she got the glasses she needed in order to read comfortably.
   d. her parents rewarded with special treats for learning to read.

10. When Grabiner finally started reading, she
    a. sang the words to her mother.
    b. whispered the words to her mother.
    c. shouted the words to her mother.
    d. said nothing to her mother.

1. What similarities and differences did you notice between Grabiner's experience and your own? For example, were you put off by reading lessons in school as she was? Did a favorite book suddenly change your attitude in the way that *Green Eggs and Ham* got Grabiner excited about reading?

    (Answers will vary.) _____

    _____

    _____

2. How did Grabiner try to keep herself from learning to read? Do you ever remember trying to actively not learn something?

    (Answers will vary.) _____

    _____

    _____

3. What part of the reading did you particularly like or dislike? Explain your choice.

    (Answers will vary.) _____

    _____

    _____

4. What recommendations would you make about how to make early reading experiences as positive as they can be?

    (Answers will vary.) _____

    _____

    _____

5. Due to some bad experiences, Grabiner put up mental barriers to stop herself from reading. What barriers get in your way as you try to connect with a reading?

    (Answers will vary.) _____

    _____

    _____

CONNECT NOW

1 | Get a quick first impression of the topic.

2 | Relate your experience and feelings to the topic.

3 | Understand your purpose for reading and the author's purpose for writing.

PRACTICE PAGES

Chapter 1

Instructor Tip
Practice Pages contain an extra set of exercises and a practice reading, which by the end of the book include Vital Vocabulary, Objective Operations, and Quick Questions (a short-answer section). These can be used for homework prior to your giving the Mastery Test.

For practice finding an author's purpose, complete the following exercises.

PRACTICE EXERCISE 1

Each of the following selections is written to inform, to persuade, or to entertain. Read the selection and circle the answer that states the author's purpose. (The answer to the riddle is on page 20 of the Practice Pages.)

1. What's greater than God
    But more evil than the devil?
    The rich want it.
    The poor have it.
    If you eat it, you die.

    What is the author's purpose?

    a. to inform

    b. to persuade

    c. to entertain

2. The library will deliver items during business hours Monday through Friday and from 8:00 a.m. until 12:00 p.m. on Saturdays. Items are delivered in an insulated envelope (to protect items such as CDs and DVDs) that may be used for returns (patron must pay postage) and protected in a plastic bag in case of inclement weather. Items are left on porches or doorsteps at the patron's home address. It is the patron's responsibility to return the items on time. If the insulated envelope is not used for the return, please return it to the library with other returns.

    What is the author's purpose?

    a. to inform

    b. to persuade

    c. to entertain

3. Volunteering is an excellent activity. Working for an afternoon or a Saturday morning at a homeless shelter, food bank, or donation store may not seem like much, but for those few hours, people can really help. Organizations need people who are willing to give their time; if several people give a few hours each week, entire shifts can be covered. During those shifts, volunteers find beds for homeless people during cold spells, feed the hungry and provide households with groceries, and sort and organize items to sell for charity. Volunteers receive a sense of well-being and learn about themselves. Volunteering can changes hearts.

What is the author's purpose?

a. to inform

(b.) to persuade

c. to entertain

PRACTICE EXERCISE 2

Each of the following selections is written to inform, to persuade, or to entertain. Read the selection and circle the answer that states the author's purpose.

1. Tarantulas have hairs called urticating hairs that have several uses. The hairs can detect heat; this means a tarantula can sense small animals such as mice or birds without actually seeing them. Also, the hairs are used for defense; tarantulas kick them off in the face of their attacker. The hairs are small and barbed and easily embed in the nasal membranes and eyes of animals. They also are irritating due to chemicals in the hairs. Finally, tarantulas drop these hairs around the webbed burrows they create; the hairs mark the territory of individual tarantulas.

What is the author's purpose?

(a.) to inform

b. to persuade

c. to entertain

People, pay attention to your gut instincts on a first date. Do not let the date come to your house to pick you up–you may not want that person to know where you live!

2. People, pay attention to your gut instincts on a first date. Do not let the date come to your house to pick you up—you may not want that person to know where you live! Meet your date at a popular place instead. If the date says anything uncomfortable or that makes your hair stand up or gives you goosebumps, end the date as soon as you can. Something is wrong, and these physical reactions are your body's way of trying to let you know. If you sense that something is not quite right with the person or your gut tells you the person is off, listen to your gut—you are probably correct. The person may be a liar, a thief, or a homicidal maniac, and you really don't want a second date. Pay attention to your gut instinct!

What is the author's purpose?

a. to inform

(b.) to persuade

c. to entertain

3. A: Knock, knock.
    B: Who's there?
    A: Juana.
    B: Juana who?
    A: Juana come out and play?

    What is the author's purpose?

    a. to inform

    b. to persuade

    c. to entertain

    Note: The answer to the riddle in Practice Exercise 1, number 1, on page 18 is "Nothing."

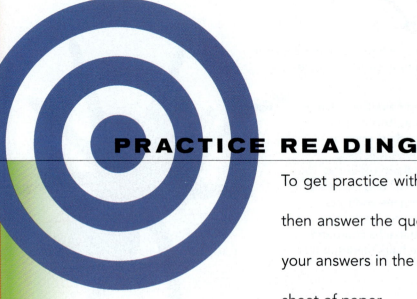

PRACTICE READING

To get practice with reading, read the passage, and then answer the questions that follow. You may write your answers in the spaces provided or on a separate sheet of paper.

The One-Room Schoolhouse of the Nineteenth Century

Students in individual grades weren't always separated from each other in different classrooms. Learning used to take place in one large room. This excerpt is from *Timed Readings Plus in Social Studies*, Book 1, Jamestown Education (Columbus: Glencoe McGraw-Hill, 2003), 33.

1   In the United States in the nineteenth century, many children were taught in one-room schoolhouses. Grades one through eight shared the same classroom. A typical one-room schoolhouse was built of wood and painted white or red.

2   To get to school, children walked, rode a horse, or rode in a buggy. When it was time for school to begin, the teacher rang a bell, and the children went inside. Sometimes they stopped in a small room to wash their hands; they poured water from a pitcher into a bowl, called a basin. They hung their coats

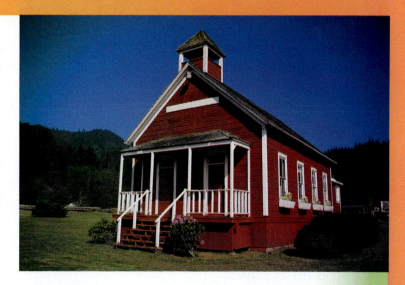

on hooks in a cloakroom and then went to their desks. They stood to recite the Pledge of Allegiance. The smallest children sat in the smallest desks at the front of the room, nearest the teacher's desk while the tallest children sat in the back. In the middle of the room stood a potbellied stove used for heat on cold days. Those near the stove may have felt too warm, but those farthest away may have felt cold. The stove burned fuel, such as wood or coal.

3 The subjects taught were arithmetic, geography, science, history, reading, art, and penmanship. Students learned to write beautiful flowing script that was easy to read. Teachers wrote the lessons on a blackboard at the front of the room. That is also where students worked math problems or practiced writing. In some schools, students had their own small slates to write on. Because one teacher had to teach all grade levels, the children were often taught one at a time.

4 Children were expected to be well behaved. Those who were not were punished by the teacher. The teacher may have used a leather strap, wooden cane, or wooden paddle for this purpose. Sometimes a child who had misbehaved would have to cut a switch from a tree, which the teacher would use on him or her. At noon, there was a recess. The children played and ate lunch. Students often carried their lunch to school in metal pails. In very cold weather, the teacher might cook something hot on the stove. Lessons resumed in the afternoon. When school let out, the children went home. There was rarely homework. Children were expected to help at home or do farm chores. Only a few children owned books. Books carried to and from school were wrapped by a leather strap and carried by the loose end of the strap.

Children were expected to be well behaved. Those who were not were punished by the teacher. The teacher may have used a leather strap, wooden cane, or wooden paddle for this purpose.

ACTIVE READERS RESPOND

After you've finished reading, use these questions to respond to "The One-Room Schoolhouse of the Nineteenth Century." You may write your answers in the spaces provided or on a separate sheet of paper.

OBJECTIVE OPERATIONS

1. What is the author's purpose?
   a. to inform
   b. to persuade
   c. to entertain

2. In a one-room schoolhouse, children in grades one through eight
   a. had different teachers.
   b. shared the same classroom.
   c. were taught the same lessons.
   d. taught each other lessons.

3. The word "basin" in paragraph 2, line 4, most nearly means
   a. sink.
   b. plate.
   c. bowl.
   d. pitcher.

4. Students often carried their lunches to school in
   a. metal pails.
   b. paper sacks.
   c. wooden buckets.
   d. plastic bags.

5. A student who had books carried them
   a. in a metal pail.
   b. inside of a basin.
   c. by a leather strap
   d. in a backpack.

6. Which of the following sentences best tells what the whole passage is about?
   a. The blackboard was an important teaching tool.
   b. In the nineteenth century, many children were taught in one-room schoolhouses.
   c. In the United States, classrooms have changed a great deal over time.
   d. Schools are important in the United States.

7. The smallest children sat in the front of the classroom so that
   a. different age groups could be separated.
   b. the oldest children could be the first to leave.
   c. the smallest children would be the closest to the stove.
   d. all students could see the blackboard.

8. According to the passage, a potbellied stove
   a. kept everyone comfortable.
   b. did not heat the room very evenly.
   c. was used mostly for cooking during the school day.
   d. was a type of pig.

9. The word "script" in paragraph 3, line 4, most nearly means
   a. print.
   b. acting.
   c. cursive.
   d. singing.

10. Students in a one-room school often studied
    a. in a group.
    b. on their own.
    c. with partners.
    d. with their parents.

1. A typical one-room schoolhouse was made of bricks. True or (False)

2. Several teachers taught together in a one-room schoolhouse. True or (False)

3. Some subjects taught were arithmetic, geography, science, _____ ,
   and history. _____ (Answers may vary.) _____

4. Students stood to recite the Pledge of Allegiance. _____
   _____

5. Why was there rarely any homework assigned? (Answers will vary.) _____
   _____
   _____

6. What were some punishments of children who misbehaved? (Answers will vary.) _____
   _____
   _____

Stay Connected and Respond

RESPOND

1 | Act as an audience member.

2 | Respond while you're reading and after you've finished reading.

3 | Make a place or space to respond.

4 | Ask questions and read to look for answers to your questions.

5 | Link ideas from other readings or sources and talk with others.

imagine this

When you and your friend go to a movie that you both have wanted to see for several days, you are excited. You sit down with your popcorn and soda, shut off your cell phone, pull off the crinkly wrappers of your candy, and shake up your popcorn. You don't want to miss any dialogue due to silly noises.

Before the movie begins, you and your friend talk about what the movie is about, who is starring in it, and whether it is supposed to be a good film. You talk about other movies that the same actors are in and whether this movie seems like it will be similar to their other films. During the movie, you sigh at the love scenes, gasp at dangerous moments, and laugh at funny events. You and your friend respond to what is happening on the screen.

When the movie is over, you immediately discuss it. You rehash scenes, question characters' motives, and make connections to other films. All in all, you respond as an involved audience member.

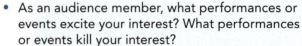

Think FIRST >

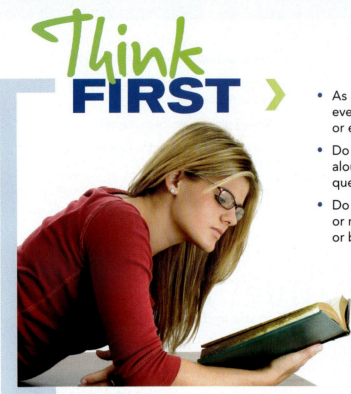

- As an audience member, what performances or events excite your interest? What performances or events kill your interest?

- Do you mumble, grumble, laugh, or comment aloud at the movies or a ballgame? Do you ask questions or predict what will happen next?

- Do you make connections after you see a movie or read a book and compare it to other movies or books?

INTRODUCTION TO THE NEW STRATEGY
Respond

Instructor Tip
Ask students if they respond audibly when they read. Do they know someone who does? Ask why they think people do this and whether responding out loud helps people to recall what they have read.

Connect Now, Strategy 1, gets you involved before you actually start to read. Strategy 2—*Respond*—keeps you involved in the process as you read.

Reading starts with you, the reader. It begins when you make a connection. You find the subject and pause to see what you think and feel about it before you begin to read. Then, you read. Now the reading process involves you and the writer. As you read what the writer has to say, you come back to what you think. What do you understand? What is your opinion about the writer's ideas?

In other words, you respond.

Remember that reading is a conversation between you (the reader) and the writer. The conversation begins as you make connections, continues as you read, and goes on after you've read, as you think about what the writer said.

How do audience behaviors change depending on the event, such as at a movie or a ball game?

You, the Audience

connect now

When we talk with different types of people, we adjust what we say and how we say it to meet the needs of our listeners. When you are eating lunch with your friends, you may use slang, but when you are having tea with your grandmother, you speak more carefully. In the same way, how writers communicate depends on the readers they expect to reach—their

Fans of music bands are some of the strangest audience members. In 1965, folk/rock band the Grateful Dead emerged on the scene and instantly earned a huge following. In 1980, Rolling Stones writer Charles Perry tried to figure out what kept the band's audience so interested, an interest that enticed Deadheads to follow the band's tours all over the country for thirty years until the death of the lead singer, Jerry Garcia, in 1995. In addition, the Deadhead's fanaticism has influenced the way fans act and respond to music.

Deadheads are not like other rock & roll fans. For one thing, in its thirteen years of recording, the band they follow has never had a Top Forty hit. For another, Deadheads are the most dedicated and exclusive fans in rock & roll.

To outsiders, the Grateful Dead are unlikely objects of devotion. Jerry Garcia, the lead singer and guitarist, is a bushy avuncular figure with no particular stage act and not the slightest inclination toward flashy costuming. His beard is even turning gray. His solos have a rambling, why-not-this-note quality, and the lyrics are obscure in a rambling why-not-this-meaning way.

Same with the Deadheads. Outsiders usually consider them hippie holdovers, nostalgic for the 1967 Summer of Love, when the Dead played legendary free concerts in the Haight-Ashbury to aimless, druggy aesthetes in tattered gypsy rags.

But to an insider, Garcia is *magic.* The Dead's music is positive, electric, high energy. The obscure lyrics, by Bob Hunter, ("Just a box of rain, wind and water/Believe it if you need it, if you don't, just pass it on"), are on the order of prophecy, and their very obscurity shows a kindly respect for the listener's spiritual growth. Deadheads usually see themselves as searching souls on a journey that's a little hard to explain, except that it's definitely with the Dead.

The Dead's audience has been like that from the start. In 1965 the Grateful Dead were the house band of the Acid Tests, where everybody was encouraged to act exactly as weird as they felt. One of the principles of the Acid Tests was that there was no *show* that you came and watched—everyone in attendance was part of the performance. From the beginning, the Dead and their audience had a communal identity, a huge formless organism with sensed but unstated aims.

Perry, Charles. "The Deadhead Phenomenon." *Garcia.* New York: Rolling Stone Press, 1995. 148.

intended audience. Frequently, writers speak to a general audience, everyday people in everyday situations. Newspapers, for instance, are written for a general audience.

Sometimes, writers use specialized language to speak to a specific audience; this specialization happens in trade journals or magazines. For example, an architect describing a better way to build a structure will use all of the jargon that an architect should use. If you read that paper, you may not understand all of it because it wasn't written for you. The architect had a very special audience in mind.

Here is another way to think about audience. Suppose you have a group writing project due in science class. You are assigned to complete the project with two other students. The three of you meet in the library one day, and everyone decides to do his or her own research first. In a few days, you will meet again to present your research to the rest of the group, and after that meeting, you will decide how to write the paper.

First, consider how you take notes as you research. Your notes are written for you, so you are your own audience. You probably abbreviate words, use slang,

Hot or Not?

Should a writer worry about engaging the audience?

Instructor Tips

Have students write two short letters. First, ask them to write a note to a pretend roommate and request that the roommate return a borrowed item (a book, a pair of jeans, etc.). Then, have the students write to the President of the United States to request the return of the borrowed item. Have the students read a few of their sets of letters aloud. Discuss the differences between the letters and how audience affected the way the students wrote.

Have students bring in magazines, books, and newspapers. Have the students randomly pick an article and read a few paragraphs. When they are finished reading, have them write down the purpose of the article and the intended audience. Have students swap articles and repeat the steps. When everyone has an answer, let the students discuss with each other the purpose and the audience and what clues made them think that.

SARAH JESSICA PARKER

The History of Love
by Nicole Krauss

The History of Love spans over 60 years and takes readers from Nazi-occupied eastern Europe to present day Brighton Beach. At the center of the novel are issues of loneliness and the need to fill a void left empty by lost love.

Sarah Jessica Parker, who became famous through her role in *Sex in the City*, has been keeping a copy of *The History of Love* on her nightstand.

If you liked *The History of Love*, you might also like:

Love Is a Mix Tape, Robert Sheffield

Stardust, Neil Gaiman

Things I've Learned from Women Who've Dumped Me, Ben Karlin, ed.

use emoticons, and write fragments. You know taking notes this way is fine because the only one who has to figure them out is you, but you can't present these notes to your group. Your second task then is to type them up to make them legible and to clarify your ideas. You still use some slang and a few fragments because only your fellow group mates will see the result, but you do want them to understand. Finally, after your last meeting when the group has collaborated on notes, you decide to write the first draft of the research paper. At this stage, you know your audience is your professor, so you write more carefully and formally to ensure you are clear (and you get a good grade). As you moved from your written notes to your typed notes to your completed paper, you made adjustments in your word choice and sentence structure to fit your audience.

As a reader, you are the audience. As a college student, you will read many pieces, and not all of those pieces were written with you, the college student, as the intended audience.

For example, in your introduction to education course, you may read a section in your textbook on identifying learning disabilities. The writer of your textbook had you in mind as the audience, but to show you different opinions, the writer may have also chosen sections from scholarly papers on identifying learning disabilities. These papers might be written by educators or psychologists whose intended audience is not *you* but other educators, psychologists, student aides, or counselors working with students. You, however, have become a temporary member of that intended audience because you are required to read parts of these papers.

Connect now

When you read any piece of writing, recognize that writers have an intended audience, and become a member of that audience. Usually, the piece will be written to a general audience, which includes you. By acting as an audience member, you will feel more inclined to participate in what you are reading. Already, you are reading with purpose, so act with purpose—think about what writers tell you, consider whether you agree or disagree, and ask them questions. The more you respond to a reading, the more likely you will remember it.

What are some ways you respond to different types of writers?

For practice identifying an author's audience, complete the following exercises.

Each of the following selections is written to an intended audience. Read the selection and circle the answer that best describes the intended audience.

1. The first day of school was always exciting to Ben. New freshmen wandered the halls and searched aimlessly for lockers, the lock combinations long since forgotten in the frenzy and confusion. The freshmen stopped and stared at the other students, but dazed, they never asked for help. Ben could easily spot the sophomores, too. Their backpacks weren't as fresh and clean as their lower classmen's, and their shoulders were hunched forward, stooping toward the highly polished linoleum floors. Sophomores also noticed the lost freshmen, and embarrassed, they tried not to let their empathy show and made no eye contact, instead staring at the toes of their Cons. Finally, there were the juniors, which Ben was; aloof students, they noticed no one because they intently studied class schedules with concerned faces. They worried their courses weren't strong enough for a phenomenal college application, and their brains ticked away, filling in times with extracurricular activities—a dance group, the football team, debate club—anything to make them seem more well-rounded. The seniors? Where were they? They're seniors, thought Ben. They're smart. Not a darn one was going to get to school early on the first day!

    Who is the author's intended audience?

    a. general audience

    b. high school teachers

    c. teenagers and young adults

    d. adults

2. Writing students must be careful when editing. They must ensure that they have chosen the correct words. For example, a sentence such as this, "Pick up the cloths off the floor," might confuse a reader if a writer continues with details involving jeans, tee shirts, and socks. One word, 'cloths,' creates confusion because it is not the word 'clothes.' Another common error is using the word 'posses' when the word 'possess' is wanted. For instance, "My friends posses a great deal of sports equipment." A quick read might cause a reader to wonder about a pal's gang affiliation until the reader realizes the word choice error. During the editing process, writing students need to remember to read the word that has been written, and not the word they want to see.

    Who is the author's intended audience?

    a. writing students

    b. high school students

    c. general audience

    d. writing instructors

3. A hermit crab's mouth is not where most people think a mouth should be. The crab's mouth is underneath its body, behind its front legs, eyestalks, and antennae. The mouth is a tiny hole at the center of where its leg sections meet. (A hermit crab is a decapod, which means it has ten legs, six legs at the front of its body and four used to anchor itself in a shell.) When it wants a snack, the crab uses its larger claw to crush, tear, or break up food. It then drops the snack on the ground. With its smaller claw, the crab picks up the crushed morsels and reaches underneath and back to its mouth to feed itself. The crab also has three sets of additional appendages, called maxillipeds, which it uses to push food into its mouth.

Who is the author's intended audience?

a. adults

b. boys

c. biologists

d. general audience

Time for Responding

All readers need a few moments to respond to what they read. As you read, pause and think about what you've just read. Ask questions and notice things you like or don't like. Depending on the reading, you will pause at different points. Sometimes, you might stop after a few sentences. Other times, you'll read a group of paragraphs before pausing.

Once you come to the last sentence, don't stop responding. Continue asking questions, making more comments, or looking back to make sure you have the main ideas.

Space for Responding

Readers have different places for responding as they read. Some write on a sheet of paper; others write in their books. Your choice depends on what you prefer as a reader.

Your Own Mind

The conversation between you and the writer takes place in your own mind. While you read and after you've finished reading, think about what the writer has said.

Margin Notes

Mark places in the margin where you find yourself responding. These are **margin notes.** Just put a pencil mark next to the sentence or paragraph you responded to. If what you read puzzles you, put a question mark; if it amazes you, put an exclamation point (!). You can draw a smiley face or a frown or jot a key word that will help you remember.

Journal or Log

A **journal** or **reading log** is useful for jotting down responses as you go along and after you've finished reading. Some people divide a notebook into two columns, one column for writing a few words from the reading and the other column for a personal response to them.

connect now

Have you ever written in your textbook before? Did you doodle or write important notes?

THE READER'S EDGE: BOOK TWO

Reading Partner

You can also try reading with a partner. In a "joint reading" you each read the same text silently. After each paragraph, you pause to say how each of you responds. Then read the next paragraph, and so on. This technique is especially useful for difficult readings.

Questions and Comments

Questions

As in a conversation, you sometimes need to ask questions to make sure you haven't misunderstood. You can often find the answer to a question just by looking more closely at what you've read. If you can't, don't get discouraged. Instead, keep in mind what you do understand, and identify what other information you need. You can work on these questions or get help with them later.

Agreements and Disagreements

Connecting with the writer doesn't mean you have to agree with what the writer is saying. Notice when you agree or disagree. For example, after reading "Forbidden Reading," do you agree with what Manguel says about the power of reading?

Likes and Dislikes

This reading is a good one for noticing your likes and dislikes. Manguel describes cruelty experienced by slaves, so you probably didn't "like" what he says. However, you might like learning about the slaves' cleverness for finding secret ways to learn to read. You might find some examples interesting, but you might be frustrated by the old-fashioned language in statements by former slaves. What specific things did you like in this reading? What didn't you like?

Looking for Answers

Readers are always questioning the pieces that they read. They can't help it. Audience members love to participate, and they will grumble, argue, concur, disagree, cheer, or consider as they read. As an audience member, you need to know that it is safe and appropriate to question and to respond to what you are reading. As you read, look for answers to questions that you have. Engage yourself in what the writer is telling you, and see if writers have done their jobs and answered all of your questions. Stay connected, and respond.

Connections with Other Ideas

Compare the information a writer gives with what you know from other sources—from seeing a film or TV program on the subject or from another reading. Seeing relationships between ideas, what we call **linking ideas,** helps you identify what different writers have in common as well as what makes each writer's ideas unique.

Hot or Not?

Do you think before you speak? How is this similar to responding to reading?

connect now

How do you keep yourself engaged when you read?

Instructor Tips

To extend the previous activity, have students exchange articles and write a response; when responses are complete, allow students time to exchange responses with each other, read them, and discuss the similarities or differences. Ask them to also discuss favorite parts of the reading.

Students should have a dictionary with them at all times during class and should be encouraged to use it. Encourage students to highlight each word that they look up in their dictionaries so that they can see how their vocabulary develops throughout the semester. If words in the margins of the reading are new to them, remind them to use their dictionaries later so that they can highlight the word.

For example, Grabiner (Reading 2, pp. 14–15) and Manguel each describe the process of learning to read. How are the readings different? What is Grabiner's purpose? What is Manguel's purpose?

Talking with Others

Connect now

Writers want you to talk back to them, but they also want you to talk about their ideas with other readers. A writer's ideas really come to life in the discussions readers have about what they've read. (This is why book clubs are so popular.)

Readers also find that a reading means much more after they've talked about it with others. Even when readers have different opinions, they help each other to get more out of the reading.

Do you talk about books or articles with friends? Do you share an article you find interesting?

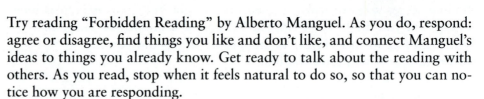

APPLY THE NEW STRATEGY
▌Respond

Try reading "Forbidden Reading" by Alberto Manguel. As you do, respond: agree or disagree, find things you like and don't like, and connect Manguel's ideas to things you already know. Get ready to talk about the reading with others. As you read, stop when it feels natural to do so, so that you can notice how you are responding.

Connect with the Reading

- What could the title of this reading mean? Were you ever forbidden to read something?

- The first sentence hints at the subject. What do you already know about this subject?

- Be aware of any strong feelings you might have about the subject.

Forbidden Reading

READING 3 — ALBERTO MANGUEL

Alberto Manguel is a writer, translator, and editor, with a wide-ranging knowledge of literatures of the world. Born in Buenos Aires, Manguel is now a citizen of Canada. In his book *A History of Reading* (1990), he explores what has drawn people throughout history to want to read, even when, as in this excerpt, they are forbidden to.

1   For centuries, Afro-American slaves learned to read against extraordinary odds, risking their lives in a process that, because of the difficulties set in their way, sometimes took several years. The accounts of their learning are many and heroic. Ninety-year-old Belle Myers Carothers—interviewed by the Federal Writers' Project, a commission set up in the 1930s to record, among other things, the personal narratives of former slaves—recalled that she had learned her letters while looking after the plantation owner's baby, who was playing with alphabet blocks. The owner, seeing what she was doing, kicked her with his boots. Myers persisted, secretly studying the child's letters as well as a few words in a speller she had found. One day, she said, "I found a hymn book . . . and spelled out 'When I Can Read My Title Clear.' I was so happy when I saw that I could really read, that I ran around telling all the other slaves."

2   Leonard Black's master once found him with a book and whipped him so severely "that he overcame my thirst for knowledge, and I relinquished its pursuit until after I absconded." Doc Daniel Dowdy recalled that "the first time you was caught trying to read or write you was whipped with a cowhide, the next time with a' cat-o-nine-tails and the third time they cut the first joint off your forefinger." Throughout the South, it was common for plantation owners to hang any slave who tried to teach the others how to spell.

3   Under these circumstances, slaves who wanted to be literate were forced to find devious methods of learning, either from other slaves or from sympathetic white teachers, or by inventing devices that allowed them to study unobserved. The American writer Frederick Douglass, who was born into slavery and became one of the most eloquent abolitionists of his day, as well as founder of several political journals, recalled in his autobiography: "The frequent hearing of my mistress reading the Bible aloud . . . awakened my curiosity in respect to this mystery of reading, and roused in me the desire to learn. Up to this time I had known nothing whatever of this wonderful art, and my ignorance and inexperience of what it could do for me, as well as my confidence in my mistress, emboldened me to ask her to teach me to read. . . . In an incredibly short time, by her kind assistance, I had mastered the alphabet and could spell words of three or four letters. . . . [My master] forbade her to give me any further instruction . . . [but] the determination which he expressed to keep me in ignorance only rendered me the more resolute to seek intelligence.

[S]laves who wanted to be literate were forced to find devious methods of learning, either from other slaves or from sympathetic white teachers, or by inventing devices that allowed them to study unobserved.

4   "In learning to read, therefore, I am not sure that I do not owe quite as much to the opposition of my master as to the kindly assistance of my amiable mistress." Thomas Johnson, a slave who later became a well-known missionary preacher in England, explained that he had learned to read by studying the letters in a Bible he had stolen. Since his master read aloud a chapter from the New Testament every night, Johnson would coax him

. . . : a series of dots show some words have been left out

"When I Can Read My Title Clear": *title* here means a deed showing ownership

absconded: ran away and hid

cat-o-nine tails: a whip made with nine knotted cords

devious: sly, indirect

abolitionist: someone who campaigned to do away with slavery

rendered me the more resolute: made me more determined

> Learning to read was, for slaves, not an immediate passport to freedom but rather a way of gaining access to one of the powerful instruments of their oppressors: the book.

Illicit: illegitimate, unlawful

to read the same chapter over and over, until he knew it by heart and was able to find the same words on the printed page. Also, when the master's son was studying, Johnson would suggest that the boy read part of his lesson out loud. "Lor's over me," Johnson would say to encourage him, "read that again," which the boy often did, believing that Johnson was admiring his performance. Through repetition, he learned enough to be able to read the newspapers by the time the Civil War broke out, and later set up a school of his own to teach others to read.

Learning to read was, for slaves, not an immediate passport **5** to freedom but rather a way of gaining access to one of the powerful instruments of their oppressors: the book. The slave-owners (like dictators, tyrants, absolute monarchs and other illicit holders of power) were strong believers in the power of the written word. They knew, far better than some readers, that reading is a strength that requires barely a few first words to become overwhelming. Someone able to read one sentence is able to read all; more important, that reader has now the possibility of reflecting upon the sentence, of acting upon it, of giving it a meaning.

ACTIVE READERS RESPOND

After you've finished reading use these activities to respond to "Forbidden Reading." You may write your answers in the spaces provided or on a separate sheet of paper.

OBJECTIVE OPERATIONS

1. What is the author's purpose?
   a. to inform *(circled)*
   b. to persuade
   c. to entertain

2. Who is the intended audience?
   a. history teachers
   b. historians
   c. students
   d. general audience *(circled)*

3. The word "persisted" in paragraph 1, line 11, most nearly means
   a. continued. *(circled)*
   b. gave up.
   c. insisted.
   d. sweat.

4. Plantation owners tried to keep their slaves from reading or teaching others to read by
   a. keeping all reading material hidden and locked away.
   b. whipping them or even hanging them. *(circled)*
   c. whipping them or selling them to other masters.
   d. threatening them with the branding iron.

5. Who read first "When I Can Read My Title Clear"?
   a. Belle Myers Carothers *(circled)*
   b. Thomas Johnson
   c. Frederick Douglass
   d. Doc Daniel Dowdy

6. One of the slaves praised his master's son's reading of a biblical passage and asked him to read it over and over. Doing this was an example of

a. an attempt to flatter the master's son so that he would break the rules and teach the slave to read.

b. an attempt to keep the boy reading so that the slave could put off doing his hard labor as long as possible.

c. a device that allowed the slave to learn to read without being caught.

d. a device for learning Bible passages in order to say them in times of trouble.

7. It's possible to teach yourself to read whole books just by learning the alphabet and a few words because

a. when you know how to sound out a few words in English, you can figure out the system for sounding out all English words.

b. each letter of the alphabet has a unique shape that allows you to remember it when you see it in words.

c. books for beginners have very few words, and therefore require learning only a small number of words.

d. when you know how to sound out a few words in English, you can memorize those words and skip over the other words.

8. The word "oppressors" in paragraph 5, line 3, most nearly means

a. people who hold you back.

b. people who encourage you.

c. people who press you.

d. people who impress you.

9. Frederick Douglass was motivated to learn to read first when he heard his mistress reading the Bible aloud and then when

a. his mistress refused to help him.

b. his mistress praised him for learning to spell words of three and four letters.

c. his master tried to keep him from learning.

d. he was able to see the alphabet blocks of his mistress' baby.

10. By the time the Civil War broke out, Thomas Johnson was able to read:

a. a few letters.

b. the entire alphabet.

c. whole words.

d. newspapers.

11. According to the passage,

a. if you can read a few letters, you can read all letters.

b. if you can read one sentence, you can read all sentences.

c. if you can read one word, you can read all words.

d. if you can't read, you will never be able to.

12. Slave owners were afraid to have slaves learn to read because they knew that

a. once slaves could read, they had access to knowledge, and through knowledge they could gain power.

b. once slaves could read, they became more involved in stories and fantasy that lead them away from working hard.

c. slaves did not have the mental capacity to learn to read.

d. slaves might learn to read in their native African languages and be better able to communicate with one another.

READERS WRITE

1. How did plantation owners try to keep slaves from learning to read?

(Answers will vary.)

_____

_____

2. How can people teach themselves to read whole books just by learning the alphabet and a few words?

(Answers will vary.)

_____

_____

3. What two things motivated Frederick Douglass to learn to read?

(Answers will vary.)

_____

_____

4. Why did plantation owners want to keep slaves from reading?

(Answers will vary.)

_____

_____

5. What part of the history of slaves learning to read seemed most unjust to you?

(Answers will vary.)

_____

_____

1. Share your ideas about the reading with someone else or with a group. What similarities and differences do you find in your responses?

(Answers will vary.)

_____

_____

2. Now that you've thought more about "Forbidden Reading" and discussed it, what is your opinion about it? How did your response change from your first impressions?

(Answers will vary.)

_____

_____

_____

STRATEGY 2

RESPOND

1 | Act as an audience member.

2 | Respond while you're reading and after you've finished reading.

3 | Make a place or space to respond.

4 | Ask questions and read to look for answers to your questions.

5 | Link ideas from other readings or sources and talk with others.

Summary

CHAPTER TWO

HOW DOES STRATEGY 2 HELP YOU BECOME AN ENGAGED READER?

When you begin a reading, you prepare yourself to *make a connection*. As you read and after you've finished reading, you continue making that connection by *responding* with your own questions, comments, and ideas.

HOW DOES THE RESPOND STRATEGY WORK?

Strategy 2 reminds you to keep the conversation going between you and the writer. Strategy 2 reminds you that you are the audience. Most authors write to a general audience, but sometimes, they write to a specific type of audience. Recognizing your role as an audience member helps you to respond.

Strategy 2 teaches you to respond to what you are reading. It encourages you to *ask questions* and consider ideas as you read and to continue asking and considering after you have finished reading a piece.

Strategy 2 shows you how to make a place or space for responding. Not only do you need to clear your mind to focus on what a writer is saying, but you should also jot ideas either on a sheet of paper or in the margins of the text.

Strategy 2 allows you to ask questions and respond to a writer's ideas. You can agree or disagree and like or dislike what a writer is telling you. Strategy 2 encourages you to look for answers to your questions as you read. The more engaged you are, the more you will remember what you read.

Strategy 2 reminds you to connect this reading with other readings or information you have about the topic. In addition, Strategy 2 encourages you to share with others what you think.

Key Terms

journal or reading log: a place for writing your personal responses to a reading

linking ideas: seeing relationships among ideas in different readings or other sources

margin notes: marks or very brief notes in the margin showing your response

Think AGAIN ❯

At a ballgame, certain behaviors are appropriate. The audience can yell, scream, and act a bit crazy without anyone thinking it odd. This is their way of responding to the action, but this sort of behavior would be intolerable at a ballet or an opera. Why do audiences respond so differently?

With regard to reading, when is it okay to respond aloud and when should you be quiet? When is it okay to act a little crazy about a reading and when should you maintain decorum?

MASTERY TEST

Now that you understand Strategy 2, put it into practice with Reading 4, "'See Spot Run': Teaching My Grandmother to Read." Respond—in your mind, on paper, or in discussion with others. Respond by asking questions, saying what you like or don't like, and agreeing or disagreeing with the writer's ideas. Link ideas from this reading with others you've read about the subject.

Connect with the Reading

- Have you known any adults who could not read? What do you imagine it would be like to live in today's society without knowing how to read?

- What kind of relationship have you had with grandparents? Can you imagine teaching a grandparent or other older relative how to read or do some other basic skill?

- What feelings—positive or negative—do you bring to this subject?

"See Spot Run": Teaching My Grandmother to Read

READING 4   ELLEN TASHIE FRISINA

Ellen Tashie Frisina is a journalism professor at Hofstra University on Long Island. In this reading she remembers herself as a young teenager following an unusual desire: to teach the basics of reading to her grandmother, who never had the opportunity to learn when she was young.

1   When I was 14 years old, and very impressed with my teenage status (looking forward to all the rewards it would bring), I set for myself a very special goal—a goal that so differentiated me from my friends that I don't believe I told a single one. As a teenager, I was expected to have deep, dark secrets, but I was not supposed to keep them from my friends.

2   My secret was a project that I undertook every day after school for several months. It began when I stealthily made my way into the local elementary school—horror of horrors should I be seen; I was now in junior high. I identified myself as a graduate of the elementary school, and being taken under wing by a favorite fifth grade teacher, I was given a small bundle from a locked storeroom—a bundle that I quickly dropped into a bag, lest anyone see me walking home with something from the "little kids" school.

stealthily: secretly

3   I brought the bundle home—proudly now, for within the confines of my home, I was proud of my project. I walked into the living room, and one by one, emptied the bag of basic reading books. They were thin books with colorful covers and large print. The words were monosyllabic and repetitive. I sat down to the secret task at hand.

monosyllabic: having only one syllable

4   "All right," I said authoritatively to my 70-year-old grandmother, "today we begin our first reading lesson."

5   For weeks afterward, my grandmother and I sat patiently side by side—roles reversed as she, with a bit of difficulty, sounded out every word, then read them again, piece by piece, until she understood the short sentences. When she slowly repeated the full sentence, we both would smile and clap our hands—I felt so proud, so grown up.

6   My grandmother was born in Kalamata, Greece, in a rocky little farming village where nothing much grew. She never had the time to go to school. As the oldest child, she was expected to take care of her brother and sister, as well as the house and meals, while her mother tended to the gardens, and her father scratched out what little he could from the soil.

7   So, for my grandmother, schooling was out. But she had big plans for herself. She had heard about America. About how rich you could be. How people on the streets would offer you a dollar just to smell the flower you were carrying. About how everyone lived in nice houses—not stone huts on the sides of mountains—and had nice clothes and time for school.

8   So my grandmother made a decision at 14—just a child, I realize now—to take a long and sickening 30-day sea voyage alone to the United States. After lying about her age to the passport officials, who would shake their heads vehemently at anyone under 16 leaving her family, and after giving her favorite gold earrings to her cousin, saying "In America, I will have all the gold I want," my young grandmother put herself on a ship. She landed in New York in 1916.

9   No need to repeat the story of how it went for years. The streets were not made of gold. People weren't interested in smelling flowers held by strangers. My grandmother was a foreigner. Alone. A young girl who worked hard doing piecework to earn enough money for meals. No leisure time, no new gold earrings—and no school.

> Here was this old woman slowly and carefully sounding out each word, moving her lips, not saying anything aloud until she was absolutely sure, and then, loudly, proudly, happily saying, "Look at Spot. See Spot run."

She learned only enough English to help her in her daily business as she 10 traveled about Brooklyn. Socially, the "foreigners" stayed in neighborhoods where they didn't feel like foreigners. English came slowly.

My grandmother had never learned to read. She could make out a menu, 11 but not a newspaper. She could read a street sign, but not a shop directory. She could read only what she needed to read as, through the years, she married, had five daughters, and helped my grandfather with his restaurant.

So when I was 14—the same age that my grandmother was when she 12 left her family, her country, and everything she knew—I took it upon myself to teach my grandmother something, something I already knew how to do. Something with which I could give back to her some of the things she had taught me.

And it was slight repayment for all she taught me. How to cover the fig 13 tree in tar paper so it could survive the winter. How to cultivate rose bushes and magnolia trees that thrived on her little piece of property. How to make baklava, and other Greek delights, working from her memory. ("Now we add some milk." "How much?" "Until we have enough.") Best of all, she had taught me my ethnic heritage.

First, we phonetically sounded out the alphabet. Then, we talked about 14 vowels—English is such a difficult language to learn. I hadn't even begun to explain the different sounds "gh" could make. We were still at the basics.

Every afternoon, we would sit in the living room, my grandmother with 15 an afghan covering her knees, giving up her crocheting for her reading lesson. I, with the patience that can come only from love, slowly coached her from the basic reader to the second-grade reader, giving up my telephone gossiping.

Years later, my grandmother still hadn't learned quite 16 enough to sit comfortably with a newspaper or magazine, but it felt awfully good to see her try. How we used to laugh at her pronunciation mistakes. She laughed more heartily than I. I never knew whether I should laugh. Here was this old woman slowly and carefully sounding out each word, moving her lips, not saying anything aloud until she was absolutely sure, and then, loudly, proudly, happily saying, "Look at Spot. See Spot run."

When my grandmother died and we faced the sad task of 17 emptying her home, I was going through her night-table drawer and came upon the basic readers. I turned the pages slowly, remembering. I put them in a paper bag, and the next day returned them to the "little kids" school. Maybe someday, some teenager will request them again, for the same task. It will make for a lifetime of memories.

baklava: pastry made of many layers of paper-thin dough with a filling of ground nuts and honey

afghan: type of blanket or shawl

Abraham Lincoln moved his lips when he read. Do you?

ACTIVE READERS RESPOND

After you've finished reading use these activities to respond to " 'See Spot Run': Teaching My Grandmother to Read." You may write your answers in the spaces provided or on a separate sheet of paper.

OBJECTIVE OPERATIONS

1. What is the author's purpose?

   a. to inform

   b. to persuade

   (c.) to entertain

2. Who is the intended audience?

   a. educators

   b. students teaching people to read

   c. granddaughters

   (d.) general audience

3. The word "bundle" in paragraph 2, line 6, most nearly means

   (a.) a group of items.

   b. many.

   c. a package.

   d. few.

4. Frisina's grandmother wanted to come to the United States all by herself at age 14 because

   (a.) her life in Greece promised only hard work and poverty, and she thought everyone could get rich in America.

   b. she was expected to marry at 14, and she wanted to escape the arranged marriage.

   c. she had to take care of her brother and sister and thought she could give them better care by sending back money to them from America.

   d. she felt she could return to Greece if things didn't work out, which is why she gave her gold earrings to her cousin for safekeeping.

5. The grandmother was now

   (a.) 70 years old.

   b. 50 years old.

   c. 40 years old.

   d. 90 years old.

6. Frisina's grandmother met with disappointments and difficulties that were typical of immigrants' experiences. These included

   a. being forced to go to school and learn English.

   b. finding pieces of bouquets and trying to sell these flowers to strangers.

   c. being labeled a foreigner and restricted by city law to staying in her own neighborhood.

   (d.) having to work hard just to have money to eat and having no time for school.

7. Frisina is most grateful for what she had learned from her grandmother about

   a. covering trees with tar paper.

   b. cooking without a recipe.

   c. the ways of immigrant life in a brand new culture.

   (d.) the ways of her ethnic heritage.

8. The word "cultivate" in paragraph 13, line 2, most nearly means

   (a.) grow.

   b. school.

   c. kill.

   d. sell.

9. During these reading lessons, Frisina's grandmother

   a. became upset when Frisina laughed at her pronunciation mistakes.

   (b.) laughed hard at her own pronunciation mistakes.

   c. wanted to give up trying when she still couldn't read the newspaper.

   d. became upset when Frisina wanted to stop and go back to telephone gossiping.

10. When her grandmother made mistakes and laughed, Frisinia felt

    a. comfortable laughing with her grandmother.

    (b.) uncomfortable laughing with her grandmother.

    c. embarrassed for her grandmother.

    d. pleased with her grandmother.

11. Both the author and her grandmother felt the importance of these reading lessons because the lessons

    a. finally allowed her grandmother to sit comfortably with a newspaper or magazine.

    b. were evidence that her grandmother was more intelligent than people had given her credit for.

    (c.) were evidence of the love the author felt for her grandmother.

    d. finally allowed her grandmother to give up the crocheting she'd had to do for so many years.

12. Which of the following statements is true?

    a. After her grandmother's death, Frisina found the books and returned them to the school.

    b. After her grandmother's death, Frisina found the books and kept them.

    c. After her grandmother's death, Frisina regretted teaching her grandmother to read.

    d. After her grandmother's death, Frisina taught others to read.

READERS WRITE

1. What led Frisina's grandmother to want to come to the United States all by herself at such a young age?

(Answers will vary.)

2. Frisina suggests that her grandmother's difficulties upon arriving in this country were typical for most immigrants. What were these difficulties?

(Answers will vary.)

3. What had the grandmother taught the author that inspired the author to want to teach her grandmother in return?

(Answers will vary.)

4. How did these reading lessons affect the relationship between the author and her grandmother? Why do you think the lessons seemed so important to both of them?

(Answers will vary.)

5. Do you think many teenagers would want do what Frisina did? Why or why not?

(Answers will vary.)

READERS DISCUSS

1. What does this reading show about what it is like to be an immigrant or a member of an immigrant family? Compare what you learned to what you already knew about the immigrant experience.

(Answers will vary.)

2. Now that you've thought more about "'See Spot Run': Teaching My Grandmother to Read," what is your opinion of it? Of the four readings in Chapters 1 and 2, which one appeals to you most? Why?

(Answers will vary.)

RESPOND

1 | Act as an audience member.

2 | Respond while you're reading and after you've finished reading.

3 | Make a place or space to respond.

4 | Ask questions and read to look for answers to your questions.

5 | Link ideas from other readings or sources and talk with others.

PRACTICE PAGES

Chapter 2

For practice identifying an author's audience, complete the following exercises.

PRACTICE EXERCISE

Each of the following selections is written to an intended audience. Read the selection and circle the answer that best describes the intended audience.

1. To make eyelashes look luscious when you use your mascara, first dust the lashes lightly with baby powder and blot away the excess powder. Then, curl the lashes with an eyelash curler—one quick squeeze should be enough. Now, apply a thin even coat of mascara. Using an eyelash comb, gently comb through the lashes to separate them and let the mascara dry for a few seconds. Apply a second thin coat and comb gently. Finally using an eyelash brush, brush the lashes upwards to fluff them. Voila! Totally winkable!

   Who is the intended audience?

   a. general audience

   b. women

   c. females

   d. males

2. Sitting in the hospital's surgical conference room with the door propped halfway open, I was waiting for two students and jotting in my journal. My CPR manikins were out and ready to go, the infant manikin resting on the table next to me and the adult torso laying on the floor on top of his "body bag." I heard the main hallway doors click open and footsteps on the tiles. Suddenly, a voice exclaimed, "Oh no!" I looked up as the conference room door slammed into the wall.

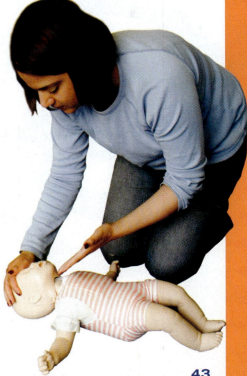

A nurse barged in, recovered by clearing her throat, and said, "Ahem. Excuse me." Her face was slightly pale but a huge grin spread across it; she shrugged as the start of an apology and said, "I, uh, I thought someone collapsed. I saw the bald head, and the door wasn't open all the way." She shook her head. "It's early."

About 5:49 a.m., I thought. I said, "I'm glad to see you on alert. No worries though! He'll stay dead for most of the day, but at least he won't complain."

The nurse laughed and continued down the hall.

Who is the author's intended audience?

a. nurses

b. CPR students

c. general audience

d. doctors

3. Parents, need a quick cheap summer treat for your kids? If you have a blender that crushes or shaves ice, this recipe for snow-cone syrup is perfect for you. You'll need one cup of water, two cups of sugar, and a packet of Kool-Aid, whatever flavor your kids like the best. Mix the water and the sugar in a pot and heat (on high) on the stove. As soon as the sugar water comes to a rolling boil, remove it from the stove and mix in the Kool-Aid packet. Let the mixture come to room temperature, pour into recyclable bottles, and refrigerate until the next hot, sunny day. When the kids need a treat, shave some ice in your blender and pour the syrup over top. A quick cool treat for cheap!

Who is the author's intended audience?

a. parents

b. teenagers

c. children

d. general audience

PRACTICE READING

To get practice responding, read the passage, and

then jot down questions and comments within the text.

You may write your answers in the spaces provided or

on a separate sheet of paper.

Connect with the Reading

- What kind of memories do you have of bringing home report cards to your parents?

- Who helped you to believe in your own abilities when you were a child? How did they help you?

- What feelings does this subject bring up for you?

Think Big!

BEN CARSON, M.D., WITH CECIL MURPHEY

Ben Carson is a neurosurgeon at Johns Hopkins University Hospital in Baltimore. This reading is an excerpt from his book *Think Big* (1992), in which he describes how he was able to meet the challenge of poverty and early academic failure and climb to the top of his profession.

1   "Benjamin, is this your report card?" my mother asked as she picked up the folded white card from the table.

2   "Uh, yeah," I said, trying to sound casual. Too ashamed to hand it to her, I had dropped it on the table, hoping that she wouldn't notice until after I went to bed.

3   It was the first report card I had received from Higgins Elementary School since we had moved back from Boston to Detroit, only a few months earlier.

4   I had been in the fifth grade not even two weeks before everyone considered me the dumbest kid in the class and frequently made jokes about me. Before long I too began to feel as though I really was the most stupid kid in the fifth grade. Despite Mother's frequently saying, "You're smart, Bennie. You can do anything you want to do," I did not believe her.

5   No one else in school thought I was smart, either.

6   Now, as Mother examined my report card, she asked, "What's this grade in reading?" (Her tone of voice told me that I was in trouble.) Although I was embarrassed, I did not think too much about it. Mother knew that I wasn't doing well in math, but she did not know I was doing so poorly in every subject.

7   While she slowly read my report card, reading everything one word at a time, I hurried into my room and started to get ready for bed. A few minutes later, Mother came into my bedroom.

8   "Benjamin," she said, "are these your grades?" She held the card in front of me as if I hadn't seen it before.

9   "Oh, yeah, but you know, it doesn't mean much."

10   "No, that's not true, Bennie. It means a lot."

11   "Just a report card."

12   "But it's more that that."

13   Knowing I was in for it now, I prepared to listen, yet I was not all that interested. I did not like school very much and there was no reason why I should.

Inasmuch as I was the dumbest kid in the class, what did I have to look forward to? The others laughed at me and made jokes about me every day.

"Education is the only way you're ever going to escape poverty," she said. **14** "It's the only way you're ever going to get ahead in life and be successful. Do you understand that?"

"Yes, Mother," I mumbled. **15**

"If you keep on getting these kinds of grades you're going to spend the **16** rest of your life on skid row, or at best sweeping floors in a factory. That's not the kind of life that I want for you. That's not the kind of life that God wants for you."

I hung my head, genuinely ashamed. My mother had been rais- **17** ing me and my older brother, Curtis, by herself. Having only a third-grade education herself, she knew the value of what she did not have. Daily she drummed into Curtis and me that we had to do our best in school.

"You're just not living up to your potential," she said. "I've got **18** two mighty smart boys and I know they can do better."

I had done my best—at least I had when I first started at Hig- **19** gins Elementary School. How could I do much when I did not understand anything going on in our class?

In Boston we had attended a parochial school, but I hadn't learned **20** much because of a teacher who seemed more interested in talking to another female teacher than in teaching us. Possibly, this teacher was not solely to blame—perhaps I wasn't emotionally able to learn much. My parents had separated just before we went to Boston, when I was eight years old. I loved both my mother and father and went through considerable trauma over their separating. For months afterward, I kept thinking that my parents would get back together, that my daddy would come home again the way he used to, and that we could be the same old family again—but he never came back. Consequently, we moved to Boston and lived with Aunt Jean and Uncle William Avery in a tenement building for two years until Mother had saved enough money to bring us back to Detroit.

Mother kept shaking the report card at me as she sat on the side of my **21** bed. "You have to work harder. You have to use that good brain that God gave you, Bennie. Do you understand that?"

"Yes, Mother." Each time she paused, I would dutifully say those words. **22**

"I work among rich people, people who are educated," she said. "I watch **23** how they act, and I know they can do anything they want to do. And so can you." She put her arm on my shoulder. "Bennie, you can do anything they can do—only you can do it better!"

Mother had said those words before. Often. At the time, they did not **24** mean much to me. Why should they? I really believed that I was the dumbest kid in fifth grade, but of course, I never told her that.

"I just don't know what to do about you boys," she said. "I'm going to **25** talk to God about you and Curtis." She paused, stared into space, then said (more to herself than to me), "I need the Lord's guidance on what to do. You just can't bring in any more report cards like this."

> I did not like school very much and there was no reason why I should. Inasmuch as I was the dumbest kid in the class, what did I have to look forward to? The others laughed at me and made jokes about me every day.

26   As far as I was concerned, the report card matter was over.

27   The next day was like the previous ones—just another bad day in school, another day of being laughed at because I did not get a single problem right in arithmetic and couldn't get any words right on the spelling test. As soon as I came home from school, I changed into play clothes and ran outside. Most of the boys my age played softball, or the game I liked best, "Tip the Top."

28   We played Tip the Top by placing a bottle cap on one of the sidewalk cracks. Then taking a ball—any kind that bounced—we'd stand on a line and take turns throwing the ball at the bottle top, trying to flip it over. Whoever succeeded got two points. If anyone actually moved the cap more than a few inches, he won five points. Ten points came if he flipped it into the air and it landed on the other side.

29   When it grew dark or we got tired, Curtis and I would finally go inside and watch TV. The set stayed on until we went to bed. Because Mother worked long hours, she was never home until just before we went to bed. Sometimes I would awaken when I heard her unlocking the door.

30   Two evenings after the incident with the report card, Mother came home about an hour before our bedtime. Curtis and I were sprawled out, watching TV. She walked across the room, snapped off the set, and faced both of us. "Boys," she said, "you're wasting too much of your time in front of that television. You don't get an education from staring at television all the time."

31   Before either of us could make a protest, she told us that she had been praying for wisdom. "The Lord's told me what to do," she said. "So from now on, you will not watch television, except for two preselected programs each week."

32   "Just *two* programs?" I could hardly believe she would say such a terrible thing. "That's not—"

33   "And *only* after you've done your homework. Furthermore, you don't play outside after school, either, until you've done all your homework."

34   "Everybody else plays outside right after school," I said, unable to think of anything except how bad it would be if I couldn't play with my friends. "I won't have any friends if I stay in the house all the time—"

35   "That may be," Mother said, "but everybody else is not going to be as successful as you are—"

36   "But, Mother—"

37   "This is what we're going to do. I asked God for wisdom, and this is the answer I got."

38   I tried to offer several other arguments, but Mother was firm. I glanced at Curtis, expecting him to speak up, but he did not say anything. He lay on the floor, staring at his feet.

39   "Don't worry about everybody else. The whole world is full of 'everybody else,' you know that? But only a few make a significant achievement."

40   The loss of TV and play time was bad enough. I got up off the floor, feeling as if everything was against me. Mother wasn't going to let me play with my friends, and there would be no more television—almost none, anyway. She was stopping me from having any fun in life.

41   "And that isn't all," she said. "Come back, Bennie."

I turned around, wondering what else there could be. **42**

"In addition," she said, "to doing your homework, you have to read two **43** books from the library each week. Every single week."

"Two books? Two?" Even though I was in fifth grade, I had never read a **44** whole book in my life.

"Yes, two. When you finish reading them, you must write me a book re- **45** port just like you do at school. You're not living up to your potential, so I'm going to see that you do."

Usually Curtis, who was two years older, was the more rebellious. But **46** this time he seemed to grasp the wisdom of what Mother said. He did not say a word.

She stared at Curtis. "You understand?" **47**

He nodded. **48**

"Bennie, is it clear?" **49**

"Yes, Mother." I agreed to do what Mother told me—it wouldn't have oc- **50** curred to me not to obey—but I did not like it. Mother was being unfair and demanding more of us than other parents did.

The following day was Thursday. After school, Curtis and I walked to **51** the local branch of the library. I did not like it much, but then I had not spent that much time in any library.

We both wandered around a little in the children's section, not having **52** any idea about how to select books or which books we wanted to check out.

The librarian came over to us and asked if she could help. We explained **53** that both of us wanted to check out two books.

"What kind of books would you like to read?" the librarian asked. **54**

"Animals," I said after thinking about it. "Something about animals." **55**

"I'm sure we have several that you'd like." She led me over to a section **56** of books. She left me and guided Curtis to another section of the room. I flipped through the row of books until I found two that looked easy enough for me to read. One of them. *Chip, the Dam Builder*—about a beaver—was the first one I had ever checked out. As soon as I got home, I started to read it. It was the first book I ever read all the way through even though it took me two nights. Reluctantly I admitted afterward to Mother that I really had liked reading about Chip.

Within a month I could find my way around the children's section like **57** someone who had gone there all his life. By then the library staff knew Curtis and me and the kind of books we chose. They often made suggestions. "Here's a delightful book about a squirrel," I remember one of them telling me.

As she told me part of the story, I tried to appear indifferent, but as **58** soon as she handed it to me, I opened the book and started to read.

Best of all, we became favorites of the librarians. When new books came **59** in that they thought either of us would enjoy, they held them for us. Soon I became fascinated as I realized that the library had so many books—and about so many different subjects.

After the book about the beaver, I chose others about animals—all **60** types of animals. I read every animal story I could get my hands on. I read books about wolves, wild dogs, several about squirrels, and a variety of animals that lived in other countries. Once I had gone through the animal books, I started reading about plants, then minerals, and finally rocks.

61   My reading books about rocks was the first time the information ever became practical to me. We lived near the railroad tracks, and when Curtis and I took the route to school that crossed by the tracks, I began paying attention to the crushed rock that I noticed between the ties.

62   As I continued to read more about rocks, I would walk along the tracks, searching for different kinds of stones, and then see if I could identify them.

63   Often I would take a book with me to make sure that I had labeled each stone correctly.

64   "Agate," I said as I threw the stone. Curtis got tired of my picking up stones and identifying them, but I did not care because I kept finding new stones all the time. Soon it became my favorite game to walk along the tracks and identify the varieties of stones. Although I did not realize it, within a very short period of time, I was actually becoming an expert on rocks.

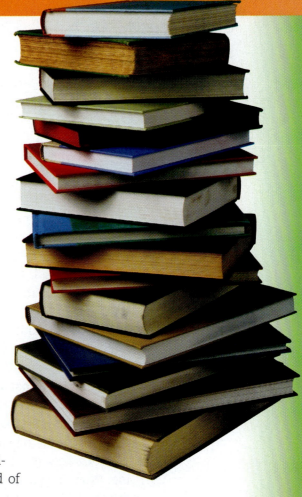

65   Two things happened in the second half of fifth grade that convinced me of the importance of reading books.

66   First, our teacher, Mrs. Williamson, had a spelling bee every Friday afternoon. We'd go through all the words we'd had so far that year. Sometimes she also called out words that we were supposed to have learned in fourth grade. Without fail, I always went down on the first word.

67   One Friday, though, Bobby Farmer, whom everyone acknowledged as the smartest kid in our class, had to spell "agriculture" as his final word. As soon as the teacher pronounced his word, I thought, I can spell that word. Just the day before, I had learned it from reading one of my library books. I spelled it under my breath, and it was just the way Bobby spelled it.

68   If I can spell "agriculture," I'll bet I can learn to spell any other word in the world. I'll bet I can learn to spell better than Bobby Farmer.

69   Just that single word, "agriculture," was enough to give me hope.

70   The following week, a second thing happened that forever changed my life. When Mr. Jaeck, the science teacher, was teaching us about volcanoes, he held up an object that looked like a piece of black, glass-like rock. "Does anybody know what this is? What does it have to do with volcanoes?"

71   Immediately, because of my reading, I recognized the stone. I waited, but none of my classmates raised their hands. I thought. *This is strange. Not even the smart kids are raising their hands. I raised my hand.*

"Yes, Benjamin," he said. 72

I heard snickers around me. The other kids probably 73 thought it was a joke, or that I was going to say something stupid.

"Obsidian," I said. 74

"That's right!" He tried not to look startled, but it 75 was obvious he hadn't expected me to give the correct answer.

"That's obsidian," I said, "and it's formed by the su- 76 percooling of lava when it hits the water." Once I had their attention and realized I knew information no other student had learned, I began to tell them everything I knew about the subject of obsidian, lava, lava flow, super-cooling, and compacting of the elements.

When I finally paused, a voice behind me whispered, "Is that Bennie 77 Carson?"

"You're absolutely correct," Mr. Jaeck said and he smiled at me. If he had 78 announced that I'd won a million-dollar lottery, I couldn't have been more pleased and excited.

"Benjamin, that's absolutely, absolutely right," he repeated with enthu- 79 siasm in his voice. He turned to the others and said, "That is wonderful! Class, this is a tremendous piece of information Benjamin has just given us. I'm very proud to hear him say this."

For a few moments, I tasted the thrill of achievement. I recall think- 80 ing, Wow, look at them. They're all looking at me with admiration. Me, the dummy! The one everybody thinks is stupid. They're looking at me to see if this is really me speaking.

Maybe, though, it was I who was the most as- 81 tonished one in the class. Although I had been reading two books a week because Mother told me to, I had not realized how much knowledge I was accumulating. True, I had learned to enjoy reading, but until then I hadn't realized how it connected with my schoolwork. That day—for the first time—I realized that Mother had been right. Reading is the way out of ignorance, and the road to achievement. I did not have to be the class dummy anymore.

For a few moments, I tasted the thrill of achievement. I recall thinking, Wow, look at them. They're all looking at me with admiration. Me, the dummy! 82

For the next few days, I felt like a hero at school. The jokes about me stopped. The kids started to listen to me. *I'm starting to have fun with this stuff.*

As my grades improved in every subject, I asked myself, 83 "Ben, is there any reason you can't be the smartest kid in the class? If you can learn about obsidian, you can learn about social studies and geography and math and science and everything."

84   That single moment of triumph pushed me to want to read more. From then on, it was as though I could not read enough books. Whenever anyone looked for me after school, they could usually find me in my bedroom—curled up, reading a library book—for a long time, the only thing I wanted to do. I had stopped caring about the TV programs I was missing; I no longer cared about playing Tip the Top or baseball anymore. I just wanted to read.

85   In a year and a half—by the middle of sixth grade—I had moved to the top of the class.

ACTIVE READERS RESPOND

After you've finished reading, use these questions to respond to "Think Big!" You may write your answers in the spaces provided or on a separate sheet of paper.

OBJECTIVE OPERATIONS

1. Who is the writer's intended audience?

   a. general audience

   b. young people

   c. parents

   d. teachers

2. What is the author's purpose?

   a. to inform

   b. to persuade

   c. to entertain

3. Carson got off to a bad start in his fifth grade class because

   a. he'd had poor teaching in his previous school, and he was upset over his parents' recent separation.

   b. he was so shy and afraid of speaking in class that he never answered the teacher.

   c. he felt that he was so much in his older brother's shadow that he didn't want to try to do well.

   d. he been known as "dumbest kid in class" in his previous school, and he had come to accept the label.

4. The word "skid row" in paragraph 16, line 2, most nearly means

   a. the last row in the classroom.

   b. a dangerous place, prone to landslides.

   c. a run-down place for drunks and the homeless.

   d. a small, cramped row house.

5. In order to improve Carson's and his brother's school performance, their mother made them read two library books a week in addition to requiring them to

   a. stop watching any TV.

   b. watch only two TV programs a week.

   c. cut back on their TV viewing and get all their homework done before watching any TV.

   d. go to the after-school program and watch the educational TV programs provided there.

6. Carson's mother was able to get her boys to follow her strict plan because

   a. she promised them that they would move back to their old house if they did what she said.

   b. the boys were afraid that they would be severely beaten if they didn't do what their mother told them to do.

   c. they had been aware that they were failing, and they were eager to follow a plan designed to improve their learning.

   d. it didn't occur to the boys not to obey their mother.

7. Carson begin to realize that his reading could be of practical use as well as be entertaining when

  a. he was able to fix the kitchen sink for his mother by reading a simple book about plumbing.

  b. he finally got a good grade on his reading test.

  c. he could help his older brother learn the names of rocks they found along the railroad tracks.

  d. he was able to tell the class what he'd learned about obsidian from reading books about rocks.

8. According to the passage, Carson's mother was

  a. uncertain of how to help her sons improve in school due to her own limited education.

  b. certain of her plan to help her boys improve in school because it had come to her through prayer.

  c. unreasonably strict, using harsh physical punishment to get the boys to follow her plan.

  d. compassionate and flexible, allowing her boys to follow their own version of her plan for helping them improve in school.

9. What did the boys love to play?

  a. video games

  b. Tip the Top

  c. math games

  d. baseball

10. The word "tenement" in paragraph 20, line 11, most nearly means

  a. two-story.

  b. antiquated.

  c. public housing.

  d. skyscraper.

11. What was the first book Carson brought home?

  a. a book about beavers

  b. a book about rocks

  c. *Bambi*

  d. *Chip, the Dam Builder*

12. When Carson realized how much he knew,

  a. he was disappointed in himself.

  b. other students were jealous of him.

  c. he was proud of himself.

  d. he taught the class for the rest of the week.

1. Carson did not have a bad start in his fifth grade class. True or (False)

2. Carson was known as the "dumbest kid in class." (True) or False

3. The boys were allowed to watch two television programs a week.

   _____

4. Carson checked out books about beavers, squirrels, and rocks.

   _____

5. Carson tells us that his success in explaining *obsidian* in class "forever changed his life." How could that single event have had such a profound effect on him?

   (Answers will vary.)

   _____

   _____

6. What do the words and actions of Carson's mother show about her character? How was she able to get her boys to follow her strict plan to improve their school performance?

   (Answers will vary.)

   _____

   _____

3

Vital Vocabulary

VITAL VOCABULARY

1 | Recognize the tone of the sentence.

2 | Pay attention to context clues.

3 | Make the dictionary work for you.

4 | Use word parts to figure out words and build vocabulary.

5 | Create a system for learning new words.

imagine this

Not knowing the definitions to many words is very similar to learning to read graffiti on walls and bridges. Sometimes, the graffiti artist has made his or her words so large that the words make very little sense to you. It isn't until you step back several feet and look at the art in different ways that suddenly it makes sense, and you understand.

If you don't have a large vocabulary, you may shy away from reading. You may skip words, call yourself names because you don't understand, or give up almost as soon as you start. Words, though, don't have to control you. They are small things made up of little letters. They only appear big and scary because you haven't learned the right tricks to help you figure out a word's definition. You haven't learned to back up and consider the word in different ways.

Think FIRST

- What clues do you use to get the gist of something? Do you consider examples or contrasts or use logic?

- Do you and your friends add parts of words to other words, such as saying, "He is such a pseudo-boyfriend"? Do you ever use parts of words to create new words?

- What are some fun new words you have found in the dictionary? Have you used them in a sentence yet?

Instructor Tip
Ask students whether they ask someone what a word means if they do not know. Ask whether how not knowing a word makes them feel. If they do not know a word and they do not ask about it, how does that make them feel? What can they do to change this?

INTRODUCTION TO THE NEW STRATEGY
Vital Vocabulary

Instructor Tip
Ask students whether, when told to look something up, they actually do. If they do, why? (Was the dictionary conveniently nearby? Did they "google" it?) If they don't, why?

Have you ever misunderstood something because you weren't familiar with the words?

connect now

Connect Now, Strategy 1, and *Respond,* Strategy 2, help you to be *involved* in a reading. However, difficult vocabulary can get in the way of your responding to the writer. When you're in the middle of reading something for a college course, every other word may seem unfamiliar to you. Strategy 3— *Vital Vocabulary*—gives you a process for dealing with unfamiliar words so that you can understand what the writer is saying.

This strategy helps you understand unfamiliar vocabulary so that you can remove "language barriers" between you and the writer. First, the strategy teaches you about the sound of the author's words, also known as tone. Then it gives you three ways to figure out word meanings. It also shows you how to develop your own system for expanding your vocabulary.

Tone, or the Author's Voice

Consider this phrase: "What are you going to do now?" It probably has very little meaning to you as it is. However, suppose that your friend asks this of you after you have won a million dollars in the lottery: "What are you going to do now?" Or, suppose that your friend asks this after you have failed your algebra test, again, and you have to tell your parents: "What are you going to do now?" Or, suppose that you say this to a nurse who is about to give you an injection: "What are you going to

The tone used by people in customer service has affected writer Nancy Friedman's shopping experiences. Have you ever experienced anything similar?

Your Mom was right. It's not what you say, but how you say it. Several times while out shopping recently, I've been told things that, frankly, weren't that bad, but the tone of voice was *so* wrong. I walked away not wanting to do business with that company anymore. It reminded me of that game we played a long time ago. You take one sentence and emphasize each word one at a time every time you say the sentence. Something like this:

> *I* love my job.
> I *love* my job.
> I love *my* job.
> I love my *job.*

You can take most sentences and do that. Point being, the way we emphasize and use our tone of voice means a whole lot in the customer service arena. Think of all the 'tones' and deliveries we can use. A few that come to mind are:

Bored
Happy
Sad
Angry
Terrified
Worried
Unconcerned
Hurt
Inconsiderate
Shocked

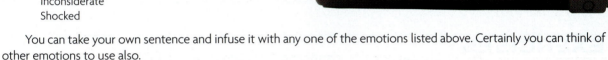

You can take your own sentence and infuse it with any one of the emotions listed above. Certainly you can think of other emotions to use also.

Obviously, there are various tones we don't want to use in certain situations. As basic as this sounds, we cannot forget that our voice is a key instrument delivering customer service.

Let's go back to the opening paragraph—and my true story. I had gone into a store and purchased an item. When the clerk told me the amount, I wrote out a check. He took it and looked up my account. Without even looking up at me he said, "If you're *gonna* write a check, I *have* to see a picture ID." The tone he used was rather threatening in my perception. I'd been a customer there a long time and this was the first time I'd been asked for ID. I immediately made a decision not to return there any more.

There were several ways he could have told me he needed ID. Especially since he saw from the database, which he found prior to my handing him the check, that I had been a frequent customer.

He *could* have said, "Mrs. Friedman, I see you're on the database and shop here often. Most clerks know you. However, I've only been here three days and haven't met everyone yet. If I can get your ID this time, next time I'll recognize you."

That's just one way. Gosh, you even feel the difference just by reading the words. See the difference? More importantly, I'm sure you could hear the difference.

At the other end of the customer service spectrum, I went into a jewelry store the other day to pick up an item. When I said to the owner, who does know me, that I was here to pick up my watch, I could sense he seemed to blank out on my name. With a big smile he said, "Good, glad to get it. By the way, which name will that be under?" A class act.

So practice using your most positive tone with which to talk to customers. Then, practice saying positive things. It works wonders.

Friedman, Nancy. "Watch That Tone of Voice." *My Article Archive.com.* 2005. 4 June 2009. Available: www.myarticlearchive.com/articles/6/206.htm

do now?" Each time, the phrase was said with a different tone, or voice. You may not have paid as much attention to the words as to the way those words sounded. Tone, or voice, reveals a person's true feelings and attitude.

When was the last time you made a mistake at your job? A coworker may have seen you make that mistake, such as spilling dirty mop water all

Instructor Tip
Have students say this sentence aloud: "I don't have to go to school today." Have them repeat the sentence but put emphasis on a different word each time: *I* don't have to. . . . ; I *don't* have . . . ; I don't *have* . . . Ask them how changing the emphasis on each word affects the tone, or the sound, of the sentence.

over his clean floor or dropping a tray full of plates he needed. Your coworker might have said, "Great job, you clodhopper!" You recognized from his tone that he was displeased, and although you weren't quite sure of the word "clodhopper," you're pretty sure it means "klutz" based on that tone and your clumsiness.

In a reading, tone tells you how writers feel about a topic, but it also tells you how writers feel about their readers. Your coworker's tone let you know that you had really messed up. Similarly, writers will choose specific details and words to let you know how they feel about their subject matter. Generally, after you have read a piece, you can sum up this feeling in one adjective, a word that describes the tone.

Words that describe tone include: ironic, critical, funny, comical, angry, cheerful, apologetic, optimistic, pessimistic, nostalgic, scolding, disgusted, happy, humorous, witty, formal, and cruel. As you may have noticed, all of these words are adjectives, so you may assume that any adjective may be used to describe a piece's tone.

Tone, a writer's voice, can add meaning to the words used in a statement.

EXERCISES

PRACTICE

To get practice identifying tone, complete the following exercises.

Read the following statements and ask yourself how each one "sounds." This will help you identify the tone of the statement. Choose the word that best describes the tone.

1. "Oh my! Where did you get that black eye?!"
   a. astonished
   b. lighthearted
   c. sweet

2. "Turn off the television right now, and get to bed!"
   a. commanding
   b. negative
   c. convincing

3. "Your bedroom is so wonderful. It is so nice and cozy. You have wonderful taste!"
   a. optimistic
   b. admiring
   c. enticing

4. "The bus is coming. Hurry! You'll be late, and it won't wait! Hurry!"
   a. urgent
   b. encouraging
   c. critical

5. "The weather looks wonderful. It will be a good day for the picnic. Even though it looks like rain, we won't let that ruin anything."

    a. ambivalent

    b. optimistic

    c. pessimistic

6. "Failing an exam is my favorite school activity."

    a. arrogant

    b. sarcastic

    c. displeased

7. "You will be arrested for disorderly conduct if you don't behave yourself in this courtroom."

    a. straightforward

    b. harsh

    c. informative

8. "I don't care what we do or where we go. I just don't care at all."

    a. pessimistic

    b. apathetic

    c. whining

9. "What do you mean I lost millions in the stock market crash?!"

    a. inquisitive

    b. amazed

    c. alarmed

10. "Will you please stop whining and behave yourself? You should be ashamed."

    a. scolding

    b. sad

    c. apologetic

Context Clues

Context clues refer to the surrounding words and ideas that give you hints about word meanings. Context clues helped you figure out your coworker's insult, that "clodhopper" meant "klutz." Your use of the context will be most effective if you learn to recognize four different types of context clues: logic, example, contrast, and definition.

Logic Clues

You can often guess the meaning of a word just from the sense of the sentence, or from the logic of the rest of the sentence and perhaps the sentences around it. In the example, the meaning of the word "prevaricate" is suggested by logic clues.

Oscar had been known to prevaricate *so often that no one ever believed him anymore; his word was simply not trustworthy.*

Instructor Tips

Discuss with students how context clues influence their everyday lives. How would they know school was closed if they showed up on campus on a day they forgot the school was closed? Just coming home, how do they know a roommate is also home even if they haven't seen the person yet? How do they know there is an accident ahead of them on a busy road without actually having seen the accident?

Discuss how example clues influence their everyday lives. Do they use examples to help others understand what they are trying to say? For example, if a student goes on a blind date that went bad, what examples might be offered to prove the date was awful?

The sentence shows that Oscar doesn't tell the truth, so you can guess that "prevaricate" means "to lie."

Example Clues

> **Signal words and phrases for examples**
> for example, for instance, e.g., such as, to illustrate, included are, that is (to say), like, like the following

Sometimes the context gives specific examples that provide clues. Examples are given to help you understand a word or an idea. Phrases that signal an example include "for example," "for instance," or "such as." Sometimes, just a list of examples is given as with the following:

The inn has added new amenities *(an exercise room, a sauna, a whirlpool, and new lounge chairs on the balcony).*

All the words in the parentheses are examples of something that would bring a guest more comfort, so the word "amenities" probably refers to comforts or features.

Contrast Clues

> **Signal words and phrases for contrast**
> but, however, in contrast, on the other hand, whereas, while, contrary to, although, yet, instead, even though, on the contrary, conversely

Sometimes a contrast between a word you already know and one you don't know will tell you that one is the opposite of the other. For example, contrast clues indicate the meaning of "deciduous" in this sentence: "Deciduous trees turn color in the fall, but evergreen trees stay green all year long." The word "but" points to a contrast, and the sentence shows that "deciduous" means the opposite of "evergreen."

Contrast clues are probably the least obvious clues. For this reason, your learning them can make the biggest improvement in your ability to find meaning from the context. Consider the following example:

Dad gave credence *to my story, while Mom's reaction was one of total disbelief.*

The opposing ideas here suggest that "credence" must have to do with believing, since the opposite idea is disbelief.

Definition Clues

> **Signal words and phrases for definition**
> that is, that is to say, or, also known as, to define this, to say what this means, this means that, namely, in other words
>
> **Punctuation clues**
> dashes, commas, and parentheses

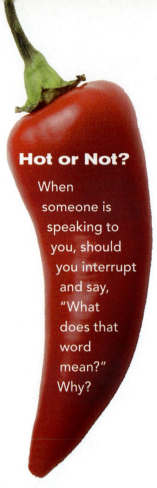

Hot or Not?

When someone is speaking to you, should you interrupt and say, "What does that word mean?" Why?

Instructor Tips

Discuss how students use contrast clues to make decisions. Why do they choose to drive a car rather than ride a motorcycle to school? Why do they shop at discount stores rather than high-end boutiques?

Ask whether students believe the phrase "Opposites attract." If they believe it is true, can they cite specific examples? (Tell them to think about their best friends or their boyfriends and girlfriends while considering this.) Discuss as a class.

Ask the students whether they do anything that requires specialized vocabulary. For example, someone might be a veterinary technician or a certified nursing assistant. What are some terms that people in these jobs use? What terms would have to be defined so everyone would understand? When do students find the need to define certain terms?

THE READER'S EDGE: BOOK TWO

Sometimes words are defined by the writer. For example, a word like "defenestration" is not a common word; therefore, a writer will probably define it for you: "Defenestration, or throwing yourself out of a window, is not an option when your high rise is on fire."

Other times, a word might be defined with a **synonym**—a word that means the same thing. The synonym "everyday" defines "quotidian" in this sentence: "Eating and sleeping are quotidian, or everyday, activities."

Also, punctuation clues and certain phrases signal that a definition is coming. In this example, the writer uses dashes before and after the definition.

He was known for his performance of the fado—*a type of Portuguese folk song—and gained fame throughout the early part of this century.*

How Writers Use Context Clues

Very rarely will you find that a piece uses only one type of context clues, such as contrast or example. Instead, you will find that one paragraph may contain several new words and that writers expect you to recognize the types of context clues used in order to define those new words.

A "blob" face shield looks like an inflated plastic donut that seals well when positioned over the mouth and nose of a patient, unlike a "sheet" face shield, a thin plastic sheet that, when the gauze center is positioned over the patient's mouth and nose, does not seal well because rescuers must remember to pinch the patient's nose themselves to prevent air leaks.

Here, the writer defines a "blob" face shield as "an inflated plastic donut that seals well when positioned over the mouth and nose of a patient"; furthermore, the writer contrasts a "blob" to a "sheet" face shield, thus offering another context clue.

Writers love using words, and they love to show off their vocabularies. They expect their readers to use context clues in order to fully understand a paragraph.

COURTNEY LOVE

Trading Up
by Candace Bushnell

Rock musician and actress Courtney Love, who has been called "the most controversial woman in the history of rock," has been reading *Trading Up* by Candace Bushnell. In this novel, the main character, Janey, makes a habit of sleeping with extremely rich men, hoping that their wealth will help improve her own life (or at least her financial outlook).

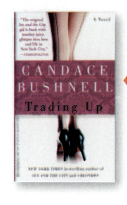

If you liked *Trading Up*, you might also like:

Confessions of a Shopaholic,
Sophie Kinsella

Delivery Man,
Joe McGinniss Jr.

Fight Club,
Chuck Palahniuk

WHAT ARE THEY READING?

EXERCISES

PRACTICE

To get practice using context clues, do this exercise. Write out your answers, and don't use the dictionary!

For each of the following sentences, look for the context clues that suggest the meaning of the italicized word. Then state what kind of context clue you used: logic, example, contrast, or definition. Don't use the dictionary!

> **EXAMPLE**
>
> He was a *landlubber* while his companion had grown up on boats and knew all about the sea.
>
> *someone who knows nothing about being on boats or at sea*   clue: *contrast*

1. The effects over time of too much alcohol can be extremely *deleterious*: there can be a steep drop in job performance, an increase in health risks, and a gradual onset of deep depression.

   harmful _____ clue: example _____

2. The *novice* scuba diver knew he might need help in the water because this was his first time diving.

   new, beginner _____ clue: logic _____

3. He tried to *ingratiate* himself (make himself pleasing to us) to no avail.

   make himself pleasing _____ clue: definition _____

4. The professor's *nefarious* activities became well known to the public, whereas his brother's excellent and helpful works went unnoticed.

   wicked and evil _____ clue: contrast _____

5. The parents *munificently* rewarded the child for any good behavior, giving him expensive presents and large amounts of spending money.

   generously _____ clue: example _____

6. She grew frightened at the *insouciance* of the tourists who allowed their children to climb high on the rocks without seeming to notice the danger of falling.

   indifference _____ clue: logic _____

7. Some people express their thoughts using few words; others are *verbose*.

   wordy _____ clue: contrast _____

8. Some instances of the *harrowing* experiences faced by all parents are losing a child in a crowded store, finding her playing with matches, or suddenly seeing her at the top of a tall tree.

   distressing _____ clue: example _____

9. After the long drought all the crops died, and a *dearth* of food for the inhabitants spread across the land.

   scarcity _____ clue: logic _____

10. Although the priceless vase seemed to be in a *precarious* position near the edge of the mantel, it was actually made quite secure by the special wax on the bottom that held it in place.

    unstable, not secured _____ clue: contrast _____

62   THE READER'S EDGE: BOOK TWO

11. Her entire speech was made up of one *bromide* (trite saying) after another.

    trite saying _____ clue: definition _____

12. Ben is fearless, but his brother Jim never tries anything and is as *timorous* as can be.

    fearful _____ clue: contrast _____

The Dictionary

Make sure you have a desk or collegiate dictionary. Pocket dictionaries can be useful as a quick reference, but they have too few words and limited information about each word. *Merriam-Webster's Collegiate Dictionary*, *The American Heritage Dictionary*, and *The Random House Dictionary* are three widely used collegiate dictionaries.

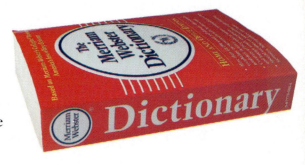

When to Look Up a Word

You may occasionally need to look up a new word while you are reading. Usually, though, you won't want to interrupt your response to the writer's ideas. As you read, keep track of unknown words. Underline them or make a list. After reading, look the words up so that you can understand the reading.

Dictionary Entries

Dictionary entries are packed with information. Study the sample dictionary entry for *afghan*, a word from Reading 4, " 'See Spot Run': Teaching My Grandmother to Read," to see what it can tell you.

connect now

Do your parents or teachers ever tell you to look up a word? Do you? Why or why not?

The Right Definition for the Context

Many words have multiple meanings, so you need to depend on the context to choose the one that fits. In Reading 4, "afghan" was used in this context: ". . . we would sit in the living room, my grandmother with an afghan covering her knees. . . ."

The sample entry gives four definitions. In this case, the context makes it fairly easy to determine. We can be sure "afghan" is a noun because it is a thing covering the grandmother's knees.

#1. *A native of Afghanistan?* Unlikely!

#2: *Pashto,* we know from the etymology (language history), is a language, so we can eliminate that one.

#3 *A coverlet of wool, knitted or crocheted.* This one makes the most sense. Notice, too, that this version of the word is not capitalized, matching the way the word is used in the reading.

#4 *An Afghan hound?* Not impossible, but there would probably be other references to a dog besides that mention.

"Upside-down e"[b]

Abbreviations[c]
Pronunciation[a]   Parts of speech[d]

Multiple meanings

Af·ghan (ăf'găn' –gən) *n.* **1.** A native of Afghanistan. **2.** Pashto. **3.** afghan. A coverlet of wool, knitted or crocheted in colorful geometric designs. **4.** An afghan hound. —*adj.* Of or pertaining to Afghanistan, its people, or their language. [Pashto *afghănī.*]

Etymology[e]
(the language history of the word)

a. **Pronunciation**—sometimes two possibilities are given. If so, the first is "preferred"; the second is acceptable. The pronunciation key is always given at the bottom of the page.

b. **Upside-down e symbol**—appears repeatedly as the unaccented vowel like **a** in *alone* or **o** in *gallop.*

c. **Abbreviations**—used to save space. Get to know a few common ones like *L* for *Latin, OE* for *Old English,* or *usu.* for *usually.* You'll find a key to abbreviations at the beginning of the dictionary.

d. **Parts of speech**—*n.* for *noun,* **v.** for *verb,* **adj.** for *adjective,* etc. Look also for plurals of some nouns and tenses for irregular verbs.

e. **Etymology**—in brackets, gives you the origins of the word, including what language it came from. Now at least you know that Pashto is a language. This part can also give you a word part like **-logy** in *etymology* (meaning *the study of*) that helps you with the word's meaning.

Many dictionary entries also include a synonym—a word that has the same, or close to the same, meaning as the entry word. Examples of synonyms are: *contented* for happy; *automobile* for car; *argue* for fight.

ă pat / ā pay / âr care / ä father / b bib / ch church / d deed / ĕ pet / ē be / f fife / g gag / h hat / hw which / ĭ pit / ī pie / îr pier / j judge / k kick / l lid, needle / m mum / n no, sudden / ng thing / ŏ pot / ō toe / ô paw, for / oi noise / ou out / ŏŏ look / ōō boot / p pop / r roar / s sauce / sh ship, dish / t tight / th thin, path / th this, bathe / u cut / û urge / v valve / w with / y yes / z zebra, size / zh vision / ə about, item, edible, gallon, circus / œ *Fr.* feu, *Ger.* schön / ü *Fr.* tu, *Ger.* über / кн *Ger.* ich, *Scot.* loch / N *Fr.* bon.

Instructor Tip
Discuss with students connotation and denotation and ask them to give examples of words with different connotations and denotations. For example, saying a book was "cool" doesn't mean the book's temperature has fallen below room temperature; usually, it means the book was good to read.

Sign up to be e-mailed a new word to learn every day. The e-mail will have the word, a definition, and a sample sentence.

connect now

Denotation

Denotation, or denotative meaning, is a word's basic or literal meaning. This is the definition you find in the dictionary. However, we use words in certain ways when we talk to people, and writers do the same. Words can be used in ways other than just their dictionary definition, or literal meaning. Sometimes, a word might have a different connotation than you would expect.

Connotation

Connotation, or connotative meaning, refers to the cluster of suggestions or emotional responses a word may carry with it. These connotations add to the denotative meaning of the word. The added meaning may be positive, negative, or specialized in some way and creates a tone for the piece.

To understand denotation and connotation, consider some popular slang terms such as "smooth" or "hot." If a friend says, "I have the smoothest girlfriend," the girlfriend is not necessarily smooth to touch, as you might expect from the denotation of the word "smoothest." Instead, you pay attention to the connotation of the word, that is that the girlfriend is suave or clever.

Be aware that writers often imply meaning through their choice of words. Watch for words with special connotations. The words with special connotations will help you figure out the author's tone, or voice in a reading. The author's tone will tell you how the author feels about the subject being written about.

EXERCISES

PRACTICE

To get practice using the dictionary, do this exercise. Write out your answers.

> ### EXAMPLE
>
> Read this paragraph and see which definition best fits the context.
>
> Americans have always welcomed some immigrants more readily than others. Not surprisingly, those have been the immigrants who have been most easily *assimilated* into this country's culture. Others, those who have not had that same kind of warm greeting are especially resistant to the notion of America as a kind of melting pot.
>
> *Sample Entry from* American Heritage Dictionary
>
> **as·sim·i·late** (e-sĭm′e-lāt′) *v.* **-lat-ed, -lat-ing, -lates.** —*tr.* **1.** *Physiol.* **a.** To consume and incorporate into the body; digest. **b.** To transform (food) into living tissue; metabolize constructively. **2.** To absorb and incorporate (knowledge, for example) into the mind. **3.** To make similar; cause to assume a resemblance. **4.** *Ling.* To alter (a sound) by assimilation. **5.** To absorb (an immigrant or culturally distinct group) into the prevailing culture. —*intr.* To become assimilated. [ME *assimilaten* < Lat. *assimilare*, to make similar to: *ad-*, to + *similis*, like.] —**as·sim′i·la′tor** *n.*
>
> Definition 5 is the best definition because it clarifies the special use of "assimilate" in relation to immigrants and makes it the best choice out of the five definitions.

Now, read/review the following entries from The American Heritage Dictionary, College Edition *for the meaning of the word in bold in the following sentences. Choose the definition that fits the way the word was used.*

1. There was a **profusion** of anger at the newspaper article that belittled Barack Obama.

    1: The state of being profuse; abundance

    2: Lavish or unrestrained expense

    (3:) A profuse outpouring or display

2. The **quotidian** display of affection by Julie's boyfriend was growing dull.

    (1:) Recurring daily

    2: Everyday; commonplace

3. The **upheaval** of cumulous clouds is what starts a rainstorm.

   (1:) The process or instance of growing upward

   2: A sudden and violent disruption or upset: "The psychic upheaval caused by war" (Wallace Fowlie)

   3: *Geol.* A lifting up of the earth's crust by the movement of stratified or other rocks

Now read another paragraph about the experience of elderly immigrants coming to this country. After you've read the paragraph, choose the correct definition for each italicized word as it is used in this context.

Elderly parents who are brought here by their immigrant children may sometimes seem *recalcitrant* about learning the ways of American culture, preferring instead to *steep* themselves in memories of their homeland. In reality, they *pine* for the home and friends they left behind. They miss what they were used to, such as the special bread, pastry, or other *delicacy* that they could find in any small shop back home. The foods they find at our supermarkets are an *affront* to their taste buds. To make matters worse, many of these older people are not *fluent* in English, and their difficulty in communicating adds to the impression they give of being unfriendly and *remote*.

1. **recalcitrant** definition 1 _____

   1: *adj.* Stubbornly resistant to authority, domination, or guidance, refractory

   2: *n.* A recalcitrant person

2. **steep** definition 2 _____

   1: To soak in liquid in order to cleanse, soften, or extract a given property from

   2: To infuse or subject thoroughly to

3. **pine** definition 1 _____

   1: To suffer intense longing or yearning: *pined for her family*

   2: To wither or waste away from longing or grief: *pined away and died*

4. **delicacy** definition 1 _____

   1: Something pleasing and appealing, esp. a choice food

   2: Exquisite fineness or daintiness of appearance or structure

   3: Frailty of bodily constitution or health

5. **affront** definition 2 _____

   1: *v.* To insult intentionally, esp. openly

   2: *n.* An open or intentional offense, slight, or offense

6. **fluent** definition 1 _____

   1: Having facility in the use of language: *fluent in three languages*

   2: **a.** Flowing effortlessly; polished. **b.** Flowing smoothly; graceful: *fluent curves*

7. **remote** definition 3 _____

   1: Located far away; relatively distant in space

   2: Distant in time: *the remote past*

   3: Distant in manner; aloof

Word Parts

Sometimes a long word contains a familiar "little" word that gives clues to the long word's meaning. You could guess the meaning of *smokescreen* from the two smaller words that make up the longer one: *smoke* and *screen*.

Latin and Greek word parts, known as prefixes, roots, and suffixes, are the building blocks for thousands of English words. By learning some of these word parts, you greatly increase the number of words you know.

Prefixes

Prefixes come at the beginning of a word. Some prefixes add meanings, such as *in, out, back, before, across,* or *not*. Others add a number or an amount. Here are some common examples:

pre (before): preview, pretest

re (back; again): return, review

un (not): unhappy, unabridged

tri (three): tricycle, triangle

Knowing just a few prefixes gives you a head start on understanding hundreds of new words.

Roots

The **root** of a word gives its core meaning. The root can often produce a clear picture in your mind, especially if you recognize it from a familiar word. For example, **biographers** contains the root *graph*, meaning "writing." *Graph* is the root for familiar words such as "autograph" or "telegraph."

A word's **etymology**—its origin and history—is given in the dictionary entry. Look at the entry to see if a Greek or Latin root makes the word's meaning clearer. Here are two more common roots:

port: (carry) *portable* = able to be carried; *export* = carry out; *port* = place where ships carry things in and out;

dict: (say, speak), *predict* = say before; *diction* = style of speaking; *dictate* = tell someone what to do or to write

Suffixes

Suffixes, which come at the end of words, tell you how the word is used, whether it is a noun, verb, adjective, or adverb. Here are some common suffixes:

-ize shows action: criticize, sanitize, baptize.

-ist indicates a *person* who does something: *artist or violinist*

-ful indicates an adjective: colorful, helpful, grateful

-ly is the usual suffix for adverbs

See the charts on pages 82–83 for lists of common prefixes, roots, and suffixes. These lists will help you immensely in recognizing word parts.

Instructor Tip
Have students look up the words "monetary" and "admonition" in the dictionary. These words share a root, but they have very different meanings. Over time, words sometimes move away from their original definitions.

connect now

What words do you know that have origins in other languages? Spaghetti? Burro? Boudoir? Schadenfreude?

PRACTICE

To get practice using word parts, complete the following exercise.

Each of the following ten words contains at least one prefix, root, or suffix found in the charts on pages 82–83. Follow these steps to figure out their meanings:

- Give the meaning of each prefix, root, or suffix found in the charts.
- Say what the whole word means

> **EXAMPLE**
>
> *synchronize:* syn = "together or with" and chron = "time"; word means "to check to see that you have the same time."

1. retrospect   back, look = to look back
2. intervene   between, come = to come between
3. apathy   without, feeling or suffering = emotionless
4. graphology   writing, the study of = the study of writing
5. fusion   blend, act of = to blend together
6. circumvent   around, come = to go around
7. pseudonym   false, name = a fake name or pen name
8. monotheism   one, god = the belief there is one god
9. biocide   life, to kill = the killing of life
10. telepathy   far, feeling or suffering = to communicate from afar with the mind

A System for Learning New Words

Words don't become part of your vocabulary until you make them your own. Here's a system for doing that.

Deciding What Words to Learn

Your instructor may assign vocabulary lists for you to learn, but you can also choose new words to learn:

- words you've seen several times
- words you are likely to find again in your reading or that you can imagine using in writing or conversation
- words that relate to subjects that interest you

Vocabulary Cards for Studying Words

On the front of a 3 x 5 index card, write the word in context (plus pronunciation symbols if needed). On the back, write the definition, along other helpful information such as you see on the sample cards: simple drawings or diagrams (*profusion*), associations with the sound of the word (*perceive*), or word parts that connect it to related words (*lexicographer*).

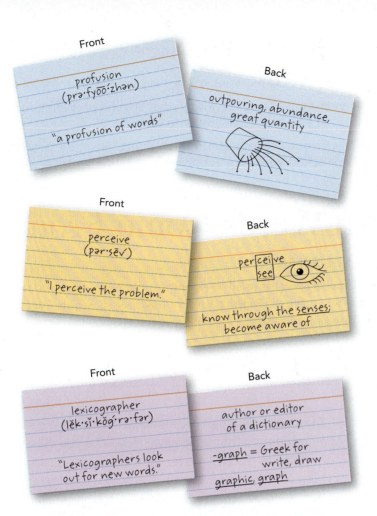

Instructor Tip
Have students write on index cards every new vocabulary word in this chapter. Tell them to learn the words. Tell students that you will have a pop vocabulary quiz on the new words in each chapter. Tell them their best way to study is to learn the information on their index cards. Try to have a vocabulary quiz at least once a week.

What are the advantages of using cards over lists in a notebook?

- It's easier to test yourself without "cheating" when the definition of the word is on the back of the card.
- You can carry a pack of these cards with you to look over whenever you have a free moment or are stuck waiting in a line.
- You don't waste time going over words you've already learned. Once you know the word on a card, you put it aside.
- You don't become dependent on learning words in a set order, as you do with a list of words in a notebook.

connect now

Where can you put your cards so that you see them daily? How about taping them to the bathroom mirror?

APPLY THE NEW STRATEGY
Vital Vocabulary

Now that you understand Strategy 3, put it into practice with the following reading. Use context clues, the dictionary, and word parts to help you understand new words.

Connect with the Reading

- What has been your experience of learning English as a school subject?

- Is English your native tongue? If not, what special problems and frustrations do you find when you're reading?

- Do you have strong feelings about this subject? If so, be aware of how your feelings affect your connection with what the writer is saying.

Where English Words Come From

READING 5   DEBORAH SILVEY

As an author Deborah Silvey has relied on experiences that have worked well for many years with students in her reading and English classes at Diablo Valley College in California. Students in her classes have enjoyed knowing a little bit about how events in the past helped make English the way it is today.

respond

Textbooks and academic writers give credit for material borrowed or quoted from others. Here the parentheses point you to a full credit at the end of the reading, called "Works Cited."

Snail mail, whazzup, chill, e-commerce—these are just a few of the newcomers that lexicographers—the people who compile dictionaries—added to the 2000 edition of *Merriam-Webster's Collegiate Dictionary*. These words join past years' new entries, such as *chain smoker* (1930s), *desegregation* (1950s), *yuck* (1960s), and *heavy metal* (1970s) (Wright 37). While some words fall out of use—and therefore out of dictionaries—English speakers show no sign of losing their enthusiasm for using a great wealth of words. **1**

Over its long history, the English language developed an unusual facility for incorporating new words. By now unabridged dictionaries contain from 450,000 to 600,000 words, far more than are in other languages. There is a special word to express almost anything. Although it makes our language extremely flexible, this profusion of possibilities may seem like an overabundance when you're confronted with so many new words. **2**

Where did all of these words come from? A brief glance at the history of English will provide some answers. **3**

Talking with an Englishman from the Year 1000

The English language developed among the Germanic tribes who invaded England centuries before the first millennium. By around the year 1000, the inhabitants of England were speaking what we now call Old English. With its Germanic roots, Old English would seem like a foreign language to us. For a modern English speaker, trying to talk with an Englishman of the year 1000 would be pretty frustrating. **4**

But if you stuck to the basic words of everyday life, you and the Englishman might do all right. A hundred or so of our most frequently used **5** words have been around for at least 1000 years. These include many of our words for family relationships, such as *mother, father, husband, wife, child, brother,* and *sister,* as well as many words for our quotidian activities, such as *wake, eat, drink, fight, love,* and *sleep.* You and the man from 1000 would also understand the same basic function words: *to, for, but, and, in,* and so on. But your conversation would be limited. Apart from these basic words, you would find little in common between today's English and Old English. What happened to change the language so drastically?

The Battle That Transformed English

6   The biggest transformation in English came as a result of a French victory over England in 1066. For the next several generations, French became the language of the court and the upper echelons of society, but the lower classes—the peasants—"continued to eat, drink, work, sleep, and play in English" (Bryson 54). Thus English acquired a vast new collection of French words but held onto many Old English words for the basics of everyday life.

7   In many cases English doubled its vocabulary—using both an Old English word and a French word for almost the same thing. One of the clearest examples of how this doubling added a helpful distinction can be seen in the words for farm animals and the meat they provide. The animals tended by the peasants kept their English names (*sheep, cow, calf*), while the meat served to the upper classes was given the French names (*mutton, beef, veal*). English gained that distinction, while French did not.

A Borrowing Language

8   The English language never went through such an upheaval again. Believe it or not, the English of Shakespeare's time—the sixteenth century—is considered modern English, because the changes that have occurred since that time have been so minor compared to the earlier transformations in the language.

9   But English never stopped adding new words from other languages. Wherever English people have traveled and traded and colonized, they have taken in new words. From Native American languages came *moccasin* and *raccoon*; from India came *pajamas* and *shampoo*; and from the Tagalog language of the Philippines came *boondocks.*

> English never stopped adding new words from other languages. Wherever English people have traveled and traded and colonized, they have taken in new words.

Borrowing from the Past: Greek and Latin Word Parts

10   The largest number of new words have been borrowed from two ancient languages—Latin and Greek. Latin word parts (prefixes, roots, and suffixes) came into English by way of French, itself a direct descendant of Latin. But right up to the present, English has gone on making up words with Latin and Greek word parts. Why?

11   The answer is in part that for hundreds of years these were the languages of scholarship and learning. Scholars throughout Europe communicated with one another in Greek or Latin. Even up until the beginning of the twentieth century, students at a university were supposed to know Greek and Latin.

For this reason, these languages have been the basis for words to name **12** hundreds of discoveries, inventions, or new ideas. For example, when space travel was first considered more than just a fantasy, scientists needed a name for the people who would do the traveling. The term *astronaut* was coined from *astro,* Latin for star and *naut,* Latin for sailor. Although "star sailor" might have done just as well to name an explorer of space, to some it would have seemed too fanciful, while the Latin-based word sounded sufficiently technical.

Because so many new words in English have come from Latin and Greek, **13** learning the most common word parts from these languages is a good way to expand your vocabulary.

What's the Future of English?

As you can see, English has always embraced new words to commu- **14** nicate both new ideas and slight variations of old ideas. And our society is now changing so fast that we can expect an even greater increase of new words to express the changes in our lives.

These words won't necessarily be borrowed from other languages. New **15** words like those we started off with—*whazzup, chill, snail mail, e-commerce*— are now often derived from home-grown slang or from new technologies.

Where will the new English words come from? Just listen (and read)! **16** If enough people use a word enough times—whether it comes from street slang, the computer business, or the Brazilian dance scene or—you can be sure the lexicographers will be on to it. Watch to see which ones make it into the next Merriam-Webster's Collegiate.

Works Cited

Bryson, Bill. (1990). *Mother Tongue: English and How It Got That Way.* New York: William Morrow and Company.
Wright, Karen. (2000). Keepers of words. *Discover* (March): 37–39.

ACTIVE READERS RESPOND

After you've finished reading, use these questions to respond to "Where English Words Come From." You may write your answers in the spaces provided or on a separate sheet of paper.

VITAL VOCABULARY

Some words in this reading may be unfamiliar to you. Use the methods of Strategy 3 to explain what the listed words mean.

USE CONTEXT CLUES

a. lexicographers (paragraph 1) (use definition clues)

_____

b. profusion (paragraph 2) (use logic clues)

_____

c. unabridged (paragraph 2) (use contrast clues)

_____

d. quotidian (paragraph 5) (use example clues)

_____

USE WORD PARTS

a. upheaval (paragraph 8) (note that the word contains two parts: heave and up.)

_____

b. home-grown (paragraph 15) (note the two words)

_____

c. express (paragraph 14) (note the prefix _ex_)

_____

USE THE DICTIONARY

Choose the correct definition of these words as they are used in the context of this reading.

a. echelons (paragraph 6)

_____

b. doubling (paragraph 7)

_____

OBJECTIVE OPERATIONS

1. Who is the writer's intended audience?
   a. general audience
   b. linguists
   c. professors
   d. wordsmiths
2. What is the author's purpose?
   a. to inform
   b. to persuade
   c. to entertain
3. What is the tone of the passage?
   a. objective
   b. admiring
   c. apathetic
   d. enraged
4. Words such as _child, eat, fight,_ and _sleep_
   a. come from two ancient languages, Greek and Latin.
   b. came into the language due to the French invasion in 1066.

   c. were spoken in the English of a thousand years ago.
   d. were first spoken in the English of Shakespeare's day.
5. The term "compile" in paragraph 1, line 2, most nearly means
   a. put together.
   b. take away.
   c. make a pile.
   d. be with a pile.
6. After the French invasion in 1066, English changed because
   a. so many new words came into the language from the French words used by the French ruling classes.
   b. so many peasants were forced to leave England to work in France.
   c. everyone in England was forced to speak French.
   d. Old English was not considered up-to-date enough for the French ruling classes.

7. According to the article, an unabridged dictionary contains
   a. 450 to 600 words.
   b. 4,500 to 6,000 words.
   c. 45,000 to 60,000 words.
   d. 450,000 to 600,000 words.

8. The word "inhabitants" in paragraph 4, line 3, most nearly means
   a. people who live.
   b. people who live in an area.
   c. places to live in an area.
   d. to live in an area.

9. According to the article, the largest number of new words has been borrowed from
   a. English and French.
   b. English and Latin.
   c. Latin and Greek.
   d. Latin and Tagalog.

10. According to the reading, slang is
    a. prohibited from being included in the dictionary.
    b. the source of problems in communication.
    c. constantly changing and therefore cannot be included in the dictionary.
    d. the source of many new words included in the dictionary.

11. The word "colonized" in paragraph 9, line 3, most nearly means
    a. stolen.
    b. settled.
    c. contaminated.
    d. traded.

12. The English language continues to incorporate new words in many different ways. Which one of the following is not one of these ways?
    a. New words from slang become part of mainstream English.
    b. New words are created by an official committee of English and American lexicographers.
    c. New words come from Asia and Africa, as well as Europe.
    d. New words come from recent developments in technology.

13. The word "scholarship" in paragraph 11, line 2, most nearly means
    a. study or learning.
    b. an award to attend school.
    c. status.
    d. diligence.

14. Scientists came up with the word "astronauts" which roughly translates to
    a. sailor stars.
    b. star sailors.
    c. star ship.
    d. traveler among the stars.

15. Based on this reading, you can assume that there are so many words of Greek and Latin origin in your textbooks because
    a. Greek and Latin words provide the best structures for creating new words.
    b. for centuries Greek and Latin were the languages of scholarship and learning.
    c. for centuries Greeks and Romans wrote most of the books used in the universities of Europe.
    d. even today, university professors write their textbooks in Greek or Latin before translating them into English.

READERS WRITE

1. What kinds of words do we still use today that are basically the same as the ones used in Old English? What are some examples of these words?
   (Answers will vary.)
   _____
   _____
   _____

2. How did the French language influence English after the French victory in 1066?
   (Answers will vary.)
   _____
   _____
   _____

3. Why are so many of the new words you find in college textbooks derived from Greek or Latin?

(Answers will vary.)

_____

_____

4. What was most surprising to you about how English developed?

(Answers will vary.)

_____

_____

5. Why does it make sense to learn some common prefixes, roots, and suffixes?

(Answers will vary.)

_____

_____

READERS DISCUSS

1. What new slang word, word from technology, or word from another language do you hear being used more and more often? Is it in the dictionary yet? Bring the word to class to discuss where it comes from and how you use it.

(Answers will vary.)

_____

_____

2. If you know another language, compare it to English. What words has it borrowed from English?

(Answers will vary.)

_____

_____

Summary

CHAPTER 3

HOW DOES STRATEGY 3 HELP YOU BECOME A MORE ENGAGED READER?

By *responding,* you connect to the writer's ideas. However, that connection may get interrupted when you run into too many new words. Strategy 3—*Vital Vocabulary*—gives you ways to understand unfamiliar words so that you can continue to stay involved with what the writer is saying.

HOW DOES THE VITAL VOCABULARY STRATEGY WORK?

Strategy 3 teaches you to pay attention to tone. How something sounds can add meaning to your understanding.

Strategy 3 shows you how to use context clues to help you figure out words. Using logic, examples, contrasts, and definitions will enable you to decipher the meanings of words that you don't know.

Strategy 3 teaches you how to use the dictionary. In addition, it shows you how to find the right definition based on the context clues of the word in question.

VITAL VOCABULARY

1 | Recognize the tone of the sentence.

2 | Pay attention to context clues.

3 | Make the dictionary work for you.

4 | Use word parts to figure out words and build vocabulary.

5 | Create a system for learning new words.

STRATEGY 3

Strategy 3 offers you a new way of figuring out words using their parts. Identifying the prefix, root, and suffix will help you get a sense of a word's definition.

Strategy 3 gives you ways to learn new vocabulary. This helps you create your own way for learning and remembering new words. An increased vocabulary is empowering.

Key Terms

context: the surroundings in which you find a word

etymology: the origin and history of a word

prefix: the word part that comes at the beginning of a word; it shows such information as direction (in, out, under) and number

root: the word part that gives the core meaning of a word

suffix : the word part that comes at the end of a word: it shows the word's part of speech (verb, noun, adjective, adverb)

synonym: a word that has the same meaning

Think AGAIN >

A logomachy is a fight or dispute over words. From the Greek, the word is made of two parts, "logo" which means "word" and "machy" which means "battle." People fight over words for many reasons, including arguing over the denotation or connotation of a word or its proper pronunciation. Have you and your friends ever engaged in a logomachy, perhaps over how to use a slang word or its precise definition? What strategies did you use to end the argument?

Connect with the Reading

- **What do you know about children who grow up in Africa?**

- **Should people go into poor communities and hand out items such as cameras, computers, etc.?**

Point. Shoot. See.

JESSE BLUMBERG

READING **6**

What happens when you give a group of young African children their own cameras to record their lives? Miracles. Written by Jesse Blumberg, this article first appeared in the November issue of *Smithsonian* in 2007.

1   Klaus Schoenwiese traveled down the road eight miles north of Lusaka, Zambia, through soft hills, still lush from the rainy season, and fields of <u>maize</u> that were beginning to dry. Charcoal sellers <u>whizzed</u> by on bikes. His Land Cruiser turned at a sign marked CCHZ. Along this <u>rutted</u>, dirt road were a few small farmhouses, open fields of tomatoes and a fluttering flock of blue finches.

respond

2   Another turn took him to the Chishawasha Children's House of Zambia, an orphanage and school. In a yard shaded by low trees, Schoenwiese barely had time to step outside of his SUV before he was <u>bombarded</u> with hugs. "Uncle Klaus!" the kids shouted.

Schoenwiese, a 43-year-old native of Germany who lives in New York City, is a photographer specializing in travel and portrait work. He went to Chishawasha this past May with the backing of the New York City-based Kids with Cameras, which sponsors photography workshops for disadvantaged children. The organization was made famous by the Oscar-winning documentary "Born into Brothels," about its work with the children of Calcutta prostitutes.

The Chishawasha facility and its sister non- **3** profit organization, the Zambian Children's Fund, were founded in 1999 by Kathe Padilla of Tucson, Arizona, to serve children orphaned by AIDS. Chishawasha's three new concrete and mud-brick residences—the name Chishawasha means "that which lives on" in the local Bemba language—currently house 40 children, ages 3 to 19; another 50 children attend the school, which goes through the sixth grade. Zambia is one of the world's poorest nations, with about two-thirds of its population of 11 million subsisting on less than a dollar a day. One out of every six adults is HIV positive or has AIDS. More than 700,000 children have lost one or both parents to the disease.

At Chishawasha, Schoenwiese gave the entire orphanage an introduc- **4** tory lesson in photography; but mainly he worked with a dozen students, ages 11 to 18. He said he chose the most introverted children, to "get them out of their shell." He provided them with 35-millimeter point-and-shoot cameras he bought on eBay; and developed and printed the film at a photo lab in Lusaka. Many of the kids had never used a camera, so there was some initial confusion about which side of the viewfinder to look through, and it was a while, he says, before most of the kids were able to "envision" a picture before creating it. Over three weeks, Schoenwiese gave the kids several assignments, asking them to document their surroundings and to take pictures of friends and family members. They also went on a mini safari at a resort hotel's game preserve, snapping away at elephants and zebras and then lingering by the hotel pool and laughing as they daintily pretended to drink tea out of china cups the waiters hadn't yet cleared away.

The idea of the photography workshop, **5** in part, was to help the kids look at their world afresh. Peter, 11, who shepherds goats and likes to build toy cars out of wire, said he loved learning something completely different. Mary, 15, now thinks she wants to be a journalist. "I like the way they inform the world on what is happening in other countries," she said. "And I also hear that journalists speak proper English." Charles, 18, who has a knack for electronic gadgets—he'd rigged up a CD player in his room from discarded old parts—said he would rather be behind the camera than in front of it. Annette, 14, said she hoped that her photographs might someday appear in a magazine. Schoenwiese remembers an intense aesthetic debate with Amos, 13, who really liked a certain photograph he'd taken of a goat. Schoenwiese tried to convince the boy that a different photograph he'd taken of the goat was technically superior—sharper, with better contrast and exposure. Amos was unmoved. "One forgets that in our hyper-visual world these ideas are very subjective," Schoenwiese says.

6   In another assignment, a Chishawasha student would go to a family member's home, and another student would photograph him with his relatives. Schoenwiese placed those pictures in albums for the kids to keep, part of an effort to add to their meager stock of mementos. "As orphans, many of the students have an incomplete knowledge of or are not quite in possession of their own personal history, presence and immediate relationships reflected in photographs." The kids went through the album pages in awe," recalls Mary Hotvedt, Chishawasha's development director. "With all the loss and prevalence of death in Zambia," she says, "these photos showed the kids that they really matter, that they really exist."

7   At the end of the workshop, the school exhibited 250 of the kids' pictures in a large classroom. More than 100 people showed up to gaze at the mounted 4-by-6-inch prints, many pinned from clotheslines. "The kids had a new way of seeing their families," Hotvedt says. "You could see how proud they were to say 'these are my people.'"

8   Schoenwiese features the students' work in an online gallery (tribeofman.corn/zambia), and he's planning to sell prints of the students' work to support future photography workshops at Chishawasha. He's been a professional photographer for nearly two decades, but he says the youngsters—whose jubilant farewell party for him included dancing, singing, drumming and poetry—opened his eyes. "Despite their difficult past and their most certainly challenging future," he says, they "have an especially wonderful ability to live in the present. In that they have taught me plenty."

> "The kids went through the album pages in awe," recalls Mary Hotvedt, Chishawasha's development director. "With all the loss and prevalence of death in Zambia," she says, "these photos showed the kids that they really matter, that they really exist."

ACTIVE READERS RESPOND

After you've finished reading, use these questions to respond to "Point. Shoot. See." You may write your answers in the spaces provided or on a separate sheet of paper.

VITAL VOCABULARY

Some words in this reading may be unfamiliar to you. Use the methods of Strategy 3 to explain what the listed words mean.

USE CONTEXT CLUES

a.   whizzed (paragraph 1) (use logic clues)

_____

b.   rutted (paragraph 1) (use logic clues)

_____

c.   introverted (paragraph 4) (use contrast clues)

_____

d.   daintily (paragraph 4) (use example clues)

_____

USE WORD PARTS

a.   viewfinder (paragraph 4) (note the two words put together)

_____

b.   hyper-visual (paragraph 5) (note the prefix "hyper")

_____

USE THE DICTIONARY

Choose the correct definition of these words as they are used in the context of this reading.

a.   maize (paragraph 1)

_____

b.   bombarded (paragraph 2)

_____

OBJECTIVE OPERATIONS

1. Who is the writer's intended audience?
    a. general audience
    b. audiovisual students
    c. professors
    d. journalists

2. What is the author's purpose?
    a. to inform
    b. to persuade
    c. to entertain

3. What is the tone of the passage?
    a. subjective
    b. negative
    c. informative
    d. pessimistic

4. According to the passage,
    a. many children of Zambia have parents who have AIDS or have died from AIDS.
    b. many children of Zambia are abandoned and live in orphanages.

    c. the photographer wasted his time when he donated the cameras.
    d. the photographer donated cameras but did not help the children.

5. The word "aesthetic" in paragraph 5, line 14, most nearly means
    a. caustic.
    b. numbing.
    c. beauty.
    d. pleasure.

6. How much of the population survives on less than a dollar a day?
    a. about one-half
    b. about one-third
    c. about two-thirds
    d. about three-fourths

7. According to the article,
    a. one out of every six adults is HIV positive or has AIDS.
    b. fewer than 700,000 children have lost their parents to HIV/AIDS.

c. Chishawasha is a boarding school.

d. the children were upset about receiving the cameras.

8. The word "meager" in paragraph 6, line 4, most nearly means

a. few.

b. weak.

c. plentiful.

d. avid.

9. Zambia has a population of roughly

a. 8 million people.

b. 9 million people.

c. 11 million people.

d. 18 million people.

10. After receiving the cameras, the children

a. became more aware of themselves and their hopes and dreams.

b. became less aware of themselves and their hopes and dreams.

c. decided to pursue careers in photography.

d. moved out of Zambia.

11. The word "prevalence" in paragraph 6, line 10, most nearly means

a. something that is rare.

b. something that is common.

c. something that is a preference.

d. something that is gallant.

12. Photographer Schoenwiese believes that

a. art is subjective.

b. art is objective.

c. art is the same all around the world.

d. art is not important to children in Africa.

13. The word "jubilant" in paragraph 8, line 5, most nearly means

a. judging.

b. magic.

c. joyful.

d. sadness.

14. A conclusion that can be drawn from the passage is that

a. the cameras helped the children to express themselves.

b. the cameras were useless gifts to children.

c. the children live very sad lives.

d. hardships make a child very strong.

15. Which sentence best states the main idea of the passage?

a. Teaching impoverished children about art is good.

b. Teaching impoverished children about art, such as photography, improves their lives.

c. Teaching impoverished children about art, such as photography, disrupts their lives.

d. Photography is an art which helps poor children.

READERS WRITE

1. Why motivated Schoenwiese to give cameras to the children at the orphanage?

(Answers will vary.)

2. How did the children react when they first were introduced to the camera? Why were they unfamiliar with cameras?

(Answers will vary.)

3. How has HIV/AIDS impacted these children's lives? Why is HIV/AIDS so prevalent in Zambia?

(Answers will vary.)

4. What are some of the hopes and dreams of the children? What are their current activities?

(Answers will vary.) _____

_____

_____

5. What did the school do with the photographs when the children were finished? How do the children feel about art?

(Answers will vary.) _____

_____

_____

READERS DISCUSS

1. Suppose you could give gifts such as cameras, books, or computers to a community in need. What would you choose to give? Which community would you choose? Why would that particular gift benefit the community?

(Answers will vary.) _____

_____

_____

2. Certain diseases have drastically impacted societies throughout human existence. Sadly, Zambia is no exception. What can be done to prevent the spread of diseases? How can you help?

(Answers will vary.) _____

_____

_____

COMMON PREFIXES		
a (or *ab*): without or not	*ex* (or *e*): out or out of	*peri*: around
anti: against	*hetero*: other, different	*poly*: many
auto: self	*homo*: same	*post*: after
bene: good	*hyper*: over	*pre*: before
bi: two; *tri*: three	*hypo*: under	*pro*: forward
cata: down or away	*in* (or *il, im, ir*): in OR not	*pseudo*: false
centro, centri: around or center	*inter*: between OR among	*re*: again or back
circ (or *circum*): round or around	*macro*: large	*retro*: back
co (or *con*): together or with	*mal*: bad	*semi*: half
contra (or *con*): against	*meta*: beyond	*sub*: under
counter: opposing or opposite to	*micro*: small	*sur, super*: over or above
de: down or showing a reversal	*mono*: one	*syn* (or *sym*): with or together
dia: through or across	*neo*: new	*tele*: far
dis: not, away	*non*: not	*trans*: across
eu: happy	*para*: false	*ultra*: beyond

COMMON SUFFIXES

SUFFIXES FOR NOUNS (PERSON)
-*agog*, -*agogue* (one who leads or rules)

-*ee* (one who is)

-*er*, -*or* (one who takes part in)

-*ist* (one who believes in)

SUFFIXES FOR NOUNS
-*(o)logy* (study of)

-*ance*, -*ence* (state or quality of)

-*ation* (act of)

-*cide* (killing of)

-*ent*, -*ant* (condition of)

-*graphy* (writing of or describing of)

SUFFIXES FOR NOUNS (continued)
-*ics* (things having to do with)

-*ion* (act of)

-*ism* (the belief in)

-*ity* (state or quality of)

-*ness* (state or quality of)

-*oid* (shaped like)

-*phobia* (fear of)

-*sis* (condition of)

SUFFIXES FOR ADJECTIVES
-*able*, -*ible* (capable of)

-*al* (relating to)

-*en* (made of)

SUFFIXES FOR ADJECTIVES (continued)
-*ent*, -*ant* (pertaining to)

-*ful* (full of)

-*ic* (having to do with)

-*ive* (the nature of)

-*less* (without)

-*ous* (full of)

SUFFIXES FOR VERBS
-*ate*

-*en*

-*ify*, -*fy*

-*ize*

COMMON ROOTS

act: do

anthropo: human

aqua, *aque*: water

arch: chief or leader

aster: star

aud: sound

biblio: book

bio: life

cap: take or seize

carn: meat or flesh

chron: time

cogn: know

cosm: world or order

cred: belief

crypt: hidden

culp: guilt

cycl: wheel or circle

dei: god

dem(o): people

dent: tooth

derm: skin

dict: word or say

duc(t): lead

equ: equal

frag, *fract*: break

frater: brother

fus: pour or blend as if by melting

geo: earth

grad, *gress*: step

graph: writing or drawing

jud: judge

leg, *lect*: read or choose

liter: letter

loc: place

log(o): word

log: knowledge or record

lumen, *lumin*: light

magn: large

man(u): hand

mater: mother

morph: form or structure

mort: death or dying

nomen, *nomin*: name

octo: eight

omni: all

pater: father

path: feeling or suffering

pend: hang or weigh

phil(o): like (or lover of)

phon(o): sound or voice

pod: feet

port: carry

psych(o): mind

quer, *quis*: ask

rupt: break

sang: blood

scent, *scend*: climb

sci: know

sciss: cut

scrib, *script*: write

sed, *sess*: sit

sens, *sent*: feel

sequ, *secu*: follow

serv: serve

simil: same

sol: sun

son: sound

spec(t): look or see

spond, *spons*: promise or answer for

tang, *tact*: touch

terr: earth

theo: God or gods

therm: heat

uni: one

vac: empty

ven (or *vent*): come

vit: life

zoo: animal

VITAL VOCABULARY

1 | Recognize the tone of the sentence.

2 | Pay attention to context clues.

3 | Make the dictionary work for you.

4 | Use word parts to figure out words and build vocabulary.

5 | Create a system for learning new words.

PRACTICE PAGES

Chapter 3

To get practice identifying tone, complete the following exercises.

PRACTICE EXERCISE 1

Read the following statements and ask yourself how each one "sounds." This will help you identify the tone of the statement. Choose the word that best describes the tone.

1. "I just learned the best new word. I can't wait to use it!"

   a. encouraging

   b. apathetic

   c. excited

2. "That can't be true! That just can't be!"

   a. admiring

   b. approving

   c. disbelieving

3. "You look glorious, my dear. As sweet as an angel. Here, let me get that door for you. Such an angel shouldn't have to work so hard."

   a. charming

   b. nice

   c. endearing

4. "I bet you can learn how to do it if you try. You are such a smart, resourceful person that you can do anything you set your mind to."

   a. ambivalent

   b. sarcastic

   c. encouraging

5. "Seven people are in the hospital with serious injuries. Two others are in intensive care and have little chance of a full recovery."

   a. mean

   b. grim

   c. ambivalent

6. "I just adore spending this much money on gas for my car!"

   a. displeased

   b. sarcastic

   c. humorous

7. "The library is down this corridor, the first door on the left."

   a. condescending

   b. rushed

   (c.) informative

8. "I have broken my leg before, so I know how bad it can be. The itchy cast, the pain, the crutches. It's awful."

   (a.) sympathetic

   b. stressed

   c. cautious

9. "You are useless and ignorant. I never want to talk to someone as pathetic as you again."

   a. unconcerned

   b. optimistic

   (c.) cruel

10. "I'd had that cat for eighteen years. I can't believe she is gone! What will I do without her?"

   a. teasing

   (b.) sad

   c. angry

To get practice using context clues, do this exercise. Write out your answers, and don't use the dictionary!

PRACTICE EXERCISE 2

For each of the following sentences, look for the context clues that can suggest the meaning of the italicized word. Then state what kind of context clue you used: logic, example, contrast, or definition. Don't use the dictionary!

> **EXAMPLE**
>
> Before I left the psychic reading, the psychic gave me one last *caveat*, a warning not to trip on the step on my way out.
>
> *a warning* _____ clue: *definition*

1. The summer rain was *ephemeral;* it lasted for only a few minutes.

   short-lived _____ clue: logic

2. My *indolent* brother does nothing: He never cleans his room, does his homework, or goes to work.

   lazy _____ clue: example

3. One juror was *reticent* about the case during the break, but the others had no problems talking about it as much as they wanted, despite warnings from the judge.

   inclined to keep quiet _____ clue: contrast

4. Without letting any of the other staff members know or asking their opinions, the boss made a *unilateral* decision and changed the Friday dress code.

   having only one side _____ clue: logic

5. Cheerleaders have a *verve*, an energy and enthusiasm, that keeps them upbeat even when their teams are down.

   an energy and enthusiasm _____ clue: definition

6. Lovebugs are *ubiquitous* in Florida during May and September, but they can't be found anywhere during other months.

   everywhere _____ clue: contrast

7. I realized her requests were *inane* when she asked for some colder ice, a less hoarse horse, and larger rain drops on the trail ride.

   silly, senseless _____ clue: example

8. *Pernicious* is too long of a word to use on the poison bottle; just use 'deadly'—it means the same thing.

deadly   clue: definition

9. The children have *finite* attention spans; even television can't keep them occupied longer than ten minutes or so.

limited   clue: logic

10. Lotty has the same, methodical routine every morning, but her *capricious* sister Lois never does the same thing the same way twice.

flighty   clue: contrast

11. Her comments were *superfluous,* just completely needless.

needless   clue: definition

12. At nineteen years of age, Carl still has some *puerile* behaviors—he whines or cries if he doesn't get his way, sucks his thumb to fall asleep, and stamps his feet when he is angry.

childish   clue: example

To get practice using the dictionary, do this exercise. Write out your answers.

PRACTICE EXERCISE 3

Read this paragraph and see which definition of the italicized word best fits the context.

The Amish are descendents of the Anabaptists, a sect that rejected infant baptism. It *emerged* at the time of the Protestant Reformation. A leader of the Anabaptists was Jacob Amman, who lived in Switzerland in the early sixteenth century. Amman and his followers opposed any kind of state church. They were pacifists, so many refused to fight in wars. Some believed it immoral to vote or take part in government. The modern Amish continue to organize their lives around spirituality and to separate themselves from worldly concerns such as politics and modern technology.

Definitions from www.dictionary.com:

1. to come forth into view or notice, as from concealment or obscurity: *a ghost emerging from the grave; a ship emerging from the fog*
2. to rise or come forth from or as if from water or other liquid
3. to come up or arise, as a question or difficulty
4. to come into existence; develop
5. to rise, as from an inferior or unfortunate state or condition

   Definition 4 is the best definition because it can mean a group's coming into existence.

Now, read/review the following entries from www.dictionary.com for the meaning of the words in bold in the following sentences. Choose the definition that fits the way the word was used.

1. Tired, Lucy made a **fatuous** comment that it was a good idea to put dark clothing in a bleach wash.

   (1:) foolish or inane, esp. in an unconscious, complacent manner; silly

   2: unreal; illusory

2. Parents are supposed to **inculcate** their children with a desire to be polite, but many fail.

   1: to implant by repeated statement or admonition; teach persistently and earnestly

   (2:) to cause or influence (someone) to accept an idea or feeling (usually followed by with)

3. After she broke up with her boyfriend, Maria made a **feckless** attempt at her homework, but she just didn't care about English.

    1: ineffective; incompetent; futile

    (2:) having no sense of responsibility; indifferent; lazy

Now read a paragraph about fascism. After you've read the paragraph, choose the correct definition for each italicized word as it is used in this context.

Fascism is a form of government in which the needs of the state are thought to *outweigh* the rights of citizens. Under fascism, freedoms are *suppressed* so that order can be maintained. Change is discouraged. A fascist government controls almost all *aspects* of life. Such a government, one might say, is the exact opposite of democracy. It stresses nationalism and racial *identity* and regards other cultures with distrust. It is *militaristic* in outlook and quick to declare war.

1. *outweigh* definition 1

    1: to exceed in value, importance, influence, etc.

    2: to exceed in weight

    3: to be too heavy or burdensome for

2. *suppress* definition 2

    1: to put an end to the activities of (a person, body of persons, etc.)

    2: to do away with by or as by authority; abolish; stop

    3: to keep in or repress

    4: to withhold from disclosure or publication

    5: to stop or arrest

    6: to vanquish or subdue

3. *aspect* definition 4

    1: appearance to the eye or mind; look

    2: nature; quality; character

    3: a way in which a thing may be viewed or regarded; interpretation; view

    4: part; feature; phase

    5: facial expression; countenance

    6: bearing; air; mien

4 *identity* definition 7

    1: the state or fact of remaining the same one or ones, as under varying aspects or conditions

    2: the condition of being oneself or itself, and not another

    3: Frailty of bodily constitution or health

    4: condition or character as to who a person or what a thing is

    5: the state or fact of being the same one as described

    6: The collective aspect of the set of characteristics by which a thing is definitively recognizable or known

    7: The set of behavioral or personal characteristics by which an individual is recognizable as a member of a group

5. *militaristic* definition 2

    1: Glorification of the ideals of a professional military class

    2: Predominance of the armed forces in the administration or policy of the state

    3: A policy in which military preparedness is of primary importance to a state

To get practice using word parts, complete the following exercise.

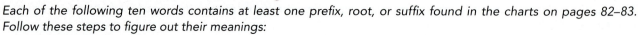

PRACTICE EXERCISE 4

Each of the following ten words contains at least one prefix, root, or suffix found in the charts on pages 82–83. Follow these steps to figure out their meanings:
- Give the meaning of each prefix, root, or suffix found in the charts.
- Say what the whole word means

> **EXAMPLE**
>
> *chronology: chron = time and ology = the study of; word means "the study of time"*

1. culpable _____ guilt, capable of = able to be guilty, blameworthy _____

2. interrupt _____ between, break = to break in between _____

3. audible _____ sound, capable of = able to be heard _____

4. cosmic _____ world or order, having to do with = having to do with the world _____

5. infusion _____ in, blend, act of = a blending in together _____

6. pseudopod _____ false, foot = a false foot (on a snail) _____

7. hyperactive _____ over, do, the nature of = being overactive _____

8. anthropomorphism _____ human, form, belief in = the belief in taking a human form, as in a god _____

9. science _____ know, pertaining to = the study of knowing _____

10. teleport _____ far, carry = to carry from afar _____

PRACTICE READING

To get practice with reading, read the passage, and then answer the questions that follow. You may write your answers in the spaces provided or on a separate sheet of paper.

- **What do you think of the movie and TV violence you grew up seeing? What kind of effect do you think it had on you and other children?**

- **What is your current attitude toward seeing violence in the media?**

Does Media Violence Desensitize Children to Violence?

MADELINE LEVINE

Madeline Levine is a clinical psychologist and former instructor in child development. This reading is from *See No Evil: A Guide to Protecting Our Children from Media Violence* (1998), a discussion of recent research about the effects of media violence on children.

 **respond**

1   Perhaps the greatest concern that parents have about media violence is that their children seem increasingly desensitized to violence. Given the large amounts of violence witnessed under the <u>guise</u> of entertainment, it seems reasonable to ask whether children's feelings as well as their behaviors are affected by the thousands of acts of violence they have seen. Parents, educators, and therapists are appalled that so many children seem to take even the most horrifyingly graphic depictions of violence in stride. As we have seen . . . there is no question that media violence encourages real-life violence among some children. The question of desensitization to violence is equally compelling and more complex, and it probably affects larger numbers of children.

2   A mother consulted me after taking her two sons, ages eleven and thirteen, to see the popular action movie *Demolition Man*. She accompanied her sons because she wanted to see "what all the fuss is about." In a particularly gruesome scene, Simon Phoenix, played by Wesley Snipes, holds up a bloody eye that he has just gouged out of another man's head. The mother reflexively let out a scream and covered her eyes with her hands. Both sons turned to her in disgust and embarrassment and told her, "Be quiet! It's just a movie." Neither son seemed the least bit upset by what he had just seen. The mother wanted to know whether this was a "normal" reaction or whether her sons had become desensitized to media violence. She was worried that their lack of concern about violence on the screen would translate into a general lack of concern about people and a reluctance to be helpful to others.

3   This mother, along with the many <u>stricken</u> parents who find that their children seem strangely unaffected by even the most sickeningly graphic

> Depictions of violence in the media have become so routine that normal people no longer recognize it.

scenes, has good reason to be <u>concerned</u>. Two decades of research on the question of whether media violence can desensitize people have consistently shown that repeated exposure to violence blunts emotional reactions and makes people less likely to intervene or seek help for victims.

University researchers find that their experiments dealing with aggression are being delayed because their student assistants are unable to identify aggressive acts. Graduate students hired to help code aggression on television do not always record pushing, shoving, hitting, and in some instances using a gun as acts of aggression. Research assistants need to be educated that physical assault of one person by another is by definition an act of aggression. Depictions of violence in the media have become so routine that normal people no longer recognize it.   4

What exactly is desensitization? It is a type of learning that makes us increasingly less likely to react to something. When we are first exposed to a new situation, whether to a violent movie, an upsetting argument, or an attractive member of the opposite sex, our bodies respond automatically. Scientists who study <u>arousal</u> and its opposite, desensitization, use physiological measures, such as heart rate, and psychological measures, such as attitude checklists, to determine level of arousal.   5

The relationship between desensitization and learning is easy to see. If we are sitting at home working on a project and it begins to rain heavily, it may startle us at first, but we quickly become accustomed to the sound and are able to go on with our work. If the rain continued to demand our attention, raised our heart rate, and made us anxious, we would accomplish very little. By itself, desensitization is neither good nor bad but simply a type of learning.   6

Very young children are aroused by aggressive scenes on television. Research studies have shown that preschoolers show higher levels of emotion when watching aggressive television programs as compared to more neutral programs.[1] Much like the preadolescent who finds himself hacking and choking after his first cigarette drag, young children are initially distressed by threatening and violent images. This arousal diminishes with repeated exposure as the child becomes desensitized to the violence.   7

The little (superscript) numbers, like [1], refer to sources listed at the end of the reading.

Numerous studies have shown that the more people watch media violence, the less sensitive they become to it.[2] This explains why children seem increasingly capable of tolerating more and more explicit scenes of violence in the media. Over and over, in <u>gruelingly</u> graphic movies such as *Natural Born Killers, Seven,* or *Interview with the Vampire,* it is inevitably adults who walk out in distress or disgust. The large numbers of teenagers in the audience stay put. This is partly because one of the rites of passage of adolescence is to remain unfazed by horror movies. However, it also reflects a lessening of the impact of violence on those who have been exposed to a steady diet of visual abuse from the time they could talk. The more we watch violence, and the less distressed we are by it, the more we risk becoming tolerant of real-life violence.   8

Are Desensitized Children More Likely to Behave Violently?

9   The phenomenon of desensitization has been studied for many years. Public outrage over several well-publicized events in the 1960s and 1970s accelerated scientific study in this area. In 1964 Kitty Genovese was raped and murdered outside her New York apartment building. Although more than forty people were aware of her distress, no one came to her aid. The My Lai trials in 1971 revealed that during the Vietnam War, American soldiers witnessed and participated in the killing of unarmed civilians and children with a shocking level of unconcern. Researchers became increasingly interested in the question of whether people who have been exposed to a great deal of prior violence, either directly or vicariously through the media, might eventually exhibit a kind of psychological and physiological tuning out of the normal emotional responses to violent events.

10   In an early study of desensitization, a team of researchers exposed their subjects to films of a tribal ritual involving painful and bloody genital mutilation.[3] Though initially very distressed, the subjects became less emotionally responsive with repeated viewing of the film. Repeatedly exposing a person to a frightening stimulus in order to lessen anxiety is called systematic desensitization, and it is frequently used to treat individuals with phobias. It is a process all parents are familiar with as they try to coax a frightened child into approaching a feared situation or object. Many a mother, with a fearful child attached to her leg, has slowly approached a neighborhood dog while reassuring her child, "You don't have to touch the doggy, just watch Mommy touch her. See, that wasn't so bad." Over time, the parent's patience and reassurance, as well as the child's repeated exposure to the animal, help the child to be less fearful. Desensitization then can help children engage in activities that were previously anxiety-provoking.

11   Unlike the beneficial effects of desensitization described, desensitization to violence works against healthy development. One particular study can serve as a model for the many done on this subject.[4] This study was designed to determine whether children who watched a

Repeatedly exposing a person to a frightening stimulus in order to lessen anxiety is called systematic desensitization, and it is frequently used to treat individuals with phobias.

lot of television were less likely to be aroused by violence than children who watched little television. Researchers divided the children into two groups: heavy viewers and light viewers. The children watched several neutral films and a brutal boxing scene from the Kirk Douglas movie *Champion*. The choice of a boxing scene is important because scenes of violence alternated with nonviolent scenes as each round came to an end and the boxers returned to their corners.

Heavy and light viewers showed no differences in arousal to **12** the neutral films. However, when both groups were exposed to the filmed violence, the low-viewing group became more emotionally aroused than the high-viewing group. Interestingly, even during the nonviolent segments of the boxing movie, children who watched little television tended to be somewhat more aroused than the frequent viewers. It seems that it was harder for them to recover from having witnessed violence. The scientific literature as well as common sense tells us that it's easier to participate in an activity that doesn't make us anxious than in one that does.[5] It may be exactly this decreased anxiety about aggression that encourages aggressive behavior after watching violent media. Kids who no longer feel anxious about violence are more likely to participate in it.

Does Desensitization Diminish the Capacity to Show Care and Concern for Others?

Studies by psychologists Ronald Drabman and Margaret Thomas show **13** that children who have been exposed to more violent programming are less likely to help younger children who are in trouble.[6] In a study with third- and fourth-graders, children were randomly divided into two groups; one group watched a violent television program and the other did not. The children were then led to believe that they were responsible for monitoring the behavior of a group of younger children whom they could observe on a videotape monitor. The children on the videotape played quietly at first and then became progressively more angry and destructive with each other. Whereas 58 percent of the children who had not seen a violent program sought adult help before the angry children began physically fighting with each other, only 17 percent of the children who had seen a violent film sought adult help before actual physical fighting broke out. The researchers concluded that children who are exposed to media violence may be more likely to consider fighting a normal way to resolve conflict or may be more desensitized to and less aroused by violence.

Arousal is highly correlated with swift intervention in an emergency **14** situation.[7] An experiment that examined how bystanders respond to emergencies found that an increased heart rate and the speed of intervention in a staged emergency situation were substantially underlined. More aroused people came to the aid of others in trouble more quickly than those who were less aroused. As we have seen, repeated viewing of media violence lowers arousal level.[8]

15 In a world in which <u>genocide</u> still comes to us on our nightly news, where random violence has become the most common form of murder in this country, and where handguns are the leading cause of death of large segments or our population, desensitization is perhaps the greatest threat of all. We are losing our awareness of what it means to be human as we become less responsive to human suffering. Although we may never engage in violent acts or endorse violence ourselves, we may not dislike it nearly as much as we should.

Summarized Research Findings

True or false?
- Media violence encourages children to act more aggressively.
- Media violence encourages attitudes that are distorted, fearful, and pessimistic.
- Media violence desensitizes children to real-life violence.
- Desensitized children are more likely to be aggressive than children who are not desensitized.
- Desensitization interferes with a child's capacity for empathy.

ALL OF THESE STATEMENTS ARE TRUE!

Notes

1. D. K. Osborn and R. C. Endsley, "Emotional Reactions of Young Children to TV Violence," *Child Development,* 1971, 42, 321-331.
2. R. E. Goranson, "Media Violence and Aggressive Behavior: A Review of Experimental Research," in L. Berkowitz (ed.). *Advances in Experimental Social Psychology,* Vol. 5 (Orlando, Fla.: Academic Press, 1970).
3. R. Lazarus, J. Speisman, A. Mordkoff, and L. Davison, "A Laboratory Study of Psychological Stress Produced by a Motion Picture Film," *Psychological Monographs,* 1962, 76.
4. V. B. Cline, R. G. Croft, and S. Courrier, "Desensitization of Children to Television Violence," *Journal of Personality and Social Psychology,* 1973, 27, 360-365.
5. A. Bandura, E. B. Blanchard, and B. Ritter, "The Relative Efficacy of Desensitization and Modeling Approaches for Inducing Behavioral, Affective, and Attitudinal Changes," *Journal of Personality and Social Psychology,* 1969, 13, 173-199.
6. R. S. Drabman and M. H. Thomas, "Does Media Violence Increase Children's Toleration of Real-Life Aggression?" *Developmental Psychology,* 1974, 10, 418-421.
7. S. L. Gaertner and J. F. Dovidio, "The Subtlety of White Racism, Arousal, and Helping Behavior," *Journal of Personality and Social Psychology,* 1977, 35, 691-707.
8. M. H. Thomas, R. Horton, E. Lippincott, and R. S. Drabman, "Desensitization to Portrayals of Real-Life Aggression as a Function of Exposure to TV Violence," *Journal of Personality and Social Psychology,* 1977, 35.

ACTIVE READERS RESPOND

After you've finished reading, use these questions to respond to "Does Media Violence Desensitize Children to Violence?" You may write your answers in the spaces provided or on a separate sheet of paper.

VITAL VOCABULARY

Some words in this reading may be unfamiliar to you. Use the methods of Strategy 3 to explain what the listed words mean.

USE CONTEXT CLUES

a. arousal (paragraph 5) (use logic clues)

_____

b. vicariously (paragraph 9) (use logic clues)

_____

c. concerned (paragraph 3) (use logic clues)

_____

USE WORD PARTS

a. desensitize (title) (note the prefix *de-* and the suffix *–ize*)

_____

b. phobia (paragraph 10) (check the prefix, root, and suffix list)

_____

c. genocide (paragraph 15) (See the list for *-cide; gen* comes from *genus*, meaning *race* or *kind*.)

_____

d. stricken (paragraph 3) (Relate this word to *struck,* since it comes originally from the verb *to strike*.)

_____

USE THE DICTIONARY

Choose the correct definition of these words as they are used in the context of this reading.

a. guise (paragraph 1)

_____

b. gruelingly (paragraph 8)

_____

c. correlated (paragraph 14)

_____

OBJECTIVE OPERATIONS

1. Who is the writer's intended audience?

   a. general audience

   b. parents

   c. children

   d. people who study violence

2. What is the author's purpose?

   a. to inform

   b. to persuade

   c. to entertain

3. What is the tone of the passage?

   a. critical

   b. negative

   c. biased

   d. ambivalent

4. In paragraph 4 Levine tells us that graduate student research assistants needed to be taught how to identify aggressive acts because

   a. media violence has become so routine that normal people don't always recognize pushing, shoving, or hitting as aggression.

   b. graduate students are under such pressure that their own aggressive thoughts prevent them from looking objectively at what would normally be called aggression.

   c. pushing, shoving, or hitting are not defined by the researchers as real acts of aggression.

   d. the graduate students had spent most of their childhood and adolescence reading books and studying and were unfamiliar with normal childhood acts of aggression.

5. The term "arousal" in paragraph 5, line 5, most nearly means

   a. fear.

   b. impression.

   c. taking away.

   d. stimulation.

6. A psychologist who helps a person overcome an unreasonable and deep-seated fear may

   a. help the person to see the irrationality of the fears.

   b. use a process of gradually exposing the person to the frightening stimulus.

   c. help the person to forget the fear by substituting good thoughts and feelings.

   d. place the person in an situation that will shock him out of his fear.

7. According to the article,

   a. young children are not affected by violence on television.

   b. young children are aroused by violence on television.

   c. young children do not respond to violence on the playground.

   d. young children do not watch television.

8. The word "desensitize" in the title most nearly means

   a. make one descend.

   b. make one more violent.

   c. make one less sensitive.

   d. make one more sensitive.

9. According to the article,

   a. if we become less sensitive to each other, we become less sensitive to violence.

   b. if we become less sensitive to violence, we become less sensitive to each other.

   c. violence has no effect on our humanity.

   d. violence is acceptable.

10. In the study described in paragraphs 11 and 12, two groups of children watched television violence. The study showed all of the following except

    a. the heavy TV viewers were less anxious after seeing aggressive acts than the light TV viewers.

    b. the light TV viewers were more aroused than the heavy viewers even during nonviolent segments of the boxing movie.

    c. the light TV viewers were less anxious after seeing aggressive acts than the heavy TV viewers.

    d. it was harder for the light TV viewers to recover from having seen the TV violence.

11. The word "correlated" in paragraph 14, line 4, most nearly means

    a. corrected.

    b. connected.

    c. unrelated.

    d. partnered.

12. Researchers Ronald Drabman and Margaret Thomas studied children's capacity to show care and concern for others. In this study they found that

    a. children who grow up in households where parents fight a lot are likely to ignore the fighting that other children do.

    b. after watching TV violence children are likely to seek help from an adult when they see other children fighting.

    c. children who come from stable, loving households are likely to be less influenced by TV violence than those who come from unstable homes.

    d. children who are exposed to more violent TV programming may be more likely to think that fighting is a normal way to resolve conflict.

13. The word "genocide" in paragraph 15, line 1, most nearly means

    a. deliberate extermination of a whole racial or ethnic group.

    b. bloodbath caused by a mass murderer.

    c. dying out of a whole racial or ethnic group.

    d. mass suicide.

14. According to the article, which statement is true?

    a. Media violence does not encourage children to act more aggressively.

    b. Children who are desensitized to violence are more sensitive to personal relationships.

    c. Media violence encourages children to act more aggressively.

    d. Children who are desensitized to violence are less likely to commit violent acts.

15. Levine suggests that one result of our becoming less sensitive to violence is that we

    a. are more likely to become aggressive with others when we become impatient over minor annoyances.

    b. may be less likely to fear blood and gore, and so be better equipped to help out in a medical emergency.

    c. may be less likely to recognize an emergency situation when it comes up in real life.

    d. become more withdrawn and depressed because of our lack of trust of others.

1. Desensitization does not work in combating phobias. True or (False)

2. Children who grow up in a violent household are always violent themselves. True or (False)

3. Before watching a violent program, <u>58 percent</u>_____ of children told adults that a fight was about to occur on the playground.

4. Although teenagers have stayed, adults have walked out of movies such as <u>Natural Born Killers</u>_____ and <u>Seven.</u>_____ (Answers may vary.)_____

5. What new information about the effects of media violence did you find in the essay?

   <u>(Answers will vary.)</u>_____

   _____

   _____

   _____

   _____

6. Why do university researchers have a hard time finding graduate students who can identify aggressive acts? What do research assistants need to be taught?

   <u>(Answers will vary.)</u>_____

   _____

   _____

   _____

   _____

Operation Overview

GET AN OVERVIEW

1 | Use the title as a key to finding the subject.

2 | Flip through pages to learn more about the subject.

3 | Skim paragraphs if you need more information.

4 | Predict what the writer will say.

imagine this

Imagine you are looking at a wall or bulletin board covered with notices. Do you take the time to read each and every bulletin? Probably not. Instead, you quickly look over all of the notices, and if a heading or title catches your attention, you read that bulletin more carefully. Maybe you are looking for a job, a used car, or a place to go dancing. You apply similar skills as you scan the classified section of the newspaper or scroll through a webpage and look for information you need.

When you find a notice that seems to suit you, you make guesses about that job, car or place. (Similarly, when you look someone over, you might "size them" up and make guesses about that person.) When you give a reading an overview, you are doing the same task. Using the big picture to help give you an idea of what's happening in the little picture comes naturally to you.

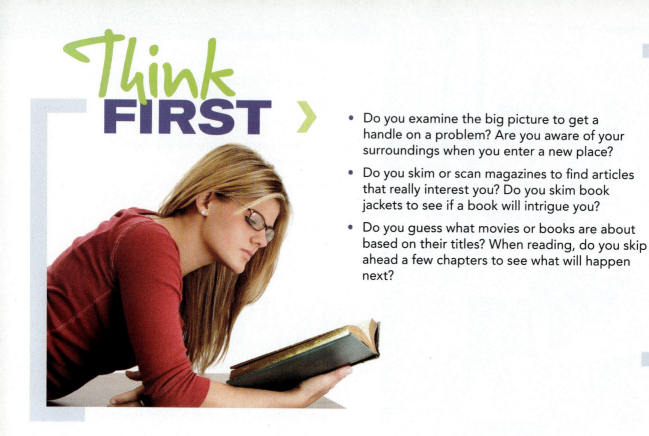

Think FIRST 〉

- Do you examine the big picture to get a handle on a problem? Are you aware of your surroundings when you enter a new place?

- Do you skim or scan magazines to find articles that really interest you? Do you skim book jackets to see if a book will intrigue you?

- Do you guess what movies or books are about based on their titles? When reading, do you skip ahead a few chapters to see what will happen next?

INTRODUCTION TO THE NEW STRATEGY
Get an Overview

Instructor Tip
Ask students why they feel uncomfortable questioning what they read. If it is fear of ridicule or ignorance, remind them that reading will reduce that ignorance. If it is fear of hard work, remind them that reading takes practice.

Instructor Tip
Ask students whether flipping through a magazine to become familiar with it makes the reading material less "scary." Ask them whether they flip through their textbooks before school starts. Why do they flip through reading material? Does it help to ease anxieties about reading?

Getting an **overview** of something means looking at the "big picture" so that you don't get lost in the details. It's the kind of view you get from a skyscraper as you look down over an entire city. You don't see each neighborhood. Instead you get a general—or overall—sense of all the major locations in the area. In the same way, an overview gives you a general sense of the entire reading. You're then able to predict what will be meaningful and important so that you get involved in the reading right from the start and can follow the writer's ideas more easily.

The Title: The Author's Key to the Subject

The title indicates the subject of the reading. Everything in the reading will be about that subject. When you *make connections,* you look at the title to think about what that subject might mean to you. However, when you *get an overview,* you use the title as a key for finding what the writer will say about the subject.

For example, the title of Reading 7 is "What Deprived Children Tell Us about Human Nature." The subject of the reading involves both deprived children and human nature. The title shows that the writer's main concern is to explain what we can learn from deprived children about what makes us human—our human nature. When you start looking through the reading for more information, be sure you see how it is related to or connected to the information you get from the title.

Other Important Clues

Take some time before reading to flip through the pages looking for other important **reading clues.** Various parts of the reading will direct your attention to the writer's ideas. These parts include the introduction, illustrations, and the conclusion.

The time you'll need to flip through the pages will vary. Complex material that you will be tested on may require several minutes. Easier or more familiar material may take just a few seconds. However, an overview saves you time later because it helps you to concentrate and to understand the reading.

Here are the clues you are likely to find in many different kinds of writing. (The following will guide you through an overview of Reading 7 on page 107.)

Headnotes

Headnotes—notes that appear before the reading—often appear in books made up of a collection of readings, like this textbook. Headnotes give helpful information about the author and often tell you what to expect in the reading. For example, the headnote for Reading 7 suggests that the social aspects of human nature will be discussed, since the reading comes from the chapter titled "Socialization" in a sociology textbook.

Headings

Headings tell you what will be discussed, as with Reading 7's headings, which show that both isolated and institutionalized children are part of the essay. Deprived animals will be discussed, too. You might predict that deprived children will be compared to deprived animals so we can understand what makes us human.

Introduction

Look at the first few sentences or paragraphs of Reading 7. Here, the shocking example of Isabelle suggests what happens when a child is isolated. You can expect the reading to tell you more about what happened to Isabelle under the heading "Isolated Children."

How does this example relate to the word "deprived" in the title? What was this child deprived of?

Conclusion

The final paragraph (paragraph 20), following the heading "In Sum," gives a summary of the ideas in the reading. How does the summary relate to the title and the other information you have already gained from the headings and the introduction?

connect now

Have you ever summed up the overall point of a movie or a book to a friend? How many sentences did you use?

MADONNA

The Night Listener
by Armistead Maupin

Given her roles as singer, songwriter, actress, businesswoman, and mom, it's hard to know when Madonna finds the time to read, but she does. Not long ago, she was seen carrying a copy of *The Night Listener*. This novel by Armistead Maupin is about a San Francisco radio personality who develops a cult following, but suffers writer's block after a breakup with his long-time partner.

If you liked *The Night Listener*, you might also like:

The Graveyard Book, Neil Gaiman

Maurice, E. M. Forester

The Catcher in the Rye, J. D. Salinger

Illustrations

In many types of writing—especially in textbooks—authors use visual information to illustrate their ideas. Look for drawings or photographs. They can stimulate your interest and clarify the subject. In textbooks look for charts and tables that help you visualize information. (See, for example, the table in this chapter, on page 103 about what to look for in an overview.)

Don't forget the captions under the illustrations. They often add important pieces of information.

In this reading, what does the photograph of the monkey (p. 111) tell you about this subject? What has the monkey been deprived of? How does the information in the caption relate to what you discovered from the rest of your overview?

One of the best ways to keep track of all of this information is to make a quick list on a sheet of paper.

First, write down the various parts that you considered in your overview.

Notes before reading

Headings

Introduction

Conclusion

Illustration

Visual features

Captions

Then, fill in the information, like this:

Notes before reading *suggest that the social aspects of human nature will be discussed, since the reading comes from the chapter titled "Socialization" in a sociology textbook.*

Headings *show both isolated and institutionalized children and deprived animals are part of the essay.*

Introduction *The example of Isabelle suggests what happens when a child is isolated.*

Conclusion *The final paragraph gives a summary of the ideas in the reading.*

Illustration *the photograph of the monkey (fig. 4.1)*

Visual features *Only the photo*

Captions *Shows monkeys need nurturing like humans*

A quick list like this one can help you with your overview. In addition, a list like this one will enable you to skim more efficiently and predict what a reading will be about.

Skimming

Skimming is the high-speed reading that you do when you skip over many words and sentences—even paragraphs—in order to grasp the broad outlines of a reading. You often do this when you pick up a magazine and look at the table of contents page to see what this month's issue is about. This skimming gives you information quickly. Likewise, for your overview, you may need to skim the paragraphs in a reading to get more information. Here are some guidelines for efficient skimming:

- Look for information related to the title and subject. (Eyeball captions, photographs, and visual features like boxed or bulleted information.)

Hot or Not?

Should you read or skim over legal contracts such as leases or car loans?

WHAT TO LOOK FOR IN AN OVERVIEW		
WHAT	**WHERE**	**WHY**
Title	Just before the reading	Tells (or suggests) subject of entire reading
Headnotes	Usually before the reading (mainly in magazines or collections of readings by many authors)	Gives information about the author and the reading
Headings	Spaced throughout a reading	Tells the subject of a specific section of the reading
Introduction	The first paragraph (or first few paragraphs)	1) Gets your interest and/or 2) Lets you know the overall point
Conclusion	The last paragraph (or last few paragraphs)	1) Gives a final example or comment and/or 2) Sums up the information
Visual features (illustration, photos, charts, tables, maps)	Usually near a relevant piece of information	Shows examples to help you picture ideas; adds interest
Captions for visual features	Under or beside the feature	Explains visual feature; often adds important pieces of information

> *In this excerpt, Thomas Kida, a professor at the University of Massachussetts, considers our love of predictions, especially those of Nostradamus, even though he thinks that we predict as well as we guess.*

Our history shows that we have always had a desire to predict future events. Written records from five thousand years ago indicate that the ancient world was attempting to foretell the future by using everything from animal entrails to celestial patterns.[1] Alexander the Great had his psychics read the insides of slaughtered animals to ascertain future events. This desire still finances a number of activities, from reading tarot cards, palms, tea leaves, and crystal balls, to listening to mediums who supposedly receive messages from the dead or some unseen power. Many people believe that psychics and astrologers who've been dead for centuries, like the sixteenth-century French astrologer Nostradamus, can predict today's and future events, while others listen to a host of more current foretellers. Major companies have even employed psychics in their personnel hiring decisions, and some police departments have used them in attempting to solve crimes.[2]

So is there any value to psychic predictions? People point to some pretty amazing success stories. For example, Jeanne Dixon supposedly foretold the assassinations of John Kennedy and Martin Luther King, while many people believe that Nostradamus predicted both world wars, the atom bomb, Hitler, and the 9/11 tragedy. When evaluating these predictions, a couple of things must be kept in mind. First, we have to ask ourselves, are the predictions unambiguous, and second, are the predictions more accurate than what we would expect from chance.

Consider the following prophecy of Nostradamus that many people believe predicted the 9/11 disaster:

> Earthshaking fire from the centre of the earth,
> Will cause tremors around a new city,
> Two great rocks will war for a long time,
> Then arethusa will redden a new river.[3]

It certainly seems applicable to the Twin Towers collapse in New York City, referring to "two great rocks" and "a new city." In fact, researchers found that 68 percent of people surveyed thought that the verses might have predicted 9/11.[4] But is that because they were looking for such evidence? To find out, the researchers gave the same prophecy to another group of people and asked if it might have predicted the London blitz, where Germany bombed London for fifty-seven straight nights during World War II. It turned out that 61 percent thought the prophecy referred to the London blitz, where "earthshaking fires" and "tremors" were experienced throughout the city." The bottom line is that the prophecy is ambiguous enough to allow multiple interpretations. To further prove the point, the researchers *randomly* selected lines from different prophecies. Amazingly, 58 percent of the people surveyed thought that this scrambled version accurately predicted World War II!

Even Nostradamus experts can't agree on the meanings of his predictions. For example, two noted experts have interpreted the same verses in very different ways. One expert thought that a certain prophecy predicted the role of

---

Kida, Thomas. *Don't Believe Everything You Think: The Six Basic Mistakes We Make in Thinking.* New York: Prometheus Books, 2006. 134-135.
Notes
1. W. Sherden, *The Fortune Sellers: The Big Business of Buying and Selling Predictions* (New York: John Wiley and Sons, 1998), 2.
2. E. Marshall, "Police Science and Psychics," *Science* 210 (1980): 994.
3. M. Yafeh and C. Heath, "Nostradamus's Clever 'Clairvoyance,'" *Skeptical Inquirer* (September/October 2003): 38.

Instructor Tip
To extend the last activity, have students skim the articles to see what they are about. Have them jot down what they think the article is about. Remind them that they should not read the article, just "eyeball" it.

- Read some first and/or last sentences, where the main idea of the paragraph is often given. (This will help you get the gist of the reading.)

- Skip most sentences, even paragraphs. (Look, but don't read!)

- Avoid turning skimming into reading. (Set a time limit, and keep your focus on the center of the page.)

connect now Do you skim the back of a DVD to find out what the movie is about? When do you slow down and actually read the text?

Skimming Reading 7 can help you find out what happens to a child who is isolated. You might skim until you come to the first paragraph under "Isolated Children." There you learn that children like Isabelle are unable to speak.

Emperor Haile Selassie in World War II, while the other said it referred to Henry IV and the siege of Malta in 1565.[6] In effect, the verses are so ambiguous and open to interpretation that anyone can read whatever they want into them, and so, they are veridically worthless.

In addition to considering their ambiguity, we also have to question whether psychic predictions are more accurate than what we would expect from mere guessing. Thousands of forecasters make millions of predictions every year. With such a large number, some of the predictions will be right some of the time. As we have seen, coincidences happen quite often because of the sheer number of events that occur. In some instances, a coincidence will take place when a psychic foretells an event and the event actually occurs. Many people interpret that happenstance as proof of psychic ability. Why? When we test the hypothesis—psychics can predict the future—we naturally attend to evidence that confirms the hypothesis. Thus, we focus on the few times that psychics may have been somewhat right, and disregard the vast number of times they were wrong.

Psychologists Scott Madey and Tom Gilovich interestingly demonstrated this biased reaction to data. They gave subjects a diary of a student who supposedly had prophetic dreams. The diary contained a number of the student's dreams, along with events that occurred later on in her life. Half of the dreams appeared to come true, while half did not. When subjects were later asked to remember as many of the dreams as they could, they remembered many more that came true. When it comes to prophecies and fortune telling, we remember the hits and forget the misses.[7]

4. Ibid.
5. Ibid.
6. T. Schick and L. Vaughn, *How to Think about Weird Things* (New York: McGraw-Hill, 2002), 61.
7. S. Madey and T. Gilovich, "Effects of Temporal Focus on the Recall of Expectancy—Consistent and Expectancy—Inconsistent Information," *Journal of Personality and Social Psychology* 65, no. 3 (1993): 458.

Predicting

Putting together the title and other clues. Once you've become familiar with the reading's organization and various parts, you can make a good **prediction** about what the reading will cover. Use the title as the key to what is most important, but then factor in other ideas you had during your overview. For Reading 7, a quick overview might offer some ideas that connect to the title, "What Deprived Children Tell Us About Human Nature":

- The isolated child, Isabelle, had no contact with other human beings.

- Isolated children don't know how to interact with others and have no language.

- Institutionalized children are also discussed. Probably they have similar problems because of little or no human contact.

Instructor Tip

To extend the previous activity about skimming articles, write this question on the chalkboard: From your prediction, what do you think is the point of what you will read? Tell students that their answer must be one sentence only.

- Baby animals deprived of contact with their mothers can't interact with others.

- Humans need contact with others as they grow up in order to develop normally.

The Overall Point

By putting together the ideas in the title and the information from your overview, you can predict the writer's **overall point** about the subject. The overall point of a reading is the writer's most important message. Just as an overview looks over a whole area or subject, the "overall" point covers—or includes—all those ideas, or major points, of a reading. The overall point can be summed up in a general statement about the subject.

Try using your own words, as if you were talking to a friend, to predict the overall point in one or two sentences. For Reading 7 you could predict the overall point in this way:

> If children don't have contact with other people, they don't learn how to talk or to relate to others. Deprived children show that what makes us human—our human nature—has to be learned from other people.

> Then, as you read the passage, keep the overall point in mind; this will keep you engaged as you determine whether you are correct about the overall point and your predictions.

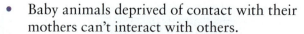

connect now

How often do you make predictions about things like whether it will rain or how well you did on a test?

APPLY THE NEW STRATEGY
Get an Overview

Apply this strategy with the next reading, "What Deprived Children Tell Us about Human Nature," which begins on page 107. Try to make a connection with the article, and then try getting an overview of the reading on your own. See what the title says about the subject, and keep the title in mind as you flip through the pages to find more information. If you need to know more, skim through paragraphs. Then, based on what you find, try to predict what the writer will say about the subject.

EXERCISE: OPERATION OVERVIEW

1. Gather information from the following parts of the article for your overview:

   a. Notes before reading (Answers will vary.) _____

   _____

   b. Headings (Answers will vary.) _____

   _____

c. Introduction (Answers will vary.) _____

_____

d. Conclusion (Answers will vary.) _____

_____

e. Illustration (Answers will vary.) _____

_____

f. Visual features (Answers will vary.) _____

_____

g. Captions (Answers will vary.) _____

_____

2. Skim the article.

3. What do you predict is the overall point? (Answers will vary.) _____

_____

Connect with the Reading

- If children are described as deprived, what does that mean? What do children need that they could be deprived of?

- What gives us our "human" nature? What makes us different from animals?

- What feelings does this subject bring up for you?

What Deprived Children Tell Us about Human Nature

JAMES M. HENSLIN   READING **7**

James Henslin is a sociology professor at Southern Illinois University. This reading comes from the chapter called "Socialization" in his textbook *The Essentials of Sociology* (2000). In this section from the chapter, the author uses specific cases of deprived children to investigate what people need in order to become truly human.

➤ respond

1   The old man was horrified when he found out. Life never had been good since his daughter lost her hearing when she was just two years old. She couldn't even talk—just fluttered her hands around trying to tell him things. Over the years, he had gotten used to that. But now he shuddered at the thought of her being pregnant. No one would be willing to marry her, he knew that. And the neighbors, their tongues would never stop wagging. Everywhere he went, he could hear people talking behind his back.

2   If only his wife were still alive, maybe she could come up with something. What should he do? He couldn't just kick his daughter out into the street.

After the baby was born, the old man tried to shake his feelings, but **3** they wouldn't let loose. Isabelle was a pretty name, but every time he looked at the baby he felt sick to his stomach.

He hated doing it, but there was no way out. His daughter and her baby **4** would have to live in the attic.

. . . Unfortunately, this is a true story. Isabelle was discovered in Ohio **5** in 1938 when she was about 6 1/2 years old, living in a dark room with her deaf-mute mother. Isabelle couldn't talk, but she did use gestures to communicate with her mother. An inadequate diet and lack of sunshine had given Isabelle a disease called *rickets*. Her legs

> were so bowed that as she stood erect the soles of her shoes came nearly flat together, and she got about with a skittering <u>gait</u>. Her behavior toward strangers, especially men, was almost that of a wild animal, manifesting much fear and hostility. In lieu of speech she made only a strange croaking sound. (Davis 1940/1999:138)

When the newspapers reported this case, sociologist Kingsley Davis de- **6** cided to find out what happened to Isabelle after her discovery. We'll come back to that later, but first let's use the case of Isabelle to gain some insight into human nature.

What Is Human Nature?

For centuries, people have been intrigued with the question of what is **7** human about human nature. How much of people's characteristics comes from "<u>nature</u>" (heredity) and how much from "<u>nurture</u>" (the *social environment*, contact with others)? One way to answer this question is to study identical twins who have been reared apart. . . . Another way is to study children who have had little human contact. Let's begin with the case of Isabelle.

Isolated Children

Cases like Isabelle's surface from time to time. What can they tell us **8** about human nature? We certainly can conclude that humans have no natural language, for Isabelle, and others like her, are unable to speak.

But maybe Isabelle was not normal. This is what people first thought, **9** for she scored practically zero on an intelligence test. But in a few months, after intensive language training, Isabelle was able to speak in short sentences. In about a year, she could write a few words, do simple addition, and retell stories after hearing them. Seven months later, she had a vocabulary of almost 2,000 words. It took only two years for Isabelle to reach the normal intellectual level for her age. She then went on to school, where she was "bright, cheerful, energetic . . . and participated in all school activities as normally as other children." (Davis 1940/1999:139)

Institutionalized Children

But what besides language is required if a child is to develop into what **10** we consider a healthy, balanced, intelligent human being? We find part of the answer in an interesting experiment from the 1930s. Back then, orphanages dotted the United States, and children reared in orphanages tended to have difficulty establishing close bonds with others—and to have lower IQs. "Common sense" (which . . . is unreliable) told everyone that the cause of mental retardation is biological ("They're just born that way"). Two psychologists, H. M. Skeels and H. B. Dye (1939), however, began to suspect another cause. For background on their experiment, Skeels (1966) provides this account of a "good" orphanage in Iowa during the 1930s, where he and Dye were consultants:

> Until about six months, they were cared for in the infant nursery. The babies were kept in standard hospital cribs that often had protective sheeting on the sides, thus effectively limiting visual stimulation; no toys or other objects were hung in the infants' lines of vision. Human interactions were limited to busy nurses who, with the speed born of practice and necessity, changed diapers or bedding, bathed and medicated the infants, and fed them efficiently with propped bottles.

11   Perhaps, thought Skeels and Dye, the absence of stimulating social interaction was the basic problem, not some biological incapacity on the part of the children. To test their controversial idea, they placed thirteen infants whose mental retardation was so obvious that no one wanted to adopt them in an institution for the mentally retarded. Each infant, then about 19 months old, was assigned to a separate ward of women ranging in mental age from 5 to 12 and in chronological age from 18 to 50. The women were pleased with this arrangement. They not only did a good job taking care of the infants' basic physical needs—diapering, feeding, and so on—but also they loved to play with the children, to cuddle them, and to shower them with attention. They even competed to see which ward would have "its baby" walking or talking first. Each child had one woman who became particularly attached to him [or her] and figuratively "adopted" him [or her]. As a consequence, an intense one-to-one adult-child relationship developed, which was supplemented by the less intense but frequent interactions with the other adults in the environment. Each child had some one person with whom he [or she] was identified and who was particularly interested in him [or her] and his [or her] achievements. (Skeels 1966)

12   The researchers left a control group of twelve infants at the orphanage. These infants also were retarded but were higher in intelligence than the other thirteen. They received the usual care. Two and a half years later, Skeels and Dye tested all the children's intelligence. Their findings were startling: Those assigned to the retarded women had gained on an average of 28 IQ points while those who remained in the orphanage had lost 30 points.

13   What happened after these children were grown? Did these initial differences matter? Twenty-one years later, Skeels and Dye did a follow-up study. Those in the control group who had remained in the orphanage had, on average, less than a third grade education. Four still lived in state institutions, while the others held low-level jobs. Only two had married. In contrast, the average level of education for the thirteen individuals in the experimental group was twelve grades (about normal for that period). Five had completed one or more years of college. One had not only earned a B.A. but had also gone on to graduate school. Eleven

Their findings were startling: Those assigned to the retarded women had gained on an average of 28 IQ points while those who remained in the orphanage had lost 30 points.

had married. All thirteen were self-supporting and had higher-status jobs or were homemakers (Skeels 1966). Apparently, then, one characteristic we take for granted as being a basic "human" trait—high intelligence—depends on early close relations with other humans.

Let's consider one other case, the story of Genie: **14**

> In 1970, California authorities found Genie, a 13-year-old girl who had been kept locked in a small room and tied to a chair since she was 20 months old. Apparently her 70-year-old father hated children, and had probably caused the death of two of Genie's siblings. Her 50-year-old mother was partially blind and was frightened of her husband. Genie could not speak, did not know how to chew, and was unable to stand upright. On intelligence tests, she scored at the level of a 1-year-old. After intensive training, Genie learned to walk and use simple sentences (although they were garbled). As she grew up, her language remained primitive, she took anyone's property if it appealed to her, and she went to the bathroom wherever she wanted. At the age of 21, Genie went to live in a home for adults who cannot live alone. (Pines 1981)

From this pathetic story, we can conclude that not only intelligence but **15** also the ability to establish close bonds with others depends on early interaction. In addition, apparently there is a period prior to age 13 in which language and human bonding must occur for humans to develop high intelligence and the ability to be sociable and follow social norms.

Deprived Animals

A final lesson can be learned by looking at animals that have been **16** deprived of normal interaction. In a series of experiments with rhesus monkeys, psychologists Harry and Margaret Harlow demonstrated the importance of early learning. The Harlows (1962) raised baby monkeys in isolation. They gave each monkey two artificial mothers, shown in the photograph on page 111. One "mother" was only a wire frame with a wooden head, but it did have a nipple from which the baby could nurse. The frame of the other "mother," which had no bottle, was covered with soft terrycloth. To obtain food, the baby monkeys nursed at the wire frame.

When the Harlows (1965) frightened them with a mechanical **17** bear or dog, the babies did not run to the wire frame "mother." Instead, they clung pathetically to their terrycloth "mother." The Harlows concluded that infant-mother bonding is due not to feeding but, rather, to what they termed "intimate physical contact." To most of us, this phrase means cuddling.

In one of their many experiments, the Harlows isolated baby **18** monkeys for different lengths of time. They found that when monkeys were isolated for short periods (about three months), they were able to overcome the effects of their isolation. When they were isolated for six months or more, however, they were unable to adjust to normal monkey life. They could not play or engage in pretend fights, and the other monkeys rejected them. In other words, as in the case of Genie, the longer

The Harlows concluded that infant-mother bonding is due not to feeding but, rather, to what they termed "intimate physical contact." To most of us, this phrase means cuddling.

Like humans, monkeys also need interaction to thrive. Those raised in isolation are unable to interact satisfactorily with others. In this photograph, we see one of the monkeys described in the text. Purposefully frightened by the experimenter, the monkey has taken refuge in the soft terrycloth draped over an artificial "mother."

the isolation, the more difficult it is to overcome its effects. In addition, a critical learning stage may exist; if that stage is missed, it may be impossible to compensate for what has been lost.

19   Because humans are not monkeys, we must always be careful about extrapolating from animal studies to human behavior. The Harlow experiments, however, strongly support what we know about children who are reared in isolation.

In Sum: Society Makes Us Human

20   Apparently, babies do not develop "naturally" into human adults. Although their bodies grow, if raised in isolation they become little more than big animals. Without the concept of language, they can't experience or even grasp relations between people (the connections we call brother, sister, parent, friend, teacher, and so on). And without warm, friendly interaction, they aren't "friendly" in the accepted sense of the term; nor do they cooperate with others. In short, it is through human contact that people learn to be members of the human community. This process by which we learn the ways of society (or of particular groups), called *socialization*, is what sociologists have in mind when they say "Society makes us human."

Works Cited

Davis, Kingsley, "Extreme Social Isolation of a Child." *American Journal of Sociology,* 45, 4 Jan. 1940:554–565.

Harlow, Harry F., and Margaret K. Harlow, "Social Deprivation in Monkeys," *Scientific American*, 207, 1962:137–147.

Harlow, Harry F., and Margaret K. Harlow, "The Affectional Systems." In *Behavior of Nonhuman Primates: Modern Research Trends*, Vol. 2, Allan M. Schrier, Harry F. Harlow, and Fred Stollnitz, eds. New York: Academic Press, 1965:287–334.

Pines, Maya, "The Civilizing of Genie." *Psychology Today*, 15, September 1981:28–34.

Skeels, H. M., and H. B. Dye, "A Study of the Effects of Differential Stimulation on Mentally Retarded Children." *Proceedings and Addresses of the American Association on Mental Deficiency*, 44, 1939:114–136.

Skeels, H. M., *Adult Status of Children with Contrasting Early Life Experiences: A Follow-Up Study*. Monograph of the Society for Research in Child Development, 31, 3, 1966.

ACTIVE READERS RESPOND

After you've finished reading, use these activities to respond to "What Deprived Children Tell Us about Human Nature." You may write your answers in the spaces provided or on a separate sheet of paper.

EXERCISE: OPERATION OVERVIEW

Now that you've finished the article, how accurate was your overview? Did you miss any important information?

1. Add any information from the following parts of the article that you may have overlooked in your overview:

    a. Notes before reading (Answers will vary.)

    b. Headings (Answers will vary.)

    c. Introduction (Answers will vary.)

    d. Conclusion (Answers will vary.)

    e. Illustration (Answers will vary.)

    f. Visual features (Answers will vary.)

    g. Captions (Answers will vary.)

2. What did you predict as the overall point? How close was your prediction, now that you have completed the reading?

    (Answers will vary.)

Some words in this reading may be unfamiliar to you. Use the methods of Strategy 3 to explain what the listed words mean.

USE CONTEXT CLUES

a.   nature; nurture (paragraph 7) (use contrast clues) _____

b.   trait (paragraph 13) (use logic clues) _____

USE WORD PARTS

a.   controversial (paragraph 11) (note "contra," meaning against)

_____

b.   norms (paragraph 15) ("norm" is the root word for the word "normal")

_____

USE THE DICTIONARY

Choose the correct definition of these words as they are used in the context of this reading.

a.   gait (paragraph 5) _____

b.   bond; bonding (paragraphs 15 and 17) _____

c.   compensate (paragraph 18) _____

OBJECTIVE OPERATIONS

1. Who is the writer's intended audience?
    a. sociologists
    b. general audience
    c. wild children
    d. parents

2. What is the author's purpose?
    a. to inform
    b. to persuade
    c. to entertain

3. What is the tone of the passage?
    a. serious
    b. positive
    c. sympathetic
    d. critical

4. Isabelle lived in isolation until she was
    a. two years old.
    b. three years old.
    c. four and a half years old.
    d. six and a half years old.

5. Isabelle was able to catch up with her peers in her intellectual and social development. Genie, on the other hand, remained severely limited both intellectually and socially because
    a. she had less natural intelligence than Isabelle.
    b. at 13, she had already missed the critical period for language and social development.
    c. lack of proper food caused lasting physical and mental problems.
    d. the training she received was not as intensive and thorough as Isabelle's.

6. In the 1930s, the "common sense" idea about the reason for orphanage children's low intelligence and poor social skills was that
    a. they needed better nutrition and exercise.
    b. they needed better training and education.
    c. they lacked human love and contact.
    d. they were born with lower intelligence and an inability to interact with others.

7. In the "good" orphanage visual stimulation was limited and so was
    a. physical stimulation.
    b. human interaction.
    c. basic care.
    d. infant growth.

8. The word "incapacity" in paragraph 11, line 2, most nearly means

   a. lack of love.

   b. lack of stability.

   c. lack of ability.

   d. lack of mobility.

9. According to the passage, children get rickets due to

   a. lack of sunlight and nutrition.

   b. lack of sunlight.

   c. lack of nutrition and love.

   d. lack of nutrition.

10. When the women in the institution for the mentally retarded spent time holding and playing with the orphaned babies, those babies grew into adults who

    a. succeeded in school and lived normal lives.

    b. had minimal schooling and were happy with low-level jobs.

    c. sounded and acted like the retarded women who had cared for them.

    d. dedicated their lives to helping other orphaned babies.

11. The word "compensate" in paragraph 18, line 10, most nearly means

    a. take away from.

    b. make up for.

    c. compete with.

    d. pass through.

12. The Harlow's experiment proved that when monkeys were isolated for six months or more,

    a. they developed equally to other monkeys.

    b. they easily adjusted to normal monkey life.

    c. they died at young ages.

    d. they could not adjust to normal monkey life.

13. The Harlows' experiment showed that, like human children, young animals' social development depends most on

    a. good nutrition.

    b. a quiet, protected environment.

    c. close physical contact with a mother or mother substitute.

    d. frequent pretend fights with their peers.

14. According to the passage, without warm interactions, babies aren't

    a. nice.

    b. warm.

    c. friendly.

    d. natural.

15. Henslin tells us that "society makes us human." He supports his statement by showing that children raised in isolation

    a. can survive even under horrifying conditions.

    b. are unable to learn adequate language or to interact normally with others.

    c. depend on the rest of society to get along in life.

    d. must have superior intelligence in order to make up for being isolated.

READERS WRITE

1. Why was Isabelle able to catch up with her peers in her intellectual and social development, whereas Genie remained severely limited both intellectually and socially?

   (Answers will vary.)

   _____

   _____

   _____

2. What was the "common sense" reason in the 1930s for orphanage children's low intelligence and poor social skills?

   (Answers will vary.)

   _____

   _____

   _____

3. What did the women in the institution for the mentally retarded provide for the babies that the standard orphanages did not? What effect did this different treatment have on the babies' later development?

(Answers will vary.)

_____

_____

4. Why did the baby monkeys prefer the "mother" that was covered with terrycloth even though the wire-covered "mother" was the one with the food? How is this animal experiment related to the other ideas in this reading about human children's needs?

(Answers will vary.)

_____

_____

5. Paragraph 7 asks, "How much of people's characteristics comes from "nature" (heredity) and how much from "nurture" (the social environment, contact with others)?" What do the cases of deprived children tell us about the role of "nurture" in developing the characteristics that make us most human?

(Answers will vary.)

_____

_____

_____

READERS DISCUSS

1. Did this reading change your ideas about what children need in order to become fully developed human beings? Explain why or why not.

(Answers will vary.)

_____

_____

_____

2. Henslin concludes by saying, "Society makes us human." How does this reading support that statement?

(Answers will vary.)

_____

_____

_____

Summary

CHAPTER 4

HOW DOES STRATEGY 4 HELP YOU BECOME A MORE ENGAGED READER?

When you **make connections,** you take a quick look at yourself and the experiences you bring to the subject of the reading. When you **get an overview,** you take a quick look at information in the pages of the reading. The overview tells you what to expect ahead of time so that you become more involved in a dialogue with the writer as you read. Your predictions help you follow the writer's ideas and stimulate you to **respond** to them.

HOW DOES THE GET AN OVERVIEW STRATEGY WORK?

Getting an overview gives you ways to glance over an entire reading in a short time and get a good sense of what the writer will cover.

GET AN OVERVIEW

1 | Use the title as a key to finding the subject.

2 | Flip through pages to learn more about the subject.

3 | Skim paragraphs if you need more information.

4 | Predict what the writer will say.

Strategy 4 teaches you to use the title to find the subject of the reading. The title should tell you what the reading is about.

Strategy 4 reminds you to flip through a reading to become familiar with it. Thumbing through the pages lets you know where you can find important information such as headings, captions, or photographs.

Strategy 4 shows you how to skim through a reading to gather information quickly. Skimming gives you more information for your overview.

Strategy 4 teaches you to predict what a writer will say. By using information from your overview, you can make a guess as to what the overall point will be.

Key Terms

headnotes: notes before a reading about the author and the reading

overall point: the writer's most important message that covers—or includes—all the other ideas in the reading

overview: a general sense of an entire subject, indicating what will be important in a reading

prediction: using all the elements in the reading to see what to expect

reading clues: parts of the reading, such as the title, headings, introduction, and conclusion, that point to important information

skimming: high-speed reading just to grasp the broad outlines of a reading

Think AGAIN ›

When a friend lends you a book, you flip through it almost immediately. You read the book jacket, check the author's page, look at the blurbs on the back, or peruse the table of contents. You get a quick idea about the book, but you might also ask your friend questions like, "Did you like it? Was it similar to the other book you told me about? Do the characters live through to the end?" You make predictions, such as, "I bet it will be better than the last book" or "I hope the villain gets it this time." You probably get similar overviews of movies or albums. Where else are overviews beneficial?

MASTERY TEST

Before reading "The Good Person," Reading 8,

connect with the text and get an overview.

Skimming should be a part of your overview this time, since the meaning of the headings in Reading 8 is not as obvious as in Reading 7. For example, a quick skimming of the first page will give you the following pieces of information:

- Children were discussing what makes a good person.
- These were children in an elementary school where the author taught.
- He used a story, called "Starry Time" to think about "goodness."
- The story has to do with there being no stars in the sky.

Now, put together information from skimming and the rest of your overview to see what Coles will say about the subject. Try using your own words to predict the overall point of the reading.

EXERCISE: OPERATION OVERVIEW

1. Using the article, gather the following information for your overview:

   a. Notes before reading (Answers will vary.)

   b. Headings (Answers will vary.)

   c. Introduction (Answers will vary.)

   d. Conclusion (Answers will vary.)

   e. Illustration (Answers will vary.)

   f. Visual features (Answers will vary.)

   g. Captions (Answers will vary.)

2. Skim the article.

3. What do you predict is the overall point? (Answers will vary.)

Connect with the Reading

- How would you define "a good person"?

- How did you learn about being "a good person" as a child? What kind of moral lessons did you get at home, at school, or with your friends?

- What feelings do you have about the whole idea of teaching children to be "good"?

The Good Person

READING 8

ROBERT COLES

Robert Coles, a professor of psychiatry at Harvard Medical School, writes frequently about child psychology. This reading comes from *The Moral Intelligence of Children* (1997), in which Coles analyzes the ways in which children develop their ideas about moral behavior.

respond

For many years I have been asking children to tell me their ideas about what makes for a good person. Rather obviously, those children have varied in their responsive definitions, some emphasizing a person's interest in reaching out to and assisting others, some putting stress on a person's religious beliefs, some pointing out the importance of certain secular values such as independence of mind, civic responsibility, commitment to work, to a solid family life.

In an elementary school class I taught, twenty-eight children sat before me, their desks lined up row upon row; I remember how they reacted when we had a discussion of "goodness." We exchanged moral scenarios. At one point I told the children a story; it had been written by a college student of mine, Howie Axelrod, a young man of great intelligence and heart, both. The story, a moral fable, if you will, was called "Starry Time," and it went like this:

> Once upon a time, there were no stars in the sky.
> Only the lonely moon shone at night. And since it was sad and alone, it gave off very little light.
> One person had all the stars. He was not a powerful king. And she was not an evil witch. But a little girl named Stella. When Stella's mother turned off her lights at night, Stella's ceiling turned into sparkles brighter than any Christmas tree.
> Sometimes she felt as though she was looking down from an airplane over a city of lights.
> Stella loved falling asleep under her starry ceiling. She always had bright and wonderful dreams. One day in school, she overheard some boys and girls talking. One boy said, "I can't sleep at night. My room is very dark and I get scared."
> A girl agreed, "Me too. That sad old moon doesn't do any good. My room is as dark as a closet."

Stella felt bad. She hadn't known that she was the only one with stars in her room.

That night, when her mother turned off the lights, her ceiling lit up like the lights of a city. But Stella could not sleep. She thought about all of the boys and girls who were lying awake in the dark, and she felt sad.

She climbed out of bed, and opened her window. The moon hung sadly in the sky.

"Moon, why don't you give off more light?" Stella asked.

"Because I am lonely. I have to spend the whole night out here by myself. Sometimes I get scared."

"I'm sorry," Stella said. She was surprised that something as big and beautiful as the moon could get scared just like little boys and girls.

"Plus, I get tired," said the moon. "It's a big job to light the whole sky."

Stella thought for a while.

"Moon," she said, "Would my stars help to keep you company?"

"Yes," said the moon.

"And would they make the sky brighter?"

"Yes, and they would make me happy."

Stella stood back from her window. She looked up at her stars.

"You should go and help the moon," she said. "I will miss you, but every night I will look out my window and see you in the sky." She wiped a tear from her eye. "Now, go."

With that, the stars burst from her ceiling and whirled around with a dazzling glow until they gained enough speed to shoot towards the moon. They streamed out of her window, and fanned out across the sky. It was the most beautiful sight Stella had ever seen.

From then on, the nights were brighter. The moon had many friends, and he beamed with happiness.

And with the light of the new night sky, grandmothers and grandfathers sat outside on their porches telling stories about the old days. And young couples strolled hand in hand along the streets.

And best of all, Stella could sit outside with a friend, and they could watch the stars together.

3   The children were enchanted. They wanted to hear the story again. They wanted me to make copies of the story, so that they could take it home, read it to their parents, or ask their parents to read it aloud to them. They were anxious to discuss the story, <u>glean</u> from it a message, a line of thinking. Most of all, they were touched by Stella's gesture, and by her capacity, her willingness, to think of others, and more than that, to give of her world so that the world of others would be brighter. Stella's generosity prompted them to marvel at their own humanity. A girl said, "She was being—she was being good. It was natural—it's what you'd want to do, if you could." Another girl took immediate issue, wondered whether "natural"

is quite the word to use, since, she observed, "Lots of people wouldn't want to share those stars with anyone else, probably." In no time, these ten-year-olds were having a spirited discussion of the extent and limits of generosity, an aspect of the subject of "goodness" that we had been exploring with some considerable and (for all of us, I thought) quite instructive determination.

Moreover, I soon learned, "Starry Time," starring Stella, had a **4** stirring life in home after home for several weeks. Parents read it, read it to their children, and talked of it, so that when we addressed it once more (I asked several children to divide it up and read aloud to us their chosen segments), their exchanges were even more lively, knowing, at times passionate. These children began to think of what *they* had in their closets (in their lives, really), that they might want to share with others—and, also very important, of what the consequences would be of so doing.

Words into Action

That last word, "consequences," needless to say, was quite impor- **5** tant: it is one thing to make a list of qualities that in their sum make for a good person or child; it is something else to try to picture oneself enacting this or that virtue, to live it out in daily life—to turn nouns such as generosity, kindness, thoughtfulness, sensitivity, compassion into verbs, words of action.

When that class was over, I thought I'd finally stumbled into some old- **6** fashioned "advice" that I could offer to the parents of children I teach or work with as a doctor—and all of us parents have our moments of hungry eagerness for such advice. Take those nouns that denote good moral traits, and with the help of your sons and daughters try to convert them into verbs: tasks to accomplish, plans for action, to be followed by the actual work of doing. An imagined plan or plot is a mere prelude to a life's day-to-day behavior, yet over the long run of things, the sum of imagined plans turned into action becomes one's "character." With imagined scenarios we are quite possibly setting the stage for later actions, whereas lists of good qualities, of values and virtues, can be rather quickly forgotten, as quickly as they are memorized.

At one point in the discussion of "Starry Time" a boy wondered whether **7** the story might help us figure out how to describe a "good child"—as I've mentioned, I'd been pressing those children and others for some time to help me come up with some useful specifications. "If you read the story," the boy declared, "and you go give something to someone, and it's a good thing you've done—you've given the world a star, and that means you're better than you were before. But you could fall back and forget about the next guy, so you have to keep sharing with others, or you'll be good for one day, and then the next, you're not doing what's good, and that's a missed chance, my mom said." As I listened I thought of the myth of Sisyphus in Greek mythology—with its image of a man condemned to rolling a heavy rock up a hill, only to have it fall down each time, just as he nears the top, and its reminder of the constant struggle to lift up ourselves, as it were, with backsliding an ever-present possibility. And I thought of Emerson's

*These children began to think of what *they* had in their closets (in their lives, really), that they might want to share with others—and, also very important, of what the consequences would be of so doing.*

notion of each day as a god, his way of emphasizing the enormous moral possibilities a given span of time can offer. All of that worked into a child's worried, yet vigorously demanding ethical speculation.

A Good Person

8   Good children are boys and girls who in the first place have learned to take seriously the very notion, the desirability, of goodness—a living up to the Golden Rule, a respect for others, a commitment of mind, heart, soul to one's family, neighborhood, nation—and have also learned that the issue of goodness is not an abstract one, but rather a concrete, expressive one: how to turn the rhetoric of goodness into action, moments that affirm the presence of goodness in a particular lived life.

9   Another child's testimony—he was thirteen, in middle school, when he told me this: "My dad says a lot of people talk and talk a good line—but their scorecard isn't so good, because talk is cheap. If you just try to remember to be polite, and help someone, if you can; if you try to be friendly to folks, and not be a wise guy, always knocking them down in what you think of them, and what you say, then you're off to a start, because it's on your mind (you see?), it's on your mind that you should be out there doing something about it, what you believe is right, is good, and not just talking it up, the subject [of goodness], and to tell you what I believe: if you do a lot of that [talking it up], you're really talking yourself up, I mean, if you don't match your words with what you end up doing." A silence, a few seconds long, and then a brief, pointed—stunning, even—afterthought: "You know, a guy who's out there, being a good guy, that guy (even him!) could ruin everything; he could keep on calling attention to himself, and all he's doing, all the good, and he comes off as a big ego, someone looking for everyone's applause."

10   An accomplished righteousness that has turned self-righteous, self-serving is a risk, surely, for many of us, who can be tempted to wag our finger at others, and not so subtly point at ourselves with a good deal of self-satisfaction. In further remarks, that boy worried out loud and at some length about becoming a "goody-goody" person, his cautionary spin on the subject of "goodness," as we were pursuing it. I still remember that moment, that expressed concern, that time of moral alarm: wait a minute, buddy, give this subject another round of consideration, lest you become smug, priggish, all too full of yourself, drunk on your self-congratulatory goodness, even your enacted goodness, all of which can, Sisyphus-like, come tumbling down morally. Yet another of life's ironies that can await any of us around any corner, even an apparently promising one.

ACTIVE READERS RESPOND

After you've finished reading, use these questions to respond to "The Good Person." You may write your answers in the spaces provided or on a separate sheet of paper.

SKILLS TEST: OPERATION OVERVIEW

Now that you've finished the article, how accurate was your overview? Did you miss any important information?

1. Add any information from the following parts of the article that you may have overlooked in your overview:

   a. Notes before reading (Answers will vary.)

   _____

   b. Headings (Answers will vary.)

   _____

   c. Introduction (Answers will vary.)

   _____

   d. Conclusion (Answers will vary.)

   _____

   e. Illustration (Answers will vary.)

   _____

   f. Visual features (Answers will vary.)

   _____

   g. Captions (Answers will vary.)

   _____

2. What did you predict as the overall point? How close was your prediction, now that you have completed the reading?

   (Answers will vary.)

   _____

   _____

VITAL VOCABULARY

Some words in this reading may be unfamiliar to you. Use the methods of Strategy 3 to explain what the listed words mean.

USE CONTEXT CLUES

a. secular (paragraph 1) (use contrast clues)

_____

b. rhetoric (paragraph 8) (use logic clues)

_____

c. priggish (paragraph 10) (use logic clues)

_____

USE WORD PARTS

a. scenario (paragraph 2) (note the familiar root word, *scene*)

_____

b. prelude (paragraph 6) (note the prefix)

_____

c. speculation (paragraph 7) (note that this word has the same root as *inspect: look* or *see*)

_____

Choose the correct definition of these words as they are used in the context of this reading.

a.   glean (paragraph 3)

_____

b.   ethical (paragraph 7)

_____

OBJECTIVE OPERATIONS

1. Who is the writer's intended audience?
   a. children
   b. adults
   c. general audience *(circled)*
   d. parents

2. What is the author's purpose?
   a. to inform *(circled)*
   b. to persuade
   c. to entertain

3. What is the tone of the passage?
   a. curious *(circled)*
   b. subjective
   c. polite
   d. apathetic

4. The children related the message of the story, "Starry Time," to their own lives by
   a. bringing items to school to share with others.
   b. asking their parents to be more generous to others.
   c. wondering what they would be willing to share with others. *(circled)*
   d. deciding that no one could be as good as Stella was.

5. A moral to "Starry Time" could be:
   a. You should keep what you own to yourself.
   b. Sometimes things are better when they are shared. *(circled)*
   c. The girl had a lot of stars.
   d. The moon will always shine on.

6. Coles' heading, "Words into Action," refers to his idea that
   a. words are harder to remember than actions.
   b. it's easier to list qualities that make up goodness than to act them out in daily life. *(circled)*
   c. it's easier to act like a good person than to really be one.
   d. turning nouns into verbs teaches children about grammar.

7. After hearing the story, the children
   a. decided to never listen to the story again.
   b. wrote their own stories.
   c. found things they could give away. *(circled)*
   d. asked their parents to become volunteers.

8. The word "glean" in paragraph 3, line 4, most nearly means
   a. pick over in search of relevant ideas. *(circled)*
   b. gather grain.
   c. shine.
   d. erase from memory.

9. Cole suggests turning certain nouns into action; these words include
   a. compassion, sincerity, and kindness.
   b. thoughtfulness, sincerity, and generosity.
   c. thoughtfulness, sensitivity, and kindness. *(circled)*
   d. sincerity, kindness, and generosity.

10. The thirteen-year-old boy referred to in paragraphs 9–10 comes to the realization that "a good guy" could ruin everything by calling attention to himself; that's a problem because then he
    a. starts pretending to be good, instead of really being good.
    b. can become so involved in self-congratulation that he starts doing bad things.
    c. can become more involved in self-congratulation than in actually doing good. *(circled)*
    d. only cares about pointing out the faults of others.

11. The word "denote" in paragraph 6, line 4, most nearly means

a. to indicate.

b. to improve.

c. to find meaning.

d. to conceal.

12. According to the passage,

a. everyone should aim to be pure.

b. everyone should aim to be a goody-goody.

c. everyone should move forwards.

d. everyone is at risk of slipping backwards.

13. Under the heading, "A Good Person," Coles defines good children as those who

a. sincerely believe in the desirability of goodness but understand that life doesn't always allow you to be good.

b. understand the ideas of goodness and realize the importance of holding onto these abstract ideas.

c. understand the Golden Rule and can help others to understand its meaning.

d. sincerely believe in the desirability of goodness and understand that goodness must be lived through one's actions.

14. In paragraph 7, Coles compares the boy's description of being good to the myth of Sisyphus because

a. you can never give a person something without that person wanting even more from you.

b. being good is a constant struggle and it's always possible to backslide.

c. being good is like rolling a rock that's too heavy for you.

d. human beings are condemned to fail at being good.

15. According to the thirteen-year-old child's father, a lot of people

a. talk the talk but don't walk the walk.

b. talk the talk and walk the walk.

c. do nothing.

d. help others to score points.

READERS WRITE

1. What was the message of the story, "Starry Time"? How did the children relate that message to their own lives?

(Answers will vary.)

_____

_____

_____

2. What does Coles mean by turning "words into action"?

(Answers will vary.)

_____

_____

_____

3. What are the two parts that make up Coles' definition of good children in the section called "A Good Person"?

(Answers will vary.)

_____

_____

_____

4. In paragraphs 9–10, Coles refers to the discussion of a thirteen-year-old boy about the challenges we all face in trying to be good. What are these challenges?

(Answers will vary.)

_____

_____

_____

5. What did you think of the story called "Starry Time?" Why do you think it affected the children so much?

(Answers will vary.)

_____

_____

_____

READERS DISCUSS

1. What is your definition of a good person? How does yours compare with Coles'? How does it compare with that of other students?

(Answers will vary.)

_____

_____

_____

2. Describe briefly a story or film that worked for you in the way "Starry Time" did for the children.

(Answers will vary.)

_____

_____

_____

GET AN OVERVIEW

1 | Use the title as a key to finding the subject.

2 | Flip through pages to learn more about the subject.

3 | Skim paragraphs if you need more information.

4 | Predict what the writer will say.

PRACTICE PAGES

Chapter 4

Managing Workforce Diversity

RONALD J. EBERT AND RICKY W. GRIFFIN

Ronald Ebert teaches business at the University of Missouri, Columbia, and Ricky Griffin teaches business at Texas A & M University. This reading comes from the chapter called "Managing Human Resources and Labor Relations" in their textbook, *Business Essentials* (2000). Here the authors discuss the challenges of managing workers in a multicultural society.

get an overview

affirmative action: encouragement of increased representation of women and minorities

1 An extremely important set of human resource challenges centers on workforce diversity—the range of workers' attitudes, values, beliefs, and behaviors that differ by gender, race, and ethnicity. The diverse workforce is also characterized by individuals of different ages and physical abilities. In the past, organizations tended to work toward *homogenizing* their workforces, getting everyone to think and behave in similar ways. Partly as a result of affirmative action efforts, however, many U.S. organizations are now creating workforces that are more diverse, thus embracing more women, more ethnic minorities, and more foreign-born employees than ever before.

2 Figures 1 and 2 help put the changing U.S. workforce into perspective. Figure 1 shows changes in the percentages of different groups of workers—white males, white females, blacks, Hispanics, and Asians and others—in the total workforce in the years 1980, 1993, and (as projected) 2005. Figure 2

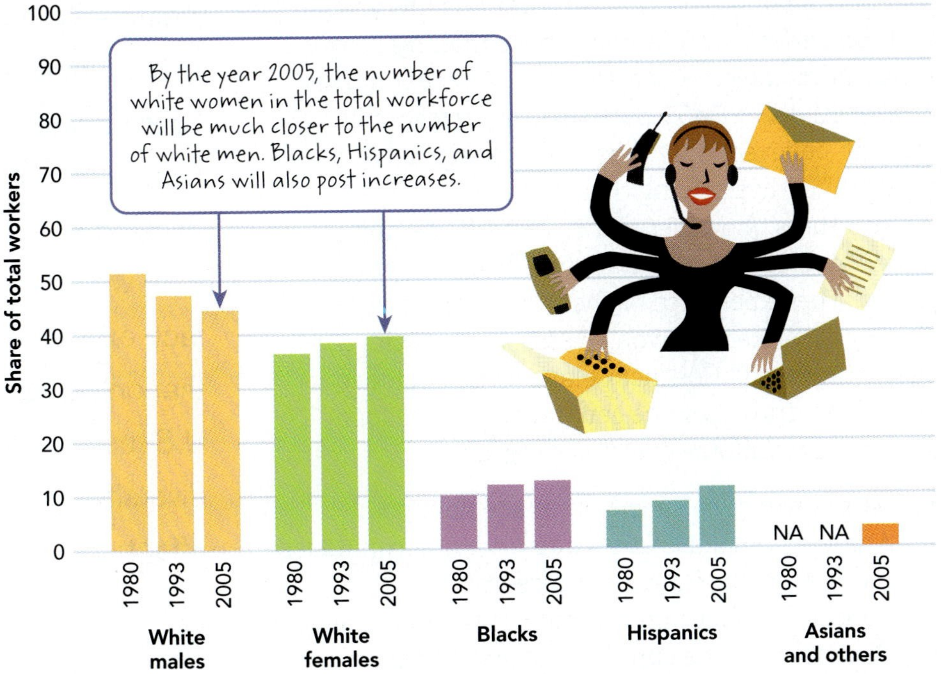
By the year 2005, the number of white women in the total workforce will be much closer to the number of white men. Blacks, Hispanics, and Asians will also post increases.
Share of total workers
100
90
80
70
60
50
40
30
20
10
0
NA
NA
1980
1993
2005
White males
White females
Blacks
Hispanics
Asians and others

Figure 1

shows changes among managerial and professional workers for blacks and Hispanics between 1983 and 1997. The first picture is one of increasing diversity over the past decade. The second is one of a slower but steady trend toward diversity. By 2005, says the Labor Department, half of all workers entering the labor force will be women and more than one-third will be blacks, Hispanics, Asian Americans, and others.

Diversity as a Competitive Advantage

3 Today, organizations are recognizing not only that they should treat everyone equitably, but also that they should acknowledge the individuality of each person they employ. They are also recognizing that diversity can be a competitive advantage. For example, by hiring the best people available from every single group rather than hiring from just one or a few groups, a firm can develop a higher-quality labor force. Similarly, a diverse workforce can bring a wider array of information to bear on problems and can provide insights on marketing products to a wider range of consumers. Says the head of workforce diversity at IBM: "We think it is important for our customers to look inside and see people like them. If they can't . . . the prospect of them becoming or staying our customers declines."

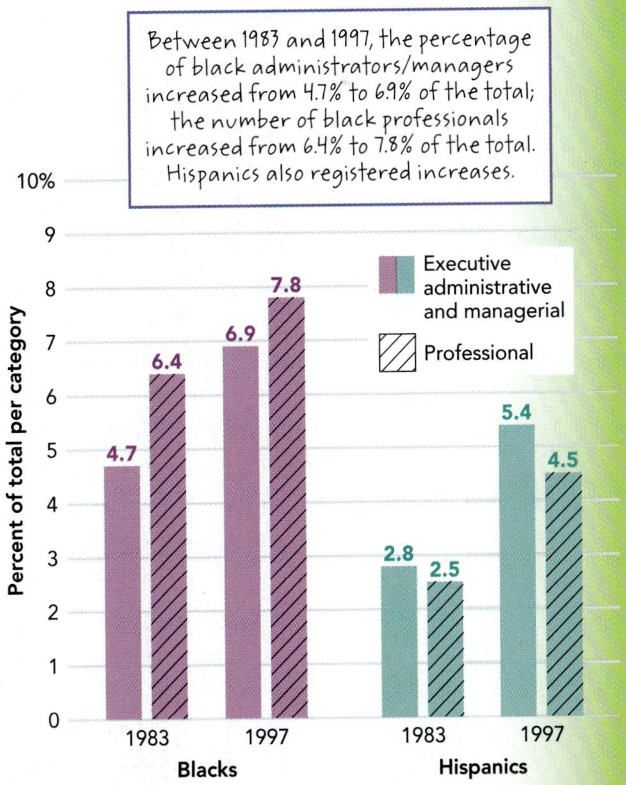
Between 1983 and 1997, the percentage of black administrators/managers increased from 4.7% to 6.9% of the total; the number of black professionals increased from 6.4% to 7.8% of the total. Hispanics also registered increases.
Percent of total per category
10%
9
8
7
6
5
4
3
2
1
0
Executive administrative and managerial
Professional
4.7
6.4
6.9
7.8
2.8
2.5
5.4
4.5
1983
1997
Blacks
Hispanics

Figure 2

4 Admittedly, not all U.S. companies have worked equally hard to adjust their thinking and diversify their workforces. In fact, experts estimate

human resources: a company's workforce

that only a handful of U.S. corporations are diversifying with any effect. Even among those making progress, it has nevertheless been slow.[1] In a recent survey of executives at 1,405 participating firms, only 5 percent believed that they were doing a "very good job" of diversifying their human resources. Many others, however, have instituted—and, more importantly, maintained—diversity programs. The experience of these companies (including IBM, Xerox, Avon, AT&T, Burger King, Levi Strauss, and Hoechst Celanese) has made it possible to draw up some general guidelines for a successful workforce diversity program:

> Admittedly, not all U.S. companies have worked equally hard to adjust their thinking and diversify their workforces. In fact, experts estimate that only a handful of U.S. corporations are diversifying with any effect.

- Make diversity a specific management goal.
- Analyze compensation scales and be scrupulously fair in tracking individual careers.
- Continue to focus on diversity in the midst of downsizing.
- Contribute to the supply of diverse workers.
- Celebrate diversity.
- Respond to the concerns of white males.

compensation scales: amounts and ranges of salaries and other benefits

Diversity Training

Another guideline calls for companies to use *diversity training*—programs designed to improve employees' understanding of differences in attitudes and behavior patterns among their coworkers. However, there is no consensus yet on how to *conduct* such programs—on exactly what to teach and how to do it. 5

Not surprisingly, there are sometimes repercussions to such an approach. Indeed, some recent studies have shown that focusing strictly on such issues as race and gender can arouse deep feelings and be almost as divisive as ignoring negative stereotyping in the first place. Other studies suggest that too many training programs are limited to correcting affirmative action problems: Backlash occurs when participants appear to be either "winners" (say, black women) or "losers" (white men) as a result of the process. 6

Many companies therefore try to go beyond mere awareness training. Du Pont, for example, offers a course for managers on how to seek and use more diverse input before making decisions. Sears offers what it calls diversity-friendly programs: bus service for workers who must commute from the inner city to the suburbs and leaves of absence for foreign-born employees to visit families still living overseas. Finally, one consultant emphasizes that it is extremely important to integrate training into daily routines: "Diversity training," he says, "is like hearing a good sermon on Sunday. You must practice what you heard during the week." 7

Note

1. M. Adams, "Building a Rainbow, One Stripe at a Time," *HR Magazine* (August 1998): 72-78.

Now that you've finished the article, how accurate was your overview? Did you miss any important information?

1. Using the article, add any information from the following sections that you may have overlooked in your overview:

    a. Notes before reading (Answers will vary.) _____

    _____

    b. Headings (Answers will vary.) _____

    _____

    c. Introduction (Answers will vary.) _____

    _____

    d. Conclusion (Answers will vary.) _____

    _____

    e. Illustration (Answers will vary.) _____

    _____

    f. Visual features (Answers will vary.) _____

    _____

    g. Captions (Answers will vary.) _____

    _____

2. What did you predict as the overall point? How close was your prediction, now that you have

    completed the reading?

    (Answers will vary.) _____

ACTIVE READERS RESPOND

After you've finished reading, use these activities to respond to "Managing Workforce Diversity." You may write your answers in the spaces provided or on a separate sheet of paper.

VITAL VOCABULARY

Some words in this reading may be unfamiliar to you. Use the methods of Strategy 3 to explain what the listed words mean.

USE CONTEXT CLUES

a. workforce diversity (paragraph 1) (use logic clues) _____

b. diversity training (paragraph 5) (use logic clues) _____

USE WORD PARTS

a. equitably (paragraph 3) (Note that part of the word "equal" begins this word.)

    _____

b. diversify (paragraph 4) (Note that the suffix for this word modifies its meaning.)

    _____

c.   divisive (paragraph 6) (Note that the suffix for this word modifies its meaning.)

_____

d.   downsizing (paragraph 4) (Note that this word is made of two words.)

_____

e.   backlash (paragraph 6) (Note that this word is made of two words.)

_____

USE THE DICTIONARY

Choose the correct definition of each word as it is used in the context of this reading.

a.   array (paragraph 3) _____

b.   scrupulously (paragraph 4) _____

c.   consensus (paragraph 5) _____

d.   repercussions (paragraph 6) _____

OBJECTIVE OPERATIONS

1. Who is the writer's intended audience?
   a. employers
   b. general audience
   c. employees
   d. companies

2. What is the author's purpose?
   a. to inform
   b. to persuade
   c. to entertain

3. What is the tone of the passage?
   a. persuasive
   b. critical
   c. condescending
   d. impartial

4. In addition to gender, race, and ethnicity as categories of difference, the authors also mention
   a. people of different educational backgrounds and intellectual abilities.
   b. people from different parts of the country who have different accents.
   c. people from other countries who need special work visas.
   d. people of different ages and physical abilities.

5. According to the passage, by 2005 how many workers entering the workforce will be blacks, Hispanics, Asian Americans and others?
   a. one-half
   b. one-third
   c. two-thirds
   d. three-fourths

6. The word "homogenizing" in paragraph 1, line 5, most nearly means
   a. blending.
   b. separating.
   c. portraying.
   d. conditioning.

7. One reason that organizations find it advantageous to have a diverse workforce is
   a. they can reach a wider range of consumers.
   b. they can get cheaper labor.
   c. workers from different groups can share their customs and traditions with one another.
   d. workers from different groups can be pitted against each other during battles between management and workers.

8. According to the passage, hiring the best people from every single group will

a. send people from minorities to other companies.

b. create a higher-quality workforce. *(circled)*

c. bring equality to the workplace.

d. help to market products to more people.

9. Of the 1,405 companies surveyed, what percent felt they were doing well?

a. 2 percent

b. 3 percent

c. 5 percent *(circled)*

d. 7 percent

10. The word "instituted" in paragraph 4, line 10, most nearly means

a. argued.

b. schooled.

c. experienced.

d. established. *(circled)*

11. In reporting on the progress U.S. companies are making toward greater diversity of their workforce, the authors say that

a. most companies have made good headway on diversifying their workforce.

b. there are new, general guidelines about how to diversify that companies must follow.

c. most companies have diversified so well that white males are very concerned about their jobs.

d. very few companies have successfully diversified their workforce. *(circled)*

12. One of the guidelines for a successful workforce diversity program is to

a. downsize minorities.

b. offer many parties and celebrations.

c. suppress diversity.

d. respond to the concerns of white males. *(circled)*

13. The purpose of diversity training is to

a. help employees from diverse groups learn to blend in with the attitudes and behaviors of the corporate culture.

b. let employees from diverse groups get specialized training in new technologies.

c. improve employees' understanding of differences in attitudes and behaviors among the people they work with. *(circled)*

d. help managers hire the best people from diverse groups.

14. According to the passage,

a. many companies go beyond awareness training. *(circled)*

b. many companies remain limited by their awareness training.

c. many companies offer more incentives to minorities.

d. many companies are not diverse.

15. The reason some diversity training programs have negative repercussions may be that they have focused too much on

a. issues such as race or gender. *(circled)*

b. the backlash against women.

c. ending affirmative action.

d. integrating training into daily routines.

QUICK QUESTIONS

1. In 1980 white males made up just a little over 50% of the workforce. **True** or False

2. Workforce diversity includes categories of difference such as gender and race. **True** or False

3. One guideline for a successful workforce diversity program is *(Answers will vary.)* _____

_____

4. When participants appear to be _____winners_____ or _____losers_____ , backlash occurs.

5. What is the purpose of diversity training programs? *(Answers will vary.)* _____

6. Why are there repercussions to the diversity programs? What are some of these repercussions?

(Answers will vary.) _____

Interesting Inquiries

ASK QUESTIONS

1 | Ask questions about what catches your interest.

2 | Ask questions that help you get an overview and predict main ideas.

3 | As you read, try to find answers to your questions and continue to ask more questions.

4 | After reading, ask and answer questions, especially about main ideas.

imagine this

Standing at a magazine rack, you pick up a magazine that has an interesting cover. You might look at the article titles or the celebrity photographs on the cover and wonder what the article is about or what other celebrities are being discussed. You might see that your favorite car magazine has an article on how to fix a radiator hose and wonder whether the article will help you figure out your car's problem. You might notice that the latest fashion magazine has models in spring dresses, and you might be curious whether you will like any of them.

All you are doing while standing next to the magazine rack is asking questions, but those questions are helping you to get a general overview of the magazine and its articles. Each question that you ask leads you to another question. After a few moments, you realize there is only one way to get the answers you seek: Read the magazine.

Think FIRST

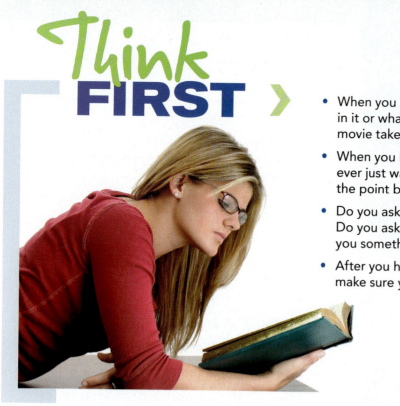

- When you go to the movies, do you ask who is in it or what it is about? Do you ask when the movie takes place or where it is located?

- When you listen to someone tell a story, do you ever just want the overall point? Do you ever get the point before the story is over?

- Do you ask questions in the middle of a movie? Do you ask questions when someone is telling you something new?

- After you hear a story, do you ask questions to make sure you got the point?

INTRODUCTION TO THE NEW STRATEGY
Ask Questions

Instructor Tip
Ask students whether they asked any questions about this course before taking it. Did they read a course description or did they talk to a friend? How did they find out information about this course and others? What kinds of questions did they ask?

Any time that you read something, you have to ask questions, and asking questions works well with any of the reading strategies. However, Strategies 4 and 5 work especially well together. You've seen how the *overview* gives you information about what to expect from the reading, just as you do when you ask a friend about a movie you haven't seen. *Asking questions* while looking over that information will help you predict important ideas the reading will cover.

Try this strategy when you read Reading 9, "How Babies Use Patterns to See," by Laura E. Berk, on pages 139–143. Asking questions before, during, and after reading will help keep you *connected* to the reading. Questions will also help guide you as you look for the reading's most important ideas.

Questions for Connecting to the Reading

When you make a connection, you focus on yourself and your ideas about the subject. The questions you ask all come down to this basic one: How does the subject relate to me? For example, a question you could ask about the title of Reading 9, "How Babies

Hot or Not?

Many people don't ask enough questions, but questions can be life saving. How?

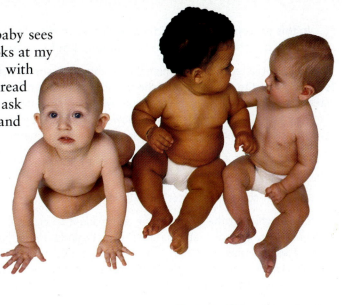

Use Patterns to See," is: "How does the way a baby sees compare to the way I see?" or "When a baby looks at my face, what is she seeing?" Your own connection with the writer's ideas remains important while you read and after you've finished reading. So, continue to ask about any ideas in the reading that interest you, and read to find the answers.

Questions for Predicting the Overall Point and Main Ideas

When you get an overview, you turn your attention to what the writer is saying about the subject. Your overview should help you predict the writer's overall point and main ideas. The questions you ask should help you predict that point and those ideas.

Instructor Tip
Ask students if they have ever heard a joke and beaten the teller to the punch line. How did they predict what the punch line was going to be? How is a punch line similar to an overall point?

The Title and the Overall Point

When you get an overview, you use the title as a key for finding the overall point. Now, turn the title into a question. It will become an even more effective key. Use the "5Ws+H" formula to jog your brain. Think in terms of *who, what, when, where, why,* and *how.* Reading 9's title is "How Babies Use Patterns to See." You could easily turn that title into a question:

- How do babies use patterns to see?

In addition, you could restate the question in a couple of different ways:

- What makes patterns important for the way babies see?
- Why are patterns important for the way babies see?

connect now

What stories that your friends share make you ask *who, what, when, where, why,* and *how?*

Any of those questions could work as an **overall-point question.** The overall-point question acts like an umbrella over the reading's main ideas because it covers all the ideas in the reading. A reading's overall point is commonly called the **thesis** or **thesis statement.**

The Headings and the Main Ideas

The **main ideas** of a reading are those that are central to the thesis statement. For the writer, main ideas support the thesis statement. For the reader, main ideas are important for understanding the writer's message. The headings suggest a reading's main ideas. Reading 9's two headings are: "Contrast Sensitivity" and "Combining Pattern Elements." Headings like these are easier to understand if you relate them to the title. You can then turn the headings into questions that will help you find the main ideas, which are part of the thesis.

Here is how you could turn these headings into questions:

CULTURE WIRE

> *In this excerpt, Thomas Kida, a professor at the University of Massachussetts, shows how psychics use genial questions to gather information about the people they wish to fool.*

Cold reading is a technique in which the psychic asks general questions about the deceased until she gets some useful feedback from the subject. When she obtains useful information, she becomes more specific in her comments. If the listener responds positively, she continues with the line of inquiry and comment. If she's wrong, she makes it sound as if she were right. For example, statistics show that most people die of an illness somewhere in the chest area, like a heart attack. A standard technique for the psychic would be something like the following:

PSYCHIC: You lost a loved one. I'm getting a pain in the chest. Was it a heart attack?

SUBJECT: It was lung cancer.

PSYCHIC: Of course, that explains the pain in the chest.

The psychic got the illness wrong, but made it sound as if she was right. Is this what the radio show psychic did with her callers? Exactly! Listening closely, you begin to realize that she asks a number of rapid-fire, general questions. In many cases, the caller doesn't even have a chance to respond—instead, the psychic quickly jumps in and says something like, "You know what I mean," giving the impression that she was right. When callers respond negatively, she deflects the inaccuracies with a few common ploys. Some of the interactions that I heard went like this:

PSYCHIC: Your father died of a heart condition?

CALLER: No, he didn't.

PSYCHIC: Then it must be his sister that's coming through with him.

Or in another case:

PSYCHIC: Was she in a wheelchair?

CALLER: No.

PSYCHIC: If it's not her, it's on her mother's side of the family.

When she's wrong about the deceased with whom she's supposedly communicating, she deflects attention by saying she's picking up some other relative that's with the deceased. In some cases, she even had the audacity to suggest that the caller simply doesn't know the truth about what she's uncovering. For example:

PSYCHIC: Who wore the pin striped suits?

CALLER: No one.

PSYCHIC: If you don't get what I'm saying, write it down and ask your other relatives.

Or in another case:

Kida, Thomas. *Don't Believe Everything You Think: The Six Basic Mistakes We Make in Thinking.* New York: Prometheus Books, 2006. 61–64.

- Contrast Sensitivity: "What is contrast sensitivity, and how does it help babies use patterns to see?"
- Combining Pattern Elements: "How does combining elements (parts) of patterns help babies learn to see?

Asking questions as part of your overview helps you predict the writer's main ideas. Putting those main ideas together into one statement will give you the writer's thesis. Questions can guide you to things to look for as you read and help you figure out the reading's overall point.

Questions That Get Useful Answers

It's not always easy to come up with a good question. Prompt yourself with *who, what, when, where, why,* and *how* to make generating questions easier. Consider these points to ask effective questions:

PSYCHIC: Where are the twins?

CALLER: There are no twins.

PSYCHIC: He says there are twins. Either that or someone lost a baby very young with another one. Ask your mother.

As can be seen, the psychic's technique is to ask a number of leading questions and look for answers where she's on the right track. If she happens to hit one, she pursues it. If not, she deflects her error, attributing it to some other spirit coming through from the other side, or to the fact that the caller doesn't have the knowledge and has to ask his relatives. Invariably, she keeps it positive, with comments like, "Your father has the nicest smile," "He's with his grandmother now," and "I'm going to give you a big hug from your mother." Without fail, the deceased wants the caller to know that he's not suffering and that he loves the caller very much.

So, can cold reading really be the reason that people think they're talking with their deceased relatives? Can we be fooled so easily? A considerable amount of data says that we can. Researchers have known for years that we interpret very general comments as applying directly to ourselves. That is, we have a tendency to accept vague personality descriptions as uniquely describing ourselves, without realizing that the identical description could apply to others as well. It's called the "Forer effect." Also, you have to remember that people who seek out a psychic are those who desperately want to talk with their loved ones. As we will see, our perceptions can be clouded by what we want to see and believe. Cold reading works because people want it to work. They want to talk with their loved ones, and they don't want to be disappointed. And so, they are inclined to believe, and are therefore more than willing to overlook any errors in the psychic's comments as long as the end result assures them that their deceased relatives are okay and say they love them.

If we truly want to believe something, we'll remember the hits and forget the misses. As an example of this phenomenon, consider a reading that another renowned psychic did for nine people who had lost loved ones. Michael Shermer observed the readings. According to Shermer, the psychic applied a number of standard cold reading techniques, such as rubbing his chest or head and saying, "I'm getting a pain here," and looking for feedback. In the first two hours, Shermer said he counted over a hundred misses and about a dozen hits. Even with this poor hit rate, all nine people still gave the psychic a positive evaluation. If we want to believe it, we will.

- Generating questions can be difficult, but it is easier with a group of people. Why? *Why, how,* or *what* (for example, why do babies see patterns differently?)—make the most useful questions for asking about main ideas and getting a complete answer. (Use *who* to substitute for *what,* if identifying a person.) This is the best way to start an overall-point question.

- *When* and *where* questions (for example, when do babies see patterns or where do babies look?)—may be useful for asking about details of time and place, but they don't usually lead to main ideas.

- *Yes-No questions* (for example, do babies see patterns?)—stimulate interest and can help you connect to the reading, but they don't get at information beyond one word: "yes" or "no." They're usually not helpful in finding main ideas or details.

connect now

Children are obsessed with questions, especially those that begin with the word "why." Why?

Instructor Tip
Ask student about the 5Ws+H. When do they want this information as quickly as possible? Remind them of a party invitation, and the kinds of questions people ask before going. Besides parties, when else are the 5Ws+H the questions to ask for essential information?

KRISTIN CAVALLARI

Love Me, Hate Me: Barry Bonds and the Making of an Anti-Hero, by Jeff Pearlman

Reality TV star Kristin Cavallari is reading a biography of Major League Baseball outfielder Barry Bonds. It must provide interesting reading. Bonds' career has included a record-setting 7 MVP awards and the all-time home run record, but also a role in baseball's steroids scandal.

If you liked *Love Me, Hate Me*, you might also like:

Blood of My Blood, Marjorie Kinnan Rawlings

The Good, the Bad, and the Mad, E. Randall Floyd

A Childhood: The Biography of a Place, Harry Crews

Answers and New Questions

Looking for answers to your questions and asking new questions should be a continuous process as you read.

- **Mark in the margins.** Put check marks by the sentences and paragraphs where you find answers to your questions. Notice especially when ideas or information seem to relate directly to your overall-point question.

- **Ask new questions.** Notice when your reading brings up new questions. Read to answer those new questions. Put a question mark in the margins if you aren't able to find an answer.

- **Use headings, introduction, conclusion, and illustrations.** Continue to use the reading cues to help you answer your questions. Illustrations can be especially helpful for understanding textbook material. For example, use Figure 5.1, on page 140, to get an idea of the way babies see contrast in a checkerboard pattern. Use Figure 5.2, on page 141, to see how babies from birth to two months interpret the pattern of a human face.

When you finish reading, see how well your overall-point question worked. Did the main ideas of the reading answer the question you asked? If so, your question worked well to guide your reading. If not, see how you might modify your question to fit the reading more closely.

Look over the reading. See if the parts you noted with a question mark are now clearer after completing the reading. If not, plan to ask other students or your instructor about them.

Finally, take advantage of the questions provided for you in the Active Readers Respond section of the chapter. You'll find that they all deal with main ideas—the ideas that relate most closely to the overall-point question. For example, for Reading 9 you could use the overall-point question: "How do babies use patterns to see?" You'll see

Instructor Tip

Give all students a copy of the same reading, preferably an article with headnotes, headings, and subheadings. Tell the students to get an overview and write down what they think the overall point will be. Then have the students read the article and write down the questions they have as they read in the margins or on a sheet of paper. After they read, tell them to answer their own questions if they can, and see if their predicted overall point is correct.

that all the questions in the Active Readers Respond section relate to that overall question.

APPLY THE NEW STRATEGY
Ask Questions ❚

First, get an overview of the reading. Then, get your pencil ready. Review the question samples that you have already seen throughout the chapter. This will help you feel more comfortable about asking questions. Your own questions can be about anything that interests you, but for reviewing main ideas, be sure your questions also relate to the overall-point question.

Connect with the Reading

- **What would it be like to see without understanding what you're seeing?**

- **Do you have any negative feelings about this subject? If so, can you put them aside?**

How Babies Use Patterns to See

LAURA E. BERK

READING **9**

Laura Berk is a professor of psychology at Illinois State University, where she teaches child-development courses. This reading comes from the chapter about infant learning in her textbook *Child Development* (2000). Earlier in the chapter, Berk tells us that babies aren't born seeing the world as you and I do. At birth, the other senses—touch, hearing, and so on—are more highly developed than the sense of sight. It takes babies about a year to fully develop the complex eye-brain system of vision. In this excerpt from the chapter, you'll find out how babies develop one important element of vision—the ability to find meaningful patterns in what they see.

Be sure to make good use of the visual features in this reading (Figures 5.1–5.4) in order to understand the somewhat technical explanations about babies' vision. Textbooks frequently use visual features like these (the illustrations, tables, charts, and so on, referred to in the table in Chapter 4). This visual information gives you a clearer picture of the written material. It can be as important as the text itself. As you read this excerpt, look at each figure, read the captions, and connect what you see in the picture to the explanation given in the text.

➤ respond

1   Are young babies sensitive to the pattern, or form, of things they see, and do they prefer some patterns to others? Early research revealed that even newborns prefer to look at patterned rather than plain stimuli—for example, a drawing of the human face or one with scrambled facial features to a black-and-white oval (Fantz, 1961).

perception: awareness that comes through the senses

stimuli: plural of stimulus (something that causes a reaction)

Use the visual features to help you predict ideas.

Since then, many studies have shown that as infants **2** get older, they prefer more complex patterns. For example, when shown black-and-white checkerboards, 3-week-old infants look longest at ones with a few large squares, whereas 8- and 14-week-olds prefer those with many squares (Brennan, Ames, & Moore, 1966). Infant preferences for many other patterned stimuli have been tested—curved versus straight lines, connected versus disconnected elements, and whether the pattern is organized around a central focus (as in a bull's eye), to name just a few.

vital vocabulary

contrast sensitivity: ability to see contrast between light and dark areas

adjacent: next to or bordering

resolve: distinguish between

Contrast Sensitivity

For many years, investigators did not understand why babies of differ- **3** ent ages find certain patterns more attractive than others. Then a general principle was discovered that accounts for early pattern preferences: *contrast sensitivity* (Banks & Ginsburg, 1985). *Contrast* refers to the difference in the amount of light between adjacent regions in a pattern. If babies *are sensitive to* (can detect) the contrast in two or more patterns, they prefer the one with more contrast.

To understand this idea, look at the two checkerboards in the top row **4** of Figure 5.1. To the mature viewer, the one with many small squares has more contrasting elements. Now look at the bottom row, which shows how these checkerboards appear to infants in the first few weeks of life. Because of their poor vision, very young babies cannot resolve the small features in more complex patterns. To them, the large, bold checkerboard has more contrast, so they prefer to look at it. By 2 months of age, detection of fine-

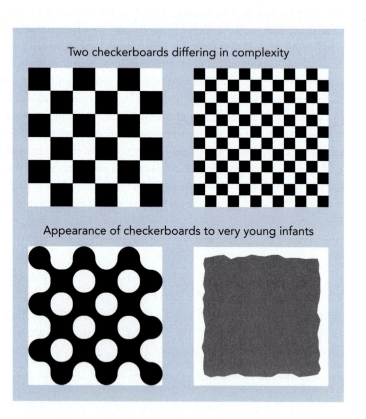

Two checkerboards differing in complexity

Appearance of checkerboards to very young infants

Figure 5.1 The way two checkerboards differing in complexity look to infants in the first few weeks of life. Because of their poor vision, very young infants cannot resolve the fine detail in the more complex checkerboard. It appears blurred, like a gray field. The large, bold checkerboard appears to have more contrast, so babies prefer to look at it.

(Adapted from M. S. Banks & P. Salapetek (1983) "Infant Visual Perception," in M. M. Haith and J. J. Campos eds., Handbook of Child Psychobiology: Vol. 2 Infancy and Developmental Psychology, 4th ed., New York: Wiley, 504. Copyright © 1983 John Wiley & Sons.)

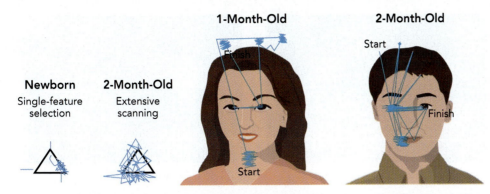

Newborn
Single-feature selection

2-Month-Old
Extensive scanning

1-Month-Old

2-Month-Old

Figure 5.2 Visual scanning of simple and complex patterns by young infants. When scanning a simple triangle, newborns focus only on a single feature, whereas 2-month-olds scan the entire border. When patterns are complex, such as a human face, 1-month-olds limit their scanning to single features on the outskirts of the stimulus, whereas 2-month-olds examine internal features.

grained detail has improved considerably. As a result, infants become sensitive to the contrast in complex patterns and start to spend much more time looking at them (Dodwell, Humphrey, & Muir, 1987).

Combining Pattern Elements

5   In the early weeks of life, infants respond to the separate parts of a pattern. For example, when shown a triangle or a drawing of the human face, very young babies look at the outskirts of the stimulus and stare at single high-contrast features—one corner of the triangle or the hairline and chin of the face (see Figure 5.2). At about 2 months, when scanning ability and contrast sensitivity have improved, infants inspect the entire border of a geometric shape. And they explore the internal features of complex stimuli like the human face, pausing briefly to look at each salient part (Bronson, 1991).

6   Once babies can take in all aspects of a pattern, at 2 to 3 months they start to combine pattern elements, integrating them into a unified whole. By 4 months, they are so good at detecting pattern organization that they even perceive subjective boundaries that are not really present. For example, look at Figure 5.3. Four-month-olds perceive a square in the center of this pattern, just as you do (Ghim, 1990).

7   Older Infants carry this responsiveness to subjective form even further. Nine-month-olds can detect the organized, meaningful pattern in a series of moving lights that resemble a person walking, in that they look much longer at this display than they do at upside-down or disorganized versions. Although 3- to 5-month-olds can tell the difference between these patterns, they do not show a preference for one with both an upright orientation and a humanlike movement pattern (Bertenthal et al., 1985; Bertenthal et al., 1987).

8   By the end of the first year, infants extract meaningful patterns on the basis of very little information. For example, 12-month-olds can figure out an object's shape from a succession of partial views as it passes behind a small opening (Arterberry, 1993). They can also recognize a shape by

Figure 5.3 Subjective boundaries in a visual pattern. Do you perceive a square in the middle of this figure? By 4 months of age, infants do, too.

(Figure adapted from Ghim, 1990; Rose, Jankowski & Senior, 1997.)

subjective form: shape or structure constructed in the mind

upright orientation: right-side-up direction

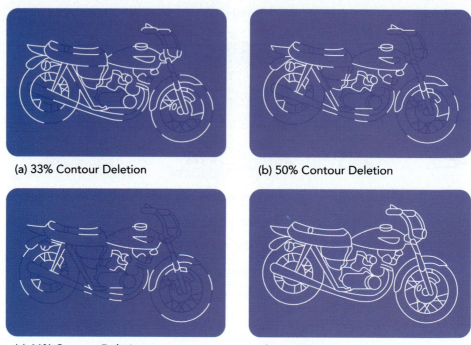

(a) 33% Contour Deletion

(b) 50% Contour Deletion

(c) 66% Contour Deletion

(d) Intact Figure

Figure 5.4 Contour-deleted versions of a figure of a motorcycle, used to test whether infants can extract meaningful patterns on the basis of very little visual information. After 12-month-olds habituated to 33 percent (a), 50 percent (b), or 66 percent (c) contour deletions, the intact figure (d) was paired with a novel figure. Infants recognized the corresponding intact figure, since they dishabituated to (looked longer at) the novel form.

(Figure adapted from Ghim, 1990, Rose, Jankowski & Senior, 1997.)

global representation: overall image

watching a moving light trace its outline. Finally, 12-month-olds can even detect objects represented by incomplete figures—ones missing as much as two-thirds of their contour (see Figure 5.4; Rose, Jankowski, & Senior, 1997). These findings suggest that by 1 year of age, a global representation is sufficient for babies to perceive the similarity between two forms.

Works Cited

Arterberry, M. E., "Development of Spatial Temporal Integration in Infancy." *Infant Behavior and Development, 16,* 1993:343–364.

Bertenthal, B. I., D. R. Profitt, S. J. Kramer, and N. B. Spetner, "Infants' Encoding of Kinetic Displays Varying in Relative Coherence." *Developmental Psychology, 23,* 1987:171–178.

Bertenthal, B. I., D. R. Profitt, N. B. Spetner, and M. A. Thomas, "The Development of Infant Sensitivity to Biomechanical Motions." *Child Development, 56,* 1985:531–543.

Brennan, W. M., E. W. Ames, and R. W. Moore, "Age Differences in Infants' Attention to Patterns of Different Complexities." *Science, 151,* 1966:354–356.

Bronson, G. W., "Infant Differences in Rate of Visual Encoding." *Child Development, 62,* 1991:44–54.

Dodwell, P. C., G. K. Humphrey, and D. W. Muir, "Shape and Pattern Perception." In P. Salapated & L. Cohen (Eds.), *Handbook of Infant Perception* (vol. 2, pp. 1–77). Orlando, FL: Academic Press, 1987.

Fantz, R. L., "The Origin of Form Perception." *Scientific American, 204,* 1961:66–72.

Ghim, H. R., "Evidence for Perceptual Organization in Infants: Perception of Subjective Contours by Young Infants." *Infant Behavior and Development, 13,* 1990:221–248.

Rose, S. A., J. J. Jankowski, and G. J. Senior, "Infants' Recognition of Contour-Deleted Figures." *Journal of Experimental Psychology: Human Perception and Performance, 23,* 1997:1206–1216.

ACTIVE READERS RESPOND

After you've finished reading, use these questions to respond to "How Babies Use Patterns to See." You may write your answers in the spaces provided or on a separate sheet of paper.

EXERCISE: OPERATION OVERVIEW

Now that you've finished the article, how accurate was your overview? Did you miss any important information?

1. Add any information from the following parts of the article that you may have missed in your overview:

    a. Notes before reading (Answers will vary.)

    b. Headings (Answers will vary.)

    c. Introduction (Answers will vary.)

    d. Conclusion (Answers will vary.)

    e. Illustration (Answers will vary.)

    f. Visual features (Answers will vary.)

    g. Captions (Answers will vary.)

2. What were your three questions? Did your questions help you predict the overall point?

    (Answers will vary.)

3. What is the overall point, now that you have completed the reading?

    (Answers will vary.)

VITAL VOCABULARY

Some words in this reading may be unfamiliar to you. Use the methods of Strategy 3 to explain what the listed words mean.

USE CONTEXT CLUES

a. detection (paragraph 4)

b. subjective boundaries (paragraph 6)

c. contour (paragraph 8)

_____

d. intact (caption for Fig. 5.4)

_____

USE WORD PARTS

a. outskirts (paragraph 5)

_____

b. extract (paragraph 8)

_____

c. habituate/dishabituate (caption for Fig. 5.4) (Note the word "habit" in these words.)

_____

USE THE DICTIONARY

Choose the correct definition of these words as they are used in the context of this reading.

a. scanning (paragraph 5)

_____

b. salient (paragraph 5)

_____

c. succession (paragraph 8)

_____

d. novel (caption for Fig. 5.4)

_____

OBJECTIVE OPERATIONS

1. Who is the writer's intended audience?
    a. scientists
    b. psychologists
    c. general audience
    d. parents
2. What is the author's purpose?
    a. to inform
    b. to persuade
    c. to entertain
3. What is the tone of the passage?
    a. interested
    b. ambiguous
    c. serious
    d. subjective

4. The word "detection" in paragraph 4, line 7, most nearly means
    a. acknowledgement.
    b. recollection.
    c. solution.
    d. recognition.
5. Very young infants prefer to look at black-and-white checkerboards with a few large squares instead of the checkerboard with many small squares, because they
    a. see only the central squares of the checkerboard.
    b. haven't learned to appreciate contrast.
    c. can't tell the difference between curved and straight lines.
    d. can't see the fine detail in the smaller checkerboard.

6. Figure 5.2 tells you that when a newborn looks at a pattern, such as a geometric shape, the baby
   a. examines the internal features.
   b. stares at a point beyond the shape.
   c. stares at a single point on the shape.
   d. blinks several times a second.

7. By what age does the ability to see fine-grained detail improve?
   a. three weeks.
   b. eight weeks.
   c. fourteen weeks
   d. two years

8. At two or three months, babies can combine pattern elements and
   a. eliminate the patterns.
   b. find a parent's face.
   c. integrate the pattern into a unified whole.
   d. perceive squares.

9. Once a baby is one year-old, it recognizes
   a. similarities between two forms.
   b. its parents' faces.
   c. shapes and colors.
   d. exactly what it sees.

10. By the end of the first year, babies can
    a. figure out the shape of an object even when only shown incomplete views of it.
    b. figure out the shape of an object when its image is flashed only once.
    c. use a light to create original shapes.
    d. use contrast sensitivity to figure out the shape of an object.

11. According to the article, one-month-olds
    a. scan single features on a person's face.
    b. scan a person's face but do not see it.
    c. focus on a triangular area of the face.
    d. focus on a person's eyes.

12. The ability of 4-month-old babies to perceive subjective boundaries that are not really present comes from their learning
    a. to scan an entire border of a shape.
    b. to see more contrast.
    c. to use their imagination.
    d. to detect pattern organization.

13. Nine-month-olds detect
    a. no patterns.
    b. nothing.
    c. very large patterns.
    d. organized patterns.

14. The word "succession" in paragraph 8, line 4, most nearly means
    a. sequence.
    b. type.
    c. connection.
    d. accomplishment.

15. Based on the reading, we can assume a newborn would prefer to look at a circle that is painted
    a. in one pastel color, such as pink or baby blue.
    b. with broad black-and-white stripes.
    c. in one bright color, such as red or yellow.
    d. with tiny white dots all over a black background.

READERS WRITE

1. How does Figure 5.1 help you understand why very young infants prefer to look at black-and-white checkerboards that have a few large squares instead of the checkerboard with many small squares? What does this preference demonstrate about the idea of contrast sensitivity?

   (Answers will vary.)

   _____

   _____

2. What does Figure 5.2 tell you about the way a newborn baby looks at a pattern, such as a geometric shape or a human face? What does it tell you about how a two-month-old looks at a geometric shape or a human face?

   (Answers will vary.)

   _____

   _____

3. What have babies learned by about 4 months that enables them to perceive the square in the middle of Figure 5.3, "just as you do"?

(Answers will vary.)

_____

_____

4. How does this ability demonstrate the baby's ability to combine pattern elements?

(Answers will vary.)

_____

_____

5. What is one example of how infants at the end of their first year can see meaningful patterns even when given very little information?

(Answers will vary.)

_____

_____

READERS DISCUSS

1. How were you able to connect to the information in this reading? For example, did you find out a little about how your own visual perception works? Or were you more interested in the babies' learning? Discuss your responses with others.

(Answers will vary.)

_____

_____

2. How were you able to understand the somewhat technical information in this reading? Did the illustrations clarify the ideas for you? What other strategies did you use? Discuss with others what worked best.

(Answers will vary.)

_____

_____

ASK QUESTIONS

1 | Ask questions about what catches your interest.

2 | Ask questions that help you get an overview and predict main ideas.

3 | As you read, try to find answers to your questions, and continue to ask more questions.

4 | After reading, ask and answer questions, especially about main ideas.

Summary

CHAPTER 5

HOW DOES STRATEGY 5 HELP YOU BECOME A MORE ENGAGED READER?

Asking questions starts a dialogue between you and the writer, in which you read actively to find answers. Any questions you ask can be good for stimulating your interest. Strategy 5 shows you how to ask questions that connect your interests and ideas on a subject and the writer's ideas.

HOW DOES THE ASK QUESTIONS STRATEGY WORK?

Asking questions reminds you to ask about what interests you. However, for getting the overall point and main ideas, it suggests turning the title, headings, and other cues from the reading into questions. By using *who, what, when, where, why,* and *how* with these cues, you create your own questions and read to find the answers.

Strategy 5 teaches you to start with your own interest. What catches your eye about a reading? This question will engage you as you prepare to ask other questions.

Strategy 5 shows you ways to ask questions that help you to predict a writer's main ideas. This is important in determining the thesis statement, or the overall point of the reading.

Strategy 5 reminds you to seek answers as you read. This will help to keep you engaged with the reading.

Strategy 5 teaches you to continue to ask questions, especially about main ideas. This will encourage you to read more deeply.

Key Terms

main ideas: ideas in a reading that are central to the overall point

overall-point question: the question that asks about the writer's overall point; it covers all the ideas in the reading to help you predict the thesis

thesis (or **thesis statement**): the overall point of a reading; the sum of the main ideas in one sentence

Think AGAIN >

During a movie, you and your friends may ask questions. You may wonder why the killer chose that person or whether the girl will marry the awful boyfriend. At the end of the film, you and your friends may rehash the film and discuss what happened. Some of you may ask more questions to get deeper meaning from the characters or the plot. In fact, you hear other audience members making comments and asking similar questions. Why is this?

Where else do you ask questions to gain a deeper understanding of something?

MASTERY TEST

Now that you understand Strategy 5, put it into practice

with Reading 10, "talking back."

Connect with the Reading

Before beginning to read, **connect** with the text. Then practice getting an overview and **asking questions**. Take special note of these elements for this reading. Think of a question for each of the cues you find here.

- Ask and answer a question of your own about what the title, "talking back," means to you.

- How does this title relate to the kind of responding you've been doing with the readings in this book?

- What feelings do you have about "talking back"?

- **Headnote.** The headnote tells you that this reading comes from the writer's book, *talking back*, subtitled *thinking feminist, thinking black*. You can assume that the writer is a black feminist. Sample question: How might being a black feminist relate to ideas about talking back?

- **Introduction.** The author grew up in a southern black community where children weren't supposed to have their own opinion. Sample question: What was it like for her to grow up that way?

- **Conclusion.** The very last sentence of the reading is complicated, but see how it relates to the title. What is your question?

- **Skim a few paragraphs.** Here are sample main ideas you can get from the first sentences of various paragraphs: Paragraph 2. "Speaking out was an act of risk and daring." Paragraph 8. "Madness was the punishment for a female who talked too much." What are your questions?

- Finally, you may have already noticed that the author doesn't use capital letters for her name or for the title of the reading. Why? Ask a question about this unusual style. What might this suggest? See if you find the answer as you read "talking back."

talking back

bell hooks is a writer and has been a professor at Yale University, Oberlin College, and City College in New York. This reading is a chapter titled "talking back" from her 1988 book, also titled *talking back*, subtitled *thinking feminist, thinking black*. In this reading the author tells what "talking back" means to her, and why it is so important to her.

> **respond**

1   In the world of the southern black community I grew up in, "back talk" and "talking back" meant speaking as an equal to an authority figure. It meant daring to disagree and sometimes it just meant having an opinion. In the "old school," children were meant to be seen and not heard. My great-grandparents, grandparents, and parents were all from the old school. To make yourself heard if you were a child was to invite punishment, the back-hand lick, the slap across the face that would catch you unaware, or the feel of switches stinging your arms and legs.

> **get an overview**

2   To speak then when one was not spoken to was a courageous act—an act of risk and daring. And yet it was hard not to speak in warm rooms where heated discussion began at the crack of dawn, women's voices filling the air, giving orders, making threats, fussing. Black men may have excelled in the art of poetic preaching in the male-dominated church, but in the church of the home, where the everyday rules of how to live and how to act were established, it was black women who preached. There, black women spoke in a language so rich, so poetic, that it felt to me like being shut off from life, smothered to death if one were not allowed to participate.

3   It was in that world of woman talk (the men were often silent, often absent) that was born in me the craving to speak, to have a voice, and not just any voice but one that could be identified as belonging to me. To make my voice, I had to speak, to hear myself talk—and talk I did—darting in and out of grown folks' conversations and dialogues, answering questions that were not directed at me, endlessly asking questions, making speeches. Needless to say, the punishments for these acts of speech seemed endless. They were intended to silence me—the child—and more particularly the girl child. Had I been a boy, they might have encouraged me to speak believing that I might

> To speak then when one was not spoken to was a courageous act—an act of risk and daring.

someday be called to preach. There was no "calling" for talking girls, no legitimized rewarded speech. The punishments I received for "talking back" were intended to suppress all possibility that I would create my own speech. That speech was to be suppressed so that the "right speech of womanhood" would emerge.

Within feminist circles, silence is often seen as the sexist "right speech **4** of womanhood"—the sign of woman's submission to patriarchal authority. This emphasis on woman's silence may be an accurate remembering of what has taken place in the households of women from WASP backgrounds in the United States, but in black communities (and diverse ethnic communities), women have not been silent. Their voices can be heard. Certainly for black women, our struggle has not been to emerge from silence into speech but to change the nature and direction of our speech, to make a speech that compels listeners, one that is heard.

Our speech, "the right speech of womanhood," was often the soliloquy, **5** the talking into thin air, the talking to ears that do not hear you—the talk that is simply not listened to. Unlike the black male preacher whose speech was to be heard, who was to be listened to, whose words were to be remembered, the voices of black women—giving orders, making threats, fussing—could be tuned out, could become a kind of background music, audible but not acknowledged as significant speech. Dialogue—the sharing of speech and recognition—took place not between mother and child or mother and male authority figure but among black women. I can remember watching fascinated as our mother talked with her mother, sisters, and women friends. The intimacy and intensity of their speech—the satisfaction they received from talking to one another, the pleasure, the joy. It was in this world of woman speech, loud talk, angry words, women with tongues quick and sharp, tender sweet tongues, touching our world with their words, that I made speech my birthright—and the right to voice, to authorship, a privilege I would not be denied. It was in that world and because of it that I came to dream of writing, to write.

Writing was a way to capture speech, to hold onto it, keep it close. And so **6** I wrote down bits and pieces of conversations, confessing in cheap diaries that soon fell apart from too much handling, expressing the intensity of my sorrow, the anguish of speech—for I was always saying the wrong thing, asking the wrong questions. I could not confine my speech to the necessary corners and concerns of life. I hid these writings under my bed, in pillow stuffings, among faded underwear. When my sisters found and read them, they ridiculed and mocked me—poking fun. I felt violated, ashamed, as if the secret parts of my self had been exposed, brought into the open, and hung like newly clean laundry, out in the air for everyone to see. The fear of exposure, the fear that one's deepest emotions and innermost thoughts will be dismissed as mere nonsense, felt by so many young girls keeping diaries, holding and hiding speech, seems to me now one of the barriers that women have always needed and still need to destroy so that we are no longer pushed into secrecy or silence.

Despite my feelings of violation, of exposure, I continued to speak and **7** write, choosing my hiding places well, learning to destroy work when no safe place could be found. I was never taught absolute silence. I was taught that it was important to speak but to talk a talk that was in itself a silence. Taught to speak and yet beware of the betrayal of too much heard speech, I experienced intense confusion and deep anxiety in my efforts to speak and write. Reciting poems at Sunday afternoon church service might be rewarded. Writing a poem (when one's time could be "better" spent sweeping, ironing, learning to cook) was luxurious activity, indulged in at the expense of others. Questioning authority, raising issues that were not deemed appropriate subjects brought pain, punishments—like telling mama I wanted to die before her because I could not live without her—that was crazy talk, crazy speech, the kind that would lead you to end up in a mental institution. "Little girl," I would be told, "if you don't stop all this crazy talk and crazy acting you are going to end up right out there at Western State."

8   Madness, not just physical abuse, was the punishment for too much talk if you were female. Yet even as this fear of madness haunted me, hanging over my writing like a monstrous shadow, I could not stop the words, making thought, writing speech. For this terrible madness which I feared, which I was sure was the destiny of daring women born to intense speech (after all, the authorities emphasized this point daily), was not as threatening as imposed silence, as suppressed speech.

9   Safety and sanity were to be sacrificed if I was to experience defiant speech. Though I risked them both, deep-seated fears and anxieties characterized my childhood days. I would speak but I would not ride a bike, play hardball, or hold the gray kitten. Writing about the ways we are traumatized in our growing-up years, psychoanalyst Alice Miller makes the point in *For Your Own Good* that it is not clear why childhood wounds become for some folk an opportunity to grow, to move forward rather than backward in the process of self-realization. Certainly, when I reflect on the trials of my growing-up years, the many punishments, I can see now that in resistance I learned to be vigilant in the nourishment of my spirit, to be tough, to courageously protect that spirit from forces that would break it.

10   While punishing me, my parents often spoke about the necessity of breaking my spirit. Now when I ponder the silences, the voices that are not heard, the voices of those wounded and/or oppressed individuals who do not speak or write, I contemplate the acts of persecution, torture—the terrorism that breaks spirits, that makes creativity impossible. I write these words to bear witness to the primacy of resistance struggle in any situation of domination (even within family life); to the strength and power that emerges from sustained resistance and the profound conviction that these forces can be healing, can protect us from dehumanization and despair.

11   These early trials, wherein I learned to stand my ground, to keep my spirit intact, came vividly to mind after I published *Ain't I A Woman* and the book was sharply and harshly criticized. While I had expected a climate of critical dialogue, I was not expecting a critical avalanche that had the power in its intensity to crush the spirit, to push one into silence. Since that time, I have heard stories about black women, about women of color, who write and publish (even when the work is quite successful) having nervous breakdowns, being made mad because they cannot bear the harsh

responses of family, friends, and unknown critics, or becoming silent, unproductive. Surely, the absence of a humane critical response has tremendous impact on the writer from any oppressed, colonized group who endeavors to speak. For us, true speaking is not solely an expression of creative power; it is an act of resistance, a political gesture that challenges politics of domination that would render us nameless and voiceless. As such, it is a courageous act—as such, it represents a threat. To those who wield oppressive power, that which is threatening must necessarily be wiped out, annihilated, silenced.

12   Recently, efforts by black women writers to call attention to our work serve to highlight both our presence and absence. Whenever I peruse women's bookstores, I am struck not by the rapidly growing body of feminist writing by black women, but by the paucity of available published material. Those of us who write and are published remain few in number. The context of silence is varied and multi-dimensional. Most obvious are the ways racism, sexism, and class exploitation act to suppress and silence. Less obvious are the inner struggles, the efforts made to gain the necessary confidence to write, to re-write, to fully develop craft and skill—and the extent to which such efforts fail.

13   Although I have wanted writing to be my life-work since childhood, it has been difficult for me to claim "writer" as part of that which identifies and shapes my everyday reality. Even after publishing books, I would often speak of wanting to be a writer as though these works did not exist. And though I would be told, "you are a writer," I was not yet ready to fully affirm this truth. Part of myself was still held captive by domineering forces of history, of familial life that had charted a map of silence, of right speech. I had not completely let go of the fear of saying the wrong thing, of being punished. Somewhere in the deep recesses of my mind, I believed I could avoid both responsibility and punishment if I did not declare myself a writer.

14   One of the many reasons I chose to write using the pseudonym bell hooks, a family name (mother to Sarah Oldham, grandmother to Rosa Bell Oldham, great-grandmother to me), was to construct a writer-identity that would challenge and subdue all impulses leading me away from speech into silence. I was a young girl buying bubble gum at the corner store when I first really heard the full name bell hooks. I had just "talked back" to a grown person. Even now I can recall the surprised look, the mocking tones that informed me I must be kin to bell hooks—a sharp-tongued woman, a woman who spoke her mind, a woman who was not afraid to talk back. I claimed this legacy of defiance, of will, of courage, affirming my link to female ancestors who were bold and daring in their speech. Unlike my bold and daring mother and grandmother, who were not supportive of talking back, even though they were assertive and powerful in their speech, bell hooks as I discovered, claimed, and invented her was my ally, my support.

15   That initial act of talking back outside the home was empowering. It was the first of many acts of defiant speech that would make it possible for me to emerge as an independent thinker and writer. In retrospect, "talking

back" became for me a rite of initiation, testing my courage, strengthening my commitment, preparing me for the days ahead—the days when writing, rejection notices, periods of silence, publication, ongoing development seem impossible but necessary.

16   Moving from silence into speech is for the oppressed, the colonized, the exploited, and those who stand and struggle side by side a gesture of defiance that heals, that makes new life and new growth possible. It is that act of speech, of "talking back," that is no mere gesture of empty words, that is the expression of our movement from object to subject—the liberated voice.

ACTIVE READERS RESPOND

After you've finished reading, use these activities to respond to "talking back." You may write your answers in the spaces provided or on a separate sheet of paper.

OPERATION OVERVIEW TO INTERESTING INQUIRIES

Now that you've finished the article, how accurate was your overview? Did you miss any important information?

1. Add any information from the following parts of the article that you may have missed in your overview:
    a. Notes before reading (Answers will vary.)
    b. Headings (Answers will vary.)
    c. Introduction (Answers will vary.)
    d. Conclusion (Answers will vary.)
    e. Illustration (Answers will vary.)
    f. Visual features (Answers will vary.)
    g. Captions (Answers will vary.)

2. What were your questions about the essay? Did you find answers in the reading? (Answers will vary.)

3. What is the overall point, now that you have completed the reading? (Answers will vary.)

VITAL VOCABULARY

Some words in this reading may be unfamiliar to you. Use the methods of Strategy 3 to explain what the listed words mean.

USE CONTEXT CLUES

a. soliloquy (paragraph 5) (Use example clues from the sentence the word is in.)

b. paucity (paragraph 12) (Note the contrast clues: "not by the rapidly growing body of . . . writing, but by the *paucity*.")

_____

USE WORD PARTS

a. primacy (paragraph 10)

_____

b. pseudonym (paragraph 14)

_____

c. retrospect (paragraph 15)

_____

d. dehumanization (paragraph 10) (Starting with the root *human*, what new word do the prefix *de* and two suffixes *-ize* and *–tion* create?)

_____

USE THE DICTIONARY

Choose the correct definition of these words as they are used in the context of this reading.

a. vigilant (paragraph 9)

_____

b. annihilated (paragraph 11)

_____

c. defiant (paragraph 9); defiance (paragraph 14)

_____

d. legacy (paragraph 14)

_____

OBJECTIVE OPERATIONS

1. Who is the writer's intended audience?
   a. women
   b. teenagers
   c. people who need to express themselves
   d. general audience
2. What is the author's purpose?
   a. to inform
   b. to persuade
   c. to entertain

3. What is the tone of the passage?
   a. exploratory
   b. informative
   c. angry
   d. revealing
4. The word "vigilant" in paragraph 9, line 10, most nearly means
   a. reckless.
   b. sensible.
   c. painstaking.
   d. on your guard.

5. In the black small-town, Southern community of hooks' childhood

   a. men dominated in the church, but women were the authorities in the home.

   b. women were not allowed in the men's church, but preached and worshipped in their own church.

   c. women spoke a different language in the home, so they would not be understood by the men.

   d. women had no role in establishing rules for behaving in everyday life.

6. hooks felt she had

   a. never talked back.

   b. no need to speak.

   c. to speak and to hear herself talk.

   d. to keep quiet to be polite.

7. The "right speech of womanhood" was a sign

   a. of adulthood.

   b. of women's submission to men.

   c. of a woman's power.

   d. of intimacy.

8. The "right speech of womanhood" that hooks was supposed to learn as a child is

   a. speaking out for women's rights.

   b. talking that can be ignored by others.

   c. talking in a special code only to other women.

   d. dialogue between equals.

9. According to hooks, women's tongues were

   a. sweet and kind.

   b. mean and angry.

   c. shy and sensitive.

   d. quick and sharp.

10. Although hooks has published, what she has been taught causes her to struggle to see herself as

    a. a woman.

    b. a mother.

    c. a daughter.

    d. a writer.

11. Too much talking back for a female might bring both

    a. scolding and ridicule.

    b. physical punishment and the threat that she'll be turned out of the home.

    c. ruin to her family and the threat that she will end up crazy.

    d. physical punishment and the threat of being considered crazy.

12. hooks' mother and grandmother were

    a. supportive of talking back.

    b. not supportive of talking back.

    c. angered at hooks' name change.

    d. surprised by her defiance.

13. As a girl, hooks turned to writing because

    a. she had a great-grandmother who was a writer.

    b. she needed to write to others who might help her.

    c. she wanted to try to capture what she heard and to ask the questions she wasn't supposed to ask.

    d. she wanted to practice writing so that she could one day become a writer.

14. The word "legacy" in paragraph 14, line 10, most nearly means

    a. gift given in a will.

    b. something passed on from ancestors.

    c. donation.

    d. payment.

15. Based on what you've read and on what you know about the segregated South of the 1950s, why would hooks' parents feel that children had to learn to be quiet and obedient above all else? The answer is probably that

    a. black people still felt fearful about doing or saying anything that could anger white people.

    b. the parents and grandparents themselves had been taught that disobedient children might grow up to be crazy.

    c. black people were moving to Northern cities and wanted to take with them their traditional ways of raising children.

    d. black people were beginning to demand their civil rights, and they wanted their children to know how to speak without getting into trouble.

1. What were the different roles for boys and men, as opposed to girls and women, in hooks' world?

    (Answers will vary.)

    _____

    _____

2. In paragraph 5, hooks talks about the kind of speech she grew up with and loved. What was that talking like? What made hooks love it so much?

    (Answers will vary.)

    _____

    _____

3. What were some of the specific threats and punishments made to hooks to keep her from talking back?

    (Answers will vary.)

    _____

    _____

    _____

4. The author's parents felt "the necessity of breaking [her] spirit." Why would they feel that need? Remember that their world has to be seen within the context of the white, mainstream society of the South of the 1950s.

    (Answers will vary.)

    _____

    _____

5. How does hooks respond in defiance? What does she do?

    (Answers will vary.)

    _____

    _____

READERS DISCUSS

1. The author explains why she chose her great-grandmother's name to give herself a "writer's identity." But we never learn why she doesn't use capitals for her name or for the title of her book. Based on what she's written here, what can you guess about why she avoids capital letters? Discuss your ideas as a group.

    (Answers will vary.)

    _____

    _____

2. Do you agree or disagree with hooks about the importance of talking back? Discuss your response with other students.

    (Answers will vary.)

    _____

    _____

    _____

ASK QUESTIONS

1 | Ask questions about what catches your interest.

2 | Ask questions that help you get an overview and predict main ideas.

3 | As you read, try to find answers to your questions, and continue to ask more questions.

4 | After reading, ask and answer questions, especially about main ideas.

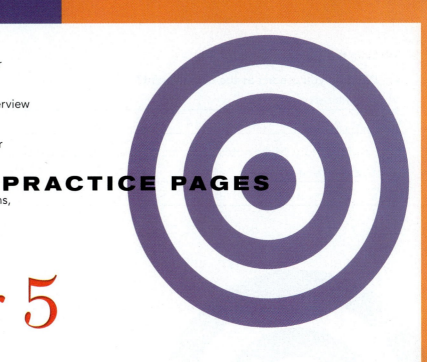

PRACTICE PAGES

Chapter 5

To get practice with reading, read the passage, and then answer the questions that follow. Before reading, take a few minutes to get an overview and ask questions. You may write your answers in the spaces provided or on a separate sheet of paper.

PRACTICE EXERCISE

1. Using the story, gather information from the following sections for your overview:

   a. Notes before reading (Answers will vary.)

   b. Headings (Answers will vary.)

   c. Introduction (Answers will vary.)

   d. Conclusion (Answers will vary.)

   e. Illustration (Answers will vary.)

   f. Visual features (Answers will vary.)

   g. Captions (Answers will vary.)

2. Write three questions beginning with *who, what, why,* or *how* that will help you generate an overall-point question.

   a. (Answers will vary.)

   b. (Answers will vary.)

   c. (Answers will vary.)

3. Skim the story.

4. What do you predict as the overall point?

    (Answers will vary.)

    _____

    _____

5. Read the story. Make notes in the margins, ask more questions, and seek answers.

    (Answers will vary.)

    _____

    _____

PRACTICE READING

Connect with the Reading

- How do you think this father compares with yours?

- How does the relationship between the father and mother compare to your parents' relationship?

- Note any other experiences or feelings at the beginning of the story.

Powder

TOBIAS WOLFF

Tobias Wolff is a novelist and short story writer. "Powder" comes from a collection of his short stories called *The Night in Question* (1996). The story shows the way a child can feel two things at once: excited and fearful, full of happiness and full of dread.

1   Just before Christmas my father took me skiing at Mount Baker. He'd had to fight for the privilege of my company, because my mother was still angry with him for sneaking me into a nightclub during his last visit, to see Thelonious Monk.

Thelonious Monk (1917–1982): jazz pianist and composer

2   He wouldn't give up. He promised, hand on heart, to take good care of me and have me home for dinner on Christmas Eve, and she <u>relented</u>. But as we were checking out of the lodge that morning it began to snow, and in this snow he observed some rare quality that made it necessary for us to get in one last run. We got in several last runs. He was indifferent to my <u>fretting</u>. Snow whirled around us in bitter, blinding <u>squalls</u>, hissing like sand, and still we skied. As the lift bore us to the peak yet again, my father looked at his watch and said, "Criminy. This'll have to be a fast one."

3   By now I couldn't see the trail. There was no point in trying. I stuck to him like white on rice and did what he did and somehow made it to the bottom without sailing off a cliff. We returned our skis and my father put chains on the Austin-Healey while I swayed from foot to foot, clapping my mittens and wishing I was home. I could see everything. The green table-cloth, the plates with the holly pattern, the red candles waiting to be lit.

Austin-Healy: sports car

4   We passed a diner on our way out. "You want some soup?" my father asked. I shook my head. "Buck up," he said. "I'll get you there. Right, doctor?"

→ respond

5   I was supposed to say, "Right, doctor," but I didn't say anything.

6   A state trooper waved us down outside the resort. A pair of sawhorses were blocking the road. The trooper came up to our car and bent down to my father's window. His face was bleached by the cold. Snowflakes clung to his eyebrows and to the fur trim of his jacket and cap.

7   "Don't tell me," my father said.

8   The trooper told him. The road was closed. It might get cleared, it might not. Storm took everyone by surprise. So much, so fast. Hard to get people moving. Christmas Eve. What can you do.

9   My father said, "Look. We're talking about five, six inches. I've taken this car through worse than that."

10   The trooper straightened up. His face was out of sight but I could hear him. "The road is closed."

11   My father sat with both hands on the wheel, rubbing the wood with his thumbs. He looked at the barricade for a long time. He seemed to be trying to master the idea of it. Then he thanked the trooper, and with a weird, old-maidy show of caution turned the car around. "Your mother will never forgive me for this," he said.

12   "We should have left before," I said. "Doctor."

13   He didn't speak to me again until we were in a booth at the diner, waiting for our burgers. "She won't forgive me," he said. "Do you understand? Never."

"I guess," I said, but no guesswork was required; she wouldn't forgive **14** him.

"I can't let that happen." He bent toward me. "I'll tell you what I want. I **15** want us all to be together again. Is that what you want?"

"Yes, sir." **16**

He bumped my chin with his knuckles. "That's all I needed to hear." **17**

When we finished eating he went to the pay phone in the back of the **18** diner, then joined me in the booth again. I figured he'd called my mother, but he didn't give a report. He sipped at his coffee and stared out the window at the empty road. "Come on, come on," he said, though not to me. A little while later he said it again. When the trooper's car went past, lights flashing, he got up and dropped some money on the check. "Okay. Vamanos."

The wind had died. The snow was falling straight down, less of it now **19** and lighter. We drove away from the resort, right up to the barricade. "Move it," my father told me. When I looked at him he said, "What are you waiting for?" I got out and dragged one of the sawhorses aside, then put it back after he drove through. He pushed the door open for me. "Now you're an <u>accom-plice</u>," he said. "We go down together." He put the car into gear and gave me a look. "Joke, son."

Down the first long stretch I watched the road behind us, to see **20** if the trooper was on our tail. The barricade vanished. Then there was nothing but snow: snow on the road, snow kicking up from the chains, snow on the trees, snow in the sky; and our trail in the snow. Then I faced forward and had a shock. The lay of the road behind us had been marked by our own tracks, but there were no tracks ahead of us. My father was breaking virgin snow between a line of tall trees. He was humming "Stars Fell on Alabama." I felt snow brush along the floorboards under my feet. To keep my hands from shaking I clamped them between my knees.

My father grunted in a thoughtful way and said, "Don't ever try **21** this yourself."

"I won't." **22**

"That's what you say now, but someday you'll get your license and **23** then you'll think you can do anything. Only you won't be able to do this. You need, I don't know—a certain instinct."

"Maybe I have it." **24**

"You don't. You have your strong points, but not this. I only mention it **25** because I don't want you to get the idea this is something just anybody can do. I'm a great driver. That's not a virtue, okay? It's just a fact, and one you should be aware of. Of course you have to give the old heap some credit, too. There aren't many cars I'd try this with. Listen!"

I did listen. I heard the slap of the chains, the stiff, jerky rasp of the wip- **26** ers, the purr of the engine. It really did purr. The old heap was almost new. My father couldn't afford it, and kept promising to sell it, but here it was.

I said, "Where do you think that policeman went to?" **27**

Down the first long stretch I watched the road behind us, to see if the trooper was on our tail.

28 "Are you warm enough?" He reached over and cranked up the blower. Then he turned off the wipers. We didn't need them. The clouds had brightened. A few sparse, feathery flakes drifted into our slipstream and were swept away. We left the trees and entered a broad field of snow that ran level for a while and then tilted sharply downward. Orange stakes had been planted at intervals in two parallel lines and my father steered a course between them, though they were far enough apart to leave considerable doubt in my mind as to exactly where the road lay. He was humming again, doing little scat riffs around the melody.

scat riffs: jazz singing with nonsense syllables

29 "Okay then. What are my strong points?"

30 "Don't get me started," he said. "It'd take all day."

31 "Oh, right. Name one."

32 "Easy. You always think ahead."

33 True. I always thought ahead. I was a boy who kept his clothes on numbered hangers to insure proper rotation. I bothered my teachers for homework assignments far ahead of their due dates so I could draw up schedules. I thought ahead, and that was why I knew that there would be other troopers waiting for us at the end of our ride, if we even got there. What I did not know was that my father would wheedle and plead his way past them—he didn't sing "O Tannenbaum," but just about—and get me home for dinner, buying a little more time before my mother decided to make the split final. I knew we'd get caught; I was resigned to it. And maybe for this reason I stopped moping and began to enjoy myself.

O Tannenbaum: Christmas carol

34 Why not? This was one for the books. Like being in a speedboat, only better. You can't go downhill in a boat. And it was all ours. And it kept coming, the laden trees, the unbroken surface of snow, the sudden white vistas. Here and there I saw hints of the road, ditches, fences, stakes, but not so many that I could have found my way. But then I didn't have to. My father was driving. My father in his forty-eighth year, rumpled, kind, bankrupt of honor, flushed with certainty. He was a great driver. All persuasion, no coercion. Such subtlety at the wheel, such tactful pedalwork. I actually trusted him. And the best was yet to come—switchbacks and hairpins impossible to describe. Except maybe to say this: if you haven't driven fresh powder, you haven't driven.

ACTIVE READERS RESPOND

After you've finished reading, use these questions to respond to "Powder." You may write your answers in the spaces provided or on a separate sheet of paper.

OPERATION OVERVIEW TO INTERESTING INQUIRIES

Now that you've finished the story, how accurate was your overview? Did you miss any important information?

1. Add any information from the following sections that you may have missed in your overview:
   a. Notes before reading (Answers will vary.)
   b. Headings (Answers will vary.)
   c. Introduction (Answers will vary.)
   d. Conclusion (Answers will vary.)
   e. Illustration (Answers will vary.)
   f. Visual features (Answers will vary.)
   g. Captions (Answers will vary.)

2. What were your three questions? Did your questions help you predict the overall point?
   (Answers will vary.)

3. What is the overall point, now that you have completed the reading?
   (Answers will vary.)

VITAL VOCABULARY

Some words in this reading may be unfamiliar to you. Use the methods of Strategy 3 to explain what the listed words mean.

USE CONTEXT CLUES

a. relented (paragraph 2)

b. accomplice (paragraph 19)

c. wheedle (paragraph 33)

d. bankrupt (of honor) (paragraph 34)

USE THE DICTIONARY

Choose the correct definition of these words as they are used in the context of this reading.

a. fretting (paragraph 2)

b. squalls (paragraph 2)

c. coercion (paragraph 34)

   (Before using the dictionary, note the contrast clue: *persuasion* in contrast to *coercion*.)

1. Who is the writer's intended audience?

   a. parents

   b. teenagers

   c. skiers

   d. general audience

2. What is the author's purpose?

   a. to inform

   b. to persuade

   c. to entertain

3. What is the tone of the passage?

   a. tense

   b. confused

   c. humorous

   d. apathetic

4. The word "squalls" in paragraph 2, line 6, most nearly means

   a. screams.

   b. gusts.

   c. flakes.

   d. storms.

5. The first half of the story shows the following strengths and weaknesses that seem characteristic of the father:

   a. amusing and loving toward his son, but lacking in intelligence and common sense.

   b. devoted husband and father, but devious and prone to illegal activity.

   c. fun-loving, devoted to his son, but immature and impulsive.

   d. intelligent and responsible, but with a cruel streak.

6. The boy tries to persuade his father to

   a. stop skiing and return home.

   b. continue skiing and stay another night at the lodge.

   c. stop skiing and stay another night at the lodge.

   d. go to the diner.

7. When his father says to the boy, "Now, you're an accomplice . . . we go down together,"

   a. he is being sarcastic with his son in order to get back at the boy for wanting to be home with his mother on Christmas Eve.

   b. he is just kidding with his son, knowing that the boy is a little afraid to go against what the state trooper told them.

   c. he is gently warning the boy that there may be serious trouble ahead.

   d. he is trying to make his son feel bad by scaring him that there will be trouble ahead.

8. From the way the father reacts after calling the mother, the boy

   a. knows his mother has accepted the situation.

   b. knows his mother is very upset.

   c. knows his mother is pleased that he is enjoying time with his father.

   d. knows his mother has invited the father for Christmas Eve dinner.

9. The fact that the father is driving this particular car is important in portraying his character because it shows that

   a. the immediate pleasure of driving a wonderfully made, expensive sports car is more important to him than keeping his promise to sell it.

   b. the father wants to show off his driving in front of his son, hoping to make his son more like him.

   c. the father often needs to have a car that handles extremely well in order to get away from the police.

   d. the father has been careful and wise to keep a car that handles well in snowy conditions.

10. As the father drives, he acts

    a. in a worried and nervous manner.

    b. in a scared and confused manner.

    c. in an uptight and strange manner.

    d. in a nonchalant and relaxed manner.

11. In contrast to the father, the boy acts

    a. in a worried and uptight manner.

    b. in a scared and confused manner.

    c. in a nervous and strange manner.

    d. in a nonchalant and relaxed manner.

12. Because one of his main strengths is to "think ahead," the boy

    a. becomes resigned to being caught by the state troopers and so begins to relax.

    b. becomes more and more anxious about being caught by the state troopers.

    c. thinks about what his mother will say when they get home late.

    d. worries about how he'll get his homework assignments done, since he and his father will get home so late.

13. After the concert, the skiing episode, and now the driving incident, the boy can conclude that

    a. his father will never do such a thing again.

    b. his father will continue to act immaturely and upset his mother.

    c. his father loves him very much.

    d. his father will try to get away with anything.

14. The word "wheedle" in paragraph 33, line 6, most nearly means

    a. sing.

    b. chatter.

    c. coax.

    d. inform.

15. The final paragraph of the story shows

    a. the fear and anxiety the boy feels about driving through "the unbroken surface of the snow."

    b. the author creating a magical ending for the story, when the car turns into a boat that can go downhill in the snow.

    c. the admiration and love the boy has for his father and the pleasure he takes in being driven through the snow.

    d. the love and sadness the boy feels for his father, knowing that soon after this Christmas Eve, his mother will split up with his father.

1. The boy acts more maturely than his father does. (True) or False

2. Due to love, the boy's mother forgives the father.   True or (False)

3. At the start of the drive, the boy and his father
   pass a diner but don't stop.

4. The father's previous outing included taking the boy to
   a Thelonius Monk concert.

5. What examples of the boy's maturity does the author give?
   (Answers will vary.)

6. How does the boy resolve what he is feeling by the end of the story?
   (Answers will vary.)

6

Find and Mark
Main Ideas

FIND AND MARK MAIN IDEAS

1 | Read with a pen or pencil in your hand.

2 | Find the overall point and the main topics of the reading.

3 | Find the main topic and main idea of each paragraph.

4 | Look for supporting ideas.

5 | Adjust your marking.

imagine this

Imagine that you and a friend are trying out different video games. You know what a good video game needs. You know it needs an overall objective, such as saving a princess or rescuing a city. You know it must have general levels that will help you earn points so that you can save the princess or rescue the city. You know it must have specific tasks for you to accomplish to earn those points. If the game you're trying doesn't have these features, you'll lose interest and do something else.

A reading is very similar to a video game. It has an overall point, or thesis statement. It has main topics that contain main ideas. For the reading to be interesting, it must also contain major and minor details. It must have specific details to help you understand difficult concepts and make connections. If a reading doesn't have these features, you might lose interest and stop reading!

Think FIRST

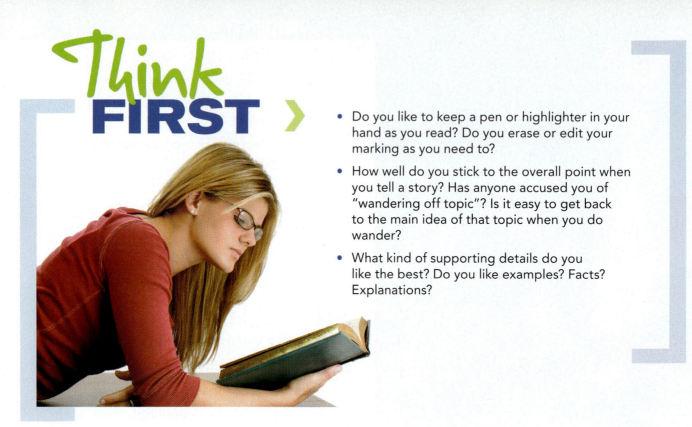

- Do you like to keep a pen or highlighter in your hand as you read? Do you erase or edit your marking as you need to?

- How well do you stick to the overall point when you tell a story? Has anyone accused you of "wandering off topic"? Is it easy to get back to the main idea of that topic when you do wander?

- What kind of supporting details do you like the best? Do you like examples? Facts? Explanations?

INTRODUCTION TO THE NEW STRATEGY
Find and Mark Main Ideas

Note: MI will be used as an abbreviation for main idea throughout the chapter.

Strategy 4—*Get an Overview*—and Strategy 5—*Ask Questions*—give you predictions and questions that prepare you to connect with what the writer has to say. Strategy 6—*Find and Mark Main Ideas*—uses this preparation to help you find the writer's main ideas while you read and after you have finished reading. These main ideas are essential to your comprehension of the reading. You need to recognize and grasp the writer's main ideas to understand the reading's **thesis,** or overall point.

Strategy 6—*Find and Mark Main Ideas*—gives you a way to understand the writer's main ideas. As you read, you keep in mind your overall-point question from your overview. You can then find main ideas that answer that overall question. The strategy also helps you find the important **support**—supporting ideas that explain each of the main ideas. Marking main ideas with a pen or pencil helps you keep your focus as you read. It also gives you a clear record of ideas that you can come back to when you need to study them.

Marking Ideas

Instructor Tip
Remind students that it is all right to mark in a textbook. If it is a book they plan on selling back, highlights and markings can help the next student out. If they feel uncomfortable writing in the book, tell them to use pencil and to mark very lightly so that the marks can be easily erased.

Reading with a pen or pencil in hand is the first step to finding and marking ideas. With these tools you can check a part of the reading that answers one of your questions; you can add a new question mark next to a puzzling part; you can mark unfamiliar words; and you can briefly note your response to an idea. Marking in your book helps you stay focused on finding main ideas.

The next steps in this strategy will help you use these tools to zero in on the main ideas in a reading. When you're sure about these ideas, you can use your own system for marking them.

1. **Underlining.** Underlining is a good way to begin marking ideas. You can use a pencil to mark so that you can erase errors as you change your mind, but pen is clearer and less likely to smudge. Until you're sure which ideas to mark, hold off on using a highlighter. Highlighting makes ideas really stand out, and sometimes, you get "highlighter happy" and highlight too much.

2. **Annotating. Annotating** means making notes. Taking brief margin notes—an occasional word or two next to your underlining—helps you to clarify the meaning of a sentence or paragraph and gives you a reference point for finding the idea again. You'll see some margin notes in the sample marking for Reading 11 on page 192.

connect now

Which books should not be written in? In which books should you write only with pencil?

3. **Reviewing.** With practice, you will learn to mark and annotate a reading so that you focus on main ideas and important points. When you have a test to study for, you'll have a record of the ideas that you can **review,** or look back over, so that you won't have to reread all of the material.

General and Specific Ideas

A general idea is one that covers, or includes, many others. The thesis, or overall point, is the general idea of the whole reading. A **main idea** is more specific than the thesis because it refers to just one part of that thesis. Similarly, a **supporting idea** is more specific than a main idea, but the main idea must be general enough to cover the supporting ideas.

Remember that **general** refers to a large category (for example: fruit or vehicles). **Specific** refers to a particular type or part within the larger category (for example: fruit includes bananas, grapes, and apples; vehicles include cars, buses, and planes). Frequently, specific ideas will contain reasons, examples, names, numbers, or words related to the five senses. Consider these three sentences:

At the restaurant, I ate the cake.

At Judy's Pie-o-Rama, I ate carrot cake.

At Judy's Pie-o-Rama while in a booth, I devoured a thick slice of moist carrot cake, topped with a white cream cheese icing and sprinkled with chopped walnuts.

Which sentence is general? Which sentence is more specific? Which sentence is most specific? (Or, which one makes your mouth water?) The first sentence is very general, but the second sentence is more specific because it names the restaurant and the type of cake. The third sentence contains very specific information: the restaurant's name, the type of cake, the cake's size and quality, the kind of icing, and the cake's topping. A thesis or

Hot or Not?

Have you ever noticed that, at the end of a movie, characters frequently recap the main events of the film?

CULTURE WIRE

Making sure someone understands what you are trying to say is important. When someone asks, "What's your point?" that person has missed the main idea of your thoughts. In this piece, writer F. John Reh offers tips on how to get your point across.

Getting Your Point Across

When we're trying to get a point across to someone else we often think long and hard about what we want to say. That is the wrong way to go about it. Instead of focusing on what you want to say to get your point across, you should focus on what you want the other person to hear.

What Do I Want to Say?

Whether you are giving instructions to an employee, ordering food at a drive-through, or writing a memo explaining the new dress code you want to be sure to get your point across. You want to say just the right thing so the other person understands your point. Sometimes you practice what you are going to say. Often we write drafts of our memos and speeches to make sure we use the right words. All this is done to make sure we send the right message.

Countless books and articles have been written that explain why sending the right message is so important and teach you how to send exactly the message you want to send. Their authors stress the importance of being concise, precise, and specific in choosing your words, regardless of whether you write them or speak them. They tell you that this is the best way to get your point across to your audience.

Who Is My Audience?

We all know how important our audience is in deciding what we are going to say and how we are going to say it. Explaining the value of a new phone system is different if you are speaking to the finance department than if you are addressing the telesales staff. The better you know your audience the easier it is for you to tailor your message to them. The more your message is tailored to your audience the more likely it is that you will get your point across.

How Do I Reach Them?

While the message you send is important, the message the receiver hears is even more important. If you know your audience you usually have an idea of how they will interpret or filter what you say. You can use this to your advantage to make sure they receive the message you are trying to send.

We all know, for instance, that if we are addressing a group of first-graders we can't use "big words" because they won't get it. They won't understand our message. So we choose words they will understand. Rather than using "big words" that convey the message we want to send, we use words we think they will understand. That way they will hear our message and understand it.

Don't try to explain technology concepts to accountants using technical terms. Don't use a financial analogy to get a point across to the Creative Department. If you want your service department to handle more calls per day, tell them that. Don't tell them they need to "reduce the time interval between customer-interface opportunities."

Manage This Issue

To increase your chances of getting your point across, focus more on the receiver than on the sender. Tailor your message to your audience to improve their comprehension. Don't worry so much about what you want to say as about what you want them to hear and understand.

Reh, F. John. "Getting Your Point Across." About.com.: Management. 6 July 2009. Available: http://management.about.com/cs/communication/a/GetPointOver702.htm

overall point will be like the first sentence, very general, while a main idea sentence is like the second sentence, a little more specific but still general. A support statement will be like the third sentence, very specific and full of details.

To get practice with general versus specific ideas, complete the following exercise.

Each of these pairs of sentences has been taken from a paragraph in Reading 11. The sentences have been shortened slightly. Which sentence is the more general statement? Which sentence is the more specific statement? Write your answer on the line.

1. First pair:

   Most adults, to varying degrees, ask themselves, "What will the neighbors think? What will my family think?" when they are making choices.

   specific
   _____

   Peer pressure is a powerful force in shaping attitudes and behavior.

   general
   _____

2: Second pair:

   People along the way may have told you that you were a great musician or a terrific actor.

   general
   _____

   You struck out with a couple of bands; you didn't get the starring role in a local stage production.

   specific
   _____

3: Third pair:

   One woman . . . never thought of herself as a maverick until she realized she was the first woman to successfully complete an engineering degree at a male-dominated institution.

   specific
   _____

   Sometimes, through this self-observation, we discover strengths that encourage us to assume new labels.

   general
   _____

Overall Point and Main Topics in a Reading

Your questions and predictions from your overview show you what to look for in a reading. Your questions help you establish general ideas about a reading, but your reading will provide more specific ideas. You can start with the most general question, your overall-point question, to help you find a rough thesis of the reading. As you read and find main ideas, you can fine-tune your rough thesis so that it covers all of the points the writer makes.

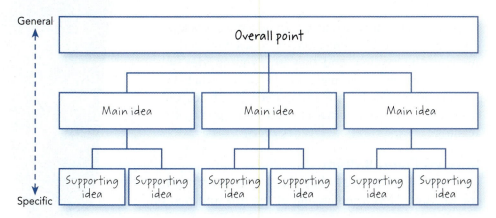

Overall-Point Question

The overall-point question from your overview is an especially important guide. It reminds you to look at how each part of a reading relates to the whole message. For example, Reading 11 is titled "How the Self-Concept Develops." An overall-point question for Reading 11—"How *does* the self-concept develop?"—will start you looking for answers about where our sense of ourselves comes from.

Stated Overall Point

In some readings the overall point stands out immediately as a clear-cut answer to your overall-point question. In Reading 11, the writers state their overall point in their introduction (paragraph 1):

> Some psychologists and sociologists have advanced theories that suggest we learn who we are through four basic means: (1) our communication with other individuals, (2) our association with groups, (3) roles we assume, and (4) our self-labels.

This sentence answers the question of how "we learn who we are (our self-concept)," and it covers four different "means," or ways, we have of learning about ourselves.

Main Topics

A reading is really a series of topics that relate to the thesis. A main **topic** is what one paragraph or one entire section of the reading is about. Like a subject of the reading as a whole, a topic can be stated in a word or phrase. In Reading 11, for example, the heading "Communication with Others" names the topic of the first section. If you ask yourself, "What is this paragraph about?" or "What are these paragraphs about?", your answer is the topic.

connect now

Do you glance at the title and headings of web pages to get an overall idea as to whether these pages will be useful to you?

Headings and Main Topics

Headings in a reading usually give you a good idea of the main topics. The four headings for Reading 11 announce four main topics:

- Communication with Others
- Association with Groups
- Assumed Roles
- Self-Labels

Each topic refers to one way in which we develop our self-concept. Headings make it easier to find the thesis of the reading, and they give you an idea of what the stated thesis might be. However, what do you do when the thesis is *not* stated? What do you do if the writer only hints at the overall point of a reading?

Implied Overall Point

You may have noticed that the stated overall point for Reading 11 is a rephrasing of the title and the four

Instructor Tip
Have students bring in articles that have headings and subheadings. In groups, have students write down the title, the heading, and the subheadings. Using this information, the students should then generate an overall-point statement. Have them read the article and test their overall point against that of the authors.

headings for the main topics. In some readings, you may have to figure out the overall point because it is not stated. If the reading has headings, you should be able to get an idea of the overall point based on the title and the headings. (Readings without headings will be discussed later.)

Figure out the overall point using the title and the headings, and then write a sentence that covers everything, and you will have written a rough thesis statement for the reading. To get a clearer idea of how to do this, look at the title and the headings for the reading below, but do not read the passage:

THE GREAT FLU EPIDEMIC

The New Threat

As the horrors of World War I drew to a close, a new threat arose. In March of 1918, hundreds of U.S. soldiers at Fort Riley, Kansas, fell ill with influenza, or flu. The outbreak was swift and harsh. About one in nine ill soldiers died. Despite the number of deaths, the public did not take notice. The horrors soldiers faced on the front in Europe seemed to surpass this isolated illness. Soon, soldiers from Fort Riley joined the Allied forces in Europe. Within months, the illness had spread throughout Europe, killing millions of people. Experts believe that the mass movement of troops aided the spread of the disease.

The Spread of the Disease

In September, as soldiers began to return home, the illness attacked the U.S. public. It struck first in Boston, Massachusetts, a city with a busy international port. People died within hours of falling ill. The death toll grew so high nationwide that there was a shortage of caskets. To block the spread of the disease, states restricted gatherings and travel. They closed saloons and prohibited stores from having sales. They even limited funerals to 15 minutes. Nevertheless, the flu claimed the lives of more than a half-million Americans, 10 times as many as had died in the war. Worldwide, it was the worst epidemic ever, killing between 20 and 40 million people.

> The death toll grew so high nationwide that there was a shortage of caskets.

What is the title of the reading?

The Great Flu Epidemic

What are the headings?

The New Threat and _The Spread of the Disease_

Write a sentence that combines the title and the headings:

Flu was the new threat, and the disease spread during the Great Flu Epidemic.

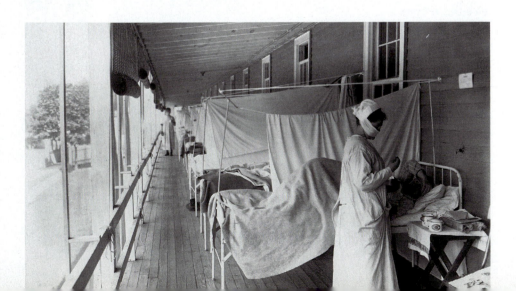

Now, go back and read the passage to see if your sentence covers all of the main topics. Your rough thesis statement should cover the contents of the paragraphs, and after you are finished reading, you can fine-tune the thesis if necessary. Read the revised thesis below:

Toward the end of World War I, influenza became a new threat as soldiers throughout the world fell ill, and the disease spread, causing a terrible epidemic known as the Great Flu Epidemic.

This thesis covers all of the main topics discussed in the passage.

EXERCISES

PRACTICE

To get practice writing a thesis statement, complete the following exercise.

Look at the title and the headings for the reading below, but do not read the passage. Answer the questions that follow the passage.

ARETHA FRANKLIN, QUEEN OF SOUL

The Church Choir

Aretha Franklin, the "queen of soul," grew up singing in the choir at church. Her father was a preacher and her mother a gospel singer. In her youth, Franklin worked with some of gospel music's greatest stars, such as Mahalia Jackson and Clara Ward. By the age of 12, Franklin was singing solos. These highlighted the beauty and power of her voice. By the age of 14, Franklin had recorded her first gospel album.

Stifled in New York

At the age of 18, Franklin moved to New York to pursue her career as a singer. Talent scouts offered her several contracts, and she signed with one of the companies. Franklin made many albums over the next few years, but her talents were not fully expressed. Instead of rhythm and blues, Franklin was performing only pop and jazz.

A New Company, a New Career

In 1966, when her contract expired, Franklin signed with another company. Now she was able to focus on her rhythm and blues roots while weaving in gospel and rock. The styles mixed well with her natural talents and provided a showcase for her soulful voice. Over the next few years, Franklin sold millions of albums. She recorded many hits such as "Respect" and "Chain of Fools." In 1987 Franklin was inducted into the Rock and Roll Hall of Fame. She was the first woman to receive this tribute.

1. What is the title of the reading?

   Aretha Franklin, Queen of Soul

2. What are the headings?

   The Church Choir, Stifled in New York, and A New Company, A New Career

3. Write a sentence that combines the title and the headings:

Aretha Franklin, Queen of Soul, sang in a church choir, was stifled in New York, and signed with a new company to start a new career.

4. Read the passage. Once you have read the passage, review your thesis statement and revise it if necessary.

Aretha Franklin, Queen of Soul, began singing in a church choir and moved to New York to sing but felt stifled; however, when she signed with a new company, she started a career that made her famous.

_____

_____

Main Ideas in Paragraphs

Headings can help you find main topics, and once you find a main topic, you want to look for what the writer says about that topic. For example, in Reading 11 the first topic is "Communication with Others," but you don't know what the writers say about communication with others until you read.

Stated Main Ideas

Every paragraph of a reading will have a main idea, and each paragraph will somehow support a main topic of the reading, which in turn supports the thesis. As you read, look for a stated main idea sentence that gives a general, or overall, idea about an individual paragraph. Often that sentence appears near the beginning of the paragraph. However, a stated main idea can be found anywhere in a paragraph. For example, the main idea about the topic of communicating with others is found in the third sentence in paragraph 2 of Reading 11.

> We learn who we are by *communicating with others*, receiving their feedback, making sense out of it, and internalizing or rejecting all or part of it, such that we are altered by the experience.

The italicized part of the sentence repeats the topic. The first part of the sentence states the idea that links communication to our self-concept. The rest of the sentence tells more precisely how we use this communication. This sentence is unusual because it covers all of the ideas of paragraph 2, but it also covers all of the ideas of this particular section of the reading. So, not only is it the stated main idea of the paragraph, it is also the stated main idea of the main topic.

Finding a stated main idea is easier if you first figure out the topic of the paragraph by using the heading or by reading the paragraph, asking yourself, "What is this paragraph about?" and jotting your answer in the margin. Then, read to find what the writer says about that topic (ask yourself, "What are these paragraphs about?"). Remember, the main idea will be more general and cover major points of the paragraph.

Instructor Tip

Using scissors, cut a paragraph up so that sentences are separated on individual slips of paper (you can use any of the example or exercise paragraphs in this book). Place slips into an envelope. Using different paragraphs, make several envelopes like this. In groups, have students arrange the sentences into what they think is the proper order for the paragraph. Then have students identify the main idea.

To get practice finding main ideas, complete the following exercise.

Read the passage below and answer the questions in the margins. When you find a sentence that states the main idea of the paragraph, underline it. Then, answer the questions that follow the passage.

FOOD FROM THE 'HOOD

The Los Angeles Riots

In 1992, students at Crenshaw High School turned a garden into a business. Food from the 'Hood began as a response to violent Los Angeles riots. One cause of the riots was the verdict in the Rodney King trial, in which an all-white jury acquitted four police officers accused of beating an African American man. The students also saw another reason for the riots: lack of economic opportunity.

Students Respond

The students responded by forming their own natural-foods business. A teacher and a volunteer adviser helped them make a plan. In October, the student-owners planted crops in a garden behind the school. By late December, they had donated their first harvest to a neighborhood food bank.

The next year, they developed their quarter-acre garden into a business asset. They sold their produce at a local farmer's market. They also started a line of salad dressings. Half of the profits were used to expand their company. The rest went into a scholarship fund.

Today's Market

Today students still learn business skills by managing Food from the 'Hood. They give one-quarter of their produce to the needy. Their products bring in $250 thousand a year.

As students expand the company, they also cultivate their futures. More than 70 students who were once at risk of dropping out have gone on to college.

> Today students still learn business skills by managing Food from the 'Hood.

What is this paragraph about? Food from the 'Hood and the LA Riots

What is this paragraph about? The students' business

What is this paragraph about? a business asset

What are these paragraphs about? how the students responded to the lack of economic opportunity that contributed to the riots

What is this paragraph about? the business today

1. What is the title of the reading?

    Food from the 'Hood

2. What are the headings?

    The Los Angeles Riots, Students Respond, and Today's Market

3. What is the stated main idea of paragraph 1?

    Food from the 'Hood began as a response to the lack of economic opportunity that contrib-

    uted to the violent Los Angeles riots.

    What is the stated main idea of paragraph 2?

    The students responded by forming their own natural-foods business.

    What is the stated main idea of paragraph 3?

    The next year, they developed their quarter-acre garden into a business asset.

    What is the main idea of the topic "Students Respond" (paragraphs 2 and 3)?

    The students created a profitable business.

    What is the main idea of paragraph 4?

    Today students still learn business skills by managing Food from the 'Hood.

4. Write a sentence that combines the main ideas and states the thesis of the
    reading.

    As a response to the Los Angeles riots, students created a natural-food business

    called Food from the 'Hood, developed the business, and still manage it today.

Implied Main Ideas

Sometimes, the main idea of a paragraph or main topic is implied. This means the writer has not stated the point but hinted at it, assuming the reader is intelligent enough to figure it out. And you are. Remember, a stated main idea contains a topic and its major points, so an implied main idea must contain the same information.

Let's consider a paragraph with an implied main idea. First, read the paragraph.

New wireless technologies have cut the cord that bound people to telephones in their homes and workplaces and to telephones in stationary telephone booths. The sounds of telephone signals are everywhere— from boulevards and department stores to restaurants and theaters. Many of these conversations are taking place in cars. Anecdotal evidence suggests that talking on the phone while driving causes accidents, but it takes more than a few personal tales to establish a link between cell phones and problems on the road. Scientists, however, are examining this relationship that drivers are more likely to wander from lane to lane and collide with another vehicle when using cell phones. Drivers using phones are also more likely

> One study demonstrates that drivers are more likely to wander from lane to lane and collide with another vehicle when using cell phones.

to strike pedestrians. "Hands-free" phones appear to be no safer than hand-held phones, and using phones in cars appears to be more dangerous for older people than for younger people. In addition, drivers on the phone seem to respond more slowly to changes in traffic or unexpected events. In fact, drivers who talk while they drive are four times as likely to be in an accident as drivers who do not. Drivers using the phone at the time of an accident, moreover, are more likely to suffer a serious or fatal injury than those who focus only on driving.

Then, ask yourself, "What is this paragraph about?" Next, mark in the margin or underline the major points discussed in the paragraph.

What is this paragraph about?

cell phones everywhere and driving accidents

use causes accidents

New wireless technologies have cut the cord that bound people to telephones in their homes and workplaces and to telephones in stationary telephone booths. The sounds of telephone signals are everywhere—from boulevards and department stores to restaurants and theaters. Many of these conversations are taking place in cars. Anecdotal evidence suggests that talking on the phone while driving causes accidents, but it takes more than a few personal tales to establish a link between cell phones and problems on the road. Scientists, however, are examining this relationship.

dangerous distraction; accident more likely

One study demonstrates that drivers are more likely to wander from lane to lane and collide with another vehicle when using car phones. Drivers using phones are also more likely to strike pedestrians. "Hands-free" phones appear to be no safer than hand-held phones, and using phones in cars appears to be more dangerous for older people than for younger people. In addition, drivers on the phone seem to respond more slowly to changes in traffic or unexpected events. In fact, drivers who talk while they drive are four times as likely to be in an accident as drivers who do not. Drivers using the phone at the time of an accident, moreover, are more likely to suffer a serious or fatal injury than those who focus only on driving.

Now, write a sentence that contains the paragraph's topic and its major points, but ensure your sentence covers all of the points.

Talking on a cell phone while driving a car causes accidents; the phone is a dangerous distraction that makes an accident more likely.

_____

_____

_____

Instructor Tip
To extend the previous paragraph activity, make copies of a few new paragraphs with stated main ideas. Cut a paragraph up so that sentences are separated on individual slips of paper (you can use any of the example or exercise paragraphs in this book). Place all the slips *except the main idea* into an envelope. Have students get into groups, rearrange the paragraph into its proper order, and figure out the implied main idea. Have them write their own main idea sentence. When they are complete, you show the students the original main idea so they may compare it to theirs.

As you can see, it is not very difficult to generate a main idea sentence for a paragraph. What happens when you cannot find a stated main idea for a main topic? If this is the case, first figure out the main ideas of the individual paragraphs, and then figure out the main idea for the main topic. Suppose you read the following selection in a book on how to get into college. The heading for this section is "Student Loans: Getting the Education You Want"; the title of the book is *College and You.*

STUDENT LOANS: GETTING THE EDUCATION YOU WANT

The cost of a four-year college education is escalating daily. Current figures suggest that in 2002, a typical student will pay more than $26,000 per year at a private school and almost $12,000 at a public one and that those numbers will increase by about 6 percent per year.

Whatever the size of one's college savings account, additional sources of funds (including government grants, private scholarships, and a variety of loan programs) are available to students. The first step a student must take to find the money needed is to fill out a FAFSA form (free application for federal student aid), because all government and most private lending agencies use the information provided on it. Students can get these forms from their high school or college counselor or from the Internet.

College loans typically are granted either to the student or to the parents. Student loans—such as the Stafford Loan—are sponsored by the government and have a low interest rate. They do not have to be repaid until the student has graduated or left school. The most common loan for parents is a government-sponsored, low-interest Plus Loan, which the borrower must begin to repay immediately. Some parents also seek alternative loans and may, for example, take out a second mortgage on their home.

Where do you start? Easy. Look for stated main ideas in each paragraph. If you cannot find them, ask yourself, "What is each paragraph about?" Next, mark in the margin or underline the major points discussed in each paragraph.

STUDENT LOANS: GETTING THE EDUCATION YOU WANT

The cost of a four-year college education is escalating daily. Current figures suggest that in 2002, a typical student will pay more than $26,000 per year at a private school and almost $12,000 at a public one and that those numbers will increase by about 6 percent per year.

What is this paragraph about?

tuition increases

Whatever the size of one's college savings account, additional sources of funds (including government grants, private scholarships, and a variety of loan programs) are available to students. The first step a student must take to find the money needed is to fill out a FAFSA form (free application for federal student aid), because all government and most private lending agencies use the information provided on it. Students can get these forms from their high school or college counselor or from the Internet.

What is this paragraph about?

additional sources for college funds

no stated MI but types of loans discussed

College loans typically are granted either to the student or to the parents. Student loans—such as the Stafford Loan—are sponsored by the government and have a low interest rate. They do not have to be repaid until the student has graduated or left school. The most common loan for parents is a government-sponsored, low-interest Plus Loan, which the borrower must begin to repay immediately. Some parents also seek alternative loans and may, for example, take out a second mortgage on their home.

What is this paragraph about?

info on student loans

Now, write a sentence that contains the heading of the selection and the main ideas of each paragraph, but ensure your sentence covers all of the points.

Tuition has increased, so to get the education you want, you may need to find additional

college funds and know the types of loans available to you.

_____

_____

You may have noticed that working with the above selection was like working with a reading that has no headings. So, what do you do with a reading without headings, such as Reading 12?

Readings without Headings

First, get an overview and ask questions about the reading you are working with. Skim the introduction and the conclusion for a stated thesis. If you find a stated thesis, mark it. Then, read the passage for its main topics and look for main idea sentences in individual paragraphs. Ask yourself, "What is this paragraph about?" and "What are these paragraphs about?", and "How do these paragraphs relate to my overall-point question?" Mark major points in paragraphs. Then, add up the information.

You have learned how to find implied main ideas for paragraphs and main topics. Working through a reading without headings applies the same skills. The writer does not include headings because she knows that you, an intelligent reader, will figure out the main topics. Figure out the main ideas for individual paragraphs to figure out the main ideas for the main topics. Figure out the main ideas for main topics to figure out the thesis of the reading.

Supporting Ideas

You already know that main ideas support the thesis. Now you need to recognize that supporting ideas explain and clarify—or support—a main idea, whether that main idea is part of a paragraph or a main topic.

Types of Supporting Ideas

Supporting details are often referred to as major or minor details. A major detail is more general, and a minor detail is more specific. Consider these two sentences:

The children made a mess of the living room.

They turned over chairs, wrote on walls, spilled juice on the floor, and tore up the couch cushions.

If these sentences were supporting ideas in a paragraph, one would be considered major, and one would be considered minor. The first statement is a general idea, telling you the children made a mess, while the second statement gives specific examples of the mess the children made.

There are many ways to give specific support for a more general idea. Here are some of the kinds of supporting ideas you'll find:

- explanations
- examples (such as the example you just saw about the children)
- details about people, places, things
- facts
- statistics
- quotations

Supporting and Main Ideas

To find supporting ideas that explain or clarify a main idea, it's useful to turn the main idea into a question. For example, for the first main idea of Reading 11, you could ask the question, "How does communication with others develop our self-concept?" Here are two specific ideas in the section that clearly answer that question:

- From birth on, the most important communication that influences our self-concept comes from parents and siblings; later we're also influenced by friends, teachers, and co-workers. (paragraph 4)
- A woman whose sense of herself was damaged by her overly critical mother demonstrates how the influence of others affects our self-concept. (paragraph 5).

These two supporting ideas clearly answer the question of how communication with others affects us. The sample marking for Reading 11 on page 192 shows the supporting ideas for this main idea and for the other three main ideas.

You don't usually read a single paragraph of a reading. Instead, you see how ideas in a reading move logically from one paragraph to the next. Reading with the overall point and main ideas in mind helps you understand each paragraph and see how details support those main ideas.

KIRSTEN DUNST

The Varieties of Scientific Experience: A Personal View of the Search for God

by Carl Sagan

Working on the *Spider-Man* trilogy seems to have gotten Kirsten Dunst thinking about some serious questions. She's exploring the intersection of science and religion by reading Carl Sagan's *The Varieties of Scientific Experience: A Personal View of the Search for God.*

If you liked **The Varieties of Scientific Experience,** you might also like:

The Stuff of Thought, Steven Pinker

Cosmos, Carl Sagan

The Day the Universe Changed, James Burke

Instructor Tip
Have students get into groups and give each group a main-idea sentence. Have the group brainstorm and generate supporting ideas for that main idea. Have them write a paragraph using the main-idea sentence and the supporting ideas they generated during the group discussion.

connect now

What kind of details do you use to support your ideas in a conversation? Do you use facts or statistics to prove a point?

Sometimes you run into a challenging paragraph. In that case, use the same steps for finding the main idea and supporting ideas in the paragraph that you use for implied ideas and readings without headings:

1. Find the topic of the paragraph.
2. Look for the main idea about the topic.
3. See how the specific ideas support the main idea.

Try these steps with paragraph 10 in Reading 11.

1. The topic is gender, since every sentence in the paragraph points to gender or sex differences.
2. The main idea about gender can be found in the first sentence. You could turn that idea into a question: "How does gender influence our self-concept from birth on?"
3. The specific supporting ideas answer the question about this influence. From the beginning, parents put children into gender groups. By ages three to five children, encouraged by parents, begin to understand their gender roles. By adulthood our self-concept is very influenced by our gender.

Hot or Not?

Have you ever quoted someone to support your ideas? Who did you quote?

EXERCISES

To get practice with marking main ideas and supporting details, complete the following exercise.

Read the passage below and answer the questions in the margins. When you find a sentence that states the main idea of the paragraph, underline it. Then, answer the questions that follow the passage.

CHANGING HEMLINES: THE STOCK MARKET AND FASHION

Through the years, some economic analysts have hypothesized that the stock market takes its cue from fashion magazines: that it goes up or down along with hemlines; that when times are good and spending expands, fabric shrinks. A mathematician might express the idea as an inverse ratio and say that when more money buys less clothing, good times will surely follow.

Individuals can weigh the facts that follow and decide for themselves whether the "hemline theory" has any merit and whether it is true that widespread wealth is related to risqué fashion.

At the beginning of the twentieth century, the market suffered brief downturns following the assassination of President William McKinley in 1901 and the San Francisco earthquake in 1907. Hemlines hovered at the ankle, but an improved economy in the years just before World War I was accompanied by a more relaxed approach to fashion. More comfortable undergarments also replaced the stiff corsetry of the nineteenth century.

During the Roaring Twenties, flappers bobbed their hair and shortened their skirts, exposing a considerable length of leg encased in modern, sheer ho-

Hemlines stayed patriotically short throughout the war to help conserve fabric.

What is this paragraph about? economy and fashion

What is this sentence? The overall point

What is this paragraph about? pre-WWI economy and its effect on fashion

What is this paragraph about? 1920's economy and its effect on fashion

siery. The Dow Jones Industrial Index saw a rise of 350 percent. Then, on October 29, 1929, the market crashed, sending the United States into the Great Depression. Hemlines slipped below the calf.

As the business picture improved, feminine knees came back into view for the first time in years. Soon, the market responded with nationalistic fervor to the entrance of the United States into World War II after the bombing of Pearl Harbor. Hemlines stayed patriotically short throughout the war to help conserve fabric.

During the prosperous 1960s, shorts shrank into hotpants, and skirts went to mini and then to micromini length, heading higher and higher along with the stock market and the astronauts. There is a saying, however, that "what goes up must come down." The market turned decidedly bearish, declining along with hemlines as the country moved into the 1970s. Skirts again began to descend modestly.

Except for a few insignificant setbacks, the 1980s and 1990s represented the longest sustained bull market the country had ever seen, and the Dow Jones average rose from less than 1,000 points to a high that reached almost 12,000 points. Hemlines shot up; tops were cropped almost out of existence; "less" clothing turned into "more" fashion as computers and the Internet put millions of dollars into uncounted pockets.

Is there a stated main idea? If not, what kind of supporting details are there? __No stated MI; details are examples__ _____ _____

What are these paragraphs about? __fashion and economy before and after WWII__ _____

What kinds of details are used here? __more examples__ _____

1. What is the title of the reading?

   Changing Hemlines: The Stock Market and Fashion _____

2. What are the headings?

   There are no headings. _____
   _____

3. What is the implied main idea of paragraph 1?

   As stock markets fluctuate, so do clothing hemlines. _____
   _____

   What is the stated main idea of paragraph 3?

   Hemlines hovered at the ankle, but an improved economy in the years just before

   World War I was accompanied by a more relaxed approach to fashion.

   What is the implied main idea of paragraph 4?

   At the beginning of the 1920s when the market was good, hemlines were short, but when

   the market crashed in 1929, the hemlines were lengthened.

   What is the implied main idea of the main topic of paragraphs 5 and 6?

   Before and after World War II, hemlines changed as much as the economy changed.
   _____

4. What is the stated or implied thesis of this reading?

Individuals can weigh the facts that follow and decide for themselves whether the

"hemline theory" has any merit and whether it is true that widespread wealth is related

to risqué fashion.

Adjust Your Marking

When you've found and marked the overall point, main ideas, and a few supporting ideas, look over your marking. You may need to make some changes once you have a clearer picture of the relationship of ideas in the reading. The overall point you've marked should be general enough to cover all the main ideas in the reading; each main idea should support the overall point.

APPLY THE NEW STRATEGY
Find and Mark Main Ideas

Before reading "How the Self-Concept Develops," make a connection, get an overview, and ask questions. The title of this reading is already close to being a question. We can frame the overall-point question in this way: "How does the self-concept develop?" As you read, try finding and underlining main ideas that answer this question. Look for supporting ideas that explain each main idea.

How the Self-Concept Develops

READING 11   **STEVEN A. BEEBE, SUSAN J. BEEBE, AND DIANA K. IVY**

Steven and Susan Beebe teach communication courses at Southwest Texas University; Diana Ivy teaches communication at Texas A & M University–Corpus Christi. This reading comes from the chapter called "Self-Awareness and Communication," from their textbook *Communication: Principles for a Lifetime* (2001). In this section from the chapter, the authors discuss how each of us develops a sense of our own identity.

connect ◄──────────────────────────────────

Some psychologists and sociologists have advanced theories that sug-   1
gest we learn who we are through four basic means: (1) our communication with other individuals, (2) our association with groups, (3) roles we assume, and (4) our self-labels.

Communication with Others

get an overview and ask questions

Be sure to see the "Recap" (summary) at the end of this reading.

2   A valued colleague of ours often says, when he teaches communication courses, that every time you lose a relationship you lose an opportunity to see yourself. What he means is that we don't come to know and understand ourselves in a vacuum. We learn who we are by communicating with others, receiving their feedback, making sense out of it, and internalizing or rejecting all or part of it, such that we are altered by the experience. For example, probably someone in your life has told you that you have a good sense of humor. But think about it for a moment: How would you know if you're funny if it were not for others laughing at humorous things you say or do? Sure, you can crack yourself up, but the real test of a sense of humor is how it manifests itself with others.

respond

3   In 1902, scholar Charles Norton Cooley first advanced the notion that we form our self-concepts by seeing ourselves in a figurative looking glass: We learn who we are by interacting with others, much as we look into a mirror and see our reflection.[1] Like Cooley, George Herbert Mead, author of the important work *Mind, Self, and Society,* also believed that our sense of who we are is a consequence of our relationship with others.[2] So when we form new relationships and sustain the old ones, we gain opportunities to know ourselves better.

vital vocabulary

4   Self-concept development begins at birth. Names and nicknames reveal how we are viewed by important others; thus they are some of our earliest indicators of identity. During the early years of our lives, our parents and siblings are the key individuals who reflect who we are. Sometimes it seems like, as much as we try or might like to, we cannot escape those early messages we received from our families—messages that shaped our view of self more than any other influence. As we become less dependent on family members, friends become highly influential in shaping our attitudes, beliefs, and values. Your earliest peer groups have had a pronounced effect on who you have become. Friends, teachers, and later, co-workers provide feedback on how well we perform certain tasks. This, in turn, helps us shape our sense of identity as adults. The media also has an effect on our view of self, although this indirect effect has less impact than the people in our lives.

5   Haven't you met people whom you just wished you could hand a decent self-concept? They're nice people, but they seem to suffer from a self-concept formed out of years of criticism from important others. We recall the story of one colleague who was quite an accomplished dancer as an undergraduate. She'd known an upbringing of never being quite good enough, never being able to please her demanding mother, hard as she tried. She

remembered one particular dance recital, where she felt she had danced the performance of her life. She just knew her mother would be proud, but when her mother joined her backstage after the performance, amidst the accolades of her friends, her mother had only one thing to say: She pointed out one moment in the dance when the woman's arm should have been straight up instead of out to the side. That's all the feedback she got from her mother—stinging criticism about one brief moment in a brilliant evening's worth of performance.

6　　Sometimes it's upsetting, as teachers, to meet students who seem to have taken such an emotional pummeling from their parents in their early years that they seem beaten down by life at a very early age. We can recover from such early warping of our self-concepts, but it is quite an undertaking. Fortunately, we see many more students who have well-balanced, fully developed self-concepts. You can tell that they were raised in a supportive, loving environment.

Association with Groups

7　　I'm a native New Yorker. I'm a soccer player. I'm a rabbi. I'm a real estate agent. I'm a member of the Young Democrats. Each of these self-descriptive statements answers the "Who am I" question by providing identification with a group or organization. Our awareness of who we are is often linked to who we associate with. How many of these kinds of group-associated terms could you use to describe yourself? Religious groups, political groups, ethnic groups, social groups, study groups, and occupational and professional groups play important roles in shaping your self-concept. Some of these groups we are born into; others we choose on our own. Either way, group associations are significant parts of our identities.

8　　As we alluded to earlier, peer pressure is a powerful force in shaping attitudes and behavior, and adolescents are particularly susceptible to it. But adolescents are not alone in allowing the attitudes, beliefs, and values of others to shape their expectations and behaviors. Most adults, to varying degrees, ask themselves, "What will the neighbors think? What will my family think?" when they are making choices.

> Our awareness of who we are is often linked to who we associate with.

Assumed Roles

9　　A large part of most people's answers to the "Who am I" question reflects roles they assume in their lives. Mother, aunt, brother, uncle, manager, salesperson, teacher, spouse, and student are labels that imply certain expectations for behavior, and they are important in shaping self-concept.

10　　Gender asserts a powerful influence on the self-concept from birth on. As soon as parents know the sex of their child, many begin associating their children into a gender group by adhering to cultural rules. They give children sex-stereotypical toys, such as catcher's mitts, train sets, or guns for boys, and dolls, tea sets, and "dress-up" kits for girls. These cultural conventions and expectations play a major role in shaping our self-concept and our behavior.[3] Research Indicates that up until the age of three, children are not acutely aware of sex roles. Between the ages of three and five, however, masculine and feminine roles begin to emerge (as encouraged by parents), and they are usually solidified between the ages of five and seven.[4] Research shows that by the time we reach adulthood, our self-concepts are quite distinguishable by gender, with men describing themselves more in terms of giftedness, power, and invulnerability, and women viewing themselves in terms of likeability and morality.[5]

Self-Labels

11 Although our self-concept is deeply affected by others, we are not blank slates for them to write on. The labels we use to describe our own attitudes, beliefs, values, and actions also play a role in shaping our self-concept. From where do we acquire our labels? We interpret what we experience; we are self-reflexive. *Self-reflexiveness* is the human ability to think about what we're doing while we're doing it. We talk to ourselves about ourselves. We are both participants and observers in all that we do. This dual role encourages us to use labels to describe who we are.

12 When you were younger, perhaps you dreamed of becoming a rocker or a movie star. People along the way may have told you that you were a great musician or a terrific actor, but as you matured, you probably began observing yourself more critically. You struck out with a couple of bands; you didn't get the starring role in a local stage production. So you self-reflexively decided that you were not, deep down, a rocker or an actor, even though others may have labeled you as "talented." Sometimes, through this self-observation, we discover strengths that encourage us to assume new labels. One woman we know never thought of herself as a "maverick" until she realized that she was the first woman to successfully complete an engineering degree at a male-dominated institution.

Recap

How the Self-Concept Develops

Communication with Others	The self-concept develops as we communicate with others, receive their feedback, make sense out of it, and internalize or reject all or part of it.
Association with Groups	We develop our self-concept partly because of and through our identification with groups or organizations.
Assumed Roles	The self-concept is affected by roles we assume, such as son or daughter, employee, parent, spouse, student.
Self-Labels	The terms we use to describe our attitudes, beliefs, values, and actions play a role in shaping the self-concept.

Notes

1. C. H. Cooley, *Human Nature and the Social* Order (New York: Scribner's, 1912).
2. G. H. Mead, *Mind, Self, and Society* (Chicago: University of Chicago Press, 1934).
3. D. K. Ivy and P. Backlund, *Exploring GenderSpeak: Personal Effectiveness in Gender Communications,* 2nd ed. (New York: McGraw-Hill, 2000).

4. J. C. Pearson, L. Turner, and W. T. Mancillas, *Gender and Communications*, 3rd ed. (Dubuque, Ia.: William C. Brown, 1995).
5. J. E. Stake, "Gender Differences and Similarities in Self-Concept Within Everyday Life Contexts," *Psychology of Women Quarterly 6* (1992): 349–363.

ACTIVE READERS RESPOND

After you've finished reading, use these activities to respond to "How the Self-Concept Develops." You may write your answers in the spaces provided or on a separate sheet of paper.

VITAL VOCABULARY

Some words in this reading may be unfamiliar to you. Use the methods of Strategy 3 to explain what the listed words mean.

USE CONTEXT CLUES

a. accolades (paragraph 5) (Two context clues help define this word.)

_____

b. pummeling (paragraph 6) (In "such an emotional pummeling," the word "such" is an example clue.)

_____

USE WORD PARTS

a. adhering (paragraph 10) (The word "adhere" is related to the word "adhesive" (sticking to).)

_____

USE THE DICTIONARY

Choose the correct definition of each word as it is used in the context of this reading.

a. assume (paragraph 9)

_____

b. alluded to (paragraph 8)

_____

c. maverick (paragraph 12)

_____

SKILLS EXERCISE: THE OVERALL POINT AND MAIN IDEAS

1. What is the title of the reading?

   How the Self-Concept Develops
   _____

2. What are the headings?

   Communication with Others, Association with Groups, Assumed Roles, Self-Labels
   _____

   _____

3. What is the stated main idea of paragraph 7?

   Our awareness of who we are is often linked to who we associate with.
   _____

   _____

What is the implied main idea of paragraph 12?

You may not know who are you until you examine yourself critically.

What is the main idea of the main topic for paragraphs 11 and 12?

The labels we use to describe our own attitudes, beliefs, values, and actions also play a role in shaping our self-concept.

4. What is the stated or implied thesis of this reading?

Some psychologists and sociologists have advanced theories that suggest we learn who we are through four basic means: (1) our communication with other individuals, (2) our association with groups, (3) roles we assume, and (4) our self-labels.

OBJECTIVE OPERATIONS

1. Who is the writer's intended audience?

   a. communication students
   b. sociologists
   c. general audience
   d. psychologists

2. What is the author's purpose?

   a. to inform
   b. to persuade
   c. to entertain

3. Which sentence is the stated main idea of the passage?

   a. "Some psychologists and sociologists have advanced theories that suggest we learn who we are through four basic means: (1) our communication with other individuals, (2) our association with groups, (3) roles we assume, and (4) our self-labels."
   b. "A valued colleague of ours often says, when he teaches communication courses, that every time you lose a relationship you lose an opportunity to see yourself."
   c. "What he means is that we don't come to know and understand ourselves in a vacuum."
   d. "We learn who we are by communicating with others, receiving their feedback, making sense out of it, and internalizing or rejecting all or part of it, such that we are altered by the experience."

4. The word "accolades" in paragraph 5, line 10, most nearly means

   a. credits.
   b. expressions of surprise.
   c. great compliments.
   d. expressions of dismay.

5. What is the topic of paragraphs 5 and 6?

   a. self-concept
   b. forming a self-concept
   c. how criticism affects self-concept
   d. forming a decent self-concept

6. Our self-concept is influenced most by

   a. our current relationships with peers.
   b. our early experiences with teachers.
   c. our early experiences with peers.
   d. our early experiences with parents and siblings.

7. If someone has been harshly criticized as a child,

   a. he or she will not be able to gain a good self-concept as an adult.
   b. he or she will have to work hard to gain a good self-concept.
   c. the criticism makes the person tougher and thus strengthens the person's self-concept.
   d. you can assume that the parents were treated the same way as children.

8. The word "maverick" in paragraph 12, line 9, most nearly means

a. revolutionary.

b. individualist.

c. unbranded range animal.

d. untamed.

9. What is the topic of paragraphs 7 and 8?

a. Who am I?

b. how peer pressure shapes us

c. association with groups

d. self-awareness

10. Our awareness of who we are is often connected with groups we associate with. These are groups that

a. we are born into or choose on our own.

b. we choose after we've learned to know what we think is important to us.

c. we have to work hard to join.

d. we are born into or have friends or family as members.

11. The word "alluded" in paragraph 8, line 1, most nearly means

a. related.

b. referred to.

c. submitted.

d. passed on.

12. Which sentence is the stated main idea of paragraph 4?

a. "Self-concept development begins at birth."

b. "During the early years of our lives, our parents and siblings are the key individuals who reflect who we are."

c. "As we become less dependent on family members, friends become highly influential in shaping our attitudes, beliefs, and values."

d. "Friends, teachers, and later, co-workers provide feedback on how well we perform certain tasks."

13. What is the implied main idea of paragraph 5?

a. Mothers who criticize are harmful.

b. Harsh criticism can affect the development of a decent self-concept.

c. A demanding mother can affect whether a person has a decent self-concept.

d. Criticism hurts.

14. Self-reflexiveness shapes our self-concept by

a. changing what we think of ourselves to better reflect societal norms and conventions.

b. giving us a chance to adapt to other people's concept of us.

c. allowing us to describe who we are as we observe ourselves doing things.

d. allowing us to do things by instinct, as if by reflex.

15. Based on the information about gender roles in the reading, you could assume that

a. babies are born with a strong awareness of gender roles.

b. until age three, children have no strong awareness of gender roles.

c. as we grow into adult men and women, our self-concept is less and less dependent on strong identification with a gender role.

d. from birth on, parents exert a powerful influence on a child's awareness of gender roles.

16. According to the authors, who first proposed the idea that we learn who we are by how we are reflected by others?

a. George Herbert Mead

b. Charles Norton Cooley

c. the woman who sought her mother's approval

d. the woman who saw herself as a maverick

17. If friends have an effect on you in childhood, then who is most likely to have an effect on you in adulthood?

a. teachers

b. new friends

c. co-workers

d. parents

18. What is the overall tone of the passage?

a. concerned

b. informative

c. critical

d. objective

1. How do our early experiences with family influence our self-concept? Give some examples the authors use.

   (Answers will vary.)

2. How do the kinds of groups we associate with contribute to our awareness of who we are?

   (Answers will vary.)

3. What is the effect of gender on the roles we assume?

   (Answers will vary.)

4. What is meant by self-reflexiveness? How does it help shape our self-concept?

   (Answers will vary.)

5. How closely did this reading match your own understanding about how you developed a sense of "who you are"?

   (Answers will vary.)

READERS DISCUSS

1. What group association terms could you come up with to help identify yourself? What roles do you play in your life that help identify you?

   (Answers will vary.)

2. What are the most important things you learned about yourself from this reading? Discuss with others the kinds of information each of you gained.

   (Answers will vary.)

SAMPLE MARKING:
How the Self-Concept Develops

overall point

Some psychologists and sociologists have advanced theories that sug- **1** gest we learn who we are through four basic means: (1) our communication with other individuals, (2) our association with groups, (3) roles we assume, and (4) our self-labels.

Communication with Others

A valued colleague of ours often says, when he teaches communication **2** courses, that every time you lose a relationship you lose an opportunity to see yourself. What he means is that we don't come to know and understand ourselves in a vacuum. <u>We learn who we are by communicating with others, receiving their feedback, making sense out of it</u>, and <u>internalizing or rejecting all or part of it</u>, such that we are <u>altered by the experience</u>. For

MI

example, probably someone in your life has told you that you have a good sense of humor. But think about it for a moment: <u>How would you know if you're funny if it were not for others laughing at humorous things you say or do?</u> Sure, you can crack yourself up, but the real test of a sense of humor is how it manifests itself with others.

ex.

In 1902, scholar Charles Norton Cooley first advanced the notion that **3** we form our self-concepts by seeing ourselves in a figurative looking glass: <u>We learn who we are by interacting with others</u>, much as we <u>look into a mirror and see our reflection</u>.[1] Like Cooley, George Herbert Mead, author of the important work *Mind, Self, and Society*, also believed that our sense of who we are is a consequence of our relationship with others.[2] So when we form new relationships and sustain the old ones, we gain opportunities to know ourselves better.

<u>Self-concept development begins at birth</u>. Names and nicknames reveal **4** how we are viewed by important others; thus they are some of our earliest indicators of identity. During the <u>early years of our lives, our parents and siblings are the key individuals who reflect who we are</u>. Sometimes it seems like, as much as we try or might like to, we cannot escape those early messages we received from our families—messages that shaped our view of self more than any other influence. As we become less dependent on fam-

early

later

ily members, <u>friends become highly influential</u> in shaping our attitudes, beliefs, and values. Your earliest peer groups have had a pronounced effect on who you have become. <u>Friends, teachers, and later, co-workers provide feedback</u> on how well we perform certain tasks. This, in turn, helps us shape our sense of identity as adults. The media also has an effect on our view of self, although this indirect effect has less impact than the people in our lives.

Haven't you met people whom you just wished you could hand a decent **5** self-concept? They're nice <u>people</u>, but they seem to <u>suffer from a self-concept formed out of years of criticism</u> from important others. We recall the story of one colleague who was quite an accomplished dancer as an undergraduate. She'd known an upbringing of never being quite good enough, never being able to please her demanding mother, hard as she tried. She remembered one particular dance recital, where she felt she had danced the performance of her life. She just knew her mother would be proud, but when her mother joined her backstage after the performance, amidst the accolades of her friends, her mother had only one thing to say: She pointed out one moment in the dance when the woman's arm should have been straight up instead of out to the side. That's all the feedback she got from her mother—stinging criticism about one brief moment in a brilliant evening's worth of performance.

ex.—effects of demanding mother

6 Sometimes it's upsetting, as teachers, to meet students who seem to have taken such an emotional pummeling from their parents in their early years that they seem beaten down by life at a very early age. We can recover from such early warping of our self-concepts, but it is quite an undertaking. Fortunately, we see many more students who have well-balanced, fully developed self-concepts. You can tell that they were raised in a supportive, loving environment.

Association with Groups

7 I'm a native New Yorker. I'm a soccer player. I'm a rabbi. I'm a real estate agent. I'm a member of the Young Democrats. Each of these self-descriptive statements answers the "Who am I" question by providing identification with a group or organization. Our awareness of who we are is often linked to who we associate with. How many of these kinds of group-associated terms could you use to describe yourself? Religious groups, political groups, ethnic groups, social groups, study groups, and occupational and professional groups play important roles in shaping your self-concept. Some of these groups we are born into; others we choose on our own. Either way, group associations are significant parts of our identities.

MI

many possible groups

8 As we alluded to earlier, peer pressure is a powerful force in shaping attitudes and behavior, and adolescents are particularly susceptible to it. But adolescents are not alone in allowing the attitudes, beliefs, and values of others to shape their expectations and behaviors. Most adults, to varying degrees, ask themselves, "What will the neighbors think? What will my family think?" when they are making choices.

Assumed Roles

9 A large part of most people's answers to the "Who am I" question reflects roles they assume in their lives. Mother, aunt, brother, uncle, manager, salesperson, teacher, spouse, and student are labels that imply certain expectations for behavior, and they are important in shaping self-concept.

MI

roles

10 Gender asserts a powerful influence on the self-concept from birth on. As soon as parents know the sex of their child, many begin associating their children into a gender group by adhering to cultural rules. They give children sex-stereotypical toys, such as catcher's mitts, train sets, or guns for boys, and dolls, tea sets, and "dress-up" kits for girls. These cultural

→parents put child into gender role

conventions and expectations play a major role in shaping our self-concept and our behavior.[3] Research Indicates that up until the age of three, children are not acutely aware of sex roles. Between the ages of three and five, however, masculine and feminine roles begin to emerge (as encouraged by parents), and they are usually solidified between the ages of five and seven.[4] Research shows that by the time we reach adulthood, our self-concepts are quite distinguishable by gender, with men describing themselves more in terms of giftedness, power, and invulnerability, and women viewing themselves in terms of likeability and morality.[5]

diffs. betw. men + women

Self-Labels

Although our self-concept is deeply affected by others, we are not blank slates for them to write on. The labels we use to describe our own attitudes, beliefs, values, and actions also play a role in shaping our self-concept. From where do we acquire our labels? We interpret what we experience; we are self-reflexive. *Self-reflexiveness* is the human ability to think about what we're doing while we're doing it. We talk to ourselves about ourselves. We are both participants and observers in all that we do. This dual role encourages us to use labels to describe who we are.

MI

talk about self to self

11

When you were younger, perhaps you dreamed of becoming a rocker or a movie star. People along the way may have told you that you were a great musician or a terrific actor, but as you matured, you probably began observing yourself more critically. You struck out with a couple of bands; you didn't get the starring role in a local stage production. So you self-reflexively decided that you were not, deep down, a rocker or an actor, even though others may have labeled you as "talented." Sometimes, through this self-observation, we discover strengths that encourage us to assume new labels. One woman we know never thought of herself as a "maverick" until she realized that she was the first woman to successfully complete an engineering degree at a male-dominated institution.

ex.— change in self-label

12

Recap

How the Self-Concept Develops

Communication with Others	The self-concept develops as we communicate with others, receive their feedback, make sense out of it, and internalize or reject all or part of it.
Association with Groups	We develop our self-concept partly because of and through our identification with groups or organizations.
Assumed Roles	The self-concept is affected by roles we assume, such as son or daughter, employee, parent, spouse, student.
Self-Labels	The terms we use to describe our attitudes, beliefs, values, and actions play a role in shaping the self-concept.

Summary

CHAPTER 6

HOW DOES STRATEGY 6 HELP YOU BECOME AN ENGAGED READER?

When you find main ideas, you improve your comprehension of the writer's ideas. The strategy helps you to see the writer's overall point and to recognize the ideas that support it. Marking those ideas creates an easy reference point for when you need to review.

HOW DOES THE FIND AND MARK MAIN IDEAS STRATEGY WORK?

You use your overall-point question from your *overview* to guide you in *finding main ideas.* As you read, you look for the thesis and main ideas as answers to your question. Often you find the main ideas by identifying a series of main topics. You also look for supporting ideas that explain each main idea. You mark these ideas according to a system that works for you.

Strategy 6 teaches you how to read with a pen or pencil in your hand. You will be more likely to mark a text if you are prepared.

Strategy 6 shows you how to hunt for the thesis, or overall point, of a reading and its main topics first. This will help you find the main ideas of individual paragraphs and of main topics. Sometimes the thesis is stated, and sometimes it is implied.

Strategy 6 teaches you how to find the main ideas of individual paragraphs and main topics. Sometimes the main ideas are stated, and sometimes they are implied.

Strategy 6 shows you how to look for supporting details. Supporting details include explanations, examples, details, facts, statistics, and quotations and other specific information that support main ideas.

Strategy 6 reminds you to adjust your markings. Be flexible. Just as a rough thesis can be fine-tuned, so can your markings of a text. Change them to fit your needs.

1 | Read with a pen or pencil in your hand.

2 | Find the overall point and the main topics of the reading.

3 | Find the main topic and main idea of each paragraph.

4 | Look for supporting ideas.

5 | Adjust your marking.

Key Terms

annotating: writing notes in the margin to supplement underlining

general: refers to a large category that includes several items (for example, fruit)

main idea: a general idea of a paragraph or a topic; it supports the thesis

review: go over again to study and remember

specific: refers to a particular type or part within the larger category (for example, type of fruit, including bananas, grapes, apples)

support: the information used to explain or clarify the overall point or a main idea

supporting idea: a more specific idea that supports a main idea

thesis: the overall point of a reading

topic: what a main part of a reading is about

Think AGAIN ›

Think about the last DVD box that you looked at. Did you look at the title? Did you read the scenes' chapter titles? The title of the movie gives you a clue to its overall point, and each chapter title is like a scene's main topic. What do you think are the supporting details? How do individual scenes support a movie's overall point? Can you name a movie as an example? How do an overall point and main topics apply to other media, such as books or music albums?

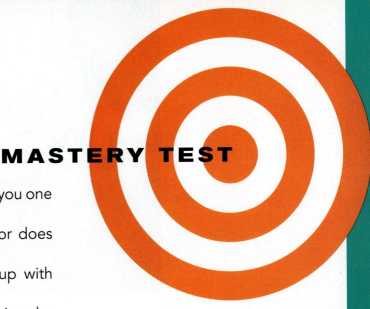
Unlike Reading 11, Reading 12 does not give you one clear-cut statement of the overall point. Nor does this reading have headings. Try to come up with your own overall-point statement by combining the two main ideas. Make sure you mark in the margins and underline.

After you've read "School Is Bad for Children," complete your marking in the sample provided on page 206.

School Is Bad for Children

JOHN HOLT

READING 12

John Holt (1923–1985) was a teacher and commentator on education who believed children should be allowed to discover their own paths to learning. His unusual ideas about school have been the subject of debate ever since "School Is Bad for Children" was first published in 1969 in a popular magazine of that time, *The Saturday Evening Post*.

> connect

1   Almost every child, on the first day he sets foot in a school building, is smarter, more curious, less afraid of what he doesn't know, better at finding and figuring things out, more confident, resourceful, persistent and independent than he will ever be again in his schooling—or, unless he is very unusual and very lucky, for the rest of his life. Already, by paying close attention to and interacting with the world and people around him, and without any school-type formal instruction, he has done a task far more difficult, complicated and abstract than anything he will be asked to do in school, or than any of his teachers has done for years. He has solved the mystery of language. He has discovered it—babies don't even know that language exists—and he has found out how it works and learned to use

it. He has done it by exploring, by experimenting, by developing his own model of the grammar of language, by trying it out and seeing whether it works, by gradually changing it and refining it until it does work. And while he has been doing this, he has been learning other things as well, including many of the "concepts" that the schools think only they can teach him, and many that are more complicated than the ones they do try to teach him.

get an overview and ask questions ◀

In he comes, this curious, patient, determined, energetic, skillful learner. 2 We sit him down at a desk, and what do we teach him? Many things. First, that learning is separate from living. "You come to school to learn," we tell him, as if the child hadn't been learning before, as if living were out there and learning were in here, and there were no connection between the two. Secondly, that he cannot be trusted to learn and is no good at it. Everything we teach about reading, a task far simpler than many that the child has already mastered, says to him, "If we don't make you read, you won't, and if you don't do it exactly the way we tell you, you can't." In short, he comes to feel that learning is a passive process, something that someone else does to you, instead of something you do for yourself.

respond ◀

In a great many other ways he learns that he is worthless, untrustworthy, 3 fit only to take other people's orders, a blank sheet for other people to write on. Oh, we make a lot of nice noises in school about respect for the child and individual differences, and the like. But our acts, as opposed to our talk, say to the child, "Your experience, your concerns, your curiosities, your needs, what you know, what you want, what you wonder about, what you hope for, what you fear, what you like and dislike, what you are good at or not so good at—all this is of not the slightest importance, it counts for nothing. What counts here, and the only thing that counts, is what we know, what we think is important, what we want you to do, think and be." The child soon learns not to ask questions—the teacher isn't there to satisfy his curiosity. Having learned to hide his curiosity, he later learns to be ashamed of it. Given no chance to find out who he is—and to develop that person, whoever it is—he soon comes to accept the adults' evaluation of him.

vital vocabulary

4   He learns many other things. He learns that to be wrong, uncertain, confused, is a crime. Right Answers are what the school wants, and he learns countless strategies for prying these answers out of the teacher, for conning her into thinking he knows what he doesn't know. He learns to dodge, bluff, fake, cheat. He learns to be lazy. Before he came to school, he would work for hours on end, on his own, with no thought of reward, at the business of making sense of the world and gaining competence in it. In school he learns, like every buck private, how to <u>goldbrick</u>, how not to work when the sergeant isn't looking, how to know when he is looking, how to make him think you are working even when he is looking. He learns that in real life you don't do anything unless you are bribed, bullied or conned into doing it, that nothing is worth doing for its own sake, or that if it is, you can't do it in school. He learns to be bored, to work with a small part of his mind, to escape from the reality around him into daydreams and fantasies—but not like the fantasies of his preschool years, in which he played a very active part.

5   The child comes to school curious about other people, particularly other children, and the school teaches him to be indifferent. The most interesting thing in the classroom—often the only interesting thing in it—is the other children, but he has to act as if these other children, all about him, only a few feet away, are not really there. He cannot interact with them, talk with them, smile at them. In many schools he can't talk to other children in the halls between classes; in more than a few, and some of these in stylish suburbs, he can't even talk to them at lunch. Splendid training for a world in which, when you're not studying the other person to figure out how to do him in, you pay no attention to him.

6   In fact, he learns how to live without paying attention to anything going on around him. You might say that school is a long lesson in how to turn yourself off, which may be one reason why so many young people, seeking the awareness of the world and responsiveness to it they had when they were little, think they can only find it in drugs. Aside from being boring, the school is almost always ugly, cold, inhuman—even the most stylish, glass-windowed, $20-a-square-foot schools.

7   And so, in this dull and ugly place, where nobody ever says anything very truthful, where everybody is playing a kind of role, as in a <u>charade</u>, where the teachers are no more free to respond honestly to the students than the students are free to respond to the teachers or each other, where the air practically vibrates with suspicion and anxiety, the child learns to live in a daze, saving his energies for those small parts of his life that are

He learns that in real life you don't do anything unless you are bribed, bullied or conned into doing it, that nothing is worth doing for its own sake, or that if it is, you can't do it in school.

too trivial for the adults to bother with, and thus remain his. It is a rare child who can come through his schooling with much left of his curiosity, his independence or his sense of his own dignity, competence and worth.

So much for criticism. What do we need to do? Many things. Some are **8** easy—we can do them right away. Some are hard, and may take some time. Take a hard one first. We should abolish <u>compulsory</u> school attendance. At the very least we should modify it, perhaps by giving children every year a large number of authorized absences. Our compulsory school-attendance laws once served a humane and useful purpose. They protected children's rights to some schooling, against those adults who would otherwise have denied it to them in order to exploit their labor, in farm, store, mine or factory. Today the laws help nobody, not the schools, not the teachers, not the children. To keep kids in school who would rather not be there costs the schools an enormous amount of time and trouble—to say nothing of what it costs to repair the damage that these angry and resentful prisoners do every time they get a chance. Every teacher knows that any kid in class who, for whatever reason, would rather not be there not only doesn't learn anything himself but makes it a great deal tougher for anyone else. As for protecting the children from exploitation, the chief and indeed only exploiters of children these days *are* the schools. Kids caught in the college rush more often than not work 70 hours or more a week, most of it on paper busywork. For kids who aren't going to college, school is just a useless time waster, preventing them from earning some money or doing some useful work, or even doing some true learning.

Objections. "If kids didn't have to go to school, they'd all be out in the **9** streets." No, they wouldn't. In the first place, even if schools stayed just the way they are, children would spend at least some time there because that's where they'd be likely to find friends; it's a natural meeting place for children. In the second place, schools wouldn't stay the way they are, they'd get better, because we would have to start making them what they ought to be right now—places where children would *want* to be. In the third place, those children who did not want to go to school could find, particularly if we stirred up our brains and gave them a little help, other things to do—the things many children now do during their summers and holidays.

There's something easier we could do. We need to get kids out of the **10** school buildings, give them a chance to learn about the world at first hand. It is a very recent idea, and a crazy one, that the way to teach our young people about the world they live in is to take them out of it and shut them up in brick boxes. Fortunately, educators are beginning to realize this. In Philadelphia and Portland, Oregon, to pick only two places I happen to have heard about, plans are being drawn up for public schools that won't have any school buildings at all, that will take the students out into the city and help them to use it and its people as a learning resource. In other words, students, perhaps in groups, perhaps independently, will go to libraries, museums, exhibits, courtrooms, legislatures, radio and TV stations, meetings, businesses and laboratories to learn about their world and society at first hand. A small private school in Washington is already doing this. It makes sense. We need more of it.

11   As we help children get out into the world, to do their learning there, we can get more of the world into the schools. Aside from their parents, most children never have any close contact with any adults except people whose sole business is children. No wonder they have no idea what adult life or work is like. We need to bring a lot more people who are not full-time teachers into the schools, and into contact with the children. In New York City, under the Teachers and Writers Collaborative, real writers, working writers—novelists, poets, playwrights—come into the schools, read their work, and talk to the children about the problems of their craft. The children eat it up. In another school I know of, a practicing attorney from a nearby city comes in every month or so and talks to several classes about the law. Not the law as it is in books but as he sees it and encounters it in his cases, his problems, his work. And the children love it. It is real, grown-up, true, not *My Weekly Reader,* not "social studies," not lies and baloney.

12   Something easier yet. Let children work together, help each other, learn from each other and each other's mistakes. We now know, from the experience of many schools, both rich-suburban and poor-city, that children are often the best teachers of other children. What is more important, we know that when a fifth- or sixth-grader who has been having trouble with reading starts helping a first-grader, his own reading sharply improves. A number of schools are beginning to use what some call Paired Learning. This means that you let children form partnerships with other children, do their work, even including their tests, together, and share whatever marks or results this work gets—just like grownups in the real world. It seems to work.

> We now know, from the experience of many schools, both rich-suburban and poor-city, that children are often the best teachers of other children.

13   Let the children learn to judge their own work. A child learning to talk does not learn by being corrected all the time—if corrected too much, he will stop talking. *He* compares, a thousand times a day, the difference between language as he uses it and as those around him use it. Bit by bit, he makes the necessary changes to make his language like other people's. In the same way, kids learning to do all the other things they learn without adult teachers—to walk, run, climb, whistle, ride a bike, skate, play games, jump rope—compare their own performance with what more skilled people do, and slowly make the needed changes. But in school we never give a child a chance to detect his mistakes, let alone correct them. We do it all for him. We act as if we thought he would never notice a mistake unless it was pointed out to him, or correct it unless he was made to. Soon he becomes dependent on the expert. We should let him do it himself. Let him figure out, with the help of other children if he wants it, what this word says, what is the answer to that problem, whether this is a good way of saying or doing this or that. If right answers are involved, as in some math or science, give him the answer book, let him correct his own papers. Why should we teachers waste time on such donkey work? Our job should be to help the kid when he tells us that he can't find a way to get the right answer. Let's get rid of all this nonsense of grades, exams, marks. We don't know now, and we never will know, how to measure what another person knows or understands. We certainly can't find out by asking him questions. All we find out

is what he doesn't know—which is what most tests are for, anyway. Throw it all out, and let the child learn what every educated person must someday learn, how to measure his own understanding, how to know what he knows or does not know.

We could also abolish the fixed, required curriculum. People remember **14** only what is interesting and useful to them, what helps them make sense of the world, or helps them get along in it. All else they quickly forget, if they ever learn it at all. The idea of a "body of knowledge," to be picked up in school and used for the rest of one's life, is nonsense in a world as complicated and rapidly changing as ours. Anyway, the most important questions and problems of our time are not *in* the curriculum, not even in the hotshot universities, let alone the schools.

Children want, more than they want anything else, and even after years **15** of miseducation, to make sense of the world, themselves, and other human beings. Let them get this job, with our help if they ask for it, in the way that makes most sense to them.

ACTIVE READERS RESPOND

After you've finished reading, use these activities to respond to "School Is Bad for Children." You may write your answers in the spaces provided or on a separate sheet of paper.

VITAL VOCABULARY

Some words in this reading may be unfamiliar to you. Use the methods of Strategy 3 to explain what the listed words mean.

USE CONTEXT CLUES

a. goldbrick (paragraph 4) (Use logic clues and synonyms.)

_____

USE WORD PARTS

a. miseducation (paragraph 15) (Note the prefix.)

_____

b. compulsory (paragraph 8) (Use the stronger verb form of this word, "compel" (to force), to help you

remember this adjective.)

_____

USE THE DICTIONARY

Choose the correct definition of this word as it is used in the context of this reading.

a. charade (paragraph 7)

_____

SKILLS TEST: THE OVERALL POINT AND MAIN IDEAS

1. What is the title of the reading?

School Is Bad for Children _____

2. What are the headings?

There are no headings.

3. What is the main idea of first main topic?

Children naturally want to learn, but school destroys their confidence in their own ability and turns off their curiosity.

What is the main idea of the second main topic?

The general solution: Find ways to let children learn on their own, giving them help when they need it.

4. What is the stated or implied thesis of this reading?

Children naturally want to learn, but school destroys their confidence in their own ability and turns off their curiosity, so we should find ways to let children learn on their own, giving them help when they need it.

OBJECTIVE OPERATIONS

1. Who is the writer's intended audience?

   a. students

   b. teachers

   c. general audience

   d. parents

2. What is the author's purpose?

   a. to inform

   b. to persuade

   c. to entertain

3. Which sentence best states the main idea of the passage?

   a. Children are not learning what they are supposed to in the current school system.

   b. The current school system stifles children's curiosity about learning and their confidence in their own abilities, so we should find ways to let children learn on their own and offer help as needed.

   c. Children want to learn, but school destroys their ability to learn and their curiosity.

   d. Learning is separate from living.

4. The word "compulsory" in paragraph 8, line 3, most nearly means

   a. protective.

   b. important.

   c. essential.

   d. required.

5. What is the topic of paragraph 2?

   a. what children are taught at school

   b. two lessons children are taught at school

   c. learning versus living

   d. learning as a passive process

6. What is the stated main idea of paragraph 2?

   a. "In he comes, this curious, patient, determined, energetic, skillful learner."

   b. "We sit him down at a desk, and what do we teach him? Many things."

   c. "Everything we teach about reading, a task far simpler than many that the child has already mastered, says to him, 'If we don't make you read, you won't, and if you don't do it exactly the way we tell you, you can't.'"

   d. "In short, he comes to feel that learning is a passive process, something that someone else does _to_ you, instead of something you do for yourself."

7. Holt gives several important negative lessons that he says school teaches children from the very beginning. Which of the following is not one of those negative lessons?

   a. getting correct answers from children is the school's main concern

   b. learning for its own sake is more important than getting good grades

   c. appearing to be busy and productive is what counts

d. teachers are not there to answer children's questions

8. The word "exploitation" in paragraph 8, line 16, most nearly means

    a. development.

    b. utilization.

    c. manipulation.

    d. management.

9. What is the topic of paragraph 5?

    a. what school teaches

    b. other children

    c. being cut off from others

    d. training

10. Holt says that "school is a long lesson in how to turn yourself off" because

    a. the only way children can get correct answers is by ignoring what their peers are doing.

    b. the only way children can hold onto their individual interests is by escaping into their own daydreams.

    c. children ignore what interests them in order to do well in school.

    d. children are not allowed to turn on the electronic games they like to play.

11. The word "charade" in paragraph 7, line 2, most nearly means

    a. reproduction.

    b. guessing game.

    c. fake situation.

    d. ignorance.

12. What is the implied main idea of paragraph 10?

    a. Children need to go out into the community and learn about the world firsthand.

    b. Educators are realizing students need to be part of a community.

    c. Children will go to public places to learn.

    d. We need an easy solution.

13. Which sentence is the stated main idea of paragraph 13?

    a. "We don't know now, and we never will know, how to measure what another person knows or understands."

    b. "A child learning to talk does not learn by being corrected all the time—if corrected too much, he will stop talking."

    c. "Let the children learn to judge their own work."

    d. "Let's get rid of all this nonsense of grades, exams, marks."

14. Holt knows people would object to his proposals for abolishing required schooling. One answer he gives to answer these objections is that schools would have to

    a. improve in order to attract children to come.

    b. get jobs for children that would pay them to go to schools.

    c. improve their monitoring to tell which children were not attending.

    d. encourage teachers and students to become friends.

15. Holt says that children can learn on their own, without teachers giving them lessons and grades. He supports his idea by saying that if left alone, children

    a. compare what they do with what they see more skilled people doing.

    b. become more sensitive to their own needs and fear being judged by teachers.

    c. get answers in such subjects as math and science by trial and error.

    d. become dependent on the experts they come in contact with.

16. According to the author, another solution is to

    a. abolish the required curriculum.

    b. let children learn as they are currently learning.

    c. let children get jobs.

    d. let children make friends.

17. Holt says in the second-to-last paragraph that "the most important questions of our time are not *in* the curriculum, not even in the hotshot universities. . . ." Given Holt's concerns in this reading, we can assume that one of these "most important questions" would be:

    a. How can we have a well-trained workforce for our future economy?

    b. What technologies can be used in schools to improve children's learning?

    c. What historical events led to the adoption of compulsory school attendance?

    d. How can we get along well with others in our families, in our neighborhoods, and in our larger communities?

18. What is the overall tone of the passage?
    a. condescending
    b. admiring
    (c.) critical
    d. supportive

1. According to Holt, what negative lessons does school teach children from the very beginning?
(Answers will vary.)
_____

2. Why does he say, in paragraph 6, that "school is a long lesson in how to turn yourself off"?
(Answers will vary.)
_____

3. How does Holt answer the objections he knows people would make about abolishing required schooling?
(Answers will vary.)
_____

4. What are some of the ways that children could learn without depending so much on adults? What would the advantages be for this kind of learning?
(Answers will vary.)
_____

5. How does Holt's description of school match your own experience? If you had to choose sides in a debate on this reading, which side would you be on?
(Answers will vary.)
_____

1. Discuss with other students your final response to this reading. There will almost certainly be disagreements about Holt's ideas, so be sure to listen carefully to what people on each side have to say.
(Answers will vary.)
_____

2. Notice that this reading was written in 1969. Include in your discussion of Holt's ideas how much or how little things have changed in over thirty years.
(Answers will vary.)
_____

SAMPLE MARKING:
School Is Bad for Children

JOHN HOLT

General Problem

child starting school

already knows

Almost every child, on the first day he sets foot in a school building, is **1** smarter, more curious, less afraid of what he doesn't know, better at finding and figuring things out, more confident, resourceful, persistent and independent than he will ever be again in his schooling—or, unless he is very unusual and very lucky, for the rest of his life. Already, by paying close attention to and interacting with the world and people around him, and without any school-type formal instruction, he has done a task far more difficult, complicated and abstract than anything he will be asked to do in school, or than any of his teachers has done for years. He has solved the mystery of language. He has discovered it—babies don't even know that language exists—and he has found out how it works and learned to use it. He has done it by exploring, by experimenting, by developing his own model of the grammar of language, by trying it out and seeing whether it works, by gradually changing it and refining it until it does work. And while he has been doing this, he has been learning other things as well, including many of the "concepts" that the schools think only they can teach him, and many that are more complicated than the ones they do try to teach him.

@ school child learns
① ②

In he comes, this curious, patient, determined, energetic, skillful learner. **2** We sit him down at a desk, and what do we teach him? Many things. First, that learning is separate from living. "You come to school to learn," we tell him, as if the child hadn't been learning before, as if living were out there and learning were in here, and there were no connection between the two. Secondly, that he cannot be trusted to learn and is no good at it. Everything we teach about reading, a task far simpler than many that the child has already mastered, says to him, "If we don't make you read, you won't, and if you don't do it exactly the way we tell you, you can't." In short, he comes to feel that learning is a passive process, something that someone else does *to* you, instead of something you do for yourself.

his exp. etc. not imp.

distrust self

In a great many other ways he learns that he is worthless, untrustworthy, **3** fit only to take other people's orders, a blank sheet for other people to write on. Oh, we make a lot of nice noises in school about respect for the child and individual differences, and the like. But our acts, as opposed to our talk, say to the child, "Your experience, your concerns, your curiosities, your needs, what you know, what you want, what you wonder about, what you hope for, what you fear, what you like and dislike, what you are good at or not so good at—all this is of not the slightest importance, it counts for nothing. What counts here, and the only thing that counts, is what we know, what we think is important, what we want you to do, think and be." The child soon learns not to ask questions—the teacher isn't there to satisfy his curiosity. Having learned to hide his curiosity, he later learns to be ashamed of it. Given no chance to find out who he is—and to develop that person, whoever it is—he soon comes to accept the adults' evaluation of him.

4   He learns many other things. He learns that to be wrong, uncertain, confused, is a crime. (Right Answers) are what the school wants, and he learns
countless strategies for prying these answers out of the teacher, for conning
her into thinking he knows what he doesn't know. He learns to dodge, bluff,
fake, cheat. He learns to be lazy. Before he came to school, he would work
for hours on end, on his own, with no thought of reward, at the business of
making sense of the world and gaining competence in it. In school he learns,
like every buck private, how to goldbrick, how not to work when the sergeant
isn't looking, how to know when he is looking, how to make him think you
are working even when he is looking. He learns that in real life you don't do
anything unless you are bribed, bullied or conned into doing it, that nothing
is worth doing for its own sake, or that if it is, you can't do it in school. He
learns to be bored, to work with a small part of his mind, to escape from the
reality around him into daydreams and fantasies—but not like the fantasies
of his preschool years, in which he played a very active part.

learns more:

only do what have to

5   The child comes to school curious about other people, particularly other
children, and the school teaches him to be indifferent. The most interesting
thing in the classroom—often the only interesting thing in it—is the other
children, but he has to act as if these other children, all about him, only a
few feet away, are not really there. He cannot interact with them, talk with
them, smile at them. In many schools he can't talk to other children in
the halls between classes; in more than a few, and some of these in stylish
suburbs, he can't even talk to them at lunch. Splendid training for a world
in which, when you're not studying the other person to figure out how to do
him in, you pay no attention to him.

he's cut off from other kids.

6   In fact, he learns how to live without paying attention to anything going
on around him. You might say that school is a long lesson in how to turn
yourself off, which may be one reason why so many young people, seeking
the awareness of the world and responsiveness to it they had when they
were little, think they can only find it in drugs. Aside from being boring, the
school is almost always ugly, cold, inhuman—even the most stylish, glass-
windowed, $20-a-square-foot schools.

7   And so, in this dull and ugly place, where nobody ever says anything
very truthful, where everybody is playing a kind of role, as in a charade,
where the teachers are no more free to respond honestly to the students
than the students are free to respond to the teachers or each other, where
the air practically vibrates with suspicion and anxiety, the child learns to
live in a daze, saving his energies for those small parts of his life that are
too trivial for the adults to bother with, and thus remain his. It is a rare
child who can come through his schooling with much left of his curiosity,
his independence or his sense of his own dignity, competence and worth.

school-boring, ugly, distrusting atmosph.

8   So much for criticism. What do we need to do? Many things. Some are
easy—we can do them right away. Some are hard, and may take some time.
Take a hard one first. (We should abolish compulsory school attendance.) At
the very least we should modify it, perhaps by giving children every year
a large number of authorized absences. Our compulsory school-attendance
laws once served a humane and useful purpose. They protected children's
rights to some schooling, against those adults who would otherwise have denied it to them in order to exploit their labor, in farm, store, mine or factory.

solutions (paragraphs 8–15)

end compuls. school

Today the laws help nobody, not the schools, not the teachers, not the children. To keep kids in school who would rather not be there costs the schools an enormous amount of time and trouble—to say nothing of what it costs to repair the damage that these angry and resentful prisoners do every time they get a chance. Every teacher knows that any kid in class who, for whatever reason, would rather not be there not only doesn't learn anything himself but makes it a great deal tougher for anyone else. As for protecting the children from exploitation, the chief and indeed only exploiters of children these days *are* the schools. Kids caught in the college rush more often than not work 70 hours or more a week, most of it on paper busywork. For kids who aren't going to college, school is just a useless time waster, preventing them from earning some money or doing some useful work, or even doing some true learning.

Objections. "If kids didn't have to go to school, they'd all be out in the streets." No, they wouldn't. In the first place, even if schools stayed just the way they are, children would spend at least some time there because that's where they'd be likely to find friends; it's a natural meeting place for children. In the second place, schools wouldn't stay the way they are, they'd get better, because we would have to start making them what they ought to be right now—places where children would *want* to be. In the third place, those children who did not want to go to school could find, particularly if we stirred up our brains and gave them a little help, other things to do—the things many children now do during their summers and holidays.

There's something easier we could do. We need to get kids out of the school buildings, give them a chance to learn about the world at first hand. It is a very recent idea, and a crazy one, that the way to teach our young people about the world they live in is to take them out of it and shut them up in brick boxes. Fortunately, educators are beginning to realize this. In Philadelphia and Portland, Oregon, to pick only two places I happen to have heard about, plans are being drawn up for public schools that won't have any school buildings at all, that will take the students out into the city and help them to use it and its people as a learning resource. In other words, students, perhaps in groups, perhaps independently, will go to libraries, museums, exhibits, courtrooms, legislatures, radio and TV stations, meetings, businesses and laboratories to learn about their world and society at first hand. A small private school in Washington is already doing this. It makes sense. We need more of it.

As we help children get out into the world, to do their learning there, we can get more of the world into the schools. Aside from their parents, most children never have any close contact with any adults except people whose sole business is children. No wonder they have no idea what adult life or work is like. We need to bring a lot more people who are not full-time teachers into the schools, and into contact with the children. In New York City, under the Teachers and Writers Collaborative, real writers, working writers—novelists, poets, playwrights—come into the schools, read their work, and talk to the children about the problems of their craft. The children eat it up. In another school I know of, a practicing attorney from a nearby city comes in every month or so and talks to several classes about the law. Not the law as it is in books but as he sees it and encounters it in his cases, his

outgrew purpose

school useless/ costly if <u>not</u> wanted or needed

how work?
① ② ③

Get kids into community.

resources

bring working adults into classrm.

9

10

11

problems, his work. And the children love it. It is real, grown-up, true, not *My Weekly Reader,* not "social studies," not lies and baloney.

12   Something easier yet. Let children work together, help each other, learn from each other and each other's mistakes. We now know, from the experience of many schools, both rich-suburban and poor-city, that children are often the best teachers of other children. What is more important, we know that when a fifth- or sixth-grader who has been having trouble with reading starts helping a first-grader, his own reading sharply improves. A number of schools are beginning to use what some call Paired Learning. This means that you let children form partnerships with other children, do their work, even including their tests, together, and share whatever marks or results this work gets—just like grownups in the real world. It seems to work.

13   Let the children learn to judge their own work. A child learning to talk does not learn by being corrected all the time—if corrected too much, he will stop talking. *He* compares, a thousand times a day, the difference between language as he uses it and as those around him use it. Bit by bit, he makes the necessary changes to make his language like other people's. In the same way, kids learning to do all the other things they learn without adult teachers—to walk, run, climb, whistle, ride a bike, skate, play games, jump rope—compare their own performance with what more skilled people do, and slowly make the needed changes. But in school we never give a child a chance to detect his mistakes, let alone correct them. We do it all for him. We act as if we thought he would never notice a mistake unless it was pointed out to him, or correct it unless he was made to. Soon he becomes dependent on the expert. We should let him do it himself. Let him figure out, with the help of other children if he wants it, what this word says, what is the answer to that problem, whether this is a good way of saying or doing this or that. If right answers are involved, as in some math or science, give him the answer book, let him correct his own papers. Why should we teachers waste time on such donkey work? Our job should be to help the kid when he tells us that he can't find a way to get the right answer. Let's get rid of all this nonsense of grades, exams, marks. We don't know now, and we never will know, how to measure what another person knows or understands. We certainly can't find out by asking him questions. All we find out is what he doesn't know—which is what most tests are for, anyway. Throw it all out, and let the child learn what every educated person must someday learn, how to measure his own understanding, how to know what he knows or does not know.

child corrects self in learning lang. etc.

let child evaluate self

14   We could also abolish the fixed, required curriculum. People remember only what is interesting and useful to them, what helps them make sense of the world, or helps them get along in it. All else they quickly forget, if they ever learn it at all. The idea of a "body of knowledge," to be picked up in school and used for the rest of one's life, is nonsense in a world as complicated and rapidly changing as ours. Anyway, the most important questions and problems of our time are not *in* the curriculum, not even in the hotshot universities, let alone the schools.

learn what needs + wants

15   Children want, more than they want anything else, and even after years of miseducation, to make sense of the world, themselves, and other human beings. Let them get this job, with our help if they ask for it, in the way that makes most sense to them.

general solution

FIND AND MARK MAIN IDEAS

1 | Read with a pen or pencil in your hand.

2 | Find the overall point and the main topics of the reading.

3 | Find the main topic and main idea of each paragraph.

4 | Look for supporting ideas.

5 | Adjust your marking.

PRACTICE PAGES

Chapter 6

To get practice with general versus specific ideas, complete the following exercise.

PRACTICE EXERCISE 1

Read the passage below. More directions will follow the passage.

ROUTE 66: THE MAIN STREET OF AMERICA

Some places take on a mythic quality, entering the lore of a culture and becoming legendary. Route 66, the first highway to link Chicago to Los Angeles, has such a legendary place in American lore.

Unlike roads that went directly west and over the high passes of the Rocky Mountains, Route 66 cut a diagonal course southwest. Route 66 crossed flat prairie lands and offered mild temperatures and more dependable weather than comparable roads. Thus it became a favorite road of truck drivers and travelers, linking communities along its way that in turn gave the road its distinctive character.

In the early 1960s, a television program, *Route 66*, gave this highway a special position in the American imagination. For four seasons, viewers watched Tod and Buzz travel down Route 66's twists and turns in search of adventure. The ordinary people and eccentric personalities they met along the way seemed to personify the country in all its diversity.

Eventually, the need for speed and efficiency spelled doom for that unique road. As new superhighways were constructed, parts of the original Route 66 fell into disuse and then disrepair. It finally disappeared. In 1984 Interstate 40 in Arizona replaced the last segment of the road sometimes called the "Main Street of America." Today signposts proclaiming "Historic Route 66" are found alongside the roads that replaced it.

Each of these pairs of sentences has been taken from the passage. Which sentence is the more general statement? Which is the more specific statement? Write your answer on the line.

1. First pair:

   Route 66 crossed flat prairie lands and offered mild temperatures and more dependable weather than comparable roads. specific

   Unlike roads that went directly west and over the high passes of the Rocky Mountains, Route 66 cut a diagonal course southwest. general

2. Second pair:

   In the early 1960s, a television program, *Route 66*, gave this highway a special position in the American imagination. general

   For four seasons, viewers watched Tod and Buzz travel down Route 66's twists and turns in search of adventure. specific

3. Third pair:

   As new superhighways were constructed, parts of the original Route 66 fell into disuse and then disrepair. specific

   Eventually, the need for speed and efficiency spelled doom for that unique road. general

To get practice writing a thesis statement, complete the following exercise.

PRACTICE EXERCISE 2

Look at the title and the headings for the reading below, but do not read the passage. Answer the questions that follow the passage.

A MORE NATURAL APPROACH: DRESS REFORM IN THE VICTORIAN ERA

Victorian Era Fashion

The Victorian Era was a time of high morals and modest behavior and dress. Although fashionable men and women both adhered to rules that governed their attire, menswear was relatively comfortable. By contrast, the fashionable woman could hardly move. Her figure was squeezed into an hourglass shape with whalebone corsets. Undergarments—which first included petticoats and later a crinoline or underskirt reinforced with wood or wire—could weigh up to fourteen pounds. The trailing skirts and long, tight sleeves of a woman's outer dress impeded activity. Etiquette books offered instruction on how to manage this costume so as to walk, sit, and dance with modesty and decorum.

Thank Goodness for Bloomers!

In the United States, Mrs. Amelia Bloomer (1818–1894) designed baggy pants cuffed at the ankle that could be worn under a knee-length skirt, a style now called "bloomers." Bloomers gave women more freedom of movement and lightened the number of pounds of clothing a woman wore. Although few women adopted the look, Bloomer's ideas won the approval of many progressive thinkers in the United States and abroad.

A Society of Support

In 1881 socially prominent British women formed the Rational Dress Society in London. They believed that no woman should have to wear more than seven pounds of undergarments and decried the use of corsets that "deformed the figure." They also advocated a "bifurcated garment" suitable for athletic exercise, gardening, housework, or the workplace. In addition, they admired Mrs. Bloomer's costume.

Today women are not restricted by the morals and rules of the Victorian Era, and the clothing that women choose reflects this freedom.

1. **What is the title of the reading?**

   A More Natural Approach: Dress Reform in the Victorian Era

2. **What are the headings?**

   Victorian Era Fashions, Thank Goodness for Bloomers!, and A Society of Support

3. **Write a sentence that combines the title and the headings:**

   Due to Victorian Era fashions, dress was reformed for a more natural approach, bloomers came about, and a society formed.

4. **Read the passage. Once you have read the passage, review your thesis statement and revise it if necessary.**

   Victorian Era fashions for women were restrictive and confining, so as a response, bloomers were invented, and a society

   formed that advocated more suitable dress.

To get practice finding main ideas, complete the following exercise.

PRACTICE EXERCISE 3

Read the passage below and answer the questions in the margins. When you find a sentence that states the main idea of the paragraph, underline it. Then, answer the questions that follow the passage.

RAOUL WALLENBERG: THE HERO WHO DISAPPEARED

A Hero

What is this paragraph about? Raoul Wallenberg, a hero

Raoul Wallenberg, a Swedish envoy, has been called an "angel" who saved the lives of thousands of Jews during World War II. In 1944 Wallenberg traveled to Hungary in an effort to save Jews from Nazi persecution. He designed a flashy but official-looking pass and used it to bring countless Jews out of the country. He also established some 30 "Swedish houses" in Budapest, where 15,000 refugees found sanctuary at one time or another.

Tricking the Nazis to Save Lives

What is this paragraph about? saving Jews in World War II

For a year, Wallenberg gave out his passes, even stuffing them through the windows of trains headed to death camps. He forced Nazi officials to honor them, using threats, bribery, and the sheer force of his personality. Altogether, using his trickery, Wallenberg may have saved 100,000 lives. By the time the Russians arrived in Budapest in 1945, however, only 97,000 Jews were still living in the ghettos.

Vanished!

What is this paragraph about? Wallenberg disappears

Wallenberg disappeared in January 1945, before World War II ended. He was on his way to Soviet headquarters in Hungary and told friends that he would be back in about eight days. In 1957 the Soviet government stated that Wallenberg had died in one of its prisons in 1947. There has never been any reasonable explanation for why he was arrested or conclusive proof of his death. Today, the circumstances surrounding his disappearance are unknown, and his whereabouts (if, indeed, he is still alive) remain a mystery.

1. What is the title of the reading?

   Raoul Wallenberg, the Hero Who Disappeared

2. What are the headings?

   A Hero, Tricking the Nazis to Save Lives, and Vanished!

3. What is the main idea of paragraph 1?

   Raoul Wallenberg, a Swedish envoy, has been called an "angel" who saved the lives of thousands of Jews during World War II.

   What is the main idea of paragraph 2?

   Altogether, using his trickery, Wallenberg may have saved 100,000 lives.

   What is the main idea of paragraph 3?

   Today, the circumstances surrounding his disappearance are unknown, and his whereabouts (if, indeed, he is still alive) remain a mystery.

4. Write a sentence that combines the main ideas and states the thesis of the reading.

   Raoul Wallenberg has been called an angel because using trickery he saved the lives of thousands of Jews during World War II until he mysteriously disappeared.

To get practice with marking main ideas and supporting details, complete the following exercise.

PRACTICE EXERCISE 4

Read the passage below and answer the questions in the margins. When you find a sentence that states the main idea of the paragraph, underline it. Then, answer the questions that follow the passage.

INDONESIA'S MINANGKABAU

The modern nation of Indonesia is an archipelago of 17,000 islands clustered around the equator, between the Indian and Pacific Oceans and the South China Sea. The climate is tropical, and geological instability can cause earthquakes and destructive tsunamis. A region rich with natural resources from spices to minerals, Indonesia has been the crossroads of many cultures. The dominant religion on the islands was Hinduism until the rise of Islam in the thirteenth century. Colonized by the Dutch in the seventeenth century, Indonesia spent time under both British and Japanese rule and achieved independence in 1949.

What is this paragraph about? Indonesia

What is the stated or implied thesis? Indonesia is a country with many cultures, but the most distinctive is the Minangkabau group.

What is this paragraph about? Minangkabau family

What is this paragraph about? adat and the female line

Is there a stated main idea? If not, what kind of supporting details are there? No stated MI; details are examples

What is this paragraph about? the origin of the name Minangkabau

What kinds of details are used here? An explanation

Among the most distinctive of Indonesia's cultures is the Minangkabau group, which lives on the island of Sumatra. This is the largest matrilineal society in the modern world. (In a matrilineal society, descent is traced through the maternal, or mother's, line.) The Minangkabau follow a set of traditional practices called *adat.* Each family, for instance, has a *rumah adat,* or a "house for all adat." In this building, people related to each other through the mother's family gather together to rejoice or for sorrow, to make decisions or perform rituals.

Among the Minangkabau, the female line is called *suku,* and children take their mother's family name. Ancestral lands are passed down from mother to daughter. According to adat, a young man must wait for a marriage proposal from the families of eligible girls and on his wedding day he is brought to the home of his bride. Also according to adat, a young man must leave his village to seek his fortune. Once a man has achieved financial success, he returns to his wife's village and her home. Although adat may be the normal way of life in the village, in the cities the Minangkabau tend to adopt a more traditional Islamic pattern.

The name Minangkabau comes from an old David-and-Goliath-type story. A king on the nearby island of Java threatened to invade. Instead of a war, however, the groups staged a fight between two buffalo. The buffalo belonging to the Javanese was defeated; the other smaller one became known as the minang kabau, or "victorious buffalo." Buffalo fights are still popular entertainment for the Minangkabau. Each buffalo is linked by a rope to its owner, who murmurs quiet words, telling it how to fight. The contest, therefore, like the ancient battle against Java, is ultimately between the men and not the animals.

1. **What is the title of the reading?**
   Indonesia's Minangkabau

2. **What are the headings?**
   There are no headings.

3. **What is the stated main idea of paragraph 2?**
   Among the most distinctive of Indonesia's cultures is the Minangkabau group, which lives on the island of Sumatra.

   What is the implied main idea of paragraph 3?
   The family line is through the female, and males must prove themselves worthy in order to become family.

   What is the stated main idea of paragraph 4?
   The name Minangkabau comes from an old David-and-Goliath-type story.

4. **What is the stated or implied thesis of this reading?**
   Indonesia is a country with many cultures, but the most distinctive is the Minangkabau group.

To get practice with reading, read the passage, and then answer the questions that follow. You may write your answers in the spaces provided or on a separate sheet of paper.

Learning the River

MARK TWAIN

Mark Twain (1835–1910) loved writing about the Mississippi River he knew as a child and young man. Born Samuel Clemens, he even derived his pen name from the riverman's term for measuring the water's depth (*mark* meaning measurement and *twain* meaning two). The Mississippi is the setting for Twain's most famous adventurers, Tom Sawyer and Huckleberry Finn. The river takes on even more importance in *Life on the Mississippi,* Twain's memoir of his youthful career as a steamboat pilot.

This excerpt from *Life on the Mississippi* shows Twain's early lessons on how to steer a steamboat—with a load of passengers and 200 tons of cargo—up and down the Mississippi (see Figure 1). The river is full of hazards because silting and rainfall cause constant changes in the depth. A river pilot has to know exactly where the steamboat should go to avoid going aground in the shallows or on a sandbar, but the water everywhere looks the same (see Figure 2, page 217). As the reading begins, Twain mentions the features of the river he's already learned, including its bars (sandbars at or near the surface of the water) and bends (curves in the river). This early stage of learning has given him a feeling of complacency (smug confidence) that Mr. Bixby, his pilot-teacher, will soon "fetch down" (put down), by giving him even harder lessons to learn.

connect

lumber: miscellaneous useless articles

settler: hard question

protoplasm: liquid substance of cells, used here as an incomprehensible term

placable: calmed down

smooth-bore: old-fashioned gun with less fire power than a rifle

get an overview and ask questions

Look over the picture and map to get an idea of what the reading will be about.

At the end of what seemed a tedious while, I had managed to pack my **1** head full of islands, towns, bars, "points," and bends; and a curiously inanimate mass of lumber it was, too. However, inasmuch as I could shut my eyes and reel off a good long string of these names without leaving out more than ten miles of river in every fifty, I began to feel that I could take a boat down to New Orleans if I could make her skip those little gaps. But of course my complacency could hardly get start enough to lift my nose a trifle into the air, before Mr. Bixby would think of something to fetch it down again. One day he turned on me suddenly with this settler—

"What is the shape of Walnut Bend?" **2**

He might as well have asked me my grandmother's opinion of proto- **3** plasm. I reflected respectfully, and then said I didn't know it had any particular shape. My gunpowdery chief went off with a bang, of course, and then went on loading and firing until he was out of adjectives.

I had learned long ago that he only carried just so many rounds of am- **4** munition, and was sure to subside into a very placable and even remorseful old smooth-bore as soon as they were all gone. That word "old" is merely affectionate; he was not more than thirty-four. I waited. By and by he said,—

"My boy, you've got to know the *shape* of the river perfectly. It is all there **5** is left to steer by on a very dark night. Everything else is blotted out and gone. But mind you, it hasn't the same shape in the night that it has in the day-time."

"How on earth am I ever going to learn it, then?" **6**

"How do you follow a hall at home in the dark? Because you know the **7** shape of it. You can't see it."

Figure 1: Illustration of a steamboat on the Mississippi.

8 "Do you mean to say that I've got to know all the million trifling variations of shape in the banks of this interminable river as well as I know the shape of the front hall at home?"

9 "On my honor, you've got to know them *better* than any man ever did know the shapes of the halls in his own house."

10 "I wish I was dead!"

11 "Now I don't want to discourage you, but"—

12 "Well, pile it on me; I might as well have it now as another time."

> **respond**

13 I went to work now to learn the shape of the river; and of all the <u>eluding</u> and ungraspable objects that ever I tried to get mind or hands on, that was the chief. I would fasten my eyes upon a sharp, wooded point that projected far into the river some miles ahead of me, and go to laboriously photographing its shape upon my brain; and just as I was beginning to succeed to my satisfaction, we would draw up toward it and the exasperating thing would begin to melt away and fold back into the bank! If there had been a <u>conspicuous</u> dead tree standing upon the very point of the <u>cape</u>, I would find that tree inconspicuously <u>merged</u> into the general forest, and occupying the middle of a straight shore, when I got <u>abreast</u> of it! No <u>prominent</u> hill would stick to its shape long enough for me to make up my mind what its form really was, but it was as dissolving and changeful as if it had been a mountain of butter in the hottest corner of the tropics. Nothing ever had the same shape when I was coming down-stream that it had borne when I went up. I mentioned these little difficulties to Mr. Bixby. He said,—

> **vital vocabulary**

14 "That's the very main virtue of the thing. If the shapes didn't change every three seconds they wouldn't be of any use. Take this place where we are now, for instance. As long as that hill over yonder is only one hill, I can boom right along the way I'm going; but the moment it splits at the top and forms a V, I know I've got to scratch to starboard in a hurry, or I'll bang this

scratch: move quickly

starboard: righthand direction (nautical term)

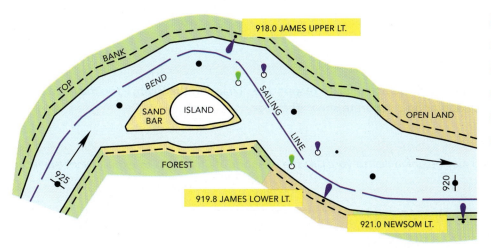

Figure 2: Present-day map of a section of the Mississippi, showing a sandbar, a bend in the river, and identifying the safe sailing line.

larboard: lefthand direction (old-fashioned nautical term)

keelson: structure on the bottom of a boat

"thortships": athwartships, from one side of the ship or boat to another

leadsman: sailor who measures depth of water using a heavy line

shoal: of little depth

soundings: measurements of water's depth

roustabout: unskilled laborer

boat's brains out against a rock; and then the moment one of the prongs of the V swings behind the other, I've got to waltz to larboard again, or I'll have a misunderstanding with a snag that would snatch the keelson out of this steamboat as neatly as if it were a sliver in your hand. If that hill didn't change its shape on bad nights there would be an awful steamboat graveyard around here inside of a year."

It was plain that I had got to learn the shape of the river in all the different ways that could be thought of,—upside down, wrong end first, inside out, fore-and-aft, and "thortships,"—and then know what to do on gray nights when it hadn't any shape at all. So I set about it. In the course of time I began to get the best of this knotty lesson, and my self-complacency moved to the front once more. Mr. Bixby was all fixed, and ready to start it to the rear again. He opened on me after this fashion: 15

"How much water did we have in the middle crossing at Hole-in-the-Wall, trip before last?" 16

I considered this an outrage. I said:— 17

"Every trip, down and up, the leadsmen are singing through that tangled place for three quarters of an hour on a stretch. How do you reckon I can remember such a mess as that?" 18

"My boy, you've got to remember it. You've got to remember the exact spot and the exact marks the boat lay in when we had the shoalest water, in every one of the five hundred shoal places between St. Louis and New Orleans; and you mustn't get the shoal soundings and marks of one trip mixed up with the shoal soundings and marks of another, either, for they're not often twice alike. You must keep them separate." 19

When I came to myself again, I said,— 20

"When I get so that I can do that, I'll be able to raise the dead, and then I won't have to pilot a steamboat to make a living. I want to retire from this business. I want a slush-bucket and a brush; I'm only fit for a roustabout. I haven't got brains enough to be a pilot; and if I had I wouldn't have strength enough to carry them around, unless I went on crutches." 21

"Now drop that! When I say I'll learn[1] a man the river, I mean it. And you can depend on it. I'll learn him or kill him." 22

---

[1]"Teach" is not in the river vocabulary.

ACTIVE READERS RESPOND

After you've finished reading, use these activities to respond to "Learning the River." You may write your answers in the spaces provided or on a separate sheet of paper.

VITAL VOCABULARY

Some words in this reading may be unfamiliar to you. Use the methods of Strategy 3 to explain what the listed words mean.

USE CONTEXT CLUES

a. cape (paragraph 13)

_____

b. merged (paragraph 13)

_____

c. abreast (paragraph 13)

_____

USE WORD PARTS

a. prominent (paragraph 13) (Use the prefix *pro-* to help you remember this word.)

_____

b. fore-and-aft (paragraph 15)

_____

c. knotty (paragraph 15)

_____

USE THE DICTIONARY

Choose the correct definition of this word as it is used in the context of this reading.

a. subside (paragraph 4)

_____

b. remorseful (paragraph 4)

_____

c. eluding (paragraph 13)

_____

d. conspicuous (paragraph 13)

_____

e. snag (paragraph 14)

_____

OBJECTIVE OPERATIONS

1. Who is the writer's intended audience?
    a. students
    b. boaters
    c. general audience
    d. riverfolk
2. What is the author's purpose?
    a. to inform
    b. to persuade
    c. to entertain
3. Which sentence best states the main idea of the passage?
    a. Although knowledgeable about rivers, Twain has not learned how rivers change

and how to navigate in the dark, skills pilots must have.
    b. Although knowledgeable about rivers, Twain has to be taught how to navigate by Bixby.
    c. Twain is complacent about the river, but Bixby will end that.
    d. Learning the river and its changes is very important to a pilot.

4. The word "remorseful" in paragraph 4, line 2, most nearly means
    a. pathetic.
    b. regretful.
    c. shameful.
    d. sad.

5. What is the topic of paragraph 5?

   a. the shape of the river

   b. the shoals of the river

   c. Mr. Bixby teaching Twain

   d. learning the river

6. What is the stated main idea of paragraph 13?

   a. "I went to work now to learn the shape of the river; and of all the eluding and un-graspable objects that ever I tried to get mind or hands on, that was the chief."

   b. "I would fasten my eyes upon a sharp, wooded point that projected far into the river some miles ahead of me, and go to laboriously photographing its shape upon my brain; and just as I was beginning to succeed to my satisfaction, we would draw up toward it and the exasperating thing would begin to melt away and fold back into the bank!"

   c. "If there had been a conspicuous dead tree standing upon the very point of the cape, I would find that tree inconspicuously merged into the general forest, and occupying the middle of a straight shore, when I got abreast of it!"

   d. "Nothing ever had the same shape when I was coming down-stream that it had borne when I went up."

7. When Twain says he didn't know Walnut Bend had "any particular shape" Mr. Bixby got so mad that

   a. his gun went off accidentally.

   b. he told Twain he was fired.

   c. he used every swear word he could think of.

   d. he went off to do some shooting practice to get over his anger.

8. The word "subside" in paragraph 4, line 2, most nearly means

   a. settle down.

   b. build up.

   c. collapse.

   d. immerse.

9. What is the topic of paragraph 14?

   a. the river

   b. Bixby talking to Twain

   c. the changing river and how to navigate it

   d. navigating

10. Mr. Bixby explains to Twain that it's actually an advantage that the shapes he sees along the river change "every three seconds," because

    a. the changing shapes keep the pilot from getting bored and losing concentration.

    b. if the shapes changed more slowly, they could be confused with other steamboats approaching.

    c. by knowing exactly how and where the shape will change, you can know where to steer the boat.

    d. when one shape splits into two parts, you can steer the boat between the two parts.

11. The word "merged" in paragraph 13, line 9, most nearly means

    a. escaped.

    b. mingled.

    c. grown.

    d. blended.

12. What is the implied main idea of paragraph 14?

    a. Learning to navigate means that, by being observant, a pilot should expect and antici-pate changes in the river.

    b. Learning to navigate a river is tricky and cumbersome.

    c. Learning to navigate a river in the dark means a pilot uses all of his skills.

    d. The river constantly changes.

13. According to Twain,

    a. going down river was the same as coming up.

    b. the river never changes.

    c. going down river was never the same as coming up.

    d. all rivers are extremely different.

14. Once Twain learns the shape of the river, he is shocked to find out that Mr. Bixby has yet an-other type of information that must be memo-rized. He must also know

    a. the speed of the current at each point.

    b. the depth of the water at each point.

c. the speed of each steamboat as it approaches the boat he is on.

d. the names of each farm and plantation along the river.

15. When Twain finds out he must learn this new type of information, he says

a. he'd have to be a miracle worker and a genius to be able to learn all that.

b. he might as well become a stage magician and leave the steamboat business.

c. he might as well try to become a famous painter and artist as learn all that.

d. he's not strong enough to carry all the books he'd need to learn all that.

16. According to Bixby, Twain will

a. never learn how to navigate.

b. be taught how to navigate no matter what.

c. let Bixby take the helm.

d. teach others how to navigate.

17. From what we see of Mr. Bixby in this excerpt, we can see that he's the kind of teacher who is basically

a. mean-spirited and determined to make his apprentice feel bad.

b. lazy and determined to make his apprentice do all the work.

c. bad-tempered and unwilling to apologize when he loses control of his temper.

d. good-hearted and dedicated to getting his apprentice to learn.

18. What is the overall tone of the passage?

a. humorous

b. admiring

c. confused

d. questioning

QUICK QUESTIONS

1. Twain says in the second-to-last paragraph that he wouldn't have enough strength to carry around the brains of a pilot. True or False

2. Once Twain learns the shape of the river, he is shocked to find out that Mr. Bixby has yet another type of information that must be memorized. True or False

3. Mr. Bixby says he'll _____ "learn" _____ a man the river.

4. Some examples of the "little difficulties" Twain has in learning the shape of the river include
   navigating in the dark and learning the shallow spots. (Answers will vary.)
   _____
   _____

5. What does Twain want to do once he knows he must learn a new set of details about the river?
   Answers will vary.
   _____
   _____

6. What were the advantages of the way Twain learned the river? What were the disadvantages? What could a teacher learn about how to teach a challenging subject from this reading?
   Answers will vary.
   _____
   _____

7

Patterns of Thought

PATTERNS OF THOUGHT

1 | Look for common patterns of thought.

2 | Connect these patterns to the overall point and main ideas.

3 | Watch for signal words and phrases.

imagine this

As you stroll down the sidewalk, you see a new café has opened. Will it have items that you are familiar with? Will it sell tea, coffee, and snacks? Will it be different from the café that is only four blocks down the street? You look at the chalkboard with the day's specials; you see that breakfast is served all day, and the café offers vegetarian dishes. The café four blocks away serves neither, and although it does serve coffee and tea, you do not know whether it is fair trade.

As you ponder what is written on the chalkboard, you make comparisons and contrasts, think of items you might like to try, or wonder what "fair trade" is. These patterns of thought, the comparisons, contrasts, examples, and definitions, come naturally to you. These patterns, and a few others, are part of your everyday thoughts. You use them to help you make decisions. In a reading, patterns of thought will help you understand the author's ideas and make it easier to find the overall point and the main ideas.

Think FIRST >

- Do you notice when people give examples or contrasts when explaining something to you? Do you compare or classify ideas? Do you define ideas when people need to understand?

- Do you ever hear people support a point by giving examples or comparisons? Do you support your main ideas with contrasts or definitions?

- Before you explain an idea, do you say, "For example . . . ," "However," "In addition," etc.? Do you hear people use these transitions?

INTRODUCTION TO THE NEW STRATEGY
Patterns of Thought

Patterns of thought are structures our minds use all the time. All of our thinking and communicating depend on **patterns of thought** such as reasons—"I was late because my car broke down"—or comparisons—"I had the same problems with my last car!" Recognizing these familiar patterns as you read helps you comprehend the writer's overall point and the purpose of the main ideas.

Before reading "Optimism: The Great Motivator," Reading 13, learn to recognize common patterns of thought in passages from readings in other parts of the book.

Common Patterns

You have already seen how the patterns of examples, contrast, and definition help you to get the meaning of a word from the context. They can also help you understand the writer's meaning in a reading as a whole. There are also other common patterns of thought: cause-and-effect reasoning and sequence.

Examples
Examples show specific cases or instances of a general idea. The pattern of examples makes a general idea easier to understand by connecting it to specifics.

> **Signal words and phrases for examples**
> for example, for instance, e.g., such as, to illustrate, to be specific, that is (to say), namely, another instance, another example

See how examples are used in this passage from Reading 11, "How the Self-Concept Develops."

Instructor Tip
Have students bring in a variety of reading materials. In groups, ask them to find examples of sentences/paragraphs that use examples.

We learn who we are by communicating with others, receiving their feedback, making sense of it, and internalizing or rejecting all or part of it, such that we are altered by the experience. For example, probably someone in your life has told you that you have a good sense of humor. But think about it for a moment: How would you know if you're funny if it were not for others laughing at humorous thing you say or do?

Even without the signal phrase, "for example," you can pick out the examples pattern here. The first sentence gives the general idea that others' views influence our self-concept. The second sentence shows you just one specific case that demonstrates that general idea.

connect now

Are you more likely to be convinced if a salesman offers examples of a product's benefits?

Try picking out the examples in the following passage from "How Conscious Is Thought?" (Reading 14).

The mindless processing of information has benefits: If we stopped to think twice about everything we did, we would get nothing done ("I'm reaching for my toothbrush; now I'm putting toothpaste on it; now I'm brushing my right molars"). But mindlessness can also lead to errors and mishaps, ranging from the trivial (putting the butter in the dishwasher or locking yourself out of your apartment) to the serious (driving carelessly while on "automatic pilot").

In this case, the examples, all located within the parentheses, show specific instances of mindlessness.

Often a single, longer example—sometimes called an illustration—is used to demonstrate a general statement. Look for the extended example in this passage from Reading 11, in "How the Self-Concept Develops." State it in your own words.

Haven't you met people whom you just wished you could hand a decent self-concept? They're nice people, but they seem to suffer from a self-concept formed out of years of criticism from important others. We recall the story of one colleague who was quite an accomplished dancer as an undergraduate. She'd known an upbringing of never being quite good enough, never being able to please her demanding mother, hard as she tried. She remembered one particular dance recital, where she felt she had danced the performance of her life. She just knew her mother would be proud, but when her mother joined her backstage after the performance, amidst the accolades of her friends, her mother had only one thing to say: She pointed out the moment in the dance when the woman's arm should have been straight up instead of out to the side. That's all the feedback she got from her mother—stinging criticism about one brief moment in a brilliant evening's worth of performance.

Comparison/Contrast

To **compare** (to give similarities) and to **contrast** (to give differences) may be seen as separate patterns. However, they often work together.

> **Signal words and phrases for comparison**
> as, like, similarly, in a similar manner, likewise, in comparison, in a like manner, both

> *Comparison shopping is a very common practice in the United States, but when it comes to tattoos, author Karen Hudson gives many reasons not to shop around. What other patterns do you notice?*

At least if you live in the United States, you've probably seen it. The auto insurance television commercial that shows a girl sitting on a couch while her parents are shaking their heads in disappointment and expressing shock and outrage. At this point, we think we see the reason for the upset as the young girl sticks out her tongue revealing a huge barbell. The "punch line" of the commercial, however, is that the parents are not upset that she got a tongue piercing, but that she didn't shop around for the best price!

Cute. At least for once, in a commercial, the body art wasn't the object of disdain. However, the very idea that people should be shopping for a bargain when getting a piercing or tattoo is about as pleasant as a root canal.

What's the Big Deal?

I think it's safe to say that most of us are not rich, and we all appreciate a good deal. Why not? Blowing money unnecessarily is just a waste, and most of us enjoy finding a bargain even if we can afford to spend more. When shopping for cars, electronics, furniture or even food, frugal living is the way of the wise these days. Grabbing up freebies and samples are at the core of our very survival. So, why the big deal about shopping around when looking for a tattoo or piercing?

"The bitterness of a poor-quality tattoo will linger long after the sweetness of a cheap price is forgotten."—Unknown

You Get What You Pay For

Ever heard the saying, "You get what you pay for"? Yeah, well, the body art industry is one place you won't find a better example of the prudence of that advice. Quality in the body art world can range anywhere from absolute crap to jaw-dropping fantastic—and everywhere in between. And although it may not always be this way, in most cases you're going to get exactly what you pay for.

Hudson, Karen L. "You'd Better (Not!) Shop Around: Why Tattoos and Piercings Shouldn't Be Bargains." About.com. 7 July 2009. Available at: http://tattoo.about.com/cs/articles/a/nobargain.htm

Instructor Tip
Have students bring in a variety of reading materials. In groups, ask them to find examples of sentences/paragraphs that use comparison and contrast.

Signal words and phrases for contrast
but, however, in contrast, on the other hand, whereas, while, contrary to, although, yet

Why did you choose your best friend? Was it due to your similarities?

In "Why Men Don't Last" (Reading 18), Natalie Angier finds a striking contrast in the ways that men and women deal with depression and suicidal thoughts.

By standard measures, men have less than half the rate of depression seen in women. When men do feel depressed, they tend to seek distraction in an activity, which, many psychologists say, can be a more effective technique for dispelling the mood than is a depressed woman's tendency to turn inward and ruminate. In the United States and many other industrialized nations, women are about three times more likely than men to express suicidal thoughts or to attempt to kill themselves.

connect now

Mark the supporting details that show the contrast between men's and women's ways of dealing with depression in this paragraph.

Now read the paragraph that follows:

What about piercings? Guy 1 charges $15 for a tongue piercing, and Guy 2 down the street charges $50. Why do you think Guy 1 can charge so much less? Possibly it's because he doesn't spend the money to sterilize his equipment properly? Or maybe he never spent the money to even be trained in how to pierce properly? Or maybe he uses inferior quality jewelry, which can lead to pain, infection, healing difficulties and a lot of hassles. Do you really want to have Guy 1 sticking a needle through you just to save 35 bucks? Come on!

"Good tattoos ain't cheap, and cheap tattoos ain't good!"—Unknown

The Price You Pay for a Bargain

I'd be rich if I had a dime for every time I heard someone say, "I really want a tattoo from so-and-so, but they're so expensive!" If you really want a tattoo from a particular artist, why are you going to let a price tag hold you back? You do realize you'll be wearing this tattoo for the rest of your life, right? If you don't think that's worth a few extra dollars, don't get it! "But I can get the same tattoo from my buddy for half that price!" Fine—you go see your buddy and don't come looking for a shoulder to cry on when you end up with a lousy tattoo or get some kind of disease or infection from improper sterilization.

This does not mean that every quality artist charges an arm and a leg. There are some that genuinely do good work but also don't charge a lot. There are also some charging more than their work is worth. This is where research comes in. Don't choose any artist based on price alone. Look at the portfolio. Ask around to see if they have a good reputation for good work. Check out the competition and compare quality, not prices!

Some Things Never Change

"A guy came into Charlie [Wagner's] shop and said, 'I want to get me a good tattoo!' Charlie said, 'I do cheap tattoos, I don't do real good tattoos. Now, if you want a real good tattoo you go to my friend Lew Alberts. You'll get a real good tattoo but you're going to pay for it. This 25-cent tattoo will cost you three or four dollars.'"—Fun City Tattoo: History

Cutting the Right Corners

Does this mean I'm totally apathetic toward people that can't afford a $200/hour tattoo? No, of course not. But if you really want a tattoo you're going to be proud of for the rest of your life, you're going to have to pay for it. Get over the "too expensive" mentality. There are other ways you can cut corners and save for the exact tattoo you want. But from now on, save the bargain hunting for your next TV, not your next tattoo.

And yet . . . men don't last. They die off in greater numbers than women do at every stage of life, and thus their average life span is seven years shorter. Women may attempt suicide relatively more often, but in the United States, four times more men than women die from the act each year.

Mark the supporting details in this paragraph. Did you take note of all the details in the table that follows?

MEN	WOMEN
less than half the rate of depression reported in women	more than twice the rate of depression reported in men
when depressed seek distraction in activity	when depressed turn inward and think; more likely to feel suicidal and attempt suicide
life span seven years shorter	life span seven years longer
four times more likely to succeed in killing themselves	attempt suicide more often, but less likely to succeed

EXERCISES

To practice identifying the example, comparison, and contrast patterns, do this exercise.

Each of the following excerpts is from one of the readings in this book. Read the selection and underline signal words if they are used. If signal words are not used, underline the details that helped you determine the pattern. Then decide which pattern is used.

1. But maybe Isabelle was not normal. This is what people first thought, for she scored practically zero on an intelligence test. But in a few months, after intensive language training, Isabelle was able to speak in short sentences. In about a year, she could write a few words, do simple addition, and retell stories after hearing them. Seven months later, she had a vocabulary of almost 2,000 words. It took only two years for Isabelle to reach the normal intellectual level for her age. She then went on to school, where she was "bright, cheerful, energetic . . . and participated in all school activities as normally as other children."

   Excerpt from Reading 7: What Deprived Children Tell Us about Human Nature

   What pattern does this selection use? _____ Contrast _____

2. At Child's School in Bloomington, Indiana, I quickly discovered that, in spite of my two-handed turkey-drawing ability, I was very much behind the other children. My classmates laughed when they saw me carefully printing my name all in uppercase, when I thought that the more Elmer's glue you used the better it stuck, and when I didn't know the Pledge of Allegiance, even though it was printed on the inside of my pencil-box lid.

   Excerpt from Reading 2: I Do Not Like to Read—Sam-I-Am!

   What pattern does this selection use? _____ Comparison _____

3. At one point in the discussion of "Starry Time" a boy wondered whether the story might help us figure out how to describe a "good child"—as I've mentioned, I'd been pressing those children and others for some time to help me come up with some useful specifications. "If you read the story," the boy declared, "and you go give something to someone, and it's a good thing you've done—you've given the world a star, and that means you're better than you were before. But you could fall back and forget about the next guy, so you have to keep sharing with others, or you'll be good for one day, and then the next, you're not doing what's good, and that's a missed chance, my mom said." As I listened I thought of the myth of Sisyphus in Greek mythology—with its image of a man condemned to rolling a heavy rock up a hill, only to have it fall down each time, just as he nears the top, and its reminder of the constant struggle to lift up ourselves, as it were, with backsliding an ever-present possibility. And I thought of Emerson's notion of each day as a god, his way of emphasizing the enormous moral possibilities a given span of time can offer. All of that worked into a child's worried, yet vigorously demanding ethical speculation.

   Excerpt from Reading 8: The Good Person

   What pattern does this selection use? _____ Example _____

Definition and Classification

Definition explains the meaning of a word or idea. Writers give a longer, more detailed definition of a word when they want to introduce a new term or to reexamine the meaning of a word. Definition often includes **classification**—a pattern that shows how a word or idea belongs as one type within a larger category.

> **Signal words and phrases for definition**
> that is, that is to say, or, also known as, to define this, to say what this means, this means that, namely

Instructor Tip
Have students bring in a variety of reading materials. In groups, ask them to find examples of sentences/paragraphs that use definition and classification.

> **Signal words and phrases for definition and classification**
> types, kinds, category, elements of, traits, characteristics, features, parts

In the passage below, for example, the definition includes classifying optimism as one type within the category of attitudes. Extended definitions also use comparison/contrast, examples, and further explanation.

Paragraph 3 of "Optimism: The Great Motivator," Reading 13, is an extended definition of optimism.

Optimism, like hope, means having a strong expectation that, in general, things will turn out all right in life, despite setbacks and frustrations. From the standpoint of emotional intelligence, optimism is an attitude that buffers people against falling into apathy, hopelessness, or depression in the face of tough going. And, as with hope, its near cousin, optimism pays dividends in life (providing, of course, it is a realistic optimism; a too-naïve optimism can be disastrous).

connect now

Vehicles are classified in many ways, such as model, color, or type. What other items can you think of that have classifications?

This definition says what the word means (in the first sentence). After classifying the word, the definition gives the word's special characteristics (what kind of attitude it is). Finally, optimism is compared to hope, "its near cousin."

Cause-and-Effect Reasoning

Cause-and-effect reasoning gives logical reasons that answer why or how. A cause is the reason for something happening; an effect is the result or outcome.

Instructor Tip
Have students bring in a variety of reading materials. In groups, ask them to find examples of sentences/paragraphs that show cause and effect.

> **Signal words and phrases for cause-and-effect reasoning**
> because, thus, therefore, as a result, for this reason, to explain, consequently, hence, then, if . . . then, accordingly

You can see how this pattern works in this section of paragraph 8 from "Optimism: The Great Motivator."

Just why optimism makes such a difference in sales success speaks to the sense in which it is an emotionally intelligent attitude. Each no a salesman gets is a small defeat. The emotional reaction to that defeat is crucial to the ability to marshal enough motivation to continue. As the noes mount up, morale can deteriorate, making it harder and harder to pick up the phone for the next call. Such rejection

OPRAH WINFREY

Their Eyes Were Watching God

by Zora Neale Hurston

When Oprah Winfrey started her book club in 1996, she used her celebrity status to build a community of readers. Over the years, she's proven that she has an eye for dramatic plots, courageous success stories, and fascinating characters. Her selections have ranged from classics like Toni Morrison's novel *Sula*, to contemporary bestsellers like David Wroblewski's *The Story of Edgar Sawtelle*. Oprah credits Zora Neale Hurston's novel *Their Eyes Were Watching God* as inspiring her love of books, as well as her desire to share that passion. No matter what direction she decides to take her star power on television, one thing is sure, Oprah's audience will follow eagerly awaiting to see what she reads next.

If you liked *Their Eyes Were Watching God*, you might also like:

The Color Purple, Alice Walker

I Know Why the Caged Bird Sings, Maya Angelou

Push, Sapphire

is especially hard to take for a pessimist, who interprets it as meaning. "I'm a failure at this; I'll never make a sale"—an interpretation that is sure to trigger apathy and defeatism, if not depression.

The paragraph answers the question why optimism makes such a difference in sales success. It begins by showing the cause of emotional difficulty—the rejection that is an inevitable part of sales work.

Mark the phrases that show the general effects of rejection. Then mark the phrases that show the specific effects of rejection on a pessimist.

Now, take a look at the rest of the paragraph.

Optimists, on the other hand, tell themselves, "I'm using the wrong approach," or "That last person was just in a bad mood." By seeing not themselves but something in the situation as the reason for their failure, they can change their approach in the next call. While the pessimist's mental set leads to despair, the optimist's spawns hope.

Mark the phrases that show the specific effects of rejection on an optimist.

Note the way the pattern of comparison/contrast is used in this passage, along with cause-and-effect reasoning.

See the summary of the passage in the table below.

CAUSE	EFFECT ON OPTIMISTS	EFFECT ON PESSIMISTS	MAIN IDEA (RESULTS)
Rejection	Look at specific situation as reason for failure	Look at themselves as failures	Optimists have much more success in making sales
	Reevaluate their approach	Become defeated, depressed	

To practice identifying the definition, classification, and cause-and-effect reasoning patterns, do this exercise.

Each of the following excerpts is from one of the readings in this book. Read the selection and underline signal words if they are used. If signal words are not used, underline the details that helped you determine the pattern. Then decide which pattern is used.

1. When the Harlows (1965) frightened them with a mechanical bear or dog, the babies did not run to the wire frame "mother." Instead, they clung pathetically to their terrycloth "mother." The Harlows concluded that infant-mother bonding is due not to feeding but, rather, to what they termed "intimate physical contact." To most of us, this phrase means cuddling.

   Excerpt from Reading 7: What Deprived Children Tell Us about Human Nature

   What pattern does this selection use? _____ Cause and effect _____

2. No need to repeat the story of how it went for years. The streets were not made of gold. People weren't interested in smelling flowers held by strangers. My grandmother was a foreigner. Alone. A young girl who worked hard doing piecework to earn enough money for meals. No leisure time, no new gold earrings—and no school.

   Reading 4: "See Spot Run": Teaching My Grandmother to Read

   What pattern does this selection use? _____ Classification _____

3. For many years I have been asking children to tell me their ideas about what makes for a good person. Rather obviously, those children have varied in their responsive definitions, some emphasizing a person's interest in reaching out to and assisting others, some putting stress on a person's religious beliefs, some pointing out the importance of certain secular values such as independence of mind, civic responsibility, commitment to work, to a solid family life.

   Excerpt from Reading 8: The Good Person

   What pattern does this selection use? _____ Definition _____

Order in Time or Space

The **sequence** pattern is used to give details in a certain order. The sequence or order of details matters when telling stories, giving the history of events, explaining how something works (how plants turn sunlight into food, for example), giving instructions where one step must be completed before beginning the next, or giving details as to where something or someone is located.

Instructor Tip
Have students bring in a variety of reading materials. In groups, ask them to find examples of sentences/paragraphs that show sequence.

> **Signal words and phrases for time order**
> First, before, after, afterward, at last, during, now, at that time, since, until, finally, next, when, then, while, throughout

> **Signal words and phrases for process order**
> First, second, third, before, after, afterward, further, last, finally, next, then

Look at this sequence of events from Reading 2, "I Do Not Like to Read—Sam-I-Am!"; this paragraph is written in time order:

> My mother was taking forever to finish her work, so I began to flip through the pages, looking for my favorite picture, the one with the goat in it. What happened next was really an accident. . . . Almost without realizing it, I found myself reading the entire page, and liking it.

Notice that first the author flipped through the pages, looking for a picture, but then she tells you "what happened next."

Frequently items in a sequence are numbered. If not, you might add your own numbers to make the items easier to remember.

Why is telling a story in its proper sequence important? What happens if details are out of order?

Connect now

EXERCISES

PRACTICE

To practice identifying the individual sequence patterns (time order, process, and spatial order), do this exercise.

Each of the following excerpts is from one of the readings in this the book. Read the selection and underline signal words if they are used. If signal words are not used, underline the details that helped you determine the pattern. Then decide which pattern is used.

1. Since his master read aloud a chapter from the New Testament every night, Johnson would coax him to read the same chapter over and over, until he knew it by heart and was able to find the same words on the printed page. Also, when the master's son was studying, Johnson would suggest that the boy read part of his lesson out loud. "Lor's over me," Johnson would say to encourage him, "read that again," which the boy often did, believing that Johnson was admiring his performance. Through repetition, he learned enough to be able to read the newspapers by the time the Civil War broke out, and later set up a school of his own to teach others to read.

   Excerpt from Reading 3: Forbidden Reading

   What pattern does this selection use? _____ Process

2. Klaus Schoenwiese traveled down the road eight miles north of Lusaka, Zambia, through soft hills, still lush from the rainy season, and fields of maize that were beginning to dry. Charcoal sellers whizzed by on bikes. His Land Cruiser turned at a sign marked CCHZ. Along this rutted, dirt road were a few small farmhouses, open fields of tomatoes and a fluttering flock of blue finches.

   Excerpt from Reading 6: Point. Shoot. See.

   What pattern does this selection use? _____ Spatial order

3. Older Infants carry this responsiveness to subjective form even further. Nine-month-olds can detect the organized, meaningful pattern in a series of moving lights that resemble a person walking, in that they look much longer at this display than they do at upside-down or disorganized ver-

sions. Although 3- to 5-month-olds can tell the difference between these patterns, they do not show a preference for one with both an upright orientation" and a humanlike movement pattern. . . .

Excerpt from Reading 9: How Babies Use Patterns to See

What pattern does this selection use? _____time order_____

Patterns and the Overall Point

Recognizing patterns in a reading can help you understand the overall point. As you get an overview, see if the title, headings, or other clues from skimming suggest patterns of thought. Then, as you read, continue to look for patterns that the writer uses to support the overall point.

Titles

The title of Reading 12, "School Is Bad for Children," tells you to expect cause-and-effect reasoning about the bad effects of school on children. On the other hand, the title of Reading 8, "The Good Person," suggests that the writer will define what it is to be a good person or give you an example of someone who is good.

connect now

What do the titles of some movies tell you about the movie's organization? For example, what do the titles *When Harry Met Sally* or *How to Lose a Guy in Ten Days* tell you about the movie?

Headings

What can you learn from the first two headings of Reading 15, "Why People Don't Help in a Crisis": (1) "The Unseeing Eye" and (2) "Seeing Is Not Necessarily Believing"? The headings suggest a pattern of statement and clarification—the first stating that we don't see what we should in a crisis and clarifying why, and the second stating that seeing is not believing and then further explaining why.

Skimming

The title of Reading 18, "Why Men Don't Last," suggests the pattern of cause-and-effect reasoning (why don't they last?). Skimming confirms that overall pattern, but shows a second major pattern—the contrast between men and women—as part of the writer's overall point about men.

Patterns and Main Ideas

Patterns can often help you *find and mark main ideas.* Be especially watchful for patterns while using these steps from Strategy 6.

Grouping the Reading into Topics

Look for patterns as you divide the reading into topics that relate to the overall point. The title of Reading 11, "How the Self-Concept Develops," gives us our overall-point question: "How does it develop?" The question implies the cause-effect reasoning pattern. In addition, each of the four topics (revealed in the headings) refers to one cause for our self-concept developing in a certain way.

Finding Main Ideas about the Topic

Look for patterns as you find and mark main ideas about the topic. For example, the first topic of the same reading continues the pattern: it shows

the effect on us of communicating with others. The main idea sentence (sentence 4) gives a general statement of these effects.

Finding Supporting Ideas for a Main Idea

Look for patterns as you mark important supporting ideas related to a main idea. The main idea of the last topic in Reading 11, "Self-Labels," also has a cause-effect pattern: the effect of our own attitudes, beliefs, values and actions. However, definition is another helpful pattern in pointing out the new term, "self-reflexiveness."

Look for patterns when you're stuck on a difficult paragraph. The pattern of examples is especially helpful for clarifying a hard topic. However, don't apply the strategy rigidly. Not all readings, not even all paragraphs, fall neatly into one pattern. Instead, you'll often find combinations of patterns.

Signal Words and Phrases

Signal words and phrases help you determine which pattern a writer uses. By learning certain words and phrases associated with each pattern and understanding how transitions work in a paragraph, you will be better able to pick out the thought pattern.

Signals for Patterns

Signal words and phrases are listed with each pattern in the boxes. Get used to picking up these signals.

Signals for Transitions

Writers often signal a change in topic with a **transition** word or phrase that serves as a link or bridge from one thought to the next. Sometimes, these are the same words and phrases that are used with common patterns. Or they may signal clarification, additional information, or summary.

Hot or Not?

Where else do you look for patterns besides reading? Do you look for your teachers' patterns or traffic patterns?

> **Signal words for clarification**
> in other words, indeed, clearly, in fact, certainly, obviously, without a doubt, of course, apparently, surely, evidently

> **Signal words and phrases for addition**
> in addition, what's more, also, and, furthermore, moreover, besides, as well as, additionally, further

> **Signal words and phrases for summary**
> in brief, in conclusion, in short, to summarize, to sum up, on the whole, conclusively, overall, generally speaking, mainly, lastly

Now that you understand Strategy 7, put it into practice with Reading 13, "Optimism: The Great Motivator." When you read "Optimism: The Great Motivator," you will find several examples of signal words and phrases. Try to identify as many examples as you can, and notice how they're used.

Try looking for patterns of thought as you determine the overall point and find main ideas. You've already seen the pattern of definition and cause-and-effect reasoning in passages from this reading. See if the title suggests an overall pattern. Then skim the reading to see what other patterns you recognize. Let these patterns help you identify the topics of the reading.

Optimism: The Great Motivator

DANIEL GOLEMAN

READING 13

Daniel Goleman is a professor of psychology at Harvard University. This reading comes from his book *Emotional Intelligence: Why It Can Matter More Than IQ* (1995). Emotional intelligence, according to Goleman, means our ability to respond emotionally in appropriate, productive ways to life's challenges.

get an overview and ask questions

1   Americans who follow swimming had high hopes for Matt Biondi, a member of the U.S. Olympic Team in 1988. Some sportswriters were touting Biondi as likely to match Mark Spitz's 1972 feat of taking seven gold medals. But Biondi finished a heartbreaking third in his first event, the 200-meter freestyle. In his next event, the 100-meter butterfly, Biondi was inched out for the gold by another swimmer who made a greater effort in the last meter.

respond

2   Sportscasters speculated that the defeats would <u>dispirit</u> Biondi in his successive events. But Biondi rebounded from defeat and took a gold medal in his next five events. One viewer who was not surprised by Biondi's comeback was Martin Seligman, a psychologist at the University of Pennsylvania, who had tested Biondi for optimism earlier that year. In an experiment done with Seligman, the swimming coach told Biondi during a special event meant to showcase Biondi's best performance that he had a worse time

than was actually the case. Despite the downbeat feedback, when Biondi was asked to rest and try again, his performance—actually already very good—was even better. But when other team members who were given a false bad time—and whose test scores showed they were pessimistic—tried again, they did even worse the second time.[1]

Optimism, like hope, means having a strong expectation that, in general, things will turn out all right in life, despite setbacks and frustrations. From the standpoint of emotional intelligence, optimism is an attitude that buffers people against falling into apathy, hopelessness, or depression in the face of tough going. And, as with hope, its near cousin, optimism pays dividends in life (providing, of course, it is a realistic optimism; a too-naïve optimism can be disastrous).[2]

3

[O]ptimism is an attitude that buffers people against falling into apathy, hopelessness, or depression in the face of tough going.

vital vocabulary

◀━━━━━━━━━━━━━━━━━━━━━━━

Seligman defines optimism in terms of how people explain to themselves their successes and failures. People who are optimistic see a failure as due to something that can be changed so that they can succeed next time around, while pessimists take the blame for failure, ascribing it to some lasting characteristic they are helpless to change. These differing explanations have profound implications for how people respond to life. For example, in reaction to a disappointment such as being turned down for a job, optimists tend to respond actively and hopefully, by formulating a plan of action, say, or seeking out help and advice; they see the setback as something that can be remedied. Pessimists, by contrast, react to such setbacks by assuming there is nothing they can do to make things go better the next time, and so do nothing about the problem; they see the setback as due to some personal deficit that will always plague them.

4

find and mark main ideas

◀━━━━━━━━━━━━━━━━━━━━━━━

Use patterns to help you mark main ideas.

explanatory style: way of explaining successes or failures

As with hope, optimism predicts academic success. In a study of five hundred members of the incoming freshman class of 1984 at the University of Pennsylvania, the students' scores on a test of optimism were a better predictor of their actual grades freshman year than were their SAT scores or their high-school grades. Said Seligman, who studied them, "College entrance exams measure talent, while explanatory style tells you who gives up. It is the combination of reasonable talent and the ability to keep going in the face of defeat that leads to success. What's missing in tests of ability is motivation. What you need to know about someone is whether they will keep going when things get frustrating. My hunch is that for a given level

5

of intelligence, your actual achievement is a function not just of talent, but also of the capacity to stand defeat."[3]

6   One of the most telling demonstrations of the power of optimism to motivate people is a study Seligman did of insurance salesmen with the MetLife company. Being able to take a rejection with grace is essential in sales of all kinds, especially with a product like insurance, where the ratio of noes to yeses can be so discouragingly high. For this reason, about three quarters of insurance salesmen quit in their first three years. Seligman found that new salesmen who were by nature optimists sold 37 percent more insurance in their first two years on the job than did pessimists. And during the first year the pessimists quit at twice the rate of the optimists.

7   What's more, Seligman persuaded MetLife to hire a special group of applicants who scored high on a test for optimism but failed the normal screening tests (which compared a range of their attitudes to a standard profile based on answers from agents who have been successful). This special group outsold the pessimists by 21 percent in their first year, and 57 percent in the second.

8   Just why optimism makes such a difference in sales success speaks to the sense in which it is an emotionally intelligent attitude. Each 'no' a salesperson gets is a small defeat. The emotional reaction to that defeat is crucial to the ability to marshal enough motivation to continue. As the noes mount up, morale can deteriorate, making it harder and harder to pick up the phone for the next call. Such rejection is especially hard to take for a pessimist, who interprets it as meaning, "I'm a failure at this; I'll never make a sale"—an interpretation that is sure to trigger apathy and defeatism, if not depression. Optimists, on the other hand, tell themselves, "I'm using the wrong approach," or "That last person was just in a bad mood." By seeing not themselves but something in the situation as the reason for their failure, they can change their approach in the next call. While the pessimist's mental set leads to despair, the optimist's spawns hope.

9   One source of a positive or negative outlook may well be inborn temperament; some people by nature tend one way or the other. But . . . temperament can be tempered by experience. Optimism and hope—like helplessness and despair—can be learned. Underlying both is an outlook psychologists call *self-efficacy*, the belief that one has mastery over the events of one's life and can meet challenges as they come up. Developing a competency of any kind strengthens the sense of self-efficacy, making a person more willing to take risks and seek out more demanding challenges. And surmounting those challenges in turn increases the sense of self-efficacy. This attitude makes people more likely to make the best use of whatever skills they may have—or to do what it takes to develop them.

10   Albert Bandura, a Stanford psychologist who has done much of the research on self-efficacy, sums it up well: "People's beliefs about their abilities have a profound effect on those abilities. Ability is not a fixed property; there is a huge variability in how you perform. People who have a sense of self-efficacy bounce back from failures; they approach things in terms of how to handle them rather than worrying about what can go wrong."[4]

Optimism and hope— like helplessness and despair—can be learned.

Notes

1. Optimistic swimmers: Martin Seligman, *Learned Optimism* (New York: Knopf, 1991).
2. A realistic vs. naïve optimism: see, for example, Carol Whalen et al., "Optimism in Children's Judgments of Health and Environmental Risks," *Health Psychology* 13 (1994).
3. I interviewed Martin Seligman about optimism in *The New York Times* (Feb. 3, 1987).
4. I interviewed Albert Bandura about self-efficacy in *The New York Times* (May 8, 1988).

ACTIVE READERS RESPOND

After you've finished reading, use these questions to respond to "Optimism: The Great Motivator." You may write your answers in the spaces provided or on a separate sheet of paper.

VITAL VOCABULARY

Some words in this reading may be unfamiliar to you. Use the methods of Strategy 3 to explain what the listed words mean.

USE CONTEXT CLUES

a. formulating (paragraph 4)

_____

b. surmounting (paragraph 9)

_____

USE WORD PARTS

a. dispirit (paragraph 2)

_____

b. apathy (paragraph 3)

_____

c. defeatism (paragraph 8)

_____

USE THE DICTIONARY

Choose the correct definition of this word as it is used in the context of this reading.

a. naïve (paragraph 3)

_____

b. marshal (paragraph 8)

_____

c. tempered (paragraph 9) (Be sure to get the right part of speech.)

_____

d. property (paragraph 10)

_____

Find the sentence or sentences that demonstrate the specific pattern listed for each of these paragraphs. Explain briefly how the pattern is used.

1. Paragraphs 1 and 2 (the introduction): examples and contrast

   (Answers will vary.)

   _____

2. Paragraph 5: cause-and-effect reasoning

   (Answers will vary.)

   _____

3. Paragraph 6: cause-and-effect reasoning

   (Answers will vary.)

   _____

4. Paragraph 9: definition

   (Answers will vary.)

   _____

OBJECTIVE OPERATIONS

1. Who is the writer's intended audience?

   a. psychologists

   b. general audience ✓

   c. students

   d. optimists

2. What is the author's purpose?

   a. to inform ✓

   b. to persuade

   c. to entertain

3. What is the tone of the passage?

   a. joyful

   b. encouraging ✓

   c. unhappy

   d. serious

4. Biondi rebounded from the bad news about his performance whereas his teammates did not because

   a. he had trained more consistently and was therefore stronger.

   b. he had a healthier attitude that allowed him to learn from his mistakes. ✓

   c. he had better luck in the successive events than his teammates did.

   d. his too-naïve optimism gave him the illusion that he couldn't fail.

5. The word "surmounting" in paragraph 9, line 9, most nearly means

   a. overdoing.

   b. suffering.

   c. overcoming. ✓

   d. suppressing.

6. Which sentence best states the main idea of the passage?

   a. What you believe you can do has an effect on what you can do.

   b. What you believe about your abilities has a profound effect on those abilities, and you can change the outcomes depending on your attitude. ✓

   c. As an optimist you will always succeed; as a pessimist, you won't.

   d. Optimism is better than pessimism.

7. What is the stated main idea of paragraph 3?

   a. "Optimism, like hope, means having a strong expectation that, in general, things will turn out all right in life, despite setbacks and frustrations." ✓

   b. "From the standpoint of emotional intelligence, optimism is an attitude that buffers people against falling into apathy, hopelessness, or depression in the face of tough going."

c. "And, as with hope, its near cousin, optimism pays dividends in life (providing, of course, it is a realistic optimism; a too-naïve optimism can be disastrous)."

d. "Seligman defines optimism in terms of how people explain to themselves their successes and failures."

8. Goleman shows that optimism is "an emotionally intelligent attitude" because

a. optimists analyze a failure to see what specific things they could do better next time, whereas pessimists assume there is nothing they can do to improve.

b. optimists overlook their failures and pretend they didn't happen, whereas pessimists dwell on the things they can do to improve.

c. pessimists, in general, tend to have lower intelligence than optimists and to do more poorly on tests than optimists do.

d. optimists don't expect to face any failures and therefore they are usually able to avoid disappointment.

9. Which sentence provides support for this sentence (paragraph 4, lines 5–6): "These differing explanations have profound implications for how people respond to life."?

a. "Seligman defines optimism in terms of how people explain to themselves their successes and failures."

b. "People who are optimistic see a failure as due to something that can be changed so that they can succeed next time around, while pessimists take the blame for failure, ascribing it to some lasting characteristic they are helpless to change."

c. "For example, in reaction to a disappointment such as being turned down for a job, optimists tend to respond actively and hopefully, by formulating a plan of action, say, or seeking out help and advice; they see the setback as something that can be remedied."

d. "Pessimists, by contrast, react to such setbacks by assuming there is nothing they can do to make things go better the next time, and so do nothing about the problem; they see the setback as due to some personal deficit that will always plague them."

10. The author's claim that optimists have a strong expectation that generally everything will be all right in life (paragraph 3, line 2) is

a. adequately supported with details.

b. inadequately supported with details.

11. What is the topic of paragraph 6?

a. a study of insurance salesmen

b. how optimism affects the job

c. a study of insurance salesmen and their attitudes

d. pessimism

12. Martin Seligman's study of incoming freshmen at the University of Pennsylvania showed that success in college

a. depends on your having a good explanatory style for convincing professors to raise your grade when necessary.

b. comes from being highly motivated no matter what level of ability or talent you have.

c. depends on a combination of high SAT scores and good high school grades.

d. comes from a combination of reasonable intelligence and the ability to keep going after experiencing defeat.

13. Identify the relationship between these two sentences from paragraph 8.

"Such rejection is especially hard to take for a pessimist, who interprets it as meaning, 'I'm a failure at this; I'll never make a sale'—an interpretation that is sure to trigger apathy and defeatism, if not depression. Optimists, on the other hand, tell themselves, 'I'm using the wrong approach,' or 'That last person was just in a bad mood.'" (lines 6–11)

a. definition

b. addition

c. example

d. contrast

14. For paragraph 8, the author uses an overall organization pattern that

a. compares.

b. explains.

c. defines.

d. summarizes.

15. You can strengthen your self-efficacy by

a. becoming apathetic in any endeavor, which in turn allows you to avoid correcting mistakes.

b. making yourself more efficient by organizing your activities and practicing more self-discipline.

c. becoming more competent in any endeavor, which in turn gives you the confidence to take on greater challenges.

d. being willing to say no to new things you have never tried before.

16. The word "tempered" in paragraph 9, line 3, most nearly means

    a. irritated.

    b. enraged.

    c. moderated.

    d. characterized.

17. What is the relationship between the following sentences (from paragraph 6)?

    "Being able to take a rejection with grace is essential in sales of all kinds, especially with a product like insurance, where the ratio of noes to yeses can be so discouragingly high. For this reason, about three quarters of insurance salesmen quit in their first three years." (lines 3–6)

    a. statement and clarification

    b. definition

    c. cause and effect

    d. contrast

18. According to the passage, a positive or negative outlook may be

    a. inborn.

    b. enjoyed.

    c. renewed.

    d. permanent.

19. What is the relationship between the parts of the following sentence (from paragraph 8)?

    "Such rejection is especially hard to take for a pessimist, who interprets it as meaning, 'I'm a failure at this; I'll never make a sale'—an interpretation that is sure to trigger apathy and defeatism, if not depression." (lines 6–9)

    a. addition

    b. clarification

    c. comparison

    d. contrast

20. You can assume from this reading that one of the following people would be an example of a "too-naïve" optimist:

    a. a student in first-year chemistry who expects to get a higher grade on her next test by going to the campus tutoring center.

    b. an insurance salesman who expects to find a certain percentage of his clients in a good mood.

    c. an artist who expects to sell some of the paintings that were chosen for a local art show.

    d. a sixteen-year-old skater who just started skating two months ago expects to enter the Olympics next year.

READERS WRITE

1. Why did Biondi rebound from the bad news about his performance, whereas his teammates did not?

    (Answers will vary.)

2. What did Martin Seligman's study of incoming freshmen at the University of Pennsylvania show about the effects of optimism?

    (Answers will vary.)

3. What is the meaning of self-efficacy? Why does becoming more competent at anything you do strengthen your self-efficacy?

    (Answers will vary.)

4. If optimism has such beneficial effects, why would a "too-naïve optimism" be "disastrous"?

    (Answers will vary.)

5. From your reading, has the author convinced you of the value of optimism? Explain your answer.

    (Answers will vary.)

1. How would you classify your explanatory style? Is it basically optimistic or pessimistic? Discuss with other students what they think about their explanatory style.

   (Answers will vary.)

   _____

   _____

2. Goleman says that people's temperament can be modified (paragraph 9). Do you agree or disagree? How much change could you see taking place in your basic sense of optimism or pessimism?

   (Answers will vary.)

   _____

   _____

STRATEGY 7

PATTERNS OF THOUGHT

1 | Look for common patterns of thought.

2 | Connect these patterns to the overall point and main ideas.

3 | Watch for signal words and phrases.

Summary

CHAPTER 7

HOW DOES STRATEGY 7 HELP YOU BECOME AN ENGAGED READER?

When you look for **Patterns of Thought** in a reading, you use your own familiar way of thinking to understand the writer's ideas. Recognizing these common patterns sharpens your focus, so that you can more easily find and understand the author's ideas.

HOW DOES THE PATTERNS OF THOUGHT STRATEGY WORK?

Strategy 7 teaches you how to look for common patterns. Writers use example, comparison, contrast, definition, classification, and sequence to help readers understand ideas.

Strategy 7 shows you how to connect patterns to the writer's overall point and main ideas. Recognizing patterns makes it easier for you to find the important points the writer is making.

Strategy 7 teaches you common signal words or phrases that help you identify patterns. In addition, this strategy teaches you what transitions, or connector words, to look for when reading.

Key Terms

cause-and-effect reasoning: explains why or how one event brings about another

compare and contrast: give similarities and/or differences

definition and classification: explains the meaning of a word and show the category it belongs in

examples: show specific cases or instances of a general idea

patterns of thought: structures we use to think, such as reasons or examples

sequence: gives events or items in a particular order

transition: a word or phrase that serves as a bridge from one thought to another

Think AGAIN

Readers expect certain patterns of thought to support a writer's ideas. For example, suppose you were reading instructions on how to change the oil in your car. You would expect the writer to use process to teach you the steps to do an oil change. Or, imagine you were reading a pamphlet on an illness that you have; you might expect to read about the types of treatments available. What other examples can you think of?

TABLE 7.1 SUMMARY TABLE OF PATTERNS OF THOUGHT		
(Numbers in parentheses refer to pages in this chapter where the pattern is discussed.)		
PATTERN	**DESCRIPTION**	**SIGNAL WORDS**
Examples	Show specific instances of a general idea. (224–225)	for example, e.g., to illustrate, for instance, to be specific, that is to say, namely
Comparison	Gives similarities between two or more things. (225–227)	as, like, similarly, in a similar way, compared with, in like manner
Contrast	Gives differences between two or more things. (225–227)	but, yet, however, nevertheless, nonetheless, while, whereas, on the other hand, contrary to, although
Definition	Explains the meaning of a word or an idea. (228–229)	that is, to define this, means Punctuation clues: parentheses, brackets, dashes
Classification	Shows how a word or idea belongs as one type within a larger category. (228–229)	category, elements of, characteristics, features, types, kinds, parts
Cause-and-effect reasoning	Explains why or how one event brings about another. (229–230)	for this reason, because, to explain, as a result, consequently, hence, therefore, thus, then
Sequence (for time order)	Gives events in the order they took place in time. (231–232)	first, before, after, afterward, at last, during, now, at that time, since, until, while
Sequence (for process)	Gives items in the order in which they should be done (231–232)	first, second, third, next, the next step, further, then, before, after that, finally, last
Location/spatial order	Shows the place where items are found. (232)	above, below, next to, opposite, within, elsewhere, beyond, close by, adjacent to
Clarification	Makes a statement clearer by saying it in other words or discussing it further. (234)	clearly, in fact, certainly, obviously, without a doubt, or course
Addition	Provides more information. (234)	in addition, also, as well as, finally, furthermore, moreover, besides, what's more
Summary	Brief, condensed statement of the previous ideas. (234)	in brief, in short, in conclusion, to sum up, to summarize, on the whole

MASTERY TEST

Now that you understand Strategy 7, put it into practice with Reading 14, "How Conscious Is Thought?" Try using patterns along with all the appropriate strategies for getting started. Then, as you read, use patterns for finding main ideas.

How Conscious Is Thought?

READING 14   CAROLE WADE AND CAROL TAVRIS

Carole Wade is a professor of psychology at Dominican College in California. Carol Tavris is author of *The Mismeasure of Woman* and has coauthored several books with Carole Wade, including *Psychology* (2000), the textbook from which this reading comes. In this excerpt from their chapter on thinking and intelligence, the authors discuss how our minds work even when we are not actually aware of thinking.

connect

When we think about thinking, we usually have in mind those mental 1 activities, such as solving problems or making decisions, that are carried out in a deliberate way with a conscious goal in mind. However, a great deal of mental processing occurs without conscious awareness.

get an overview and ask questions

Subconscious and Nonconscious Thinking

Subconscious processes lie outside of awareness but can be brought into 2 consciousness when necessary. These processes allow us to handle more information and to perform more complex tasks than if we depended entirely on conscious thought, and they enable us to perform more than one task simultaneously (Kahneman & Treisman, 1984). Consider all the automatic routines performed "without thinking," though they might once have required careful, conscious attention: knitting, typing, driving a car, decoding the letters in a word in order to read it. Because of the capacity for automatic processing, people can, with proper training, even learn to perform simultaneously such complex tasks as reading and taking dictation (Hirst, Neisser, & Spelke, 1978).

respond

3   Nonconscious processes, in contrast, remain outside of awareness. For example, you have no doubt had the odd experience of having a solution to a problem "pop into mind" after you have given up trying to find one. With sudden insight, you see how to solve an equation, assemble a cabinet, or finish a puzzle, without quite knowing how you managed to find the solution. Similarly, people will often say they rely on "intuition"—hunches and gut feelings—rather than conscious reasoning to make decisions.

vital
vocabulary

4   Insight and intuition probably involve two stages of mental processing (Bowers et al., 1990). In the first stage, clues in the problem automatically activate certain memories or knowledge, and you begin to see a pattern or structure in the problem, although you cannot yet say what it is. This nonconscious process guides you toward a hunch or a hypothesis. Then, in the second stage, your thinking becomes conscious, and you become aware of a possible solution. This stage may feel like a sudden revelation ("Aha, I've got it!"), but considerable nonconscious mental work has already occurred.

find and
mark main
ideas

5   Imagine that you are given four decks of cards and are told that you will win or lose money depending on which cards you turn over. Unbeknownst to you, two of the decks are stacked so that they will produce payoffs at first but will make you lose in the long run, whereas the other two pay less at first but cause you to win in the long run. Every so often, someone stops you and asks whether you have figured out the best strategy for winning. Most people, when presented with this problem, start to show physiological signs of anxiety before picking cards from the losing decks and begin avoiding those decks *before* they consciously realize which decks are riskier. And some learn to make good choices without *ever* consciously discovering the rules for winning. Interestingly, people with damage in part of the prefrontal cortex have trouble learning that two of the decks are stacked against them; they seem to lack the sort of intuition that most people take for granted (Bechara et al., 1997).

prefrontal cortex: location of subconscious thinking in brain

Usually, of course, much of our thinking is conscious, but we may not be thinking very *hard*. . . . We may act, speak, and make decisions out of habit, without stopping to analyze what we are doing or why we are doing it.

Mindlessness

Usually, of course, much of our thinking is conscious, but we may **6** not be thinking very *hard*. . . . We may act, speak, and make decisions out of habit, without stopping to analyze what we are doing or why we are doing it. This sort of mental <u>inertia</u>, which Ellen Langer (1989) has called *mindlessness*, keeps people from recognizing when a change in context requires a change in behavior.

In one study by Langer and her associates, a researcher ap- **7** proached people as they were about to use a photocopier and made one of three requests: "Excuse me, may I use the Xerox machine?" "Excuse me, may I use the Xerox machine, because I have to make copies?" or "Excuse me, may I use the Xerox machine, because I'm in a rush?" Normally, people will let someone go before them only if the person has a legitimate reason, as in the third request. In this study, however, people also complied when the reason sounded like an authentic explanation but was actually meaningless ("because I have to make copies"). They heard the form of the request, but not its content, and they mindlessly stepped aside (Langer, Blank, & Chanowitz, 1978).

The mindless processing of information has benefits: If we stopped **8** to think twice about everything we did, we would get nothing done ("I'm reaching for my toothbrush; now I'm putting toothpaste on it; now I'm brushing my upper-right molars"). But mindlessness can also lead to errors and mishaps, ranging from the trivial (putting the butter in the dishwasher or locking yourself out of your apartment) to the serious (driving carelessly while on "automatic pilot").

Jerome Kagan (1989) has argued that fully conscious awareness is **9** needed only when we must make a deliberate choice, when events happen that cannot be handled automatically, and when unexpected moods and feelings arise. "Consciousness," he says, "can be likened to the staff of a fire department. Most of the time, it is quietly playing pinochle in the back room; it performs [only] when the alarm sounds." That may be so, but most of us would probably benefit if our mental firefighters paid a little more attention to their jobs. <u>Cognitive</u> psychologists have, therefore, devoted a great deal of study to mindful, conscious thought and the capacity to reason.

pinochle: a card game

Works Cited

Bechara, Antoine, et al., "Deciding advantageously before knowing the advantageous strategy." *Science, 275,* 1997: 1293–1294.

Bowers, Kenneth S., et al., "Intuition in the context of discovery." *Cognitive Psychology, 22,* 1990:72–110.

Hirst, William; Ulric Nesser; and Elizabeth Spelke, "Divided attention." *Human Nature, 1,* January 1998:54–61.

Kagan, Jerome, *The Nature of the Child.* New York: Basic Books, 1984.

Kahneman, Daniel, and Anne Treisman, "Changing Views of Attention and Automaticity." In R. Parasuraman, D. R. Davies, and J. Beatty, eds., *Varieties of Attention.* New York: Academic Books, 1984.

Langer, Ellen J., *Mindfulness*. Reading, Mass.: Addison Wesley, 1984.

Langer, Ellen J.; Arthur Blank; and Benzion Chanowitz, "The mindfulness of ostensibly thoughtful action: The role of placebic information in interpersonal interaction." *Journal of Personality and Social Psychology, 36,* 1978:635–642.

ACTIVE READERS RESPOND

After you've finished reading, use these questions to respond to "How Conscious Is Thought?" You may write your answers in the spaces provided or on a separate sheet of paper.

VITAL VOCABULARY

Some words in this reading may be unfamiliar to you. Use the methods of Strategy 3 to explain what the listed words mean.

USE CONTEXT CLUES

a. intuition (paragraph 3)

_____

b. inertia (paragraph 6) (Use logic clues and example clues.)

_____

USE WORD PARTS

a. hypothesis (paragraph 4) (If "thesis" means "theory or proposition," how does the prefix *hypo* modify that meaning? Note that this is *hypo*, not *hyper*.)

_____

b. revelation (paragraph 4) (Use the familiar verb form of this word—"reveal"—to remember it.)

_____

USE THE DICTIONARY

Choose the correct definition of each word as it is used in the context of this reading.

a. cognitive (paragraph 9) (Based on the context, what is the correct definition of this word?)

_____

SKILLS TEST: PATTERNS OF THOUGHT

Find the sentence or sentences that demonstrate the specific pattern listed for each of these paragraphs. Explain briefly how the pattern is used.

1. Paragraph 2: definition and classification.

   (Answers will vary.)
   _____

2. Paragraph 3: definition and classification.

   (Answers will vary.)
   _____

3. Paragraph 4: process.

(Answers will vary.)

4. Paragraph 7: example

(Answers will vary.)

OBJECTIVE OPERATIONS

1. Who is the writer's intended audience?

   a. psychology students

   b. thinkers

   c. general audience

   d. women

2. What is the author's purpose?

   a. to inform

   b. to persuade

   c. to entertain

3. What is the tone of the passage?

   a. condescending

   b. insightful

   c. irritated

   d. subjective

4. We can handle automatic routines, such as knitting, driving a car, and typing, "without thinking," because our minds can perform "subconscious processes." These subconscious processes

   a. require us to do more than one thing at one time.

   b. require our constant attention.

   c. are those that deal with childhood experiences.

   d. can be brought into consciousness when necessary.

5. The word "intuition" in paragraph 3, line 7, most nearly means

   a. payment for college.

   b. feelings of extrasensory perception.

   c. quick and ready insight.

   d. foreboding.

6. Which sentence(s) is (are) the best stated main idea(s) of the passage?

   a. "These processes allow us to handle more information and to perform more complex tasks than if we depended entirely on conscious thought, and they enable us to perform more than one task simultaneously."

   b. "When we think about thinking, we usually have in mind those mental activities, such as solving problems or making decisions, that are carried out in a deliberate way with a conscious goal in mind. However, a great deal of mental processing occurs without conscious awareness."

   c. "Because of the capacity for automatic processing, people can, with proper training, even learn to perform simultaneously such complex tasks as reading and taking dictation."

   d. "Cognitive psychologists have, therefore, devoted a great deal of study to mindful, conscious thought and the capacity to reason."

7. What is the stated main idea of paragraph 4?

   a. "Insight and intuition probably involve two stages of mental processing."

   b. "In the first stage, clues in the problem automatically activate certain memories or knowledge, and you begin to see a pattern or structure in the problem, although you cannot yet say what it is."

   c. "This nonconscious process guides you toward a hunch or a hypothesis."

   d. "This stage may feel like a sudden revelation ("Aha, I've got it!"), but considerable nonconscious mental work has already occurred."

8. Nonconscious processes are defined as those that

   (a.) remain outside our awareness.

   b. babies are born with, but lose within the first three years.

   c. can easily be brought into consciousness.

   d. are performed as we sleep.

9. Which sentence provides support for this sentence (paragraph 3, lines 1–2): "Nonconscious processes, in contrast, remain outside of awareness."?

   a. "Because of the capacity for automatic processing, people can, with proper training, even learn to perform simultaneously such complex tasks as reading and taking dictation."

   (b.) "For example, you have no doubt had the odd experience of having a solution to a problem "pop into mind" after you have given up trying to find one."

   c. "With sudden insight, you see how to solve an equation, assemble a cabinet, or finish a puzzle, without quite knowing how you managed to find the solution."

   d. "Similarly, people will often say they rely on "intuition"—hunches and gut feelings—rather than conscious reasoning to make decisions."

10. The authors' claim that people often rely on hunches for decisions (paragraph 3, lines 6–8) is

   (a.) adequately supported with details.

   b. inadequately supported with details.

11. What is the topic of paragraph 8?

   a. disadvantages of mindlessness

   (b.) advantages of mindlessness

   c. mindlessness

   d. reasons for mindlessness

12. The authors tell us that intuition probably goes through two stages. In the first stage, a problem sets off certain memories and/or knowledge in your mind that you're not yet aware of and leads you to a "good guess." In the second stage

   a. you lose consciousness and wait for the solution come to you.

   (b.) your thinking becomes more conscious as a possible solution presents itself.

   c. your thinking becomes more conscious as you develop a hypothesis.

   d. your memory of the correct answer becomes clear to you.

13. Identify the relationship between these two sentences from paragraph 7.

"Normally, people will let someone go before them only if the person has a legitimate reason, as in the third request. In this study, however, people also complied when the reason sounded like an authentic explanation but was actually meaningless ('because I have to make copies')." (lines 6–10)

   a. definition

   b. addition

   c. example

   (d.) contrast

14. For paragraph 7, the author uses an overall organization pattern that

   a. compares.

   b. explains.

   c. defines.

   (d.) illustrates.

15. According to Ellen Langer, mindlessness is a kind of "mental inertia." She says that mindlessness causes problems because it keeps people from

   a. seeing that we can accomplish more tasks by learning to do them without engaging all parts of our mind.

   (b.) noticing when something in a situation has changed and thus requires us to change our behavior.

   c. understanding that we must become conscious of each part of the tasks we take on in daily life.

   d. focusing on their feelings and emotions rather than relying so much on mental activities.

16. The word "inertia" in paragraph 6, line 4, most nearly means

   (a.) laziness.

   b. energy.

   c. exhaustion.

   d. solidity.

17. What is the relationship between the parts of the following sentence (from paragraph 5)?

"Every so often, someone stops you and asks whether you have figured out the best strategy for winning." (lines 5–7)

a. time order

(b.) addition

c. process

d. contrast

18. A disadvantage of mindlessness is that it

a. can help you solve problems.

(b.) can lead to mishaps.

c. can cause laziness.

d. can create false hunches.

19. What is the relationship between the parts of the following sentence (from paragraph 9)?

"That may be so, but most of us would probably benefit if our mental firefighters paid a little more attention to their jobs." (lines 6–8)

a. addition

b. definition

c. comparison

(d.) contrast

20. Three of the four following activities are ones that people often do "mindlessly." Which is the one activity most people would not do "mindlessly"?

a. brush teeth.

b. drive a car.

(c.) give an oral report in front of a class.

d. copy notes from the blackboard.

READERS WRITE

1. What is the basic difference between subconscious and nonconscious processes?

(Answers will vary.)

_____

_____

_____

2. What is automatic processing? Why is it introduced in the section on subconscious thought?

(Answers will vary.)

_____

_____

_____

3. What stages does the mind go through when we have an insight or an intuition? Describe each stage in your own words.

(Answers will vary.)

_____

_____

_____

4. What problems are caused by the "mental inertia" that Ellen Langer calls mindlessness?

(Answers will vary.)

_____

_____

_____

5. What are some of the activities you do that have become automatic routines? When do you become aware that you are doing them?

(Answers will vary.)

_____

_____

_____

READERS DISCUSS

1. In which of your courses are you most apt to use insight or intuition? How might your knowledge of the two-stage mental process help you to study better?

(Answers will vary.)

_____

_____

_____

_____

_____

2. What activities do you do "mindlessly" that you might need to become more aware of? What activities would you like to do more automatically? Discuss with others what you would need to make these modifications.

(Answers will vary.)

_____

_____

_____

_____

_____

PATTERNS OF THOUGHT

1 | Look for common patterns of thought.

2 | Connect these patterns to the overall point and main ideas.

3 | Watch for signal words and phrases.

PRACTICE PAGES

Chapter 7

To practice identifying the example, comparison, and contrast patterns, do this exercise.

PRACTICE EXERCISE 1

Each of the following excerpts is from one of the readings in this book. Read the selection, and underline signal words. If signal words are not used, underline the details that helped you determine the pattern. Then decide which pattern, if any, is used.

1. . . . I had just "talked back" to a grown person. Even now I can recall the surprised look, the mocking tones that informed me I must be kin to bell hooks—a sharp-tongued woman, a woman who spoke her mind, a woman who was not afraid to talk back. I claimed this legacy of defiance, of will, of courage, affirming my link to female ancestors who were bold and daring in their speech. Unlike my bold and daring mother and grandmother, who were not supportive of talking back, even though they were assertive and powerful in their speech, bell hooks as I discovered, claimed, and invented her was my ally, my support.

    Excerpt from Reading 10: talking back

    What pattern does this selection use? _____Comparison_____

2. Recently, efforts by black women writers to call attention to our work serve to highlight both our presence and absence. Whenever I peruse women's bookstores, I am struck not by the rapidly growing body of feminist writing by black women, but by the paucity of available published material. Those of us who write and are published remain few in number. The context of silence is varied and multi-dimensional. Most obvious are the ways racism, sexism, and class exploitation act to suppress and silence. Less obvious are

the inner struggles, the efforts made to gain the necessary confidence to write, to re-write, to fully develop craft and skill—and the extent to which such efforts fail.

Excerpt from Reading 10: talking back

What pattern does this selection use? _____Contrast_____

3. Since then, many studies have shown that as infants get older, they prefer more complex patterns. For example, when shown black-and-white checkerboards, 3-week-old infants look longest at ones with a few large squares, whereas 8- and 14-week-olds prefer those with many squares. Infant preferences for many other patterned stimuli have been tested—curved versus straight lines, connected versus disconnected elements, and whether the pattern is organized around a central focus (as in a bull's eye), to name just a few.

Excerpt from Reading 9: How Babies Use Patterns to See

What pattern does this selection use? _____Example_____

To practice identifying the definition, classification, and cause-and-effect reasoning patterns, do this exercise.

PRACTICE EXERCISE 2

Each of the following excerpts is from one of the readings in this book. Read the selection, and underline signal words if they are used. If signal words are not used, underline the details that helped you determine the pattern. Then decide which pattern is used.

1. Leonard Black's master once found him with a book and whipped him so severely "that he overcame my thirst for knowledge, and I relinquished its pursuit until after I absconded." Doc Daniel Dowdy recalled that "the first time you was caught trying to read or write you was whipped with a cow-hide, the next time with a' cat-o-nine-tails and the third time they cut the first joint off your forefinger." Throughout the South, it was common for plantation owners to hang any slave who tried to teach the others how to spell.

Excerpt from Reading 3: Forbidden Reading

What pattern does this selection use? _____Classification_____

2. In the world of the southern black community I grew up in, "back talk" and "talking back" meant speaking as an equal to an authority figure. It meant daring to disagree and sometimes it just meant having an opinion. In the "old school," children were meant to be seen and not heard. My great-grandparents, grandparents, and parents were all from the old school. To make yourself heard if you were a child was to invite punishment, the back-hand lick, the slap across the face that would catch you unaware, or the feel of switches stinging your arms and legs.

Excerpt from Reading 10: talking back

What pattern does this selection use? _____Definition_____

3. The researchers left a control group of twelve infants at the orphanage. These infants also were retarded but were higher in intelligence than the other thirteen. They received the usual care. Two and a half years later, Skeels and Dye tested all the children's intelligence. Their findings were startling: Those assigned to the retarded women had gained on an average of 28 IQ points while those who remained in the orphanage had lost 30 points.

Excerpt from Reading 7: What Deprived Children Tell Us about Human Nature

What pattern does this selection use? _____Cause and effect_____

4. But if you stuck to the basic words of everyday life, you and the Englishman might do all right. A hundred or so of our most frequently used words have been around for at least 1000 years. These include many of our words for family relationships, such as *mother, father, husband, wife, child, brother,* and *sister,* as well as many words for our quotidian activities, such as *wake, eat, drink, fight, love,* and *sleep.* You and the man from 1000 would also understand the same basic function words: *to, for, but, and, in,* and so on. But your conversation would be limited. Apart from these basic words, you would find little in common between today's English and Old English. What happened to change the language so drastically?

Reading 5: Where English Words Come From

What pattern does this selection use? _____Classification_____

To practice identifying the individual sequence patterns (time order, process order, and spatial order), do this exercise.

PRACTICE EXERCISE 3

Each of the following excerpts is from one of the readings in this book. Read the selection, and underline signal words if they are used. If signal words are not used, underline the details that helped you determine the pattern. Then decide which pattern is used.

1. First, we phonetically sounded out the alphabet. Then, we talked about vowels—English is such a difficult language to learn. I hadn't even begun to explain the different sounds "gh" could make. We were still at the basics.

Reading 4: "See Spot Run": Teaching My Grandmother to Read

What pattern does this selection use? _____Process order_____

2. . . . In Philadelphia and Portland, Oregon, to pick only two places I happen to have heard about, plans are being drawn up for public schools that won't have any school buildings at all, that will take the students out into the city and help them to use it and its people as a learning resource. In other words, students, perhaps in groups, perhaps independently, will go to libraries, museums, exhibits, courtrooms, legislatures, radio and TV stations, meetings, businesses and laboratories to learn about their world and society at first hand. A small private school in Washington is already doing this. It makes sense. We need more of it.

Reading 12: School Is Bad for Children

What pattern does this selection use? _____Spatial order_____

3. Once babies can take in all aspects of a pattern, at 2 to 3 months they start to combine pattern elements, integrating them into a unified whole. By 4 months, they are so good at detecting pattern organization that they even perceive subjective boundaries that are not really present. For example, look at Figure 5.3. Four-month-olds perceive a square in the center of this pattern, just as you do . . .

Excerpt from Reading 9: How Babies Use Patterns to See

What pattern does this selection use? _____Time order_____

4. My mother was taking forever to finish her work, so I began to flip through the pages, looking for my favorite picture, the one with the goat in it. What happened next was really an accident . . . Almost without realizing it, I found myself reading the entire page, and liking it.

Excerpt from Reading 2: I Do Not Like to Read—Sam-I-Am!

What pattern does this selection use? _____Process order_____

PRACTICE READING

To get practice with reading, read the passage, and then answer the questions that follow. You may write your answers in the spaces provided or on a separate sheet of paper.

Connect with the Reading

Before reading "Traveling," think about the strategies you'll need to get started and to read. The margin notes give you reminders, but by this time you are skilled and secure enough in reading to decide which strategies to use. It is helpful to note the sequence pattern in this reading; see how the writer moves from one time period to another.

Traveling

GRACE PALEY

Grace Paley is known as a master of the short story. Her best-known collections of short stories are *The Little Disturbances of Man* (1959), *Enormous Changes at the Last Minute* (1974), and *Later the Same Day* (1985). In "Traveling," first published in the *New Yorker* in 1997, Paley tells the true story of travels that had an impact on her entire family.

→ get an overview and ask questions

1   My mother and sister were traveling South. The year was 1927. They had begun their journey in New York. They were going to visit my brother, who was studying at the Medical College of Virginia, in Richmond. Their bus was an express and had stopped only in Philadelphia, Wilmington, and now Washington. Here the darker people who had got on in Philadelphia or New York rose from their seats, put their bags and boxes together, and moved to the back of the bus. People who boarded in Washington knew where to seat themselves. My mother had heard that something like this would happen. My sister had heard of it, too. They had not lived in it. This reorganization of

passengers by color happened in silence. My mother and sister remained in their seats, which were about three-quarters of the way back.

respond

Negroes and colored: these are terms used for African Americans during the time period the writer describes.

When everyone was settled, the bus driver began to collect tickets. My sister saw him coming. She pinched my mother—"Ma! Look!" Of course, my mother saw him, too. What frightened my sister was the quietness. The white people in front, the black people in back—silent. **2**

The driver sighed, said, "You can't sit here, ma'am. It's for them"— waving over his shoulder at the Negroes, among whom they were now sitting. "Move, please." **3**

My mother said, "No." **4**

He said, "You don't understand, ma'am. It's against the law. You have to move to the front." **5**

My mother said, "No." **6**

When I first tried to write this scene, I imagined my mother saying, "That's all right, mister. We're comfortable. I can't change my seat every minute." I read this invention to my sister. She said it was nothing like that. My mother did not try to be friendly or pretend innocence. While my sister trembled in the silence, my mother said for the third time—quietly—"No." **7**

Somehow, finally, they were in Richmond. There was my brother, in school among so many American boys. After hugs and my mother's anxious looks at her young son, my sister said, "Vic, you know what Mama did?" **8**

My brother remembers thinking, What? Oh! She wouldn't move? He had a classmate, a Jewish boy like him, but from Virginia, who had had a public confrontation with a Negro man. He had punched that man hard, knocked him down. My brother couldn't believe it. He was stunned. He couldn't imagine a Jewish boy wanting to knock anyone down. He had never wanted to. But he thought, looking back, that he had been set down to work and study in a nearly foreign place, and had had to get used to it. Then he told me about the Second World War, when the disgrace of black soldiers forced to sit behind white German P.O.W.s shook him. Shamed him. **9**

About fifteen years later, in 1943, in early summer, I rode the bus for about three days from New York to Miami Beach, where my husband and hundreds of other boys in sweaty fatigues were trudging up and down the streets and beaches to prepare themselves for war. **10**

By late afternoon of the second long day, we were well into the South, beyond Richmond, maybe in South Carolina or Georgia. My excitement about travel in **11** the wide world was damaged a little by a sudden fear that I might not recognize Jess, or he me. We hadn't seen each other for two months. I took a photograph out of my pocket; yes, I would know him.

12   I had been sleeping, waking, reading, writing, dozing, waking. So many hours, the movement of the passengers was like a tide that sometimes ebbed and now seemed to be noisily rising. I opened my eyes to the sound of people brushing past my aisle seat. And looked up to see a colored woman holding a large sleeping baby, who, with the heaviness of sleep, his arms tight around her neck, seemed to be pulling her head down. I looked around and noticed that I was in the last white row. The press of new travelers had made it impossible for her to move farther back. She seemed so tired, and I had been sitting and sitting for a day and a half at least. Not thinking, or maybe refusing to think, I offered her my seat.

13   She looked to the right and left as well as she could. Softly, she said, "Oh, no." I became fully awake. A white man was standing right beside her, but on the other side of the invisible absolute racial border. Of course, she couldn't accept my seat. Her sleeping child hung mercilessly from her neck. She shifted a little to balance the burden. She whispered to herself, "Oh, I just don't know." So I said, "Well, at least give me the baby." First, she turned, barely looking at the man beside her. He made no move. Then, to my surprise, but obviously out of sheer exhaustion, she disengaged the child from her body and placed him on my lap. He was deep in child-sleep. He stirred, but not enough to bother himself or me. I liked holding him, aligning him along my twenty-year-old young woman's shape. I thought ahead to that holding, that breathing together that would happen in my life if this war would ever end. I was so comfortable under his nice weight. I closed my eyes for a couple of minutes but suddenly opened them to look up into the face of a white man talking. In a loud voice, he addressed me: "Lady, I wouldn't of touched that thing with a meat hook."

14   I thought, Oh, this world will end in ice. I could do nothing but look straight into his eyes. I did not look away from him. Then I held that little boy a little tighter, kissed his curly head, pressed him even closer, so that he began to squirm. So sleepy, he reshaped himself inside my arms. His mother tried to narrow herself away from that dangerous border, too frightened at first to move at all. After a couple of minutes, she leaned forward a little, placed her hand on the baby's head, and held it there until the next stop. I couldn't look up into her mother face.

15   I write this remembrance more than fifty years later. I look back at that mother and child. I see how young she is. Her hand on his head is quite small, though she tries by spreading her fingers wide to hide him from the white man. But the child I'm holding, his little face as he turns toward me, is the dark-brown face of my *own* grandson, my daughter's boy, the open mouth of the sleeper, the full lips, the thick little body of a child who runs wildly from one end of the yard to the other, leaps from dangerous heights with experienced caution, muscling his body, his mind, for coming realities.

this world will end in ice: refers to Robert Frost's lines about hate in his poem "Fire and Ice."

find and mark main ideas

Of course, when my mother and sister returned from Charlottesville **16** the family at home wanted to know: How was Vic doing in school among all those Gentiles? Was the long bus ride hard? Was the anti-Semitism really bad or just normal? What happened on the bus? I was probably present at that supper, the attentive listener and total forgetter of information that immediately started to form me.

Then, last year, my sister, casting the net of old age (through which re- **17** cent experience easily slips), brought up that old story. First, I was angry. How come you never told me about your bus ride with Mama? I mean, really, so many years ago.

I don't know, she said. Anyway, you were only about four years old and, **18** besides, maybe I did.

I asked my brother why we'd never talked about that day. He said he **19** thought now that it had had a great effect on him: he had tried unraveling its meaning for years—then life, family, work happened. So I imagined him, a youngster, really, a kid from the Bronx in Virginia in 1927—why, he was a stranger there himself.

In the next couple of weeks, we continued to talk about our mother, the **20** way she was principled, adamant, and at the same time so shy. What else could we remember. . . Well, I said, I have a story about those buses, too. Then I told them: how it happened on just such a journey, when I was still quite young, that I first knew my grandson, first held him close but could protect him for only about twenty minutes fifty years ago.

ACTIVE READERS RESPOND

After you've finished reading, use these questions to respond to "Traveling." You may write your answers in the spaces provided or on a separate sheet of paper.

VITAL VOCABULARY

Most of the words in this reading are probably familiar to you. However, the writer uses some words in unexpected ways. Explain the way the italicized words are used.

a. "Here *the darker people* who had got on in Philadelphia or New York . . . moved to the back of the bus." (paragraph 1)

_____

_____

b. "A white man was standing right beside her, *but on the other side of the invisible absolute racial border.*" (paragraph 13)

_____

_____

c. "Lady, I wouldn't of *touched that thing with a meat hook.*" (paragraph 13)

_____

_____

d. "Oh, this *world will end in ice*" refers to a poem by Robert Frost, "Fire and Ice" that begins, "Some say the world will end in fire/Some say in ice." What makes Paley say the world will end in ice? (paragraph 14)

_____

_____

_____

e. ". . . I told them: how it happened on just such a journey, when I was still quite young, that I first knew my *grandson.*" (paragraph 20)

_____

_____

f. ". . . the movement of the passengers was like a *tide* that sometimes ebbed and now seemed noisily to be *rising.*" (paragraph 12)

_____

_____

g. ". . . my sister, *casting the net of old age (through which recent experience easily slips)* brought up that old story." (paragraph 17)

_____

_____

OBJECTIVE OPERATIONS

1. Who is the writer's intended audience?
   a. students
   b. Southerners
   c. general audience
   d. historians

2. What is the author's purpose?
   a. to inform
   b. to persuade
   c. to entertain

3. What is the tone of the passage?
   a. understanding
   b. insightful
   c. objective
   d. sad

4. The time periods of this reading are:
   a. the 1920s, the 1930s, and the 1940s.
   b. the 1920s, the 1940s, and the 1990s.
   c. the 1920s and the 1940s.
   d. the 1940s and the 1990s.

5. The word "disengaged" in paragraph 13, line 8, most nearly means
   a. detached.
   b. attached.
   c. paid attention.
   d. ignored.

6. Which sentence states the implied main idea of the passage?
   a. Resisting racism and prejudice is good for a person.
   b. Sometimes, going against accepted social norms and accepting others help a person define and discover herself.
   c. A long time ago, the busses were divided by race.
   d. Going against social norms and accepting others defines a family.

7. What is the implied main idea of paragraph 7?

   a. Paley's mother refused to cooperate.

   b. Although Paley wishes to make her mother seem more heroic, Paley's sister helps Paley realizes her mother's quiet resistance is heroic.

   c. Paley's sister believes only the truth should be told.

   d. Paley's mother is heroic in her quiet resistance to the conductor.

8. Paley's mother was supposed to change seats once the bus got to Washington because

   a. she was getting out at the next stop and needed to make room for incoming passengers.

   b. she was seen as being too friendly with black people and would have to be separated from them.

   c. she was sitting in the back of the bus, where only black people were supposed to sit.

   d. she hadn't paid for a first-class seat.

9. Which sentence provides support for this sentence (paragraph 12, line 1): "I had been sleeping, waking, reading, writing, dozing, waking."?

   a. "So many hours, the movement of the passengers was like a tide that sometimes ebbed and now seemed to be noisily rising."

   b. "I opened my eyes to the sound of people brushing past my aisle seat."

   c. "And looked up to see a colored woman holding a large sleeping baby, who, with the heaviness of sleep, his arms tight around her neck, seemed to be pulling her head down."

   d. "I looked around and noticed that I was in the last white row."

10. The author's claim that the woman with the baby seemed tired (paragraph 12, line 8) is

    a. adequately supported with details.

    b. inadequately supported with details.

11. What is the topic of paragraph 11?

    a. excitement and worry about seeing her husband

    b. disappointment about her husband

    c. remembering her husband's face

    d. her husband

12. On her own bus trip, Paley was going

    a. to New York to see her grandson.

    b. to Miami Beach to see her husband who was in the military.

    c. to Virginia to see her brother who was in the military.

    d. to South Carolina or Georgia depending on where the military had sent her husband.

13. Identify the relationship between the parts of the following sentence from paragraph 12.

    "The press of new travelers had made it impossible for her to move farther back." (lines 7–8)

    a. definition

    b. cause and effect

    c. example

    d. statement and clarification

14. For paragraph 2, the author uses an overall organization pattern that

    a. compares.

    b. explains.

    c. describes.

    d. contrasts.

15. When Paley was on the bus trip and held the young mother's baby on her lap

    a. she felt uncomfortable at first about holding a baby of a different race.

    b. the baby cried, so she had to give him back to his mother.

    c. the baby reminded her of holding her younger brother when he'd been small.

    d. she thought about what it would be like to hold her own baby.

16. The word "fatigues" in paragraph 10, line 5, most nearly means

    a. tires.

    b. energizes.

    c. camouflage uniform.

    d. worries.

17. What is the relationship among the following sentences (from paragraph 9)?

"He couldn't imagine a Jewish boy wanting to knock anyone down. He had never wanted to. But he thought, looking back, that he had been set down to work and study in a nearly foreign place, and had had to get used to it." (lines 4–8)

   a. time order

   b. statement and clarification

   c. addition

   d. definition and example

18. In the following sentence, what does the italicized phrase most nearly mean?

"A white man was standing right beside her, *but on the other side of the invisible absolute racial border.*" (paragraph 13)

   a. the unseen line, known as the Mason-Dixon line, that divided the North and the South

   b. the mental line drawn due to prejudice against black people

   c. the border between Mexico and the United States

   d. the line in the bus dividing the black section from the white section

19. What is the relationship between the parts of the following sentence (from paragraph 12)?

"She seemed so tired, and I had been sitting and sitting for a day and a half at least." (lines 8–9)

   a. addition

   b. definition

   c. comparison

   d. contrast

20. The most obvious qualities we see in both Paley's mother and Paley in this reading are:

   a. creativity, intelligence, and imagination.

   b. efficiency, intelligence, and broadmindedness.

   c. resilience, determination, and practicality.

   d. compassion, courage, and broadmindedness.

QUICK QUESTIONS

1. The first incident in this reading takes place in 1927. True or False

2. Paley's mother calmly obeys the conductor and changes seats. True or False

3. Virginia in 1927 is "a nearly foreign place" for Paley's brother Vic because he is _____Jewish_____ .

4. The baby Paley holds makes her think of her _____future child_____ .

5. Why was the Paley's mother supposed to change seats once the bus got to Washington? What was the situation in the southern part of the United States during both bus trips that she describes?

(Answers will vary.)

_____

_____

6. What happens when Paley tries to help an exhausted black woman by holding the woman's sleeping baby on her lap? How does she feel about the baby?

(Answers will vary.)

_____

_____

8

Map Main Ideas

MAP MAIN IDEAS

1 | Place the overall point in a map or an outline.

2 | Place the main ideas and supporting ideas in relation to the overall point.

imagine this

You're watching a classmate draw a graph on a board. You think back to the math class in high school when you learned to draw graphs. Line graphs, bar graphs, Venn diagrams, and $f(x)$ diagrams gave you something visual to remember as you worked on math problems. These visual interpretations helped you to see how an equation worked, how to figure out a problem, or whether your understanding was correct.

You can also "draw" a picture of a reading by mapping its main point and ideas. This process is called outlining or drawing a box or cluster map. When you mark and map ideas for a reading, you understand more about the reading than you would expect. In addition, using visual images such as box map will help you remember what you read, and this recall will help you on tests or during class. Once you have read a piece of writing, you can test your understanding of it by drawing a picture.

Think FIRST

- Have you ever filled in a friend who was absent from a conversation? Did you explain the overall point of the conversation, such as "After a bit of debate, we decided to go to the movies on Friday" or "We think our friend Jazmine needs help"?

- Do you sum up in one sentence what you are about to tell someone, such as, "Oh, I had the worst reading class today," before you give details, such as, "I failed my test, I made the instructor mad, I forgot my book, and my homework was incomplete"? Do you ever write thoughts like these down?

INTRODUCTION TO THE NEW STRATEGY

Map Main Ideas

Strategy 8 gives you steps for making a visual map of ideas that is easy to refer to and remember. A *map of ideas* is a skeleton of a reading's organization. You *find the main ideas* of the reading and show on a separate sheet of paper how they relate to each other and to the overall point. Working with the writer's ideas in this way makes the ideas more familiar and meaningful to you.

connect now

With Strategy 8—*Map Main Ideas*—you clarify your understanding by putting main ideas down on paper in a simple format that works for you. Some readers like to sketch outlines, but you may find that a cluster map is best for clarifying a reading's overall point and main ideas.

Have you and a friend ever created an itinerary for a road trip? What did you include on your schedule?

Placing the Overall Point, the Main Ideas, and the Supporting Ideas

Mapping main ideas builds on Strategy 6, *Find and Mark Main Ideas.* You transfer the ideas from the reading to a clean sheet of paper where there is plenty of space for you to show the relationships among the ideas. To get started, read the following passage:

HONDURAS AND HURRICANE MITCH

In 1998 Hurricane Mitch, the deadliest Atlantic hurricane since 1780, took a devastating toll on Central America. Among the countries hardest hit was Honduras. Mitch's fury battered the area from October 26 to November 4, generating sustained winds of 155 miles per hour and gusts reaching well beyond 200 miles per hour. As the storm moved slowly westward across Honduras, it picked up moisture from both the Caribbean Sea and the Pacific Ocean. Up to two feet of rain per day fell in the mountains, creating floods and mudslides that swept away entire villages.

Honduras was once part of the far-reaching Maya civilization. Its indigenous populations declined precipitously after Spain colonized the country in the sixteenth century. On the north, Honduras meets the Caribbean Sea along a 400-mile coastline. Its interior is a landscape of fertile plains broken up by deep valleys and high mountains. Honduran natural resources include forests and mineral deposits. The clear-cutting of trees to make a profit and to create farmlands—as well as aggressive mining for silver and zinc—has left the land exposed to erosion. Rivers and lakes have been polluted by chemical runoff. Honduras is a relatively poor country with a turbulent political history: even before Hurricane Mitch, it had long battled such problems as malnutrition, disease, and poor housing. These factors heightened Honduras's vulnerability to Mitch's attack.

Although exact numbers were never determined with total certainty, the final death toll from the hurricane exceeded 11,000. Three million Hondurans were severely affected or left homeless, prompting Honduran President Carlos Flores Facusse to describe the damage as the destruction of 50 years of progress. Whole villages were washed away. Also, perhaps 75 percent of the country's transportation infrastructure—including most of its bridges and secondary roads—was destroyed. Mitch also ruined most of Honduras's valuable export crops of coffee and bananas. The financial cost of the storm was set at more than five billion American dollars.

Recovery from this disaster is ongoing and time consuming. Problems include epidemics of diseases carried by foul water and sewage, food shortages, and the influx of millions of people—who come in search of food, shelter, and work—from the country to the cities. Among the countries providing disaster assistance are the United States, Mexico, Spain, Canada, and Japan. Two former U.S. presidents, George H. W. Bush and Jimmy Carter, visited Central America after the storm.

> Three million Hondurans were severely affected or left homeless, prompting Honduran President Carlos Flores Facusse to describe the damage as the destruction of 50 years of progress.

265

> Writing an idea down makes it real and helps you to remember it. This article, "The Importance of Getting Your Ideas Down on Paper," from a website for amateur digital artists, stresses the importance of writing thoughts down.

This is so unbelievably important that I shouldn't even have to tell you. But I've fallen victim to letting my thoughts go unwritten or unsketched myself, so I figure some of you might have the same problem.

The human brain is an amazing piece of evolutionary creation. It can do things no other organ in the history of the planet has been able to do. You can thank it for being essentially everything that you are and make.

But it's far from perfect.

Your brain (and I guess your mind, if you can even make that distinction) sees or hears or senses some things, combines them together with other things and with some of your memories and thoughts, and there's your idea. A great story or character concept, a design for something that fits perfectly into one of your projects, a song or part of a song, a music video, a striking image, a game or some other form of interactive artwork, anything. It's your idea, yours and yours alone. Conceived by some beautiful chemical reactions in your brain, your idea is now floating in the vast ocean of your mind, like a small collection of driftwood.

I haven't yet described the exact vastness of this ocean. It's pretty vast. Really vast. But also busy. Even when sleeping, your brain is an active little thing. Neurons are flashing about a bajillion times per second, and that small collection of driftwood can get lost pretty quickly.

The point is that your brain is always on, and always looking for more room, and if you don't write or sketch down your idea, your brain will replace, morph, or forget your original idea entirely.

Keep a notebook on you at all times, even if it's just a small notepad. Some people like to go all fancy and get one of those Moleskine things, but the quality of a notebook has very little to do with the quality of the ideas within it. Any scrap of paper will do, really. If you're on your computer at the time of conception, open up your text editor of choice and write it all down.

Again, the point is that you create a connection from your mind to the 'real' world, and through that connection both strengthen the original idea in your mind, and have a reference for the idea outside of it.

I'm sure you've had great ideas disappear into the depths of your mind before. Do yourself a favor and do the one thing you need to do to ensure it won't happen again.

Write them down.

"The Importance of Getting Your Ideas Down on Paper." *Superluminal* website. 3 February 2009. 1 July 2009. Available: http://superlumi.nl/the-importance-of-getting-your-ideas-down-on-paper/

Mapping after Marking

Your first step in outlining or mapping is to shorten the overall point and transfer it to paper, so you might have to do some marking in order to figure out the overall point. For example, in "Why People Don't Help in a Crisis," the overall point is not stated in one sentence. However, you can pull out the overall point from the last two paragraphs of the reading. These paragraphs sum up the main ideas—the answers about why people don't help.

For the passage you have just read on Hurricane Mitch, your marking might look like this:

HONDURAS AND HURRICANE MITCH

Overall Point

In 1998 Hurricane Mitch, the deadliest Atlantic hurricane since 1780, took a devastating toll on Central America. Among the countries hardest hit was Honduras. Mitch's

THE READER'S EDGE: BOOK TWO

fury battered the area from October 26 to November 4, generating sustained winds of 155 miles per hour and gusts reaching well beyond 200 miles per hour. As the storm moved slowly westward across Honduras, it picked up moisture from both the Caribbean Sea and the Pacific Ocean. Up to two feet of rain per day fell in the mountains, creating floods and mudslides that swept away entire villages.

Honduras was once part of the far-reaching Maya civilization. Its indigenous populations declined precipitously after Spain colonized the country in the sixteenth century. On the north, Honduras meets the Caribbean Sea along a 400-mile coastline. Its interior is a landscape of fertile plains broken up by deep valleys and high mountains. Honduran natural resources include forests and mineral deposits. The clear-cutting of trees to make a profit and to create farmlands—as well as aggressive mining for silver and zinc—has left the land exposed to erosion. Rivers and lakes have been polluted by chemical runoff. Honduras is a relatively poor country with a turbulent political history: even before Hurricane Mitch, it had long battled such problems as malnutrition, disease, and poor housing. These factors heightened Honduras's vulnerability to Mitch's attack.

Although exact numbers were never determined with total certainty, the final death toll from the hurricane exceeded 11,000. Three million Hondurans were severely affected or left homeless, prompting Honduran President Carlos Flores Facusse to describe the damage as the destruction of 50 years of progress. Whole villages were washed away. Also, perhaps 75 percent of the country's transportation infrastructure—including most of its bridges and secondary roads—was destroyed. Mitch also ruined most of Honduras's valuable export crops of coffee and bananas. The financial cost of the storm was set at more than five billion American dollars.

Recovery from this disaster is ongoing and time consuming. Problems include epidemics of diseases carried by foul water and sewage, food shortages, and the influx of millions of people—who come in search of food, shelter, and work—from the country to the cities. Among the countries providing disaster assistance are the United States, Mexico, Spain, Canada, and Japan. Two former U.S. presidents, George H. W. Bush and Jimmy Carter, visited Central America after the storm.

PRESIDENT BARACK OBAMA

Self-Reliance by Ralph Waldo Emerson

President Barack Obama's reading list is a popular topic during interviews. An accomplished writer himself, Obama is as comfortable speaking about children's classics like Maurice Sendak's *Where the Wild Things Are* as Ernest Hemingway's novel, *For Whom the Bell Tolls.* In his first 100 days in office he was spotted toting books on a variety of topics. Obama often credits *Self-Reliance*, by Ralph Waldo Emerson, and Gandhi's autobiography as influencing his character, as well as his passion, for literature. While critics and supporters may clash on his politics, Obama's hobby gives them something to agree on—this president loves to read.

If you liked *Self-Reliance*, you might also like:

Walden, Henry David Thoreau

The Scarlet Letter, Nathaniel Hawthorne

As I Lay Dying, William Faulkner

Main Idea

No stated Main Idea, but main idea is: Hurricane Mitch killed thousands, left many homeless, and destroyed crops.

Main Idea

Instructor Tip
Bring in copies of an article and distribute it to students. Have them read the article and mark the overall points, the main ideas, and the supporting details. Tell them to make a note if a paragraph does not contain a stated main idea.

Condensing and Simplifying Wording

As you outline or map ideas, shorten the wording to just the essentials, as you do when you take notes. This means summarizing the overall point into one sentence and focusing on only the essential information.

For example, the first heading of "Why People Don't Help in a Crisis" is "The Unseeing Eye." The main idea for that topic can be found in paragraph 10. The underlining shows the essential parts of the main idea sentence. These are the parts you would put in note form on your map.

In a crowd, then, each person is less likely to notice a potential emergency than when alone.

The passage on Hurricane Mitch is summed up in its first two sentences; the parts you would put in note form are underlined:

In 1998 Hurricane Mitch, the deadliest Atlantic hurricane since 1780, took a devastating toll on Central America. Among the countries hardest hit was Honduras.

Summed up in one sentence, the overall point of the passage about Hurricane Mitch is this:

In 1998 Hurricane Mitch took a devastating toll on Honduras.

connect now

Formats for Mapping

Once you have shortened the overall point to one sentence, you will need to decide how you wish to map; that is, will you use an informal outline, a box map, or a cluster map?

Outlining

With an informal **outline,** the overall point is placed at the top of the outline, and the main ideas are listed under it. Likewise, supporting details are listed under main ideas. For example, here is an informal outline for the Hurricane Mitch passage:

Overall Point: In 1998 Hurricane Mitch, the deadliest Atlantic hurricane since 1780, took a devastating toll on Honduras, a country in Central America.

Have you heard anyone say, "Let me outline the situation for you"?

Main Idea: Honduras is a relatively poor country with a turbulent political history: even before Hurricane Mitch, it had long battled such problems as malnutrition, disease, and poor housing.

Main Idea: Hurricane Mitch killed thousands, left many homeless, and destroyed crops.

Main Idea: Recovery from this disaster is ongoing and time consuming.

Instructor Tip
To extend the previous activity, have students create an outline from their condensed overall point and main ideas.

EXERCISES

PRACTICE

For practice outlining, complete the following exercise.

Read the following passage and mark in the margins as you identify the overall point and the main ideas. Complete the outline that follows.

THE CONFEDERATED TRIBES OF THE UMATILLA INDIAN RESERVATION

The area encompassing southeastern Washington, northeastern Oregon, and western Idaho is known as the Columbia Plateau. The Plateau covers more than 6.4 million acres of rivers, forested mountains, and lush valleys. Before 1855, it was home to various Native American groups. The Cayuse, Umatilla, and Walla Walla people spoke different but related languages, and they followed similar ways of life but had different customs and traditions. They traveled with the seasons of the year. They fished for salmon in the spring, hunted deer and elk and harvested roots and berries in the summer, and sought the mild climate of the valleys in the winter.

Tribal names, which grouped certain bands together, were an invention of nonnative explorers and settlers who identified family groups or bands living near one another with a place name.

In the mid-1840s, with the opening of the Oregon Trail, the number of settlers who had been seeking opportunity along the Pacific coast increased dramatically. To promote settlement and bring these territories into the Union, the United States government reserved for Native American groups some smaller areas as permanent homelands. Native Americans could avoid conflicts with incoming settlers by moving.

Through the Treaty of 1855, the Cayuse, Umatilla, and Walla Walla people accepted a property, the Umatilla Indian Reservation, in northeast Oregon. They also reserved the right to fish, hunt, and gather traditional foods both on and off their land. Later laws that were passed by the U.S. government reduced the size of the reservation. Today the Umatilla Indian Reservation includes about 172,000 acres of land.

The idea of a reservation was not the only thing new to these Native Americans. Also unfamiliar was the concept of the *confederation of tribes*. The bands that made up the Cayuse, Umatilla, and Walla Walla nations had camped together during the winter but had gone their separate ways during the

food-gathering season. These small bands, each with its own leader, did not regard themselves as members of a larger nation. Tribal names, which grouped certain bands together, were an invention of nonnative explorers and settlers who identified family groups or bands living near one another with a place name. Thus, the unique bands living in the Umatilla area became known as the Umatilla Nation.

The Confederated Tribes of the Umatilla Reservation wrote and adopted a constitution and a set of by-laws that was approved by the U.S. Secretary of the Interior in 1949. After years of intermarriage and social and economic integration, distinctions between the three main groups of the confederation have decreased.

Overall Point: _The Cayuse, Umatilla, and Walla Walla people spoke different languages and followed similar ways of life but had different customs and traditions, and when forced to live on the same reservation, the three bands joined to become the Confederation of Tribes._

Main Idea: _To promote settlement and bring these territories into the Union, the United States government reserved for Native American groups some smaller areas as permanent homelands._

Main Idea: _Through the Treaty of 1855, the Cayuse, Umatilla, and Walla Walla people accepted a property, the Umatilla Indian Reservation, in northeast Oregon._

Main Idea: _Tribal names, which grouped certain bands together, were an invention of nonnative explorers and settlers who identified family groups or bands living near one another with a place name._

Instructor Tip
To extend the previous outline activity, have students create a box map from their condensed overall point and main ideas.

Box Map

You can also use a box map. For a box map, place the overall point at the top of the page. Each main idea is then placed in its own box beneath the overall point, and supporting details are placed in their own boxes beneath the main ideas that they support. The following is a box map for the passage on Hurricane Mitch.

Hot or Not?

How is a theater playbill similar to an outline for the play?

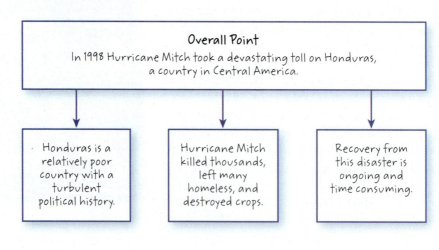

Overall Point
In 1998 Hurricane Mitch took a devastating toll on Honduras, a country in Central America.

| Honduras is a relatively poor country with a turbulent political history. | Hurricane Mitch killed thousands, left many homeless, and destroyed crops. | Recovery from this disaster is ongoing and time consuming. |

THE READER'S EDGE: BOOK TWO

For practice making a box map, complete the following exercise.

Read the following passage and mark in the margins as you identify the overall point and the main ideas. Complete the box map that follows.

THREE WRITERS OF WORLD WAR I

People called World War I "the war to end all wars." Hostilities began in Western Europe and included European colonies in Asia and Africa. Russia was involved, as were Australia, New Zealand, Canada, and the United States.

Writers from every literary field documented their war experiences. Many who died on the battlefields were immortalized in poetry and prose. Others survived to publish some of the most compelling descriptions of war ever penned. Among the latter were German novelist Erich Maria Remarque, English poet and critic Robert Graves, and American journalist Thomas M. Johnson.

Remarque's 1929 novel, *All Quiet on the Western Front,* is perhaps the best-known story of World War I. Drawing heavily on Remarque's own experience as a German soldier, this story of friendships, hardships, and the human cost of all wars was adapted as a film in 1930.

When Graves published his memoir *Good-bye to All That* in 1929, it drew criticism as unpatriotic. Graves was 19 years old when he enlisted in the British army at the outbreak of World War I. Commissioned as an officer, Graves led his men through unimaginable horror in the battlefields—gas attacks, foul conditions in the trenches, and inept leadership by superior officers. Graves almost died after being wounded by shrapnel. His book is notable for its cynical tone, its sympathetic attitude toward the enlisted men, and its mockery of the English military system.

A newspaper correspondent rather than a soldier, Johnson, coauthor of *The Lost Battalion* (1938), reported on the war for the *New York Sun. The Lost Battalion* describes the fate of a group of soldiers under the command of Major Charles W. Whittlesey. The unit belonged to the American Expeditionary Forces, as the U.S. troops were called, and had been assigned to take and hold a position deep in German-held territory in France. The soldiers succeeded in reaching the position, but they had lost contact with headquarters. Misinformed about the soldiers' precise location, American airplane pilots dropped food and ammunition over German positions instead.

An American artillery unit then attacked "the lost battalion" where they had hunkered down; more than 80 men died from this "friendly fire." Fewer than 200 of the original 554 men in the battalion survived the five-day ordeal.

These three works, along with many others, illustrated aspects of World War I from different perspectives and helped to present a broad view of the war experience.

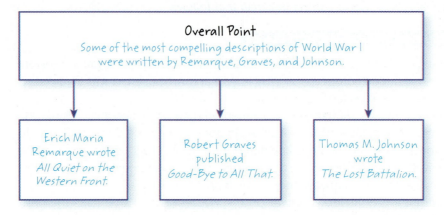

Cluster Map

Finally, you can use a **cluster map,** with the overall point in the center and the main ideas branched around it. For a cluster map, write notes about the overall point in the center of the page, and circle them. The main ideas come out from the central circle like branches. In a cluster map, the main ideas are branched around the overall point in a counterclockwise order. Your map may give you enough information with just the overall point and main ideas. However, if you need a supporting idea to make one or more of the main ideas clearer to you, put it down as a branch coming out of the main idea it clarifies. It is helpful to include the paragraph numbers on your map. Consider the cluster map for the reading on Hurricane Mitch below:

**Cluster Map
"Hurricane Mitch"**

Honduras is a relatively poor country with a turbulent political history.

Overall Point
In 1998 Hurricane Mitch took a devastating toll on Honduras, a country in Central America.

Hurricane Mitch killed thousands, left many homeless, and destroyed crops.

Recovery from this disaster is ongoing and time consuming.

Instructor Tip
To extend the previous box map activity, have students create a cluster map from their condensed overall point and main ideas.

THE READER'S EDGE: BOOK TWO

For practice making a cluster map, complete the following exercise.

Read the following passage and mark in the margins as you identify the overall point and the main ideas. Complete the cluster map that follows.

PICTURING THE AMERICAN WEST

In 1867 the United States faced the task of rebuilding after the ravages of the Civil War, so it looked westward for the raw materials needed to fuel industrial growth. Geological surveys and mapping expeditions were set forth to explore this unfamiliar territory. These groups, in turn, hired mapmakers, scientists, cooks, drivers, and doctors. They also hired painters and photographers as part of the teams. Painters needed few supplies, making it relatively easy for them to travel in the wilderness, but photographers were not so lucky; they had to transport a fully stocked darkroom on these expeditions.

Until the late 1870s, most photographers used the difficult wet-collodion process. The first step was to wash a clean sheet of glass with a sticky mixture of *collodion* and chemicals. (Collodion or "gun-cotton" was a recent medical discovery used to cover wounds because the viscous solution turned into a protective film when dry.) After it was washed, the plate went into another bath that stopped the picture from getting darker. Finally, the glass negative was rinsed clean with fresh water. Printing a photograph from the negative had to wait until the photographer went back to the studio. The size of the negative depended on the size of the camera. Mammoth-plate negatives could be as large as 20 by 24 inches.

Imagine the challenge of taking photographs in the 1860s and 1870s in the remote western wilderness! Photographers jolted over rocky mountains and through rushing rivers. They baked in the blazing desert heat, with cameras, sheets of glass, and vats of chemicals. Bad weather, equipment failures, and accidents were frequent problems. Success in creating a negative did not guarantee the production of a photograph; plates still had to be safely transported back to the studio before the image could be printed on paper. A photographer could lug 120 pounds of equipment many miles to capture a magnificent view or an unusual formation only to have the fragile plate destroyed in transit.

When photographers were successful, however, the results were exquisite and much admired. Photographs were put on exhibition, and people bought albums filled with pictures by Timothy O'Sullivan, Carleton Watkins, and William Henry Jackson, among others. Jackson's photographs of Yellowstone's natural wonders, along with the paintings of fellow expeditionary Thomas Moran, even helped persuade Congress to preserve thousands of acres of this land in 1872 as the nation's first national park.

> Success in creating a negative did not guarantee the production of a photograph; plates still had to be safely transported back to the studio before the image could be printed on paper.

Overall Point: Expeditions to the American West hired photographers who traveled with a great deal of equipment in harsh conditions.

_____

_____

_____

Main Idea: Until the late 1870s, most photographers used the difficult wet-collodion process.

_____

Main Idea: Bad weather, equipment failures, and accidents were frequent problems.

_____

Main Idea: When photographers were successful, however, the results were exquisite and much admired.

_____

Cluster Map
"Picturing the American West"

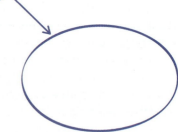

Until the late 1870s, most photographers used the difficult wet-collodion process.

Bad weather, equipment failures, and accidents were frequent problems.

Overall Point
Expeditions to the American West hired photographers who traveled with a great deal of equipment in harsh conditions.

When photographers were successful, however, the results were exquisite and much admired.

Hot or Not?

Would you take a cross-country trip without a map? Why or why not?

Keeping the Order of Ideas

For any format, be sure to place the ideas in the same order in which they are given in the reading. This way you are less likely to become confused, and you can see how each idea builds from the one that precedes it.

Consider including the introduction and conclusion on your map if they are long and give helpful examples or other information, as is the case with "Why People Don't Help in a Crisis."

(When working with the readings for this chapter, you will focus on the cluster map, but you will see a sample of an informal outline and a box map for Reading 15 on pages 284–285.)

Mapping before Marking

Sometimes a reading is especially challenging. Or it may have no headings that show how it is divided into topics. In these cases, you may want to do some preliminary outlining or mapping and then go back to mark main ideas in the reading. You start with the overall question, as you do in finding and marking main ideas. Then you sketch possible main topics on paper to see whether they answer the overall-point question. For Reading 15, for example, your overall-point question is easy to form from the title: "Why don't people help in a crisis?" And the reading's headings name the topics for you. This preliminary stage of mapping is shown on page 283. There, the central circle for the overall point has a question mark in it, and the surrounding circles show the topics that partially answer that question. When you're confident that you've selected the main topics, you can mark them in your book and find the main ideas for the topics and/or complete your map.

connect now

Why do DVDs often call the place where you select a scene the chapter map?

APPLY THE NEW STRATEGY
Map Main Ideas

Before reading "Why People Don't Help in a Crisis," think about the strategies you'll need to get started and to read. The margin notes give you reminders, but by this time you are skilled and secure enough in reading to decide which strategies you'll use. In the margin, write down two or three other strategies that you think will help you.

For this reading, as you get an overview and ask questions, see how the title suggests the cause-and-effect reasoning pattern of thought. It will also be important to find and mark ideas. You may find it helpful to collaborate with other students in looking for this reading's main ideas.

Why People Don't Help in a Crisis

JOHN M. DARLEY AND BIBB LATANÉ

READING 15

John M. Darley is a professor of psychology at Princeton University. He has written frequently about the way adults and children form their moral judgments. Bibb Latané has served as professor of psychology at the University of North Carolina and as director of the Behavioral Sciences Laboratory at Ohio State University. In this reading the authors explore why people may be reluctant to help others in an emergency.

get an overview and ask questions

1   Kitty Genovese is set upon by a maniac as she returns home from work at 3 A.M. Thirty-eight of her neighbors in Kew Gardens, N.Y., come to their windows when she cries out in terror; not one comes to her assistance, even though her assailant takes half an hour to murder her. No one so much as calls the police. She dies.

2   Andrew Mormille is stabbed in the head and neck as he rides in a New York City subway train. Eleven other riders flee to another car as the 17-year-old boy bleeds to death; not one comes to his assistance, even though his attackers have left the car. He dies.

Eleanor Bradley trips and breaks **3** her leg while shopping on New York City's Fifth Avenue. Dazed and in shock, she calls for help, but the hurrying stream of people simply parts and flows past. Finally, after 40 minutes, a taxi driver stops and helps her to a doctor.

How can so many people watch **4** another human being in distress and do nothing? Why don't they help?

Since we started research on by- **5** stander responses to emergencies, we have heard many explanations for the lack of intervention in such cases. "The megalopolis in which we live makes closeness difficult and leads to the alienation of the individual from the group," says the psychoanalyst. "This sort of disaster," says the sociologist, "shakes the sense of safety and sureness of the individuals involved and causes psychological withdrawal." "Apathy," say others. "Indifference."

find and mark main ideas and look for patterns of thought

All of these analyses share one characteristic: they set the indifferent **6** witness apart from the rest of us. Certainly not one of us who reads about these incidents in horror is apathetic, alienated, or depersonalized. Certainly these terrifying cases have no personal implications for us. We needn't feel guilty, or re-examine ourselves, or anything like that. Or should we?

If we look closely as the behavior of witnesses to these incidents, the **7** people involved begin to seem a little less inhuman and a lot more like the rest of us. They were not indifferent. The 38 witnesses of Kitty Genovese's murder, for example, did not merely look at the scene once and then ignore it. They continued to stare out of their windows, caught, fascinated, distressed, unwilling to act but unable to turn away.

Why, then, didn't they act? **8**

There are three things the bystander must do if he is to intervene in **9** an emergency: *notice* that something is happening; *interpret that* event as an emergency; and decide that he has *personal responsibility for* intervention. As we shall show, the presence of other bystanders may at each stage inhibit his action.

The Unseeing Eye

Suppose that a man has a heart attack. He clutches his chest, staggers **10** to the nearest building, and slumps sitting to the sidewalk. Will a passerby come to his assistance? First, the bystander has to notice that something is happening. He must tear himself away from his private thoughts and pay attention. But Americans consider it bad manners to look closely at other people in public. We are taught to respect the privacy of others, and when among strangers we close our ears and avoid staring. In a crowd, then, each person is less likely to notice a potential emergency than when alone.

11   Experimental evidence corroborates this. We asked college students to an interview about their reactions to urban living. As the students waited to see the interviewer, either by themselves or with two other students, they filled out a questionnaire. Solitary students often glanced idly about while filling out their questionnaires; those in groups kept their eyes on their own papers.

12   As part of the study, we staged an emergency: smoke was released into the waiting room through a vent. Two-thirds of the subjects who were alone noticed the smoke immediately, but only 25 percent of those waiting in groups saw it as quickly. Although eventually all the subjects did become aware of the smoke—when the atmosphere grew so smoky as to make them cough and rub their eyes—this study indicates that the more people present, the slower an individual may be to perceive an emergency and the more likely he is not to see it at all.

Seeing Is Not Necessarily Believing

13   Once an event is noticed, an onlooker must decide if it is truly an emergency. Emergencies are not always clearly labeled as such; "smoke" pouring into a waiting room may be caused by fire, or it may merely indicate a leak in a steam pipe. Screams in the street may signal an assault or a family quarrel. A man lying in a doorway may be having a coronary—or he may simply be sleeping off a drunk.

14   A person trying to interpret a situation often looks at those around him to see how he should react. If everyone else is calm and indifferent, he will tend to remain so; if everyone else is reacting strongly, he is likely to become aroused. This tendency is not merely slavish conformity; ordinarily we derive much valuable information about new situations from how others around us behave. It's a rare traveler who, in picking a roadside restaurant, chooses to stop at one where no other cars appear in the parking lot.

15   But occasionally reactions of others provide false information. The studied nonchalance of patients in a dentist's waiting room is a poor indication of their inner anxiety. It is considered embarrassing to "lose your cool" in public. In a potentially acute situation, then, everyone present will appear more unconcerned than he is in fact. A crowd can thus force inaction on its members by implying, through its passivity, that an event is not an emergency. Any individual in such a crowd fears that he may appear a fool if he behaves as though it were.

16   To determine how the presence of other people affects a person's interpretation of an emergency, Latane and Judith Rodin set up another experiment. Subjects were paid $2 to participate in a survey of game and puzzle preferences conducted at Columbia University by the Consumer Testing Bureau. An attractive young market researcher met them at the door and took them to the testing room, where they were given questionnaires to fill out. Before leaving, she told them that she would be working next door in her office, which was separated

> A person trying to interpret a situation often looks at those around him to see how he should react. If everyone else is calm and indifferent, he will tend to remain so; if everyone else is reacting strongly, he is likely to become aroused.

from the room by a folding room-divider. She then entered her office, where she shuffled papers, opened drawers and made enough noise to remind the subjects of her presence. After four minutes she turned on a high-fidelity tape recorder.

On it, the subjects heard the researcher climb up on a chair, perhaps to [17] reach for a stack of papers on the bookcase. They heard a loud crash and a scream as the chair collapsed and she fell, and they heard her moan, "Oh, my foot. . . I . . . I , . . can't move it. Oh, I . . . can't get this . . . thing . . . off me." Her cries gradually get more subdued and controlled.

Twenty-six people were alone in the waiting room when the "accident" [18] occurred. Seventy percent of them offered to help the victim. Many pushed back the divider to offer their assistance; others called out to offer their help.

Among those waiting in pairs, only 20 percent—eight out of forty—of- [19] fered to help. The other 32 remained unresponsive. In defining the situation as a nonemergency, they explained to themselves why the other member of the pair did not leave the room; they also removed any reason for action themselves. Whatever had happened, it was believed to be not serious. "A mild sprain," some said. "I didn't want to embarrass her." In a "real" emergency, they assured us, they would be among the first to help.

The Lonely Crowd

Even if a person defines an event as an emergency, the presence of other [20] bystanders may still make him less likely to intervene. He feels that his responsibility is diffused and diluted. Thus, if your car breaks down on a busy highway, hundreds of drivers whiz by without anyone's stopping to help— but if you are stuck on a nearly deserted country road, whoever passes you first is likely to stop.

To test this diffusion-of-responsibility theory, we simulated an emer- [21] gency in which people overheard a victim calling for help. Some thought they were the only person to hear the cries; the rest believed that others heard them, too. As with the witnesses to Kitty Genovese's murder, the subjects could not see one another or know what others were doing. The kind of direct group inhibition found in the other two studies could not operate.

For the simulation we recruited 72 students at New York University to [22] participate in what was referred to as a "group discussion" of personal problems in an urban university. Each student was put in an individual room equipped with a set of headphones and a microphone. It was explained that this precaution had been taken because participants might feel embarrassed about discussing their problems publicly. Also, the experimenter said that he would not listen to the initial discussion, but would only ask for reactions later. Each person was to talk in turn.

The first to talk reported that he found it difficult to adjust to New [23] York and his studies. Then, hesitantly and with obvious embarrassment, he mentioned that he was prone to nervous seizures when he was under stress. Other students then talked about their own problems in turn. The number of people in the "discussion" varied. But whatever the apparent size of the group—two, three, or six people—only the subject was actually present; the others, as well as the instructions and the speeches of the victim-to-be, were present only on a pre-recorded tape.

THE READER'S EDGE: BOOK TWO

24   When it was the first person's turn to talk again, he launched into the following performance, becoming louder and having increasing speech difficulties: "I can see a lot of er of er how other people's problems are similar to mine because er I mean er they're not er e-easy to handle sometimes and er I er um I think I I need er if if could er er somebody er er er give me give me a little er give me a little help here because er I er *uh* I've got a a one of the er seiz-er er things coming *on* and and er uh uh (choking sounds). . . ." Eighty-five percent of the people who believed themselves to be alone with the victim came out of their room to help. Sixty-two percent of the people who believed there was one other bystander did so. Of those who believed there were four other bystanders, only 31 percent reported the fit. The responsibility-diluting effect of other people was so strong that single individuals were more than twice as likely to report the emergency as those who thought other people also knew about it.

The Lesson Learned

25   People who failed to report the emergency showed few signs of the apathy and indifference thought to characterize "unresponsive bystanders." When the experimenter entered the room to end the situation, the subject often asked if the victim was "all right." Many of them showed physical signs of nervousness; they often had trembling hands and sweating palms. If anything, they seemed more emotionally aroused than did those who reported the emergency. Their emotional behavior was a sign of their continuing conflict concerning whether to respond or not.

26   Thus, the <u>stereotype</u> of the unconcerned, depersonalized *homo urbanus*, blandly watching the misfortunes of others, proves inaccurate. Instead, we find that a bystander to an emergency is an anguished individual in genuine doubt, wanting to do the right thing but compelled to make complex decisions under pressure of stress and fear. His reactions are shaped by the actions of others—and all too frequently by their inaction.

27   And we are that bystander. Caught up by the apparent indifference of others, we may pass by an emergency without helping or even realizing that help is needed. Once we are aware of the influence of those around us, however, we can resist it. We can choose to see distress and step forward to relieve it.

ACTIVE READERS RESPOND

After you've finished reading, use these questions to respond to "Why People Don't Help in a Crisis." You may write your answers in the spaces provided or on a separate sheet of paper.

VITAL VOCABULARY

Some words in this reading may be unfamiliar to you. Use the methods of Strategy 3 to explain what the listed words mean.

USE CONTEXT CLUES

a.   assailant (paragraph 1)

_____

b. nonchalance (paragraph 15) (Use the contrast clue suggested by "poor indication of the inner anxiety.")

_____

c. inhibition (paragraph 21) (Use the example clue suggested by the phrase "the kind of," and referring back to the researchers' studies.)

_____

USE WORD PARTS

a. megalopolis (paragraph 5) (Look for the meaning of *mega* and *polis* in the dictionary's etymology for this word.)

_____

b. alienated (paragraph 6)

_____

c. intervene (paragraph 9)

_____

USE THE DICTIONARY

Choose the correct definition of each word as it is used in the context of this reading.

a. corroborates (paragraph 11)

_____

b. diffusion (paragraph 21)

_____

c. simulation (paragraph 22)

_____

d. stereotype (paragraph 26)

_____

SKILLS EXERCISE: CLUSTER MAP
Complete the cluster map on page 284.

OBJECTIVE OPERATIONS

1. Who is the writers' intended audience?
    a. general audience
    b. psychology students
    c. bystanders
    d. people who need assistance
2. What is the author's purpose?
    a. to inform
    b. to persuade
    c. to entertain
3. What is the tone of the passage?
    a. cautious
    b. demanding
    c. objective
    d. personal
4. Before the research done by Darley and Latané, the explanations given about why people don't help in a crisis included that
    a. we now live in such large urban areas that crime can easily go undetected.
    b. television violence has caused people to become insensitive to the needs of others.
    c. bystanders to emergencies are different from the rest of us.
    d. we now live in such large urban areas that we lose our sense of connection with others.

5. The word "nonchalance" in paragraph 15, line 2, most nearly means

   a. lack of concern.

   b. anxiety.

   c. informality.

   d. lack of desire.

6. Which sentence states the implied main idea of the passage?

   a. During an emergency, a bystander will not help anyone unless the bystander is alone.

   b. If other people are not reacting to an emergency, then individuals are less likely to help someone.

   c. We need to learn to recognize an emergency in order to help someone out.

   d. In order to be able to help someone in an emergency, we must recognize the emergency and realize we need to help, despite what others may or may not be doing.

7. What is the stated main idea of paragraph 10?

   a. "Suppose that a man has a heart attack."

   b. "Will a passerby come to his assistance?"

   c. "But Americans consider it bad manners to look closely at other people in public."

   d. "We are taught to respect the privacy of others, and when among strangers we close our ears and avoid staring."

8. Compared to being alone, a person in a crowd is less likely to even notice that there is an emergency because

   a. people try to appear more calm and more unconcerned than they are feeling in order not to seem foolish for being too anxious.

   b. people have become so alienated by today's urban society that they ignore any crisis around them.

   c. with so many people in the way, it's difficult to see the details of what is going on.

   d. people try to appear more calm and unconcerned than they are feeling to avoid helping out.

9. Which sentence provides support for this sentence (paragraph 10, lines 3–4): "First, the bystander has to notice that something is happening."?

   a. "He clutches his chest, staggers to the nearest building, and slumps sitting to the sidewalk."

   b. "Will a passerby come to his assistance?"

   c. "He must tear himself away from his private thoughts and pay attention."

   d. "We are taught to respect the privacy of others, and when among strangers we close our ears and avoid staring."

10. The authors' claim that people look to others to determine their own reactions (paragraph 14, line 1–4) is

   a. adequately supported with details.

   b. inadequately supported with details.

11. What is the topic of paragraph 20?

   a. a person's responsibility in an emergency

   b. why hundreds of drivers don't stop when your car breaks down

   c. who will stop in an emergency

   d. how others affect a person's feelings of responsibility in an emergency

12. The diffusion-of-responsibility theory is based on the idea that

   a. people have lost their sense of responsibility as a result of their poor upbringing.

   b. the presence of others makes people feel that they don't need to help because someone else in the group will help.

   c. the presence of others makes people feel embarrassed to show any concern or anxiety.

   d. people would rather escape responsibility than face it.

13. Identify the relationship between the parts of the following sentence from paragraph 9.

   "There are three things the bystander must do if he is to intervene in an emergency: *notice* that something is happening; *interpret that* event as an emergency; and decide that he has *personal responsibility for* intervention." (lines 1–3)

   a. definition

   b. cause and effect

   c. example

   d. statement and clarification

14. For paragraph 25, the author uses an overall organization pattern that

   a. compares.

   b. explains.

   c. describes.

   d. illustrates.

15. The people who failed to report that an individual they heard on tape was apparently having a seizure

   a. were more upset than the people who did report the emergency.

b. were callous and unconcerned about what they had heard.

c. showed some few signs of concern or nervousness about what they had heard.

d. were examples of the unconcerned, depersonalized *homo urbanus*.

16. The word "corroborates" in paragraph 11, line 1, most nearly means

a. confirms.

b. corrects.

c. settles.

d. disputes.

17. What is the relationship among the following sentences (from paragraph 16)?

"An attractive young market researcher met them at the door and took them to the testing room, where they were given questionnaires to fill out. Before leaving, she told them that she would be working next door in her office, which was separated from the room by a folding room-divider." (lines 5–9)

a. time order

b. process order

c. addition

d. example

18. According to the reading, which of the following statements is true?

a. People will always help others in an emergency.

b. When alone, a person is less likely to help someone else.

c. People must decide something is wrong and is an emergency and feel responsible before being able to help.

d. People in a crowd are more likely to assist someone in an emergency.

19. What is the relationship between the parts of the following sentence (from paragraph 14)?

"If everyone else is calm and indifferent, he will tend to remain so; if everyone else is reacting strongly, he is likely to become aroused." (lines 2–4)

a. addition

b. definition

c. comparison

d. contrast

20. We can infer from the last paragraph that the intent of the authors is to show that

a. we must begin training our children to take care of themselves, because they can't expect help from others.

b. the influence of the crowd can give us confidence and strength when we're facing an emergency.

c. we can resist the influence of the crowd and help out in an emergency.

d. we can resist the influence of the crowd and keep from looking foolish in an emergency.

READERS WRITE

1. What were some of the explanations given about why people don't help in a crisis before Darley and Latané completed their research?

(Answers will vary.)

2. Why are people less likely to even notice that there is an emergency if they are in a crowd than if they are alone?

(Answers will vary.)

3. Why are people apt to appear less concerned about a potential crisis if they are in a crowd than if they are alone? Which of the experiments helped to demonstrate this tendency?

(Answers will vary.)

4. What useful patterns of thought did you find in this reading? For example, what common pattern did you find in the lengthy introduction (paragraphs 1–9)?

    (Answers will vary.)

5. From the description in "The Lesson Learned" of the people who failed to report the emergency, what kinds of thoughts can you imagine were going through their minds as they heard the victim's increasing difficulties?

    (Answers will vary.)

READERS DISCUSS

1. How might "The Lesson Learned" in this reading affect your own behavior during a crisis? Share your ideas with other classmates.

    (Answers will vary.)

2. How can you make others more aware of their behaviors in a crisis and prompt them to help? How would you take control of an emergency situation and get others to assist you? Share your ideas with classmates.

    (Answers will vary.)

**Preliminary Stage for Cluster Map
"Why People Don't Help in a Crisis"**

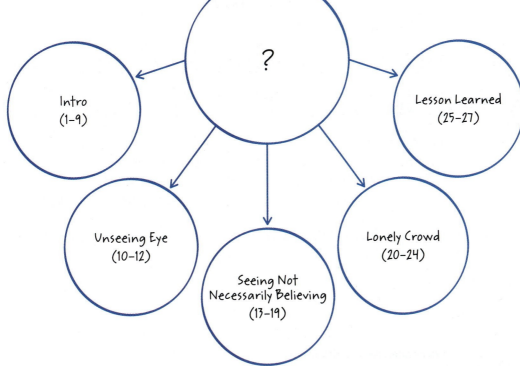

?

Intro
(1–9)

Lesson Learned
(25–27)

Unseeing Eye
(10–12)

Seeing Not
Necessarily Believing
(13–19)

Lonely Crowd
(20–24)

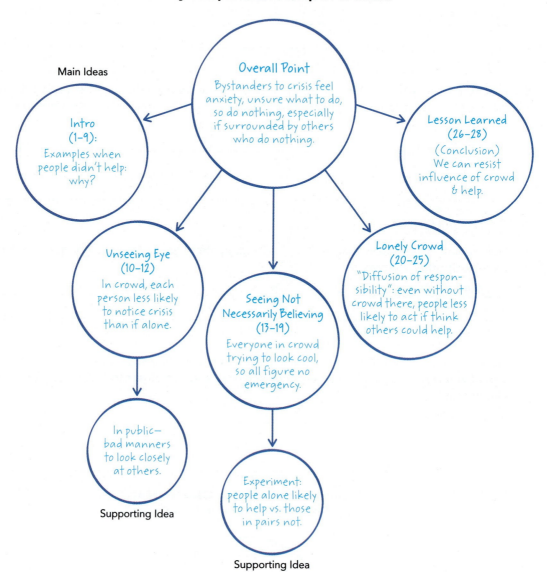

Sample Informal Outline and Box Map:
"Why People Don't Help in a Crisis"

(Overall point) Bystanders to crisis feel anxiety, unsure what to do, so do nothing, especially if surrounded by others who do nothing.

Intro (1–9): Examples when people didn't help: why?

1. Unseeing Eye (10–12): In crowd, each person less likely to notice crisis than if alone.
   - In public—bad manners to look closely at others.

2. Seeing Not Necessarily Believing (13–19): Everyone in crowd trying to look cool, so all figure no emergency.
   • Experiment showed people alone likely to help vs. those in pairs not.
3. Lonely Crowd (20–24): "Diffusion of responsibility": even without crowd there, people less likely to act if think others could help.
4. Lesson Learned (25–27, Conclusion): We can resist influence of crowd and help.

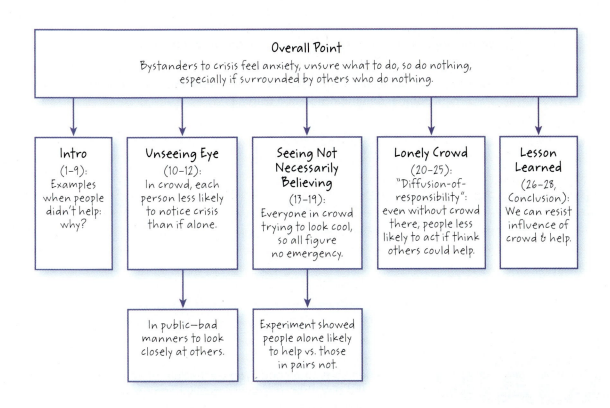

CHAPTER 8

HOW DOES STRATEGY 8 HELP YOU BECOME AN ENGAGED READER?

Mapping main ideas gets you actively involved with the writer's ideas. You work with the writer's ideas and think about how to put them into a clear format. Your map can later be the basis for your own summary of the reading's ideas. This greater involvement with the writer's ideas helps you *respond* more fully.

HOW DOES THE MAP MAIN IDEAS STRATEGY WORK?

This strategy shows you how to make a simple visual representation of a reading's overall point and main ideas. The suggested version of the map has a central circle for the overall point, with a few surrounding circles for each

MAP MAIN IDEAS

1 | Place the overall point in a map or an outline.

2 | Place the main ideas and supporting ideas in relation to the overall point.

STRATEGY 8

of the main ideas. However, there are other formats for mapping or outlining you can choose from.

Strategy 8 teaches you how to map your ideas by mapping or outlining a reading. You start by writing down the overall point or thesis of the reading and building your map or outline from there.

Strategy 8 shows you how to continue building your map or outline. Placing main ideas and supporting details onto the map or in the outline shows you how these ideas support the overall point.

Key Terms

cluster map: a cluster or boxed grouping of the overall point and main ideas in a reading

outline: a vertical listing, with indents, that shows the relationship of ideas—the overall point and main ideas—in a reading

Think AGAIN ›

When someone hands you a schedule of activities for the day, that person is actually handing you an outline or a map. If you went on a tour in another state or country, the tour guide might use a schedule to let everyone know the point of the day's tour and its major highlights. For example, a tour of Michigan during the autumn might include a trip to an apple orchard. At the orchard, you might pick apples, attend a bonfire, go on a hay ride, or make apple cider as the highlights of the day's activities. Often at conferences or during business meetings, people are handed an outline for the day. Where else have you used an outline or a map? Were you given one at your job or school orientation? Did a camp you attend have a set itinerary?

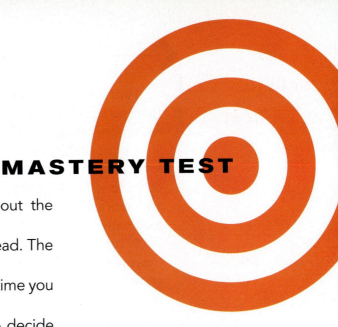

Before reading "Mother Tongue," think about the strategies you'll need to get started and to read. The margin notes give you reminders, but by this time you are skilled and secure enough in reading to decide which strategies you'll use. Write down two or three other strategies that you think will help you.

Since this reading has no headings, try mapping the main topics in pencil first before marking main ideas. You will see from your overview that Tan covers both the problems and the benefits of growing up with her mother's "limited" English. Make sure your overall-point question also covers both the problems and the benefits. Then, as you map the main topics, make sure your topics help answer your question.

Mother Tongue

AMY TAN

READING 16

Amy Tan is the daughter of Chinese immigrants, and grew up in California. Her first novel, *The Joy Luck Club* (1989), was made into a popular film about the difficult relationships between Chinese mothers and their American-born daughters. This reading explores what Tan learned about language from her relationship with her mother.

I am not a scholar of English or literature. I cannot give you much more **1** than personal opinions on the English language and its variations in this country or others.

I am a writer. And by that definition, I am someone who has always **2** loved language. I am fascinated by language in daily life. I spend a great deal of my time thinking about the power of language—the way it can evoke an emotion, a visual image, a complex idea, or a simple truth. Language is the tool of my trade. And I use them all—all the Englishes I grew up with.

Recently, I was made keenly aware of the different Englishes I do use. **3** I was giving a talk to a large group of people, the same talk I had already given to half a dozen other groups. The nature of the talk was about my writing, my life, and my book, *The Joy Luck Club*. The talk was going along well enough, until I remembered one major difference that made the whole talk sound wrong. My mother was in the room. And it was perhaps the first time she had heard me give a lengthy speech, using the kind of English I have never used with her. I was saying things like, "The intersection of memory upon imagination" and "There is an aspect of my fiction that re-lates to thus-and-thus"—a speech filled with carefully wrought grammatical phrases, burdened, it suddenly seemed to me, with nominalized forms, past perfect tenses, conditional phrases, all the forms of standard English that I had learned in school and through books, the forms of English I did not use at home with my mother.

nominalized form: *phrase that functions like a noun*

Just last week, I was walking down the street with my mother, and I **4** again found myself conscious of the English I was using, the English I do use with her. We were talking about the price of new and used furniture and I heard myself saying this: "Not waste money that way." My husband was with us as well, and he didn't notice any switch in my English. And then I realized why. It's because over the twenty years we've been together I've often used that same kind of English with him, and sometimes he even uses it with me. It has become our language of intimacy, a different sort of English that relates to family talk, the language I grew up with.

So you'll have some idea of what this family talk I heard sounds like, **5** I'll quote what my mother said during a recent conversation which I vid-eotaped and then transcribed. During this conversation, my mother was talking about a political gangster in Shanghai who had the same last name as her family's, Du, and how the gangster in his early years wanted to be adopted by her family, which was rich by comparison. Later, the gangster became more powerful, far richer than my mother's family, and one day showed up at my mother's wedding to pay his respects. Here's what she said in part:

"Du Yusong having business like fruit stand. Like off the street kind. **6** He is Du like Du Zong—but not Tsung-ming Island people. The local people call putong, the river east side, he belong to that side local people. That man want to ask Du Zong father take him in like become own family. Du Zong father wasn't look down on him, but didn't take seriously, until that man big like become a mafia. Now important person, very hard to inviting him. Chinese way, came only to show respect, don't stay for dinner. Respect for making big celebration, he shows up. Mean gives lots of respect. Chinese custom. Chinese social life that way. If too important won't have to stay too long. He come to my wedding. I didn't see, I heard it. I gone to boy's side, they have YMCA dinner. Chinese age I was nineteen."

7   You should know that my mother's expressive command of English belies how much she actually understands. She reads the *Forbes* report, listens to *Wall Street Week,* converses daily with her stockbroker, reads all of Shirley MacLaine's books with ease—all kinds of things I can't begin to understand. Yet some of my friends tell me they understand 50 percent of what my mother says. Some say they understand 80 to 90 percent. Some say they understand none of it, as if she were speaking pure Chinese. But to me, my mother's English is perfectly clear, perfectly natural. It's my mother tongue. Her language, as I hear it, is vivid, direct, full of observation and imagery. That was the language that helped shape the way I saw things, expressed things, made sense of the world.

8   Lately, I've been giving more thought to the kind of English my mother speaks. Like others, I have described it to people as "broken" or "fractured" English. But I wince when I say that. It has always bothered me that I can think of no way to describe it other than "broken," as if it were damaged and needed to be fixed, as if it lacked a certain wholeness and soundness. I've heard other terms used, "limited English," for example. But they seem just as bad, as if everything is limited, including people's perceptions of the limited English speaker.

9   I know this for a fact, because when I was growing up, my mother's "limited" English limited *my* perception of her. I was ashamed of her English. I believed that her English reflected the quality of what she had to say. That is, because she expressed them imperfectly her thoughts were imperfect. And I had plenty of empirical evidence to support me: the fact that people in department stores, at banks, and at restaurants did not take her seriously, did not give her good service, pretended not to understand her, or even acted as if they did not hear her.

10   My mother has long realized the limitations of her English as well. When I was fifteen, she used to have me call people on the phone to pretend I was she. In this guise, I was forced to ask for information or even to complain and yell at people who had been rude to her. One time it was a call to her stockbroker in New York. She had cashed out her small portfolio and it just so happened we were going to go to New York the next week, our very first trip outside California. I had to get on the phone and say in an adolescent voice that was not very convincing. "This is Mrs. Tan."

11   And my mother was standing in the back whispering loudly, "Why he don't send me check, already two weeks late. So mad he lie to me, losing me money."

It has always bothered me that I can think of no way to describe it other than "broken," as if it were damaged and needed to be fixed, as if it lacked a certain wholeness and soundness.

And then I said in perfect English, "Yes, I'm getting rather concerned. **12** You had agreed to send the check two weeks ago, but it hasn't arrived."

Then she began to talk more loudly. "What he want, I come to New **13** York tell him front of his boss, you cheating me?" And I was trying to calm her down, make her be quiet, while telling the stockbroker, "I can't tolerate any more excuses. If I don't receive the check immediately, I am going to have to speak to your manager when I'm in New York next week." And sure enough, the following week there we were in front of this astonished stockbroker, and I was sitting there red-faced and quiet, and my mother, the real Mrs. Tan, was shouting at his boss in her <u>impeccable</u> broken English.

We used a similar routine just five days ago, for a situation that was far **14** less humorous. My mother had gone to the hospital for an appointment, to find out about a <u>benign</u> tumor a CAT scan had revealed a month ago. She said she had spoken very good English, her best English, no mistakes. Still, she said, the hospital did not apologize when they said they had lost the CAT scan and she had come for nothing. She said they did not seem to have any sympathy when she told them she was anxious to know the exact diagnosis, since her husband and son had both died of brain tumors. She said they would not give her any more information until the next time and she would have to make another appointment for that. So she said she would not leave until the doctor called her daughter. She wouldn't budge. And when the doctor finally called her daughter, me, who spoke in perfect English—lo and behold—we had assurances the CAT scan would be found, promises that a conference call on Monday would be held, and apologies for any suffering my mother had gone through for a most regrettable mistake.

I think my mother's English almost had an effect on limiting my pos- **15** sibilities in life as well. Sociologists and linguists probably will tell you that a person's developing language skills are more influenced by peers. But I do think that the language spoken in the family, especially in immigrant families which are more insular, plays a large role in shaping the language of the child. And I believe that it affected my results on achievement tests, IQ tests, and the SAT. While my English skills were never judged as poor, compared to math, English could not be considered my strong suit. In grade school I did moderately well, getting perhaps B's, sometimes B-pluses, in English and scoring perhaps in the sixtieth or seventieth percentile on achievement tests. But those scores were not good enough to override the opinion that my true abilities lay in math and science, because in those areas I achieved A's and scored in the ninetieth percentile or higher.

This was understandable. Math is precise; there is only one correct an- **16** swer. Whereas, for me at least, the answers on English tests were always a judgment call, a matter of opinion and personal experience. Those tests were constructed around items like fill-in-the-blank sentence completion, such as, "Even though Tom was _____, Mary thought he was _____." And the correct answer always seemed to be the most <u>bland</u> combinations of thoughts, for example, "Even though Tom was shy, Mary thought he was charming," with the grammatical structure "even though" limiting the correct answer to some sort of semantic opposites, so you wouldn't get answers like, "Even though Tom was foolish, Mary thought he was ridiculous."

Well, according to my mother, there were very few limitations as to what Tom could have been and what Mary might have thought of him. So I never did well on tests like that.

17   The same was true with word analogies, pairs of words in which you were supposed to find some sort of logical, semantic relationship—for example, "*Sunset* is to *nightfall* as _____ is to _____." And here you would be presented with a list of four possible pairs, one of which showed the same kind of relationship: *red* is to *stoplight, bus* is to *arrival, chills* is to *fever, yawn* is to *boring*. Well, I could never think that way. I knew what the tests were asking, but I could not block out of my mind the images already created by the first pair, "*sunset* is to *nightfall*"—and I would see a burst of colors against a darkening sky, the moon rising, the lowering of a curtain of stars. And all the other pairs of words—red, bus, stoplight, boring—just threw up a mass of confusing images, making it impossible for me to sort out something as logical as saying: "A sunset precedes nightfall" is the same as "a chill precedes a fever." The only way I would have gotten that answer right would have been to imagine an associative situation, for example, my being disobedient and staying out past sunset, catching a chill at night, which turns into feverish pneumonia as punishment, which indeed did happen to me.

18   I have been thinking about all this lately, about my mother's English, about achievement tests. Because lately I've been asked, as a writer, why there are not more Asian Americans represented in American literature. Why are there few Asian Americans enrolled in creative writing programs? Why do so many Chinese students go into engineering? Well, these are broad sociological questions I can't begin to answer. But I have noticed in surveys—in fact, just last week—that Asian students, as a whole, always do significantly better on math achievement tests than in English. And this makes me think that there are other Asian-American students whose English spoken in the home might also be described as "broken" or "limited." And perhaps they also have teachers who are steering them away from writing and into math and science, which is what happened to me.

19   Fortunately, I happen to be rebellious in nature and enjoy the challenge of disproving assumptions made about me. I became an English major my first year in college, after being enrolled as pre-med. I started writing nonfiction as a freelancer the week after I was told by my former boss that writing was my worst skill and I should hone my talents toward account management.

20   But it wasn't until 1985 that I finally began to write fiction. And at first I wrote using what I thought to be wittily crafted sentences, sentences that would finally prove I had mastery over the English language. Here's an example from the first draft of a story that later made its way into *The Joy Luck Club,* but without this line: "That was my mental quandary in its nascent state." A terrible line, which I can barely pronounce.

21   Fortunately, for reasons I won't get into today, I later decided I should envision a reader for the stories I would write. And the reader I decided upon was my mother, because these were stories about mothers. So with

this reader in mind—and in fact she did read my early drafts—I began to write stories using all the Englishes I grew up with: the English I spoke to my mother, which for lack of a better term might be described as "simple"; the English she used with me, which for lack of a better term might be described as "broken"; my translation of her Chinese, which could certainly be described as "watered down"; and what I imagined to be her translation of her Chinese if she could speak in perfect English, her internal language, and for that I sought to preserve the essence, but neither an English nor a Chinese structure. I wanted to capture what language ability tests can never reveal: her intent, her passion, her imagery, the rhythms of her speech and the nature of her thoughts.

Apart from what any critic had to say about my writing, I knew I had 22 succeeded where it counted when my mother finished reading my book and gave me her verdict: "So easy to read."

ACTIVE READERS RESPOND

After you've finished reading, use these questions to respond to "Mother Tongue." You may write your answers in the spaces provided or on a separate sheet of paper.

VITAL VOCABULARY

Some words in this reading may be unfamiliar to you. Use the methods of Strategy 3 to explain what the listed words mean.

USE CONTEXT CLUES

a. hone (paragraph 19)

_____

USE WORD PARTS

a. intersection (paragraph 3)

_____

USE THE DICTIONARY

a. wrought (paragraph 3)

_____

b. impeccable (paragraph 13)

_____

c. benign (paragraph 14)

_____

d. bland (paragraph 16)

_____

Complete the cluster map on page 296.

OBJECTIVE OPERATIONS

1. Who is the writer's intended audience?

   a. students

   b. English speakers

   c. general audience

   d. Chinese

2. What is the author's purpose?

   a. to inform

   b. to persuade

   c. to entertain

3. What is the tone of the passage?

   a. interested

   b. insightful

   c. regretful

   d. joyous

4. The "different Englishes" Amy Tan tells us about in this reading include all of the following except

   a. the baby talk she uses with little children.

   b. the way she speaks with her mother.

   c. the way she writes her books.

   d. the way speaks to business professionals.

5. The word "hone" in paragraph 19, line 5, most nearly means

   a. center on.

   b. whet.

   c. prepare.

   d. perfect.

6. Which sentence states the implied main idea of the passage?

   a. Tan learned to speak English correctly although her mother did not.

   b. Learning everyone else's English was difficult for Tan due to her mother's use of English.

   c. Despite the difficulties of growing up with the "limited" English of her mother, Tan came to appreciate all the Englishes she grew up with, especially her mother's.

   d. Tan became a well-spoken English major and writer because she wished to master the language better than her mother had.

7. What is the implied main idea of paragraph 4?

   a. Tan needs to work on her English.

   b. Tan uses a broken English with her family members, yet she knows she is doing it.

   c. Tan speaks in broken English only when she wishes to have an intimate conversation with her husband.

   d. No one in Tan's family speaks English well.

8. Tan sees problems with the term "limited" English for the kind of English her mother speaks because

   a. the term doesn't convey the richness and complexity of her mother's speech.

   b. the term doesn't convey the severe difficulties her mother has had with English.

   c. "limited" implies that her mother can never improve her English.

   d. "limited" applies to the English of all immigrants, so it doesn't convey the way the Chinese learn to speak the language.

9. Which sentence provides support for this sentence (paragraph 7, lines 1–2): "You should know that my mother's expressive command of English belies how much she actually understands."?

   a. "She reads the *Forbes* report, listens to *Wall Street Week*, converses daily with her stockbroker, reads all of Shirley MacLaine's books with ease—all kinds of things I can't begin to understand."

   b. "Yet some of my friends tell me they understand 50 percent of what my mother says."

   c. "Some say they understand 80 to 90 percent. Some say they understand none of it, as if she were speaking pure Chinese."

   d. "But to me, my mother's English is perfectly clear, perfectly natural."

10. The authors' claim that some of her friends understand fifty percent of her mother's English (paragraph 7, lines 5–6) is

   a. adequately supported with details.

   b. inadequately supported with details.

11. What is the topic of paragraph 10?

    a. Tan's mother's inadequacies

    b. Tan's mother's understanding of her limitations in English

    c. limitations of English

    d. Tan's imitation of her mother on the phone

12. Tan's experiences translating for her mother taught her that if you speak limited English,

    a. stockbrokers and medical personnel are particularly insensitive to you.

    b. you will win friends due to your charming accent.

    c. people don't take you as seriously as if you speak "perfect" English.

    d. people will automatically refuse to do business with you.

13. Identify the relationship between the following sentences from paragraph 9.

    "I believed that her English reflected the quality of what she had to say. That is, because she expressed them imperfectly her thoughts were imperfect." (lines 3–5)

    a. definition

    b. cause and effect

    c. example

    d. statement and clarification

14. For paragraph 14, the author uses an overall organization pattern that

    a. compares.

    b. contrasts.

    c. defines.

    d. illustrates.

15. Tan had a slow start in writing fiction partly because her schools

    a. expected her to excel in English and criticized her when she did not.

    b. she was not allowed to take the school's tests with fill-in-the-blank sentence completions.

    c. expected her to do well in math and science, not in English.

    d. encouraged her to learn to write in Chinese rather than English.

16. The word "impeccable" in paragraph 13, line 8, most nearly means

    a. unsoiled.

    b. embarrassing.

    c. unpronounceable.

    d. flawless.

17. What is the relationship between the following sentences (from paragraph 16)?

    "Math is precise; there is only one correct answer. Whereas, for me at least, the answers on English tests were always a judgment call, a matter of opinion and personal experience." (lines 1–3)

    a. comparison

    b. statement and clarification

    c. contrast

    d. definition and example

18. What is the relationship between the following sentences (from paragraph 18)?

    "I have been thinking about all this lately, about my mother's English, about achievement tests. Because lately I've been asked, as a writer, why there are not more Asian Americans represented in American literature." (lines 1–3)

    a. cause and effect

    b. addition

    c. contrast

    d. time order

19. What is the relationship between the parts of the following sentence (from paragraph 17)?

    "The only way I would have gotten that answer right would have been to imagine an associative situation, for example, my being disobedient and staying out past sunset, catching a chill at night, which turns into feverish pneumonia as punishment, which indeed did happen to me." (lines 14–18)

    a. addition

    b. definition

    c. example

    d. sequence

20. From what Tan tells us we can infer that

    a. she is still bitter about the disgrace she felt when translating for her mother.

    b. she now looks back with fondness and values what her mother gave her as she grew up.

    c. she has learned to get over caring about what her mother thinks of her.

    d. she has decided that she would rather write just for her mother and ignore a wider reading public.

1. What does Tan mean by the "language of intimacy" she talks about in paragraph 4? What are the other "different Englishes" Amy Tan speaks about?

    (Answers will vary.)

    _____

    _____

    _____

2. Why does Tan see problems with the term "limited" English for the kind of English her mother speaks?

    (Answers will vary.)

    _____

    _____

    _____

3. What did Tan's experiences translating for her mother teach her about the way people regard speakers of "limited" English?

    (Answers will vary.)

    _____

    _____

    _____

4. Explain the title "Mother Tongue." What is the double meaning in these words?

    (Answers will vary.)

    _____

    _____

    _____

5. What useful patterns of thought did you find in this reading? For example, what pattern do you see in paragraphs 18–20 when Tan discusses becoming a writer?

    (Answers will vary.)

    _____

    _____

    _____

    _____

READERS DISCUSS

1. If you have had some of the same difficulties that Tan encountered, write briefly about your experience. Share with other classmates something about your experience.

    (Answers will vary.)

    _____

    _____

    _____

2. If you and your parents are native speakers of English, explain briefly what you learned about the problems people have speaking English as a second language. Compare your experiences with other classmates.

    (Answers will vary.)

    _____

    _____

    _____

3. All families have their own way of talking among themselves—with inside jokes and special words and phrases. What examples of "family language" can you think of? How is the way you communicate inside your family different from the way you talk outside the family setting?

(Answers will vary.)

_____

_____

_____

Cluster Map
"Mother Tongue"

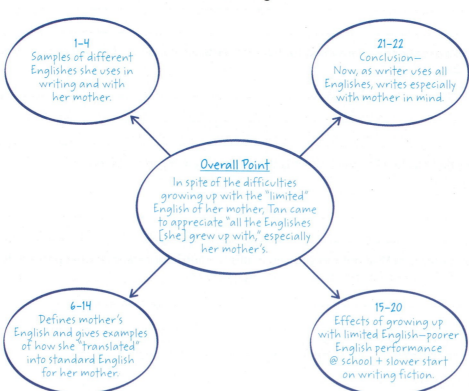

1–4
Samples of different Englishes she uses in writing and with her mother.

21–22
Conclusion—
Now, as writer uses all Englishes, writes especially with mother in mind.

Overall Point
In spite of the difficulties growing up with the "limited" English of her mother, Tan came to appreciate "all the Englishes [she] grew up with," especially her mother's.

6–14
Defines mother's English and gives examples of how she "translated" into standard English for her mother.

15–20
Effects of growing up with limited English—poorer English performance @ school + slower start on writing fiction.

MAP MAIN IDEAS

1 | Place the overall point in a map or an outline.

2 | Place the main ideas and supporting ideas in relation to the overall point.

PRACTICE PAGES

Chapter 8

For practice outlining, complete the following exercise.

PRACTICE EXERCISE 1

Read the following passage and mark in the margins as you identify the overall point and the main ideas. Complete the outline that follows.

HEROINES OF THE AMERICAN REVOLUTION

The first shots of the American Revolution were fired in Massachusetts in April 1775. Even before those shots rang out, women were part of the push for independence; scholars provide much evidence of women's involvement in political and economic acts as well as in combat and espionage.

Some colonial women were vocal in their opposition to British rule. Mercy Otis Warren, for instance, published seditious works that presented British rule as greedy, corrupt, and brutal. Other women organized boycotts of British goods, devising homemade substitutes for such imports as linen cloth, tea, and coffee. During the war, not only did women perform "traditional" female tasks such as nursing the wounded and sewing uniforms; they also took over traditionally male occupations, becoming weavers, carpenters, and blacksmiths. Patriotic societies such as the Daughters of Liberty raised money and made clothing for the Continental Army.

The daring and physical courage of many women put them in harm's way. Paul Revere was not the only one to ride through the countryside warning citizens of the approach of British troops. Sixteen-year-old Sybil Ludington was just as heroic. In 1777 she rode 40 miles in the black of night to rouse the militia following the British assault on a supply depot in Danbury, Connecticut. Women gathered intelligence on British movements and found ways to get this information to their local militias. Lydia Barrington Darragh, a mother of nine, sneaked through enemy lines to warn General George Washington of an ambush that

> During the war, not only did women perform "traditional" female tasks such as nursing the wounded and sewing uniforms; they also took over traditionally male occupations, becoming weavers, carpenters, and blacksmiths.

had been planned. Teenager Susanna Bolling crossed the Appomattox River alone and at night to alert General Joseph Lafayette about an attack.

Some women even fought alongside the men. Among the most famous of these was Deborah Samson, who joined the fourth Massachusetts Regiment disguised as Robert Shirtliffe. She was wounded twice during three years of fighting, and her sex remained secret until she became ill with a brain fever. When Fort Washington, New York, was attacked in 1776, Margaret Cochran Corbin assisted her husband, John, in taking over a cannon from a gunner who had been killed. When John was killed, Margaret became the gunner until she was badly wounded. Eventually Congress awarded her a soldier's pension for her remarkable courage. Nancy Morgan Hart defended her Georgia cabin from a small group of soldiers sympathetic to the British side. She shot and killed one of the soldiers, and her later exploits as a spy became legendary.

Overall Point: Even before those shots rang out, women were part of the push for independence; scholars provide much evidence of women's involvement in political and economic acts as well as in combat and espionage.

_____

_____

_____

Main Idea: Some colonial women were vocal in their opposition to British rule.

_____

_____

Main Idea: The daring and physical courage of many women put them in harm's way.

_____

_____

Main Idea: Some women even fought alongside the men.

_____

_____

For practice making a box map, complete the following exercise.

PRACTICE EXERCISE 2

Read the following passage and mark in the margins as you identify the overall point and the main ideas. Complete the box map that follows.

PLAYING FOR PAY: AMATEURS, PROFESSIONALS, AND THE OLYMPIC GAMES

The modern Olympic Games, founded in 1896, began as contests between individuals, rather than among nations, with the hope of promoting world peace through sportsmanship. In the beginning, the games were open only to amateurs. An *amateur* is a person whose involvement in an activity—from sports to science or the arts—is purely for pleasure. Amateurs, whatever their contributions to a field, expect to receive no form of compensation; professionals, in contrast, perform their work in order to earn a living.

From the perspective of many athletes, however, the Olympic playing field has been far from level. Restricting the Olympics to amateurs has precluded the participation of many who could not afford to be unpaid. Countries have always desired to send their best athletes, not their wealthiest ones, to the Olympic Games.

A slender and imprecise line separates what we call "financial support" from "earning money." Do athletes "earn money" if they are reimbursed for travel expenses? What if they are paid for time lost at work or if they accept free clothing from a manufacturer or if they teach sports for a living? The runner Eric Liddell was the son of poor missionaries; in 1924 the British Olympic Committee financed his trip to the Olympics, where he won a gold and a bronze medal. College scholarships and support from the United States Olympic Committee made it possible for American track stars Jesse Owens and Wilma Rudolph and speed skater Dan Jansen to train and compete. When the Soviet Union and its allies joined the games in 1952, the definition of *amateur* became still muddier. Their athletes did not have to balance jobs and training because as citizens in communist regimes, their government financial support was not considered payment for jobs.

In 1971 the International Olympic Committee (IOC) removed the word *amateur* from the rules, making it easier for athletes to find the support necessary to train and compete. In 1986 the IOC allowed professional athletes into the games.

There are those who regret the disappearance of amateurism from the Olympic Games. For them the games lost something special when they became just another way for athletes to earn money. Others say that the designation of amateurism was always questionable; they argue that all competitors receive so much financial support as to make them paid professionals. Most agree, however, that the debate over what constitutes an "amateur" will continue for a long time.

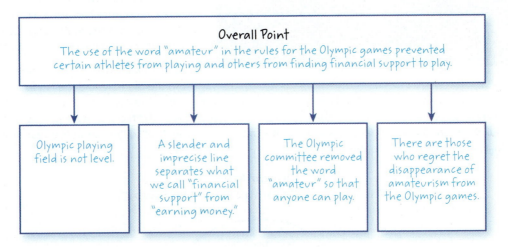

Overall Point
The use of the word "amateur" in the rules for the Olympic games prevented certain athletes from playing and others from finding financial support to play.

| Olympic playing field is not level. | A slender and imprecise line separates what we call "financial support" from "earning money." | The Olympic committee removed the word "amateur" so that anyone can play. | There are those who regret the disappearance of amateurism from the Olympic games. |

For practice making a cluster map, complete the following exercise.

PRACTICE EXERCISE 3

Read the following passage and mark in the margins as you identify the overall point and the main ideas. Complete the cluster map that follows.

THE HISTORIC COLUMBIA RIVER HIGHWAY

The Columbia River Gorge is one of the scenic wonders of the Pacific Northwest. It cuts through the Cascade mountain range separating Washington on the north from Oregon to the south. For millennia Native American groups thrived here, taking advantage of the area's abundant fish and game. In addition to the beauty of blue waters that snake between the rock bluffs of the gorge, there are meadows bright with wildflowers, dense forests, and the white spume of waterfalls.

This paradise did not escape the notice of some people who lived in nearby cities and towns. In the early twentieth century, inspired by roads he had seen along the Rhine River valley in Europe, an Oregon lawyer named Samuel Hill began to promote his vision of a highway that would serve the community and at the same time display the area's glories. Engineer and landscape architect Samuel C. Lancaster designed a modern road that linked broad vistas with glimpses of waterfalls and leafy forest glades.

Work on the highway commenced in 1913. The road itself was built to precise requirements, with such advanced materials as reinforced concrete and new safety features such as masonry guard walls. Bridges and tunnels resembled

works of art. In 1918 the Vista House, a lovely octagonal building with a copper-sheathed dome, became a popular point from which to view much of the Columbia River Gorge. In 1922 all 200 miles of concrete roadbed surfaced with asphalt opened to the public.

As automobiles became more powerful and drivers more concerned with convenience and speed than with the view through the window, Oregon's Columbia River Highway deteriorated. In the 1950s, work began on a bypass that would run straight and level on new riverbanks created from fill material dredged from the river itself. Sections of the old Columbia River Highway fell into disuse and disrepair. By the time Interstate 84 opened in 1960, the Columbia River Highway had begun to disappear.

In the 1980s, there was a resurgence of interest in the old road and the landscape around the gorge. Lost sections were identified and excavated, and a feasibility study of restoring the old Columbia River Highway to its original condition was undertaken. In 1983 surviving sections of the highway were placed on the National Register of Historic Places. The route was designated an All-American Road in 1998 and a National Historic Landmark in 2000. Preservation efforts continue to this day.

Cluster Map
"The Historic Columbia River Highway"

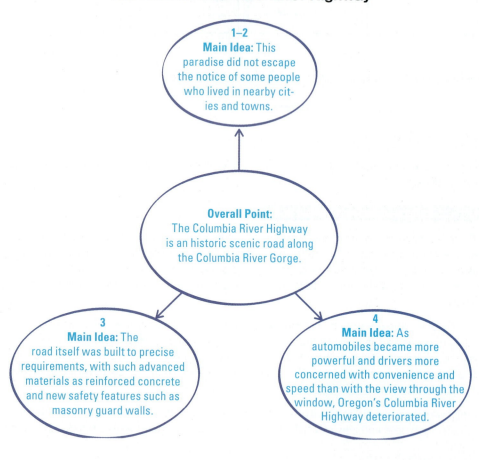

1–2
Main Idea: This paradise did not escape the notice of some people who lived in nearby cities and towns.

Overall Point: The Columbia River Highway is an historic scenic road along the Columbia River Gorge.

3
Main Idea: The road itself was built to precise requirements, with such advanced materials as reinforced concrete and new safety features such as masonry guard walls.

4
Main Idea: As automobiles became more powerful and drivers more concerned with convenience and speed than with the view through the window, Oregon's Columbia River Highway deteriorated.

To get practice with reading, read the passage, and then answer the questions that follow. You may write your answers in the spaces provided or on a separate sheet of paper.

Imprinting: A Form of Learning

ROBERT WALLACE

Robert Wallace was a professor of biology at the University of Florida until his death in 1996. He was the author of several biology textbooks and other non-fiction books on science. This reading comes from the chapter on animal behavior in his textbook *Biology: The World of Life* (1996). The reading is about the famous experiment that made a researcher the parent to a group of baby geese.

1 On your annual visits to the farm, you may have seen young ducklings waddling along after their mother, perhaps on the way to the pond. It's a quaint sight, but you're there to see where milk comes from and so you think no more about it. However, if you had visited a farm in southern Germany some years ago, you might have seen a more unusual sight—a column of young goslings following a white-haired Austrian down to the pond (Figure 1). The man was Konrad Lorenz, a future recipient of the Nobel Prize, and the following behavior of the goslings was the product of an experiment he devised.

find and mark main ideas and look for patterns of thought

2 What he did was to let them see him moving around and making noises a few hours after they had

hatched. If they had seen and heard him after that, they would have treated him like any other human. But Lorenz was the figure they encountered during their *critical period,* a window of time when the young are particularly sensitive to certain aspects of their environment. At this time, the goslings, and the young of many other <u>species</u> as well, learn the <u>traits</u> of whatever is around them. Normally, of course, this would be their mother, but these goslings developed from eggs that were artificially <u>incubated</u> and so the figure that they saw during their critical period was Konrad Lorenz, and as a result they learned to regard him as one of their own.

Lorenz called this kind of learning *imprinting,* and he defined it as learning **3** that occurs over a defined, relatively brief period of time in which the animal learns to make a specific response to certain aspects of its environment.

A great deal of research has been done on imprinting in the last few **4** decades and we have learned that it is difficult to draw hard and fast rules about its development. It is regarded, though, as a curious interaction of learned and instinctive patterns. In the case of the goslings, they learned the general characteristics of the <u>stimulus</u> for the <u>innate</u> following response.

Many animals also learn species identification during this critical period; **5** that is, they learn the image of an appropriate mate. As they approach their first breeding season, they seek out an individual with traits generally similar to those of the individual they had followed soon after hatching. If they are raised by parents of another species, they focus on individuals with traits similar to those of their foster parents when it is time to breed. Lorenz once had a tame jackdaw (a European crow) that he had hand-reared, and it would try to "courtship feed" him during mating season. On occasion when Lorenz turned his mouth away, he would receive an earful of worm pulp! . . .

Imprinting is especially important in the development of song in many **6** species. For example, for male white-crowned sparrows to be able to sing the song of their species, they must hear the song at a particular time during a brief critical period early in life. If they are exposed to the song after this period, they will produce abnormal songs, lacking the finer details. At the period during which they must hear the song, they are not yet even able to sing.

White-crowned sparrows are wide ranging, and the species forms sub- **7** populations that tend to breed among themselves and sing their own local dialects of the basic song. If young birds from different populations are isolated at hatching and reared in soundproof chambers, they all begin to sing the same rather basic song. Thus, they are apparently born with the basic pattern; the local <u>embellishments</u> of each population are learned later.

Interestingly, isolated hatchling white-crowned sparrows can learn the **8** recorded dialect of any subpopulation of the species while in their learning periods. But if they are exposed to the song of another species, they will not learn that song and will sing as if they had been reared in a soundproof cage. Finally, if a young white-crowned sparrow is deafened after it has heard the proper song but before it has had a chance to sing, it will sing only garbled passages. It apparently must hear its own song in order to match it to its inborn "<u>template</u>." The development of song in white-crowned sparrows, then, serves as an example of the interaction of learned and innate patterns in producing an adaptive response.

ACTIVE READERS RESPOND

After you've finished reading, use these activities to respond to "Imprinting: A Form of Learning." You may write your answers in the spaces provided or on a separate sheet of paper.

VITAL VOCABULARY

Some words in this reading may be unfamiliar to you. Use the methods of Strategy 3 to explain what the listed words mean.

USE CONTEXT CLUES

a. traits (paragraph 2)

_____

b. incubated (paragraph 2)

_____

c. embellishments (paragraph 7)

_____

USE THE DICTIONARY

Choose the correct definition of each word as it is used in the context of this reading.

a. species (paragraph 2)

_____

b. stimulus (paragraph 4)

_____

c. innate (paragraph 4)

_____

d. template (paragraph 8)

_____

OBJECTIVE OPERATIONS

1. Who is the writer's intended audience?
   a. students
   b. biology students
   c. general audience
   d. duck lovers

2. What is the author's purpose?
   a. to inform
   b. to persuade
   c. to entertain

3. What is the tone of the passage?
   a. subjective
   b. critical
   c. objective
   d. apathetic

4. Konrad Lorenz devised an experiment to
   a. test the ability of humans to influence the young of another species.
   b. see how the following response is developed in certain young animals.
   c. test the ability of humans to artificially incubate geese.
   d. determine what happens when young animals are trained after the critical period for learning has passed.

5. The word "traits" in paragraph 2, line 7, most nearly means
   a. characteristics.
   b. treatments.
   c. tricks.
   d. environments.

6. Which sentence states the implied main idea of the passage?

    a. All animals learn their environment through imprinting.

    b. Imprinting is a brief period of time when an animal learns how to respond to specific parts of its environment.

    c. Goslings and other birds are animals that use imprinting to learn about its environment.

    d. Imprinting is a form of learning.

7. What is the stated main idea of paragraph 6?

    a. "Imprinting is especially important in the development of song in many species."

    b. "For example, for male white-crowned sparrows to be able to sing the song of their species, they must hear the song at a particular time during a brief critical period early in life."

    c. "If they are exposed to the song after this period, they will produce abnormal songs, lacking the finer details."

    d. "At the period during which they must hear the song, they are not yet even able to sing."

8. Imprinting is defined as a kind of learning that occurs over a relatively brief period of time during which the baby animal learns

    a. to identify who its parent is.

    b. to mark out its own territory.

    c. to make embellishments in the innate patterns of its species.

    d. to make a specific response to certain aspects of the environment.

9. Which sentence provides support for this sentence (paragraph 2, lines 4–6): "But Lorenz was the figure they encountered during their critical period, a window of time when the young are particularly sensitive to certain aspects of their environment."?

    a. "What he did was to let them see him moving around and making noises a few hours after they had hatched."

    b. "If they had seen and heard him after that, they would have treated him like any other human."

    c. "At this time, the goslings, and the young of many other species as well, learn the traits of whatever is around them."

    d. "Normally, of course, this would be their mother, but these goslings developed from

eggs that were artificially incubated and so the figure that they saw during their critical period was Konrad Lorenz, and as a result they learned to regard him as one of their own."

10. The authors' claim that many species learn the image of an appropriate mate (paragraph 5, lines 1–2) is

    a. adequately supported with details.

    b. inadequately supported with details.

11. What is the topic of paragraph 4?

    a. learned responses

    b. imprinting

    c. a curious interaction

    d. imprinting and its patterns

12. The goslings regarded Lorenz as "one of their own" because

    a. he was the figure they first encountered during the critical period for imprinting.

    b. after rescuing them when their mother died, he hand fed them.

    c. they left their mother for Lorenz because he was the largest figure they saw during the critical period for imprinting.

    d. they were raised by Lorenz's lab technicians and so their preference was for male humans.

13. Identify the relationship between the following sentences from paragraph 8.

    "Interestingly, isolated hatchling white-crowned sparrows can learn the recorded dialect of any subpopulation of the species while in their learning periods. But if they are exposed to the song of another species, they will not learn that song and will sing as if they had been reared in a soundproof cage." (lines 1–4)

    a. comparison

    b. cause and effect

    c. contrast

    d. statement and clarification

14. For paragraph 1, the author uses an overall organization pattern that

    a. compares.

    b. contrasts.

    c. describes.

    d. illustrates.

15. The jackdaw's actions showed how it had learned species identification when it would
    a. follow Lorenz around the barnyard.
    b. reject all the female jackdaws in the area.
    c. try to feed Lorenz some wormy pulp.
    d. "courtship feed" a female jackdaw.

16. The word "traits" in paragraph 5, line 5, most nearly means
    a. attitudes.
    b. abilities.
    c. requirements.
    d. characteristics.

17. What is the relationship between the parts of the following sentence (from paragraph 2)?
    "If they had seen and heard him after that, they would have treated him like any other human." (lines 3–4)
    a. cause and effect
    b. statement and clarification
    c. comparison and contrast
    d. definition and example

18. What is the relationship between the parts of the following sentence (from paragraph 3)?
    "Lorenz called this kind of learning imprinting, and he defined it as learning that occurs over a defined, relatively brief period of time in which the animal learns to make a specific response to certain aspects of its environment." (lines 1–3)
    a. definition
    b. comparison
    c. example
    d. process

19. What is the relationship between the following sentences (from paragraph 7)?
    "If young birds from different populations are isolated at hatching and reared in soundproof chambers, they all begin to sing the same rather basic song. Thus, they are apparently born with the basic pattern; the local embellishments of each population are learned later." (lines 3–6)
    a. addition
    b. definition and example
    c. example
    d. cause and effect

20. If white-crowned sparrows are not exposed to the song of their species during the critical period,
    a. they will not learn to sing at all.
    b. they will sing normally, since the songs are an innate pattern in that species.
    c. they will become isolated from other birds and go into a decline.
    d. they will produce abnormal songs, lacking in finer details.

QUICK QUESTIONS

1. Imprinting is not a critical period in an animal's life. True or False

2. Konrad Lorenz became the "mother" to goslings. True or False

3. Two birds Lorenz worked with are _____jackdaws_____ and ____white-crowned sparrows____.

4. If young birds from different populations are isolated and raised in ____soundproof chambers____, they sing the same basic song.

5. What is meant by saying that animals learn "species identification"? What happened when Lorenz hand-reared a jackdaw? How did the jackdaw's actions demonstrate learning species identification?
   (Answers will vary.) _____
   _____
   _____

6. How do the experiments with white-crowned sparrows demonstrate the concept that imprinting is a "curious interaction of learned and instinctive patterns" (paragraph 4)?
   (Answers will vary.) _____
   _____
   _____

9

Make Inferences

MAKE INFERENCES

1 | Look for what is implied as well as what is stated outright.

2 | Use the logic of "putting two and two together."

3 | Notice the details.

4 | Notice the word choice.

5 | Examine your assumptions.

imagine this

When you play games with your friends, you often use inference to help you achieve your goals. You may notice one friend's scowl when he receives his hand of cards, or see another friend shake her head at an answer her partner gave. The friend's scowl lets you know that he is unhappy with what he was dealt; the head shake is a clue that your other friend's partner is incorrect in his answer. Reading these signs correctly might give you the edge you need to win the game.

When you play, you make guesses about what other players are going to do. While reading, you make similar guesses. You might make connections about things the writer does not say directly. By putting ideas together, paying attention to word choice, and using your brain to work out what the writer has *not* stated, you might find clues about the writer's meaning. You are drawing conclusions, or making inferences, about the writer's ideas.

Think FIRST >

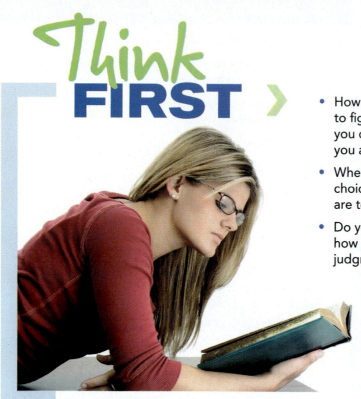

- How many times do you read between the lines to figure out what someone is really saying? Do you often make quick rational connections when you are given information?

- When do you focus on friends' details or word choice to decipher more clues about what they are telling you?

- Do you jump to conclusions? Do you recognize how your personal experience can affect your judgment?

INTRODUCTION TO THE NEW STRATEGY
Make Inferences

In our everyday life we make many well-informed guesses. We see pieces of evidence, put the pieces together, and then *make an inference*—meaning that we make connections and draw logical conclusions based on evidence. For example, if you saw a young man on campus, wearing paint-stained jeans, carrying a large canvas and paintbrushes, you would probably make an inference—or **infer**—that he is on his way to or from an art class. Strategy 9 shows you how to make similar kinds of logical connections as you read.

Before reading "A Letter to My Teacher," Reading 17, learn to make inferences by looking closely at passages from that reading. In these passages, watch for unstated as well as stated ideas. Take special note of the details and words a writer selects to get across an idea without stating it explicitly.

Inferences and Implied Ideas

Read this sentence: "When their friend crashed his car into a tree, nearly killing himself and his passengers, the students made a pact that they would always have a designated driver when they went to a party."

To get the full meaning from that sentence, your mind goes beyond the stated message. You don't have to be told

THE READER'S EDGE: BOOK TWO

that the friend had been drinking or that the students expected there would be drinking at other parties. You get that information by putting together the idea of the friend crashing the car and the students' decision to have a "designated driver" at the next party. The writer **implies**—or suggests—the meaning beyond the words. You, the reader, infer it—or make inferences about it. We sometimes use the phrase "reading between the lines" to mean that we're inferring the writer's meaning.

Logical Connections

A common expression for inferring is that we "put two and two together." In other words, we use logic to connect separate pieces of information. In the above example, we made the connection between the friend crashing the car and the drinking that often goes on at parties.

connect now

A cartoon is a good way to remind you of the kinds of connections you need to make in order to understand implied ideas. Cartoons are only funny if you make the expected connections. You use logic like this whenever you read the funny pages. To understand the humor, often you need to make a connection between the visual image and what the characters say. For example, to understand the following cartoon you need to remember that students have always given excuses for not having their homework ready. The most well-known excuse—though it may never actually have been used—was "My dog ate my homework."

Have logical connections helped you figure out how to avoid something, such as a traffic accident or a fight with a friend?

Instructor Tip
Remind students that the shoe activity relied on implied information and inferences, and explain that they use inference every day to figure out if roommates are home, the mall is busy, or a classmate is sick. Then, ask students how they know roommates are home, the mall is busy, or a classmate is sick.

"He appears to have eaten some homework."

Or you make a connection between what is shown and what you already know.

In the next cartoon, what connection can you make between the caption, "Low self-esteem," the diary entry, and the way the writer looks?

EXERCISES

PRACTICE

To practice making inferences, complete the following exercise.

Read the following introductory passage from "A Letter to My Teacher." Try "putting two and two together" by seeing what the separate pieces of information add up to.

I didn't belong in college. I should have told you that. My father dropped out of school after third grade. My mother went through twelfth grade, but her family thought she was a little uppity for doing so. Like my mother, I finished high school, and immediately got married and started having babies. A decade and a half later, I was a divorced single parent, working as a babysitter during the day and clerking part-time nights in a food store. My income fell far below the poverty level, where I'd lived for much of my life. Statisticians said I didn't belong in college. Who was I to argue?

Statisticians said I didn't belong in college. Who was I to argue?

In this introductory paragraph the author gives a lot of information about herself. Which of these sentences from that paragraph are stated ideas and which are implied? Put *S* for a stated idea, and *I* for an implied idea. If an idea is implied, what clues did you use to determine the information?

1. _S_ Her father dropped out of school after third grade.

2. _I_ She wants to be honest as she explains her background and her experience of college to this professor.

3. _I_ Her mother's family had a low opinion of education past the earlier grades.

4. _I_ Her mother was a role model for her as she grew up.

5. _S_ She got married right after high school.

6. _I_ She had more than one child by the time she was in her early twenties.

7. _S_ She was a divorced single parent.

8. _I_ She had no child support from her ex-husband.

9. _S_ She spent most of her time working and taking care of her children.

10. _S_ For much of her life her income was below the poverty level.

11. _I_ Statisticians studying poverty and single parenthood find that very few poor, single mothers make it to college.

12. _I_ At the time she describes, she didn't have confidence in her ability to succeed in college.

Details

Pay careful attention to what details the writer includes, as well as what details you might expect but that are left out.

What Details Are Included?

Ask yourself why a certain piece of information is included. For example, in the introduction to "A Letter to My Teacher," why does the writer tell you about her parents' education? Why are the details about her life immediately following high school included? What do the details about her two jobs imply about what her life is like?

connect now

What kinds of details stand out to you?

Here is another paragraph from this reading. What do the details that are included imply?

My stomach began to churn relentlessly at the thought of speaking in front of the class. "How was school today, honey?" my youngest daughter greeted me when I got home, doing a creditable imitation of my usual after-school question to her. But I was already halfway down the hall to the bathroom where I promptly lost my lunch.

Just thinking about an oral presentation made the writer feel extremely ill. That detail shows that her anxiety was quite serious.

What Expected Details Are Left Out?

Sometimes a detail that might be expected and is not included can suggest meaning. For example, notice that the writer does not mention her ex-husband, so we can infer that he is not helping to raise the children. We get an added sense of her independence, her sense of responsibility to her kids, as well as her lack of financial resources.

> *Often, we forget that we use our inference skills on a daily basis, especially when we pay attention to other people's body language. Here, author Rick Brenner gives some reasons why the message we infer may be confusing.*

Do you consider yourself a body linguist? Can you tell what people are thinking just by looking at gestures and postures? Think again. Body language is much more complex and ambiguous than many would have us believe.

Spoken language is confusing. We have words that sound alike but mean different things; we have different words that mean the same thing; and we have pauses and tones that can negate the meaning of any string of words. Still, somehow, we do tend to catch the meaning enough of the time to keep our families and relationships—and many of our major corporations—humming along. Though there is some doubt about Congress.

As confusing as spoken language is, body language is even more confusing. Here are some reasons why.

It's nonlinear.

Spoken language is largely linear. It has at least a partial time ordering, and the order greatly simplifies message extraction. By contrast, we execute the gestures and postures of body language in parallel, using different parts of our bodies and faces.

We can't turn it off.

We can stop speaking, but we can't stop body language. We're always in some kind of posture. We're always sending signals, but the signals don't always mean anything.

There is no OBD (Oxford Body-Language Dictionary).

Although spoken language has dialects and accents, the words mean more or less the same thing to anyone speaking a given language. But we learn our body language from those who rear us, and beyond the universal basics, we have no idea what our gestures and postures might mean to the outside world.

It's out of our awareness.

Even when we try to control it, or try to read it in others, we miss a lot. We have a recurring experience of suddenly realizing that we're gesturing a certain way, or that we've adopted a certain pose. And the gestures and postures of others trigger responses within us before we become aware of them.

The meanings of the "words" are very dependent on context.

Some people run cold; others run hot. Someone with arms and legs crossed might just be cold, not "closed off." Someone with flushed face and brow glistening with beads of sweat might just be hot, not "nervous." You can't tell by looking. Any one indicator just isn't enough information to make a meaning we can rely on.

Even when we've learned to read a little body language, we often see contradictions. Without realizing it, we sometimes reject contradictory interpretations, and settle on one meaning—often the one we want to see. We reach conclusions with more certainty than accuracy.

Controlling our own body language is no simpler. Trying to convey confidence and openness, a typical result is rigidity of posture and flatness of facial expression, which conveys rigidity and control, not openness or confidence. To convey how you want to feel, focus on feeling it. Your body will figure out how to tell everyone else about it.

Brenner, Rick. "Hot and Cold Running People." *Point Lookout*. Chacocanyon.com. 12 May 2004. 8 July 2009. Available: www.chacocanyon.com/pointlookout/040512.shtml

As you read the rest of "A Letter to My Teacher," you will notice that there are other details you might expect that are not there: the writer never mentions difficulties in understanding material or doing assignments. These omissions suggest that she had the ability to do well in college. She was meant to go to college after all.

Word Choice

Writers choose their words carefully, because so many words have special connotations, or implied meanings, in addition to their obvious meaning, their denotation.

Denotation

Denotation, or denotative meaning, refers to a word's explicit, or literal meaning. Consider the word "drinking," for example. The first meaning you'd find in the dictionary for that word—its literal definition—would say something about the act of swallowing liquids. However, when that word is used in other contexts, it has a very different connotation. In referring to the friend who had been drinking on page 308, we recognize the connotation of drinking alcohol.

Connotation

Connotation, or connotative meaning, refers to the cluster of suggestions, implications, or emotional responses that a word carries with it. These connotations may be positive, negative, or specialized in some way. The connotation extends the meaning of the word beyond its denotative meaning.

Some words always carry with them a special connotation. The verb "walk" is purely neutral, its denotative meaning is "to make a forward movement by taking steps." But other words that have this same denotative meaning (forward movement) can never be used in a neutral way. Each one of these verbs connotes a different kind of walk: stride, saunter, stroll, meander, glide, lumber, plod, stagger, and march.

Think of the differences in connotation between the following pairs of words, each with the same denotative meaning. Which word in each pair is neutral and which has a special, usually negative, connotation?

macho	masculine
frantic	concerned
childish	childlike
fragile	flimsy
pushy	aggressive
cheap	economical

SHIA LEBEOUF

Catcher in the Rye by J. D. Salinger

Shia LeBeouf may have started his career in Disney movies, but recently he's been stealing the show from more seasoned actors. But Shia doesn't let his success go to his head. The actor plans to take some time out of the spotlight in the near future to attend college. He's preparing for this new role in the same way he prepares for others—not just studying his lines, but reading books that set him up for the challenges with which his character will be grappling. Shia's curiosity as an actor echoes that of the main character of his favorite book, J. D. Salinger's, *Catcher in the Rye*. Hopefully Shia will keep his head in the books, and his career on track.

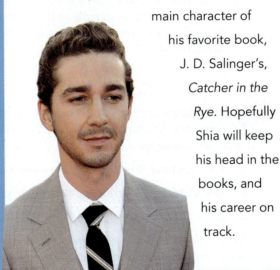

If you liked *Catcher in the Rye*, you might also like:

The Bell Jar, Sylvia Plath

The Great Gatsby, F. Scott Fitzgerald

The Perks of Being a Wallflower, Stephen Chbosky

Instructor Tip

Have students get into groups and generate a note written completely in slang. Have them write a second version, a "translated" note. Discuss the word choice in each—the denotation, the connotation, and the tone.

serious   grim

snicker   laugh

Tone is affected by a word's connotation. For example, the word "snicker" has a very negative, mean-spirited tone, but "laugh" suggests a more light-hearted tone. The connotation of a word affects the tone of the passage.

EXERCISES

PRACTICE

To further practice making inferences, complete the following exercise.

Read the following passage from Kate Boyes' "A Letter to My Teacher." Then, answer the questions.

> And I discovered something else: Taking only one course would make me eligible for student health insurance. Neither of my jobs included benefits, and every time my kids came down with a cold, I worried about what would happen to us if we were really sick. I did some careful calculations. If I took one college course each semester for a year, the cost of tuition, books and fees would be far lower than even six months of private insurance. My two kids would be covered, too. What a deal!

A. STATED VERSUS IMPLIED IDEAS

In these sentences the author gives a lot of information, both stated and implied. First, note the following stated ideas. Fill in the blanks with information that is spelled out in the passage.

1. If Boyes took one course, she could have _____ student health insurance.

2. Her children sometimes came down with _____ colds.

3. Boyes had to take ____ one college course each semester ____ to get insurance.

Now look for implied ideas in this passage. Try "putting two and two together" about the situations and people by seeing what the separate pieces of information add up to.

1. What does this sentence imply?

   ". . . [E]very time my kids came down with a cold, I worried about what would happen to us if we were really sick." (What does Boyes mean by "really sick?")

   (Answers will vary.)

   _____

2. What does this sentence imply?

   "I did some careful calculations." (What does Boyes include in her calculations?)

   (Answers will vary.)

   _____

3. Does Boyes seem very concerned with her own health? What makes you conclude that?

   (Answers will vary.)

   _____

In each of these sentences, consider the denotation of the underlined word; then, explain the connotation associated with the word choice. Finally, identify the tone of the sentence.

1. "What a deal!"

   Denotation: _____ a transaction or bargain _____

   What special meanings do the connotations of these words suggest?

   _____ This is a cheap find for the author _____

   Circle the word that best describes the tone:

   light-hearted   (excited)   upset

2. "My two kids would be covered, too."

   Denotation: _____ children _____

   What special meaning does the connotation of this word suggest?

   _____ "Kids" suggests a fondness or an affection toward the children. _____ .

   Circle the word that best describes the tone:

   (informal)   formal   informed

Your Own Assumptions

When you make an inference, you are using information you already have to make connections. It usually serves us well to make use of our assumptions as we put clues together. **Assumptions** are ideas we hold based on our previous beliefs and experience; they are ideas that we take for granted, that we no longer question. However, we need to be careful, since sometimes these assumptions may be proven wrong or not relevant for the present circumstances. For example, the young man who appeared to be an art student at your college might instead be a young art teacher. Perhaps you assumed too easily that all young people are students.

connect now

When can making an assumption cause problems?

As you read "A Letter to My Teacher," think about your own assumptions—about poverty, about single mothers. See which of your assumptions were matched by the reading and which—if any—needed to be reexamined.

APPLY THE NEW STRATEGY
Make Inferences

Now that you understand Strategy 9, put it into practice with Reading 17, "A Letter to My Teacher."

You've already looked for implied ideas in several passages from this reading. As you skim through the reading to predict what the writer's overall point will be, keep in mind the beginning of her letter: she didn't belong in college. Put that idea together with the end of her letter where she writes to say "thanks" and to say she is teaching at a university. What will your overall-point question be?

A Letter to My Teacher

READING 17 KATE BOYES

Kate Boyes lives in Smithfield, Utah. She is the author of a monthly magazine column on living simply, as well as poems and essays. She is also a writer-in-residence in public schools. This reading comes from an anthology called *Fortitude: True Stories of True Grit*, published in 2000.

Dear Professor, 1

I didn't belong in college. I should have told you that. My father dropped 2 out of school after third grade. My mother went through twelfth grade, but her family thought she was a little <u>uppity</u> for doing so. Like my mother, I finished high school, and immediately got married and started having babies. A decade and a half later, I was a divorced single parent, working as a babysitter during the day and clerking part-time nights in a food store. My income fell far below the poverty level, where I'd lived for much of my life. Statisticians said I didn't belong in college. Who was I to argue?

But one night when I was emptying the trash at the end of my shift, I 3 noticed a brightly colored catalog in the dumpster behind the store. I fished it out and wiped the ketchup drips off the cover. Flipping through the catalog later, I discovered it listed all the courses available at the local college.

And I discovered something else: Taking only one course would make 4 me eligible for student health insurance. Neither of my jobs included benefits, and every time my kids came down with a cold, I worried about what would happen to us if we were really sick. I did some careful calculations. If I took one college course each semester for a year, the cost of tuition, books and fees would be far lower than even six months of private insurance. My two kids would be covered, too. What a deal!

5   Becoming a student was a great <u>scheme</u>. But I knew, when I took my first course from you, that I was an <u>impostor</u>.

6   The very first day of that sociology class, you made an announcement that threatened to expose me. "At the end of the semester, each student will be required to make an oral presentation," you told us.

7   My stomach began to churn relentlessly at the thought of speaking in front of the class. "How was school today, honey?" my youngest daughter greeted me when I got home, doing a creditable imitation of my usual after-school question to her. But I was already halfway down the hall to the bathroom where I promptly <u>lost my lunch</u>.

8   Weeks passed before I could sit through class without nausea. I talked myself into going to class each day by telling myself, over and over, that I was doing this for my kids. I went early to claim the only safe seat—back row, aisle. Close to the door. Just in case. Back with the whisperers and the snoozers, behind the tall man who always read the student newspaper during class, I chewed the fingernails on one hand while I took notes with the other.

9   I needed three credits. I didn't need the <u>agony</u> of a presentation. I considered dropping your course and signing up for something else. Anything else. But I stayed, although I didn't know why. You were new to teaching, and your lectures certainly weren't <u>polished</u>. You gripped the <u>lectern</u> like a shield and sometimes your voice died out in the middle of a sentence. But your enthusiasm for your subject left me longing to know more. I looked forward to a few quiet hours each week—those rare times when the store was empty or my little ones were napping—that I spent reading, writing, and thinking about what I'd heard in your class.

10   One day while I was thinking, I recalled a fascinating lecture you had given on the importance of defining terms. And I noticed that your syllabus hadn't defined "oral presentation." Perhaps I had discovered a way out of the ordeal I dreaded. When the time came for my presentation at the end of the semester, I carried a tape recorder to the front of the room, pushed "play," and returned to my seat, where I listened with the other students to the oral presentation I'd taped the night before.

11   When I signed up for the next course you taught, a course on women who had shaped American culture and history, I expected you would require another oral presentation. But I figured a little agony while I started a tape recorder wouldn't be so bad.

12   In this second course, you came out from behind the lectern and moved up and down the aisles as you spoke. You often stood at the back of the room when you made an important point. Whispering and sleeping ceased when you did that; all heads turned in your direction. You spoke confidently and smoothly, and you called on us by name.

13   I was so caught up in the class that a few weeks passed before I read the syllabus carefully. Then I found your long and precise definition of "oral presentation," a definition that excluded the use of tape recorders. To be

Becoming a student was a great scheme. But I knew, when I took my first course from you, that I was an impostor.

sure I understood, you stopped by my desk one day and said, "This time, I want it live!"

College was sharpening my critical thinking skills, and I put those skills **14** to work when choosing the subject for my presentation. I would speak about Lucretia Mott, a Quaker feminist. When my turn dawned, I came to class dressed like Lucretia, in a long skirt and shawl, a black bonnet covering most of my face. Standing before the other students, I spoke in the first person. Acting a part, I felt as if someone else were giving that presentation.

By the time we met again in the classroom, I had had to admit to myself **15** that I was in college for more than my health. I'd scraped together enough credits to be one quarter away from graduation. I had a lean program of study that allowed no frills, just the courses essential for my degree. Your course didn't fit my program, but I decided to take it anyway, and I skipped lunch for weeks to pay for the extra credits.

When you handed back our first exam, mine had a note scribbled **16** alongside the grade. You said you wanted me to give my presentation for this course. Not a tape recorder. Not a persona. My body tensed and my breathing grew shallow as I felt the same panic that had gripped me during my first course with you. My only comfort came from knowing that by the time I recovered from fainting during my presentation, the quarter would be over and I would have my degree.

You didn't lecture in this course. You pushed the lectern into a corner **17** and arranged our chairs in a circle. You sat with us, your voice one among many. You gave direction to discussions that we carried on long after class periods officially ended. I came early, not to claim an escape seat but to share ideas with other students. I stayed late to be part of the continuing conversation.

Three can be a magic number. One day, toward the end of that third **18** course, you turned to me and said, "Kate, would you share with the class what you've learned about the dangers of moving elderly folks from one living place to another?" This was the subject I'd been researching for my presentation, and I knew it cold. I rose and moved to the chalkboard to draw a graph of my findings. Then I stood in front of the class, speaking in my own voice, just as I had spoken during our discussion circles. I was five minutes into my talk when it hit me: I was giving a presentation. My heartbeat accelerated, but I kept my attention on the interested faces before me, and the moment of panic passed. I remember thinking, as I walked back to my seat, that I wasn't an impostor in the classroom any more. I belonged in that room as much as anyone.

I was happy when you stopped to speak with me after class. I thought **19** you might congratulate me on surviving the presentation or on finishing the coursework for my bachelor's degree. Instead, you asked where I planned to go to graduate school.

You were doing it again! Every time I crept over the line between the **20** familiar and the unknown, you pushed the line a little farther forward. I steamed out of the classroom. *She has already forced me to talk in front of people,*

I thought resentfully—or at least, partly so. I'm getting the first college degree in my family. And now she wants more?

21   Weeks later—after graduation, after I'd read all the <u>mindless</u> magazines on the rack at work, after I'd thought about life without the stimulation of classes—I cooled down. And applied to graduate school.

22   I wonder if you knew that the only way I could finance my graduate degree would be by teaching classes as a graduate assistant, a challenge that initially cost me many a sleepless night. The first time my voice gave out in the middle of a lecture, I remembered you. I realized then that you had felt as nervous while teaching as I had felt being taught. I looked over the lectern at a room full of people, many of whom probably felt as I once had: nervous, unsure, but anxious to learn. And I stopped the lecture and arranged the chairs in a circle.

23   So I write this letter to say thanks. Thanks for opening the circle and thanks for opening my mind. And thanks for giving me a push when I needed it.

24   By the way, my graduate degree opened up a great job for me. Yes, you guessed it—I'm teaching at a university. With health insurance.

25   Gratefully, Kate Boyes

ACTIVE READERS RESPOND

After you've finished reading, use these activities to respond to "A Letter to My Teacher." You may write your answers in the spaces provided or on a separate sheet of paper.

VITAL VOCABULARY AND WORD CONNOTATIONS

Most of the words in this reading are probably familiar to you. Take this time to check your understanding of the connotation of words. The following phrases or sentences from the reading contain words with special connotations. For each italicized word, explain what that connotation is and say what meaning the writer implies by that word choice.

a.   ". . . her family thought she was a little *uppity* for doing so." (paragraph 2)

_____

b.   "I didn't need the *agony* of a presentation." (paragraph 9)

_____

c.   "Becoming a student was a great *scheme*. But I knew, when I took my first course from you, that I was an *impostor*." (paragraph 5)

_____

d.   "But I was already halfway down the hall to the bathroom where I promptly *lost my lunch*." (paragraph 7)

_____

e.   "You gripped the *lectern* like a shield . . ." (paragraph 9)

_____

f.   "I'd *scraped together* enough credits . . ." (paragraph 15)

_____

g. "I had a *lean* program of study that allowed no frills . . ." (paragraph 15)

_____

h. "This was the subject I'd been researching. . . , and I *knew it cold.*" (paragraph 18)

_____

i. "I *steamed out* of the classroom." (paragraph 20)

_____

SKILLS EXERCISE

A. STATED VERSUS IMPLIED IDEAS

In these sentences the author gives a lot of information, both stated and implied. First, note the following stated ideas. Fill in the blanks with information that is spelled out in the passage.

1. Boyes skipped lunch _____for weeks_____ to pay for a course.

2. Boyes now teaches at a _____university_____ and has _____health insurance_____ .

3. During one of her first lectures, Boyes stops and arranges _____the chairs in a circle_____ .

Now look for implied ideas in this passage. Try "putting two and two together" about the situations and people by seeing what the separate pieces of information add up to.

1. What can you infer about Boyes from the way she handled the first two oral presentations?

   (Answers will vary.) _____

   _____

2. What kind of relationship can you infer developed between Boyes and her teacher over the three

   courses? Give evidence for your answer. (For example, why was she so angry at the teacher for asking

   her about graduate school?)

   (Answers will vary.) _____

   _____

3. Boyes never explains why she had such an extreme fear of public speaking. Can you make an educated

   guess based on what she tells us about herself?

   (Answers will vary.) _____

   _____

B. WORD CHOICE

In each of these sentences, consider the denotation of the underlined word; then, explain the connotation associated with the word choice. Finally, identify the tone of the sentence.

1. "Weeks later—after graduation, after I'd read all the <u>mindless</u> magazines on the rack at work, after I'd thought about life without the stimulation of classes—I cooled down." (paragraph 21)

   Denotation:

   _____

   What special meaning does the connotation of this word suggest?

   _____

Circle the word that best describes the tone:

angry   (calm)   upset

2. "You were new to teaching, and your lectures certainly weren't <u>polished</u>." (paragraph 9)

Denotation:

_____

What special meaning does the connotation of this word suggest?

_____

Circle the word that best describes the tone:

(honest)   mean-spirited   jealous

OBJECTIVE OPERATIONS

1. Who is the writer's intended audience?
   a. general audience
   b. students
   c. teachers
   (d.) Boyes' professor

2. What is the author's purpose?
   (a.) to inform
   b. to persuade
   c. to entertain

3. What is the tone of the passage?
   (a.) grateful
   b. informative
   c. apathetic
   d. acerbic

4. Boyes decided to take her first college course primarily because
   a. she was tired of working two jobs.
   b. she found an interesting course in the catalogue she'd fished out of the trash.
   (c.) she could get health insurance for herself and her children.
   d. she wanted to prove the statisticians wrong about her not belonging in college.

5. The word "statistician" in paragraph 2, line 9, most nearly means
   a. expert in statics.
   (b.) expert in statistics.

   c. someone who doesn't move.
   d. people who hate statistics.

6. Which of the following sentences best summarizes this passage?
   a. Boyes was happy she went to college.
   b. Boyes learned a great deal when she went to college and became a teacher.
   (c.) Boyes realized that one professor had a profound impact on her education and wished to thank her.
   d. Boyes realized that one professor had a profound impact on her education.

7. What is the implied main idea of paragraph 21?
   a. Boyes became a teacher due to her professor's influence.
   (b.) Boyes realizes the importance of studies to her life and admits that grad school is a logical step.
   c. Boyes calmed herself by imitating her former professor.
   d. Boyes is her former professor.

8. Her teacher's enthusiasm made Boyes want to stay in her class, even though her teacher
   a. demanded too much homework.
   b. was boring and repetitive.
   (c.) was nervous and inexperienced.
   d. relied too much on student presentations.

9. Which sentence provides support for this sentence (paragraph 8, line 1): "Weeks passed before I could sit through class without nausea."

   a. "I talked myself into going to class each day by telling myself, over and over, that I was doing this for my kids."

   b. "I went early to claim the only safe seat—back row, aisle."

   c. "Close to the door."

   d. "Back with the whisperers and the snoozers, behind the tall man who always read the student newspaper during class, I chewed the fingernails on one hand while I took notes with the other."

10. The author's claim that she didn't belong in college (paragraph 2, line 1) is

    a. adequately supported with details.

    b. inadequately supported with details.

11. What is the topic of paragraph 17?

    a. how the professor adjusted her teaching style

    b. how Boyes controlled herself

    c. how the professor controlled herself

    d. how Boyes adjusted to being a student

12. For her first oral presentation Boyes avoided speaking in front of the class by taping her talk. For her second presentation

    a. she played a tape of Lucretia Mott speaking to a crowd of Quakers.

    b. she had to be herself, no tape, no taking on a persona.

    c. was too nervous to speak and had to leave the classroom.

    d. she pretended to be the person she was talking about.

13. Identify the relationship between the parts of this sentence from paragraph 9.

    "But your enthusiasm for your subject left me longing to know more." (lines 5–6)

    a. cause and effect

    b. time order

    c. statement and clarification

    d. contrast

14. For paragraph 8, the author organizes the information by giving

    a. examples.

    b. contrasts.

    c. definitions.

    d. comparisons.

15. The most important improvement in teaching technique that the teacher made by the third course Boyes took is that

    a. she didn't lecture; she instead engaged students in discussions.

    b. she had control over the class and prevented any whispering and sleeping.

    c. she gave up student oral presentations in favor of her own well-organized lectures.

    d. she made more demands on her students and expected class discussions to last long after the official end of class.

16. The word "relentlessly" in paragraph 7, line 1, most nearly means

    a. nonstop.

    b. nicely.

    c. mercilessly.

    d. kindly.

17. Identify the relationship between the following sentences (paragraph 10, lines 4–7): "When the time came for my presentation at the end of the semester, I carried a tape recorder to the front of the room, pushed 'play,' and returned to my seat, where I listened with the other students to the oral presentation I'd taped the night before."

    a. spatial order

    b. process order

    c. time order

    d. example

18. From the way Boyes handled the first two oral presentations, you can infer that

    a. she had been physically abused by her father for not doing an oral presentation in high school.

    b. she was clever and resourceful in meeting the demands of a course.

    c. she really was an impostor in the classroom.

    d. she was unable to fulfill the assignments and wasn't yet ready for college.

19. What is the relationship between the parts of the following sentence (from paragraph 4)?

    "If I took one college course each semester for a year, the cost of tuition, books and fees would be far lower than even six months of private insurance." (lines 5–7)

a. definition and example

b. comparison

c. cause and effect

d. classification

20. According to the author, becoming a student was a great scheme, which

a. indicates her sense that she is fooling others about her level of interest in college studies.

b. indicates her confidence in herself as a student.

c. shows her cleverness in preparing for college.

d. shows her willingness to admit that she is a liar.

READERS WRITE

1. What led Boyes to decide to take her first college course?

(Answers will vary.) _____

_____

2. Why did she stay in that first class, even though she was terrified of giving the required oral presentation? What were her teacher's strengths and weaknesses?

(Answers will vary.) _____

_____

3. You read earlier that Boyes gave her second oral presentation by playing the role of Lucretia Mott. How did she handle giving her first oral presentation? What did her teacher demand of her for her last oral presentation?

(Answers will vary.) _____

_____

4. What improvements do we see in the way the teacher taught class throughout the three courses Boyes took with her?

(Answers will vary.) _____

_____

5. Is there a statement of the overall point? If so, where? If not, write your own.

(Answers will vary.) _____

_____

READERS DISCUSS

1. Boyes had to overcome several obstacles to be a successful student. What are some of your own obstacles? What are some of your ways of overcoming them? Discuss ideas for succeeding in college with other students.

(Answers will vary.) _____

_____

2. Have you had a teacher in the past who had the kind of positive influence that Boyes' teacher had on her? If so, describe this teacher. If not, what kind of teacher can you imagine who would help you in that way? Share your ideas about good teachers with other students.

(Answers will vary.) _____

_____

1 | Look for what is implied as well as what is stated outright.

2 | Use the logic of "putting two and two together."

3 | Notice the details.

4 | Notice the word choice.

5 | Examine your assumptions.

Summary

CHAPTER 9

HOW DOES STRATEGY 9 HELP YOU BECOME AN ENGAGED READER?

Like using patterns of thought (Strategy 7), making inferences is a familiar way we have of understanding what others are doing and saying. *Making inferences* gives you a more complete understanding of a reading because you grasp ideas that are implied as well as those that are stated outright. This understanding of the reading allows you to *respond* more fully with your own ideas.

HOW DOES THE MAKE INFERENCES STRATEGY WORK?

This strategy helps you understand ideas in a reading that are implied rather than stated directly. You see pieces of evidence—often certain details or words—and put these pieces together. You then make an inference; that is, you make logical connections and draw conclusions based on that evidence.

Strategy 9 teaches you to look for implied ideas. Sometimes, a writer will state ideas, but sometimes, you must make connections and figure out ideas on your own.

Strategy 9 shows you how to "put two and two together." It reminds you to make logical connections and read between the lines to understand ideas.

Strategy 9 reminds you to pay attention to the details. A writer's choice of details, or lack of details, is important to your overall understanding of a reading.

Strategy 9 reminds you to notice word choice. A writer's word choice will give you clues about the writer's implied ideas.

Strategy 9 teaches you to think about your own assumptions. Based on your personal experience, you may make assumptions about things you know to be true. Your own knowledge enriches your understanding of a reading.

Key Terms

assumptions: ideas we take for granted, based on our previous beliefs and experience

connotation (connotative meaning): refers to the cluster of specialized associations that accompany a word

denotation (denotative meaning): the literal meaning of a word

imply: suggest meaning by using certain words, details, or other evidence

infer (make inferences): make connections and draw logical conclusions based on evidence

Think AGAIN ›

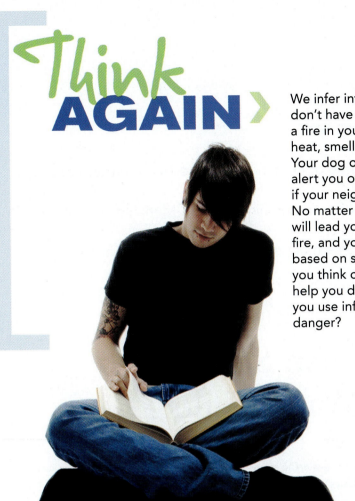

We infer information all the time. For example, you don't have to actually see flames to know there is a fire in your house during the night. You will feel heat, smell or see smoke, or hear flames crackling. Your dog or cat might paw or scratch at you to alert you of danger. You might hear response sirens if your neighbors called emergency rescue for you. No matter how sleepy you feel, all of these clues will lead you to one important inference: There is a fire, and you are in danger. Often, we infer danger based on such clues. What other examples can you think of? When have you used similar clues to help you determine there is danger? When could you use inference to help you determine there is danger?

The title of Reading 18 suggests the pattern of cause-and-effect reasoning—"*Why* Men Don't Last." Look for some main topics that give reasons or causes.

Why Men Don't Last: Self-Destruction as a Way of Life

READING 18 · NATALIE ANGIER

Natalie Angier is a Pulitzer Prize-winning science writer. Her latest book is *The Canon: A Whirligig Tour of the Beautiful Basics of Science*. In this reading, published first in the *New York Times* in 1999, the author examines what leads so many men into self-destructive behavior.

ficus trees: plants found in gyms

1 My father had great habits. Long before ficus trees met weight machines, he was a <u>dogged</u> exerciser. He did push-ups and isometrics. He climbed rocks. He went for long, vigorous walks. He ate sparingly and avoided sweets and grease. He took such good care of his teeth that they looked fake.

2 My father had terrible habits. He was chronically angry. He threw things around the house and broke them. He didn't drink often, but when he did, he turned more violent than usual. He didn't go to doctors, even when we begged him to. He let a big, ugly mole on his back grow bigger and bigger, and so he died of malignant melanoma, a curable cancer, at 51.

3 My father was a real man—so good and so bad. He was also Everyman.

4 Men by some measures take better care of themselves than women do and are in better health. They are less likely to be fat, for example; they exercise more, and suffer from fewer chronic diseases like diabetes, osteoporosis and arthritis.

osteoporosis: disorder causing brittle bones

5 By standard measures, men have less than half the rate of depression seen in women. When men do feel depressed, they tend to seek distraction in an activity, which, many psychologists say, can be a more effective technique for <u>dispelling</u> the mood than is a depressed woman's tendency to turn inward and <u>ruminate</u>. In the United States and many other industrialized nations, women are about three times more likely than men to express suicidal thoughts or to attempt to kill themselves.

6   And yet . . . men don't last. They die off in greater numbers than women do at every stage of life, and thus their average life span is seven years shorter. Women may attempt suicide relatively more often, but in the United States, four times more men than women die from the act each year.

7   Men are also far more likely than women to die behind the wheel or to kill others as a result of their driving. From 1977 to 1995, three and a half times more male drivers than female drivers were involved in fatal car crashes. Death by homicide also favors men; among those under 30, the male-to-female ratio is 8 to 1.

8   Yes, men can be impressive in their tendency to self-destruct, explosively or gradually. They are at least twice as likely as women to be alcoholics and three times more likely to be drug addicts. They have an eightfold greater chance than women do of ending up in prison. Boys are much more likely than girls to be thrown out of school for a conduct or antisocial personality disorder, or to drop out on their own surly initiative. Men gamble themselves into a devastating economic and emotional pit two to three times more often than women do.

9   "Between boys' suicide rates, dropout rates and homicide rates, and men's self-destructive behaviors generally, we have a real crisis in America," said William S. Pollack, a psychologist at Harvard Medical School and co-director of the Center for Men at McLean Hospital in Belmont, Mass. "Until recently, the crisis has gone unheralded."

10   It is one thing to herald a presumed crisis, though, and to cite a ream of gloomy statistics. It is quite another to understand the crisis, or to figure out where it comes from or what to do about it. As those who study the various forms of men's self-destructive behaviors realize, there is not a single, glib, overarching explanation for the sex-specific patterns they see.

11   A crude evolutionary hypothesis would have it that men are natural risk-takers, given to showy displays of bravado, aggression and daring all for the sake of attracting a harem of mates. By this premise, most of men's self-destructive, violent tendencies are a manifestation of their need to take big chances for the sake of passing their genes into the river of tomorrow.

crude evolutionary hypothesis: overly simple, evolution-based theory

12   Some of the data on men's bad habits fit the risk-taker model. For example, those who study compulsive gambling have observed that men and women tend to display very different methods and preferences for throwing away big sums of money.

13   "Men get enamored of the action in gambling," said Linda Chamberlain, a psychologist at Regis University in Denver who specializes in treating gambling disorders. "They describe an overwhelming rush of feelings and excitement associated with the process of gambling. They like the feeling of being a player, and taking on a struggle with the house to show that they can overcome the odds and beat the system. They tend to prefer the table games, where they can feel powerful and omnipotent while everybody watches them."

14   Dr. Chamberlain noted that many male gamblers engage in other risk-taking behaviors, like auto racing, or hang gliding. By contrast, she said, "Women tend to use gambling more as a sedative, to numb themselves and escape from daily responsibilities, or feelings of depression or alienation. Women tend to prefer the solitary forms of gambling, the slot machines or video poker, where there isn't as much social scrutiny."

anodynes: pain relievers

oncology: study of cancer

Yet the risk-taking theory does not account for why men outnumber **15** women in the consumption of licit and illicit anodynes. Alcohol, heroin and marijuana can be at least as numbing and sedating as repetitively pulling the arm of a slot machine. And some studies have found that men use drugs and alcohol for the same reasons that women often overeat: as an attempt to self-medicate when they are feeling anxious or in despair.

"We can speculate all we want, but we really don't know why men drink **16** more than women," said Enoch Cordis, the head of the National Institute on Alcohol Abuse and Alcoholism. Nor does men's comparatively higher rate of suicide appear linked to the risk-taking profile. To the contrary, Paul Duberstein, an assistant professor of psychiatry and oncology at the University of Rochester School of Medicine, has found that people who complete a suicidal act are often low in a personality trait referred to as "openness to experience," tending to be rigid and inflexible in their behaviors. By comparison, those who express suicidal thoughts tend to score relatively high on the openness-to-experience scale.

Given that men commit suicide more often than women, and women **17** talk about it more, his research suggests that, in a sense, women are the greater risk-takers and novelty seekers, while the men are likelier to feel trapped and helpless in the face of changing circumstances.

Silvia Cara Canetto, an associate professor of psychology at Colorado **18** State University in Fort Collins, has extensively studied the role of gender in suicidal behaviors. Dr. Canetto has found that cultural narratives may determine why women attempt suicide more often while men kill themselves more often. She proposes that in Western countries, to talk about suicide or to survive a suicidal act is often considered "feminine," hysterical, irrational and weak. To actually die by one's own hand may be viewed as "masculine," decisive, strong. Even the language conveys the <u>polarized</u>, weak-strong imagery: a "failed" suicide attempt as opposed to a "successful" one.

"There is indirect evidence that there is negative stigma toward men who **19** survive suicide," Dr. Canetto said. "Men don't want to 'fail,' even though failing in this case means surviving." If the "suicidal script" that identifies completing the act as "rational, courageous and masculine" can be "undermined and torn to pieces," she said, we might have a new approach to prevention.

Dr. Pollack of the Center for Men also blames many of men's self- **20** destructive ways on the persistent image of the dispassionate, resilient, action-oriented male—the Marlboro Man who never even gasps for breath. For all the talk of the sensitive "new man," he argues, men have yet to catch up with women in expanding their range of acceptable emotions and behaviors. Men in our culture, Dr. Pollack says, are pretty much limited to a menu of three strong feelings: rage, triumph, lust. "Anything else and you risk being seen as a sissy," he said.

In a number of books, most recently "Real Boys: Rescuing Our Sons From **21** the Myths of Boyhood," he proposes that boys "lose their voice, a whole half of their emotional selves," beginning at age 4 or 5. "Their vulnerable, sad feelings and sense of need are suppressed or shamed out of them," he said—by their peers, parents, the great wide televised fist in their face.

22   He added: "If you keep hammering it into a kid that he has to look tough and stop being a crybaby and a mama's boy, the boy will start creating a mask of bravado."

23   That boys and young men continue to feel confused over the proper harmonics of modern masculinity was revealed in a study that Dr. Pollack conducted of 200 eighth-grade boys. Through questionnaires, he determined their scores on two scales, one measuring their "egalitarianism"—the degree to which they think men and women are equal, that men should change a baby's diapers, that mothers should work and the like—and the other gauging their "traditionalism" as determined by their responses to conventional notions, like the premise that men must "stand on their own two feet" and must "always be willing to have sex if someone asks."

harmonics: (as used here) characteristics

24   On average, the boys scored high on both scales. "They are split on what it means to be a man," said Dr. Pollack.

25   The cult of masculinity can beckon like a siren song in baritone. Dr. Franklin L. Nelson, a clinical psychologist at the Fairbanks Community Mental Health Center in Alaska, sees many men who get into trouble by adhering to sentimental notions of manhood. "A lot of men come up here hoping to get away from a wimpy world and live like pioneers by old-fashioned masculine principles of individualism, strength and ruggedness," he said. They learn that nothing is simple; even Alaska is part of a wider, interdependent world and they really do need friends, warmth and electricity.

siren song in baritone: very attractive idea related to masculinity

26   "Right now, it's 35 degrees below zero outside," he said during a January interview. "If you're not prepared, it doesn't take long at that temperature to freeze to death."

ACTIVE READERS RESPOND

After you've finished reading, use these questions to respond to "Why Men Don't Last: Self-Destruction as a Way of Life." You may write your answers in the spaces provided or on a separate sheet of paper.

VITAL VOCABULARY

Some words in this reading may be unfamiliar to you. Use the methods of Strategy 3 to explain what the listed words mean.

USE CONTEXT CLUES

a. bravado (paragraph 11)

_____

b. enamored (paragraph 13)

_____

c. polarized (paragraph 18) (Note the example clues for this word.)

_____

USE WORD PARTS

a. dogged (paragraph 1)

_____

b. dispelling (paragraph 5)

_____

c. omnipotent (paragraph 13)

_____

USE THE DICTIONARY

Choose the correct definition of each word as it is used in the context of this reading.

a. ruminate (paragraph 5)

_____

b. glib (paragraph 10)

_____

c. premise (paragraph 11)

_____

SKILLS TEST

A. STATED VERSUS IMPLIED IDEAS

In these sentences the author gives a lot of information, both stated and implied. First, note the following stated ideas. Fill in the blanks with information that is spelled out in the passage.

1. When depressed, men use _____drugs and alcohol,_____ while women overeat.

2. Surviving a suicide is considered _____feminine._____

3. To show off their masculinity, men move to _____Alaska._____

Now look for implied ideas in this passage. Try "putting two and two together" about the situations and people by seeing what the separate pieces of information add up to.

1. Why would "displays of bravado, aggression, and daring" attract a harem of mates?

    (Answers will vary.) _____

    _____

2. In paragraph 17, the author says that "in a sense, women are the greater risk-takers and novelty seek-

    ers." In what sense would he describe women that way? (Answers will vary.) _____

    _____

3. What does Dr. Pollack imply would be the advantages for boys and men if they could express a wider

    range of emotions? (Answers will vary.) _____

    _____

B. WORD CHOICE

In each of these sentences, consider the denotation of the underlined word; then, explain the connotation associated with the word choice. Finally, identify the tone of the sentence.

1. "Given that men commit suicide more often than women, and women talk about it more, his research

    suggests that, in a sense, women are the greater risk-takers and novelty seekers, while the men are like-

    lier to feel trapped and helpless in the face of changing circumstances." (paragraph 17)

    Denotation: _____

What special meanings do the connotations of these words suggest?

_____

Circle the word that best describes the tone:

apathetic   (hopeless)   belittling

2. "The <u>cult</u> of masculinity can beckon like a siren song in baritone." (paragraph 25)

Denotation: _____

What special meaning does the connotation of this word suggest? _____

_____

Circle the word that best describes the tone:

sweet   (humorous)   condoning

OBJECTIVE OPERATIONS

1. Who is the writer's intended audience?

   a. men

   b. women

   (c.) general audience

   d. psychologists

2. What is the author's purpose?

   (a.) to inform

   b. to persuade

   c. to entertain

3. What is the tone of the passage?

   a. funny

   b. formal

   c. critical

   (d.) serious

4. In some ways men take better care of themselves than women do. They

   a. turn inward and ruminate, rather than expressing their emotions.

   b. are less likely to be overweight, to die of a chronic disease, or to die in a traffic accident.

   (c.) exercise more, are less likely to be overweight, and suffer from fewer chronic diseases.

   d. exercise more, are less likely to abuse alcohol or drugs, and suffer from fewer chronic diseases.

5. The word "dispelling" in paragraph 5, line 4, most nearly means

   a. forgetting.

   b. casting spells.

   c. cheering up.

   (d.) clearing away.

6. Which of the following sentences best summarizes this passage?

   (a.) Men don't last because their struggle with the definition of being a man causes them to take more deadly risks.

   b. Men don't live as long as women do.

   c. Men don't last because they have to act emotionless, calm, and strong at all times.

   d. Men don't last because they hide behind a mask of bravado.

7. What is the implied main idea of paragraph 18?

   a. If men fail a suicide attempt, they are considered weak.

   b. Men are considered weak if they attempt suicide and succeed.

   (c.) If men fail a suicide attempt, they are considered weak, while women's suicide attempts do not have such strong social stigmas.

   d. Women do not have social stigmas with regard to suicide.

8. The fact that men are four times as likely to die from suicide as women is used as one piece of evidence to show

   (a.) men's tendency to "self-destruct."

   b. the greater numbers of suicide attempts made by men than by women.

   c. men's ability to take better care of themselves than women do.

   d. men's tendency to distract themselves by acting rather than thinking.

9. Which sentence provides support for this sentence (paragraph 15, lines 1–2): "Yet the risk-taking theory does not account for why men outnumber women in the consumption of licit and illicit anodynes."

   a. " 'Women tend to prefer the solitary forms of gambling, the slot machines or video poker, where there isn't as much social scrutiny.' "

   b. "Alcohol, heroin and marijuana can be at least as numbing and sedating as repetitively pulling the arm of a slot machine."

   c. "And some studies have found that men use drugs and alcohol for the same reasons that women often overeat: as an attempt to self-medicate when they are feeling anxious or in despair."

   d. "Nor does men's comparatively higher rate of suicide appear linked to the risk-taking profile."

10. The author's claim that "men don't last" (paragraph 6, line 1) is

   a. adequately supported with details.

   b. inadequately supported with details.

11. What is the topic of paragraph 8?

   a. women's self-destruction

   b. controlling women

   c. men's self-destructive behaviors

   d. controlling poor behaviors

12. In paragraphs 11 through 14, Angier explains the theory that men are greater risk-takers. Then, she challenges that theory by saying that

   a. men who complete a suicide attempt tend to fit a personality profile that is relatively high on the "openness-to-experience" scale.

   b. men outnumber women in the use of alcohol and drugs that numb pain and provide escape from anxiety.

   c. men outnumber women in using food to self-medicate and avoid uncomfortable feelings.

   d. there is a negative stigma attached to men who fail at a suicide attempt.

13. Identify the relationship between the parts of this sentence from paragraph 4.

   "They are less likely to be fat, for example; they exercise more, and suffer from fewer chronic diseases like diabetes, osteoporosis and arthritis." (lines 2–4)

   a. example

   b. time order

   c. process order

   d. contrast

14. For paragraph 5, the author organizes the information by giving

   a. examples.

   b. contrasts.

   c. definitions.

   d. comparisons.

15. Dr. William S. Pollack blames "the persistent image of the dispassionate, resilient, action-oriented male—the Marlboro Man" for many of men's self-destructive tendencies. He says that this image

   a. is responsible for the great rise in lung cancer caused by smoking.

   b. limits the ways in which boys and men are allowed to experience and express their feelings.

   c. takes away a boy's or man's ability to experience any feelings.

   d. teaches them that the only response to any difficult situation is to consider suicide.

16. The word "polarized" in paragraph 18, line 8, most nearly means

   a. opposite.

   b. cold.

   c. north-south.

   d. dissimilar.

17. Identify the relationship between the following sentences (paragraph 7, lines 1–5): "Men are also far more likely than women to die behind the wheel or to kill others as a result of their driving. From 1977 to 1995, three and a half times more male drivers than female drivers were involved in fatal car crashes. Death by homicide also favors men; among those under 30, the male-to-female ratio is 8 to 1."

   a. statement and clarification

   b. comparison

   c. definition

   d. contrast

18. Dr. Pollack implies that boys and men would be better off if they could express a wider range of emotions because

   a. they would be able to rely on women more.

   b. they would be more able to treat women as equals.

   c. they would be more able to display the bravado our culture demands of them.

   d. they would be able to ask for help when they need it.

19. What is the relationship between the parts of the following sentence (from paragraph 17)?

"Given that men commit suicide more often than women, and women talk about it more, his research suggests that, in a sense, women are the greater risk-takers and novelty seekers, while the men are likelier to feel trapped and helpless in the face of changing circumstances." (lines 1–4)

a. contrast

b. comparison

c. cause and effect

d. classification

20. You can infer that

a. the author does not understand why men don't last.

b. the author feels that men will continue to go to Alaska.

c. the author believes men have more emotional control than women do.

d. the author feels men need emotional bonds just as women do.

READERS WRITE

1. In what ways do men take better care of themselves than women do?

(Answers will vary.)

2. What evidence does the author use to show men's tendency to "self-destruct"?

(Answers will vary.)

3. What does the author say is wrong with the first risk-taking theory that she refers to in paragraphs 11 through 14?

(Answers will vary.)

4. Why does Dr. William S. Pollack blame "the persistent image of the dispassionate, resilient, action-oriented male—the Marlboro Man" for many of men's self-destructive tendencies?

(Answers will vary.)

5. Where is the first theory (or hypothesis) about the causes of self-destructive behavior introduced? Where is this theory rejected as an inadequate explanation?

(Answers will vary.)

READERS DISCUSS

1. Do you agree with those in the reading who blame many of men's self-destructive tendencies on having too rigid an idea of what it means to be a man? Compare your response with other students.

(Answers will vary.)

2. Discuss this reading with male and female students. What parts of the reading seemed to have most personal relevance for each student? Do men and women have different reactions to the reading?

(Answers will vary.)

MAKE INFERENCES

1 | Look for what is implied as well as what is stated outright.

2 | Use the logic of "putting two and two together."

3 | Notice the details.

4 | Notice the word choice.

5 | Examine your assumptions.

PRACTICE PAGES

Chapter 9

To practice making inferences, complete the following exercise.

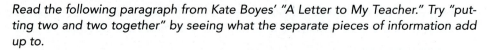

PRACTICE EXERCISE 1

Read the following paragraph from Kate Boyes' "A Letter to My Teacher." Try "putting two and two together" by seeing what the separate pieces of information add up to.

Three can be a magic number. One day, toward the end of that third course, you turned to me and said, "Kate, would you share with the class what you've learned about the dangers of moving elderly folks from one living place to another?" This was the subject I'd been researching for my presentation, and I knew it cold. I rose and moved to the chalkboard to draw a graph of my findings. Then I stood in front of the class, speaking in my own voice, just as I had spoken during our discussion circles. I was five minutes into my talk when it hit me: I was giving a presentation. My heart-beat accelerated, but I kept my attention on the interested faces before me, and the moment of panic passed. I remember thinking, as I walked back to my seat, that I wasn't an impostor in the classroom any more. I belonged in that room as much as anyone.

In this introductory paragraph the author gives a lot of information about herself. Which of these sentences from that paragraph are stated ideas and which are implied? Put "S" for a stated idea, and "I" for an implied idea. If an idea is implied, what clues did you use to determine the information?

1. __I__ The professor knows Boyes is nervous about speaking before the class.

2. __S__ Boyes speaks in the voice she used in discussion circles.

3. __I__ The professor knows Boyes would be fine giving the presentation if she didn't know that was what she was doing.

4. ___S___ Boyes knows her material so well she should have no problem with the presentation.

5. ___S___ Boyes goes to the chalkboard and draws a graph.

6. ___S___ It takes Boyes five minutes to realize she is presenting.

7. ___S___ Boyes allows her panic about giving a presentation to pass without incident.

8. ___S___ Boyes' heart rate increases.

9. ___I___ When Boyes discovers she is presenting, she becomes extremely nervous.

10. ___I___ No one in the classroom realizes that Boyes is as nervous as she is.

11. ___S___ Boyes returns to her seat and no longer feels like an impostor.

12. ___I___ Boyes feels she has earned the right to be in the classroom.

PRACTICE EXERCISE 2

To further practice making inferences, complete the following exercise.

Read the following passage from Barbara Smuts' "A Gorilla's Embrace." Then, answer the questions.

I mingled with these animals under the guise of scientific research, and, indeed, most of my activities while "in the field" were designed to gain objective, replicable information about the animals' lives. Doing good science, it turned out, consisted mostly of spending every possible moment with the animals, watching them with the utmost concentration, and documenting myriad aspects of their behavior. In this way, I learned much that I could confidently report as scientific findings. But while one component of my being was engaged in rational inquiry, another part of me, by necessity, was absorbed in the physical challenge of functioning in an unfamiliar landscape devoid of other humans or any human-created objects save what I carried on my back. When I first began working with baboons, my main problem was learning to keep up with them while remaining alert to poisonous snakes, irascible buffalo, aggressive bees, and leg-breaking pig holes. Fortunately, these challenges eased over time, mainly because I was traveling in the company of expert guides—baboons who could spot a predator a mile away and seemed to possess a sixth sense for the proximity of snakes. Abandoning myself to their far superior knowledge, I moved as a humble disciple, learning from masters about being an African anthropoid.

A. STATED VERSUS IMPLIED IDEAS

In these sentences the author gives a lot of information, both stated and implied. First, note the following stated ideas. Fill in the blanks with information that is spelled out in the passage.

1. Smuts is in the field to study the behavior of _____ baboons.

2. The baboons teach her to be alert to _____ snakes, buffalo, bees, _____ and _____ pig holes.

3. The only human-created objects available are _____ what Smuts carries herself.

Now look for implied ideas in this passage. Try "putting two and two together" about the situations and people by seeing what the separate pieces of information add up to.

1. What does this sentence from the passage imply?

   "Doing good science, it turned out, consisted mostly of spending every possible moment with the animals, watching them with the utmost concentration, and documenting myriad aspects of their behavior." (Does this science seem consistent with what Smuts has learned about science?)

   (Answers will vary.)

   _____

   _____

   _____

335

2. What does this sentence imply?

   "Fortunately, these challenges eased over time, mainly because I was traveling in the company of expert guides—baboons who could spot a predator a mile away and seemed to possess a sixth sense for the proximity of snakes." (Why does Smuts feel she must trust the baboons?)

   (Answers will vary.) _____

   _____

3. In this paragraph, why does Smuts avoid telling you what she is carrying with her?

   (Answers will vary.) _____

   _____

B. WORD CHOICE

In each of these sentences, consider the denotation of the underlined word; then, explain the connotation associated with the word choice. Finally, identify the tone of the sentence.

1. "I mingled with these animals under the guise of scientific research . . ."

   Denotation: _____a ruse_____

   What special meaning does the connotation of this word suggest

   This suggests she is not really working.

   Circle the word that best describes the tone:

         humorous   mean   wary

2. "I mingled with these animals under the guise of scientific research . . ."

   Denotation: _____ _interacted_ _____

   What special meaning does the connotation of this word suggest? _____

   "Mingled" implies that she interacted socially as though she were at a party.

   Circle the word that best describes the tone: casual   humorous   careless

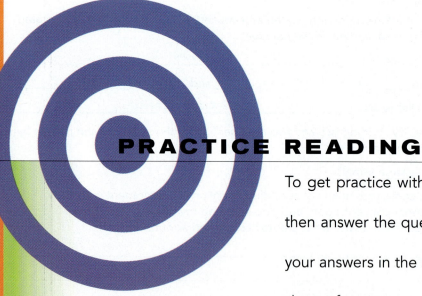

PRACTICE READING

To get practice with reading, read the passage, and then answer the questions that follow. You may write your answers in the spaces provided or on a separate sheet of paper.

Choose appropriate strategies for reading "The Gorilla's Embrace." You'll find it especially helpful to make inferences and look for patterns of thought. Finally, because this reading has no headings, try mapping main topics in pencil first, before marking main ideas.

The Gorilla's Embrace

BARBARA SMUTS

Barbara Smuts is a professor at the University of Michigan, editor of *Primate Societies,* and author of *Sex and Friendship in Baboons.* This reading was published first in the Summer 1999 issue of *Whole Earth.* In this piece Smuts shows how her extensive research on animal behavior has given her both a scientific understanding and a personal, affectionate view of the animals she's studied.

1   For the heart to truly share another's being, it must be an embodied heart, prepared to encounter directly the <u>embodied</u> heart of another. I have met the "other" in this way, not once or a few times in my life, but over and over during years spent in the company of "persons" like you and me, who happen to be nonhuman.

2   These nonhuman persons included gorillas at home in the perpetually wet, foggy mountaintops of central Africa, chimpanzees carousing in the hot, rugged hills of western Tanzania, baboons lazily strolling across the golden grass plains of highland Kenya and dolphins gliding languorously through the green, clear waters of Shark Bay. In each case, I was lucky to be accepted by the animals as a mildly interesting, harmless companion, permitted to travel amongst them, eligible to be touched by hands and fins— although I refrained, most of the time, from touching in turn.

Tanzania and Kenya: countries in East Africa

3   I mingled with these animals under the guise of scientific research, and, indeed, most of my activities while "in the field" were designed to gain objective, <u>replicable</u> information about the animals' lives. Doing good science, it turned out, consisted mostly of spending every possible moment with the animals, watching them with the utmost concentration, and documenting myriad aspects of their behavior. In this way, I learned much that I could confidently report as scientific findings. But while one component of my being was engaged in rational inquiry, another part of me, by necessity, was absorbed in the physical challenge of functioning in an unfamiliar landscape <u>devoid</u> of other humans or any human-created objects save what I carried on my back. When I first began working with baboons, my main problem was learning to keep up with them while remaining alert to poisonous snakes, irascible buffalo, aggressive bees, and leg-breaking pig holes. Fortunately, these challenges eased over time, mainly because I was traveling in the company of expert guides—baboons who could spot a <u>predator</u> a mile away and seemed to possess a sixth sense for the proximity of snakes.

anthropoid: member of primate group of apes (gorilla, chimpanzee, etc.), monkeys, humans

Emily Post: author of books on manners

intersubjectivity: whether humans and baboons have shared experiences or have anything in common such as emotions or language

I developed the knack of sweetly but firmly turning my back on the playful advances of juveniles, conveying, as did the older females, that although I found them appealing, I had more important things to do.

Abandoning myself to their far superior knowledge, I moved as a humble disciple, learning from masters about being an African anthropoid.

Thus I became (or, rather, regained my ancestral right to be) an animal, moving instinctively through a world that felt (because it was) like my ancient home. Having begun to master this challenge, I faced another one equally daunting: to comprehend and behave according to a system of baboon etiquette bizarre and subtle enough to stop Emily Post in her tracks. This task was forced on me by the fact that the baboons stubbornly resisted my feeble but sincere attempts to convince them that I was nothing more than a detached observer, a neutral object they could ignore. Right from the start, they knew better, insisting that I was, like them, a social subject vulnerable to the demands and rewards of relationship. Since I was in their world, they determined the rules of the game, and I was thus compelled to explore the unknown terrain of human-baboon intersubjectivity. Through trial and embarrassing error, I gradually mastered at least the rudiments of baboon propriety. I learned much through observation, but the deepest lessons came when I found myself sharing the being of a baboon because other baboons were treating me like one. Thus I learned from personal experience that if I turned my face away but held my ground, a charging male with canines bared in threat would stop short of attack. I became familiar with the invisible line defining the personal space of each troop member, and then I discovered that the space expands and contracts depending on the circumstances. I developed the knack of sweetly but firmly turning my back on the playful advances of juveniles, conveying, as did the older females, that although I found them appealing, I had more important things to do. After many months of immersion in their society I stopped thinking so much about what to do and instead simply surrendered to instinct, not as mindless, reflexive action, but rather as action rooted in an ancient primate legacy of embodied knowledge. **4**

Living in this way with baboons, I discovered that to be an animal is to be "full of being," full of "joy." Like the rest of us, baboons get grouchy, go hungry, feel fear and pain and loss. But during my times with them, the default state seemed to be a lighthearted appreciation of being a baboon body in baboon-land. Adolescent females concluded formal, grown-up-style greetings with somber adult males with a somersault flourish. Distinguished old ladies, unable to get a male's attention, stood on their heads and gazed up at the guy upside down. Grizzled males approached balls of wrestling infants and tickled them. Juveniles spent hours perfecting the technique of swinging from a vine to land precisely on the top of mom's head. And the voiceless, breathy chuckles of baboon play echoed through the forest from dawn to dusk. **5**

During the cool, early morning hours, the baboons would work hard to fill their stomachs, but as the temperature rose, they became prone to taking long breaks in especially attractive locales. In a mossy glade or along the white-sanded beach of an inland lake, they would shamelessly indulge a passion for lying around in the shade on their backs with their feet in the **6** air. Every now and then someone would concur about the agreeableness of the present situation by participating in a chorus of soft grunts that rippled through the troop like a gentle wave. In the early days of my fieldwork, when I was still preoccupied with doing things right, I regarded these siestas as valuable opportunities to gather data on who rested near whom. But later, I began to lie around with them. Later still, I would sometimes lie around without them—that is, among them, but while they were still busy eating. Once I fell asleep surrounded by 100 munching baboons only to awaken half an hour later, alone except for an adolescent male who had chosen to nap by my side (presumably inferring from my deep sleep that I'd found a particularly good resting spot). We blinked at one another in the light of the noonday sun and then casually sauntered several miles back to the rest of the troop, with him leading the way.

7   There were 140 baboons in the troop, and I came to know every one as a highly distinctive individual. Each one had a particular gait, which allowed me to know who was whom, even from great distances when I couldn't see anyone's face. Every baboon had a characteristic voice and unique things to say with it; each had a face like no other, favorite foods, favorite friends, favorite bad habits. Dido, when chased by an unwelcome suitor, would dash behind some cover and then dive into a pig hole, carefully peeking out every few moments to see if the male had given up the chase. Lysistrata liked to sneak up on an infant riding on its mother's back, knock it off (gently), and then pretend to be deeply preoccupied with eating some grass when mom turned to see the cause of her infant's distress. Apie, the alpha male, would carefully study the local fishermen from a great distance, wait for just the right moment to rush toward them, take a flying leap over their heads to land on the fish-drying rack, grab the largest fish, and disappear into the forest before anyone knew what was happening.

8   I also learned about baboon individuality directly, since each one approached his or her relationship with me in a slightly different way. Cicero, the outcast juvenile, often followed me and sat quietly a few feet away, seemingly deriving some small comfort from my proximity. Leda, the easygoing female, would walk so close to me I could feel her fur against my bare legs. Dakar, feisty adolescent male, would catch my eye and then march over to me, stand directly in front of me, and grab my kneecap while staring at my face intently (thanks to Dakar, I've become rather good at appearing calm when my heart is pounding). Clearly, the baboons also knew me as an individual. This knowledge was lasting, as I learned when I paid an unexpected visit to one of my study troops seven years after last being with them. They had been unstudied during the previous five years, so the adults had no recent experience with people coming close to them, and the youngsters had no such experience at all. I was traveling with a fellow scientist whom the baboons had never met, and, as we approached on foot from a distance, I anticipated considerable wariness toward both of us. When we got to within about one hundred yards, all of the youngsters fled, but the adults merely glanced at us and continued foraging. I asked my companion

to remain where he was, and slowly I moved closer, expecting the remaining baboons to move away at any moment. To my utter amazement, they ignored me, except for an occasional glance, until I found myself walking among them exactly as I had done many years before. To make sure they were comfortable with me, as opposed to white people in general, I asked my friend to come closer. Immediately, the baboons moved away. It was me they recognized, and after a seven-year interval they clearly trusted me as much as they had on the day I left.

Trust, while an important component of a friendship, does not, in and **9** of itself, define it. Friendship requires some degree of mutuality, some give-and-take. Because it was important, scientifically, for me to minimize my interactions with the baboons, I had few opportunities to explore the possibilities of such give-and-take with them. But occasional events hinted that such relations might be possible, were I encountering the baboons first and foremost as fellow social beings, rather than as subjects of scientific inquiry. For example, one day, as I rested my hand on a large rock, I suddenly felt the gentlest of touches on my fingertips. Turning around slowly, I came face-to-face with one of my favorite juveniles, a slight fellow named Damien. He looked intently into my eyes, as if to make sure that I was not disturbed by his touch, and then he proceeded to use his index finger to examine, in great detail, each one of my fingernails in turn. This exploration was made especially <u>poignant</u> by the fact that Damien was examining my fingers with one that looked very much the same, except that his was smaller and black. After touching each nail, and without removing his finger, Damien glanced up at me for a few seconds. Each time our gaze met, I wondered if he, like me, was contemplating the implication of the realization that our fingers and fingernails were so alike.

I experienced an even greater sense of intimacy when, in 1978, I had the **10** exceptional privilege of spending a week with Dian Fossey and the mountain gorillas she had been studying for many years. One day, I was out with one of her groups, along with a male colleague unfamiliar to the gorillas and a young male researcher whom they knew well. Digit, one of the young adult males, was strutting about and beating his chest in an early challenge to the leading silverback male. My two male companions were fascinated by this tension, but after a while I had had enough of the macho energy, and I wandered off. About thirty meters away, I came upon a "nursery" group of mothers and infants who had perhaps moved off for the same reasons I had. I sat near them and watched the mothers eating and the babies playing for timeless, peaceful moments. Then my eyes met the warm gaze of an adolescent female, Pandora. I continued to look at her, silently sending friendliness her way. Unexpectedly, she stood and moved closer. Stopping right in front of me, with her face at eye level, she leaned forward and pushed her large, flat, wrinkled nose against mine. I know that she was right up against me, because I distinctly remember how her warm, sweet breath fogged up my glasses, blinding me. I felt no fear and continued to focus on the enormous affection and respect I felt for her. Perhaps she sensed my attitude, because in the next moment I felt her impossibly

Dian Fossey: researcher of gorillas, subject of movie *Gorillas in the Mist*

long ape arms wrap around me, and for precious seconds, she held me in her embrace. Then she released me, gazed once more into my eyes, and returned to munching on leaves.

11   After returning from Africa, I was very lonely for nonhuman company. This yearning was greatly eased by my dog Safi. Safi and I are equals. This does not mean we are the same; we are, in fact, very different, she with the blood of wolves, me with the blood of apes. It does mean I regard her as a "person." Relating to other beings as "persons" has nothing to do with whether or not we attribute human characteristics to them. It has to do with recognizing that they are social creatures like us whose idiosyncratic, subjective experience of us plays the same role as our subjective experience of them. When Safi or the baboons relate to us as individuals, and when we relate to them as individuals, it is possible for both to have a personal relationship. If a human being relates to a nonhuman being as an anonymous object, rather than as a being with its own subjectivity, it is the human, and not the other animal, who <u>relinquishes</u> personhood.

12   The limitations most of us encounter with other animals reflect not their shortcomings, as we too often assume, but our own narrow views. Treating members of other species as persons, as beings with potential far beyond our normal expectations, will bring out the best in them. Each animal's best includes unforeseeable gifts.

ACTIVE READERS RESPOND

After you've finished reading, use these questions to respond to "The Gorilla's Embrace." You may write your answers in the spaces provided or on a separate sheet of paper.

VITAL VOCABULARY

Some words in this reading may be unfamiliar to you. Use the methods of Strategy 3 to explain what the listed words mean.

USE CONTEXT CLUES

a.   predator (paragraph 3)

_____

b.   somber (paragraph 5)

_____

c.   proximity (paragraph 8)

_____

d.   relinquishes (paragraph 11)

_____

USE WORD PARTS

a.   embodied (paragraph 1)

_____

b. intersubjectivity (paragraph 4)

_____

c. propriety (paragraph 4) The word "proper" is part of this word.

_____

USE THE DICTIONARY

Choose the correct definition of each word as it is used in the context of this reading.

a. replicable (paragraph 3)

_____

b. devoid (paragraph 3)

_____

c. rudiments (paragraph 4)

_____

d. poignant (paragraph 9)

_____

OBJECTIVE OPERATIONS

1. Who is the writer's intended audience?
    a. scientists
    b. women
    c. general audience
    d. primatologists

2. What is the author's purpose?
    a. to inform
    b. to persuade
    c. to entertain

3. What is the tone of the passage?
    a. forgiving
    b. nice
    c. objective
    d. compassionate

4. The work Smuts does is defined as "scientific research" because
    a. she documents every type of animal behavior by recording, filming, and note taking.
    b. her research is designed to gain objective information about the animals' lives that other scientists using the same methods would be likely to find.
    c. her research is designed to allow her to bring the animals out of the wild and into a scientific laboratory.
    d. she brings her equipment from her scientific laboratory into the animals' environment.

5. The word "propriety" in paragraph 4, line 14, most nearly means
    a. basics.
    b. good manners.
    c. friendliness.
    d. biology.

6. Which of the following sentences is the stated overall point of this passage?
    a. "If a human being relates to a nonhuman being as an anonymous object, rather than as a being with its own subjectivity, it is the human, and not the other animal, who relinquishes personhood."
    b. "The limitations most of us encounter with other animals reflect not their shortcomings, as we too often assume, but our own narrow views."
    c. "Treating members of other species as persons, as beings with potential far beyond our normal expectations, will bring out the best in them."
    d. "Each animal's best includes unforeseeable gifts."

7. What is the implied main idea of paragraph 9?
    a. Gorillas have friendships just as humans do.
    b. Gorillas and humans respond to the same personal experiences.

c. Recognizing baboons as fellow social beings might allow closer relations, even friendships, with baboons.

d. Smuts touched a gorilla.

8. It was hard to retain a completely detached, neutral view of the baboons she was studying because

   a. the baboons expected her to join with them as a part of their social organization.

   b. sometimes the baboons became too aggressive and threatened to attack her.

   c. she sometimes found the baboon's behavior too disgusting.

   d. the baboons frustrated her because they kept running away from her.

9. Which sentence provides support for this sentence (paragraph 8, lines 1–2): "I also learned about baboon individuality directly, since each one approached his or her relationship with me in a slightly different way."

   a. "Cicero, the outcast juvenile, often followed me and sat quietly a few feet away, seemingly deriving some small comfort from my proximity."

   b. "Leda, the easygoing female, would walk so close to me I could feel her fur against my bare legs."

   c. "Dakar, feisty adolescent male, would catch my eye and then march over to me, stand directly in front of me, and grab my kneecap while staring at my face intently (thanks to Dakar, I've become rather good at appearing calm when my heart is pounding)."

   d. all of the above

10. The author's claim that she developed intimate relationships with the gorillas (paragraph 10, lines 1–3) is

    a. adequately supported with details.

    b. inadequately supported with details.

11. What is the topic of paragraph 11?

    a. the author's dog Safi

    b. seeking nonhuman company

    c. personal relationships

    d. being nonhuman

12. The main lesson Smuts gains from the gorilla's embrace was

    a. how surprisingly sweet the breath of a gorilla could be.

    b. how impossibly long the arms of a gorilla are as they wrapped around her.

    c. how much intimacy and respect there can be between a "wild" animal and a human being.

    d. how little cause she had for feeling terrified of the gorilla.

13. Identify the relationship between the parts of this sentence from paragraph 8.

    "They had been unstudied during the previous five years, so the adults had no recent experience with people coming close to them, and the youngsters had no such experience at all." (lines 12–15)

    a. definition and example

    b. time order

    c. cause and effect

    d. contrast

14. For paragraph 6, the author organizes the information by giving

    a. examples.

    b. contrasts.

    c. steps.

    d. spatial order.

15. Smuts had proof of how well the baboons got to know and trust her as an individual human being when

    a. she visited the same group seven years later and they accepted her, while running away from the fellow scientist they'd never seen before.

    b. a female baboon came up to her and embraced her.

    c. she would return after trips into town with a fellow scientist, they would run away from him, but greet her warmly.

    d. she fell asleep among them, and they covered her with leaves.

16. The word "poignant" in paragraph 9, line 14, most nearly means

    a. upsetting.

    b. tragic.

    c. charming.

    d. touching.

17. Identify the relationship between the following sentences (paragraph 4, lines 14–18): "I learned much through observation, but the

deepest lessons came when I found myself sharing the being of a baboon because other baboons were treating me like one. Thus I learned from personal experience that if I turned my face away but held my ground, a charging male with canines bared in threat would stop short of attack."

a. statement and clarification

b. comparison

c. cause and effect

d. contrast

18. Smuts' fundamental belief about the way we should interact with animals is that we should

a. look for the human attributes in them.

b. train them so that the human attributes in them can be developed.

c. accept them as the independent, wild creatures they are.

d. treat them like individuals, using the care and respect we would like to be treated with ourselves.

19. What is the relationship between the parts of the following sentence (from paragraph 6)?

"Once I fell asleep surrounded by 100 munching baboons only to awaken half an hour later, alone except for an adolescent male who had chosen to nap by my side (presumably inferring from my deep sleep that I'd found a particularly good resting spot)." (lines 13–16)

a. time order

b. process order

c. cause and effect

d. classification

20. Based on the gorilla Pandora's hug, you can infer that

a. the author does not like gorillas.

b. the gorilla shows acceptance of Smuts.

c. the author knows the gorilla shares her experience.

d. the gorilla wants to be Smuts' friend.

1. Smuts studies animals by researching from afar and never walking or interacting among the animals. True or (False)

2. Fear made it hard to retain a completely detached, neutral view of the baboons she was studying. (True) or False

3. _____Damien_____ explored Smuts' fingers and seemed to compare them to his.

4. When not studying apes, Smuts' companion is a dog named _____Safi._____

5. What are some examples Smuts gives of the individual differences she finds among all the different baboons she gets to know? (Answers will vary.) _____
   _____
   _____
   _____

6. What incident does Smuts tell that shows how well the baboons got to know and trust her as an individual human being? (Answers will vary.) _____
   _____
   _____
   _____

10

Find Meaning in Metaphors

imagine this

When we watch children play, we often describe their actions with colorful language. For example, maybe your younger brother tears up the living room in a such a way that you can follow his path of destruction; while doing so, you may be thinking, "The little tornado! Just look at this disaster!" Or you might say that your younger sister wouldn't do harm to anyone because she is "as sweet as pie."

We often use colorful descriptions so that our audience knows what we are talking about and can visualize the description. The colorful images are called metaphors and similes. Writers use them to enrich the stories that they tell, and readers recognize that these non-literal expressions enrich their reading experience. If you've compared your brother to a tornado or your sister to a pie, you already know how to use metaphors and similes.

Think FIRST >

- Do you enjoy using colorful language and images to express your ideas? Do you like to make comparisons to ensure people understand your ideas?

- Are you intrigued when others compare unlike items, such as, "These old jeans are as soft as the skin of a peach" or "Our teacher is a wicked old ogre"? Do you recognize the deeper meaning?

INTRODUCTION TO THE NEW STRATEGY
Find Meaning in Metaphors

Strategy 10—*Find Meaning in Metaphors*—builds on what you already know by explaining how to interpret these imaginative expressions. Our everyday language is full of expressions that use words in unexpected ways to create a vivid, often visual, impression.

connect now

We know what "traffic bottlenecks" are. They are not, literally, the necks of bottles on highways. They are lanes narrowing down—just as a bottle narrows at its neck—with too much traffic trying to squeeze into too narrow a space. Used in this way, "bottleneck" is a **metaphor**, a comparison that uses an object or idea in place of another to suggest a likeness or a picture in our minds. (Clean living rooms, for instance, are often struck by tornadoes also known as younger brothers.)

What would our language be like without colorful expressions such as metaphors and similes?

A metaphor is a figure of speech, an expression that heightens the effect and meaning of language. Metaphors make our language more colorful and interesting; in addition, they help writers to express

THE READER'S EDGE: BOOK TWO

themselves and help readers understand new ideas. Strategy 10 will show you how to recognize and interpret metaphorical expressions that are not part of our ordinary speech.

Metaphorical Expressions

Metaphorical expressions are based on a surprising comparison that highlights a particular image or idea. When words are used metaphorically, you cannot take them literally. That is, these words don't have their ordinary or primary meanings. They are being used as a comparison to something else—a bottleneck to a narrow passage for traffic, for example.

Here is another example of metaphorical expression. How is "rusty" used in the following sentences?

I haven't played the piano in such a long time. I'm really rusty.

Look at the chart below to see how "rusty," which literally refers to the "reddish, brittle coating on metal left in moist air," can also describe a human being.

There are hundreds of common expressions we use metaphorically, not literally—"tip of the iceberg," "a ton of work to do," or "cool as a cucumber." What other examples can you come up with? You might be surprised by how many metaphors you use on a daily basis.

Metaphorical expressions actually come in two types—similes and metaphors. Both are **figurative expressions** or figures of speech. They are based on an imaginative comparison.

Hot or Not?

When might a metaphor seem inappropriate?

Interpret the Metaphor: How Can a Pianist Be *Rusty?*

1. What two things are being compared?

Iron tools **unused for a long time,** therefore covered with reddish, brittle coating.

Piano skills **unused for a long time.**

2. What characteristic do these two things have in common?

Lack of use over a long time.

3. What does the metaphor mean in literal terms?

"I'm rusty" in literal terms means, "I'm out of practice—I **haven't used my skills in a long time.**"

> Sarah Rice, an information architect who helps make programs and ideas more user-friendly, suggests that metaphors are necessary to help familiarize us with new technology. Without metaphors, we would have had difficulty understanding what a car, e-mail, or the Internet is.

Metaphors are used every day. We are all familiar with them and what they are. They help us understand conceptual ideas, convey complex notions and have a shared understanding so that we can talk to each other using verbal shorthand. Take electronic mail, otherwise known as email, as an example. Email seems so much like regular mail, except that there is no paper, no ink, no envelope, no postage stamp, and no postal carrier. There is, however, something familiar about composing a message and sending it to someone else.

What about the wildly popular Tivo's metaphor? I applaud the decision to use a well-known comparison to explain what the product does: the video cassette recorder. Tivo does replicate many of the VCR's abilities . . . and yet it offers so much more! We're so overjoyed to be able to pause live TV that we overlook the fact that Tivo won't play your video cassette tapes or let you transfer recorded shows from one machine to another, and it requires a monthly fee.

Metaphors help us grasp new things, but they don't necessarily account for all aspects of that idea. VCRs couldn't pause live TV; regular postal mail couldn't arrive at its destination 3.2 seconds after it had been sent. The main characteristics of the original metaphor allow us to understand the basics of the new; the rest we learn over time. Moreover, the original metaphor helps us easily understand why a product might be useful or necessary, which means we're more likely to adopt it into our daily lives.

Adoption metaphors have a lifecycle. They begin by introducing a new concept. They help us map something new to something we already understand and give us a framework in which to understand the new thing. After a while, the concept isn't new anymore, and people usually understand it pretty well without needing the original metaphor. The internet is a perfect example. Remember the term "Information Superhighway"? It was such a buzzword back in the 1990s. Although the internet had been around for a while, its introduction as an information superhighway helped frame the whole idea so that others could understand it. They could understand it because it was framed in terms of their daily lives. Do we still use the term "information superhighway"? Not much. Does this mean that we don't use the internet anymore? Is it gone from our minds the same way the term has gone away? Hardly! The internet is such a pervasive part of our culture now. It is everyday. It is mundane. It's the exception rather than the rule to have no internet connection available to you. We are offered connections at work, at home, in coffee shops, through cell phones and in most public libraries.

Rice, Sarah. "Using Adoption Metaphors to Increase Customer Acceptance." Boxes and Arrows. June 5, 2006. 15 July 2009. Available: www.boxesandarrows.com/view/using_adoption_

Simile

A **simile** is a clear-cut or explicit comparison, because it uses the words "like" or "as." "The fear was like an iron band that squeezed her chest, making it difficult to breathe" is a simile that shows how constricting fear can be.

Metaphor

A metaphor is an implied comparison that does not use like or as. See the contrast between a simile and a metaphor in the following chart:

simile	*explicit* comparison, using "like" or "as"	"Fear was like an iron band that squeezed her chest, making it difficult to breathe."
metaphor	*implied* comparison	"Fear was an iron band that squeezed her chest, making it difficult to breathe."

Literal versus Metaphorical Expressions

We make **literal** comparisons all the time between things that have obvious similarities. For example, we can better understand what our family

The concept of the internet has been so well adapted into our culture, that it is now being used as a metaphor itself for other things. The language of the net pervades our everyday lives. For example, last week I was interviewing a woman who talked about a meeting she had with her supervisor because she needed to get up to speed on a project. Two years ago, she might have said that he informed her, he briefed her, he told her everything he could about what he knew on that particular topic. However, she said, "he downloaded it to me." There was no computer in the room. No internet connection was involved. It was a verbal transaction, yet she invoked a metaphor that is widely recognized as being synonymous with online activity (the act of collecting or retrieving an electronic file from a remote location). Instead of an electronic file, it was ideas or thoughts. Instead of being retrieved from a remote server, it was retrieved from the supervisor's brain. Instead of being received onto a computer, it was received into the person's collection of thoughts. Instead of a file being "pulled" from a server and collected on one's own computer, the information was "pushed" from one person and collected by another. As you can see, not all aspects of the metaphor fit precisely, but when she said "he downloaded that information to me," I had no doubt what had happened between the supervisor and the direct report during the lifespan of that meeting.

With this example, you can see the lifecycle of an adoption metaphor, from its introduction, when it is a novel concept first being introduced to the public, to acceptance, when our understanding moves beyond the initial adoption metaphor and fully embraces the concept itself on its own merits. At that point, the metaphor has outlived its usefulness and is either discarded (information superhighway) or becomes mundane (download). You know the adoption metaphor has reached the pinnacle of success when the metaphor itself is used as a metaphor for other things ("where can I get "TiVo" for my radio?"). We don't bother to refer to cars as "horseless carriages", but we often use cars as metaphors for other things. Three quotes from recent articles: "Cops drive home seatbelt safety [in a 3-day game event aimed at high-schoolers] " "Congress Revs Its Engine." "Fitness Beginners learn how to go from zero to sixty with these workout tips."

Metaphors accompany every new technological leap. . . .

pet is like by comparing it to another member of the cat family—a tiger; we can get an idea about flying a plane by comparing it to driving another vehicle—the family car. We expect to compare two kinds of cats or two kinds of vehicles.

However, a metaphor or simile is based on an unexpected, even startling comparison. For example, saying "My younger brother eats like a tiger that's been starving on the grasslands—just look at how he tears into his food at the dinner table!" offers the unexpected comparison of the way a boy eats to the way a starving tiger eats. Or, saying "Using a sewing machine is as easy as driving a car—you just step on the pedal and stay between the lines!" compares using a sewing machine to driving a vehicle, another unusual comparison.

Which one of the following is a literal comparison, and which is a simile?

A Monterey pine leans out over the Pacific . . . and it looks like a wind-swept fir tree.

A Monterey pine leans out over the Pacific . . . and it looks like a shaggy black finger pointing out to sea.

The first is a literal comparison. Why? Because there is no unexpected comparison. The second was written by Diane Ackerman in *A Natural History of the Senses*. It is a simile—a metaphorical comparison. The surprising comparison lets us see the tree overlooking the ocean in a new way.

connect now

When should you stick to a literal explanation rather than a metaphorical one?

EXERCISES

PRACTICE

To practice identifying literal versus metaphorical expressions, complete the following exercise.

Read each of the following examples and decide which is the literal expression and which is the metaphorical expression. Place an L on the blank line if the expression is literal; place an M on the blank line if the expression is metaphorical. Underline the metaphorical expression for the sentence you identify as metaphorical.

1. __M__ . . . your voice caught in the dark cathedral of your skull . . .

   __L__ . . . your voice spoken in the filled cavity of your skull . . .

   From Reading 1: The Voice You Hear When You Read Silently

2. __M__ In a great many other ways he learns that he is worthless, untrustworthy, fit only to take other people's orders, a blank sheet for other people to write on.

   __L__ In a great many other ways he learns that he is worthless, untrustworthy, fit only to take other people's orders, someone for other people to control.

   From Reading 12: School Is Bad for Children

3. __M__ Learning to read was, for slaves, not an immediate right to freedom . . .

   __L__ Learning to read was, for slaves, not an immediate passport to freedom . . .

   From Reading 3: Forbidden Reading

4. __L__ I identified myself as a graduate of the elementary school, and being taken care of by a favorite fifth grade teacher, I was given a small bundle from a locked storeroom . . .

   __M__ I identified myself as a graduate of the elementary school, and being taken under wing by a favorite fifth grade teacher, I was given a small bundle from a locked storeroom . . .

   From Reading 4: "See Spot Run": Teaching My Grandmother to Read

5. __M__ Writing was a way to capture speech, to hold onto it, keep it close.

   __L__ Writing was a way to express oneself with words.

   From Reading 10: talking back

Interpreting Metaphors

We usually understand everyday expressions like "bottleneck" and "rusty" because we've heard them so often. However, you may have to stop and think about what a new metaphor means. Once you recognize that the expression can't be literal, but must be metaphorical, it's helpful to ask three questions to be sure what it means:

1. What two things are being compared?
2. What characteristic do these two things have in common?
3. What does the metaphor mean in literal terms?

See how these questions work to interpret the following metaphor:

There have been tornadoes. They lay their elephant trunks out in the sage until they find houses, then slurp everything up and leave.

From Gretel Ehrlich, "The Solace of Open Spaces"

1. The tornadoes are compared to elephants using their trunks to "slurp" water. This is an unexpected comparison, since a weather system and an animal are not literally alike.
2. The first characteristic they have in common is the tornado's long, funnel-shaped cloud as it touches the ground, which has the same shape as an elephant's trunk. The second characteristic is the way both the tornado and the elephant's trunk suck things up.
3. Wherever a tornado's funnel cloud touches the ground it sucks up everything in its path.

BILL GATES

A Lesson Before Dying

by Ernest Gaines

As one of the wealthiest entrepreneurs in the world, Bill Gates could spend his free time doing just about anything. But instead of jet setting, the former CEO of Microsoft commits his time to charitable causes through the Gates Foundation. Gates' efforts to help those facing injustice and oppression may very well be a reflection of his favorite books. Among others, he cites Ernest Gaines' *A Lesson Before Dying* as being hugely influential. While he is no longer writing computer code, it's good to know he is giving back to the community through donations, as well as his love of reading.

If you liked *A Lesson Before Dying*, you might also like:

The Known World, Edward P. Jones

The House on Mango Street, Sandra Cisneros

Beloved, Toni Morrison

Instructor Tip

Write up a list of common metaphors and similes on the board. You can use examples from magazines, books, newspapers, etc. Ask students the following about each: What two things are being compared? What characteristic do these two things have in common? What does the metaphor mean in literal terms?

Judging the Metaphor

You can tell how effective a metaphor is by seeing what would be lost if the same idea were written in purely literal terms. In this case we would miss the clear picture of the tornado as the elephant's trunk, along with imagining the elephant's slurping action.

EXERCISES

PRACTICE

To get practice with analyzing the metaphor, complete the following exercise.

After reading each passage, first identify the metaphorical expression, saying whether it is a metaphor or a simile. Next, interpret its meaning, using these questions:

1. What two things are being compared?

2. What characteristic do these two things have in common?

3. What does the metaphor mean in literal terms?

1. Looking over his shoulder, Victor spots the red-eyed bobo flying through the trees as if stitching together the forest with the rise and fall of its wings. If the lady is here to see the park, she should not miss the flight of the bobo.

   From Julia Alvarez, "Victor," in Off the Beaten Path: Stories of Place

   (Answers will vary.)
   _____
   _____
   _____

   bobo: bird found in forests of Dominican Republic

2. I still keep in mind a certain wonderful sunset which I witnessed when steamboating was new to me. A broad expanse of the river was turned to blood; in the middle distance the red hue brightened into gold, through which a solitary log came floating, black and conspicuous.

   From Mark Twain, *Life on the Mississippi*

   (Answers will vary.)
   _____
   _____
   _____

   jumar: a brand name for an ascender

   ascender: a device you clamp on a rope to climb up the rope

3. If, for some reason, a [mountain] climber lost his top jumar and his chest roller, he'd fall backward and end up hanging from the ascenders on his feet. There is almost no way to recover from this calamity. You simply hang there, upside down, until you freeze to death. Popsicle on a rope.

   From Tim Cahill, "Terror Unlimited"

   (Answers will vary.)
   _____
   _____
   _____

4. On March 24, 1989, a supertanker ran aground and spilled more than 10 million gallons of crude oil into Prince William Sound in Alaska. This eco-logical disaster was a shocking reminder that our technological tentacles reach far; as we burn gasoline in Los Angeles, Chicago or New York, the impact of our demand for oil is felt thousands of miles away.

   From Campbell et. al., *Biology: Concepts and Connections*

   (Answers will vary.)
   _____
   _____
   _____

5. The valley before me has darkened. I know somewhere out there, too far away to see now, long scarves of geese are riding and banking against these rising winds, and that they are aware of the snow. In a few weeks Tule Lake will be frozen and they will be gone.

From Barry Lopez, "A Reflection on White Geese," in *The Best of Outside*

banking: tilting (while flying)

(Answers will vary.)

_____

_____

6. I pause on a wind-ripped slope of Big Sur. A Monterey pine leans out over the Pacific, making a ledge for the sunset.

From Diane Ackerman, *A Natural History of the Senses*

Big Sur: dramatic part of the California coast line

(Answers will vary.)

_____

_____

APPLY THE NEW STRATEGY
Find Meaning in Metaphors

Now that you understand Strategy 10, put it into practice with Reading 19, "Terror Unlimited."

Choose appropriate strategies for reading "Terror Unlimited." To follow Cahill's ideas, you'll find it especially helpful to make inferences during and after reading. Finally, since this reading has no headings, try mapping main topics in pencil first, before marking main ideas.

Terror Unlimited

READING 19 TIM CAHILL

Tim Cahill is well known for writing about his adventures from a humorous perspective. He is one of the founding editors of the magazine *Outside* and has collected columns from the magazine in his books, such as *Pecked to Death by Ducks* and *Jaguars Ripped My Flesh*. In this reading, taken from *Outside*, he tells about an unexpected kind of terror.

1 I can't remember the host's name—only that the show was one of a series being taped for a proposed talk show on ABC. It was to be called *Stories*. I was a guest on the program. During each and every commercial break I got up and vomited in a wastebasket set discreetly off camera for this purpose.

2 Worst case of stage fright in television history, probably.

3 The format was rather formal: four guys sitting around a coffee table, complete with little cups of coffee, all of us wearing coats and ties.

4 I have never worn a tie since. It's been over ten years now. The show was filmed at seven in the morning, but we were supposed to look as if we'd just finished dinner and were having a spontaneous discussion. My impression was that some network exec had attended a dinner party in which the conversation had been about something other than television and had thought, "Hey, wow—good television."

5 The host said that one of the best episodes they'd filmed so far had to do with people who had seen or had contact with flying saucers. Those folks told good stories.

6 There were two other guests at the coffee table. One was Hugh Downs, the distinguished ABC broadcaster, a gentleman adventurer who once dove in a cage while great white sharks cruised by outside. The other interviewee was Dick Bass, the businessman-turned-mountaineer who, at the time, was the oldest man to have climbed Mount Everest. We were to tell hair-raising stories of manly courage, or so I gathered. My job was to blather on about various adventures I'd written about in the past—in other words, about my life before a sudden and vividly loathsome awareness of personal extinction had confined me to my own house for two months with a condition subsequently diagnosed as panic disorder.

7 Now, the concept of a fearless adventurer suffering panic for no reason at all is High Comedy on the face of it. I knew that. There was a part of me, just observing, that thought: This is actually the funniest story of *Stories*, happening right here on camera: big adventure guy paralyzed by fear, for no apparent reason.

8 Sometime after the second commercial break, when it became achingly obvious that I was suffering through a bout of intense emotional torment, Hugh Downs, a nice guy who is as calm and reassuring in person as he has always been on the small screen, sought to hearten and comfort me. "You know," he said, "the great Ethel Merman once said, 'Stage fright's a waste of time. What can they do, kill me?'"

9 I thought, Thank you, Hugh, you blithering simpleton. Ethel Merman is *dead*. Does that tell you something, anything at all?

10   A stagehand counted down from ten and the filming started again. The host asked, "What would you say your closest call was? Tim? Dick?" He meant, Tell me a tale about how you came face to face with death and spat in its vile face. I could taste the bile rising in the back of my throat. Steel bands tightened around my chest, and I was possessed by a sense of vertigo so intense I could barely catch my breath. I was going to die, perhaps right then and there—but if not then, sometime, sooner or later. The perception wasn't simply academic. It was visceral. Death was nigh, and despite Samuel Johnson's smug prediction, it did not concentrate my mind wonderfully.

Samuel Johnson: 18th-century writer who said that being in danger of dying makes one extremely alert

11   Panic disorder strikes at least 1.6 percent of the population. It is characterized by feelings of intense terror, impending death, a pounding heart, and a shadowy sense of unreality. My own version featured several daily attacks of ten to 30 minutes in which I felt smothered and unable to catch my breath. There were chest pains, flushes and chills, along with a looming sense of imminent insanity. The attacks struck randomly, like lightning out of a clear blue sky. The idea that people might see me in this state of helpless terror was unacceptable. I stayed home, cowering in solitude, unable to read or concentrate or write or even watch television. My overwhelming conviction was that I was going crazy. So when a producer called from ABC and asked me if I wanted to tell hairy-chested stories of virile derring-do, I told her, "You bet." I thought, this terror thing has gone on long enough. I'm going to stroll right over to the abyss and stare directly into it. And I'm going to do it on national TV. Face the fear, boyo.

12   The producer had seen a picture of me climbing El Capitan in Yosemite, on a single rope. It looked pretty scary. Could I talk about that? No problem.

El Capitan: famous, sheer cliff face in Yosemite, California

13   El Cap, I explained, is shaped rather like the prow of a ship, and my companions had anchored a mile-long rope in half a dozen places up top and tossed it over the precipice so that it fell free for 2,600 feet. A half-mile drop.

14   The rope-walking and rappelling techniques we had used are most commonly employed by cavers. Caves generally follow the course of underground rivers, and sometimes these rivers form waterfalls. Over millennia, the rivers sink deeper into the earth, and the bottoms of the waterfalls become mostly dry pits, sometimes hundreds of feet deep. Many cavers like to "yo-yo the pits," which is to say, drop a rope, rappel down, and climb back up solely for the sport of it, never mind the exploration aspect.

rappelling: descend (as from a cliff) by sliding down a rope

15   That's what we were doing at Yosemite: We were going to yo-yo El Cap. Because cavers are Calvinists, we were going to reverse the usual process: We'd climb first in order to "earn" the rappel. I recall standing on the talus slope at the bottom of the vertical granite wall with my climbing companion, photographer Nick Nichols. We calculated that the climb would take us five to six hours. Aside from the cruel weight of cameras that Nick carried, our backpacks contained some bits of spare climbing gear, a few sandwiches, and only two quarts of water. We intended to hydrate big-time before we started, and each of us choked down a gallon of water as we contemplated the cliff face.

Calvinists: Protestants who believe that, to earn a reward, they must work hard first

talus: a slope formed by rock debris

16   Nick wanted me to follow him on the rope, for photographic reasons. His professional sense of the situation told him that the better picture was shoot-

ing down, at my terrified face, with the world dropping out forever below. The alternative was six hours of my butt against the sky. And so we strapped on our gear—seat harnesses, Gibbs ascenders on our feet, a chest roller that held us tight to the rope, a top jumar for safety—and proceeded to climb the rope. There was a goodly crowd of people watching us from the road. Some of them had binoculars.

About an hour into the climb, Nick called down that he had some bad news. The water we had drunk earlier had gone directly to his bladder. I contemplated the physics of the situation and shouted up, "Can't you hold it?" **17**

"Four more hours?" he whined. "No way." **18**

"Why didn't you think of this before we started?" I yelled. I sounded like my father discussing the same subject with me as a child on a long road trip. **19**

In time, we devised a solution that might keep me dry. I climbed up to Nick, undipped my top jumar, popped the rope out of my chest roller, and climbed above the ascenders he wore on his feet before clipping back into the rope. In that position—with me directly behind Nick, my chest against his back and my arms wrapped tightly around him—he unzipped and did what he had to do. It took an <u>inordinately</u> long time to void a gallon of water. The rope was spinning ever so slowly, so that, in the fullness of time, we were facing the road, and the crowd, and the people with binoculars. I feared an eventual arrest for public <u>lewdness</u>. **20**

The television producer listened to the story and suggested the spinning yellow fountain aspect of the El Cap climb wasn't precisely what a family audience might want to hear. She wondered if there was any time during the ascent in which the choice was life or death. **21**

Well, yes, in fact, a certain lack of foresight on my part presented me with a number of unsatisfactory choices. I explained that, as Nick and I climbed, the wind came up and blew us back and forth in exciting 70-foot pendulum swings. This went on for some hours. **22**

Had we simply dropped the rope off the prow of El Cap, the sharp granite rock would have sawed it in half, snap bang splat, like that. Instead, the rope was draped over a long solid rubber tube about as big around as a basketball. Brackets at each end were bolted to the rock so that the tube was placed within an inch of the cliff wall. The final obstacle on the climb was to muscle up over the tube. This was tricky. I was affixed to the rope. The rope itself weighed several hundred pounds and was impossible to drag up over the tube. Instead, there was another rope, a short one, anchored above and dangled over the tube. It was necessary to unclip from the long rope and clip into the short one in order to make the summit—a maneuver I had neglected to consider when I clipped into the long rope on the talus slope five hours earlier. I had been contemplating the climb, not the summit, and had also been preoccupied with a different danger peculiar to this type of climbing: If, for some reason, a climber lost his top jumar and his chest roller, he'd fall backward and end up hanging from the ascenders on his feet. There is almost no way to recover from this <u>calamity</u>. You simply hang there, upside down, until you freeze to death. Popsicle on a rope. **23**

With this in mind, I'd run the long rope through the carabiner that held my seat harness together, reasoning that in a bad upside-down emergency **24**

carabiner: a metal ring used as a connector to hold a freely running rope

I might still be able to pull myself upright. What this rig meant at the summit, however, was that I was going to have to unclip my seat harness to get off the long rope and onto the short one.

25   But . . . a seat harness, as every climber knows, is the essential contrivance that marries one to the rope. Unclipping wasn't certain death, but the probabilities weren't good. I assessed my chances for over an hour. It was getting cold and late. Nick had switched ropes and summited with no problems at all. I, on the other hand, was in deep trouble.

26   The half-mile drop yawning below was sinking into darkness as the sky above burst into flame. This sunset, I understood, might well be my last, and I followed its progress as I would that of a ripening bruise on my thigh: At first the sky seemed very vividly wounded, all bright bloody reds that eventually began an ugly healing process involving pastel oranges and pinks that eventually purpled down into blue-black night. The temperature dropped. My sweat-soaked shirt was beginning to freeze to my body. I would have to do something.

27   *Stories* never made it on the air. Not the adventure segment nor even the one about flying saucers, which proves that sometimes the most fervent of our prayers are actually answered. Hugh Downs has announced his imminent retirement from ABC, and Dick Bass is no longer the oldest man to have climbed Mount Everest.

28   And me? I haven't had a panic attack in ten years, knock wood. My doctor recognized the symptoms straightaway and prescribed certain medications that had an almost immediate ameliorative effect. He suggested therapy as well, but a pamphlet he gave me about panic disorder was pretty much all I needed. There were others, I learned, who have had to deal with uncontrolled anxiety. They included scientists such as Charles Darwin and Isaac Newton; actors Laurence Olivier and Kim Basinger; writers Isaac Asimov and Alfred Lord Tennyson. Barbra Streisand and Sigmund Freud (natch) were on the list, along with the Norwegian Expressionist Edvard Munch, whose signature painting, *The Scream,* seems to me to be the perfect depiction of a panic attack.

29   The idea that I wasn't suffering alone—that the malady had a name—was strangely reassuring. Panic disorder feels like standing on the gallows, the rough rope on your neck, waiting, waiting, waiting for the floor to fall away into the never-ending night. But there is no rope, and no immediate threat. None at all.

30   Personal extinction is surely something to contemplate, but contemplating personal extinction doesn't get the grocery shopping done. In my experience, fear of collapsing into a puddle of terror at the Mini Mart—agoraphobia—feels precisely the same as real physical fear in the face of an actual threat. The difference is this: There is almost always something you can do when confronted with an authentic life-or-death situation.

31   At the summit of El Cap, for instance, my companions rigged up a pair of loops made of webbing, anchored them off, and dropped them over the rubber tube. I placed my feet in the loops and laboriously muscled the heavy

This sunset, I understood, might well be my last, and I followed its progress as I would that of a ripening bruise on my thigh: At first the sky seemed very vividly wounded, all bright bloody reds that eventually began an ugly healing process involving pastel oranges and pinks that eventually purpled down into blue-black night.

long rope up over the roller: a triumph of brute strength over clear thinking. There was no thinking at all, really, not in the ordinary sense of brooding contemplation. Risk sets its own rules, and one reacts to them instinctively, with an empty mind, in a state that some psychologists believe is akin to meditation. And, like those enlightened ones who sit cross-legged in empty rooms, uttering weenie aphorisms, risk-takers sometimes feel they've caught a glimpse into eternity, into the wisdom of the Universe, and into the curve of blinding light itself. Just a glimpse.

We didn't talk about that on *Stories*. Sitting there sweating, waiting to **32** vomit during the commercials, I was incapable of saying what I felt: that the stories we tell are the way we organize our experiences in order to understand our lives. I didn't say that risk is always a story about mortality, and that mortality is the naked and essential human condition. We put these stories together—in poems and essays and novels and after-dinner conversations—in an effort to crowbar some meaning out of the pure terror of our existence.

The stories are <u>prisms</u> through which we perceive the world. They are **33** like the lenses we look through in the optometrist's office: Put them together incorrectly, and it's all a blur. But drop in the correct stories, turn them this way and that, and—all at once—there is a sudden clarity. Call it enlightenment and admit that none of us ever get all the way there. We only see glimpses of it in a flashbulb moment when certain selected stories fall together just right. That's all. In my own case, I know that fear always feels the same, that it is about perceived mortality, and that while courage continually escapes me, appearing on one silly un-aired television show remains the purest and the bravest thing I've ever done.

ACTIVE READERS RESPOND

After you've finished reading, use these questions to respond to "Terror Unlimited." You may write your answers in the spaces provided or on a separate sheet of paper.

VITAL VOCABULARY

Some words in this reading may be unfamiliar to you. Use the methods of Strategy 3 to explain what the listed words mean.

USE CONTEXT CLUES

a. precipice (paragraph 13)

_____

b. inordinately (paragraph 20)

_____

c. lewdness (paragraph 20)

_____

d. calamity (paragraph 23)

_____

Choose the correct definition of each word as it is used in the context of this reading.

a. vertigo (paragraph 10)

_____

b. visceral (paragraph 10)

_____

c. imminent (paragraph 11)

_____

d. virile (paragraph 11)

_____

e. abyss (paragraph 11)

_____

f. prisms (paragraph 33)

_____

SKILLS EXERCISE: FIND MEANING IN METAPHOR

A. *First, read the following interpretation of a tricky metaphor from paragraph 32. Then, use Strategy 10 to identify and interpret three other metaphorical expressions in "Terror Unlimited."*

> We put these stories together . . . in an effort to crowbar some meaning out of the pure terror of our existence. (paragraph 32)

Underline the startling phrase in the sentence.

What two things are being compared?

(Answers will vary.) _____

_____

What characteristic do these two things have in common?

(Answers will vary.) _____

_____

What does the metaphor mean in literal terms?

(Answers will vary.) _____

_____

B. *Now interpret these metaphorical expressions. First identify the expression as a simile or a metaphor. Then analyze the surprising comparison.*

1. ". . . a producer . . . asked if I wanted to tell hairy-chested stories . . ." (paragraph 11)

    (Answers will vary.) _____

    _____

    _____

2. "The [panic] attacks struck randomly, like lightning out of a clear blue sky." (paragraph 11)

    (Answers will vary.) _____

    _____

    _____

3. "The stories are prisms through which we perceive the world." (paragraph 33)

(Answers will vary.)

_____

_____

_____

OBJECTIVE OPERATIONS

1. Who is the writer's intended audience?

   a. risk-takers

   b. television viewers

   c. people with panic disorders

   (d.) general audience

2. What is the author's purpose?

   a. to inform

   b. to persuade

   (c.) to entertain

3. What is the tone of the passage?

   (a.) introspective

   b. hopeless

   c. panicked

   d. serious

4. The idea for the particular episode when Cahill was asked to be on the proposed ABC talk show, called *Stories,* was that the guests would tell

   a. stories of their bouts with panic disorders.

   b. tales of experiences with flying saucers.

   (c.) tales of daring adventures.

   d. stories of being forest rangers in national parks.

5. The word "visceral" in paragraph 10, line 8, most nearly means

   a. logical.

   b. mortal.

   (c.) gut-level.

   d. intuitive.

6. Which of the following sentences is the stated overall point of the passage?

   a. "Worst case of stage fright in television history, probably."

   b. "My job was to blather on about various adventures I'd written about in the past—in other words, about my life before a sudden and vividly loathsome awareness of personal extinction had confined me to my own house for two months with a condition subsequently diagnosed as panic disorder."

   c. "We only see glimpses of it in a flashbulb moment when certain selected stories fall together just right."

   (d.) "In my own case, I know that fear always feels the same, that it is about perceived mortality, and that while courage continually escapes me, appearing on one silly un-aired television show remains the purest and the bravest thing I've ever done."

7. What is the stated main idea of paragraph 15?

   (a.) "That's what we were doing at Yosemite: We were going to yo-yo El Cap."

   b. "Because cavers are Calvinists, we were going to reverse the usual process: We'd climb first in order to 'earn' the rappel."

   c. "I recall standing on the talus slope at the bottom of the vertical granite wall with my climbing companion, photographer Nick Nichols."

   d. "We calculated that the climb would take us five to six hours."

8. Cahill agrees to tape the show and put himself through the "worst case of stage fright in television history" because

   a. he desperately needed the money, since his panic disorder had kept him from working.

   (b.) he hoped to overcome his fears by facing them directly.

   c. he had always wanted to work with the TV host, Hugh Downs.

   d. he wanted to get exposure on television for his book about ascending El Capitan in Yosemite.

9. Which sentence provides support for this sentence (paragraph 14, lines 1–2): "The rope-walking and rappelling techniques we had used are most commonly employed by cavers."

   a. "Caves generally follow the course of underground rivers, and sometimes these rivers form waterfalls."

   b. "Over millennia, the rivers sink deeper into the earth, and the bottoms of the waterfalls become mostly dry pits, sometimes hundreds of feet deep."

   (c.) "Many cavers like to 'yo-yo the pits,' which is to say, drop a rope, rappel down, and climb back up solely for the sport of it, never mind the exploration aspect."

   d. All of the above

10. The author's claim that he "hasn't had a panic attack in ten years" (paragraph 28, line 1) is

    a. adequately supported with details.

    b. inadequately supported with details.

11. What is the topic of paragraph 26?

    a. the dangerous situation looming before Cahill

    b. imminent death at the bottom of the cliff

    c. how to avoid rising panic

    d. what a rope climber does

12. When he says he and his photographer companion were going to "yo-yo" El Capitan, Cahill means that they would

    a. rappel first and then climb back up the cliff wall.

    b. use a bungee cord attached to the top of the cliff wall to bounce up and down.

    c. use special climbing equipment nicknamed "yo-yos" to keep themselves attached to each other during the climb.

    d. climb the cliff wall first, then rappel back down.

13. Identify the relationship between the following sentences from paragraph 11.

    "Panic disorder strikes at least 1.6 percent of the population. It is characterized by feelings of intense terror, impending death, a pounding heart, and a shadowy sense of unreality." (lines 1–3)

    a. definition and example

    b. process

    c. statement and clarification

    d. addition

14. For paragraph 6, the author organizes the information by using

    a. examples.

    b. contrasts.

    c. statement and clarification.

    d. comparisons.

15. The principal danger Cahill had tried to avoid by running the long rope through the carabiner that held his seat harness together was that

    a. the climber would lose his footing and fall to his death.

    b. the climber's companion would be unable to stay connected to him and help him up to the summit.

    c. the climber would fall backward and end up hanging upside down.

    d. the rope would get sawed in half by the sharp granite rock and snap in two.

16. The word "precipice" in paragraph 13, line 3, most nearly means

    a. rock face.

    b. mountain.

    c. edge.

    d. prow of a ship

17. Identify the relationship between the parts of the following sentence (paragraph 15, lines 8–10): "We intended to hydrate big-time before we started, and each of us choked down a gallon of water as we contemplated the cliff face."

    a. summary

    b. addition

    c. time order

    d. classification

18. Cahill explains that the fear that came from his panic disorder felt worse than real physical fear because

    a. when facing a real life-or-death situation, there is almost always something you can do.

    b. when dealing with uncontrolled anxiety you must avoid other people.

    c. real life-or-death situations cause such terror that you forget all your imaginary fears.

    d. a diagnosed panic disorder requires taking medication that may produce dangerous side effects.

19. What is the relationship between the parts of the following sentence (from paragraph 28)?

    "There were others, I learned, who have had to deal with uncontrolled anxiety. They included scientists such as Charles Darwin and Isaac Newton; actors Laurence Olivier and Kim Basinger; writers Isaac Asimov and Alfred Lord Tennyson." (lines 5–8)

    a. contrast

    b. comparison

    c. cause and effect

    d. classification

20. According to the passage,

    a. the author's panic disorder never improved.

    b. the author compares his panic disorder to standing on the gallows.

    c. the author no longer goes on risky adventures.

    d. the author was disappointed that *Stories* did not air.

1. What was the idea behind the proposed talk show on ABC, called *Stories*? Why was Cahill asked to be a guest on the particular episode he describes?

   (Answers will vary.)

   _____

   _____

2. In paragraph 6 Cahill reveals that he had a "condition subsequently diagnosed as panic disorder." Given the terrible effects of the disorder, what makes him agree to tape the show and put himself through the "worst case of stage fright in television history"?

   (Answers will vary.)

   _____

   _____

3. What are the rope-walking and rappelling techniques cavers use that Cahill describes in paragraph 14? What does he mean when he says he and his photographer companion were going to "yo-yo" El Capitan in Yosemite?

   (Answers will vary.)

   _____

   _____

4. What was the principal danger Cahill had tried to avoid by running the long rope through the carabiner that held his seat harness together? What new danger did that maneuver cause for him?

   (Answers will vary.)

   _____

   _____

5. What does Cahill mean by saying in paragraph 30 that "personal extinction is surely something to contemplate, but contemplating personal extinction doesn't get the shopping done"?

   (Answers will vary.)

   _____

   _____

1. Write about a time when you successfully faced a risk of some kind. How did that experience compare to either the psychological or physical risks that Cahill discusses? Share what you would like about this experience with other classmates.

   (Answers will vary.)

   _____

   _____

2. How well did Cahill help you feel the different kinds of fears he experienced? How well could you visualize his ascent up the face of El Capitan. What metaphors or other, literal descriptions were particularly successful?

   (Answers will vary.)

   _____

   _____

Summary

CHAPTER 10

HOW DOES STRATEGY 10 HELP YOU BECOME AN ENGAGED READER?

Like working with new words, *finding meaning in metaphors* helps remove "language barriers" between you and the writer's ideas. By understanding a writer's imaginative uses of familiar words or phrases, you stay in touch with the reading and the writer's ideas so you can *respond* to them with your own thoughts. You might actually find that your response is heightened by the writer's use of metaphorical expressions because they are often visual.

HOW DOES THE FIND MEANING IN METAPHORS STRATEGY WORK?

Strategy 10 teaches you to recognize a metaphor, which is when a word or phrase can not be taken literally. You see that there is some kind of implied comparison (metaphor) or explicit comparison (simile) between two things that are not normally seen as similar.

Strategy 10 encourages you to analyze the metaphor. When you're sure the language is metaphorical, look for the two unlike things that are being compared or look for the quality or characteristic these two things have in common. Then, determine what the metaphor would mean in literal terms.

Key Terms

figurative expression: a nonliteral comparison, often highly visual

literal: the ordinary or primary meaning of a word; for example, "rusty nail" uses the literal meaning of "rusty;" "rusty pianist" uses its metaphorical meaning

metaphor: an implied comparison that does not use "like" or "as"

metaphorical expression: a figure of speech that heightens the effect and meaning of language

simile: a specific kind of metaphorical expression that uses "like" or "as" to make an explicit comparison

Think AGAIN ›

Metaphors "dress up" our language and make it more colorful and interesting. When we tell stories, we frequently use metaphors and similes to express our ideas and help our listeners understand. For example, a waitress in a coffee house used to say, "Your brain is about as big as a pea rolling down a four-lane highway," if she didn't think you were very intelligent. A phrase such as "She was boring" can be made more interesting by adding a metaphor: "She was as boring as a squashed toad on a road in a rainstorm." What phrases can you dress up with a metaphor?

Buckle Up. And Behave.

WILLIAM ECENBARGER

William Ecenbarger is a former contributing editor to *Reader's Digest*. In this *Smithsonian* article, appearing in the April 2009 issue and coinciding with the seatbelt's 50th anniversary, Ecenbarger wonders whether we are more likely to take a risk when safety precautions are in place. For example, will we drive with more abandon if we know our cars have air bags?

1   In the middle of the last century, Volvo began seeking improvements to seat belts to protect drivers and passengers in its vehicles. When the Swedish automaker tried a single strap over the belly, the result was abdominal injuries in high-speed crashes. The engineers also experimented with a diagonal chest restraint. It decapitated crash-test dummies.

2   Volvo then turned to a 38-year-old mechanical engineer named Nils Bohlin, who had developed pilot ejector seats for the Saab aircraft company. Bohlin knew it would not be easy to transfer aerospace technology to the automobile. "The pilots I worked with in the aerospace industry were willing to put on almost anything to keep them safe in case of a crash," he told an interviewer shortly before he died, in 2002 "but regular people in cars don't want to be uncomfortable even for a minute."

3   After a year's research and experimentation, Bohlin had a breakthrough: one strap across the chest, another across the hips, each anchored at the same point. It was so simple that a driver or passenger could buckle up with one hand. Volvo introduced the result—possibly the most effective safety device ever invented—50 years ago; other automakers followed suit. No one can tally exactly how many lives Bohlin's three-point seat belt has spared, but the <u>consensus</u> among safety experts is at least a million. Millions more have been spared life-altering injuries.

> "The pilots I worked with in the aerospace industry were willing to put on almost anything to keep them safe in case of a crash," he told an interviewer shortly before he died, in 2002 "but regular people in cars don't want to be uncomfortable even for a minute."

But before we break out the champagne substitute to honor the three-point seat belt's demi-centennial, we might also consider the possibility that some drivers have caused accidents precisely because they were wearing seat belts.

This counterintuitive idea was introduced in academic circles several years ago and is broadly accepted today. The concept is that humans have an inborn tolerance for risk—meaning that as safety features are added to vehicles and roads, drivers feel less vulnerable and tend to take more chances. The feeling of greater security tempts us to be more reckless. Behavioral scientists call it "risk compensation."

The principle was observed long before it was named. Soon after the first gasoline-powered horseless carriages appeared on English roadways, the secretary of the national Motor Union of Great Britain and Ireland suggested that all those who owned property along the kingdom's roadways trim their hedges to make it easier for drivers to see. In response, a retired army colonel named Willoughby Verner fired off a letter to the editor of the *Times* of London, which printed it on July 13, 1908.

"Before any of your readers may be induced to cut their hedges as suggested by the secretary of the Motor Union they may like to know my experience of having done so," Verner wrote. "Four years ago I cut down the hedges and shrubs to a height of 4ft for 30 yards back from the dangerous crossing in this hamlet. The results were twofold: the following summer my garden was smothered with dust caused by fast-driven cars, and the average pace of the passing cars was considerably increased. This was bad enough, but when the culprits secured by the police pleaded that 'it was perfectly safe to go fast' because 'they could see well at the corner,' I realised that I had made a mistake." He added that he had since let his hedges and shrubs grow back.

Despite the colonel's prescience, risk compensation went largely unstudied until 1975, when Sam Peltzman, a University of Chicago economist, published an analysis of federal auto-safety standards imposed in the late 1960s. Peltzman concluded that while the standards had saved the lives of some vehicle occupants, they had also led to the deaths of pedestrians, cyclists and other non-occupants. John Adams of University College London studied the impact of seat belts and reached a similar conclusion, which he published in 1981: there was no overall decrease in highway fatalities.

There has been a lively debate over risk compensation ever since, but today the issue is not whether it exists, but the degree to which it does. The phenomenon has been observed well beyond the highway—in the workplace, on the playing field, at home, in the air. Researchers have found that improved parachute rip cords did not reduce the number of sky-diving accidents; overconfident sky divers hit the silk too late. The number of flooding deaths in the United States has hardly changed in 100 years despite the construction of stronger levees in flood plains; people moved onto the flood plains, in part because of subsidized flood insurance and federal disaster relief. Studies suggest that workers who wear back-support belts try to lift heavier loads and that children who wear protective sports equipment engage in rougher play. Forest rangers say wilderness hikers take greater risks if they know that a

THE READER'S EDGE: BOOK TWO

trained rescue squad is on call. Public health officials cite evidence that enhanced HIV treatment can lead to riskier sexual behavior.

10   All of capitalism runs on risk, of course, and it may be in this arena that risk compensation has manifested itself most calamitously of late. William D. Cohan, author of *House of Cards,* a book about the fall of Bear Stearns, speaks for many when he observes that "Wall Street bankers took the risks they did because they knew they got paid millions to do so and because they knew there would be few negative consequences for them personally if things failed to work out. In other words, the benefit of their risk-taking was all theirs and the consequences of their risk-taking would fall on the bank's shareholders." (Meanwhile investors, as Jame Surowiecki noted in a recent *New Yorker* column, tend to underestimate their chances of losing their shirts.) Late last year, 200 economists—including Sam Peltzman, who is now professor emeritus at Chicago—petitioned Congress not to pass its $700 billion plan to rescue the nation's overextended banking system in order to preserve some balance between risk, reward and responsibility. Around the same time, columnist George Will pushed the leaders of the Big Three automakers into the same risk pool.

11   "Suppose that in 1979 the government had not engineered the first bailout of Chrysler," Will wrote. "Might there have been a more sober approach to risk throughout corporate America?"

12   Now researchers are positing a risk compensation corollary: humans don't merely tolerate risk, they seek it; each of us has an innate tolerance level of risk, and in any given situation we will act to reduce—or increase—the perceived risk, depending on that level.

13   The author and principal proponent of this idea is Gerald J. S. Wilde, professor emeritus of psychology at Queen's University in Kingston, Ontario. In naming his theory "risk homeostasis," Wilde borrowed the word used for the way we humans, without knowing it, regulate our body temperature and other functions. "People alter their behavior in response to the implementation of health and safety measures," Wilde argued in his 1994 book, *Target Risk.* "But the riskiness of the way they behave will not change, unless those measures are capable of motivating people to alter the amount of risk they are willing to incur." Or, to make people behave more safely, you have to reset their risk thermostats.

14   That, he says, can be done by rewarding safe behavior. He notes that when California promised free driver's-license renewals for crash-free drivers, accidents went down. When Norway offered insurance refunds to crash-free younger drivers, they had fewer accidents. So did German truck drivers after their employers offered them bonuses for accident-free driving. Studies indicate that people are more likely to stop smoking if doing so will result in lower health and life insurance.

15   Wilde's idea remains hotly disputed, not least by members of the auto-safety establishment. "Wilde would have us believe that if you acquire a brand-new car with air bags, you will decide to drive your new car with more reckless abandon than your old one," says McCartt, a senior vice president for the Insurance Institute for Highway Safety, a nonprofit organization funded by auto insurers. "You will be unconcerned that your more

> "Wall Street bankers took the risks they did because they knew they got paid millions to do so and because they knew there would be few negative consequences for them personally if things failed to work out."

reckless driving behavior will increase chances of crashing and damaging your new car because returning to your previous level of injury risk is what you really crave! Only abstract theoreticians could believe people actually behave this way."

Still, even the institute acknowledges that drivers do compensate for 16 risk to some degree, particularly when a safety feature is immediately obvious to the driver, as with anti-lock brakes. But seat belts? No way, says McCartt. "We've done a number of studies and did not find any evidence" that drivers change their behavior while wearing them.

Questions over risk compensation will remain unresolved because be- 17 havioral change is multidimensional and difficult to measure. But it is clear that to risk is human. One reason Homo sapiens rule the earth is that we are one of history's most daring animals. So how, then, should we mark the 50th anniversary of the seat belt?

By buckling up, of course. And by keeping in mind some advice offered 18 by Tom Vanderbilt in *Traffic: Why We Drive the Way We Do (and What It Says About Us)*: "When a situation feels dangerous to you, it's probably more safe than you know; when a situation feels safe, that is precisely when you should feel on guard." Those are words even the parachutists, wilderness hikers and investors among us can live by.

ACTIVE READERS RESPOND

After you've finished reading, use these questions to respond to "Buckle Up. And Behave." You may write your answers in the spaces provided or on a separate sheet of paper.

VITAL VOCABULARY

Some words in this reading may be unfamiliar to you. Use the methods of Strategy 3 to explain what the listed words mean.

USE CONTEXT CLUES

a. compensation (paragraph 5)

_____

b. hedges (paragraph 6)

_____

c. smothered (paragraph 7)

_____

USE WORD PARTS

a. demi-centennial (paragraph 4)

_____

b. counterintuitive (paragraph 5)

_____

Choose the correct definition of each word as it is used in the context of this reading.

a. consensus (paragraph 3) _____

_____

b. hamlet (paragraph 7) _____

_____

c. prescience (paragraph 8) _____

_____

SKILLS TEST: FIND MEANING IN METAPHOR

A. First, read the following interpretation of a tricky metaphor from paragraph 6. Then, use Strategy 10 to identify and interpret three other metaphorical expressions in "Buckle Up. And Behave."

> Soon after the first gasoline-powered <u>horseless carriages</u> appeared on English roadways, the secretary of the national Motor Union of Great Britain and Ireland suggested that all those who owned property along the kingdom's roadways trim their hedges to make it easier for drivers to see. (paragraph 6)

Underline the startling phrase in the sentence.

What two things are being compared?

(Answers will vary.) _____

_____

What characteristic do these two things have in common?

(Answers will vary.) _____

_____

What does the metaphor mean in literal terms?

(Answers will vary.) _____

_____

B. Now interpret these metaphorical expressions. First identify the expression as a simile or a metaphor. Then analyze the surprising comparison.

1. ". . . overconfident sky divers hit the silk too late." (paragraph 9)

   (Answers will vary.) _____

   _____

2. "All of capitalism runs on risk, of course, and it may be in this arena that risk compensation has manifested itself most calamitously of late." (paragraph 10)

   (Answers will vary.) _____

   _____

3. "Or, to make people behave more safely, you have to reset their risk thermostats." (paragraph 13)

   (Answers will vary.) _____

   _____

1. Who is the writer's intended audience?
   a. drivers
   b. general audience
   c. transportation experts
   d. crash-test dummies

2. What is the author's purpose?
   a. to inform
   b. to persuade
   c. to entertain

3. What is the tone of the passage?
   a. wary
   b. subjective
   c. objective
   d. worried

4. Several types of seat belts were tested, but Nils Bohlin's design was the best because
   a. it had one diagonal strap that decapitated its users.
   b. it had two straps anchored at the same point and could be buckled with one hand.
   c. it had a single strap across the abdomen.
   d. it came from a pilot ejector seat.

5. The word "anchored" in paragraph 3, line 3, most nearly means
   a. a bolt.
   b. put in place.
   c. a musical note.
   d. held in place.

6. Which of the following sentences states the overall point of the passage?
   a. Security causes humans to engage in risky behavior.
   b. Greater security causes humans to engage in riskier behavior, but they still should be cautious.
   c. People take more risks if they feel safe, and humans are naturally risky.
   d. Risky behavior is typical human behavior.

7. What is the stated main idea of paragraph 9?
   a. "There has been a lively debate over risk compensation ever since, but today the issue is not whether it exists, but the degree to which it does."
   b. "The phenomenon has been observed well beyond the highway—in the workplace, on the playing field, at home, in the air."

   c. "Studies suggest that workers who wear back-support belts try to lift heavier loads and that children who wear protective sports equipment engage in rougher play."
   d. "Public health officials cite evidence that enhanced HIV treatment can lead to riskier sexual behavior."

8. What was Willoughby Verner's complaint to the *Times*?
   a. After he let his hedges grow back, drivers became more reckless.
   b. He was appalled at the *Times*' suggestion to trim his hedges.
   c. After he cut his hedges, drivers were more reckless because they could see the road better.
   d. After he cut his hedges, he had to wave at passers-by more frequently.

9. Which sentence provides support for this sentence (paragraph 14, line 1): "That, he says, can be done by rewarding safe behavior."
   a. "He notes that when California promised free driver's-license renewals for crash-free drivers, accidents went down."
   b. "When Norway offered insurance refunds to crash-free younger drivers, they had fewer accidents."
   c. "So did German truck drivers after their employers offered them bonuses for accident-free driving."
   d. All of the above

10. The author's claim that "all capitalism runs on risk" (paragraph 10, line 1) is
    a. adequately supported with details.
    b. inadequately supported with details.

11. What is the topic of paragraph 10?
    a. capitalism and risk
    b. Wall Street bankers
    c. risk-taking
    d. William D. Cohan

12. Both Sam Peltzman and John Adams concluded that
    a. safety belts were useless.
    b. safety belts sometimes saved vehicle occupants but overall did not decrease highway deaths.
    c. safety belts saved lives on a regular basis.
    d. safety belts overall increased highway deaths.

13. Identify the relationship between parts of the following sentence from paragraph 17.

   "One reason Homo sapiens rule the earth is that we are one of history's most daring animals." (lines 3–4)

   a. cause and effect
   b. process
   c. contrast
   d. addition

14. For paragraph 14, the author organizes the information by

   a. describing.
   b. contrasting.
   c. illustrating.
   d. comparing.

15. According to the passage, which of the following statements is true?

   a. People moved away from floodplains because they had flood insurance and disaster relief.
   b. If a trained rescue crew is on call, hikers take greater risks.
   c. People who skydive always pull their ripcords too late.
   d. Truck drivers who receive incentives for safe driving engage in risky behavior.

16. The word "induced" in paragraph 7, line 1, most nearly means

   a. irritated.
   b. motivated.
   c. worried.
   d. belittled.

17. Identify the relationship between the parts of the following sentence (paragraph 17, lines 1–2):

"Questions over risk compensation will remain unresolved because behavioral change is multi-dimensional and difficult to measure."

   a. addition
   b. statement and clarification
   c. cause and effect
   d. definition and example

18. By speculating that corporate America might have used "a more sober approach to risk," columnist George Will is comparing

   a. Chrysler's problems to America's problems.
   b. Wall Street's Bankers to bar patrons.
   c. the approach that was used to a drunk person's behavior.
   d. risk to corporate America.

19. What is the relationship between the following sentences (from paragraph 9)?

"Forest rangers say wilderness hikers take greater risks if they know that a trained rescue squad is on call. Public health officials cite evidence that enhanced HIV treatment can lead to riskier sexual behavior." (lines 12–14)

   a. time order
   b. comparison
   c. addition
   d. classification

20. From the story, you can infer that

   a. the author feels people should wear their safety belts.
   b. the author is a risk-taker.
   c. the author does not feel safety belts are important but wears one anyway.
   d. the author is not a risk-taker.

READERS WRITE

1. The belief that wearing a seat belt will increase risky behavior is contrary to what you might expect. Why?

   (Answers will vary.)

   _____

   _____

2. According to the author, what safety measures have increased a person's risk-taking? Why?

   (Answers will vary.)

   _____

   _____

3. According to William D. Cohan, why did Wall Street bankers feel safe taking risks?

(Answers will vary.)

_____

_____

_____

4. Although the author says that as humans we tend to seek risks, he also suggests that we should err on the side of safety. What prompts this suggestion?

(Answers will vary.)

_____

_____

_____

5. People will not engage in risky behavior if there are rewards for good behavior. What evidence does the passage provide to support this statement?

(Answers will vary.)

_____

_____

_____

READERS DISCUSS

1. Do you think safety measures increase risky behavior? What risks are you more likely to take because you feel they are safer or have been made safer?

(Answers will vary.)

_____

_____

_____

2. How has this article affected your opinion of others' risk-taking? Will you be more cautious knowing that others are more apt to engage in risky behavior? What risky behaviors do others engage in that you don't?

(Answers will vary.)

_____

_____

_____

FIND MEANING IN METAPHORS

1 | Recognize metaphors.

2 | Analyze the comparison.

PRACTICE PAGES

Chapter 10

To practice identifying literal versus metaphorical expressions, complete the following exercise.

PRACTICE EXERCISE 1

Read each of the following examples and decide which is the literal expression and which is the metaphorical expression. Place an "L" on the blank line if the expression is literal; place an "M" on the blank line if the expression is metaphorical. Underline the metaphorical expression for the sentence you identify as metaphorical.

1. __L__ While some words are no longer used—and therefore out of dictionaries—English speakers show no sign of losing their enthusiasm for using a great wealth of words.

   __M__ While some words fall out of use—and therefore out of dictionaries—English speakers show no sign of losing their enthusiasm for using a great wealth of words.

   From Reading 5: Where English Words Come From

2. __M__ In a yard shaded by low trees, Schoenwiese barely had time to step outside of his SUV before he was bombarded with hugs.

   __L__ In a yard shaded by low trees, Schoenwiese barely had time to step outside of his SUV before he was given many hugs.

   From Reading 6: Point. Shoot. See.

3. __L__ An accomplished righteousness that has turned self-righteous, self-serving is a risk, surely, for many of us, who can be tempted to wag our finger at others, and not so subtly point at ourselves with a good deal of self-satisfaction.

   __M__ An accomplished righteousness that has turned self-righteous, self-serving is like you are pointing out the pimples of others while smiling at yourself in the mirror and ignoring your own.

   From Reading 8: The Good Person

4. ___M___ As the oldest child, she was expected to take care of her brother and sister, as well as the house and meals, while her mother tended to the gardens, and her father scratched out what little he could from the soil.

   ___L___ As the oldest child, she was expected to take care of her brother and sister, as well as the house and meals, while her mother tended to the gardens, and her father earned a small living through farming.

   From Reading 4: "See Spot Run": Teaching My Grandmother to Read

5. ___M___ Sure, you can crack yourself up, but the real test of a sense of humor is how it manifests itself with others.

   ___L___ Sure, you can make yourself laugh, but the real test of a sense of humor is how it manifests itself with others.

   From Reading 11: How the Self-Concept Develops

To get practice with analyzing the metaphor, complete the following exercise.

PRACTICE EXERCISE 2

After reading each passage, first identify the metaphorical expression, saying whether it is a metaphor or a simile. Next, interpret its meaning, using these questions:

1. What two things are being compared?

2. What characteristic do these two things have in common?

3. What does the metaphor mean in literal terms?

1. She breaks it down into little pieces as if she were about to feed the word to a baby who cannot chew solid food. Her voice is clear and measured like a schoolteacher's.

   From Julia Alvarez, "Victor," in *Off the Beaten Path: Stories of Place*

   (Answers will vary.)

   _____

   _____

2. From the standpoint of emotional intelligence, optimism is an attitude that buffers people against falling into apathy, hopelessness, or depression in the face of tough going. And, as with hope, its near cousin, optimism pays dividends in life (providing, of course, it is a realistic optimism; a too-naïve optimism can be disastrous).

   From Reading 13: Optimism

   (Answers will vary.)

   _____

   _____

3. Like others, I have described it to people as "broken" or "fractured" English. But I wince when I say that. It has always bothered me that I can think of no way to describe it other than "broken," as if it were damaged and needed to be fixed, as if it lacked a certain wholeness and soundness.

   From Reading 16: Mother Tongue

   (Answers will vary.)

   _____

   _____

4. The studied nonchalance of patients in a dentist's waiting room is a poor indication of their inner anxiety. It is considered embarrassing to "lose your cool" in public. In a potentially acute situation, then, everyone present will appear more unconcerned than he is in fact.

From Reading 15: Why People Don't Help in a Crisis

(Answers will vary.)

_____

_____

_____

5. You were new to teaching, and your lectures certainly weren't polished. You gripped the lectern like a shield and sometimes your voice died out in the middle of a sentence. But your enthusiasm for your subject left me longing to know more.

From Reading 17: A Letter to My Teacher

(Answers will vary.)

_____

_____

_____

6. Yes, men can be impressive in their tendency to self-destruct, explosively or gradually.

From Reading 18: Why Men Don't Last

(Answers will vary.)

_____

_____

_____

PRACTICE READING

To get practice with reading, read the passage, and then answer the questions that follow. You may write your answers in the spaces provided or on a separate sheet of paper.

Victor

JULIA ALVAREZ

Julia Alvarez is a novelist and poet who is a writer-in-residence at Middlebury College in Vermont. Her writing, such as the novel *How the Garcia Girls Lost Their Accents* (1992), often deals with the immigrant experience of belonging to two worlds: the United States and her native country, the Dominican Republic, where she now lives part of the year. "Victor," a story that takes place in the Dominican Republic, first appeared in *Off the Beaten Path: Stories of Place* (1998).

Virgencita: Virgin Mary

Whenever Don Bernardo comes to the national park, he asks for Victor's 1
father as his guide. "And tell him to bring Victor along," he invariably adds.

Today, Don Bernardo has a strange guest with him. Victor can tell that 2
Don Bernardo is not quite at ease with this lady, as if she were here to report on his work as director of parks. But she seems harmless enough. A
skinny lady who is not Americana but looks Americana in her blue pants
and T-shirt with letters written across it. She is carrying a notebook, and
from a ribbon around her neck <u>dangles</u> a pen where the Virgencita's medal-
lion should go.

Don Bernardo looks down and notices Victor. "Ho, there, Victor! How is 3
the little man?"

As he always does when he doesn't know what to say or where to look, 4
Victor lifts his unbuttoned shirt over his head. He hides underneath it like
the lizard under the frond of the elephant fern.

"Mira, muchacho," his father <u>scolds</u> in a voice that threatens to cuff his 5
ear. After all, Don Bernardo made a point of introducing this lady as an
honored visitor who writes books and teaches in an American school. "You
can say hello like a person."

"Hello," Victor says loud and clear, like a person. 6

Don Bernardo laughs. "Victor is as smart as a pencil," he tells the lady, 7
who smiles at him and says, "Is that so?" Just as she is not americana but
looks americana, she is dominicana but speaks Spanish as if she were worried
there might be a little stone in among the words that will crack her mouthful
of white teeth. Each word is carefully spoken and cleanly finished before the
next one starts. "So tell me, Victor," she says, "what grade are you in?"

Victor glances at his father. "In the third grade," he offers. 8

"Did you complete it or are you about to start it this September?" 9

Looking over her shoulder, Victor spots the red-eyed bobo flying through 10
the trees as if stitching together the forest with the rise and fall of its wings.
If the lady is here to see the park, she should not miss the flight of the bobo.
"Look!" he points. "A bobo!"

She turns around, craning her neck to see what he sees. 11

Victor keeps pointing, but the lady is not quick enough and the bobo 12
disappears into the dark-green curtain of the rain forest.

"Bo-bo," the lady says the name slowly, writing it down in her little book. 13
"Where were we?" she asks when she looks back up.

"Lead on, Victor!" Don Bernardo commands. 14

Victor darts ahead, his shirt flapping behind him like the tail of the 15
bobo when it sits on the branch of the cedar, calling bo-bo, bo-bo, bo-bo, as
if it were trying to talk like a person, expecting an answer.

The lady walks behind him on the trail. "Wow," she says over every 16
little thing.

"Wow-oh." Victor tries out the words under his breath. "Wow-oh, 17
wow-oh." The words sound like the call of the big-eyed lechuza at night.

"Wow! Look at that flower!" The lady points. 18

"That's a campana," Victor explains. "Careful when you touch it. Wasps 19
love to build in its leaves."

20   "It's so so beautiful," the lady says, writing down the name of the flower in her notebook. "Cam-pa-na." She breaks it down into little pieces as if she were about to feed the word to a baby who cannot chew solid food. Her voice is clear and measured like a schoolteacher's. "What is *that*?" She looks up. Behind her, Don Bernardo stops to listen.

21   "That little bird singing is a barrancolf," Victor explains. "And over there is a tinaja," he adds. "You want me to cut one down for you?"

22   "Cut it down?" A scolding look spreads across the lady's face.

23   "I can cut you an orchid if you prefer." Victor hesitates. His father has taught him to figure out what will please a turista so the tip will be a good one. The ladies, when they come, always like a delicate orchid or <u>tufted</u> bromeliad to take home to the capital in their jeeps or scouts. The chauffeur, usually along carting the ice chest, carries it back in his free hand.

24   Don Bernardo catches up and wags his finger. "You know better than to disturb things in the rain forest, Victor."

25   "You know better," his father agrees. Victor recognizes the look that says, You have put your foot down beside a wasp nest. Watch out.

26   "I know better." Victor nods.

27   "Victor is as smart as a pencil," Don Bernardo repeats. "How old did you say you were, Victor?" He winks at the lady as if preparing her for a merriment.

28   Victor looks at his father. "Ten," he says solemnly.

29   "But, Victor," Don Bernardo says, eyeing him kindly, "you have been ten years old for the last three years I have been coming to the park."

30   "You mean to say he doesn't know how old he is?" the lady asks Don Bernardo. The director of parks glances at his feet. Every time he comes to the park, he teases Victor and his guests smile along with him.

31   "Don't you know how old you are, Victor?" the lady persists.

32   Victor lifts his shirt over his head and looks up at the trail. It winds through the trees and then up the incline toward the collection of white rocks the turistas like to photograph. "Nine," he tries, and then "fourteen," but none of the numbers seem to please the lady, who shakes her head at Don Bernardo.

33   "Something should be done about this," she says, making a note in her book. Don Bernardo nods gravely, his hands in his pockets. Victor glances at his father, who narrows his eyes at his son as if to say. Stand very still, boy. If you don't make a move, maybe the wasps will go away.

34   They continue down the trail, but the exploration is no fun anymore.

35   "One-two-three-four," the lady makes him slowly count out loud.

36   "What is the first month of the year, Victor?"

37   "October?"

38   "Victor! The *first* month? I already told you."

39   He tries a few more before he gets it right. They stop by a bush of bejuco de gato so the lady can write the name down.

40   "Those leaves are good for pain," Victor explains to her.

turista: woman tourist

bromeliad: family of tropical plants including pineapple and ornamentals

His father has taught him to figure out what will please a turista so the tip will be a good one.

"How do you spell bejuco anyhow?" she asks Don Bernardo, who spells 41
the word for her. That gets her started on something else. "Can you spell
your name, Victor?"

Victor feels silence tingling the inside of his mouth—as if he had taken 42
a bite of bejuco de gato and his tongue had gone numb. He looks down at
the lady's pants covered with melao and amor seco, nettles that are hard to
take out. "You want me to pick those off?" he offers her.

"V-l-C-T-O-R," she instructs him. 43

He repeats the letters after her. 44

"Well done!" Don Bernardo nods, but he does not add his usual phrase, 45
"Victor is as smart as a pencil." Perhaps he will no longer ask for Victor every
time he visits the park.

"Onetwothreefourfive!" Victor pipes up, wanting to impress them both. 46
Sure enough, Don Bernardo is laughing again!

At the fork in the trail, Don Bernardo explains to the lady that one path 47
leads to the river, the other climbs up to the white rocks. The lady decides
she wants to see the river, but then she confuses things by saying, "So take
a right, Victor."

"To the river?" he asks her just to make sure. 48

That look comes on her face again. "Which is your left, Victor, and which 50
is your right?"

"It depends," he says, outsmarting her for once. "Which way do you want 51
to go?"

This time even she laughs, little hiccup laughs that sound like the cal- 52
calf calling to the sun as it rises up in the morning.

At the river, Don Bernardo and the lady sit on the rocks and talk in low, 53
earnest voices about matters that sound important. "Thirty percent officially,"
Don Bernardo is explaining, "but it depends what you mean by illiteracy."

Victor looks over at his father, perched on a fallen log, a papagallo stem 54
in his mouth. He wishes he had picked one, too, for the sweet sap tastes so
good on a hot day. Victor can tell his father is <u>calculating</u> how much Don Bernardo will tip them for this tour. The farther the turistas go, the more they
tip. But Don Bernardo and his guest had barely gone two kilometers before
the lady discovered that Victor did not know his numbers. The walk slowed
as the lady stopped often to draw figures with a stick on the forest floor.

Beyond them, the trail cuts through to the heart of the green preserve. 55
So many things are disappearing that will never be seen again on this earth!
Or so Victor has overheard at the lodge when his father attends the <u>man-
datory</u> workshops the <u>forestry</u> service gives for the guides. But Victor sees
no sign of danger: the cocaria, whose flower stains blue and whose seeds if
chewed cure toothache, is bursting with blossoms. Beside it, the leaves of
cola de caballo bob in the slight breeze of late afternoon. The day is waning
and there is still so much to show. The bamboo knock against one another
like knuckles rapping on a desk asking for attention.

Bo-bo, bo-bo, calls the bobo. "Bo-bo, bo-bo," Victor answers back. 56

"Ho, Victor!" Don Bernardo wakes Victor from his daydreaming. 57

"Time to head back." 58

59　A soft light is falling through the canopy of thick branches. The air is cool. The forest is always so much more pleasant than the village school-house with the sun beating down on its zinc roof.

60　As they climb back up the stone steps, the lady notices a narrow foot-path that cuts away from the river in the same general direction as the trail. "Where does this go?" she wants to know.

61　"That's an old mule track up to the white rocks," Victor's father explains. "But it's too overgrown to walk."

62　"It looks fine," the lady says. "It'll give us some new things to look at. Don't you think so, Don Bernardo?" she addresses the director of parks. But it is clear from her face that her mind is already made up.

63　"There's a lot of campanas," Victor begins, seconding his father's hesitation.

64　But the lady has already sprung forward, thrashing through the under-growth so that all Victor sees through the bobbing of the fern fronds is the blue of her pants and the flash of white paper in her little book. The men exchange a look. Finally, Don Bernardo shrugs and says. "Let's go."

65　Victor has almost caught up to her when he hears the cry that comes as no surprise. She has pressed through a narrow avenue of campanas and the wasps are after her.

66　Quick, Victor looks around and snaps off a branch from a nearby guay-uyo tree. Beating a way toward her through the buzzing in the air, he yanks her by the hand back out to the river. Her notebook falls to the ground as she races beside him, Don Bernardo and his father giving them a wide berth as they jump into the water.

67　When she comes to the surface, Victor can see that one eye is already swollen shut. He searches the bank for the leaves of bejuco de gato to ease the pain and oreja de burro to keep down the swelling. Meanwhile his fa-ther and Don Bernardo are rubbing guayuyo leaves on their arms and face to keep away the few wasps who have followed the intruders to the river. The forest has gone absolutely still. Not even the bold bobo calls to find out what is going on.

68　As soon as the lady is soothed with the leaves he has brought her, Victor rubs guayuyo on his own face and arms, and runs off to retrieve the little book filled with things he has tried to teach her about the rain forest.

ACTIVE READERS RESPOND

After you've finished reading, use these questions to respond to "Victor." You may write your answers in the spaces provided or on a separate sheet of paper.

VITAL VOCABULARY

Some words in this reading may be unfamiliar to you. Use the methods of Strategy 3 to explain what the listed words mean.

USE CONTEXT CLUES

a. dangles (paragraph 2)

_____

b. scold (paragraph 5)

_____

c. calculating (paragraph 54)

_____

USE WORD PARTS

a. forestry (paragraph 55)

_____

b. undergrowth (paragraph 64)

_____

USE THE DICTIONARY

Choose the correct definition of each word as it is used in the context of this reading.

a. tufted (paragraph 23)

_____

b. mandatory (paragraph 55)

_____

c. berth (paragraph 66)

_____

OBJECTIVE OPERATIONS

1. Who is the writer's intended audience?
    a. Spanish speakers
    b. general audience
    c. nature enthusiasts
    d. children

2. What is the author's purpose?
    a. to inform
    b. to persuade
    c. to entertain

3. What is the tone of the passage?
    a. confused
    b. apathetic
    c. engaging
    d. cautionary

4. This visitor to the national park is different from the other "turistas" that Don Bernardo and Victor have been used to because

    a. she is from the United States and does not speak Spanish well, so she doesn't understand much of what they say.
    b. she was sent to find out how good a director of parks Don Bernardo is.
    c. she just wants to take home some beautiful orchids or bromeliads.
    d. she is not just coming to see the beautiful flowers and birds; she wants to "do good" by assessing Victor's education.

5. The word "frond" in paragraph 4, line 3, most nearly means
    a. a leaf.
    b. a good find.
    c. a twig.
    d. to discover.

6. Which of the following sentences states the overall point of the passage?

a. Victor is not very smart, and the tourist points that out.

b. Victor uses his knowledge of the rain forest to save the tourist.

(c.) Although he may not be formally educated, which dismays the tourist, Victor is very knowledgeable about the rain forest.

d. Victor is not formally educated, which upsets the tourist and affects her walk in the rain forest.

7. What is the implied main idea of paragraph 66?

a. Victor wishes to be stung.

(b.) Victor saves the woman from the wasps.

c. Victor helps his father save the woman from the wasps.

d. The wasps enjoy a quick swim.

8. What is the most likely reason that this turista keeps missing what Victor is trying to show her?

(a.) she is too full of her own ideas about what is important to be able to look and listen carefully to what she's being shown.

b. her purpose in coming was to tutor Victor, not to see the forest.

c. she is too distracted by her fears about getting stung by the wasps she's been warned about.

d. she is too busy trying to get Victor to pick her some flowers.

9. Which sentence provides support for this sentence (paragraph 54, lines 3–4): "Victor can tell his father is calculating how much Don Bernardo will tip them for this tour."

a. "Victor looks over at his father, perched on a fallen log, a papagallo stem in his mouth."

b. "He wishes he had picked one, too, for the sweet sap tastes so good on a hot day."

(c.) "The farther the turistas go, the more they tip."

d. "But Don Bernardo and his guest had barely gone two kilometers before the lady discovered that Victor did not know his numbers."

10. The author's claim that Victor cannot provide a satisfactory age for the woman (paragraph 32, lines 3–5) is

(a.) adequately supported with details.

b. inadequately supported with details.

11. What is the topic of paragraph 42?

a. Victor's embarrassment and avoidance

b. Victor's inability to spell his name

c. the woman's condescension

(d.) Victor's embarrassment at his inability to spell his name

12. The association between wasps and the campana flower is first mentioned

(a.) early in the story, when the lady sees it as the first flower she wants to know about.

b. in the middle of the story, when the lady decides to take the path to the river.

c. later in the story, when the lady and Don Bernardo are discussing illiteracy by the river.

d. near the end of the story, when Victor tries to warn the lady not to climb up an overgrown mule track.

13. Identify the relationship between parts of the following sentence from paragraph 4.

"As he always does when he doesn't know what to say or where to look, Victor lifts his unbuttoned shirt over his head." (lines 1–2)

(a.) cause and effect

b. process order

c. statement and clarification

d. addition

14. For paragraph 58, the author organizes the information by

a. describing.

b. contrasting.

(c.) illustrating.

d. comparing.

15. A typical way for Victor to react to being put on the spot about his lack of school knowledge is to

a. run away from the lady.

b. try to make her laugh by joking about the names of plants.

(c.) lift his unbuttoned shirt over his head and hide.

d. point out another plant, flower, or bird.

16. The word "cuff" in paragraph 5, line 1, most nearly means

a. fold upwards.

b. end of shirt sleeve.

(c.) to strike.

d. off-hand.

17. Identify the relationship between the following sentences (paragraph 23, lines 1–4): "His father has taught him to figure out what will please a turista so the tip will be a good one. The ladies, when they come, always like a delicate orchid or tufted bromeliad to take home to the capital in their jeeps or scouts."

    a. addition

    b. statement and clarification

    c. time order

    d. definition and example

18. Remember that the term irony refers to the use of words to convey meaning that is opposite to—or very different from—the literal meaning. There is irony in the last sentence of the story, when Victor runs to get the book of things "he has tried to teach [the lady] about the rain forest" because the well-educated lady

    a. was really the one who could have taught Victor what he would need to survive in the modern world.

    b. was a rain forest expert who had come to teach Don Bernardino techniques for conserving the forest.

    c. knew only book learning and was therefore unable to learn from what an illiterate boy, Victor, could have taught her.

    d. had been "taught" a harsh lesson by Victor when he made the wasps attack her.

19. What is the relationship between the parts of the following sentence (from paragraph 60)?

    "As they climb back up the stone steps, the lady notices a narrow foot-path that cuts away from the river in the same general direction as the trail." (lines 1–2)

    a. time order

    b. comparison

    c. contrast

    d. classification

20. From the story, you can infer that

    a. the woman will never respect Victor.

    b. Victor is much smarter than the woman understands.

    c. Victor is much less intelligent than the woman understands.

    d. without his father, Victor knows little about the rain forest.

1. The characters in this story are Don Bernardo, Victor, Victor's father, and the woman visitor.
   (True) or False

2. The lady turista keeps missing what Victor is trying to show her because she is not very intelligent.
   True or (False)

3. Victor warns the woman that _____ wasps _____ live in the campana flowers.

4. This visitor to the national park is different from other "turistas" because she is not American.

5. What are the different views we get of Victor? (Think about what Alvarez says about him, what the lady thinks of him, and what Don Bernardo thinks.) What is your view of him?

   (Answers will vary.) _____

   _____

   _____

   _____

6. What is the irony in the last sentence of the story when Victor runs to get the book of things "he has tried to teach [the lady] about the rain forest"?

   (Answers will vary.) _____

   _____

   _____

   _____

11

The Writer's Perspective

DETERMINE THE WRITER'S PERSPECTIVE

1 | Recognize the style of writing.

2 | Recognize the intended audience.

3 | Identify the writer's perspective.

4 | See how the tone reflects biases.

imagine this

If you have ever been skydiving, then you understand perspective. As you jump out of the plane, you notice large features of the landscape, like mountains or rivers. From this perspective, the world seems very small, and you may think that because you cannot see smaller details they do not exist. However, as you move closer to the earth, smaller features like people, cars, or houses, come into view. You get a more detailed view.

With a reading, as you get a broad overview, you might not see the smaller details: clues that point out a writer's perspective or preferences (or the attempt to sway *you* to those preferences through word choice). If like the skydiver you take in the big picture first, make sure that you realize that, on closer inspection, the small details will come into focus and offer you clues about the writer.

Think FIRST

- Do you feel that how you tell a story can make it better? Do you narrate or describe or debate to help your friends understand your point?

- Does your perspective affect the way you view the world? Should your life experience influence how you respond or react to the world around you?

- When you talk with your friends, do you reveal with the tone of your voice whether you are serious or humorous? Does your tone show whether you are informing or trying to convince? Does it reveal your preferences?

INTRODUCTION TO THE NEW STRATEGY
Determine the Writer's Perspective

Using Strategy 11 as you *get an overview* will help you get a sense of the writer's perspective before you read. A writer's perspective is the writer's point of view, and the style of writing, in addition to its audience, purpose, tone, and biases, all support this perspective. During and after reading, Strategy 11 helps you understand why writers present ideas in a certain way and how they want you to *respond* to these ideas.

Styles of Writing

Writers use different styles of writing for different **purposes,** or reasons for writing, so, as a reader, you will want to recognize these styles. Each type has a different purpose and answers a different general question.

Do you like telling stories or jokes to your friends?

connect now

Narration
Narration is used to tell a story. It answers the question: what happened? When a writer narrates, he tells a story—jokes, short stories, personal experience tales, and some historical writings are examples of narratives. You have seen narration in, Reading 2, "I Don't Like to Read—Sam-I-Am!" and the Chapter 5 Practice Reading, "Powder."

Reading 4, "See Spot Run," is an excellent example of a narrative essay; the following excerpt is from "See Spot Run":

For weeks afterward, my grandmother and I sat patiently side by side—roles reversed as she, with a bit of difficulty, sounded out every word, then read them again, piece by piece, until she understood the short sentences. When she slowly repeated the full sentence, we both would smile and clap our hands—I felt so proud, so grown up.

Description

Description creates a sensory image and can show what something, someone, or some place is like. It answers the question: what does it look, sound, feel, smell, or taste like? Descriptive writing can be found in any reading where the writer appeals to one of our five senses. Description is important for writers because it allows them to create an image for their readers. For example, in Reading 10, "talking back," bell hooks' description of the way women talked in her small town was important for showing why she loved listening to them.

In Reading 22, "Infernal Paradise," writer Barbara King-solver invites her readers in by describing part of Hawaii:

Entering the crater at dawn seemed unearthly, though Haleakala is entirely of the earth, and nothing of human artifice. The cliffs absorbed and enclosed us in a mounting horizon of bleak obsidian crags. A lake of cloud slid over the rim, wave by wave, and fell into the crater's separate atmosphere, dispersing in vapor trails. The sharp perimeter of cliffs contains a volcanic bowl three thousand feet deep and eight miles across as the crow flies (or twice that far as the hiker hikes). The depression would hold Manhattan, though fortunately it doesn't.

Exposition

Exposition—or expository writing—explains something or instructs. (Sometimes, this is called illustration, as in "to illustrate a point.") It answers the questions: what is it? why or how did it happen? Expository writing is used a great deal in textbooks where the author's purpose is to instruct students about a field of knowledge. You've read several examples of textbook writing in this book, including Reading 9, "How Babies Use Patterns to See," and Reading 14, "How Conscious Is Thought?" Though much of your college reading will be textbook reading, you will also read other writers who sometimes need to explain ideas. Examples of this kind of exposition include Reading 15, "Why People Don't Help in a Crisis," and Reading 13, "Optimism: The Great Motivator."

Lindsay Roberts, a student writer at Quinnipiac University in Hamden, Connecticut, offers her point of view on peer pressure in college in this opinion-editorial piece that was first featured in the student newspaper, the **Quinnipiac Chronicle.**

Now that the end of the year is approaching, I have been doing some reflecting on the person I was before I came to Quinnipiac and if that person has changed after this year. Everyone says college determines who you become, but what they fail to mention is that peer pressure does not die in high school.

"I love college, I love drinking." That song by Asher Roth is a perfect example of how the word "college," for many people, is synonymous with the consumption of mass amounts of alcohol. And hey, if there is ever a time to drink irresponsibly in your life, it should be in college. Because stumbling down the streets of New Haven inebriated when you are not a college student just gives off the impression you're a homeless alcoholic. However, while alcohol seems to symbolize our freedom from parents and actual society, I sometimes wonder if we take it to the next level just to live up to the college stereotype.

Sure, getting drunk can relieve stress and lead to a funny story, but I am sure there are people that sometimes don't feel like drinking, but they do because that's what everyone else is doing. For my own personal reasons I choose not to drink, and I am lucky to have found friends who completely respect and never question my decision. However, I would be lying if I said everyone is that understanding of my choice.

When I tell girls I don't drink, they'll respond with a "oh that's so good!" but I can see by their facial expression that they are making a mental note never to have too much around me because I'll remember. Guys usually give me a hard time or say "I respect that" and then ask me if I want a drink five minutes later. A lot of times I have just wanted to give in, "fine hand me a beer," and at some parties I will hold an empty Solo cup to avoid the awkward conversation.

And I know that I am not the only person who feels the pressure. The National Bureau of Economic Research has found that males that drank frequently before college who were assigned a roommate that also drank frequently had lower GPAs by two-thirds of a point. Boys are just as susceptible to peer pressure as girls; it is especially hard for guys to be studious and not be given a hard time about it. I see males in the library, so I know they study. Yet guys like to say "Oh, I actually really studied for this test. I hope I do well," which implies that in other instances they were too cool to "actually study."

Another big issue in college is weight. Everyone says that you gain the "freshman 15," but I feel like I know just as many people who picked up an eating disorder when they got to college. Look around and you can tell there are a lot of thin girls at Quinnipiac, so for those who are built differently it is hard not to feel pressure to be thin. I know a lot of girls who came to school with a love for their curves, but after living with a roommate who only eats lettuce it's hard not to scrutinize.

I also wonder if people's individual style has been altered after coming to school. What came first, The North Face or Quinnipiac? There is nothing wrong with popular clothing. I just hope that there is not a student out there that has a really unique outfit that they never wear out of fear that they might stand out too much.

Peer pressure is something we will have to deal with for the rest of our lives, and in tight living conditions it is easy to see how the behaviors of others can influence our decisions. However, the choice is up to you. You can either let those influences alter who you are or you can learn from other people's decisions and make a stronger definition of yourself.

Roberts, Lindsay. "Peer pressure: How college life can change you." *The Quinnipiac Chronicle.* 15 April 2009. 30 July 2009. Available: http://media.www.quchronicle.com/media/storage/paper294/news/2009/04/15/Oped/Peer-Pressure.How.College.Life.Can.Change.You-3711419.shtml

In the following paragraph (from Reading 3, "Forbidden Reading"), the writer explains what Thomas Johnson, a slave, had to do to learn to read:

In learning to read, therefore, I am not sure that I do not owe quite as much to the opposition of my master as to the kindly assistance of my amiable mistress." Thomas Johnson, a slave who later became a well-known missionary preacher in England, explained that he had learned to read by studying the letters in a Bible he

had stolen. Since his master read aloud a chapter from the New Testament every night, Johnson would coax him to read the same chapter over and over, until he knew it by heart and was able to find the same words on the printed page. Also, when the master's son was studying, Johnson would suggest that the boy read part of his lesson out loud. "Lor's over me," Johnson would say to encourage him, "read that again," which the boy often did, believing that Johnson was admiring his performance. Through repetition, he learned enough to be able to read the newspapers by the time the Civil War broke out, and later set up a school of his own to teach others to read.

Argument

An **argument** is written to persuade you. It answers the question: Why should you believe something or do something? You can tell that the writer's main purpose is to persuade the reader if the reading puts forward a strong position on something that not everyone will agree with. You can tell from the title that Reading 12, "School Is Bad for Children," is an argument.

connect now — Are you someone who debates or argues for the fun of it? Why do you like to play "devil's advocate"?

Reading 18, "Why Men Don't Last," is also an argument; read the following paragraph:

It is one thing to herald a presumed crisis, though, and to cite a ream of gloomy statistics. It is quite another to understand the crisis, or to figure out where it comes from or what to do about it. As those who study the various forms of men's self-destructive behaviors realize, there is not a single, glib, overarching explanation for the sex-specific patterns they see.

As you get an overview of a reading, try to determine whether the writer is narrating, describing, explaining, or arguing a point. Think about Tim Cahill's "Terror Unlimited" (Reading 19 in Chapter 10), for example. The title and first sentences of paragraphs in that reading suggest two purposes: to narrate what happened and to explain the terror he experienced.

In the next two samples, we have the kind of information we could get in an overview. What could we learn about each writer's purpose just from this small amount of information?

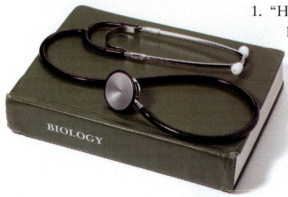

1. "How technology and the population explosion compound our impact on habitats and other species," an excerpt from a textbook, *Biology: Concepts and Connections.*

The fact that this is a textbook excerpt tells us that this reading is exposition, meant to explain or instruct. If we connect the writing type to the excerpt's title, we can predict that the reading will explain human beings' impact on the environment.

2. Reading 21, "A Global Green Deal," an article from *Time* magazine.

The first sentence of this reading is, "So what do we do?" The last paragraph begins with, "None of this will happen without an aroused citizenry," and ends with, "It's time to repeat that history on behalf of a Global Green deal." These sentences alone indicate that this reading is an *argument* to *persuade* us to do something.

The Intended Audience

Instructor Tip
Have students bring in a variety of reading materials. In groups, have them find an example of each style and state the purpose of the reading. Have students identify the author's audience and perspective, in addition to the purpose and the style. Have them state why that style fits that purpose.

A writers' perspective depends partly on the people he or she wants to reach—the **intended audience.** For example, writers for an academic journal, such as *The Journal of the American Medical Association,* write mainly to instruct or persuade fellow doctors or people in the medical professions. They use technical language to explain complex information and the formal style expected of serious, professional journals. Science writers for magazines like *Time* or *Newsweek* avoid overly technical terms and use a more informal language because the readers of these popular newsmagazines are not specialists in a particular field. They represent the **general audience.**

Type of Vocabulary

Both the biology textbook and the *Time* article, "A Global Green Deal," deal with the subject of environmental problems. However, they use very different vocabularies, because they have different intended audiences. Look at the difference in vocabulary in the very first sentences.

1. Excerpt from *Biology: Concepts and Connections*
   "*Technology and other cultural advancements have produced many benefits.* . . . But they also fuel our population explosion; and feeding, clothing, and housing billions of people even at a minimal level *strains the biosphere.*"

2. Excerpt from "A Global Green Deal"
   "*So what do we do?* Everyone knows the planet is *in bad shape,* but most people are resigned to passivity."

The italicized words and phrases demonstrate the differences between more technical, formal vocabulary in the textbook and the informal words in a popular magazine.

Sentence Structure

The sentence structures in the two excerpts are also different. Notice the longer, more complex sentences in the textbook and the shorter sentences in the magazine article.

Audience and Purpose

When considering a writer's perspective, take into account who the typical reader of the material would probably be. This can help you decide whether an author's purpose was to inform, entertain, or persuade. For example, the audience of an article in a textbook is a student taking a course on that textbook's subject; therefore, the article should include thorough enough information to serve the needs of that student. On the other hand, the audience of a credit card offer is a potential customer, so the offer's purpose is to persuade that potential customer to get the credit card. When you respond to a reading, consider whether the writer's purpose suited the intended audience. (Did the student learn? Did the potential customer fill out the credit card application?)

Perspective

Your **perspective** on a subject is your way of looking at it, or your position on it, based on your experience and beliefs. For example, you probably have a certain perspective on the effect sex in the media has on children. Your perspective depends partly on your experience. Was your experience of seeing sex in television programs and movies as a child harmful to you or not? Does your experience talking with today's kids suggest that they're getting too many sexual messages from the media or not? Your perspective on this subject may also be affected by your beliefs about appropriate sexual behavior—beliefs you've acquired from your family, your religion, and your peers.

A writer's perspective on a subject affects his or her purpose for writing. We can see how perspective affects purpose by imagining two different authors writing about drilling for oil in the Alaskan wilderness. An oil company executive would have a certain perspective based on experience and beliefs about this country's need for access to energy sources. This writer's purpose would be to persuade readers of the need to drill in Alaska. However, an environmentalist would have a different perspective, placing great value on protecting the natural

MORGAN FREEMAN

Moby Dick
by Herman Melville

Morgan Freeman never shies away from challenging roles. But recently, the actor's been lending his voice to nature documentaries. What would make this Academy Award winner give up the spotlight for a supporting role as a narrator? Well, one needs only look to his reading list for a hint. Freeman is fascinated by science, and often hits the stacks looking for books on birds. This is interesting, as Freeman's favoite book stars a large mammal—a whale, to be exact. He credits Herman Melville's *Moby Dick* as sparking his love of reading.

If you liked *Moby Dick*, you might also like:

Gulliver's Travels, Jonathan Swift

Twenty Thousand Leagues Under the Sea, Jules Verne

Robinson Crusoe, Daniel Defoe

WHAT ARE THEY READING?

Instructor Tip
Have a discussion with students about times when their point of view has affected their belief about something. For example, maybe a student broke her leg while inline skating and has never skated again because she feels the sport is dangerous whereas another student continues to skate despite having broken a leg *and* a wrist. Where else can a perspective prevent or encourage a student to do something?

environment as irreplaceable. This writer's purpose would be to persuade readers that drilling for oil in the Alaskan wilderness should be prohibited.

In this textbook, the headnotes about writers that appear after reading titles give you an idea of a writer's perspective before you begin reading. You'll need to consider the writer's perspective especially carefully when reading an argument such as we might see on either side of the oil drilling debate. By knowing the writer's perspective—where he or she is coming from—you can better evaluate the ideas, information, and reasoning that you'll find in the reading.

EXERCISES

PRACTICE

For practice identifying a writer's perspective, complete the following exercise.

For each of the following, read the notes before the excerpt and then read the excerpt. Answer the questions that follow the excerpt. (Please know that these "notes" are fictionalized.)

1. This excerpt is from a newspaper section where readers may call or write in a gripe or complaint. The letter was written by Ann Nony Maus, a former speech instructor at a community college.

I am so ticked off at people's use of English! Didn't they learn anything in school, those nitwits! I hate hearing "I seen" or "I had went"; it makes me think that I am being surrounded by a bunch of nincompoops who don't know grammar from a fly on their foreheads. All of this ignorance is due to total and utter laziness, and if it doesn't end soon, this whole country will sound like backwoods hillbillies. Go back to school and learn a thing or two!

What is the style of this paragraph? ____d____

a. narration

b. description

c. exposition

d. argument

Who is the writer's intended audience? ____b____

a. students

b. the general public

c. English teachers

d. the school board

What is the writer's purpose? ____b____

a. to inform

b. to persuade

c. to entertain

What do the notes tell you about the writer's perspective?

(Answers will vary.)

_____

_____

_____

2. This excerpt is from a textbook written for students who are in emergency services programs to become emergency medical technicians or paramedics. The description was written by Betty Breathewright, a paramedic for a local firehouse and a professor of emergency medicine at a university.

If a bag valve mask is available, first responders should use it instead of mouth-to-mouth resuscitation. Properly using a BVM delivers more oxygen to the patient than mouth-to-mouth resuscitation. Secure the blob to the patient's face and gently squeeze the BVM over two seconds. Look for chest rise and listen for air exchange. Remember that delivering too much air too forcefully will overinflate the lungs, causing the air to bypass to the stomach, and increase the likelihood of vomiting; a rumbling sound will be heard, and the stomach will swell.

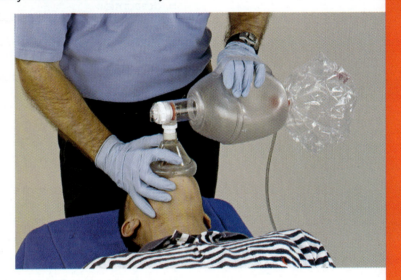

What is the style of this paragraph? __b__

a. narration

b. description

c. exposition

d. argument

Who is the writer's intended audience? __c__

a. paramedics

b. students in general courses

c. students in emergency services courses

d. the general public

What is the writer's purpose? ____a____

a. to inform

b. to persuade

c. to entertain

What do the notes tell you about the writer's perspective?

(Answers will vary.) _____

_____

_____

3. This excerpt is from a children's chapter book about a young girl named Judy who finds herself in all sorts of scrapes. It is written by I. Magi Nechild, a new children's author whose books are growing in popularity.

Judy jumped on the bed. Even though she was tall, almost four feet, she still could not jump as high as the ceiling. She tried very hard, but her train-track pajama bottoms slipped down and bunched at her feet. She tumbled across the bed with a flop and got all tangled up in her p.j.s. When her mother came in and saw her in such a confused knot of clothing, legs, and bed linens, she exclaimed, "Judy, when will you ever learn? No jumping on the bed!"

What is the style of this paragraph? ____a____

a. narration

b. description

c. exposition

d. argument

Who is the writer's intended audience? ____b____

a. the general public

b. children

c. young adults

d. fellow writers

What is the writer's purpose? ____c____

a. to inform

b. to persuade

c. to entertain

What do the notes tell you about writer's perspective?

(Answers will vary.) _____

_____

_____

4. This excerpt is from a popular lawn and garden magazine; this particular section offers information to backyard bird enthusiasts. The section is written by Wren Chaser, a woman who has a master's degree in ornithology.

A baffle will help to keep squirrels out of your birdfeeder. Find a shallow bowl that has at least a 12-inch diameter (if your birdfeeder is small, a Frisbee will do). Drill a small hole in the bottom of the bowl at the center. Before hanging your birdfeeder, turn the bowl upside-down and push the rope you will use to hang the feeder through the hole. Tie a knot to secure the baffle; attach the birdfeeder six inches below the baffle and hang the feeder. If a squirrel jumps on the baffle to get to the feeder, the baffle tips, throwing the squirrel off-balance and dropping it the ground.

What is the style of this paragraph? _____ b

a. narration

b. description

c. exposition

d. argument

Who is the writer's intended audience? _____ b

a. the general audience

b. bird enthusiasts

c. biologists

d. ornithologists

What is the writer's purpose? _____ a

a. to inform

b. to persuade

c. to entertain

What do the notes tell you about writer's perspective?

(Answers will vary.)

_____

_____

_____

Tone and Bias

Tone in writing is like the tone of voice people use when talking: both reveal attitude and mood. When we talk, changes in our voice and facial expression tell listeners a lot about the message we're conveying. Try this: say these four words out loud—"I have some news"—first in a happy tone, then in a sad, an indifferent, or an angry tone. As you change your mood, you naturally say these words very differently. You emphasize different words, vary the pitch and loudness of your voice, and use a lot or a little energy.

Inferring Tone

It's usually quite easy to identify tone in conversation, but tone in writing is not so obvious as tone of voice. Often you have to use the same kinds of evidence you use for making inferences—the logic of "putting two and two together," selection of details, and the choice of words. If the writer wants to tell a positive story about learning to read, as Rebecca Grabiner does in Reading 2, the tone will be light and lively. If a writer wants to persuade people to drill, or not to drill, in the Alaskan wilderness, the tone might be serious, perhaps upset, or it might be enthusiastic about promising solutions.

A Writer's Bias: Objective and Subjective Tones

A person who has a neutral attitude, free from emotional attachment to one or another side, is said to be objective about the subject. Being subjective is

Instructor Tip

Ask students to describe a time when someone's tone told them more than his or her words. For example, if Hannah asked Bill to the movies and Bill said, "Oh, all right, I guess we can go," what does Bill's tone really tell Hannah?

just the opposite: the person has an emotional involvement or a personal bias—or leaning—toward one side or the other. (A bias is not necessarily negative or positive; a bias merely means the author has a preference.) The chart below demonstrates the usual distinction made between kinds of writing that are expected to be either objective or subjective.

OBJECTIVE WRITING	SUBJECTIVE WRITING
newspaper reporting	newspaper editorials and opinion pieces
textbook writing	articles or books written from a certain cultural, political, or personal perspective

Instructor Tip
Ask students to describe a time when someone's bias influenced the students' behavior. For example, because Justine, the most popular girl in school, has a preference for pink polka-dot pants, her friends now wear them too.

Hot or Not?

Should a writer's biases affect your opinion of a reading?

Objective writers use words that have a neutral tone to them and are not likely to offend a general audience. Subjective writers use loaded words, words that have deep emotional connotations, and might be offensive to some members of a general audience. For example, if you overheard your instructor say, "I wish college students would be more resourceful," you might shrug and not take offense. If you overheard your instructor say, "These young brats think they should be told everything," you might be especially offended by the word "brats." "Brats" is a loaded word.

To demonstrate the difference between an objective and a subjective tone, look at two versions of roommate problems colleges try to anticipate and solve. An objective approach to the problem might be stated this way:

Colleges can no longer assume that roommates will automatically get along without some complex methods for making a match between them. For example, popular musical tastes among young people now vary far more than they did twenty-five years ago, when choosing what to play was likely to involve two clear-cut types of music: the Rolling Stones and the Bee Gees.

The same information might be presented in a far more subjective way. (Loaded words or phrases are underlined.)

Gone, gone are the days when colleges can assume that roommates will be civil to each other. Now colleges have to set up intricate questionnaires and procedures to assure that every need of every selfish and fussy young person can be met. For example, the popular musical tastes of this pampered generation have disintegrated into dozens of narrow-interest categories. In the more civil era of the previous generation, there were just two types of music—the Rolling Stones and the Bee Gees—and even those who could not agree on one or the other could get along.

The objective version simply explains the current situation. What can you see about the subjective writer? What tone of voice would she use if she were speaking? How did you pick up on her tone of voice? What biases, or preferences, do you notice from the tone?

Irony

The most familiar kind of irony is its harshest form: sarcasm. You can easily recognize the **sarcasm** when someone says, "You're a big help!" and clearly means the opposite.

Irony always depends on the opposition between the literal meaning of the words and the intended message. What makes a tone ironic is that the person uses words that apparently say one thing, while indicating that the opposite, or at least a totally different message, is intended.

It's important to recognize irony in writing so that you aren't misled into believing the writer meant the words literally. For example, Jean-Dominique Bauby's *The Diving Bell and the Butterfly* is about the limits in his life after the author suffered a paralyzing stroke. He reports being told about his condition, and his response: "Of course the party chiefly concerned is the last to hear the good news." This statement is bitterly ironic, since this news would of course be so terrible to hear. For an example of an entire reading based on irony, see Chapter 13 Practice Reading, "Memo from Coach."

For more practice recognizing bias and loaded words, do the following exercise.

Two people hired the same roofing company and had very different experiences. After the roofs were fixed, the customers decided to e-mail the manager of the company. Read the customers' e-mails, underline loaded words or phrases, and answer the questions that follow the e-mail.

1. From: Ed Anger (madman@aol.com)
   To: Stay Dry Roofs (manager@staydryroofs.com)
   Subject: My Collapsed Ceiling
   Date: April 12, 2009

Your roofing company is the <u>worst one</u> that I have ever <u>had to deal with</u>. You did a <u>crappy job</u> on my flashing, and now I have a <u>huge brown spot</u> on my ceiling where water has <u>seeped in</u> near the chimney. Last night, after a storm, that spot collapsed, so now my carpet is <u>ruined</u>. <u>Even I could have done a better job</u> than the <u>pack of hooligans</u> you sent out to fix my roof in the first place, and I would have <u>found something better</u> than the <u>black pancakes</u> you call roofing tiles. I paid <u>good money</u> for a <u>decent job</u>—all I wanted was a new roof. <u>Oh, I got one all right!</u> Along with a new ceiling and carpet!

What are some of the loaded words or phrases you identified in the e-mail?

(Answers will vary.)

_____

_____

What adjective would you use to describe the tone in this e-mail?

(Answers will vary.)

_____

_____

What biases does this writer have?

(Answers will vary.)

_____

_____

2. From: I. A. Dore (iadoreU@yahoo.com)
   To: Stay Dry Roofs (manager@staydryroofs.com)
   Subject: The Comforts of Home
   Date: April 12, 2009

When I came home and saw my new roof, I was tickled! Your company did a wonderful job creating a Spanish-style roof. I feel as though I am escaping to my private villa when I get home from work. I also had a lovely surprise when I saw the decrease in my electric bill. Your salesman promised a drop due to the excellent quality of the tiles and of the work of your expert roofers. I was so pleased—it seems the savings might even pay for the great job you did.

What are some of the loaded words or phrases you identified in the e-mail?
(Answers will vary.)

_____

_____

_____

_____

What adjective would you use to describe the tone in this e-mail?
(Answers will vary.)

_____

_____

_____

_____

What biases does this writer have?
(Answers will vary.)

_____

_____

_____

_____

APPLY THE NEW STRATEGY
Determine the Writer's Perspective

Now that you understand Strategy 11, put it into practice with Reading 21, "A Global Green Deal."

Determine the writer's purpose by considering the type of writing, the intended audience, and the writer's perspective. As you read, see how the tone reflects biases. Also, choose additional, appropriate strategies. For reading "Infernal Paradise," you'll find it especially helpful to make inferences and find meaning in metaphors. Finally, since this reading has no headings, try mapping main topics in pencil first, before marking main ideas.

A Global Green Deal

MARK HERTSGAARD

Mark Hertsgaard is a journalist who has written books and articles on a variety of subjects. He has contributed to the *New York Times,* the *New Yorker, Outside,* and numerous other publications. His book, *Earth Odyssey: Around the World in Search of Our Environmental Future* (2000), has been praised for its thorough yet readable treatment of a difficult and complicated subject. Hertsgaard wrote this argument for the *Time* Earth Day 2000 issue.

Earlier in the chapter you saw excerpts from this reading that helped you define Hertsgaard's purpose: to persuade his readers to make changes to help protect the environment. He expects his readers to be general *Time* magazine readers, not readers with special expertise or interests. To match his purpose, his tone seems positive and persuasive.

To follow Hertsgaard's ideas, you'll find it especially helpful to find meaning in metaphors—some of which may already be familiar to you. Since this reading has no headings, try mapping main topics in pencil first, before marking main ideas.

Green Deal (title): is intended to echo President Franklin Delano Roosevelt's program, the New Deal

1   So what do we do? Everyone knows the planet is in bad shape, but most people are resigned to passivity. Changing course, they reason, would require economic sacrifice and provoke stiff resistance from corporations and consumers alike, so why bother? It's easier to ignore the gathering storm clouds and hope the problem magically takes care of itself.

2   Such <u>fatalism</u> is not only dangerous but mistaken. For much of the 1990s I traveled the world to write a book about our environmental predicament. I returned home sobered by the extent of the damage we are causing and by the speed at which it is occurring. But there is nothing inevitable about our self-destructive behavior. Not only could we dramatically reduce our burden on the air, water and other natural systems, we could make money doing so. If we're smart, we could make restoring the environment the biggest economic enterprise of our time, a huge source of jobs, profits and poverty <u>alleviation</u>.

3   What we need is a Global Green Deal: a program to renovate our civilization environmentally from top to bottom in rich and poor countries alike. Making use of both market incentives and government leadership, a 21st century Global Green Deal would do for environmental technologies what government and industry have recently done so well for computer and Internet technologies: launch their commercial takeoff.

4   Getting it done will take work, and before we begin we need to understand three facts about the reality facing us. First, we have no time to lose. While we've made progress in certain areas—air pollution is down in the U.S.—big environmental problems like climate change, water scarcity and species extinction are getting worse, and faster than ever. Thus we have to change our ways profoundly—and very soon.

5   Second, poverty is central to the problem. Four billion of the planet's 6 billion people face deprivation inconceivable to the wealthiest 1 billion. To paraphrase Thomas Jefferson, nothing is more certainly written in the book of fate than that the bottom two-thirds of humanity will strive to improve

> If we're smart, we could make restoring the environment the biggest economic enterprise of our time, a huge source of jobs, profits and poverty alleviation.

their lot. As they demand adequate heat and food, not to mention cars and CD players, humanity's environmental footprint will grow. Our challenge is to accommodate this mass ascent from poverty without wrecking the natural systems that make life possible.

Third, some good news: we have in hand most of the technologies needed **6** to chart a new course. We know how to use oil, wood, water and other resources much more efficiently than we do now. Increased efficiency—doing more with less—will enable us to use fewer resources and produce less pollution per capita, buying us the time to bring solar power, hydrogen fuel cells and other futuristic technologies on line.

hydrogen fuel cells: electrochemical devices that work much like a battery

Efficiency may not sound like a rallying cry for environmental revolu- **7** tion, but it packs a financial punch. As Joseph J. Romm reports in his book *Cool Companies,* Xerox, Compaq and 3M are among many firms that have recognized they can cut their greenhouse-gas emissions in half—and enjoy 50% and higher returns on investment—through improved efficiency, better lighting and insulation and smarter motors and building design. The rest of us (small businesses, homeowners, city governments, schools) can reap the same benefits.

Super-refrigerators use 87% less electricity than older, standard models **8** while costing the same (assuming mass production) and performing better, as Paul Hawken and Amory and L. Hunter Lovins explain in their book *Natural Capitalism.* In Amsterdam the headquarters of ING Bank, one of Holland's largest banks, uses one-fifth as much energy per square meter as a nearby bank, even though the buildings cost the same to construct. The ING center boasts efficient windows and insulation and a design that enables solar energy to provide much of the building's needs, even in cloudy Northern Europe.

Examples like these lead even such mainstream voices as AT&T and **9** Japan's energy planning agency, NEDO, to predict that environmental restoration could be a source of virtually limitless profit. The idea is to retrofit our farms, factories, shops, houses, offices and everything inside them. The economic activity generated would be enormous. Better yet, it would be labor intensive; investments in energy efficiency yield two to 10 times more jobs than investments in fossil fuel and nuclear power. In a world where 1 billion people lack gainful employment, creating jobs is essential to fighting the poverty that retards environmental progress.

But this transition will not happen by itself—too many entrenched in- **10** terests stand in the way. Automakers often talk green but make only token efforts to develop green cars because gas-guzzling sport-utility vehicles are hugely profitable. But every year the U.S. government buys 56,000 new vehicles for official use from Detroit. Under the Global Green Deal, Washington would tell Detroit that from now on the cars have to be hybrid-electric or hydrogen-fuel-cell cars. Detroit might scream and holler, but if Washington stood firm, carmakers soon would be climbing the learning curve and offering the competitively priced green cars that consumers say they want.

We know such government pump-priming works; it's why so many of **11** us have computers today. America's computer companies began learning to produce today's affordable systems during the 1960s while benefiting from subsidies and guaranteed markets under contracts with the Pentagon and the space program. And the cyberboom has fueled the biggest economic expansion in history.

12   The Global Green Deal must not be solely an American project, however. China and India, with their gigantic populations and ambitious development plans, could by themselves doom everyone else to severe global warming. Already, China is the world's second largest producer of greenhouse gases (after the U.S.). But China would use 50% less coal if it simply installed today's energy-efficient technologies. Under the Global Green Deal, Europe, America and Japan would help China buy these technologies, not only because that would reduce global warming but also because it would create jobs and profits for workers and companies back home.

greenhouse gases: carbon dioxide and other gases that slow the escape of heat from Earth's surface

13   Governments would not have to spend more money, only shift existing subsidies away from environmentally dead-end technologies like coal and nuclear power. If even half the $500 billion to $900 billion in environmentally destructive subsidies now offered by the world's governments were redirected, the Global Green Deal would be off to a roaring start. Governments need to establish "rules of the road" so that market prices reflect the real social costs of clear-cut forests and other environmental abominations. Again, such a shift could be revenue neutral." Higher taxes on, say, coal burning would be offset by cuts in payroll and profits taxes, thus encouraging jobs and investment while discouraging pollution. A portion of the revenues should be set aside to assure a just transition for workers and companies now engaged in inherently antienvironmental activities like coal mining.

revenue neutral: resulting in neither profit nor loss for an organization

14   All this sounds easy enough on paper, but in the real world it is not so simple. Beneficiaries of the current system—be they U.S. corporate-welfare recipients, redundant German coal miners or cut-throat Asian logging interests—will resist. Which is why progress is unlikely absent a broader agenda of change, including real democracy: assuring the human rights of environmental activists and neutralizing the power of Big Money through campaign-finance reform.

corporate-welfare recipients: tax breaks or government money to assist corporations

15   The Global Green Deal is no silver bullet. It can, however, buy us time to make the more deep-seated changes—in our often excessive appetites, in our curious belief that humans are the center of the universe, in our sheer numbers—that will be necessary to repair our relationship with our environment.

16   None of this will happen without an aroused citizenry. But a Global Green Deal is in the common interest, and it is a slogan easily grasped by the media and the public. Moreover, it should appeal across political, class and national boundaries, for it would stimulate both jobs and business throughout the world in the name of a universal value: leaving our children a livable planet. The history of environmentalism is largely the story of ordinary people pushing for change while governments, corporations and other established interests reluctantly follow behind. It's time to repeat that history on behalf of a Global Green Deal.

ACTIVE READERS RESPOND

After you've finished reading, use these questions to respond to "A Global Green Deal." You may write your answers in the spaces provided or on a separate sheet of paper.

VITAL VOCABULARY

Some words in this reading may be unfamiliar to you. Use the methods of Strategy 3 to explain what the listed words mean.

USE CONTEXT CLUES

a. alleviation (paragraph 2)

_____

b. abominations (paragraph 13)

_____

USE WORD PARTS

Check a dictionary definition to find the meanings of these word parts.

a. retrofit (paragraph 9)

_____

b. cyberboom (paragraph 11)

_____

c. fatalism (paragraph 2) (see how the word "fate" helps you get the meaning of "fatalism")

_____

d. entrench (paragraph 10) (see how the word "trench" helps you get the meaning of "entrench")

_____

USE THE DICTIONARY

Choose the correct definition of each word as it is used in the context of this reading.

a. subsidies (paragraph 11)

_____

b. inherently (paragraph 13)

_____

c. redundant (paragraph 14)

_____

SKILLS EXERCISE

A. Answer these questions about the reading.

    1. What is the style of this reading? ___d___

       a. narration

       b. description

       c. exposition

       d. argument

2. Who is the writer's intended audience? ___c___

   a. environmentalists

   b. scientists

   c. general audience

   d. hippies

3. What is the writer's purpose? ___b___

   a. to inform

   b. to persuade

   c. to entertain

4. What do the notes tell you about writer's perspective?

   (Answers will vary.)

   _____

   _____

   _____

   _____

B. *Read the following paragraph (paragraph 5) from the reading, underline loaded words or phrases, and answer the questions that follow.* (Answers will vary.)

Second, poverty is central to the problem. Four billion of the planet's 6 billion people face deprivation inconceivable to the wealthiest 1 billion. To paraphrase Thomas Jefferson, nothing is more certainly written in the book of fate than that the bottom two-thirds of humanity will strive to improve their lot. As they demand adequate heat and food, not to mention cars and CD players, humanity's environmental footprint will grow. Our challenge is to accommodate this mass ascent from poverty without wrecking the natural systems that make life possible.

   What are some of the loaded words or phrases you identified in this paragraph?

   _____

   _____

   What adjective would you use to describe the tone in this paragraph?

   _____

   _____

   What biases does this writer have?

   _____

   _____

OBJECTIVE OPERATIONS

1. Who is the writer's intended audience?

   a. environmentalists

   b. scientists

   c. general audience

   d. hippies

2. What is the author's purpose?

   a. to inform

   b. to persuade

   c. to entertain

3. What is the tone of the passage?

   a. critical

   b. subjective

   c. serious

   d. urgent

4. According to Hertsgaard, world poverty is central to our environmental problems because

   a. poor people don't have the education they need in order to take care of the environment.

   b. the wealthier nations will send the poorer nations shoddier goods that cause more environmental pollution.

   (c.) as poor people in the rest of the world seek to improve their lives, the increased production of consumer goods will cause even more damage to the environment.

   d. the demands of poor people in the rest of the world will cause wars, resulting in more environmental damage.

5. The word "abominations" in paragraph 13, line 7, most nearly means

   a. hostilities.

   (b.) outrages.

   c. crises.

   d. activists.

6. Which of the following sentences is the stated main idea of the passage?

   (a.) "What we need is a Global Green Deal: a program to renovate our civilization environmentally from top to bottom in rich and poor countries alike."

   b. "Making use of both market incentives and government leadership, a 21st century Global Green Deal would do for environmental technologies what government and industry have recently done so well for computer and Internet technologies."

   c. "The Global Green Deal is no silver bullet."

   d. "But a Global Green Deal is in the common interest, and it is a slogan easily grasped by the media and the public."

7. What is the implied main idea of paragraph 2?

   a. Humans are damaging the environment and spreading poverty.

   b. If they were smart, humans could save the environment and make some money.

   c. Humans globally are causing damage to the planet.

   (d.) Globally, humans are damaging the environment although they could not only reduce the causes of the damage but also make a profit from environmental technologies.

8. Hertsgaard uses several examples to show that increased efficiency can help the environment

and be good for business. All these are examples he uses, except

   a. better lighting and insulation.

   b. efficient windows and use of solar energy.

   (c.) wind power for generating heat.

   d. a super-refrigerator.

9. Which sentence provides support for this sentence (paragraph 13, lines 1–3): "Governments would not have to spend more money, only shift existing subsidies away from environmentally dead-end technologies like coal and nuclear power."

   (a.) "If even half the $500 billion to $900 billion in environmentally destructive subsidies now offered by the world's governments were redirected, the Global Green Deal would be off to a roaring start."

   b. "Governments need to establish 'rules of the road' so that market prices reflect the real social costs of clear-cut forests and other environmental abominations."

   c. "Again, such a shift could be revenue neutral."

   d. "Higher taxes on, say, coal burning would be offset by cuts in payroll and profits taxes, thus encouraging jobs and investment while discouraging pollution."

10. The author's claim that China could reduce its coal usage by half is

   a. adequately supported with details.

   (b.) inadequately supported with details.

11. What is the topic of paragraph 12?

   a. the Global Green Deal

   b. international interests in the environment

   (c.) the need for international involvement in Global Green Deal

   d. Asian countries and global warming

12. According to Hertsgaard, the U.S. government could promote increased efficiency in automobiles by

   (a.) buying only hybrid-electric or hydrogen-fuel-cell cars for official government use.

   b. demanding more fuel-efficient sport utility vehicles.

   c. encouraging auto manufacturers to produce more green-colored cars to symbolize their commitment to the environment.

   d. buying only older cars rather than adding to the wasteful production of new cars.

13. Identify the relationship between the following sentences from paragraph 9.

"The economic activity generated would be enormous. Better yet, it would be labor intensive; investments in energy efficiency yield two to 10 times more jobs than investments in fossil fuel and nuclear power." (lines 4–7)

   a. cause and effect

   b. statement and clarification ✓

   c. process

   d. definition and example

14. For paragraph 8, the author organizes the information by using

   a. comparisons.

   b. contrasts.

   c. descriptions.

   d. examples. ✓

15. Hertsgaard calls the Green Deal "revenue neutral," but some people would still oppose it, including

   a. people who do not believe in any kind of government subsidies.

   b. people and corporations who benefit from the way things currently work. ✓

   c. people and corporations who fear they would fail to get government contracts.

   d. people who view environmentalists as dangerous extremists.

16. The word "subsidies" in paragraph 11, line 4, most nearly means

   a. financial support. ✓

   b. donations.

   c. scholarships.

   d. advantages.

17. Identify the relationship between the parts of the following sentence (paragraph 6, lines 3–6): "Increased efficiency—doing more with less—will enable us to use fewer resources and produce less pollution per capita, buying us the time to bring solar power, hydrogen fuel cells and other futuristic technologies on line."

   a. addition

   b. definition and example ✓

   c. contrast

   d. statement and clarification

18. At the end of the article, Hertsgaard emphasizes that this plan is a way to buy time until we can make more "deep-seated" changes. Underlying all these changes is this most important change in attitude:

   a. recognizing that environmentalism is only one factor in determining how we create a just society.

   b. understanding the importance of educating our youth in the science and technology needed to solve our environmental problems.

   c. seeing that all human beings deserve the comfortable life we have in the United States.

   d. seeing human beings as just one part of the fragile system of life on earth. ✓

19. The author shows a bias

   a. against the Global Green Deal.

   b. toward the Global Green Deal. ✓

   c. against environmentalism.

   d. toward continuing as we are.

20. According to the author,

   a. the Global Green Deal will fix the world's environmental problems.

   b. the Global Green Deal sounds like an excellent plan, but it may be extremely difficult to enact in the real world. ✓

   c. real democracy and human rights have no effect on environmental issues.

   d. Big Money needs to be reformed in order to save the environment.

READERS WRITE

1. What evidence does Hertsgaard give that our environmental problems demand immediate attention?
   (Answers will vary.)

2. According to Hertsgaard, what effect does world poverty have on our environmental future?
   (Answers will vary.)

3. What is one example that Hertsgaard gives to show that increased efficiency can help the environment and be good for business?

   (Answers will vary.)

   _____

   _____

4. How could the U.S. government promote increased efficiency in automobiles? What challenges would the government face in making this change?

   (Answers will vary.)

   _____

   _____

5. At the end of the article, Hertsgaard emphasizes that this plan is a way to buy time until we can make more fundamental changes. What changes does he refer to?

   (Answers will vary.)

   _____

   _____

READERS DISCUSS

1. Remember that Hertsgaard wrote this argument as a final piece for the *Time* Earth Day 2000 issue. It was preceded by many articles about specific environmental problems. Discuss with others how persuasive you think Hertsgaard's argument would be for the readers of that issue. Was the argument as persuasive for you? Why or why not?

   (Answers will vary.)

   _____

   _____

2. Write about an environmental problem that personally concerns you. Compare notes with others about the kinds of environmental problems they are concerned about. Discuss ways you could imagine proceeding to get more information or take some action.

   (Answers will vary.)

   _____

   _____

DETERMINE THE WRITER'S PERSPECTIVE

1 | Recognize the style of writing.

2 | Recognize the intended audience.

3 | Identify the writer's perspective.

4 | See how the tone reflects biases.

Summary

CHAPTER 11

HOW DOES STRATEGY 11 HELP YOU BECOME AN ENGAGED READER?

By determining the *writer's perspective* you know more about "where the writer is coming from." Since you know more what to expect from a reading, you get a broader view of the writer's ideas and his or her intentions in presenting them. You can then *respond* more fully, as you take into account what the writer intended as well as your personal feelings and ideas.

HOW DOES THE DETERMINE THE WRITER'S PERSPECTIVE STRATEGY WORK?

You determine the writer's perspective by asking what type of writing it is, who the intended audience is, and what the writer's experience on the subject is. You see how the tone of the writing reflects biases.

Strategy 11 shows you how to recognize the style of writing a writer uses. A writer narrates, describes, explains, or argues, and each style hints at the writer's overall perspective.

Strategy 11 reminds you to pay attention to the intended audience. Recognizing who the audience is will help you identify the writer's purpose and perspective.

Strategy 11 gives you ways to identify the writer's perspective. Knowing the writer's point of view will help you identify his or her intentions for writing.

Strategy 11 teaches you that tone can show a writer's biases. A writer's word choice can show you what his or her personal preferences are.

Key Terms

argument: persuades you to believe something or do something

bias: leaning to one or another side of a debatable question; emotional involvement

description: shows what someone or something looks like

exposition: explains something or informs

general audience: the people who have no special background in a subject

intended audience: the people a writer wants to reach

irony: use of words to convey meaning that is opposite to—or very different from—the literal meaning

narration: tells a story

objective: neutral, free from emotional attachment to one side or the other

perspective: way of looking at a subject; your position on it

purpose: the writer's reasons for writing

sarcasm: ironic use of a term to mean its opposite

subjective: having emotional involvement or bias (leaning) to one side or the other

tone: shows the writer's attitude or mood

Think AGAIN ›

Our perspective influences us in ways we do not always recognize. Maybe because you received a speeding ticket that you could not sass your way out of, you may no longer speed, and you may no longer think that sweet talk will change an officer's mind. Or perhaps you are taking a course for a second time, and you roll your eyes when a first-time student brags that she doesn't ever study because you know that she will probably be repeating the course. Your change in point of view influenced your behavior. What other examples can you think of?

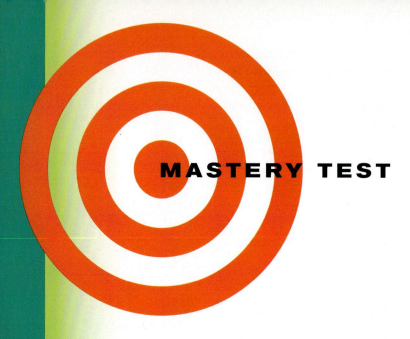

MASTERY TEST

Infernal Paradise

READING 22 BARBARA KINGSOLVER

Barbara Kingsolver is a well-known writer of novels and short stories as well as nonfiction on a wide range of subjects. She came to writing first through her career as a scientific writer and journalist. "Infernal Paradise" is excerpted from an essay in *High Tide at Tucson* (1995), a collection of her writings on common themes: family, community, and concern for the natural world.

infernal (title): hellish, fiery

Haleakala: the world's largest inactive volcano, on Maui, Hawaii
obsidian: dark, natural glass formed by cooling molten lava

1   Entering the crater at dawn seemed unearthly, though Haleakala is entirely of the earth, and nothing of human <u>artifice</u>. The cliffs absorbed and enclosed us in a mounting horizon of bleak obsidian crags. A lake of cloud slid over the rim, wave by wave, and fell into the crater's separate atmosphere, dispersing in vapor trails. The sharp <u>perimeter</u> of cliffs contains a volcanic bowl three thousand feet deep and eight miles across as the crow flies (or twice that far as the hiker hikes). The depression would hold Manhattan, though fortunately it doesn't.

2   We walked and slid down miles of gravelly slope toward the crater floor, where the earth had repeatedly <u>disgorged</u> its contents. Black sworls of bubbling lava had once flowed around red cinder cones, then cooled to a tortured standstill. I stood still myself, allowing my eye a minute to take in the <u>lunatic</u> landscape. In the absence of any human construction or familiar vegetation like, say, trees, it was impossible to judge distances. An irregular dot on the trail ahead might be a person or a house-sized boulder. Down below, sections of the trail were sketched across the valley, crossing dark lava flows and green fields, disappearing into a velvet fog that hid the crater's eastern half.

3   The strange <u>topography</u> of Haleakala Crater makes its own weather. Some areas are parched as the Sahara, while others harbor fern forests under a permanent veil of cloud. Any part of the high-altitude crater can scorch in searing sun, or be lashed by freezing rain, or both, on just about

any day of the year. Altogether it is one of the most difficult landscapes ever to host natural life. It is also one of the few places in Hawaii that looks as it did two hundred years ago—or for that matter, two thousand. Haleakala is a tiny, threatened ark.

4   To learn about the natural history of Hawaii is to understand a story of unceasing invasion. These islands, when they first lifted their heads out of the waves a million years ago, were naked, defiant rock—the most isolated archipelago in the world. Life, when it landed here, arrived only through powerful stamina or spectacular accident: a fern's spore drifting on the trade wind, a seed in the craw of a bird, the bird itself. If it survived, that was an accident all the more spectacular. Natural selection led these survivors to become new species unique in the world: the silversword, for example, a plant that lives in lava beds and dies in a giant flowery starburst; or the nene, a crater-dwelling goose that has lost the need for webbed feet because it shuns the sea, foraging instead in foggy meadows, grown languid and tame in the absence of predators. Over the course of a million years, hundreds of creatures like these evolved from the few stray immigrants. Now they are endemic species, living nowhere on earth but here. For many quiet eons they thrived in their sequestered home.

5   Then humans arrived, also through stamina and spectacular accident. The Polynesians came first, bringing along some thirty plants and animals they considered indispensable, including bananas, taro, sugar cane, pigs, dogs, chickens. And also a few stowaways: rats, snails, and lizards. All of these went forth and multiplied throughout the islands. Each subsequent wave of human immigration brought fresh invasions. Sugar cane and pineapples filled the valleys, crowding out native herbs. Logging operations decimated the endemic rain forests. Pigs, goats, and cattle uprooted and ate whatever was left. Without a native carnivore to stop them, rats flourished like the Pied Piper's dream. Mongooses were imported in a hare-brained plan to control them, but the mongoose forages by day and the rat by night, so these creatures rarely encounter one another. Both, though, are happy to feast on the eggs of native birds.

6   More species have now become extinct in Hawaii than in all of North America. At least two hundred of the islands' endemic plant species are gone from the earth for good, and eight hundred more are endangered. Of the original cornucopia of native birds, many were never classified, including fifty species that were all flightless like the dodo—and now, like the dodo, all gone. A total of only thirty endemic bird species still survive.

7   It's quite possible now to visit the Hawaiian Islands without ever laying eyes on a single animal or plant that is actually Hawaiian—from the Plumeria lei at the airport (this beloved flower is a Southeast Asian import) to the farewell bouquet of ginger (also Asian). African flame trees, Brazilian jacarandas, mangos and banyans from India, coffee from Africa, macadamia nuts from Australia—these are beautiful impostors all, but to enjoy them is to dance on a graveyard. Exotics are costing native Hawaii its life.

8   Haleakala Crater is fortified against invasion, because of its protected status as a national park, and because its landscape is hostile ground for pineapples and orchids. The endemics had millennia to adapt to their difficult

To learn about the natural history of Hawaii is to understand a story of unceasing invasion.

spore: an asexual, usually single-celled reproduction organ, usually in nonflowering plants

endemic: native to a particular place

Pied Piper's dream: main character of story about ridding a town of rats

mongoose: cat-sized mammal, known for ability to kill venomous snakes

dodo: an extinct, heavy, flightless bird

feral: wild

niche, but the balance of such a fine-tuned ecosystem is precarious, easily thrown into chaos: the plants fall prey to feral pigs and rats, and are rendered infertile by insect invaders like Argentine ants and yellow jacket wasps, which destroy native pollinators.

Humans have sated their strange appetites in Haleakala too, and while a pig can hardly be blamed for filling its belly, people, it would seem, might know better. The dazzling silverswords, which grow nowhere else on earth, have been collected for souvenirs, leis, scientific study, Oriental medicine, and—of all things—parade floats. These magical plants once covered the ground so thickly a visitor in 1873 wrote that Haleakala's slopes glowed silvery white "like winter in moonlight." But in 1911 a frustrated collector named Dr. Aiken complained that "wild cattle had eaten most of the plants in places of any access." However, after much hard work he "obtained gunny sacks full." By 1930, it was possible to count the surviving members of this species. **9**

The nene suffered an even more dire decline, nearly following the dodo. Since it had evolved in the absence of predators, nothing in this gentle little goose's ground-dwelling habits prepared it for egg-eating rodents, or a creature that walked upright and killed whenever it found an easy mark. By 1951, there were thirty-three nene geese left living in the world, half of them in zoos. **10**

Midway through the century, Hawaiians began to protect their islands' biodiversity. Today, a tourist caught with a gunny-sack of silverswords would find them pricey souvenirs—there's a $10,000 fine. The Park Service and the Nature Conservancy, which owns adjacent land, are trying to exclude wild pigs from the crater and native forests by means of a fence, though in such rugged ground it's a task akin to dividing needles from haystacks. Under this fierce protection, the silverswords are making a gradual comeback. Nene geese have been bred in captivity and reintroduced to the crater as well, but their population, numbered at two hundred and declining, is not yet considered saved. Meanwhile, the invasion creeps forward: even within the protected boundaries of a national park, 47 percent of the plant species growing in Haleakala are aliens. The whole ecosystem is endangered. If the silverswords, nene geese, and other colorful endemics of Hawaii survive this century, it will be by the skin of their teeth. It will only happen because we decided to notice, and hold on tight. **11**

ACTIVE READERS RESPOND

After you've finished reading, use these questions to respond to "Infernal Paradise." You may write your answers in the spaces provided or on a separate sheet of paper.

VITAL VOCABULARY

Some words in this reading may be unfamiliar to you. Use the methods of Strategy 3 to explain what the listed words mean.

USE CONTEXT CLUES

a. artifice (paragraph 1)

_____

b. sequestered (paragraph 4)

_____

c. carnivore (paragraph 5)

_____

d. adjacent (paragraph 11)

_____

USE WORD PARTS

You know some of these word parts. Check the etymology in your dictionary definition for the others.

a. disgorged (paragraph 2)

_____

b. topography (paragraph 3)

_____

c. ecosystem (paragraph 8)

_____

d. biodiversity (paragraph 11)

_____

USE THE DICTIONARY

Choose the correct definition of each word as it is used in the context of this reading.

a. infernal (title)

_____

b. perimeter (paragraph 1)

_____

c. lunatic (paragraph 2)

_____

d. foraging (paragraph 4)

_____

SKILLS TEST

A. Answer these questions about the reading.

   1. What is the style of this reading? ___d___
       a. narration
       b. description
       c. exposition
       d. argument

2. Who is the writer's intended audience? _____a_____

   a. general audience

   b. people concerned with the environment

   c. scientists

   d. literature students

3. What is the writer's purpose? _____b_____

   a. to inform

   b. to persuade

   c. to entertain

4. What do the notes tell you about writer's perspective?

   (Answers will vary.)

   _____

   _____

B. Read the following paragraph (paragraph 7) from the reading, underline loaded words or phrases, and answer the questions that follow.

It's quite possible now to visit the Hawaiian Islands without ever laying eyes on a single animal or plant that is actually Hawaiian—from the Plumeria lei at the airport (this beloved flower is a Southeast Asian import) to the farewell bouquet of ginger (also Asian). African flame trees, Brazilian jacarandas, mangos and banyans from India, coffee from Africa, macadamia nuts from Australia—these are beautiful impostors all, but to enjoy them is to dance on a graveyard. Exotics are costing native Hawaii its life.

What are some of the loaded words or phrases you identified in this paragraph?

(Answers will vary.)

_____

What adjective would you use to describe the tone in this paragraph?

(Answers will vary.)

_____

What biases does this writer have?

(Answers will vary.)

_____

OBJECTIVE OPERATIONS

1. Who is the writer's intended audience?

   a. general audience

   b. people concerned with the environment

   c. scientists

   d. literature students

2. What is the author's purpose?

   a. to inform

   b. to persuade

   c. to entertain

3. What is the tone of the passage?

   a. scientific

   b. informative

   c. upsetting

   d. cautionary

4. It was very hard for Kingsolver to judge distances on her walk down the volcanic crater because

   a. the trail was so steep and curved that she could hardly see what was coming.

b. it was an empty land, with no familiar land-marks, so a spot on the trail ahead could be a person or a huge boulder.

c. the high temperatures made the heat give off mirages that confused the eye.

d. the lava was still flowing, and its curving paths caused confusion to the on-looker.

5. The word "perimeter" in paragraph 1, line 5, most nearly means

a. boundary.

b. passage.

c. straight line.

d. frontier.

6. Which of the following sentences best summarizes this passage?

a. Hawaii's native plants and animals are becoming extinct, and in order for them to survive, we must do something now.

b. Hawaii's native plants and animals will not survive to the end of this century.

c. Exotic plants and animals are a problem for Hawaii's environment.

d. A tourist may never see a native plant in Hawaii.

7. What is the stated main idea of paragraph 9?

a. "Humans have sated their strange appetites in Haleakala too, and while a pig can hardly be blamed for filling its belly, people, it would seem, might know better."

b. "The dazzling silverswords, which grow no-where else on earth, have been collected for souvenirs, leis, scientific study, Oriental medicine, and—of all things—parade floats."

c. "These magical plants once covered the ground so thickly a visitor in 1873 wrote that Haleakala's slopes glowed silvery white 'like winter in moonlight.'"

d. "But in 1911 a frustrated collector named Dr. Aiken complained that 'wild cattle had eaten most of the plants in places of any access.'"

8. In paragraph 3, Kingsolver says that Hawaii's natural history is made up of a series of "unceasing invasions." During the very first of these invasions

a. the native plants and animals were crowded out by species from other parts of the world.

b. the fragile plant and animal species that had existed underwater were quickly taken over by species from other islands.

c. plants or animals arrived over sea or on the wind, and a few were able to survive on the islands' bare rock.

d. Europeans brought plant and animal species from Europe.

9. Which sentence provides support for this sentence (paragraph 5, line 1): "Then humans arrived, also through stamina and spectacular accident."

a. "The Polynesians came first, bringing along some thirty plants and animals they considered indispensable, including bananas, taro, sugar cane, pigs, dogs, chickens."

b. "And also a few stowaways: rats, snails, and lizards."

c. "All of these went forth and multiplied throughout the islands."

d. "Each subsequent wave of human immigration brought fresh invasions."

10. The author's claim that the nene geese nearly became extinct is

a. adequately supported with details.

b. inadequately supported with details.

11. What is the topic of paragraph 7?

a. Hawaii's native plants and animals

b. Hawaiians' use of exotic plants and animals

c. the absence of native plants and animals in Hawaii

d. impostors

12. Haleakala Crater still looks much as it did two thousand years ago because it is protected as national parkland and

a. the landscape there is not good for growing pineapples and orchids.

b. the federal and state governments have spent millions to restore the landscape.

c. the slopes of the crater are so steep that they can only support the native plants that thrive on steep terrain.

d. no one knew it existed until it became a national parkland.

13. Identify the relationship between the parts of the following sentence from paragraph 3.

"Some areas are parched as the Sahara, while others harbor fern forests under a permanent veil of cloud." (lines 2–3)

a. comparison

b. cause and effect

c. contrast

d. statement and clarification

14. For paragraph 2, the author organizes the information by using
    a. spatial order.
    b. contrasts.
    c. time order.
    d. comparisons.

15. According to Kingsolver, Hawaii has been losing its native species of plants at such a high rate that
    a. you can now visit Hawaii and never see a single, native Hawaiian plant.
    b. botanists are now trying to classify the species that have already been lost.
    c. researchers were called in to see what could be done to stop this mass plant extinction.
    d. tourists are required to prove that they have no native plants, such as the silversword, in their suitcases.

16. The word "adjacent" in paragraph 11, line 4, most nearly means
    a. scenic.
    b. public.
    c. far-off.
    d. neighboring.

17. Identify the relationship between the following sentences (paragraph 4, lines 4–8): "Life, when it landed here, arrived only through powerful stamina or spectacular accident: a fern's spore drifting on the trade wind, a seed in the craw of a bird, the bird itself. If it survived, that was an accident all the more spectacular."
    a. comparison
    b. addition
    c. contrast
    d. statement and clarification

18. Kingsolver tells of a creature in paragraph 10 ". . . that walked upright and killed whenever it found an easy mark." Here, "creature" refers to
    a. an egg-eating rodent.
    b. an ape.
    c. a human being.
    d. a nene goose.

19. The author shows a bias
    a. against protecting Hawaii's environment.
    b. toward protecting Hawaii's environment.
    c. against increasing tourists' awareness.
    d. toward increasing tourists' awareness.

20. According to the author,
    a. Hawaiians have done nothing to help save their state.
    b. Hawaiians have created strict laws to protect the environment.
    c. tourists may take as many silverswords as they desire.
    d. Hawaiians have been passive in creating environmental protections and national parks.

READERS WRITE

1. What made it so hard for Kingsolver to judge distances on her walk down the volcanic crater?
   (Answers will vary.)

2. Why is Haleakala Crater "one of the most difficult landscapes ever to host natural life"?
   (Answers will vary.)

3. What kind of "unceasing invasion" does Kingsolver refer to in paragraph 4? What were some of the effects of humans' arrival on the Hawaiian Islands described in paragraph 5?
   (Answers will vary.)

4. Why does Haleakala Crater still look much as it did two thousand years ago?

(Answers will vary.)

_____

_____

5. What does Kingsolver mean when she says in paragraph 9, "Humans have sated their strange appetites in Haleakala too, and while a pig can hardly be blamed for filling its belly, people, it would seem, might know better"?

(Answers will vary.)

_____

_____

READERS DISCUSS

1. How well did Kingsolver explain the threat to Hawaii's native species? Did her tone and metaphorical language work to reflect her purpose? How were you affected by what she says?

(Answers will vary.)

_____

_____

_____

2. How important do you think it is to save endangered species? Discuss your opinion with other classmates.

(Answers will vary.)

_____

_____

_____

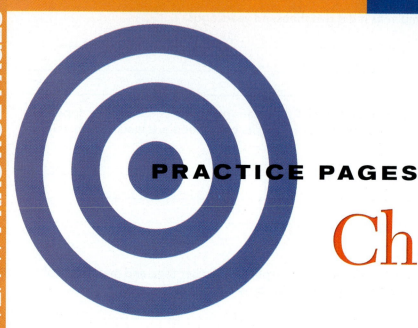

DETERMINE THE WRITER'S PERSPECTIVE

1 | Recognize the style of writing.

2 | Recognize the intended audience.

3 | Identify the writer's perspective.

4 | See how the tone reflects biases.

PRACTICE PAGES

Chapter 11

For practice identifying a writer's perspective, complete the following exercise.

PRACTICE EXERCISE 1

For each of the following, read the notes before the excerpt and then read the excerpt. Answer the questions that follow the excerpt. (Please know that these "notes" are fictionalized.)

1. This excerpt is from a young adult book about a boy named Brandon whose parents are going through a divorce. It is written by Wright Lotsof-stef, a popular author among teen audiences.

The rain fell heavily as Brandon trudged home. He should have worn his hiking boots; they were waterproof, and at least his feet would be dry. Wearing canvas sneakers during hurricane season was asinine. Why did stores even sell sneakers during hurricane season? It was stupid. So stupid Brandon fell for it when he slipped them on this morning. His mother had even said, "It's raining already. Don't you want a coat or an umbrella?" But her eyes dropped to his shoes, and the nearly imperceptible shake of her head sent him into a spasm of anger. He'd slammed out of the house without grabbing his backpack. All day, teachers asked first why he was soaked and second where his pack was. One of those crappy days from beginning to end. And now, in his sneakers, his feet ached with the cold and damp.

What is the style of this paragraph? _____ [a]

a. narration

b. description

c. exposition

d. argument

Who is the writer's intended audience? _____c_____

a. hurricane chasers

b. children

c. young adults

d. the general audience

What is the writer's purpose? _____c_____

a. to inform

b. to persuade

c. to entertain

What do the notes tell you about writer's perspective?

(Answers will vary.)

_____

_____

_____

2. This excerpt is from a popular magazine about teas and coffees; this particular excerpt comes from an essay on the proper way to brew black tea. The section is written by Assam Lieber, a man who worked as a tea connoisseur.

In order for black tea leaves to fully unfurl, the water must first come to a complete boil. Water that is 212 degrees allows the leaves to unleash their flavor. In addition, leaves that are allowed to fully unfurl also release fewer tannic acids, the cause of bitterness. Finally, steeping leaves in boiling water ensures the most delightful liquor, or color, for the tea. This will only enrich the sipper's experience.

What is the style of this paragraph? _____c_____

a. narration

b. description

c. exposition

d. argument

Who is the writer's intended audience? _____c_____

a. the general audience

b. tea drinkers

c. tea and coffee drinkers

d. people who hate tea

What is the writer's purpose? _____a_____

a. to inform

b. to persuade

c. to entertain

What do the notes tell you about writer's perspective?

(Answers will vary.)

_____

_____

_____

3. This excerpt is from a pamphlet given to people who buy hermit crabs at a local pet store. The description was written by Seg Mentedleg, a hermit crab enthusiast.

Because sand is part of a crab's natural habitat, sand is the most common strata used in a hermit crabitat. Fine sand is soft to hermit crabs and is easier to dig holes in, which is necessary during molting. In addition to being inexpensive, sand comes in a variety of colors. Natural colors, such as white or beige, are popular for crabitats designed to look like the seaside, but other colors, such as reds or browns, mimic the ground covering of tree-crab areas. Bags of sand not only vary in color, but also in size, ranging from a few pounds to a hundred pounds. Further, sand keeps a crabitat relatively odor-free as it dries and does not retain a musty smell (unless the sand has not been cleaned in months).

What is the style of this paragraph? ___b___
a. narration
b. description
c. exposition
d. argument

Who is the writer's intended audience? ___b___
a. hermit crab enthusiasts
b. new hermit crab owners
c. pet store patrons
d. the general public

What is the writer's purpose? ___a___
a. to inform
b. to persuade
c. to entertain

What do the notes tell you about the writer's perspective?
(Answers will vary.)

4. This appeal is from a local diner that is not-for-profit and does a great deal of community service. The appeal was written by owner Flowers N. Sunshine and placed in her community newspaper.

Due to the economy, HipTea Central is struggling to stay open. HipTea has always made an effort to support the community, holding fundraisers for block clean-up, volunteering employees for neighborhood watch, and donating a place to multiple groups for multiple reasons. But now HipTea really needs *your* help to stay open. In a desperate plea for community support, we are asking patrons to donate a little green to help us stay open. If HipTea has ever done anything for you in your community, even the tiniest little favor should be returned now! Donate and help this small business thrive because it helps nurture your community.

What is the style of this paragraph? ___d___
a. narration
b. description
c. exposition
d. argument

Who is the writer's intended audience? _____c_____

a. diner patrons

b. the general public

c. community members

d. hippies

What is the writer's purpose? _____b_____

a. to inform

b. to persuade

c. to entertain

What do the notes tell you about the writer's perspective?

(Answers will vary.)

_____

_____

For more practice recognizing bias and loaded words, do the following exercise.

PRACTICE EXERCISE 2

Two people applied for a job and sent a thank you after their interviews; however, each thank-you reads very differently. Read the e-mails, underline loaded words or phrases, and answer the questions that follow the e-mail.

1.   From: Bea P. Ompous (uppityme@yahoo.com)
     To: Acme World Business (manager@acmeworld.com)
     Subject: Thank You
     Date: July 12, 2009

I wish to say thank you for the interview with you today. I liked your company and the way you ran it; however, I do not feel that your offer is acceptable. Due to my experience and skills, I am more qualified than is necessary for the position, placing me in a higher salary bracket. Unfortunately, I also do not feel the position is challenging enough for an academic such as myself. However, I am grateful you took time out of your busy day to chat with me.

What are some of the loaded words or phrases you identified in the e-mail?

(Answers will vary.)

_____

_____

What adjective would you use to describe the tone in this e-mail?

(Answers will vary.)

_____

_____

What biases does this writer have?

(Answers will vary.)

_____

_____

421

2. From: Neu Hyer (novice@gmail.com)
   To: Acme World Business (manager@acmeworld.com)
   Subject: Thank you
   Date: July 12, 2009

I just wanted to say thank you for the interview today. I am excited that this job is <u>everything that I thought it would be</u>—challenging, demanding, and interesting. You described a position that is <u>fast-paced</u> and <u>requires quick-thinking</u>. Moreover, I was extremely pleased with what your company has to offer—<u>I love</u> the <u>open layout</u> of the office, the <u>pleasant family-centered atmosphere</u>, and the <u>willingness to help fellow employees</u> out. Thank you for considering me for the position. <u>I look forward</u> to hearing from you.

What are some of the loaded words or phrases you identified in the e-mail?

(Answers will vary.)

_____

_____

What adjective would you use to describe the tone in this e-mail?

(Answers will vary.)

_____

_____

What biases does this writer have?

(Answers will vary.)

_____

_____

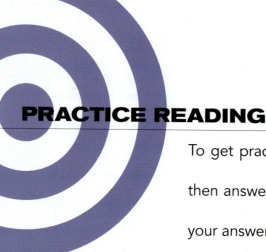

PRACTICE READING

To get practice with reading, read the passage, and then answer the questions that follow. You may write your answers in the spaces provided or on a separate sheet of paper.

Pitching Messages

JOHN VIVIAN

John Vivian is a professor of mass media at Winona State University in Minnesota. This reading comes from the chapter on advertising in his textbook *The Media of Mass Communication* (2002). Vivian discusses the various types of approaches advertisers use to reach audiences. Note the study preview that Vivian provides.

Study Preview When the age of mass production and mass markets arrived, common wisdom in advertising favored aiming at the largest possible audience of potential customers. These are called lowest common denominator approaches, and such advertisements tend to be heavy-handed so that no one can possibly miss the point. Narrower pitches, aimed at segments of the mass audience, permit more deftness, subtlety and imagination.

Importance of Brands

A challenge for advertising people is the modern-day reality that mass-produced products intended for large markets are essentially alike: Toothpaste is toothpaste is toothpaste. When a product is virtually identical to the competition, how can one toothpaste maker move more tubes?

Brand Names

By trial and error, tactics were devised in the late 1800s to set similar products apart. One tactic, promoting a product as a brand name, aims to make a product a household word. When it is successful, a brand name becomes almost the <u>generic</u> identifier, like Coke for cola and Kleenex for facial tissue.

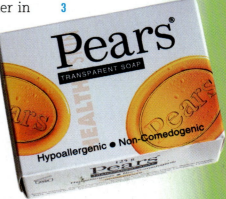

Techniques of successful brand name advertising came together in the 1890s for an English product, Pears' soap. A key element in the campaign was multimedia <u>saturation</u>. Advertisements for Pears' were everywhere— in newspapers and magazines and on posters, vacant walls, fences, buses and lampposts. <u>Redundancy</u> hammered home the brand name. "Good morning. Have you used Pears' today?" became a good-natured greeting among Britons that was still being repeated 50 years later. Each repetition reinforced the brand name.

Brand Image

David Ogilvy, who headed the Ogilvy & Mather agency, developed the brand image in the 1950s. Ogilvy's advice: "Give your product a first-class ticket through life."

Ogilvy created shirt advertisements with the distinguished Baron Wrangell, who really was a European nobleman, wearing a black eye patch—and a Hathaway shirt. The classy image was reinforced with the <u>accoutrements</u> around Wrangell: exquisite models of sailing ships, antique weapons, silver dinnerware. To some seeing Wrangell's setting, the patch suggested all kinds of exotica. Perhaps he had lost an eye in a romantic duel or a sporting accident.

Explaining the importance of image, Ogilvy once said, "Take whiskey. Why do some people choose Jack Daniels, while others choose Grand Dad or Taylor? Have they tried all three and compared the taste? Don't make me laugh. The reality is that these three brands have different images which appeal to different kinds of people. It isn't the whiskey they choose, it's the image. The brand image is 90 percent of what the distiller has to sell. Give people a taste of Old Crow, and tell them it's Old Crow. Then give them another taste of Old Crow, but tell them it's Jack Daniels. Ask them which they prefer. They'll think the two drinks are quite different. They are tasting images."

Lowest Common Denominator

Early brand-name campaigns were geared to the largest possible audience, sometimes called an LCD, or lowest common denominator approach. The term *LCD* is adapted from mathematics. To reach an audience that includes members with IQs of 100, the pitch cannot exceed their level of understanding, even if some people in the audience have IQs of 150. The opportunity for <u>deft</u> touches and even cleverness is limited by the fact they might be lost on some potential customers. **7**

LCD advertising is best epitomized in contemporary advertising by USP, short for unique selling proposition, a term coined by Rosser Reeves of the giant Ted Bates agency in the 1960s. Reeves' prescription was simple: Create a benefit of the product, even if from thin air, and then tout the benefit authoritatively and repeatedly as if the competition doesn't have it. One early USP campaign boasted that Schlitz beer bottles were "washed with live steam." The claim sounded good—who would want to drink from dirty bottles? However, the fact was that every brewery used steam to clean reusable bottles before filling them again. Furthermore, what is "live steam"? Although the implication of a competitive edge was hollow, it was done dramatically and pounded home with emphasis, and it sold beer. Just as hollow as a competitive advantage was the USP claim for Colgate toothpaste: "Cleans Your Breath While It Cleans Your Teeth." **8**

Perhaps to compensate for a lack of substance, many USP ads are heavy-handed. Hardly an American has not heard about fast-fast-fast relief from headache remedies or that heartburn relief is spelled R-O-L-A-I-D-S. USP can be unappealing as is acknowledged even by the chairman of Warner-Lambert, which makes Rolaids, who once laughed that his company owed the American people an apology for insulting their intelligence over and over with Bates's USP slogans. Warner-Lambert was also laughing all the way to the bank over the USP-spurred success of Rolaids, Efferdent, Listermint and Bubblicious. **9**

A unique selling proposition need be neither hollow nor insulting, however. Leo Burnett, founder of the agency bearing his name, refined the USP concept by insisting that the unique point be real. For Maytag, Burnett took the company's slight advantage in reliability and dramatized it with the lonely Maytag repairman. **10**

Market Segments

Rather than pitching to the lowest common denominator, advertising executive Jack Trout developed the idea of positioning. Trout worked to establish product identities that appealed not to the whole audience but to a specific audience. The cowboy image for Marlboro cigarettes, for example, established a macho attraction beginning in 1958. Later, something similar was done with Virginia Slims, aimed at women. **11**

Positioning helps to distinguish products from all the LCD clamor and noise. Advocates of positioning note that there are more and more adver- **12** tisements and that they are becoming noisier and noisier. Ad clutter, as it is called, drowns out individual advertisements. With positioning, the appeal is focused and caters to audience segments, and it need not be done in such broad strokes.

13   Campaigns based on positioning have included:
- Johnson & Johnson's baby oil and baby shampoo, which were positioned as adult products by advertisements featuring athletes.
- Alka-Seltzer, once a hangover and headache remedy, which was positioned as an upscale product for stress relief among health-conscious, success-driven people.

Redundancy Techniques

14   Advertising people learned the importance of redundancy early on. To be effective, an advertising message must be repeated, perhaps thousands of times. Redundancy is expensive, however. To increase effectiveness at less cost, advertisers use several techniques:
- *Barrages* Scheduling advertisements in intensive bursts called flights or waves.
- *Bunching* Promoting a product in a limited period, such as running advertisements for school supplies in late August and September.
- *Trailing* Running condensed versions of advertisements after the original has been introduced, as automakers do when they introduce new models with multipage magazine spreads, following with single-page placements.
- *Multimedia trailing* Using less expensive media to reinforce expensive advertisements. Relatively cheap drive-time radio in major markets is a favorite follow through to expensive television advertisements created for major events like the Super Bowl.

New Advertising Techniques

15   Inundated with advertisements, 6,000 a week on network television, double since 1983, many people tune out. Some do it literally with their remotes. Ad people are concerned that traditional modes are losing effectiveness. People are overwhelmed. Consider, for example, that a major grocery store carries 30,000 items, each with packaging that screams "buy me." More commercial messages are put there than a human being can handle. The problem is ad clutter. Advertisers are trying to address the clutter in numerous ways, including stealth ads, new-site ads and alternative media. Although not hidden or subliminal, stealth ads are subtle—even covert. You might not know you're being pitched unless you're attentive, really attentive.

Stealth Ads

Stealth ads fit so neatly into the landscape that the commercial pitch seems part of the story line. In 1996 the writers for four CBS television programs, including "Nanny" and "High Society," wrote Elizabeth Taylor into their scripts. And there she was, in over

Although not hidden or subliminal, stealth ads are subtle—even covert. You might not know you're being pitched unless you're attentive, really attentive.

425

two hours of programming one winter night, wandering in and out of sets looking for a missing string of black pearls. Hardly coincidentally, her new line of perfume, Black Pearls, was being introduced at the time.

The gradual convergence of information and entertainment, called in- 17 fotainment, has a new element: advertising. "Seinfeld" characters on NBC munched Junior Mints. The M&M/Mars candy company bought a role for Snickers in the Nintendo game *Biker Mice from Mars*. In 1997 Unilever's British brand Van den Bergh Foods introduced a video game that stars its Peperami snack sausage. In movies promotional plugs have become a big-budget item. The idea is to seamlessly work the presence of commercial products into a script without a cue—nothing like the hopelessly dated "And now a word from our sponsors."

Less subtle is the infomercial, a program-length television commer- 18 cial dolled up to look like a newscast, live-audience participation show or a chatty talk show. With the proliferation of 24-hour television service and of cable channels, airtime is so cheap at certain hours that advertisers of even offbeat products can afford it. Hardly anybody is fooled into thinking that infomercials are anything but advertisements, but some full-length media advertisements, like Liz Taylor wandering through CBS sitcoms, are cleverly disguised.

A print media variation is the 'zine—a magazine published by a manu- 19 facturer to plug a single line of products with varying degrees of subtlety. 'Zine publishers, including such stalwarts as IBM and Sony, have even been so brazen as to sell these wall-to-wall advertising vehicles at newsstands. In 1996, if you bought a splashy new magazine called *Colors*, you paid $4.50 for it. Once inside, you probably would realize it was a thinly veiled ad for Benetton casual clothes. *Guess Journal* may look like a magazine, but guess who puts it out as a 'zine: The makers of the Guess fashion brand. Stealth advertisements try "to morph into the very entertainment it sponsors," wrote Mary Kuntz, Joseph Weber and Heidi Dawley in *Business Week*. The goal, they said, is "to create messages so entertaining, so compelling—and maybe so disguised—that rapt audiences will swallow them whole, oblivi-ous to the sales component."

New-Site Ads

Ironically, solving the problem of ad clutter by going underground with 20 stealth ads contributes to the clutter. Sooner or later, it would seem, people would also tire of advertising omnipresence. Snapple stickers adorn kiwis and mangoes at the grocery. Sports stadiums named for department stores or other companies, like the Target Center in Minneapolis and the Wash-ington Redskins' FedEx Field, try to weave product names into everyday conversation and the news. Sports events galore bear the names of high-bidding sponsors. How omnipresent can advertising become? Consider the Bamboo lingerie company that stenciled messages on Manhattan side-walks: "From here, it looks like you could use some new underwear."

ACTIVE READERS RESPOND

After you've finished reading, use these questions to respond to "Pitching Messages." You may write your answers in the spaces provided or on a separate sheet of paper.

VITAL VOCABULARY

Some words may be unfamiliar to you. Use the methods of Strategy 3 to explain what the listed words mean.

USE CONTEXT CLUES

a. generic (paragraph 2)

_____

b. saturation (paragraph 3)

_____

c. covert (paragraph 15)

_____

d. rapt (paragraph 19)

_____

e. oblivious (paragraph 19)

_____

USE WORD PARTS

a. subliminal (paragraph 15)

_____

b. proliferation (paragraph 18)

_____

c. omnipresent (paragraph 20)

_____

USE THE DICTIONARY

Choose the correct definition of these words as they are used in the context of this reading.

a. redundancy (paragraph 3)

_____

b. accoutrements (paragraph 5)

_____

c. deft (paragraph 7)

_____

d. stealth (paragraph 15)

_____

e. morph (paragraph 19)

_____

OBJECTIVE OPERATIONS

1. Who is the writer's intended audience?
   a. general audience
   b. advertising students
   c. advertisers
   d. consumers

2. What is the author's purpose?
   a. to inform
   b. to persuade
   c. to entertain

3. What is the tone of the passage?
   a. compassionate
   b. informative
   c. aware
   d. cautionary

4. According to David Ogilvy, it is important to create a brand image because it
   a. helps people choose a distinctive product among others like it.
   b. makes companies imagine new products that people would like to buy.
   c. it helps keep a healthy competition among similar products.
   d. makes a product seem special though it's the same as others.

5. The word "proliferation" in paragraph 18, line 3, most nearly means
   a. demand.
   b. spreading.
   c. entertainment.
   d. nuisance.

6. Which of the following sentences best summarizes this passage?
   a. Advertisements are constantly changing to adapt to a wider audience.
   b. Advertisers market to specific groups for specific reasons, which increases their customers.
   c. Advertisers focus on the largest audience of potential customers and continuously adapt their advertisements to suit customers' needs.
   d. Customers will be overwhelmed by advertisements.

7. What is the stated main idea of paragraph 3?
   a. "Techniques of successful brand name advertising came together in the 1890s for an English product, Pears' soap."
   b. "A key element in the campaign was multi-media saturation."
   c. "Advertisements for Pears' were every-where— in newspapers and magazines and on posters, vacant walls, fences, buses and lampposts."
   d. "Redundancy hammered home the brand name."

8. The ad for the lonely Maytag repairman that dramatized the company's slight advantage in reliability was an example of
   a. the unique selling proposition (USP) with a hollow claim.
   b. the unique selling proposition (USP) that really had a unique point.
   c. a campaign to appeal to the lowest common denominator.
   d. a campaign based on positioning to blue collar workers.

9. Which sentence provides support for this sentence (paragraph 17, lines 1–2): "The gradual convergence of information and entertainment, called infotainment, has a new element: advertising."
   a. "'Seinfeld' characters on NBC munched Junior Mints."
   b. "The M&M/Mars candy company bought a role for Snickers in the Nintendo game *Biker Mice from Mars*."
   c. "In 1997 Unilever's British brand Van den Bergh Foods introduced a video game that stars its Peperami snack sausage."
   d. all of the above

10. The author's claim that "stealth ads fit so neatly into the landscape" (paragraph 16, line 1) is
    a. adequately supported with details.
    b. inadequately supported with details.

11. What is the topic of paragraph 19?
    a. Guess's 'zine and its effect
    b. the 'zine as new stealth advertisement
    c. the Benetton magazine
    d. buying advertisements

12. Two methods that advertisers use to increase the effectiveness of redundancy are
    a. trailing and positioning.
    b. barrages and bunching.

c. cluttering and posting.

d. positioning and targeting.

13. Identify the relationship between the following sentences from paragraph 6.

"The reality is that these three brands have different images which appeal to different kinds of people. It isn't the whiskey they choose, it's the image." (lines 4–6)

a. comparison

b. cause and effect

c. contrast

d. statement and clarification

14. For paragraph 8, the author organizes the information by using

a. comparisons.

b. contrasts.

c. examples.

d. descriptions.

15. The unique selling proposition (USP) claim for Colgate tooth paste was that it: "Cleans Your Breath While It Cleans Your Teeth." Vivian calls that a "hollow" claim because

a. it creates a claim out of thin air and says it repeatedly as if the competition doesn't have it.

b. it creates a product from scratch and advertises it before it's fully developed.

c. the benefits of the product are so exaggerated as to have almost no basis in fact.

d. the claims are made about defective, or "hollow," products.

16. The word "oblivious" in paragraph 19, line 12, most nearly means

a. forgetful.

b. unaware.

c. inconsiderate.

d. conscious.

17. Identify the relationship between the parts of the following sentence (paragraph 10, lines 1–2): "A unique selling proposition need be neither hollow nor insulting, however."

a. comparison

b. definition and example

c. contrast

d. cause and effect

18. Advertisers are trying new methods, such as stealth ads and alternative media to try to deal with

a. ad clutter.

b. the proliferation of 24-hour television service.

c. the lowest common denominator.

d. the ethical problems involved in advertising.

19. The author shows a bias

a. against stealth advertisements.

b. toward stealth advertisements.

c. against the adaptability of advertisers.

d. toward increasing customers' awareness.

20. According to the author,

a. customers are attentive to advertising.

b. advertisements have overwhelmed people.

c. customers will become so overwhelmed that they will cease purchasing.

d. advertisers will continue to adapt their ways to gain more customers.

1. A brand name that is successful becomes a generic identifier, such as Kleenex for tissue. True or False

2. Advertisements are omnipresent. True or False

3. Johnson & Johnson used ____athletes____ to position itself to be a product for adults.

4. The unique selling proposition (UPS) claim for Colgate tooth paste was that it:
   "Cleans Your Breath While It Cleans Your Teeth." _____

5. What are two methods advertisers can use to increase the effectiveness of "redundancy" in order to reduce their costs? How do these methods work? (Answers will vary.) _____

   _____

6. How do stealth ads address advertisers' problems with "ad clutter"? What are two major types of stealth ads? How do these types of ads work? (Answers will vary.) _____

   _____

12

Write a Summary

WRITE A SUMMARY

1 | Put the writer's ideas in your own words.

2 | Base your summary on your marking or mapping.

imagine this

During opening statements in a court trial, the prosecution and the defense present their cases to help their audience, the jurors, understand what the case is about, who it involves, and what each side will argue. Then the trial begins. The jurors are responsible for hearing both sides of the case and evaluating the findings of fact that they receive. Many jurors take brief notes throughout a case in order to remember certain details. At the end of the trial, the prosecution and defense present their closing arguments, summarizing new information discovered during the trial. The jurors are dismissed to discuss the findings and, based on that information, determine whether a law was broken.

When you paraphrase, you are acting like a juror or lawyer. You take a quotation or information from a reading, think about what you have read, and put parts of a reading in your own words. When you summarize, you consider the overall points, the main ideas, and the major details, and condense them in a few sentences. Then, you can discuss what the reading was about.

Think FIRST

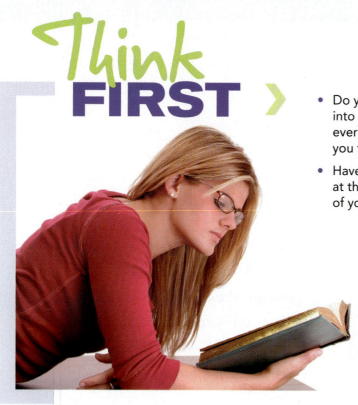

- Do you ever notice that you put a friend's story into your own words when you retell it? Do you ever rephrase something that someone has told you to make sure you understood it?

- Have you ever heard a character rehash the plot at the end of a film? Do you sum up the events of your day when you see your friends?

INTRODUCTION TO THE NEW STRATEGY
Write a Summary

When you ***write a summary,*** you increase your comprehension of the writer's ideas. A **summary** is a brief—usually one paragraph—restatement of a reading's overall point and main ideas. To create a summary you might start with your map or outline—or even with your marked text. Then restate—in your own words—the writer's overall point, main ideas, and important supporting ideas. Restating in your own words is called **paraphrasing.** If a classmate has ever asked you, "What did the professor just say?" you were probably able to answer in a short sentence in your own words. This is an example of paraphrasing.

To produce a summary, you consider the writer's ideas, and how you paraphrased them, and write a paragraph that flows logically from one sentence to the next, without distorting what the writer said. For example, you summarize when you tell someone the plot of a movie or book. In a few sentences, you explain the overall point and the main ideas of the film or book. If you are prompted, you will explain some of the supporting details. Doing this helps you remember the movie or the book better, and summarizing on paper after a reading works the same way.

Paraphrasing

Paraphrasing is a kind of translation of someone else's words into your own words. Paraphrasing the ideas in a reading helps you check your comprehension. You must thoroughly understand the writer's meaning before you can express that meaning in new words. When you paraphrase for a summary, you can start with the ideas you've already condensed into notes for your map or outline.

connect now

Have you ever "translated" a complex idea into slang for a friend?

Finding Your Own Words

Paraphrasing accurately takes practice. Start off by using language you feel comfortable with—your everyday words. (Pretend that you are going to tell your best friend about what you just read.) Then, be sure those words express the writer's meaning. When you paraphrase, you make two main kinds of changes:

- substitute new words for the writer's words (using synonyms—words that mean the same thing as the original words)

- make a different word order

Examine the sample paraphrase below taken from Reading 23, "Police and the Community." Notice the synonyms (such as "badly managed" for "mishandled") and the changes in word order.

Original sentence (paragraph 1): Yet police actions are often mishandled or misinterpreted, with the result that some people are critical of the police.

Paraphrase: Some people criticize the police because what the police do is often badly managed or misunderstood.

You may be tempted to copy the writer's words exactly, or borrow words or phrases from the writer. If you do this, you are no longer paraphrasing; instead, you are plagiarizing. **Plagiarism** is borrowing ideas that are not your own and not giving credit to whom those ideas belong. One way to force yourself to use your own words when you paraphrase is to read the passage you wish to paraphrase. Then, turn the reading over so that you cannot look at it. While you write up your paraphrase, avoid peeking at the reading. Then, review your paraphrase for accuracy. This way, you are forced to recall the details of the reading without "help" from the writer.

Instructor Tip

Have students get into groups. Write a list of titles of fairy tales on the chalkboard. Have students pick at least two fairy tales. Ask them first to decide the overall point and main ideas of the fairy tales. Remind them that a moral is similar to an overall point. Then, have the students write a short paragraph about the fairy tale, summarizing its main ideas (or main events).

Instructor Tips

#1 To extend the previous activity, have students pick another fairy tale. Have them write down a few phrases that they remember the characters in the story saying. For example, the wicked witch in "Snow White" tells Snow White to eat the apple, and the wolf threatens to blow the pigs' house down in "The Three Little Pigs." Tell them to recall at least three items that the characters say and put them into their own words. Then, remind the students that they are paraphrasing the fairy tale characters.

#2 In groups, have students work with a longer paragraph or a short multi-paragraph piece. Allow each student to read the paragraph and then have them return the copy to you. Have them write what they remember on a sheet of paper; when each student is ready, share and compare the summaries with the group. Return the paragraphs to the students to check their summaries against the paragraph. Teaching students to write about what they read without having a second look at the reading will encourage them to put their ideas into their own words.

Restating Ideas Accurately

Be accurate as you restate ideas in your own words. Don't change the meaning by changing or adding ideas. (Remember, don't copy the writer's words exactly either.) At the same time, try to keep the essential details.

Here are two examples of inaccurate paraphrasing.

Original statement: (adapted from the last sentence in paragraph 4) The relations between police and minority groups are complicated by the stereotypes they have of each other and the cultural and language differences that cause misunderstandings.

Inaccurate paraphrase: Police have problems with minority groups because of the stereotypes they have of minorities and misunderstandings of their culture and language.

What's wrong? This paraphrase makes the problem all one-sided. It leaves out the minorities' stereotypes of the police.

Another inaccurate paraphrase: The relations between police and minority groups are so stereotyped that they have no way of understanding each other, and the immigrants bring strange customs and languages that make policing impossible.

What's wrong? The first part adds a detail that changes the meaning. It says there is "no way of understanding"—an exaggeration of what Cole and Smith say. In addition, the second part changes the message by putting all the blame on the immigrants.

Including Quotations

You write a summary by paraphrasing the writer's ideas in your own words. However, it is sometimes helpful to quote directly. A quotation can call attention to an important term or phrase. For example, in a summary of Reading 16, "Mother Tongue," it would be useful to see Tan's exact words: "all the Englishes I grew up with." That phrase is an unusual and effective way to describe her different ways of speaking English. In this reading, Cole and Smith make a clear, general statement in paragraph 2—"policing in a multicultural society presents further challenges"—that is part of the overall point.

AWAITING EXAMINATION, ELLIS ISLAND   5 202-13

Hot or Not?

Have you ever confused a message that you were supposed to relate to someone else? What happened?

Instructor Tip

Give students copies of the same article. Have them pick two sentences to paraphrase. Once they have finished, have them share their sentences with the class by allowing the students to write them on the board. If a student has used exact phrasing (i.e., plagiarized), have the class help rewrite the sentence. (This way no student is singled out for mistakes, and all get a chance to learn what not to do.)

Josey Vogels, writer of the J Spot, a column for MetroNews.ca, recognizes that communication often breaks down between couples. However, her solution is what's interesting: She suggests that couples paraphrase each other in order to ensure clear communication when trying to make a point. Do you think this technique could work in other types of relationships?

You want to talk about it. He would rather stick a hot poker in his eye. You keep prodding. He leaves the room.

According to a new study in the June 2009 edition of the journal *Personal Relationships,* this kind of "demand-withdraw" communication is depressing, literally.

In relationships where a pattern develops when one spouse wants to continue discussing a marital disagreement even after the other spouse has tried to end the discussion by say, changing the topic or leaving the room (usually with the other spouse not far behind, still yakking), the study found increased levels of depressive symptoms (increased sadness, fatigue, poor sleeping and eating behaviors).

Interestingly, however, contrary to the stereotype (one I've in fact perpetuated with the above example), it's not always the woman pursuing and the man distancing.

According to the study's findings, when it comes to "demand-withdraw" communication within their relationship, husbands and wives both reported that they and their spouse took on the "demander role" and "withdrawer role" equally.

In other words, both men and women can be equally lousy communicators.

Given the impact this kind of communication clearly has upon one's mental health, it's in any couple's interest to invest some time in improving their communication style. "When relationship communication is better, we and our partners show fewer symptoms of depression," concluded the authors of the study, based out of the University of Wisconsin-Madison and the University of Notre Dame.

One of the best exercises I've ever encountered to help couples improve their communication is something called "mirroring." It's a bit like that telephone game you played at birthday parties as a kid. One partner says something to the other, and the other repeats it back and then asks if they got it right. If he or she didn't, the first partner clarifies what they said, and you repeat the exercise until the first partner is satisfied that the second partner has clearly understood.

In this way, instead of pushing each other's buttons, you're both listening and feeling heard—in other words, communicating.

It might sound tedious and artificial, but if you practice this a few times a week for several months, you'll be surprised how effective it can be in changing unhealthy communication patterns.

That is, if you can keep your partner in the room long enough to try it.

Vogels, Josey. "Communication Breakdown." The J Spot. *MetroNews.ca.* July 28, 2009. August 7, 2009. Available: www.metronews.ca/halifax/live/article/269263—communication-breakdown

When you do use the author's words, always remember to copy the words exactly and to show that you are quoting by using quotation marks. Leaving out the quotation marks might be considered plagiarism.

Setting Aside Your Own Ideas

A summary should give a fair representation of the writer's ideas. Don't include what you think until after you've summarized the ideas. You can respond to the reading with your own opinions at another time.

Instructor Tip
To extend the previous activity, have students summarize the article in their own words. Share a few examples with the class and discuss what is correct, what needs work, and what needs to be avoided.

For practice paraphrasing, do this exercise.

A. Read the following passage. Then, complete the exercise.

A Debate: The Impact of Prohibition

In the United States, the era known as Prohibition began when the Eighteenth Amendment to the Constitution went into effect in 1920. For the next 12 years, it was illegal to make, sell, or transport intoxicating beverages, defined as any drinks that were more than one half of one percent (.5%) alcohol.

Prohibition came about largely because of the growth of the Temperance Movement. For almost a century, people had praised the virtues of temperance. These reformers believed that alcohol was the main cause of disease, broken homes, poverty, and crime. Many saw "demon rum" and "John Barleycorn" as enemies of a stable and productive world. By 1916 almost half of the 48 states had passed laws that closed saloons and forbade the production of any form of alcoholic beverage.

Prohibition, therefore, was an honest effort to improve the health of all Americans, to deal with the problems associated with excessive alcohol consumption, and to lower the cost of government intervention. Some historians suggest that Prohibition enjoyed widespread support and led to a drop in some forms of crime. Others argue that it was the direct cause of increased crime, social conflict, and new forms of drug abuse. Whatever the case, the consumption of alcohol remained common throughout the United States despite the law.

It is hard to assess the impact of Prohibition. Bootlegging—the illegal manufacture and sale of liquor—was widespread and profitable, and illicit private clubs, called speakeasies, sprang up in place of the saloons that had been closed. The Customs Service and the Coast Guard struggled to stem the flood of alcohol coming in from places such as Canada and the Caribbean. The period also saw a drop in revenues for the government. Taxes could no longer be collected from the buyers and sellers of beer, wine, and spirits. Prison overcrowding was also a problem, partly because of violations of Prohibition laws.

Moreover, Prohibition-related crime quickly became organized. Individual criminals developed a network of relationships through which they could control bootlegging and provide protection to speakeasy owners. Corruption in police and government agencies also became a problem, as officers and civil servants were lured into a lucrative association with organized crime.

Prohibition ended in 1933 with the passage of the Twenty-first Amendment. The debate regarding its effectiveness continues to this day.

> **Corruption in police and government agencies also became a problem, as officers and civil servants were lured into a lucrative association with organized crime.**

B. Each of the following quotations is from the passage. Write a paraphrase for each quotation. Be sure to use your own words.

1. "For the next 12 years, it was illegal to make, sell, or transport intoxicating beverages, defined as any drinks that were more than one half of one percent (.5%) alcohol."

   Paraphrase

   (Answers will vary.)

   _____

   _____

   _____

2. "For almost a century, people had praised the virtues of temperance. These reformers believed that alcohol was the main cause of disease,

broken homes, poverty, and crime. Many saw 'demon rum' and 'John Barleycorn' as enemies of a stable and productive world."

Paraphrase

(Answers will vary.)

_____

_____

_____

3. "Some historians suggest that Prohibition enjoyed widespread support and led to a drop in some forms of crime. Others argue that it was the direct cause of increased crime, social conflict, and new forms of drug abuse."

Paraphrase

(Answers will vary.)

_____

_____

_____

4. "The period also saw a drop in revenues for the government. Taxes could no longer be collected from the buyers and sellers of beer, wine, and spirits."

Paraphrase

(Answers will vary.)

_____

_____

_____

5. "Individual criminals developed a network of relationships through which they could control bootlegging and provide protection to speak-easy owners."

Paraphrase

(Answers will vary.)

_____

_____

_____

CHRIS ROCK

The Fire Next Time

by James Baldwin

According to his website, www .chrisrock.com, comedian Chris Rock says his favorite book is *The Fire Next Time,* which became a national best-seller after its publication in 1963. Baldwin's book is part memoir, telling of his early life in Harlem, but more importantly, it is a passionate plea to Americans to embrace the multiracial character of our society and put an end to its legacy of racism.

If you liked *The Fire Next Time,* you might also like:

Their Eyes Were Watching God, Zora Neale Hurston

The Souls of Black Folk, W. E. B. DuBois

Native Son, Richard Wright

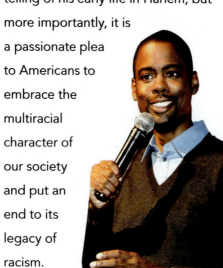

Summarizing the Overall Point and Main Ideas

Summarizing begins where marking and mapping—or outlining—leave off. When you mark and map, you identify the overall point, main ideas, and important supporting ideas. When you summarize, you put the ideas in your own words and sum up those ideas in a few sentences. It is possible to base your summary on a thorough marking of ideas in your book. However, when you're still learning to summarize, you might find it easier to start from a cluster map.

Putting the Main Ideas into a Summary

Here are some guidelines for writing a summary based on the ideas from your marking, map, or informal outline.

- Change any notes into complete sentences. A **complete sentence** has to have a subject and verb. For example, here is a note from the informal outline on page 439:

  Immigrants' different languages and cultures = more barriers.

- To turn that note into a complete sentence, you need a verb in place of the equal sign:

  Immigrants' different languages and different cultures cause more barriers.

- Paraphrase the writer's ideas, using your own words; condense the ideas if you haven't already made notes for a map or outline.

- Start with a sentence for the overall point.

- Write a sentence for each main idea and for each supporting idea you include.

connect now

Do you abbreviate when taking notes in class or do you write complete sentences? Which is more efficient?

Instructor Tip
To extend the previous activity, have students draw a cluster map of the paragraph.

- Follow the order of ideas in the reading.
- If you need a more complete summary, add more supporting ideas to each main idea.

For the following example, an informal outline for Reading 23, "Police and the Community," is still in note form. Notice that for the first main idea there are two supporting ideas given in order to explain the two aspects of police-minority relations.

"Police and the Community"

(*Overall point*) "Policing in multicultural society presents further challenges," so "community crime prevention" tries to improve police-community relations.

1. "Policing in a Multicultural Society": work made harder by stereotypes on both sides & by cultural & language differences. (2–7)
   - Immigrants' different language and culture = more barriers
   - People in inner city—esp., poor, racial-minority males—least confidence in police because of ineffective or abusive policing (8–11)

2. "Community Crime Prevention": Across country, increase in programs that involve community to help police, but results = mixed (12–16)
   - Works better in wealthier areas, but a few big cities have some success.

Even without having read "Police and the Community," you could use this outline to write up a summary. Your summary might read like this:

"Policing in a multicultural society presents further challenges," so "community crime prevention" programs try to improve community-police relations in order to involve the public in helping the police. The relations between police and minority groups are complicated by the stereotypes they have of each other and the cultural and language differences that cause misunderstandings. Immigrants' different languages and cultures cause more barriers. People in the inner city, especially those who are poor, racial-minority males, have the least confidence in the police because of ineffective or abusive policing. Across the country there has been an increase in "community crime prevention" programs that involve the community to help the police, but the results of these programs have been mixed. They work better in wealthier areas, but a few big cities have had some success in getting the community involved with the police.

See how the notes from the sample outline have been made into complete sentences. The underlining shows the slight changes and added words that make ideas clearer and more complete.

For practice summarizing, do this exercise.

A. Complete the cluster map for "A Debate: The Impact of Prohibition," the reading found on page 436.

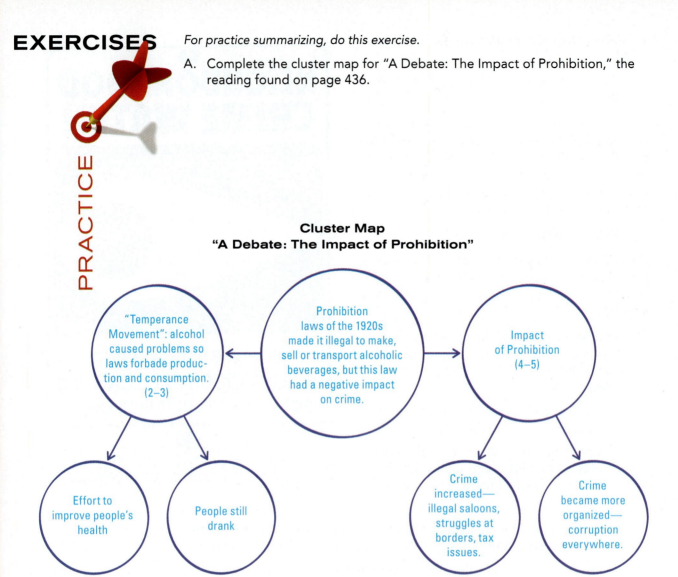

Cluster Map
"A Debate: The Impact of Prohibition"

"Temperance Movement": alcohol caused problems so laws forbade production and consumption. (2–3)

Prohibition laws of the 1920s made it illegal to make, sell or transport alcoholic beverages, but this law had a negative impact on crime.

Impact of Prohibition (4–5)

Effort to improve people's health

People still drank

Crime increased—illegal saloons, struggles at borders, tax issues.

Crime became more organized—corruption everywhere.

B. Based on your cluster map, write a summary. (Write your answers on a separate piece of paper.)

APPLY THE NEW STRATEGY
Write a Summary

Before reading "Police and the Community," think about the strategies you'll need to get started and to read. In forming your overall-point question for this reading, remember to cover both topics given in the headings: "Policing in a Multicultural Society" and "Community Crime Prevention." Notice also that the first topic is longer than the second, so you'll probably find more supporting ideas for the main idea for that topic.

Police and the Community

GEORGE F. COLE AND CHRISTOPHER E. SMITH

George F. Cole is a professor of political science at the University of Connecticut. Christopher E. Smith is a professor of criminal justice at Michigan State University. This reading comes from the chapter called "Policing: Issues and Trends" in their textbook *Criminal Justice in America*. In this reading the writers discuss ways the police try to work more effectively within a multicultural society.

1   The work of a police officer in an American city can be very hard. Hours of boring, routine work can be interrupted by short spurts of dangerous crime fighting. Although police work has always been frustrating and dangerous, officers today must deal with situations ranging from helping the homeless to dealing with domestic violence to confronting shoot-outs at drug deals gone sour. Yet police actions are often mishandled or misinterpreted, with the result that some people are critical of the police.

Policing in a Multicultural Society

2   Carrying out the complex tasks of policing efficiently and according to the law is a tough assignment even when the police have the support and cooperation of the public. But policing in a multicultural society presents further challenges.

3   In the last quarter-century the racial and ethnic composition of the United States has changed. African Americans have continued to move from the South to northern cities. Hispanic immigrants from Puerto Rico, Cuba, Mexico, and South America have become the fastest growing minority. Immigrants from Eastern Europe, Russia, the Middle East, and Asia have entered the country in greater numbers. Between 1980 and 1990, the U.S. population increased by 23 million. Sixty percent of this increase was made up of nonwhite residents, including Hispanics (6.4 million), African Americans (4.3 million), and Asians and other nonwhites (3.4 million) (Bureau of the Census, 1991. *1990 Census*).

4   Policing requires trust, understanding, and cooperation between officers and the public. People must be willing to call for help and provide information about wrongdoing. But in a multicultural society, relations between the police and minorities are complicated by stereotypes, cultural differences, and language differences.

5   Officers often attribute undesirable traits to members of minority groups: "Asian Americans are shifty," "Arab Americans are terrorists," "African Americans are lazy," "Polish Americans are stubborn." But minorities may also stereotype the police as "fascist," "dumb," or "pigs." Treating people according to stereotypes, rather than as individuals, creates tensions that harden negative attitudes.

6   New immigrants often bring with them religious and cultural practices that differ from those of the dominant culture. Many times these practices, while accepted in the home country, are viewed as deviant or are even against

> [I]n a multicultural society, relations between the police and minorities are complicated by stereotypes, cultural differences, and language differences.

Santaria: religion practiced originally in Cuba

the law in this country. The killing of animals by <u>adherents</u> of the Santaria religion has brought the police to churches in Florida. In Lincoln, Nebraska, arranged marriages of 13- and 14-year-old Iraqi-American sisters to new immigrants twice their ages brought charges of rape. In such cases the police must walk a fine line between upholding American law and respecting the customs of new residents (*New York Times*, December 2, 1996, p. A10).

Very few officers can speak a language other than English, and only 7 in large urban departments are there officers who speak any of the many languages used by new immigrants. Limited English speakers who report crimes, are arrested, or are victimized may not be understood. Language can be a barrier for the police in responding to calls for help and dealing with organized crime. Language and cultural diversity make it harder for the FBI or local police to <u>infiltrate</u> the Russian, Vietnamese, and Chinese organized crime groups now found in East and West Coast cities.

Public opinion surveys have shown that race and ethnicity are key factors shaping attitudes toward the police. Polls show that 25 percent of white Americans say they have a great deal of confidence in the police and 11 percent say they have very little or none. Surprisingly, a greater portion (26 percent) of African Americans say they have a great deal of confidence, yet 21 percent say they have very little or none (BJS, 1997. *Sourcebook:* 119). Even so, most African Americans and Hispanic Americans are similar to most white Americans in their attitudes toward the police. It is young, low-income racial-minority males who have the most negative attitudes toward the police (Walker, Spohn, and DeLone, 1996: 87, 89).

In inner-city neighborhoods—the areas that need and want effective 9 policing—there is much distrust of the police; citizens therefore fail to report crimes and refuse to cooperate with the police. Encounters between officers and members of these communities are often hostile and sometimes lead to large-scale disorders.

Why do some urban residents resent the police? Studies have shown 10 that this resentment stems from <u>permissive</u> law enforcement and police abuse of power (Dilulio, 1993a: 3). In many cities the police have been charged with failure to give protection and services to minority neighborhoods and . . . , with abusing residents physically or verbally.

Almost all studies reveal the prejudices of the police toward the poor 11 and racial minorities. These attitudes lead many officers to see all African Americans or Hispanic Americans as potential criminals, and as a result police tend to exaggerate the extent of minority crime. If both police and citizens view each other with hostility, then their encounters will be strained and the potential for conflict great.

Community Crime Prevention

There is a growing awareness that the control of crime and disorder 12 cannot be achieved solely by the police. Social control requires involvement by all members of the community. Community crime prevention can be <u>enhanced</u> if government agencies and neighborhood organizations cooperate.

Community programs to help the police have greatly increased across 13 the country. More than 6 million Americans are members of citizen crimewatch groups, which often have direct ties to police departments. Television and radio stations present the "unsolved crime of the week," and cash rewards are given for information that leads to conviction of the offender.

14   To what extent can such programs be relied upon to reduce crime and maintain social order? The results are mixed. Research on forty neighborhoods in six cities shows that while crime prevention efforts and voluntary community groups have had some success in more affluent neighborhoods, they are less likely to be found in poor neighborhoods with high levels of disorder. In such areas, "residents typically are deeply suspicious of one another, report only a weak sense of community, perceive they have low levels of personal influence on neighborhood events, and feel that it is their neighbors, not 'outsiders,' whom they must watch with care" (Skogan, 1990: 130; McGabey, 1986: 230).

15   However, Kelling and Coles have documented successful community-based crime prevention programs in Baltimore, Boston, New York, San Francisco, and Seattle (Kelling and Coles, 1996). In each city, community-based groups worked with the police and other governmental agencies to restore order and control crime. Ultimately, they say, the citizens of a community must take responsibility for maintaining civil and safe social conditions. Experience has shown that "while police might be able to *retake* a neighborhood from aggressive drug dealers, police could not *hold* a neighborhood without significant commitment and actual assistance from private citizens" (Kelling and Coles, 1996: 248).

16   Law enforcement agencies need the support and help of the community for effective crime prevention and control. They need support when they take actions designed to maintain order. They need information about wrongdoing and cooperation with investigations.

> "[W]hile police might be able to *retake* a neighborhood from aggressive drug dealers, police could not *hold* a neighborhood without significant commitment and actual assistance from private citizens."

Works Cited

BJS (Bureau of Justice Statistics). 1997. *Sourcebook of Criminal Justice Statistics, 1996.* Washington, D.C.: Government Printing Office.

Bureau of the Census. 1991. *7590 Census.* Washington, D.C.: Government Printing Office.

Dilulio, J. J., Jr. 1993a. "Rethinking the Criminal Justice System: Toward a New Paradigm," *Performance Measures for the Criminal Justice System.* Washington, D.C.: Bureau of Justice Statistics.

Kelling, G. L., and C. M. Coles. 1996. *Fixing Broken Windows: Restoring and Reducing Crime in Our Communities.* New York: Free Press.

McGabey, R. 1986. "Economic Conditions: Neighborhood Organizations and Urban Crime," *Crime and Justice: A Review of Research,* vol. 8, ed. M. Tonry and J. Petersilia. Chicago: University of Chicago Press, 427–478.

New York Times. December 2, 1996, p. A10.

Skogan, W. G. 1990. *Disorder and Decline: Crime and the Spiral of Decay in America.* New York: Free Press.

Walker, S., C. Spohn, and M. DeLone. 1996. *The Color of Justice.* Belmont, Calif.: Wadsworth, 89.

ACTIVE READERS RESPOND

After you've finished reading, use these questions to respond to "Police and the Community." You may write your answers in the spaces provided or on a separate sheet of paper.

Some words in this reading may be unfamiliar to you. Use the methods of Strategy 3 to explain what the listed words mean.

USE CONTEXT CLUES

a. deviant (paragraph 6)

_____

b. affluent (paragraph 14)

_____

USE WORD PARTS

a. permissive (paragraph 10)

_____

b. infiltrate (paragraph 7)

_____

USE THE DICTIONARY

Choose the correct definition of each word as it is used in the context of this reading.

a. dominant (paragraph 6)

_____

b. adherent (paragraph 6)

_____

c. enhanced (paragraph 12)

_____

SKILLS EXERCISE: PARAPHRASING AND SUMMARIZING

Each of the following quotations is from the passage "Police and the Community." Write a paraphrase for each quotation. Be sure to use your own words.

1. Carrying out the complex tasks of policing efficiently and according to the law is a tough assignment even when the police have the support and cooperation of the public. (paragraph 2)

    Paraphrase

    (Answers will vary.)

    _____

    _____

2. Many times these practices, while accepted in the home country, are viewed as deviant or even against the law in this country. (paragraph 6)

    Paraphrase

    (Answers will vary.)

    _____

    _____

3. In inner-city neighborhoods—the areas that need and want effective policing—there is much distrust of the police; citizens therefore fail to report crimes and refuse to cooperate with the police. (paragraph 9)
    Paraphrase
    (Answers will vary.)
    _____
    _____
    _____

4. These attitudes lead many officers to see all African Americans or Hispanic Americans as potential criminals, and as a result police tend to exaggerate the extent of minority crime. (paragraph 11)
    Paraphrase
    (Answers will vary.)
    _____
    _____
    _____

5. Research on forty neighborhoods in six cities shows that while crime prevention efforts and voluntary community groups have had some success in more affluent neighborhoods, they are less likely to be found in poor neighborhoods with high levels of disorder. (paragraph 14)
    Paraphrase
    (Answers will vary.)
    _____
    _____
    _____

Complete the cluster map for "Police and the Community."

**Cluster Map
"Police and the Community"**

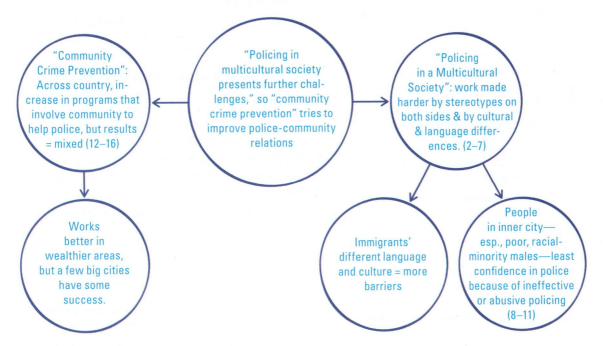

A. Based on your cluster map, write a summary.

(Answers will vary.)

_____

_____

_____

_____

_____

OBJECTIVE OPERATIONS

1. Who is the writer's intended audience?

   a. general audience

   b. people concerned with their community

   c. police officers

   d. criminal justice students

2. What is the author's purpose?

   a. to inform

   b. to persuade

   c. to entertain

3. What is the tone of the passage?

   a. condescending

   b. condemning

   c. critical

   d. fair-minded

4. According to this reading, during the last quarter century, police work has become more complicated because

   a. new types of technology are used.

   b. there is a lack of competent instructors in police academies.

   c. suburbs are growing throughout the United States.

   d. there are changes in the racial and ethnic make-up of the United States.

5. The word "affluent" in paragraph 14, line 4, most nearly means

   a. mainstream.

   b. valuable.

   c. underprivileged.

   d. prosperous.

6. Which of the following sentences best summarizes this passage?

   a. Communities need to help officers police their own neighborhoods in order to prevent crime.

   b. Language barriers prevent police officers from performing their jobs properly, especially in a multicultural society.

   c. Communities need to trust police officers and cooperate with them in order to prevent crime, but this can be difficult in a multicultural society.

   d. Police officers find their jobs especially difficult if they have prejudices.

7. What is the stated main idea of paragraph 7?

   a. "Very few officers can speak a language other than English, and only in large urban departments are there officers who speak any of the many languages used by new immigrants."

   b. "Limited English speakers who report crimes, are arrested, or are victimized may not be understood."

   c. "Language can be a barrier for the police in responding to calls for help and dealing with organized crime."

   d. "Language and cultural diversity make it harder for the FBI or local police to infiltrate the Russian, Vietnamese, and Chinese organized crime groups now found in East and West Coast cities."

8. There are often problems of communication between the police and racial and ethnic minorities because

   a. the police have stereotypes about the minorities.

   b. the minorities have stereotypes about the police.

   c. all police are prejudiced in all situations.

   d. both the police and the minorities hold onto stereotypes about one another.

9. Which sentence provides support for this sentence (paragraph 3, lines 1–2): "In the last quarter-century the racial and ethnic composition of the United States has changed."

a. "African Americans have continued to move from the South to northern cities."

b. "Hispanic immigrants from Puerto Rico, Cuba, Mexico, and South America have become the fastest growing minority."

c. "Immigrants from Eastern Europe, Russia, the Middle East, and Asia have entered the country in greater numbers."

d. all of the above

10. The author's claim that "policing requires trust" (paragraph 4, lines 1–2) is

a. adequately supported with details.

b. inadequately supported with details.

11. What is the topic of paragraph 6?

a. new immigrants

b. problems with new immigrants

c. problems with new immigrants and their cultural differences

d. cultural differences

12. One main challenge for the police in developing effective working relations with new immigrants involves

a. getting the children of immigrants to go to school and learn English.

b. learning about new immigrants' cultural practices so that they can adapt them for American holidays and celebrations.

c. dealing with strange cultural practices that are considered normal in the immigrants' homeland.

d. dealing with strange cultural practices the immigrants must learn in order to become Americans.

13. Identify the relationship between the parts of the following sentence from paragraph 9.

"In inner-city neighborhoods—the areas that need and want effective policing—there is much distrust of the police; citizens therefore fail to report crimes and refuse to cooperate with the police." (lines 1–3)

a. addition

b. cause and effect

c. summary

d. statement and clarification

14. For paragraph 11, the author organizes the information by using

a. clarification.

b. illustration.

c. comparison and contrast.

d. cause and effect.

15. Because people in inner-city neighborhoods tend to distrust the police,

a. they speak in other languages in front of the police so that the police cannot understand.

b. they do not always report crime or cooperate with the police.

c. they report crimes and cooperate as all law-abiding citizens should.

d. they abuse the police physically and verbally.

16. The word "exaggerate" in paragraph 11, line 4, most nearly means

a. to irritate.

b. to pretend.

c. to fabricate.

d. to blow out of proportion.

17. Identify the relationship between the parts of the following sentence (paragraph 8, lines 4–6): "Surprisingly, a greater portion (26 percent) of African Americans say they have a great deal of confidence, yet 21 percent say they have very little or none."

a. addition

b. definition and example

c. contrast

d. cause and effect

18. The authors say that "treating people according to stereotypes, rather than individuals, creates tensions that harden negative attitudes." This statement implies that it could ease these tensions if there were

a. less contact between individuals from hostile groups so that they can avoid hurting one another.

b. more contact between individuals from hostile groups so that they could get to know each other as individuals.

c. more contact between individuals from hostile groups so that they could confirm the stereotypes they already had.

d. less contact between people from hostile groups to allow time away from one another to heal the differences.

19. The authors show a bias
    a. against police officers.
    b. toward police officers.
    c. against police officers' avoiding stereotypes.
    d. toward police officers' using stereotypes.

20. The word "hostile" in paragraph 9, line 4, most nearly means
    a. agitated.
    b. mean.
    c. aggravated.
    d. kind.

READERS WRITE

1. What are some of the major changes in the last quarter century that have changed the racial and ethnic makeup of the United States?
   (Answers will vary.)

2. What are some of the examples of stereotypes the police and ethnic minorities have of each other?
   (Answers will vary.)

3. What are the main challenges in developing effective working relations between new immigrants and the police?
   (Answers will vary.)

4. What causes people in inner-city neighborhoods to have such strong resentment toward the police?
   (Answers will vary.)

5. Why do the writers say that "treating people according to stereotypes, rather than individuals, creates tensions that harden negative attitudes"?
   (Answers will vary.)

READERS DISCUSS

1. How does the information in this reading compare with what you know about policing in your own area—or in areas near you? Are you aware of community crime prevention programs? If so, what kind of success are they having?
   (Answers will vary.)

2. Discuss with your classmates the stereotypes about both police and minorities that complicate fair and effective policing. What kind of information or activities might improve relations between the two?

(Answers will vary.)

_____

_____

_____

Summary

WRITE A SUMMARY

1 | Put the writer's ideas in your own words.

2 | Base your summary on your marking or mapping.

CHAPTER 12

HOW DOES STRATEGY 12 HELP YOU BECOME AN ENGAGED READER?

Like *mapping, summarizing* lets you work with a writer's ideas. In a summary you get even more involved with these ideas as you "translate" them into your own words and organize them to flow logically from one sentence to the next. Summarizing increases your understanding of a reading and therefore helps you give a fair *response* to what the writer has said.

HOW DOES THE WRITE A SUMMARY STRATEGY WORK?

The information that goes into a summary comes from marking or mapping or making a simple outline. Your summary should follow the order of ideas in the reading and should represent only what the writer says. Most of the summary is made up of accurate paraphrases of the overall point, main ideas, and a few supporting ideas. Including a few appropriate quotations helps clarify ideas.

Strategy 12 teaches you to put the writer's ideas into your own words. Doing this helps you to understand what the writer has said.

Strategy 12 shows you how to summarize the writer's ideas. After mapping ideas, you can easily sum up the writer's overall point, main ideas, and supporting ideas.

Key Terms

complete sentence: a sentence that has a subject and verb and expresses a complete thought

paraphrase: a paraphrase is a kind of "translation" of others' words into your own words.

plagiarism: borrowing ideas that are not your own and not giving credit to whom those ideas belong.

summary: a brief—usually one paragraph—restatement of main ideas

Think AGAIN >

How often do you go into minute detail when recommending a movie to a friend? More than likely, you summarize the whole point of the film into one sentence: "This young girl decides she doesn't like her parents, and when she finds a secret door in the room of her new house, she ends up visiting a creepy woman known as the Other Mother." Then, as your friend asks you more about the movie, you summarize scenes and paraphrase characters. What movies have you seen recently? How did you summarize these movies for your friends? Did you paraphrase characters or quote them directly?

Now that you understand Strategy 12, put it into practice with Reading 24, "Don't Let Stereotypes Warp Your Judgments."

Since this reading has no headings, try mapping the main topics in pencil first, before marking main ideas. Let Strategy 7, Patterns of Thought, help you find topics. The reading talks about why we use stereotypes, so cause-and-effect reasoning is an important pattern. However, as you map main ideas, notice the patterns of definition and examples as well.

Don't Let Stereotypes Warp Your Judgments

ROBERT L. HEILBRONER

READING **24**

Robert L. Heilbroner is a professor emeritus of economics at the New School for Social Research. He is the author of many articles and several books, including *The Nature and Logic of Capitalism* (1985). In this reading, he shows us how our stereotypes get in the way of understanding others. As you read, think about how stereotypes limit your own thinking. (See, for example, Figure 12.1.)

1   Is a girl called Gloria apt to be better-looking than one called Bertha? Are criminals more likely to be dark than blond? Can you tell a good deal about someone's personality from hearing his voice briefly over the phone? Can

Figure 12.1 Who has the higher grade point average? Stereotypes can give us the wrong information: the brunette wearing glasses may not be getting better grades than the blonde.

a person's nationality be pretty accurately guessed from his photograph? Does the fact that someone wears glasses imply that he is intelligent?

The answer to all these questions is obviously, "No." 2

Yet, from all the evidence at hand, most of us believe these things. Ask 3 any college boy if he'd rather take his chances with a Gloria or a Bertha, or ask a college girl if she'd rather blind-date a Richard or a Cuthbert. In fact, you don't have to ask: college students in questionnaires have revealed that names conjure up the same images in their minds as they do in yours—and for as little reason.

Look into the favorite suspects of persons who report "suspicious char- 4 acters" and you will find a large percentage of them to be "swarthy" or "dark and foreign-looking"—despite the testimony of criminologists that criminals do not tend to be dark, foreign or "wild-eyed." Delve into the main asset of a telephone stock swindler and you will find it to be a marvelously confidence-inspiring telephone "personality." And whereas we all think we know what an Italian or a Swede looks like, it is the sad fact that when a group of Nebraska students sought to match faces and nationalities of 15 European countries, they were scored wrong in 93 percent of their identifications. Finally, for all the fact that horn-rimmed glasses have now become the standard television sign of an "intellectual," optometrists know that the main thing that distinguishes people with glasses is just bad eyes.

Stereotypes are a kind of gossip about the world, a gossip 5 that makes us prejudge people before we ever lay eyes on them. Hence it is not surprising that stereotypes have something to do with the dark world of prejudice. Explore most prejudices (note that the word means prejudgment) and you will find a cruel stereotype at the core of each one.

For it is the extraordinary fact that once we have typecast the 6 world, we tend to see people in terms of our standardized pictures. In another demonstration of the power of stereotypes to affect our vision, a number of Columbia and Barnard students were shown 30 photographs of pretty but unidentified girls, and asked to rate each in terms of "general lik-

> Stereotypes are a kind of gossip about the world, a gossip that makes us prejudge people before we ever lay eyes on them.

ing," "intelligence," "beauty" and so on. Two months later, the same group were shown the same photographs, this time with fictitious Irish, Italian, Jewish and "American" names attached to the pictures. Right away the ratings changed. Faces which were now seen as representing a national group went down in looks and still farther down in likeability, while the "American" girls suddenly looked decidedly prettier and nicer.

7   Why is it that we stereotype the world in such <u>irrational</u> and harmful fashion? In part, we begin to type-cast people in our childhood years. Early in life, as every parent whose child has watched a TV Western knows, we learn to spot the Good Guys from the Bad Guys. Some years ago, a social psychologist showed very clearly how powerful these stereotypes of childhood vision are. He secretly asked the most popular youngsters in an elementary school to make errors in their morning gym exercises. Afterwards, he asked the class if anyone had noticed any mistakes during gym period. Oh, yes, said the children. But it was the unpopular members of the class—the "bad guys"—they remembered as being out of step.

8   We not only grow up with standardized pictures forming inside us, but as grown-ups we are constantly having them thrust upon us. Some of them, like the half-joking, half-serious stereotypes of mothers-in-law, or country yokels, or psychiatrists, are dinned into us by the stock jokes we hear and repeat. In fact, without such stereotypes, there would be a lot fewer jokes. Still other stereotypes are <u>perpetuated</u> in the advertisements we read, the movies we see, the books we read.

9   And finally, we tend to stereotype because it helps us make sense out of a highly confusing world, a world which William James once described as "one great, blooming, buzzing confusion." It is a curious fact that if we don't know what we're looking at, we are often quite literally unable to see what we're looking at. People who recover their sight after a lifetime of blindness actually cannot at first tell a triangle from a square. A visitor to a factory sees only noisy chaos where the superintendent sees a perfectly synchronized flow of work. As Walter Lippmann has said, "For the most part we do not first see, and then define; we define first, and then we see."

10   Stereotypes are one way in which we "define" the world in order to see it. They classify the infinite variety of human beings into a convenient handful of "types" towards whom we learn to act in stereotyped fashion. Life would be a wearing process if we had to start from scratch with each and every human contact. Stereotypes economize on our mental effort by covering up the blooming, buzzing confusion with big recognizable cutouts. They save us the "trouble" of finding out what the world is like—they give it its accustomed look.

11   Thus the trouble is that stereotypes make us mentally lazy. As S. I. Hayakawa, the authority on <u>semantics</u>, has written: "The danger of stereotypes lies not in their existence, but in the fact that they become for all people some of the time, and for some people all the time, substitutes for observation." Worse yet, stereotypes get in the way of our judgment, even when we do observe the world. Someone who has formed rigid <u>preconceptions</u> of all Latins as "excitable," or all teenagers as "wild," doesn't alter his

Genoese: a person from Genoa, Italy

point of view when he meets a calm and deliberate Genoese, or a serious-minded high school student. He brushes them aside as "exceptions that prove the rule." And, of course, if he meets someone true to type, he stands triumphantly <u>vindicated</u>. "They're all like that," he proclaims, having encountered an excited Latin, an ill-behaved adolescent.

Hence, quite aside from the injustice which stereotypes do to others, they impoverish ourselves. A person who lumps the world into simple categories, who type-casts all labor leaders as "racketeers," all businessmen as "reactionaries," all Harvard men as "snobs," and all Frenchmen as "sexy," is in danger of becoming a stereotype himself. He loses his capacity to be himself—which is to say, to see the world in his own absolutely unique, <u>inimitable</u> and independent fashion. 12

Instead, he votes for the man who fits his standardized picture of what a candidate "should" look like or sound like, buys the goods that someone in his "situation" in life "should" own, lives the life that others define for him. The mark of the stereotype person is that he never surprises us, that we do indeed have him "typed." And no one fits this straitjacket so perfectly as someone whose opinions about other people are fixed and inflexible. 13

Impoverishing as they are, stereotypes are not easy to get rid of. The world we type-cast may be no better than a Grade B movie, but at least we know what to expect of our stock characters. When we let them act for themselves in the strangely unpredictable way that people do act, who knows but that many of our fondest convictions will be proved wrong? 14

Nor do we suddenly drop our standardized pictures for a blinding vision of the Truth. Sharp swings of ideas about people often just substitute one stereotype for another. The true process of change is a slow one that adds bits and pieces of reality to the pictures in our heads, until gradually they take on some of the blurriness of life itself. Little by little, we learn not that Jews and Negroes and Catholics and Puerto Ricans are "just like everybody else"—for that, too, is a stereotype—but that each and every one of them is unique, special, different and individual. Often we do not even know that we have let a stereotype lapse until we hear someone saying, "all so-and-so's are like such-and-such," and we hear ourselves saying, "Well—maybe." 15

Can we speed the process along? Of course we can. 16

First, we can become aware of the standardized pictures in our heads, in other peoples' heads, in the world around us. 17

Second, we can become suspicious of all judgments that we allow exceptions to "prove." There is no more <u>chastening</u> thought than that in the vast intellectual adventure of science, it takes but one tiny exception to topple a whole <u>edifice of ideas</u>. 18

Third, we can learn to be wary of generalizations about people. As F. Scott Fitzgerald once wrote: "Begin with an individual, and before you know it you have created a type; begin with a type, and you find you have created—nothing." 19

Most of the time, when we type-cast the world, we are not in fact generalizing about people at all. We are only revealing the embarrassing facts about the pictures that hang in the gallery of stereotypes in our own heads. 20

ACTIVE READERS RESPOND

After you've finished reading, use these questions to respond to "Don't Let Stereotypes Warp Your Judgments." You may write your answers in the spaces provided or on a separate sheet of paper.

VITAL VOCABULARY

Some words in this reading may be unfamiliar to you. Use the methods of Strategy 3 to explain what the listed words mean.

USE CONTEXT CLUES

a. perpetuated (paragraph 8)

_____

b. edifice of ideas (paragraph 18)

_____

USE WORD PARTS

a. irrational (paragraph 7)

_____

b. preconception (paragraph 11)

_____

c. inimitable (paragraph 12)

_____

USE THE DICTIONARY

Choose the correct definition of each word as it is used in the context of this reading.

a. delve (paragraph 4) _____

_____

b. semantics (paragraph 11) _____

_____

c. vindicate (paragraph 11) _____

_____

d. chastening (paragraph 18) _____

_____

SKILLS TEST: PARAPHRASING AND SUMMARIZING

A. *Each of the following quotations is from the passage "Don't Let Stereotypes Warp Your Judgments." Write a paraphrase for each quotation. Be sure to use your own words.*

   1. Look into the favorite suspects of persons who report "suspicious characters" and you will find a large percentage of them to be "swarthy" or "dark and foreign-looking"—despite the testimony of criminologists that criminals do not tend to be dark, foreign or "wild-eyed." Delve into the main asset of a telephone stock swindler and you will find it to be a marvelously confidence-inspiring telephone "personality." (paragraph 4)

Paraphrase

(Answers will vary.)

_____

_____

_____

_____

2. Why is it that we stereotype the world in such irrational and harmful fashion? In part, we begin to type-cast people in our childhood years. (paragraph 7)

Paraphrase

(Answers will vary.)

_____

_____

_____

_____

3. And finally, we tend to stereotype because it helps us make sense out of a highly confusing world, a world which William James once described as "one great, blooming, buzzing confusion." It is a curious fact that if we don't know what we're looking at, we are often quite literally unable to see what we're looking at. (paragraph 9)

Paraphrase

(Answers will vary.)

_____

_____

_____

_____

4. Worse yet, stereotypes get in the way of our judgment, even when we do observe the world. Someone who has formed rigid preconceptions of all Latins as "excitable," or all teenagers as "wild," doesn't alter his point of view when he meets a calm and deliberate Genoese," or a serious-minded high school student. (paragraph 11)

Paraphrase

(Answers will vary.)

_____

_____

_____

_____

5. Impoverishing as they are, stereotypes are not easy to get rid of. The world we type-cast may be no better than a Grade B movie, but at least we know what to expect of our stock characters. (paragraph 14)

Paraphrase

(Answers will vary.)

_____

_____

_____

_____

B. _Complete the cluster map for "Don't Let Stereotypes Warp Your Judgment."_

Cluster Map
"Don't Let Stereotypes Warp Your Judgment"

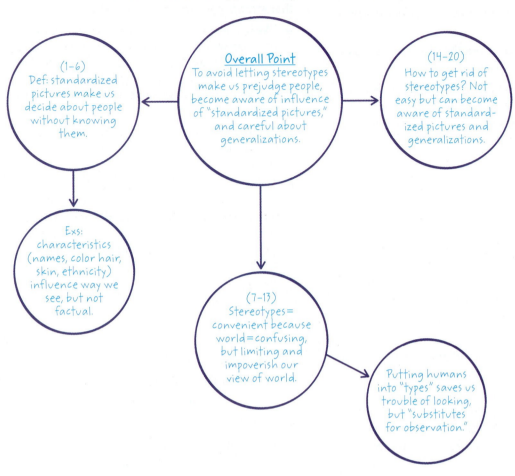

(1–6)
Def: standardized pictures make us decide about people without knowing them.

Overall Point
To avoid letting stereotypes make us prejudge people, become aware of influence of "standardized pictures," and careful about generalizations.

(14–20)
How to get rid of stereotypes? Not easy but can become aware of standard-ized pictures and generalizations.

Exs: characteristics (names, color hair, skin, ethnicity) influence way we see, but not factual.

(7–13)
Stereotypes= convenient because world=confusing, but limiting and impoverish our view of world.

Putting humans into "types" saves us trouble of looking, but "substitutes for observation."

C. Based on your cluster map, write a summary.

(Answers will vary.)

_____

_____

_____

_____

_____

OBJECTIVE OPERATIONS

1. Who is the writer's intended audience?
   a. people who are prejudiced
   b. economics professors
   c. people who are not prejudiced
   d. general audience

2. What is the author's purpose?
   a. to inform
   b. to persuade
   c. to entertain

3. What is the tone of the passage?
   a. ironic
   b. informative
   c. subjective
   d. objective

4. In the study conducted with Columbia and Bar-nard students, the students' opinions about the girls in the photos depended on whether a girl had an ethnic or an "American" name attached to her photo. This study shows that

a. the students who observed these photos had themselves been stereotyped by others.

b. stereotypes have the power to affect the way we see people.

c. stereotypes help us see the characteristics of certain groups of people.

d. the girls with ethnic backgrounds had less attractive names than the American girls.

5. The word "perpetuated" in paragraph 8, line 6, most nearly means

   a. put an end to.

   b. enabled.

   c. kept alive.

   d. appropriated.

6. Which of the following sentences best summarizes this passage?

   a. You must be aware of other's stereotypes in order to identify your own.

   b. Without stereotypes, people are less judgmental.

   c. Stereotypes influence and affect our thinking both positively and negatively.

   d. Stereotypes can influence our thinking unless we are aware of our prejudices, are suspicious of them, and are willing to change.

7. What is the implied main idea of paragraphs 10 and 11?

   a. Stereotypes are helpful, but they can make us mentally lazy.

   b. Stereotypes can be beneficial because they help us define the world, but they can be harmful because they cause us to over-generalize.

   c. Stereotypes form the way we think, but they can affect the way we think.

   d. Stereotypes help us to form judgments but make us over-generalize.

8. The main reason Heilbroner gives for the power stereotypes have to influence our thinking is that

   a. they help us to make sense of the complex and confusing world around us.

   b. they make us feel more confident about our opinions of others.

   c. they make us able to understand jokes made about certain groups.

   d. they show us the exceptions that prove the rule.

9. Which sentence provides support for this sentence (paragraph 11, lines 1): "Thus the trouble is that stereotypes make us mentally lazy."

   a. "As S. I. Hayakawa, the authority on semantics, has written: "The danger of stereotypes lies not in their existence, but in the fact that they become for all people some of the time, and for some people all the time, substitutes for observation."

   b. "Worse yet, stereotypes get in the way of our judgment, even when we do observe the world."

   c. "Someone who has formed rigid preconceptions of all Latins as 'excitable,' or all teenagers as 'wild,' doesn't alter his point of view when he meets a calm and deliberate Genoese, or a serious-minded high school student."

   d. "He brushes them aside as 'exceptions that prove the rule.' "

10. The author's claim that we can overcome our prejudices is

    a. adequately supported with details.

    b. inadequately supported with details.

11. What is the topic of paragraph 11?

    a. stereotypes

    b. how stereotypes affect our thinking

    c. the existence of stereotypes

    d. stereotypes and their exceptions

12. Heilbroner thinks it is not only harmful to the other person when you stereotype him or her, it is harmful to you because

    a. you start to see everyone as a dangerous enemy.

    b. you hurt yourself when you do harm to others.

    c. you lose your ability to be yourself and think in an independent way.

    d. you lose your ability to classify people into useful categories.

13. Identify the relationship between the parts of the following sentence from paragraph 5.

    "Stereotypes are a kind of gossip about the world, a gossip that makes us prejudge people before we ever lay eyes on them." (lines 1–2)

    a. definition

    b. illustration

    c. example

    d. clarification

14. For paragraph 8, the author organizes the information by using

    a. comparisons.

    b. contrasts.

    c. examples.

    d. definitions.

15. Heilbroner ends this reading by telling us how to avoid being too influenced by stereotypes. All of the following are guidelines he gives except

    a. become more aware of the standardized pictures in our heads.

    b. become suspicious when we think an exception has "proven" the rule.

    c. be careful of making generalizations about people.

    d. become more aware of the exception that "proves" the rule.

16. The word "inimitable" in paragraph 12, line 6, most nearly means

    a. incomparable.

    b. superior.

    c. enviable.

    d. reproducible.

17. Identify the relationship between the parts of the following sentence (paragraph 12, lines 5–7): "He loses his capacity to be himself—which is to say, to see the world in his own absolutely unique, inimitable and independent fashion."

    a. addition

    b. definition

    c. contrast

    d. illustration

18. Heilbroner says in paragraph 15, "Often we do not even know that we have let a stereotype lapse until we hear someone saying, 'all so-and-so's are like such-and-such,' and we hear ourselves saying, 'Well—maybe.'" He means by this statement that:

    a. it takes several different experiences with individuals from a group to make us certain we can know the group's characteristics.

    b. you have to agree with people when they tell you their stereotype about a group.

    c. it is impossible to let go of stereotypes because we keep hearing ourselves saying that we believe they're true.

    d. it takes several different experiences with individuals from a group to realize that our view of the group has been modified.

19. The author shows a bias

    a. against preventing stereotypes.

    b. toward protecting stereotypes.

    c. against learning from your stereotypes.

    d. toward learning not to generalize about people.

20. According to the author,

    a. you can learn to prevent your stereotypes from clouding your judgment.

    b. stereotypes are permanently ingrained in our thought patterns.

    c. stereotypes do not exist.

    d. we should never be suspicious of other people's judgments.

READERS WRITE

1. How did the study done with Columbia and Barnard students demonstrate "the power of stereotypes to affect our vision"?

(Answers will vary.)

_____

_____

2. According to Heilbroner, why do stereotypes have such power to influence our thinking?

(Answers will vary.)

_____

_____

3. Why does Heilbroner think it harms the person who does the stereotyping as well as the person being stereotyped?

   (Answers will vary.)

   _____

   _____

   _____

4. Heilbroner quotes Walter Lippmann in paragraph 9: "For the most part we do not first see, and then define; we define first, and then see." Explain how this statement relates to our need for stereotypes.

   (Answers will vary.)

   _____

   _____

   _____

5. What does Heilbroner mean when he says in paragraph 14, "Often we do not even know that we have let a stereotype lapse until we hear someone saying, 'all so-and-so's are like such-and-such,' and we hear ourselves saying, 'Well—maybe' "?

   (Answers will vary.)

   _____

   _____

   _____

READERS DISCUSS

1. Heilbroner's first recommendation is to "become aware of standardized pictures in our heads, other peoples' heads, [and] in the world around us." Try using those three categories to come up with some stereotypes: 1) that you still hold on to; 2) that people you know hold on to; 3) that we see in the world around us—especially in the media.

   (Answers will vary.)

   _____

   _____

   _____

2. Discuss with others ways that the barriers created by stereotypes can be broken down on your own campus.

   (Answers will vary.)

   _____

   _____

   _____

WRITE A SUMMARY

1 | Put the writer's ideas in your own words.

2 | Base your summary on your marking or mapping.

PRACTICE PAGES

Chapter 12

PRACTICE EXERCISE 1

For practice paraphrasing, do this exercise.

A. Read the following passage. Then, complete the exercise.

Senator Joseph McCarthy's Crusade Against the "Red Menace"

"Are you now or have you ever been a member of the Communist Party?" This question was asked repeatedly during Senator Joseph McCarthy's relentless hunt for the Communists he believed had infiltrated every aspect of American life by the 1950s. McCarthy, a Republican, won a Senate seat in Wisconsin in 1946 and gained quick attention from the media for his provocative claims. He also incurred the hostility of his Senate colleagues when he ignored the customs and written rules of the upper chamber.

McCarthy's name became a household word following a speech in West Virginia in 1950. In this speech, he claimed that the State Department and other agencies were riddled with Communists. He waved a piece of paper on which he said were written the names of 205 Communists who held jobs in the U.S. government. This was the beginning of the period now called the McCarthy era, during which panic over the "Red Menace" was pushed to new heights.

The election in 1952 brought in both a Republican president and congressional majority. McCarthy took advantage of his party's power to pursue his agenda with single-minded concentration. As chairman of the Permanent Subcommittee of Investigations, he launched a search for suspected Communists. Among his first targets was the State Department's information program, including its overseas libraries and the *Voice of America* radio broadcasts.

The hearings took a toll on those subjected to his committee's scrutiny. Famous authors and screenwriters were grilled about their beliefs, their activities, and their friends—in public and private. Many found it difficult or impossible to get their work published afterward. Members of Hollywood's film industry suffered similar problems, as McCarthy placed numerous people in the State Department under a cloud of suspicion. Many saw their careers ruined, and others had to deal with a department in disarray.

In 1954 McCarthy set his sights on the U.S. Army and began a series of televised hearings. His attacks on respected military officers and the law firm representing the Army proved to be more than the country could take. Public approval of McCarthy's search for Communists quickly turned into disapproval. Late that year, the Senate censured McCarthy for his conduct in the Senate and the tactics he used in his investigations and hearings.

Few who had been accused at the hearings were ever proved to be Communists. McCarthy died in 1957, before the end of his second term.

B. Each of the following quotations is from the passage. Write a paraphrase for each quotation. Be sure to use your own words.

1. " 'Are you now or have you ever been a member of the Communist Party?' This question was asked repeatedly during Senator Joseph McCarthy's relentless hunt for the Communists he believed had infiltrated every aspect of American life by the 1950s."

   Paraphrase

   (Answers will vary.)

   _____

   _____

   _____

2. "In this speech, he claimed that the State Department and other agencies were riddled with Communists. He waved a piece of paper on which he said were written the names of 205 Communists who held jobs in the U.S. government."

   Paraphrase

   (Answers will vary.)

   _____

   _____

   _____

3. "McCarthy took advantage of his party's power to pursue his agenda with single-minded concentration."

   Paraphrase

   (Answers will vary.)

   _____

   _____

   _____

4. "Famous authors and screenwriters were grilled about their beliefs, their activities, and their friends—in public and private. Many found it difficult or impossible to get their work published afterward. Members of Hollywood's film industry suffered similar problems, as McCarthy placed numerous people in the State Department under a cloud of suspicion. Many saw their careers ruined, and others had to deal with a department in disarray."

   Paraphrase

   (Answers will vary.)

   _____

   _____

   _____

5. "Public approval of McCarthy's search for Communists quickly turned into disapproval."

Paraphrase

(Answers will vary.)

_____

_____

_____

PRACTICE EXERCISE 2

For practice summarizing, do this exercise.

A. Complete the cluster map for "Senator Joseph McCarthy's Crusade Against the 'Red Menace,'" the reading found on page 461.

Cluster Map
"Senator Joseph McCarthy's
Crusade Against the 'Red Menace'"

"Red Menace": McCarthy believes Communism is in country. (2–3)

During the 1950s, Senator Joseph McCarthy felt that Communism had infiltrated the United States, and he launched a campaign against Communism that attacked several groups.

McCarthy hearings—many on trial (4)

McCarthy's 1950 speech—205 accused of Communism

1952 abuse of power: McCarthy uses position to launch personal agenda

Creative types: authors and screenwriters attacked.

Military: McCarthy's accusations seen as silly due to his attack of the army.

B. Based on your cluster map, write a summary.

(Answers will vary.)

_____

_____

_____

_____

_____

_____

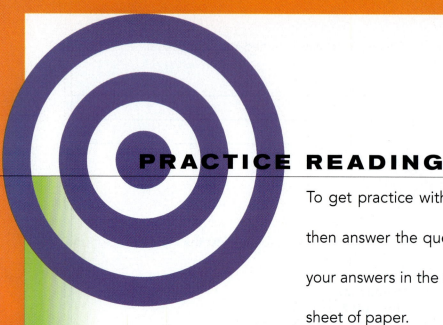

To get practice with reading, read the passage, and then answer the questions that follow. You may write your answers in the spaces provided or on a separate sheet of paper.

The Argument Culture

DEBORAH TANNEN

Deborah Tannen is a professor of linguistics at Georgetown University in Washington, D.C., and a best-selling author of many books on communication. She is best known for her analysis of the differences between men's and women's conversational styles, the subject of *You Just Don't Understand: Women and Men in Conversation* (1990). In this reading, taken from her book *The Argument Culture: Moving from Debate to Dialogue* (1998), she moves beyond gender differences into a broader area of communication.

1   Balance. Debate. Listening to both sides. Who could question these noble American traditions? Yet today, these principles have been distorted. Without thinking, we have plunged headfirst into what I call the "argument culture."

2   The argument culture urges us to approach the world, and the people in it, in an <u>adversarial</u> frame of mind. It rests on the assumption that opposition is the best way to get anything done: The best way to discuss an idea is to set up a debate; the best way to cover news is to find spokespeople who express the most extreme, <u>polarized</u> views and present them as "both sides"; the best way to settle disputes is <u>litigation</u> that pits one party against the other; the best way to begin an essay is to attack someone; and the best way to show you're really thinking is to criticize.

3   More and more, our public interactions have become like arguing with a spouse. Conflict can't be avoided in our public lives any more than we can avoid conflict with people we love. One of the great strengths of our society is that we can express these conflicts openly. But just as spouses have to learn ways of settling their differences without inflicting real damage, so we, as a society, have to find constructive ways of resolving disputes and differences.

4   The war on drugs, the war on cancer, the battle of the sexes, politicians' turf battles—in the argument culture, war metaphors <u>pervade</u> our talk and shape our thinking. The cover headlines of both *Time* and *Newsweek* one recent week are a case in point: "The Secret Sex Wars," proclaims *Newsweek*. "Starr at War," declares *Time*. Nearly everything is framed as a battle or game in which winning or losing is the main concern.

5   The argument culture pervades every aspect of our lives today. Issues from global warming to abortion are depicted as two-sided arguments, when in fact most Americans' views lie somewhere in the middle. <u>Partisanship</u> makes gridlock in Washington the norm. Even in our personal relationships, a "let it all hang out" philosophy emphasizes people expressing their anger without giving them constructive ways of settling differences.

> Even in our personal relationships, a "let it all hang out" philosophy emphasizes people expressing their anger without giving them constructive ways of settling differences.

Sometimes You Have to Fight

6   There are times when it is necessary and right to fight—to defend your country or yourself, to argue for your rights or against offensive or dangerous ideas or actions. What's wrong with the argument culture is the <u>ubiquity</u>, the knee-jerk nature, of approaching any issue, problem or public person in an adversarial way.

7   Our determination to pursue truth by setting up a fight between two sides leads us to assume that every issue has two sides—no more, no less. But if you always assume there must be an "other side," you may end up scouring the margins of science or the fringes of lunacy to find it.

8   This accounts, in part, for the bizarre phenomenon of Holocaust denial. Deniers, as Emory University professor Deborah Lipstadt shows, have been successful in gaining TV air time and campus newspaper coverage by masquerading as "the other side" in a "debate." Continual reference to "the other side" results in a conviction that everything has another side—and people begin to doubt the existence of any facts at all.

9   The power of words to shape perception has been proved by researchers in controlled experiments. Psychologists Elizabeth Loftus and John Palmer, for example, found that the terms in which people are asked to recall something affect what they recall. The researchers showed subjects a film of two cars colliding, then asked how fast the cars were going; one week later they asked whether there had been any broken glass. Some subjects were asked, "How fast were the cars going when they bumped into each other?" Others were asked, "How fast were the cars going when they smashed into each other?"

10   Those who read the question with "smashed" tended to "remember" that the cars were going faster. They were also more likely to "remember" having seen broken glass. (There wasn't any.) This is how language works. It invisibly molds our way of thinking about people, actions and the world around us.

11   In the argument culture, "critical" thinking is synonymous with criticizing. In many classrooms, students are encouraged to read someone's life work, then rip it to shreds.

When debates and fighting <u>predominate</u>, those who enjoy verbal <u>sparring</u> are likely to take part—by calling in to talk shows or writing letters to the editor. Those who aren't comfortable with oppositional discourse are likely to opt out. **12**

How High-Tech Communication Pulls Us Apart

One of the most effective ways to defuse <u>antagonism</u> between two **13** groups is to provide a forum for individuals from those groups to get to know each other personally. What is happening in our lives, however, is just the opposite. More and more of our communication is not face to face, and not with people we know. The <u>proliferation</u> and increasing portability of technology isolates people in a bubble.

Along with the voices of family members and friends, phone lines bring **14** into our homes the annoying voices of solicitors who want to sell something—generally at dinnertime. (My father-in-law startles phone solicitors by saying, "We're eating dinner, but I'll call you back. What's your home phone number?" To the nonplused caller, he explains, "Well, you're calling me at home; I thought I'd call you at home, too.")

It is common for families to have more than one TV, so the adults can **15** watch what they like in one room and the kids can watch their choice in another—or maybe each child has a private TV.

E-mail, and now the Internet, are creating networks of human connec- **16** tion unthinkable even a few years ago. Though e-mail has enhanced communication with family and friends, it also <u>ratchets</u> up the anonymity of both sender and receiver, resulting in stranger-to-stranger "flaming."

"Road rage" shows how dangerous the argument culture—and espe- **17** cially today's technologically enhanced aggression—can be. Two men who engage in a shouting match may not come to blows, but if they express their anger while driving down a public highway, the risk to themselves and others soars.

The Argument Shapes Who We Are

The argument culture has a defining impact on our lives and on our **18** culture.

It makes us distort facts, as in the Nancy Kerrigan-Tonya Harding story. **19** After the original attack on Kerrigan's knee, news stories focused on the rivalry between the two skaters instead of portraying Kerrigan as the victim of an attack. Just last month, *Time* magazine called the event a "contretemps" between Kerrigan and Harding. And a recent joint TV interview of the two skaters reinforced that skewed image by putting the two on equal footing, rather than as victim and accused.

It makes us waste valuable time, as in the case of scientist Robert Gallo, **20** who co-discovered the AIDS virus. Gallo was the object of a groundless four-year investigation into allegations he had stolen the virus from another scientist. He was ultimately exonerated, but the toll was enormous. Never mind that, in his words, "These were the most painful and horrible

contretemps: unfortunate occurrence

years of my life." Gallo spent four years fighting accusations instead of fighting AIDS.

21   *It limits our thinking.* Headlines are intentionally devised to attract attention, but the language of extremes actually shapes, and misshapes, the way we think about things. Military metaphors train us to think about, and see, everything in terms of fighting, conflict and war. Adversarial rhetoric is a kind of verbal inflation—a rhetorical boy-who-cried-wolf.

22   *It encourages us to lie.* If you fight to win, the temptation is great to deny facts that support your opponent's views and say only what supports your side. It encourages people to misrepresent and, in the extreme, to lie.

End the Argument Culture by Looking at All Sides

23   How can we overcome our classically American habit of seeing issues in absolutes? We must expand our notion of "debate" to include more dialogue. To do this, we can make special efforts not to think in twos. Mary Catherine Bateson, an anthropologist at Virginia's George Mason University, makes a point of having her class compare three cultures, not two. Then, students are more likely to think about each on its own terms, rather than as opposites.

24   In the public arena, television and radio producers can try to avoid, whenever possible, structuring public discussions as debates. This means avoiding the format of having two guests discuss an issue. Invite three guests—or one. Perhaps it is time to re-examine the assumption that audiences always prefer a fight.

25   Instead of asking, "What's the other side?" we might ask, "What are the other sides?" Instead of insisting on hearing "both sides," let's insist on hearing "all sides."

26   We need to find metaphors other than sports and war. Smashing heads does not open minds. We need to use our imaginations and ingenuity to find different ways to seek truth and gain knowledge through intellectual interchange, and add them to our arsenal—or, should I say, to the ingredients for our stew. It will take creativity for each of us to find ways to change the argument culture to a dialogue culture. It's an effort we have to make, because our public and private lives are at stake.

ACTIVE READERS RESPOND

After you've finished reading, use these questions to respond to "The Argument Culture." You may write your answers in the spaces provided or on a separate sheet of paper.

VITAL VOCABULARY

Some words in this reading may be unfamiliar to you. Use the methods of Strategy 3 to explain what the listed words mean.

USE CONTEXT CLUES

a. antagonism (paragraph 13)

_____

b. proliferation (paragraph 13)

_____

c. ratchets (paragraph 16)

_____

USE WORD PARTS

a. polarized (paragraph 2)

_____

b. partisanship (paragraph 5)

_____

c. predominate (paragraph 12)

_____

USE THE DICTIONARY

Choose the correct definition of these words as they are used in the context of this reading.

a. adversarial (paragraph 2)

_____

b. litigation (paragraph 2)

_____

c. pervade (paragraph 4)

_____

d. ubiquity (paragraph 6)

_____

e. sparring (paragraph 12)

_____

OBJECTIVE OPERATIONS

1. Who is the writer's intended audience?
   a. argumentative people
   b. people in communications
   c. general audience
   d. people who hate to argue
2. What is the author's purpose?
   a. to inform
   b. to persuade
   c. to entertain

3. What is the tone of the passage?
   a. convincing
   b. sarcastic
   c. subjective
   d. passive
4. The problem with our "argument culture," according to Tannen, is that it portrays issues as two-sided debates that
   a. give unfair advantage to one side.
   b. allow only two people to have their say.

c. have to follow strict debating format.

d. don't allow room for a middle ground. *(circled)*

5. The word "adversarial" in paragraph 2, line 2, most nearly means

a. unfriendly.

b. argumentative. *(circled)*

c. approachable.

d. dangerous.

6. Which of the following sentences best summarizes this passage?

a. We argue frequently, and it affects our ability to think clearly and intelligently.

b. Within the argument culture, we argue frequently and assume that there are two sides to every story; however, in order to develop intellectually, we need to think about the many sides of an issue. *(circled)*

c. Arguments are part of our everyday culture.

d. We argue frequently for one side or the other; therefore, we incorrectly believe there are only two sides to every argument.

7. What is the stated main idea of paragraph 4?

a. "The war on drugs, the war on cancer, the battle of the sexes, politicians' turf battles—in the argument culture, war metaphors pervade our talk and shape our thinking."

b. "The cover headlines of both *Time* and *Newsweek* one recent week are a case in point: "The Secret Sex Wars," proclaims *Newsweek*."

c. " 'Starr at War,' declares *Time*."

d. "Nearly everything is framed as a battle or game in which winning or losing is the main concern." *(circled)*

8. According to Tannen, the main reason high-tech communication "pulls us apart" is that

a. it increases the anonymity between the sender and receiver of information. *(circled)*

b. it frustrates communication because there are constant technical breakdowns.

c. there is a growing split between those people who have the latest high-tech devices and those who don't.

d. it allows so many annoying interruptions—often during dinner—that we want to withdraw from having communication with anyone.

9. Which sentence provides support for this sentence (paragraph 5, line 1): "The argument culture pervades every aspect of our lives today."

a. "Issues from global warming to abortion are depicted as two-sided arguments, when in fact most Americans' views lie somewhere in the middle."

b. "Partisanship makes gridlock in Washington the norm."

c. "Even in our personal relationships, a "let it all hang out" philosophy emphasizes people expressing their anger without giving them constructive ways of settling differences."

d. all of the above *(circled)*

10. The author's claim that there are times when it is necessary to fight is

a. adequately supported with details. *(circled)*

b. inadequately supported with details.

11. What is the topic of paragraph 7?

a. the pursuit of truth on both sides of an argument

b. the fallacy that there are always two sides *(circled)*

c. the other side of the story

d. fringes of lunacy

12. Tannen says that one of the consequences of our argument culture is that it encourages us to lie. She says this because

a. people are so overwhelmed by hearing arguments that they've become too confused to know the difference between telling the truth and lying.

b. people want to win so badly that they are willing to misrepresent facts or even lie. *(circled)*

c. arguing in order to triumph in a debate causes us to lose sight of the truth, and we lie without even realizing it.

d. people lose control of their temper during fierce arguments and are later so ashamed of their behavior that they feel they must lie about it.

13. Identify the relationship between the following sentences from paragraph 3.

"One of the great strengths of our society is that we can express these conflicts openly. But just as spouses have to learn ways of settling their differences without inflicting real damage, so we, as a society, have to find constructive ways of resolving disputes and differences." (lines 3–7)

a. comparison

b. cause and effect

c. definition

d. contrast

14. For paragraph 19, the author organizes the information by using

   a. comparisons.

   b. contrasts.

   c. examples.

   d. definitions.

15. The main way to overcome the problems caused by our argument culture is to

   a. give people more time to think about issues before expecting them to take a stand one way or the other.

   b. open up discussions to more than just two opposing sides.

   c. provide clear ground rules that give a fair hearing to both sides.

   d. make sure there is a neutral, third party in any discussion.

16. The word "sparring" in paragraph 12, line 1, most nearly means

   a. questioning.

   b. rattling.

   c. gossiping.

   d. arguing.

17. Identify the relationship between the parts of the following sentence (paragraph 16, lines 2–4): "Though e-mail has enhanced communication with family and friends, it also ratchets up the anonymity of both sender and receiver, resulting in stranger-to-stranger 'flaming.' "

a. summary

b. definition and example

c. clarification

d. cause and effect

18. In paragraph 26, Tannen changes her wording from "add them to our arsenal" to "the ingredients for our stew." She makes the change because she wants to demonstrate the need to

   a. give women more of a voice in public discourse by using more kitchen metaphors.

   b. avoid clichés and use more creative metaphors.

   c. find new metaphors other than sports and war.

   d. replace sports and war metaphors with metaphors from the kitchen.

19. The author shows a bias

   a. against presenting three sides to an argument.

   b. toward presenting only two sides to an argument.

   c. against assuming there are only two sides to an argument.

   d. toward arguing.

20. According to the author,

   a. constantly arguing causes us to distort facts.

   b. our thinking is not limited by our arguments.

   c. arguments are the only way to communicate.

   d. we are not encouraged to lie during an argument.

1. Tannen's argument relies a great deal on the use of cause-and-effect reasoning. (True) or False

2. Tannen catches herself when she uses the word "arsenal" in the last paragraph but does not change that word. True or (False)

3. Two major consequences Tannen lists to show how the argument culture influences us are:
    (Answers will vary.)
    _____
    _____
    _____
    _____

4. Tannen say that high-tech communication " pulls us apart _____."

5. Tannen disagrees with the tendency to see "critical" thinking as synonymous with criticizing. What would you infer her definition of critical thinking would be, based on this reading?
    (Answers will vary.)
    _____
    _____
    _____
    _____

6. What does Tannen mean by saying in paragraph 7 that by always assuming there is another, opposing side for every issue, "you may end up scouring the margins of science or the fringes of lunacy to find it"?
    (Answers will vary.)
    _____
    _____
    _____
    _____

13

Analyze the Information

ANALYZE THE INFORMATION

1 | Understand the uses of facts and opinions.

2 | Check the reliability of the information.

3 | Test the support.

imagine this

Magicians use prestidigitation, or sleight of hand, to create illusions and magic tricks. They let one hand wave in the air in front of them because they know that is the hand you will watch while they use their other hand to complete the trick— tug a wire you can't see to free some doves, click a switch on the table and force the bunny into the hat, or pull a card from their sleeve. They are masters of illusion.

Writers are also masters of sleight of hand. Writers sometimes hide facts within opinion statements to make the writing sound smarter. Some writers use out-dated information to support their overall point, and some writers conceal essential information that could harm their case. You need to recognize these tricks and then evaluate the reading carefully. Just because a reading has been published doesn't make it true or accurate!

Think FIRST >

- Do you know the difference between a fact and an opinion? Do you recognize when something sounds like a fact but is really an opinion?

- Do you think everything you read is the truth just because it has been published? Do you ever suspect someone's credibility?

- When you hear a bit of information, do you ever "look it up" in a dictionary or encyclopedia or on the Internet? Have you ever questioned someone's evidence?

INTRODUCTION TO THE NEW STRATEGY
Analyze the Information

Instructor Tip
Bring editorials from your local newspaper (the Ticked Off! column in the *Orlando Sentinel* is a great example and can be found online). Share a few of the editorials with students and discuss whether the arguments sound solid. What evidence do the writers give? Ask the students why they think some are strong arguments, and others are weak. What evidence can the students give?

The strategies you've learned so far help you comprehend a writer's ideas and interpret his or her language and perspective. Strategy 13—*Analyze the Information*—helps you examine how well the writer supports an overall point. Strategy 13 gives you the steps to "test" how accurately and thoroughly the author has covered a subject. This strategy is essential for judging the worth of an argument. It is also important for examining the information found in exposition—writing that explains or informs. Then, when you *respond* to the argument or explanation, you can test the writer's support.

A good argument depends on the quality of the information the writer uses to support the overall point. This information is often referred to as **evidence**—something that furnishes some proof that what the writer argues is true. A good argument also depends on the way the information is presented: evidence must be presented in a sound, logical manner. For example, we won't accept an argument in favor of changing the length of the school year without good support demonstrating how much the change would improve our children's education. And we will only be convinced if the writer presents the evidence in clear logic that leads to that overall point.

Expository writing must also use good support and a good presentation of that support in explaining a subject. An explanation of why the school year is shorter in this country than in other countries should contain accurate and complete information, presented in a clear, logical way, even though the writer is not making an argument for change.

Analyzing a writer's information depends on your understanding of the writer's purpose and overall point for the reading. In Reading 25, "Four for a Quarter," writer Kenneth Fletcher's overall point is to introduce his audience to an artist who loves photobooth photographs and their histories. His purpose in the reading is to explain the history of the photobooth from an objective—though somewhat favorable—perspective to a general *Smithsonian* magazine audience. Strategy 13 will teach you to analyze the information he uses.

Fact and Opinion

When you read, you read with a questioning mind. You don't believe everything you see in print; instead, you wonder if the writer is correct. When you do this, you question and test the writer's ideas before accepting what you read. One important part of this testing involves understanding how the writer uses facts and opinions to support the overall point. This means that you must first, be able to distinguish a fact from an opinion.

Look at the following statements. Find the statements that are not facts.

1. The United States of America is made up of fifty states.
2. The sun is 93,000,000 miles from the earth.
3. Photobooth photographs are now digital photographs.
4. Photobooth photographs show American history in a wonderful manner.
5. Many people have taken photobooth photographs, but no one really likes them.
6. Santa Claus lives at the North Pole.

Instructor Tip
In groups, have students review the fact and opinion information. Then, give them ten to fifteen examples of facts, opinions, and facts and opinions. Include myths (during a harvest moon, an alligator devours the light), legends (Bigfoot lives in Oregon), and outdated information (chocolate is bad for you). Give students time to identify whether each statement is a fact, opinion, or a combination. Allow them to use the Internet or the library to assist in verifying facts.

In 2007, a marketing group published a paper about Google.com. When the Product Management Director of Google Enterprise, Matthew Glotzbach, read the paper, he found so many inaccuracies that he had to respond by posting the following passage on GoogleEnterprise.com. Note Glotzbach's tone and his final message to his readers.

One thing we've all learned from the Internet is that just because you see something in "print," it doesn't mean that's the whole story, or that it's entirely factual. You always need to check the source and make sure it's trustworthy. I was reminded of that point recently when I received a white paper published by Autonomy, one of our enterprise search competitors.

The topic of the paper was, oddly enough, Google. Let me first note that I was surprised that the Autonomy marketing folks took the time to write a whole paper (nicely formatted and all) on our enterprise search efforts.

That notwithstanding, the more I read, the more concerned I became. The paper would lead a customer or prospect to believe a number of things about Google that are just fundamentally not true. Inaccuracies about our enterprise ranking algorithms and downright fabrications about our security and access control capabilities. The text is an amalgamation of hearsay and speculation attempting to push customers away from Google and toward their competitive product.

I decided the best course of action was to both set the record straight, and remind everyone of a key lesson. So for the record, let me call out some specific points:

1. Relevancy: The paper states that Google "relies on rich linking technology that was built for the Web to determine relevancy." This is false, and it's misleading. Google's enterprise search algorithms rely on hundreds of factors, only one of which is PageRank, to determine the most relevant content within an enterprise. We leverage the work of the largest engineering team focused on search and information retrieval in the world to solve this complex search problem.

Facts

A **fact** can be proven or verified by going to a reliable source. The first three statements are facts. Each one is either widely known to be true (as in the case of statement 1) or can be verified. You could go to an encyclopedia or any astronomy text to verify the second statement. The third statement could easily be verified as a fact; we could find the history of photobooths on the Internet or in a book.

What about the sixth statement? This statement is a fallacy. A fallacy is a false or mistaken idea. Remember, a fact is something that can be verified, and we can verify that Santa does not have a home at the North Pole. How is an opinion different from a fact?

Opinions

An **opinion** cannot be proven or disproven but is open to debate. The fourth statement is an opinion statement. This statement could not be proven to be factually true, and other reasonable

2. Reach/Aggregation: Autonomy states in their paper that "Non secure web servers can be indexed out of the box but, integrating information from databases, file systems and content management applications into Google is considerably more complex—and in some cases impossible." Google's appliance can natively reach into all content stores in an enterprise, including web servers, file servers, databases, document management systems, and business applications. All of this is offered as out of the box (or, ironically enough in the case of the appliance, "in the box") functionality. You can take a Google Search Appliance or Google Mini from its cardboard box to serving content from file systems and databases in less than 30 minutes. What's the setup time for other enterprise search systems?

3. Languages Support: The paper reports that Google's search is "language dependent technology that currently only supports 28 languages." It is true that we have a feature that supports the auto-detection of 28 languages, and if your query was in one of those 28, we'll offer you results in that language. And of course, offer you all results as well. This is a popular end-user feature on Google.com. However, our indexing and search is by no means restricted to those 28 languages.

4. Stemming: Autonomy states that "Google does not provide advanced language support such as stemming." This one is just wrong. A while back we added a query expansion feature which performs the same function as stemming, but just does it smarter. Anybody can do things like taking "park" and make it "parks"—but in a lot of cases, we've seen that unintelligent stemming actually will make results worse. Drawing off of the intelligence derived from billions of queries, we know that a good solution will detect context, and expand a query like "city park" to also include "public park" but not "city parking." So, whether you want to call what the appliance does "smart stemming" or "Context Sensitive Query Expansion" (the latter being what our marketing team chose) it's a core feature of our product.

5. Security: In perhaps the most egregious statement in the whole document, the paper states that "Google provides open access to most documents—a potential hazard for businesses needing to keep proprietary information under wraps." From the beginning, we have provided fast, accurate, and SECURE search within the enterprise. Our document-level security and access control capabilities ensure that users only see the content they are allowed to see, without requiring customers to deploy a new security system or undergo complex integrations. Google's appliances are used in the most secure environments including Fortune 500 and Global 1000 companies as well as numerous government agencies.

That's it for setting the record straight. I have by no means covered every point, but I think you get the picture. We have been working for more than 5 years with a team dedicated specifically to solving the enterprise search problem, and hold a market leadership position with over 9,000 enterprise search customers. We leverage the work and innovation of the world's largest search company, and deliver that consumer powered innovation to the enterprise. But you don't have to take my word for it: feel free to talk to any one of our thousands of delighted customers.

And about that lesson: Just because it's printed and looks official, doesn't mean it's accurate.

Glotzbach, Matthew. "Don't believe everything you read." www.googleenterprise.com. 24 July 2007. 13 August 2009. Available: http://googleenterprise.blogspot.com/2007/07/dont-believe-everything-you-read.html

people might argue strongly against this statement. This opinion is a judgment based on observations and personal beliefs.

Hiding an Opinion with a Fact

The fifth statement is a combination of fact and opinion. The first part of the sentence, "Many people have taken photobooth photographs," is factual; "Four for a Quarter" lists many different subjects of photographs. However, the last part of the sentence, that "no one really likes them," is an opinion; the artist in Fletcher's piece is actually obsessed with them.

Most writing includes both facts and opinion, sometimes, in the same sentence. Be wary of a writer who tries to hide an opinion with a fact, as with statement 5. This is one way a writer can conceal an opinion; you are more likely to focus on the fact, what you think is true, rather than the opinion, which is a personal belief.

connect now

Do you recognize when someone uses facts to hide opinions?

Analyzing Facts and Opinions

It's important to recognize factual statements so that you can see how well they support the writer's ideas. However, you need to be aware that information that is presented as factual may be wrong. The writer may present—intentionally or not—facts that are incorrect. Facts also may be so out-of-date or incomplete as to be misleading.

Opinions, on the other hand, are more complicated to analyze. Whereas we tend to reject any false statement that is presented as a fact, we can't simply reject a statement just because it's an opinion. Some opinions are more valuable than others. Opinions that are simply **personal preferences** don't carry much weight. For example, if you prefer country music over hip-hop, your preference alone would not be enough to convince others that country music is more "important" for the culture.

Other opinions to watch out for are unsupported, **sweeping generalizations**—general statements that seem overly inclusive. Since the statement that "no one really likes [photobooth photographs]" covers everyone in this country.

The value of an opinion depends on how well it is supported. Opinions that are widely held by experts in a field may be as valuable as facts. For example, that someone smoked two packs of cigarettes every day of his adult life but lived to be ninety and remained healthy is factual. However, this single fact is of little use in countering the opinion, based on years of factual evidence and shared by the entire medical community, that smoking is hazardous to the health of most people. Opinions that a writer supports through observations, reasons, or other evidence may also be valuable. Indeed, a good part of the analysis of information depends on how well the author's opinions are supported.

The following chart summarizes how to distinguish valuable from poor support provided by both facts and opinions.

Hot or Not?

Is fairness and accuracy something you consider during an argument?

	FACTS: Can be proven	**OPINIONS:** Can't be proven; open to debate
Valuable Support	Facts that you know to be true or that you could verify	Opinions that are supported by observations, reasons, or other evidence Opinions that are widely held by experts in a field
Poor Support	Incorrect "facts" Incomplete facts that are therefore misleading	Unsupported personal beliefs or preferences Unsupported, sweeping generalizations

THE READER'S EDGE: BOOK TWO

For practice with identifying facts and opinions, complete the following exercise.

For each of the following sentences, decide whether the statement is fact, opinion, or a combination of fact and opinion. If the statement is fact, place an "F" in the blank. Use "O" for opinion, and use "F/O" for statements that contain both fact and opinion.

1. __F__ Blue jays are territorial birds that will fight for food.

2. __O__ A leak in the roof will cause damage to the interior walls of a home.

3. __F/O__ The best kind of vehicle to buy in today's economy is a hybrid because they get better gas mileage.

4. __O__ Every night, people accidentally ingest eight spiders.

5. __F__ Cheese is considered a "free" food by diabetics.

6. __O__ Opening a retirement account will benefit you in the future.

7. __F/O__ All men neglect chores around the house, and women spend more time taking care of children than men.

8. __O__ The human body is the most magnificent creation in nature.

9. __O__ Green tea tastes better than coffee.

10. __F__ A cat's brainwaves are alpha waves more often than they are beta waves.

Reliable Information

Part of testing the writer's information is to check on its reliability. Is it **reliable information?** Can you rely on—or trust—the information's accuracy and thoroughness?

To answer these questions, consider the following:

1. Look at the kind of publication. Remember that a general-interest magazine provides only an introduction to a topic. For more thorough information, you would go to an academic or professional journal or to a book written by an authority in the field. These articles and books will usually include notes and a good bibliography.

2. Look at the date of publication. Some fields, such as technology or the sciences, require current information; others, such as the humanities, usually don't.

3. Find out about the author. What background, past writings, or experience does he or she have in the field? Is the author associated with a publication or a particular institution? If so, what are their views or goals? Does the writer have anything to gain from presenting certain information?

You may not realize that each time you get an overview of a reading or you consider a writer's perspective, you are testing that writer's reliability. After you have finished the reading, you can further confirm the accuracy of the information by looking at the type and date of publication and rereading the author's notes.

Testing the Support

Writers of both explanations and arguments use many different kinds of information to support an overall point. For example, in his explanation of photobooth photographs to a general audience, Fletcher uses examples, facts, and opinions to show the origins of photobooth and artist Nakki Goranin's interest in photobooths, what they are like, and their influence on Americans. He doesn't take a position for or against photobooth photographs, so this reading is not a clear-cut argument. If it were, we would want to examine his support even more critically.

Testing the writer's support applies mainly to arguments. Support for an argument should be examined closely since the writer's purpose is to convince you to believe something or do something. Here are three questions that can help determine how **credible**—believable—an argument is, that is, how well it is supported.

These are the questions to ask to test the credibility of an argument:

Instructor Tip
To extend the previous activity, have the students test the support of the article.

1. What type of support is used? (such as examples, facts, expert opinions)
2. How well does the reasoning support the argument?
3. How objective is the support?

Hot or Not?

Do you like to play devil's advocate? Why?

Type of Support
Credible arguments can be based on many different kinds of support. Writers will usually use some combination of facts and opinions as support. In addition, they may use examples—from research or observation or from personal experience.

Reasoning
Providing good evidence is not enough. The author must also use good reasoning in order to make a convincing argument. A reason given in support of a specific opinion should make sense, and the major supporting reasons should all work together to make the argument convincing.

Objectivity
An argument should be objective. You looked at the difference between being objective and subjective on page 398 under the discussion of tone. As you saw there, authors always write from a certain perspective—their way of looking at, or their position on a subject. They may even show some feelings about the subject and still write a piece that is objective overall. However, when testing the support for an argument, you need to see if the writer's

perspective prevents objectivity—or giving both sides of an argument a fair presentation. A good argument deals with ideas that the other side might state. When the writer's perspective seems too narrow-minded or limited, it is often called a bias—a leaning toward one side or another, and the argument is said to be too biased, or slanted in one direction. If you think the argument is too one-sided, refer back to the author's biography: Does he or she have anything to gain from presenting this argument?

For example, take a look at this statement from a multi-page special advertising supplement for Zocor, a cholesterol-lowering drug.

> Like diamonds, statins [cholesterol-lowering drugs] are for life. Once one begins treatment, it continues indefinitely. Most patients find the investment worthwhile. A study published in the medical journal *Circulation* in 1998 showed that statins dramatically lowered the risk of dying from heart disease.
>
> *New York Times Magazine,* December 9, 2001

The writer (or writers) of this statement represent Merck, a large drug company. We expect advertising to be one-sided—it's meant to sell us something. So, we know that the drug company representatives do have something to gain from convincing readers of the value of statins. What they say in this statement—and elsewhere in the long advertisement—may be true. As general readers, we can't easily verify what is said about statins. However, in this case, we would want to check out what a more objective medical expert might have to say as well. While you expect bias in advertising, be aware that it can appear in other writing as well.

JODI PICOULT

The Ice Queen
by Alice Hoffman

The heroine of Hoffman's book is orphaned at age 8 after angrily wishing she would never see her mother again; as an adult, she becomes an emotional "ice queen." Picoult, a writer of bestselling novels herself (*My Sister's Keeper*), commented that, "As with all Hoffman's books, I'm amazed by how she makes writing look so easy . . . and how she can cut clean to the bone of relationships between men and women."

If you liked *The Ice Queen,* you might also like:

Practical Magic, Alice Hoffman

The Handmaid's Tale, Margaret Atwood

Into the Forest, Jean Hegland

EXERCISES

PRACTICE

For practice testing reliability and support, complete the following exercise.

For the following, read the notes before the excerpt and then read the excerpt. Answer the questions that follow the excerpt. (Please know that these "notes" are fictionalized.)

This excerpt is from the introduction of a first aid course syllabus for a fall 2007 semester. The course was offered by Justine Simmons, who has been a first aid instructor for twenty years. Prior to that, she worked as an emergency medic and trauma nurse for the United States Army. She has been a tenured professor at Westover Community College in Pennsylvania since 2005.

(1) First aid courses should be required for every person. (2) First aid courses teach people how to respond in an emergency situation and the kind of help they may give during an emergency. (3) In addition to such basics as learning how to treat broken bones, sprains, shock, and dehydration, people will learn how to perform CPR and the abdominal thrust (formerly known as the "Heimlich maneuver") and how to use a defibrillator. (4) Each of these skills is invaluable in saving a person's life. (5) People who take first aid courses learn how to assist others in an emergency, but they also receive the satisfaction of knowing they can help.

1. Which sentences are facts? Number(s) ___2 and 3___

2. Which sentences are opinions? Number(s) ___1 and 4___

3. Which sentences are fact and opinions? Number(s) ___5___

4. What do the notes tell you about the writer's perspective? _(Answers will vary.)_

5. What do the notes tell you about the writer's biases? _(Answers will vary.)_

6. What adjective would you use to describe the tone in this passage?
   (Answers will vary.)

7. Is this writer reliable? Why or why not? _(Answers will vary.)_

8. How objective is this writer? _(Answers will vary.)_

APPLY THE NEW STRATEGY
Analyze the Information

Now that you understand Strategy 13, put it into practice with Reading 25, "Four for a Quarter." As you get an overview and ask questions, think about which strategies will help you most in reading "Four for a Quarter." Write down two or three strategies that you think you will help you, in addition to Strategy 13, *Analyze the Information*.

Four for a Quarter

KENNETH R. FLETCHER

Before cell phones could snap photographs, people often visited photobooths for fun photographs. Today, people still take many photographs of themselves and often post them on myspace.com or facebook.com. First published in a September 2008 *Smithsonian*, this article by Kenneth Fletcher, who has a master's degree in journalism and is a contributing writer to *Smithsonian*, examines the photobooths' effect on culture and our passion for photographing ourselves.

1   Nakki Goranin and I squeeze into a cramped photobooth in a Vermont shopping mall and practice our expressions. Goranin, a veteran, tries out some wacky poses, sticking her tongue out and squinting at the lens. I'm a bit more <u>inhibited</u> and, as the camera clicks off four shots, stick with a bemused smile. A minute later, the machine spits out a photo strip.

2   "I love them," says Goranin of the photos. "They're the real Nakki." Goranin, who lives in Burlington and has just published an illustrated history of the machine, *American Photobooth,* asks me to sign and date the back of the strip, just as she did in the late 1960s growing up in Chicago and sharing photobooth photos with her friends.

3   The routine is familiar to the generations of Americans who documented everyday moments by jumping inside a booth and popping a quarter into the slot. Still, Goranin doesn't much care for the mall's machine, which is digital—the print quality is not what it used to be. But, she says, there are only about 250 <u>authentic</u> chemical booths left in the United States, and she knows of none available to the public in Vermont.

4   As Goranin, a photographer and self-described <u>romantic</u>, sees it, photo strips tell the story of 20th-century American history from the ground up. The images in her new book, <u>culled</u> from thousands she has collected at auctions, flea markets and antiques stores, show down-at-the-heels farmers in overalls, wartime sweethearts and 1950s boys with greased hair and ducktails. She points out a photo of a World War II–era couple kissing passionately. "Day before he left," the notation reads.

5   Before the photobooth first appeared, in the 1920s, most portraits were made in studios. The new, inexpensive process made photography accessible to everyone. "For 25 cents people could go and get some memory of who they were, of a special occasion, of a first date, an anniversary, a graduation," Goranin says. "For many people, those were the only photos of themselves that they had."

6   Because there is no photographer to intimidate, photobooth subjects tend to be much less self-conscious. The result—a young boy embracing his mother or teenagers sneaking a first kiss—is often exceptionally intimate. "It's like a theater that's just you and the lens," Goranin says. "And you can be anyone you want to be."

7   Goranin's photobooth obsession began after her mother died in 1999. She needed to continue her photography, but couldn't focus on her work or bring herself to go back into the darkroom. Frequenting photobooths was the answer, she says. After a while, Goranin got the idea to publish her

collection of self-portraits—now part of the permanent collection of the International Center for Photography in New York City—along with a brief history of the machine. But she was surprised by the <u>dearth</u> of information about the machine's origins or development; she set off from her cozy white Vermont house to see what she could discover for herself. That was nine years ago.

Goranin <u>pored</u> through micro-film of old newspapers. She drove back 8 and forth across the United States and Canada interviewing anyone connected with the business that she could track down. When she telephoned the son of a long-dead early photobooth operator, she learned that only the day before, he had thrown away a trove of vintage photographs and business records. Goranin persuaded him to climb into a Dumpster to retrieve the items. Goranin even bought her own fully functioning 1960s-era photo booth and is now restoring two others that she also purchased.

The history she eventually put together chronicles the rapid rise and 9 remarkable longevity of the machine. In the 1920s, an enterprising Siberian immigrant named Anatol Josepho perfected a fully automated process that produced a positive image on paper, eliminating the need not only for negatives but for operators as well. His "Photomaton" studio, which opened in 1926 on Broadway in New York City, was an immediate hit. Crowds lined up to pay 25 cents for a strip of eight photos. Within a few years, photo booths could be found from Paris to Shanghai.

Even amid the worldwide depression of the 1930s, the photobooth continued to grow. Entrepreneurs who couldn't afford to buy the real thing built their own versions, some out of wood, then hid a photographer in the back who shot and developed the pictures and slipped them through a slot. The unsuspecting subjects were none the wiser.

By mid-century, photobooths were <u>ubiquitous</u>. Jack and Jackie Kennedy 11 stepped into one in the 1950s. Yoko Ono and John Lennon included a reproduction strip with their 1969 recording, "Wedding Album." In the 1960s, Andy Warhol shuttled models with rolls of quarters from booth to booth in New York City. A 1965 *Time* magazine cover features Warhol's photobooth portraits of "Today's Teen-Agers."

But Goranin and other purists long for the real McCoy with its distinctive smell, clanking machinery and the fraught anticipation that comes with waiting for the photos to appear.

These days digital photobooths, which became available in the 1990s, 12 let users add novelty messages and backgrounds and delete and retake shots. Allen Weisberg, president of Apple Industries, which has manufactured digital booths since 2001, says digital photobooth sales continue to grow. "Photobooths have made a tremendous resurgence," he says. "It's like apple pie and baseball. It's part of our heritage." The digital booths are being used in new ways. Lately, a number of companies have popped up offering rentals of lightweight, portable photobooths for use at weddings and parties.

But Goranin and other purists long for the real McCoy with its 13 distinctive smell, clanking machinery and the fraught anticipation that comes with waiting for the photos to appear. A Web site, Photobooth.net, documents the locations of a dwindling number of these mechanical dinosaurs.

"The old chemistry booths, which I love, are becoming harder and 14 harder to find," says Goranin. "But the [digital] booth is still a fun experience. You still get great photos. You still have a wonderful time in them. You still have the old-fashioned curtains that you can draw and that sense of mystery." Goranin smiles. "There's nothing in the world like a photobooth."

ACTIVE READERS RESPOND

After you've finished reading, use these questions to respond to "Four for a Quarter." You may write your answers in the spaces provided or on a separate sheet of paper.

VITAL VOCABULARY

Some words in this reading may be unfamiliar to you. Use the methods of Strategy 3 to explain what the listed words mean.

USE CONTEXT CLUES

a. inhibited (paragraph 1)

_____

b. ubiquitous (paragraph 11)

_____

USE WORD PARTS

a. authentic (paragraph 3)

_____

b. romantic (paragraph 4)

_____

USE THE DICTIONARY

Choose the correct definition of each word as it is used in the context of this reading.

a. culled (paragraph 4)

_____

b. dearth (paragraph 7)

_____

c. pored (paragraph 8)

_____

SKILLS EXERCISE: RELIABILITY AND SUPPORT

A. *Look at these statements from Fletcher's article and try to determine which are facts, which are opinions, and which are both.*

a. "Because there is no photographer to intimidate, photobooth subjects tend to be much less self-conscious." _____opinion_____

b. "The routine is familiar to the generations of Americans who documented everyday moments by jumping inside a booth and popping a quarter into the slot." _____fact_____

c. "The images in her new book, culled from thousands she has collected at auctions, flea markets and antiques stores, show down-at-the-heels farmers in overalls, wartime sweethearts and 1950s boys with greased hair and ducktails." _____fact_____

d. "But Goranin and other purists long for the real McCoy with its distinctive smell, clanking machinery and the fraught anticipation that comes with waiting for the photos to appear." _____opinion_____

e. "Lately, a number of companies have popped up offering rentals of lightweight, portable photobooths for use at weddings and parties." _____fact_____

B. *Answer the following questions about the reading.*

1. What do the notes tell you about the writer's perspective?

   (Answers will vary.)

   _____

   _____

2. What do the notes tell you about the writer's biases?

   (Answers will vary.)

   _____

   _____

3. What adjective would you use to describe the tone in this article?

   (Answers will vary.)

   _____

   _____

4. Is this writer reliable? Why or why not?

   (Answers will vary.)

   _____

   _____

5. How objective is this writer?

   (Answers will vary.)

   _____

   _____

OBJECTIVE OPERATIONS

1. Who is the writer's intended audience?
   a. photographers
   b. people who hate photobooths
   c. general audience
   d. people who love old photobooths

2. What is the author's purpose?
   a. to inform
   b. to persuade
   c. to entertain

3. What is the tone of the passage?
   a. abrasive
   b. depressing
   c. apathetic
   d. nostalgic

4. According to Fletcher, Nakki Goranin
   a. started working with photobooths after her mom's death.
   b. started working with photobooths before her mom's death.

   c. prefers to paint rather than photograph.
   d. had never taken an art class before.

5. The word "novelty" in paragraph 12, line 2, most nearly means
   a. dirtiness.
   b. one of many kinds.
   c. old.
   d. newness.

6. Which of the following sentences best summarizes this passage?
   a. Nakki Goranin is an artist who likes photobooths.
   b. Due to her curiosity and drive as an artist, Nakki Goranin struggles to keep the photobooth alive and encourage others to document their personal histories.
   c. Photobooths are no longer very popular, and Nakki Goranin is trying to keep them from vanishing.
   d. Photobooth photographs are part of our culture.

7. What is the stated main idea of paragraph 9?

   a. "The history she eventually put together chronicles the rapid rise and remarkable longevity of the machine."

   b. "In the 1920s, an enterprising Siberian immigrant named Anatol Josepho perfected a fully automated process that produced a positive image on paper, eliminating the need not only for negatives but for operators as well."

   c. "His 'Photomaton' studio, which opened in 1926 on Broadway in New York City, was an immediate hit."

   d. "Crowds lined up to pay 25 cents for a strip of eight photos."

8. Nakki Goranin became obsessed with photobooth photos and

   a. drove all over the United States to take photobooth photos.

   b. used her local library as the main source of her photographs.

   c. drove to Ohio to look for photobooths.

   d. drove all over the United States and Canada, looking for information about photobooths.

9. Which sentence provides support for this sentence (paragraph 7, lines 4–7): "After a while, Goranin got the idea to publish her collection of self-portraits—now part of the permanent collection of the International Center for Photography in New York City—along with a brief history of the machine."

   a. "Frequenting photobooths was the answer, she says."

   b. "But she was surprised by the dearth of information about the machine's origins or development; she set off from her cozy white Vermont house to see what she could discover for herself."

   c. "That was nine years ago."

   d. none of the above

10. The author's claim that the photobooth became increasingly popular during the twentieth century is

   a. adequately supported with details.

   b. inadequately supported with details.

11. What is the topic of paragraph 7?

   a. Nakki Goranin

   b. prior work

   c. freedom from other artists

   d. Goranin's decision to try photoboothing as new medium

12. When the Great Depression hit, people who couldn't afford to buy photobooths

   a. stopped using them.

   b. built their own photobooths.

   c. sold photobooths to make money.

   d. gave photobooths to the junkyard.

13. Identify the relationship between the following sentences from paragraph 6.

   "Because there is no photographer to intimidate, photobooth subjects tend to be much less self-conscious." (lines 1–2)

   a. cause and effect

   b. process

   c. clarification and statement

   d. definition and example

14. For paragraph 11, the author organizes the information by using

   a. addition.

   b. time order.

   c. examples.

   d. descriptions.

15. "The new, inexpensive process made photography accessible to everyone." (paragraph 5, lines 2–3)

   The above sentence is a statement of

   a. fact and opinion.

   b. opinion.

   c. fact.

16. The word "resurgence" in paragraph 12, line 5, most nearly means

   a. survival.

   b. revival.

   c. something out-dated.

   d. something brand new.

17. Identify the relationship between the parts of the following sentence (paragraph 5, lines 1–2): "Before the photobooth first appeared, in the 1920s, most portraits were made in studios."

   a. comparison

   b. process

   c. contrast

   d. time order

18. Goranin is pleased to see that photobooths are coming back, but she is disappointed that they are

   a. the same as the early models.

   b. not as popular as the early models.

   c. difficult to find.

   (d.) digital.

19. Goranin shows a bias

   a. against old-fashioned photobooths.

   (b.) toward old-fashioned photobooths.

   c. against photobooth photographs.

   d. toward photographers.

20. Identify the relationship between the parts of the following sentence (paragraph 3, lines 3–4): "Still, Goranin doesn't much care for the mall's machine, which is digital—the print quality is not what it used to be."

   (a.) contrast.

   b. comparison.

   c. definition.

   d. addition.

READERS WRITE

1. Why is Goranin's photobooth project important to American history?

(Answers will vary.)

_____

_____

2. What drove Goranin to pursue this type of project? Why does she continue to pursue it?

(Answers will vary.)

_____

_____

3. Why are people fascinated with taking photographs of themselves? What are some of the significant photographs in Goranin's collection?

(Answers will vary.)

_____

_____

4. Approximately how many of the old-fashioned photobooths exist? Why are they becoming more obscure?

(Answers will vary.)

_____

_____

5. What types of people used photobooths, and what moments did they document with photographs? Why do you think there was such a variety of people in old photobooth pictures?

(Answers will vary.)

_____

_____

READERS DISCUSS

1. Discuss with a group whether posting cellphone photographs of yourself on myspace.com or facebook.com is similar or different than going to photobooths. Are there similarities? Are their differences?

(Answers will vary.)

_____

_____

2. What events do you feel are important to record with a photograph? Have you ever taken photobooth photographs with your friends? Why was the experience different than having regular photographs taken? Discuss with others.

(Answers will vary.)

_____

_____

Summary

CHAPTER 13

HOW DOES STRATEGY 13 HELP YOU BECOME AN ENGAGED READER?

When you *analyze the information,* you use your own logical thinking to question and "test" what the writer has said. You extend your dialogue with the writer to include asking about the fairness and accuracy of the information in the reading. You can then give a fair and complete *response* to what the writer says.

HOW DOES THE ANALYZE THE INFORMATION STRATEGY WORK?

Analyzing the information shows you how to examine the reliability, fairness, and accuracy of the support in exposition and argument. It gives guidelines for looking at different types of support—such as facts, well-established opinions, examples, reasons, good, logical reasoning, and objective and complete support.

Strategy 13 helps you determine the facts and opinions the writer has used for support. It teaches you to distinguish fact from opinion and to be wary of writers who hide opinions in facts.

Strategy 13 teaches you to question the credibility of the writer. Whether or not a writer is credible helps you determine whether or not the reading is credible.

Strategy 13 shows you how to test the support. It gives you steps to determine whether the writer has adequately supported the claims made in the reading.

ANALYZE THE INFORMATION

1 | Understand the uses of facts and opinions.

2 | Check the reliability of the information.

3 | Test the support.

Key Terms

credible argument: believable argument in terms of kinds of support and reasoning

evidence: a piece of information that furnishes some proof that what the writer argues is true

fact: can be verified or proven

opinion: cannot be proven or disproven, but may be valuable support if well supported

personal preferences: opinions based only on what you like

reliable information: information you can rely on or trust to be fair, accurate, and complete

sweeping generalizations: general statements that seem overly inclusive

Think
AGAIN

Sometimes, people analyze information and consider facts and opinions without realizing that is what they are doing. For example, when you talk to a professor about an absence, you know that the professor is going to question the truthfulness of your excuse. For your experienced professor, this analysis takes seconds and may be so ingrained in the professor's habits that it becomes automatic. You may do something similar when you hear a friend's excuse as he or she cancels plans *again*. When else might you automatically analyze information you are receiving?

MASTERY TEST

Now that you understand Strategy 13, put it into

practice with Reading 26, "Buy This 24-Year-Old

and Get All His Friends Absolutely Free."

Buy This 24-Year-Old and Get All His Friends Absolutely Free

JEAN KILBOURNE   READING **26**

Jean Kilbourne is recognized internationally for her investigation of alcohol and tobacco advertising and the portrayal of women in advertising. She is best known for her award-winning documentaries, *Killing Us Softly, Slim Hopes,* and *Pack of Lies.* She is a frequent lecturer on college campuses and has twice been named Lecturer of the Year by the National Association for Campus Activities. This excerpt comes from the first chapter of her book *Can't Buy My Love: How Advertising Changes the Way We Think and Feel* (1999).

1   If you're like most people, you think that advertising has no influence on you. This is what advertisers want you to believe. But, if that were true, why would companies spend over $200 billion a year on advertising?[1] Why would they be willing to spend over $250,000 to produce an average television commercial and another $250,000 to air it?[2] If they want to broadcast their commercial during the Super Bowl, they will gladly spend over a million dollars to produce it and over one and a half million to air it.[3] After all, they might have the kind of success that Victoria's Secret did during the 1999 Super Bowl. When they paraded bra-and-panty-clad models across TV screens for a mere thirty seconds, one million people turned away from the game to log on to the Website promoted in the ad.[4] No influence?

2   Ad agency Arnold Communications of Boston kicked off an ad campaign for a financial services group during the 1999 Super Bowl that represented

1. Coen, 1999, 136.
2. Garfield, 1998, 53.
3. Reidy, 1999, D1.
4. Ryan, 1999, D1.

eleven months of planning and twelve thousand "man-hours" of work.[5] Thirty hours of footage were edited into a thirty-second spot. An employee flew to Los Angeles with the ad in a lead-lined bag, like a diplomat carrying state secrets or a courier with crown jewels. Why? Because the Super Bowl is one of the few sure sources of big audiences[6]— especially male audiences, the most precious <u>commodity</u> for advertisers. Indeed, the Super Bowl is more about advertising than football:[7] The four hours it takes include only about twelve minutes of actually moving the ball.

coattails: influence of a popular movement or candidate

Three of the four television programs that draw the largest audiences   3 every year are football games. And these games have coattails: twelve prime-time shows that attracted bigger male audiences in 1999 than those in the same time slots the previous year were heavily pushed during football games. No wonder the networks can sell this prized Super Bowl audience to advertisers for almost any price they want. The Oscar ceremony, known as the Super Bowl for women, is able to command one million dollars for a thirty-second spot because it can deliver over 60 percent of the nation's women to advertisers.[8] Make no mistake: The primary purpose of the mass media is to sell audiences to advertisers. *We* are the product. Although people are much more sophisticated about advertising now than even a few years ago, most are still shocked to learn this.

The primary purpose of the mass media is to sell audiences to advertisers. *We* are the product.

Magazines, newspapers, and radio and television programs   4 round us up, rather like cattle, and producers and publishers then sell us to advertisers, usually through ads placed in advertising and industry publications. "The people you want, we've got all wrapped up for you," declares *The Chicago Tribune* in an ad placed in *Advertising Age*, the major publication of the advertising industry, which pictures several people, all neatly boxed according to income level.

Although we like to think of advertising as unimportant, it is in fact   5 the most important aspect of the mass media. It *is* the point. Advertising supports more than 60 percent of magazine and newspaper production[9] and almost 100 percent of the electronic media. Over $40 billion a year in ad revenue is generated for television and radio and over $30 billion for magazines and newspapers.[10] As one ABC executive said, "The network is paying <u>affiliates</u> to carry network commercials, not programs. What we are is a distribution system for Procter & Gamble."[11] And the CEO of Westinghouse Electric, owner of CBS, said, "We're here to serve advertisers. That's our raison d'etre."[12]

raison d'etre: reason or justification for being

The media know that television and radio programs are simply fillers   6 for the space between commercials. They know that the programs that succeed are the ones that deliver the highest number of people to the advertisers. But not just any people. Advertisers are interested in people aged

5. Reidy, 1999, EI, E2.
6. Carter, 1999, BUI.
7. Twitchell, 1996,71.
8. Johnson, 1999, C5.
9. Twitchell, 1996, 46.
10. Endicott, 1998, S-50.
11. Collins, 1992, 13.
12. Ross, 1997, 14.

eighteen to forty-nine who live in or near a city. *Dr. Quinn, Medicine Woman,* a program that was number one in its time slot and immensely popular with older, more rural viewers, was canceled in 1998 because it couldn't command the higher advertising rates paid for younger, richer audiences.[13] This is not new: the *Daily Herald,* a British newspaper with 47 million readers, double the combined readership of *The Times, The Financial Times, The Guardian,* and *The Telegraph,* folded in the 1960s because its readers were mostly elderly and working class and had little appeal to advertisers.[14] The target audience that appeals to advertisers is becoming more narrow all the time. According to Dean Valentine, the head of the United Paramount Network, most networks have abandoned the middle class and want "very chic shows that talk to affluent, urban, unmarried, huge-disposable-income 18-to-34-year-olds because the theory is, from advertisers, that the earlier you get them, the sooner you imprint the brand name."[15]

7   "Tripod Delivers Gen-X," proclaims a sinister ad for a Website and magazine that features a delivery man carrying a corpselike consumer wrapped from neck to toe in brown paper. Several other such "deliveries" are propped up in the truck. "We've got your customers on our target," says an ad for financial services that portrays the lower halves of two people embedded in a target. "When you've got them by the ears their hearts and minds will follow," says an ad for an entertainment group. And an ad for the newspaper *USA Today* offers the consumer's eye between a knife and a fork and says, "12 Million Served Daily." The ad explains, "Nearly six million influential readers with both eyes ingesting your message. Every day." There is no humanity, no individuality in this ad or others like it—people are simply products sold to advertisers, of value only as potential consumers.

8   Newspapers are more in the business of selling audiences than in the business of giving people news, especially as more and more newspapers are owned by fewer and fewer chains. They exist primarily to support local advertisers, such as car dealers, realtors, and department store owners. A full-page ad in *The New York Times* says, "A funny thing happens when people put down a newspaper. They start spending money." The ad continues, "Nothing puts people in the mood to buy like newspaper. In fact, most people consider it almost a prerequisite to any spending spree." It concludes, "Newspaper. It's the best way to close a sale." It is especially disconcerting to realize that our newspapers, even the illustrious *New York Times,* are hucksters at heart.

9   Once we begin to count, we see that magazines are essentially catalogs of goods, with less than half of their pages devoted to editorial content (and much of that in the service of the advertisers). An ad for a custom publishing company in *Advertising Age* promises "The next hot magazine could be the one we create exclusively for your product." And, in fact, there are magazines for everyone from dirt-bike riders to knitters to mercenary soldiers, from *Beer Connoisseur* to *Cigar Aficionado.* There are plenty of magazines for the wealthy, such as *Coastal Living* "for people who live or vacation on the coast." *Barron's* advertises itself as a way to "reach faster cars, bigger

---

13. Bierbaum, 1998, 18.
14. Masterman, 1990, 3.
15. Hirschberg, 1998, 59.

houses and longer <u>prenuptial</u> agreements" and promises a readership with an average household net worth of over a million.

The Internet advertisers target the wealthy too, of course. "They give **10** you Dick," says an ad in *Advertising Age* for an Internet news network. "We give you Richard." The ad continues, "That's the Senior V.P. Richard who lives in L.A., drives a BMW and wants to buy a DVD player and a kayak." Not surprisingly there are no magazines or Internet sites or television programs for the poor or for people on welfare. They might not be able to afford the magazines or computers but, more important, they are of no use to advertisers.

This emphasis on the <u>affluent</u> surely has something to do with the in- **11** visibility of the poor in our society. Since advertisers have no interest in them, they are not reflected in the media. We know so much about the rich and famous that it becomes a problem for many who seek to emulate them, but we know very little about the lifestyles of the poor and desperate. It is difficult to feel compassion for people we don't know.

Through focus groups and depth interviews, psychological researchers **12** can zero in on very specific target audiences—and their leaders. "Buy this 24-year-old and get all his friends absolutely free," proclaims an ad for MTV directed to advertisers. MTV presents itself publicly as a place for rebels and nonconformists. Behind the scenes, however, it tells potential advertisers that its viewers are lemmings who will buy whatever they are told to buy.

The MTV ad gives us a somewhat different perspective on the concept **13** of "peer pressure." Advertisers, especially those who advertise tobacco and alcohol, are forever claiming that advertising doesn't influence anyone, that kids smoke and drink because of peer pressure. Sure, such pressure exists and is an important influence, but a lot of it is created by advertising. Kids who exert peer pressure don't drop into high school like Martians. They are kids who tend to be leaders, whom other kids follow for good or for bad. And they themselves are mightily influenced by advertising, sometimes very deliberately as in the MTV ad. As an ad for *Seventeen* magazine, picturing a group of attractive young people, says, "Hip doesn't just happen. It starts at the source: *Seventeen*." In the global village, the "peers" are very much the same, regardless of nationality, ethnicity, culture. In the eyes of the media, the youths of the world are becoming a single, seamless, soulless target audience—often cynically labeled "Generation X," or, for the newest wave of teens, "Generation Y." "We're helping a soft drink company reach them, even if their parents can't," says an ad for newspapers featuring a group of young people. The ad continues, "If you think authority figures have a hard time talking to Generation X, you should try being an advertiser," and goes on to suggest placing ads in the television sections of newspapers.

Of course, it's not only young people who are influenced by their peers, **14** *Barron's* tells its advertisers, "Reach the right bird and the whole flock will follow." The MTV ad promises advertisers that young "opinion leaders" can influence what their friends eat, drink, and wear, whereas *Barron's* sells them leaders "whose simple 'yes' can legitimize a new product, trigger eight-figure purchases, and alter the flow of cash and ideas throughout the economy." Advertisers sometimes criticize my work by saying I imply that consumers are brainwashed, stupid, and easily led. Although I never say this, it often seems that the advertisers themselves describe consumers as sitting ducks.

References

Bierbaum, T. (1998, June 8-June 14). Ailing demos bar 'Dr. Quinn.' *Variety*, 18.

Carter, B. (1999, January 30). Where the boys are. *New York Times*, BU1, BU2.

Coen, R. J. (1999). Spending spree. The Advertising Century {*Advertising* Age special issue), 126, 136.

Collins, R. (1992). Dictating content: How advertising pressure can corrupt a free press. Washington, DC: Center for Science in the Public Interest.

Endicott, R. C. (1998, November 9). Top 100 megabrands. *Advertising Age,* S-50, S-58.

Garfield, B. (1998, April 20). Fabian turns Denny's meals into side dish. *Advertising Age,* 53.

Hirschberg, L. (1998, September 20). What's a network to do? *New York Times Magazine,* 59-62.

Johnson, G. (1999, March 21). 'And the winner is . . . advertisers.' *Boston Globe,* C5.

Masterman, L. (1990, Fall). New paradigms for media education. *7e/e-medium,* 1-4.

Reidy, C. (1999, January 28). Super Bowl ad campaign goes down to wire. *Boston Globe,* D1, D5.

Reidy, C. (1999, January 30). A super bowl berth. *Boston Globe,* El, E2.

Ross, C. (1997, February 3). Jordan brings the heart of a marketer to CBS-TV. *Advertising Age,* 1,14.

Ryan, S. C. (1999, February 3). Victoria's Secret success at Super Bowl has ad world abuzz. *Boston Globe,* D1, D7.

Twitchell, J. B. (1996). Adcult USA: The triumph of advertising in American culture. New York: Columbia University Press.

ACTIVE READERS RESPOND

After you've finished reading, use these questions to respond to "Buy This 24-Year-Old and Get His Friends Absolutely Free." You may write your answers in the spaces provided or on a separate sheet of paper.

VITAL VOCABULARY

Some words in this reading may be unfamiliar to you. Use the methods of Strategy 3 to explain what the listed words mean.

USE CONTEXT CLUES

a. commodity (paragraph 2)

_____

b. affiliates (paragraph 5)

_____

USE WORD PARTS

a. prenuptial (paragraph 9)

_____

USE THE DICTIONARY

Choose the correct definition of each word as it is used in the context of this reading.

a. chic (paragraph 6)

_____

b. sinister (paragraph 7)

_____

c. hucksters (paragraph 8)

_____

d. affluent (paragraph 11)

_____

SKILLS TEST: RELIABILITY AND SUPPORT

A. *Look at these statements from Kilbourne's article and try to determine which are facts, which are opinions, and which are both.*

  a. "No wonder the networks can sell this prized Super Bowl audience to advertisers for almost any price they want." _____opinion_____

  b. "Magazines, newspapers, and radio and television programs round us up, rather like cattle, and producers and publishers then sell us to advertisers, usually through ads placed in advertising and industry publications." _____fact and opinion_____

  c. "Newspapers are more in the business of selling audiences than in the business of giving people news, especially as more and more newspapers are owned by fewer and fewer chains." _____fact_____

  d. "Once we begin to count, we see that magazines are essentially catalogs of goods, with less than half of their pages devoted to editorial content (and much of that in the service of the advertisers)." _____fact and opinion_____

  e. "Not surprisingly there are no magazines or Internet sites or television programs for the poor or for people on welfare." _____fact_____

B. *Answer the following questions about the reading.*

  1. What do the notes tell you about the writer's perspective? (Answers will vary.) _____

  _____

  2. What do the notes tell you about the writer's biases? (Answers will vary.) _____

  _____

  3. What adjective would you use to describe the tone in this article? (Answers will vary.) _____

  _____

  4. Is this writer reliable? Why or why not? (Answers will vary.) _____

  _____

  5. How objective is this writer? (Answers will vary.) _____

  _____

1. Who is the writer's intended audience?

    a. advertising students

    b. general audience

    c. advertisers

    d. consumers

2. What is the author's purpose?

    a. to inform

    b. to persuade

    c. to entertain

3. What is the tone of the passage?

    a. critical

    b. condemning

    c. passive

    d. acrid

4. According to the reading, the Oscar Ceremony is known as the Super Bowl for women because

    a. advertisers introduce clever new ads during Oscar Ceremony commercial breaks, just as they do during the Super Bowl commercial breaks.

    b. the Oscar Ceremony can deliver well over half of the nation's women to advertisers.

    c. over half of the audience who watches the Oscar Ceremony is female.

    d. women bet on which actors will win Oscars in the same way that men bet on which team will win the Super Bowl.

5. The word "sinister" in paragraph 7, line 1, most nearly means

    a. horrifying.

    b. abnormal.

    c. imaginative.

    d. ominous.

6. Which statement is the author's overall point?

    a. "Advertisers, especially those who advertise tobacco and alcohol are forever claiming that advertising doesn't influence anyone, that kids smoke and drink because of peer pressure."

    b. "The primary purpose of the mass media is to sell audiences to advertisers. *We are the product.*"

    c. "If you're like most people, you think that advertising has no influence on you. This is what advertisers want you to believe."

    d. "Advertisers sometimes criticize my work by saying I imply that consumers are brain-washed, stupid, and easily led. Although I never say this, it often seems that the advertisers themselves describe consumers as sitting ducks."

7. What is the implied main idea of paragraph 10?

    a. Advertisers only target wealthy people.

    b. Advertisers target more affluent people because poor people or people on welfare are not buyers.

    c. Poor people do not have any television shows targeted to them.

    d. Advertisers avoid poor people as a target audience.

8. In paragraph 3, Kilbourne says, "The primary purpose of the mass media is to sell audiences to advertisers." The most direct way that media producers sell audiences to advertisers is by

    a. getting consumers to buy their products.

    b. making popular radio and television programs and producing best-selling magazines and newspapers.

    c. placing ads in advertising and industry publications.

    d. developing strong relationships between the advertising departments of television, radio, and print media and their potential advertisers.

9. Which sentence provides support for this sentence (paragraph 8, lines 1–3): "Newspapers are more in the business of selling audiences than in the business of giving people news, especially as more and more newspapers are owned by fewer and fewer chains."

    a. "They exist primarily to support local advertisers, such as car dealers, realtors, and department store owners."

    b. "A full-page ad in *The New York Times* says, 'A funny thing happens when people put down a newspaper. They start spending money.'"

    c. "The ad continues, "Nothing puts people in the mood to buy like newspaper.""

    d. none of the above

10. The author's claim that "magazines are essentially catalogs of goods" (paragraph 9, lines 1–2) is

    a. adequately supported with details.

    b. inadequately supported with details.

11. What is the topic of paragraph 12?

    a. finding group leaders

    b. MTV ads

    (c.) targeting very specific audiences

    d. consumers as lemmings

12. Of the following people, the one that is most likely to find out that one of his or her favorite television programs is being canceled is

    a. an unmarried 34-year-old.

    (b.) a 40-year-old living in a rural area.

    c. an 18-year-old living in a city.

    d. a 30-year-old suburbanite.

13. Identify the relationship between the following sentences from paragraph 6.

    "The target audience that appeals to advertisers is becoming more narrow all the time. According to Dean Valentine, the head of the United Paramount Network, most networks have abandoned the middle class and want 'very chic shows that talk to affluent, urban, unmarried, huge-disposable-income 18-to-34-year-olds because the theory is, from advertisers, that the earlier you get them, the sooner you imprint the brand name.'" (lines 12–18)

    a. effect and cause

    b. time order

    (c.) statement and clarification

    d. contrast

14. For paragraph 7, the author organizes the information by using

    (a.) examples.

    b. contrasts.

    c. comparisons.

    d. definitions.

15. "*Barron's* advertises itself as a way to 'reach faster cars, bigger houses and longer prenuptial agreements' and promises a readership with an average household net worth of over a million." (paragraph 9, lines 9–11)

    The above sentence is a statement of

    (a.) fact.

    b. opinion.

    c. fact and opinion.

16. The word "chic" in paragraph 6, line 15, most nearly means

    a. well-dressed.

    b. feminine.

    (c.) stylish.

    d. traditional

17. Identify the relationship between the following sentences (paragraph 11, lines 1–3): "This emphasis on the affluent surely has something to do with the invisibility of the poor in our society. Since advertisers have no interest in them, they are not reflected in the media."

    (a.) cause and effect

    b. comparison

    c. statement and clarification

    d. contrast

18. One of the effects of the current advertising practices as Kilbourne describes them is that

    (a.) poor people are barely visible in our media.

    b. people between the ages of 18 and 24 are rarely seen in our media.

    c. children's television programming has become more violent.

    d. more and more famous people refuse to endorse products.

19. The author shows a bias

    a. against advertisements on television, radio, and the Internet.

    b. toward advertisers who treat consumers fairly.

    (c.) against advertisers in general.

    d. toward advertisers in general.

20. In paragraph 6, Kilbourne says, "The target audience that appeals to advertisers is becoming more narrow all the time." She says that this is because advertisers want to reach people who have money to spend and who

    a. are mature enough to see through the exaggerated messages that advertisements make.

    b. make the decisions about when to purchase big household items.

    c. are mature enough to want to keep to the brands that they are used to.

    (d.) are young enough so that advertisers can imprint their company's brand name on them as early as possible.

1. Why are advertisers willing to spend over a million dollars to advertise during the Super Bowl? Why is the Oscar Ceremony known as the Super Bowl for women?
    (Answers will vary.)

    _____

    _____

2. In paragraph 3, Kilbourne says, "The primary purpose of the mass media is to sell audiences to advertisers." Where and how do these media producers sell audiences to advertisers?
    (Answers will vary.)

    _____

    _____

3. Which television programs succeed, and which ones are likely to be canceled? Why?
    (Answers will vary.)

    _____

    _____

4. Describe the target audience that advertisers want. Why are people in this audience so valuable to advertisers?
    (Answers will vary.)

    _____

    _____

5. How are the poor affected by the current advertising practices as Kilbourne describes them?
    (Answers will vary.)

    _____

    _____

READERS DISCUSS

1. Before reading the excerpt, what was your opinion about advertising? Did Kilbourne's argument change your mind about the impact of advertising on our society as a whole? If so, in what ways? If not, why not?
    (Answers will vary.)

    _____

    _____

2. Choose a commercial for a program on MTV or other TV program that is aimed directly at teens and young adults. Analyze the ways in which the commercial tries to appeal to that audience. Does your analysis support what Kilbourne says about the influence of advertising or not? Explain.
    (Answers will vary.)

    _____

    _____

3. Share your opinions on the reading selection. Remember that this is an excerpt from an entire book. Discuss as a group what other information you might want from Kilbourne's book and/or from her documentaries before judging the credibility of her general argument against advertising.
    (Answers will vary.)

    _____

    _____

    _____

ANALYZE THE INFORMATION

1 | Understand the uses of facts and opinions.

2 | Check the reliability of the information.

3 | Test the support.

PRACTICE PAGES

Chapter 13

For practice with identifying facts and opinions, complete the following exercise.

PRACTICE EXERCISE 1

For each of the following sentences, decide whether the statement is fact, opinion, or a combination of fact and opinion. If the statement is fact, place an "F" in the blank. Use "O" for opinion, and use "F/O" for statements that contain both fact and opinion.

1. __F/O__ The plant lobelia is used in homeopathic remedies to ease withdrawal from nicotine, but it is not the best solution for someone who has just quit smoking.

2. __O__ The price of a pack of cigarettes is excessively high.

3. __F__ A tire with low air pressure is more likely to blow out.

4. __F__ Marijuana eases withdrawal symptoms from other drugs and can be used as an antispasmodic.

5. __O__ People should always wear aprons when they are cooking meals.

6. __F/O__ Buying a brand-new house is better than buying an older house; during the first year, there will be fewer maintenance issues for the owner of the new house.

7. __F__ Red-headed women have a higher threshold for pain than other women.

8. __O__ Live oak trees create ideal shade during the hot summer months.

9. __F/O__ A pig's squeal reaches a higher decibel than a jet engine's roar, but pigs have always been extremely noisy animals.

10. __O__ Swimming in the ocean is more pleasant than swimming in a pool.

For practice testing reliability and support, complete the following exercise.

PRACTICE EXERCISE 2

Read the notes before the excerpt and then read the excerpt. Answer the questions that follow the excerpt. (Please know that these "notes" are fictionalized.)

This excerpt is from a brochure from A Roof to You, a roofing company known for its quality. Although this company is only two years old, reviews of its services are excellent. According to a recent newspaper article, it is one of the best companies in town. All of its roofers are licensed, and each has at least ten years experience.

(1) Keeping your roof free of debris is essential to maintaining your home. (2) Leaves, branches, and debris left to sit on a roof can cause damage. (3) Areas not cleared of debris are more likely to remain damp after a rainstorm. (4) Once roofing tiles begin to rot, the roof also begins to rot, and you end up with leaks and water damage inside the house. (5) Therefore, homeowners need to have their roofs checked on a regular basis, and A Roof to You is the company to suit your needs. (6) One of our professional roofers can come to inspect your roof and offer an estimate on clearing the roof of debris, inspecting tiles and tar, and repairing damage. (7) For one of the lowest prices in town, A Roof to You offers the very best roofers and superb quality.

1. Which sentences are facts? Number(s) __2, 3, 4__

2. Which sentences are opinions? Number(s) __1__

3. Which sentences are fact and opinions? Number(s) __5 and 7__

4. What do the notes tell you about the writer's perspective?
   (Answers will vary.)

5. What do the notes tell you about the writer's biases?
   (Answers will vary.)

6. What adjective would you use to describe the tone in this passage?
   (Answers will vary.)

7. Is this writer reliable? Why or why not?
   (Answers will vary.)

8. How objective is this writer?
   (Answers will vary.)

To get practice with reading, read the passage, and then answer the questions that follow. You may write your answers in the spaces provided or on a separate sheet of paper.

Memo from Coach

CHRISTOPHER BUCKLEY

Christopher Buckley is the author of several books written from a funny, ironic perspective, such as *Little Green Men*, *Wry Martinis*, and *Thank You for Not Smoking*. His humorous writing also appears frequently in the *New Yorker* magazine. This reading is a satire—a type of writing that uses irony and humor to expose human faults or weaknesses. In this satire, Buckley takes on the role of coach for a girls' soccer team. Watch for the moment when you can first tell this is no ordinary coach writing to parents.

Welcome back! The fall Pixie League soccer season officially kicks off next week, and I'd like to take this opportunity to let you know the schedule and provide guidelines. I'm sure we all agree that, with the Grasshoppers' 1-12 record last season, there's plenty of room for improvement this fall!

With a view to maximizing our performance, this summer I attended the National Conference of Pixie League Coaches, held in King of Prussia, Pa. I did some valuable networking and came away truly "pumped."

Physical Training

Per my memo last June regarding the summer-training <u>regimen</u>, your nine-year-old daughter should now be able to: (a) run a mile in under five minutes with cinder blocks attached to each ankle (lower body); (b) bench-press the family minivan (upper body); (c) swim a hundred yards in fifty-degree water while holding her breath (wind); (d) remain standing while bowling balls are thrown at her (stamina).

Practice Schedule

4   Mondays, Wednesdays, Fridays: 5:30 A.M.

Tuesdays, Thursdays: 5:30 P.M.

Sundays: 7 A.M.

Columbus Day Weekend: 7:30 A.M.

Note: Live ammunition will be used at the Thursday practice.

Video Critique of Games

5   Mondays, 8 P.M. Parents strongly urged to attend. See "Camera Dads" sign-up list (Attachment E). Note: Professional-quality video cameras preferred.

Game Schedule

6   Saturdays, 8 A.M. Important: Please be sure to have your daughter there *at least two hours before game time* for the pregame strategy briefing and pep rally. Note: As the girls will be biting the heads off live animals, we will need lots of guinea pigs, hamsters, parakeets, etc. See sign-up list (Attachment P). No goldfish, please!

Halftime Snacks

7   Last year, there was some confusion about appropriate nourishment. According to guidelines established by the N.C.P.L.C.'s Committee on Nutrition and Performance, "snacks high in carbohydrates, sucrose, and corn syrup have been demonstrated to provide dramatic short-term metabolic gain." So save those low-fat pretzels for your cocktail parties and bring on the Twinkies and Ring Dings. Let's make sure that when the Grasshoppers hit the field they're hoppin'!

Use of Steroids

8   One of the many things I took away from the panel discussions at King of Prussia was that, contrary to medical guidelines, use of anabolic steroids by preteens is not necessarily a hundred per cent harmful. (See Attachment Q: "New Thinking on Performance Boosters and Mortality.") Grasshopper doctor dad Bill Hughes will discuss the merits of stanozolol versus fluoxymesterone and dispense prescriptions to all interested parents. (Participation encouraged!)

9   Note: If any Grasshopper parents are planning a vacation in Mexico, please see me about bringing back certain hard-to-get enhancers, like HGH (human-growth hormone) and EPO (erythropoeitin).

Parental Input on Player Substitutions

10   Much as I appreciate your enthusiasm, it is not helpful if in the middle of a tense game situation you abuse me verbally—or, as one overzealous

dad did last season, assault me physically—because I have not sent in your daughter. For this reason, I will be carrying a Taser with me at all times. These anti-assault devices deliver up to fifty thousand volts of electricity, and leave the recipient drooling and twitching for weeks. Though I will make every effort to see that each Grasshopper gets her turn on the field, if you get "in my face" about it don't be "shocked, shocked!" to find yourself flat on your back in need of cardiopulmonary resuscitation."

Injuries

If your daughter has kept up with the summer-training pro- 11
gram, there's no reason she shouldn't be able to finish out a game with minor injuries, such as hairline bone fractures or <u>subdural</u> hematomas. (Parental support needed!) Remember the Grass-hopper motto: "That which does not kill me makes me a better midfielder!"

Remember the Grasshopper motto: "That which does not kill me makes me a better midfielder!"

Cheerleading

If the coaches at K. of P. were unanimous about anything, it was 12
the key importance of parental screaming from the sidelines. This not only lets our girls know that Grasshopper parents do not accept failure but also alerts the other team that if they win you will probably "go postal" (kid talk for temporary insanity) and try to run them over in the parking lot after the game.

See you Monday morning! 13

ACTIVE READERS RESPOND

After you've finished reading, use these questions to respond to "Memo from Coach." You may write your answers in the spaces provided or on a separate sheet of paper.

VITAL VOCABULARY

Some words in this reading may be unfamiliar to you. Use the methods of Strategy 3 to explain what the listed words mean.

USE CONTEXT CLUES

a. nourishment (paragraph 7)

_____

b. dispense (paragraph 8)

_____

USE WORD PARTS

a. preteens (paragraph 8)

_____

b. enhancers (paragraph 9)

_____

USE THE DICTIONARY

Choose the correct definition of each word as it is used in the context of this reading.

a. regimen (paragraph 3)

_____

b. subdural (paragraph 11)

_____

OBJECTIVE OPERATIONS

1. Who is the writer's intended audience?

    a. soccer players

    b. parents

    c. general audience

    d. teachers

2. What is the author's purpose?

    a. to inform

    b. to persuade

    c. to entertain

3. What is the tone of the passage?

    a. informal

    b. sarcastic

    c. moody

    d. ironic

4. You first become certain that this is a satire, not a normal memo, when the coach says,

    a. "The fall Pixie League soccer season officially kicks off next week."

    b. "I did some valuable networking and came away truly 'pumped.'"

    c. ". . . your nine-year-old daughter should now be able to [a] run a mile in under five minutes with cinder blocks attached to each ankle (lower body)."

    d. "Note: Live ammunition will be used at the Thursday practice."

5. The word "maximizing" in paragraph 2, line 1, most nearly means

    a. increasing in size.

    b. using your full potential.

    c. decreasing in size.

    d. increasing in amount.

6. Which of the following sentences best summarizes this passage?

    a. Soccer is an extremely difficult sport with militant practices.

    b. Parents of soccer players need to read the memos that coaches send home.

    c. A coach is mocking the stringent guidelines placed on children's sports and the pressure to perform well.

    d. This is a letter making fun of soccer.

7. What is the implied main idea of paragraphs 1 and 2?

    a. Guidelines and schedules have been updated to help the soccer players improve.

    b. The soccer players lost many games during the previous season and need improvement.

    c. The coach went to a seminar to learn to coach more effectively.

    d. The soccer team is going to win during the coming season.

8. The memo covers normal categories of coaching activities. All of the following are included in the categories in the memo except:

    a. sportsmanship.

    b. practice schedule.

    c. nutrition.

    d. drugs.

9. Which sentence provides support for this sentence (paragraph 7, lines 2–5): "According

to guidelines established by the N.C.P.L.C.'s Committee on Nutrition and Performance, 'snacks high in carbohydrates, sucrose, and corn syrup have been demonstrated to provide dramatic short-term metabolic gain.'"

a. "Last year, there was some confusion about appropriate nourishment."

b. "So save those low-fat pretzels for your cocktail parties and bring on the Twinkies and Ring Dings."

c. "Let's make sure that when the Grasshoppers hit the field they're hoppin'!"

d. none of the above

10. The author's claim that teenagers' use of steroids is not completely harmful is

a. adequately supported with details.

b. inadequately supported with details.

11. What is the topic of paragraph 10?

a. parental input

b. parental input on player substitutions

c. player substitution

d. use of the Taser

12. Satire is a form of irony. However, the coach Buckley has created in his satire doesn't use an ironic tone. Instead, the coach's tone is

a. serious.

b. enthusiastic.

c. humorous.

d. informative.

13. Identify the relationship between the following sentences from paragraph 8.

"Grasshopper doctor dad Bill Hughes will discuss the merits of stanozolol versus fluoxymesterone and dispense prescriptions to all interested parents." (lines 4–6)

a. process

b. illustration

c. spatial order

d. definition

14. For paragraph 4, the author organizes the information by using

a. process.

b. examples.

c. spatial order.

d. time order.

15. "These anti-assault devices deliver up to fifty thousand volts of electricity, and leave the recipient drooling and twitching for weeks." (paragraph 10, lines 5–6)

The above sentence is a statement of

a. fact.

b. opinion.

c. fact and opinion.

16. The word "urged" in paragraph 5, line 1, most nearly means

a. strongly encouraged.

b. strictly mandated.

c. gently pushed.

d. secretly desired.

17. Identify the relationship between the following sentences (paragraph 10, lines 1–4): "Much as I appreciate your enthusiasm, it is not helpful if in the middle of a tense game situation you abuse me verbally—or, as one overzealous dad did last season, assault me physically—because I have not sent in your daughter. For this reason, I will be carrying a Taser with me at all times."

a. definition and example

b. statement and clarification

c. comparison and contrast

d. cause and effect

18. An example of a real behavior or attitude that Buckley makes fun of is

    a. children dreaming of become super athletes.

    b. parents wanting the best for their children.

    c. coaches' poor writing ability.

    (d.) parents putting undue pressure on their children to excel in sports.

19. The author shows a bias

    a. against soccer.

    b. toward soccer.

    (c.) against pressure on children to excel in sports.

    d. toward pressure on children to excel in sports.

20. It is probable that Buckley used nine-year-old girls for the coach's team instead of high school football players because

    a. he knew more about coaching for girls' teams.

    (b.) they add to the absurd contrast between what the players were being told to do and what they would actually be able to do.

    c. he wanted to appeal to women readers, since they are generally more sensitive to irony.

    d. they would have more appeal to the reader since they're little and cute.

QUICK QUESTIONS

1. This is a normal memo, not a satire. True or (False)

2. The coach does not believe in using a Taser to subdue parents. True or (False)

3. Two exercises that a child should now be able to do before practice begins are run a mile in under five minutes with cinder blocks attached to each ankle (lower body) and bench-press the family minivan (upper body). (Answers will vary.)

4. On Mondays and Wednesdays, practice begins at 5:30 a.m.

5. Why do you think Buckley used a team of nine-year-old girls for the coach's team? What difference would it make—if any—if he had used a team of high school football players? (Answers will vary.)

6. What is one example of a behavior or attitude that Buckley makes fun of? Explain how he uses ironic exaggeration in that example. (Answers will vary.)

14

Make an Evaluation

MAKE AN EVALUATION

1 | Think objectively.

2 | Think subjectively.

imagine this

Imagine you are witness to an angry protest march. People are waving signs, pointing fingers, chanting slogans at the top of their voices. You watch carefully to see who is provoking the conflict. Is it the punk rocker or the uniformed police officer? In trying to sort out the situation, you put together all the evidence that you have heard and seen and make a personal judgment or evaluation.

We respond to readings in the same way. After you've applied all the skills you've learned to analyze and understand a reading, you end by making an evaluation. You decide whether you agree with the writer's opinion, whether the reading was well-written, or whether the piece appealed to you. Your evaluation is your final judgment on the reading.

Think FIRST >

- Do your friends think that you are a rational, logical thinker? Do they look to you for practical answers?

- Do your friends think you wear your heart on your sleeve? Do your feelings or emotions get the best of you sometimes?

INTRODUCTION TO THE NEW STRATEGY
Make an Evaluation

Instructor Tip
Ask students whether they have ever filled out an evaluation or taken a survey. What kinds of questions were asked? What kinds of questions were about factual information? What kinds of questions were based on personal opinion? For example, a survey may ask if the soda you just tried was carbonated, and then it may ask you if the soda tasted good. What other examples can students think of?

With Strategy 14—*Make an Evaluation*—you come back to your own thoughts for a final evaluation of the writer's ideas. This final strategy introduces no new steps. Instead, it reminds you to put everything you have learned together. First, use all the strategies you've learned for comprehending and analyzing to think objectively about the reading. Then, come back to your personal *response* to think subjectively about the reading. Your final thinking—both objective and subjective—becomes your evaluation of the writer's ideas.

Strategy 14 depends on your choosing appropriate steps from among the first thirteen strategies. Those strategies will give you a thorough comprehension of what the writer says. Once you've understood the reading, you can think more objectively about it. Then you can make an evaluation by putting together this objective analysis with your subjective response.

Hot or Not?

Is it truly possible to have an objective opinion? Why or why not?

Thinking Objectively

Thinking objectively means doing more than summarizing the information in a reading. To be **objective,** you must be neutral and not attached to one side of the writer's ideas or the other. It means that you must notice techniques the writer uses and consider how reliable and accurate that information is in addition to summing up the writer's ideas.

To be an objective reader, decide how well the writer has stated his or her ideas. First, map the overall point, the main ideas, and the supporting details; create a cluster map if that helps you. This will help you begin to summarize the reading. Once you're sure you understand the reading's overall point and main ideas, use strategies (such as Strategies 11, 12 and 13) to think objectively about the writer's ideas. Then, get your paper and pen ready to write about what you have read.

You may have noticed that in the first few paragraphs of many newspaper or magazine articles writers immediately address information that includes who was involved in a situation, what happened, and when and where the situation occurred; then, writers offer an overall point for the article. In the opening paragraphs, writers are giving a **summary**—a restatement of the main ideas—but they will think more objectively throughout the rest of the article.

You should do the same thing when you write an evaluation. After you have mapped the overall point and main ideas, you should write a summary. Then begin your analysis. Notice whether the writer used a special technique to enhance the reading and include this in your analysis. For example, did the writer use a particular tone such as in Chapter 13 Practice Reading "Memo from Coach"? Or did the writer use metaphorical language such as in Reading 10, "talking back"? If there was something special about the reading, did that technique help to achieve the writer's purpose? Mention these techniques in your analysis, and give some examples to support what you say. Recognize whether a writer has communicated an idea successfully—by using a metaphor, for example, or by creating a believable character in a

LEVAR BURTON

The Road Less Travelled

by M. Scott Peck, M.D.

A best-seller in 1983, this spiritual self-help book sees personal growth as a lifelong goal. Says Burton: "This book is a 'must read' for anyone who is serious about the human journey of self-knowledge. Peck speaks to the heart in plain and easily digestible terms."

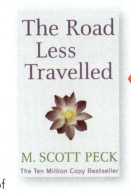

The Road Less Travelled
M. SCOTT PECK
The Ten Million Copy Bestseller

If you liked *The Road Less Travelled*, you might also like:

I'm OK, You're OK, Thomas A. Harris, M.D.

Games People Play, Eric Berne

Men Are from Mars, Women Are from Venus, John Gray

WHAT ARE THEY READING?

connect now

Why do coaches of soccer and football teams analyze different plays during and after a game?

> *The relationship between you and a roommate should be an objective relationship rather than a subjective one, more like a business partnership than a friendship. However, sometimes it is difficult to be objective about finding a roommate. ApartmentReviews.net not only helps you find an apartment, but the website also offers advice to renters. "How to Find the Right Roommate" is full of excellent suggestions.*

You're new to the city, and you can't afford to live alone. An extremely tight renters' market has forced monthly rents through the roof, so living solo is simply out of the question. But aside from a couple of old college buddies who recently moved to the area (who already have roommates), you haven't yet made friends in your new city. You've got to find a roommate fast if you want to have any chance of scoring an apartment. You'll have to take a deep breath and do what many solo renters do every day: go "potluck." It's a bit frightening, especially for those of us who saw the film "Single White Female" and are still traumatized from the experience.

So how are you supposed to find a roommate? You could always use a roommate service, but even using a professional source is no guarantee that your lifestyles and habits will be compatible. What kinds of sources can you rely upon that won't compromise your personal safety? You've got to start your search early, because it's very rare that you find a roommate immediately. It's going to take time, patience and some careful screening before you find the stranger with whom you'll be sharing living space for the immediate future.

First of all, before you even get started, abandon your illusion of finding the perfect roommate with whom you'll enjoy instant rapport and certain domestic bliss. Sure, it happens on occasion, but don't weed out potential candidates because you think they'll fall short of that ideal. All you should expect from your roommate is neatness, common courtesy, safe living habits (including the avoidance of drugs, hanging out with and inviting over a dangerous crowd and a willingness to the keep the doors locked and the keys to himself/herself) and timely payment of his/her half of the rent. If friendship develops after those ground rules have been established and respected, terrific. If not, you should still consider yourself lucky for finding yourself a good roommate, because that's exactly what you've got.

Let's say you do, in fact, have a friend in the area with whom you could consider living. Should you do it? We've all heard the advice that we should never travel with friends if we want to remain friends. In some story—but remain objective. An analysis is not the time to state your opinion or give reasons why you did not like a reading.

Finally, consider whether the information used to support the overall point was reliable and credible. Give some examples to back up your analysis. For example, Reading 27 is an argument, persuading us to see high school cliques as the source of misery for many adolescents. Thus, after you read, you can analyze objectively how persuasive Lefkowitz is. This is also a time to look again at headnotes; Lefkowitz is not a teacher, but he is someone who has worked with students. Does this affect his credibility?

cases, that's true for roommates, too. Even if you have separate bedrooms, sharing a common living space (the living room, kitchen and bathroom, in particular) can create a host of problems. You and your friend might be bosom buddies, and while you might swear that you'd remain the best of friends as roommates, avoid it if you can help it. You and your friend could start to view each other in a different light once you're sharing an apartment. New personality characteristics will suddenly come into focus in a much sharper and clearer way. The smaller the living space, the better the chance you'll be at each other's throats before long. In many cases, it's best to reside with someone who knows nothing about your history—an objective audience, so to speak.

This isn't to imply, however, that you should go grab someone off the street and ask him or her to split the rent with you. Instead, start with the local classifieds section. It's a great place to find leads for potential roommates. You'll definitely want to interview candidates; never under any circumstances should you make an offer to someone over the phone, sight unseen. Our telephone personalities can be very different than the ones we project in person. When you do start to interview candidates, have a friend or family member stay with you for two reasons: the first, for your own safety; and second, to offer a second (objective) opinion about your candidates. The sooner you start scanning the classifieds, the better. It's likely that you'll run through many duds before you find yourself a good roommate.

If you decide to place an ad yourself, set specific hours for which candidates may call. Don't print your name, or if you can help it, your sex, either. This doesn't mean your ad has to be vague, dull and straightforward, though. You can and should make it fun-spirited. Use your creativity and a touch of humor to entertain. You're more likely to receive a positive response from candidates—and a greater number of them.

A potentially safer search technique is to ask all of your friends in the area if they know anyone who's looking for a roommate. If not, or if you know a limited number of people in the area, you could try scanning the bulletin boards of reputable spots like local universities, coffee houses, your church or favorite bookstore. These are all destinations which stand a better chance of finding someone who's not only goal-oriented and moralistic, but who shares your interests, as well.

When showing your place to potential candidates, be sure that you run down the list of required utility expenses—even if the candidates don't ask (and they should). You don't want to offer someone a position as your roommate, then have them leave when they discover just how high their share of the utilities is. Also, if the building in which you live has any particular quirks—eccentric or noisy neighbors, a challenging landlord, a problem with excessive heat in the summertime—be honest and up front about it. You can counter those disclosures with positives about your building and the surrounding neighborhood.

Your most critical job as a roommate-screener is to listen to your instincts. If the red flags are waving in your brain about any one of your candidates—even if you can't put your finger on the problem—don't make that person an offer. Our instincts often prove to be our most valuable tool. They're there for our survival, so be listening.

It's not easy finding yourself a roommate—especially when time is of the essence. But you can do it safely and responsibly provided you proceed with caution as well as enthusiasm. After all, you've got to sell yourself, too.

"How to Find the Right Roommate." ApartmentReviews.net. 17 August 2009. Available: www.apartmentreviews.net/find-right-roommate.htm

EXERCISES

For practice thinking objectively, do this exercise.

A. *Read the following passage. Then, complete the exercise.*

Ellen Swallow Richards and the Science of Home Economics

Ellen Swallow Richards was the first woman to earn a bachelor's degree from the Massachusetts Institute of Technology (MIT) and later received a master's degree from Vassar. A chemist, social activist, teacher, and first woman member of the Institute of Mining and Metallurgical Engineering, she believed that housekeeping was a science. She was also a progressive thinker at a time when education for women was not widely encouraged. Women, she thought, needed to learn about money matters and have up-to-date information on cleanliness and nutrition. She also believed that education provided the best protection against greedy businesses that focused only on profits or governments that failed to keep water and food supplies safe. She encouraged women from all backgrounds to get the best education possible.

PRACTICE

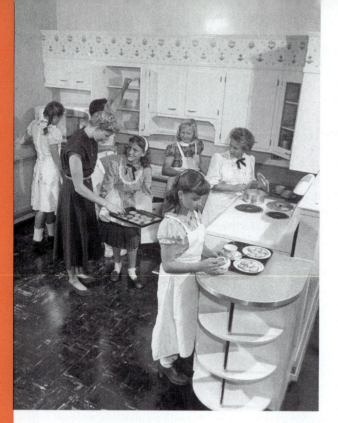

Ellen Swallow was born in 1842 and was brought up in Massachusetts in a family of modest means. After being graduated with a master's degree from Vassar College in New York, she returned to New England to attend MIT. After her marriage to Professor Robert H. Richards, she worked in a laboratory at MIT, analyzing contamination of water sources in Massachusetts. Her work led to that state's creation of the first food-inspection laws. She also focused attention on public sanitation and the importance of sanitary sewer-treatment systems. She was instructor at MIT from 1884 until her death in 1911.

Like other progressive thinkers of the era, Richards was concerned about problems of the poor and the effect of the environment, or surroundings, on society. She considered the environment a key factor in quality of life. She believed that science could help to manage finances, keep a home safe and clean, and improve quality of life. Food properly cooked could be tasty, nutritious, and inexpensive. Better and cheaper food could protect the health and improve the lives of working-class families. At the New England Kitchen in Boston, she served low-cost meals and demonstrated how to prepare them easily.

Richards created the field of domestic science, a discipline now called home economics, and elevated it to a serious college subject. She worked tirelessly for the addition of these classes to Boston's public schools. Richards was a national leader in developing academic standards, content materials, and teacher training for this new field. Her publications cover a wide range of topics—from the chemistry of cooking and cleaning to the cost of living and conservation by sanitation.

B. *Complete the cluster map for "Ellen Swallow Richards and the Science of Home Economics."*

Cluster Map
"Ellen Swallow Richards and the
Science of Home Economics"

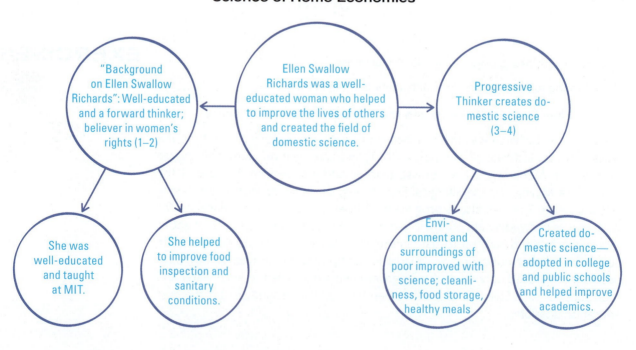

"Background on Ellen Swallow Richards": Well-educated and a forward thinker; believer in women's rights (1–2)

Ellen Swallow Richards was a well-educated woman who helped to improve the lives of others and created the field of domestic science.

Progressive Thinker creates domestic science (3–4)

She was well-educated and taught at MIT.

She helped to improve food inspection and sanitary conditions.

Environment and surroundings of poor improved with science; cleanliness, food storage, healthy meals

Created domestic science—adopted in college and public schools and helped improve academics.

C. Based on your cluster map, write an analysis.

_____

_____

_____

_____

_____

Thinking Subjectively

With each reading, you have been given a chance to respond honestly to what you've read. By making connections to a reading and responding, you apply your own personal experience to the reading as much as possible so that the reading remains lively and interesting to you. This is one way you have learned to evaluate a reading.

Thinking subjectively about a reading as part of your evaluation helps you form your own opinion about a reading. Once you're sure you comprehend the reading and can look at it objectively, you can think subjectively. To be _subjective_ means you allow your personal opinion, or your bias, to influence your evaluation of a reading. When you think subjectively, be sure to take account of your general reading likes and dislikes. You may generally dislike short stories, for example. In that case, you can recognize that a story is "well done," and you may even like some parts of it. Nevertheless, you can allow for the fact that stories are generally less appealing to you. That general, personal opinion can go in your evaluation.

In addition, take account of your own ideas on the subject before reading. For example, you don't have to change your opinion about a subject just because you think the writer did a good job of arguing. You can still have your opinion—though you may find yourself seeing things slightly differently after a good argument.

Instructor Tip
Remind students that thinking subjectively means they might rely on gut instinct rather than facts or logical clues before them. Going on gut instinct can lead to trouble. What examples can the students give where subjective thinking has caused problems, such as drinking and driving?

Instructor Tip
Have students bring in articles of their choosing. Have them pair off and exchange articles. When the students have finished reading, have them write a short analysis and an evaluation about each article. Then, have the students share their writing with each other and discuss the similarities and differences in their analyses and evaluations.

Much of your subjective thinking in the evaluation can also be based on the way you originally responded. You can note difficulties you had with comprehension. You can say what specific parts you especially liked or didn't like, and why.

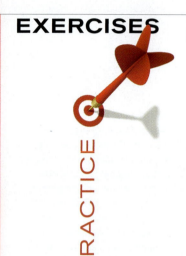

EXERCISES

For practice thinking subjectively, do this exercise.

Write an evaluation on "Ellen Swallow Richards and the Science of Home Economics," the essay found on page 513. Remember to include your opinions, parts that you like, and parts that you dislike in your evaluation. You may also wish to mention new information or ideas you learned from the reading.

(Answers will vary.)

_____

_____

_____

_____

_____

_____

APPLY THE NEW STRATEGY
Make an Evaluation

Now that you understand Strategy 14, put it into practice. Map the overall point and main ideas, and then analyze and evaluate the reading.

Don't Further Empower Cliques

READING 27   BERNARD LEFKOWITZ

Bernard Lefkowitz, an award-winning author, writes for many U.S. magazines and newspapers, and he has also written books on social issues. This reading first appeared in the *Los Angeles Times* shortly after the Columbine High School massacre in 1999. In it he examines the sometimes destructive power of popular high school cliques, using the insights he gained while researching and writing his book *Our Guys: The Glen Ridge Rape and the Secret Life of the Perfect Suburb* (1997).

While it's difficult to generate sympathy for a couple of teenagers who de-   1
cide to vent their grievances through the barrel of a gun, the carnage at Columbine High School should not eclipse an important part of this story: the power of high school cliques to make life miserable for many adolescents.

When I heard that the two young murderers in Littleton, Colorado, had   2
targeted athletes who, they said, had ridiculed them, it sounded a lot like

what young people told me ten years ago when I was researching the rape of a retarded young woman by a group of teenage athletes at Glen Ridge High School.

3   In that attractive upper-middle-class New Jersey suburb, thirteen jocks were present in the basement where the young woman's body was penetrated by a baseball bat and a broomstick. The country was sickened by the inhumanity of a bunch of guys who were among the most admired and envied young men in their community and high school.

4   After the rape, they came to school and openly boasted about what they had done. Weren't they afraid of being punished? Later, many people who knew them concluded that they had come to feel omnipotent after being treated like big-time celebrities for years by their school and by many parents in town.

5   And why shouldn't they feel omnipotent? When you walked into the high school the first thing you saw were halls lined with trophy cases celebrating the exploits of the athletes. The school held two-hour assemblies to honor the jocks. But assemblies to honor the best students rarely lasted more than twenty minutes. The school yearbook displayed ten photographs of the most mediocre football player. But the outstanding scholar was lucky to get one grainy photo.

6   The message the school sent to its impressionable students was: You don't count unless you're part of this clique or at least pay homage to it. Instead of celebrating the individuality and diversity of all its students, it chose to honor this one type of youngster—aggressive, arrogant, and intensely competitive—above all the others. This left many kids feeling alienated and isolated, and not only during this brief passage into adulthood. Ten years later, I still hear from Glen Ridge graduates who remain enraged, not only by how they were mistreated by the athletes but by the school's unqualified adulation of them.

7   After my book was published, I received hundreds of letters from people, some in their 70s and 80s, who recalled how excluded they felt when their schools anointed one group of guys as leaders. Educators are reluctant to discourage the formation of cliques because that may be considered interference in the students' "private" lives. They are disinclined to challenge parents who are proud of their child's membership in a popular group. Then, too, some educators tolerate cliques because they think they are just a passing phenomenon.

8   That's unfortunate because there is much that schools can do to demonstrate that all students, rather than the few members of favored cliques, have value. They can promote activities and projects that bring together students with diverse interests and skills. They can celebrate achievements that are intellectual and artistic as well as athletic. And they can demonstrate that there's a single standard of acceptable conduct that is applied to everyone. In Glen Ridge, as in many other schools, the athletes got away with behavior for which others were punished.

9   We don't know much about how Columbine High School responded to student cliques. But I do know that schools are not passive entities. Educators make collective judgments about which students are valuable and

> Instead of celebrating the individuality and diversity of all its students, it chose to honor this one type of youngster– aggressive, arrogant, and intensely competitive–above all the others.

which aren't. Often, educators are quick to venerate kids who are superficially attractive—who are handsome, who are athletic, who come from wealthy families. And too often they marginalize youngsters who are awkward or unsocial or iconoclastic.

Kids with supportive families and friends may ul- **10** timately succeed in life although they were treated like outcasts in school. But even they will not easily recover from the wounds they suffered as adolescents. For youngsters who already feel abandoned, the power granted to cliques by school authorities, and the inevitable abuse of that power, may be potentially devastating.

This doesn't explain the pathological behavior of **11** two kids turned killers at Columbine High School. That will require a calmer and more thoughtful investigation into how they grew up and their school lives than is possible in the heat of the moment. But we should take the opportunity that the catastrophe in Littleton offers to reflect on the damage that cliques can inflict on youngsters when they are most vulnerable.

ACTIVE READERS RESPOND

After you've finished reading, use these questions to respond to "Don't Further Empower Cliques." You may write your answers in the spaces provided or on a separate sheet of paper.

VITAL VOCABULARY

Some words in this reading may be unfamiliar to you. Use the methods of Strategy 3 to explain what the listed words mean.

USE CONTEXT CLUES

a. grievances (paragraph 1)

_____

b. anointed (paragraph 7)

_____

c. venerate (paragraph 9)

_____

USE WORD PARTS

a. omnipotent (paragraph 4)

_____

b. impressionable (paragraph 6)

_____

c. pathological (paragraph 11)

_____

Choose the correct definition of each word as it is used in the context of this reading.

a. cliques (paragraph 1)

_____

b. carnage (paragraph 1)

_____

c. adulation (paragraph 6)

_____

d. iconoclastic (paragraph 9)

_____

SKILLS EXERCISE: ANALYSIS AND EVALUATION

A. Write an analysis of the reading. (Create a cluster map if that helps you.)   (Answers will vary.)

Sample Analysis of "Don't Further Empower Cliques"

Bernard Lefkowitz' purpose in "Don't Further Empower Cliques" is to persuade us that high schools should make changes in their treatment of students. His overall point is that high schools give too much power to cliques, especially cliques of student athletes, and that those cliques make life miserable for many other students. He begins by referring to the then recent events at Columbine High School. He doesn't have sympathy for the two murderers, but he does see a connection between what happened there and what happened in the New Jersey town he wrote a book about. In both places so much power was given to the school's athletes that they came to think of themselves as "omnipotent." The author thinks this power might explain why the popular and admired young men at Glen Ridge could commit a horrible rape and brag about it. The author thinks the young men had become celebrities in their high school who could do no wrong. He says that the high school's over-valuing of school athletes sent the message that other types of students "don't count." After publishing his book about what happened in that New Jersey suburb, Lefkowitz received hundreds of letters from people saying how they had felt left out because the school only honored one type of group as leaders. He suggests ways that schools could show that all students have value, not just a few cliques. He ends by saying that we should use the "catastrophe at Littleton" to take notice of how certain privileged high school groups are given power that can be "potentially devastating" to others.

B. Write an evaluation of the reading. Remember to include your opinions, parts that you like, and parts that you dislike in your evaluation. You may also wish to mention new information or ideas you learned from the reading. (Answers will vary.)

Sample Evaluation of "Don't Further Empower Cliques"

"Don't Further Empower Cliques" is an argument that makes you think. Lefkowitz's purpose is not to make a complete, step-by-step argument to prove his overall point. If that's what he was doing, you could say he leaves a lot of things out. He concentrates only on athletes and only briefly mentions the other types of "popular kids" that tend to run schools. He also only concentrates on one school in New Jersey, so someone arguing against him could say that he's not giving enough facts about other schools. But he does have a lot of credibility, because he did such a lot of research and wrote a book about what happened in the New Jersey suburban high school. He knows the facts of that case really well. He also heard from a lot of people that said they had similar experiences of being treated like outcasts by the popular cliques. His reasoning about the causes of bad feelings in student outcasts seems good, but he doesn't try to prove that that was the cause of the Columbine massacre. His solutions of making schools be more open to more types of students also seem good. It is a pretty short reading, so he can't get into too much detail. He achieved his purpose of making people think about their own high school experience, even though the school he knows best (Glen Ridge High) may be worse than the average.

My response to the reading was mainly positive, but I did think that he exaggerated somewhat. I do think that high school is a hard experience for many, maybe most students. Athletes do get a lot of glory and the cheerleaders who they "get" also get that glory. But in my school, there were other types of cliques that were just as bad—the kids with money, clothes, cars, etc. I can see that there were kids who felt like outcasts, but a lot of us who weren't in those cliques could find ways of getting along, and there were other activities (for me the band) that were encouraged. Still, there was that image in my own mind of the athletes lording it over other kids in the hall. I hated the example of what those athletes did to that girl, and I can hardly believe any one athlete in my school would have been that bad. But it was a powerful example. I also liked the way he showed how school authorities tend to prefer certain kinds of students. It's a good thing he wasn't trying to prove that the treatment of the Columbine murderers by athletes was what caused what they did, because that's not at all clear to me. Overall I liked the reading and it did match my high school experience somewhat.

OBJECTIVE OPERATIONS

1. Who is the writer's intended audience?
   a. students
   b. parents
   c. general audience
   d. teachers

2. What is the author's purpose?
   a. to inform
   b. to persuade
   c. to entertain

3. What is the tone of the passage?
   a. critical
   b. sarcastic
   c. frank
   d. ironic

4. The people Lefkowitz interviewed in the New Jersey suburb told him they thought the young men boasted at school about raping the young mentally challenged woman because
   a. they had watched so much media violence that they had lost any sense of right and wrong.
   b. they had come to feel all-powerful because the school and parents had treated them like special celebrities for so long.
   c. they were as mentally challenged as the young woman and didn't think what they'd done was wrong.

   d. underneath their boasting, they felt tremendous guilt and wanted people to find out so they would be punished.

5. The word "carnage" in paragraph 1, line 2, most nearly means
   a. suicide.
   b. tragedy.
   c. bloodbath.
   d. terror.

6. Which of the following sentences best summarizes this passage?
   a. Cliques form in every school and cause damage to students.
   b. Cliques inflict damage on students, and educators need to learn to focus on all students rather than the cliques.
   c. Rape and carnage are results of cliques that form in schools and cause damage to students.
   d. Educators think cliques are harmless.

7. What is the stated main idea of paragraph 6?
   a. "The message the school sent to its impressionable students was: You don't count unless you're part of this clique or at least pay homage to it."
   b. "Instead of celebrating the individuality and diversity of all its students, it chose to honor this one type of youngster—aggressive, arrogant, and intensely competitive—above all the others."

c. "This left many kids feeling alienated and isolated, and not only during this brief passage into adulthood."

d. "Ten years later, I still hear from Glen Ridge graduates who remain enraged, not only by how they were mistreated by the athletes but by the school's unqualified adulation of them."

8. The assemblies at Glen Ridge High School

   a. honored their athletes far more than their good students.

   b. were held for special lectures to try to prevent what had happened to the retarded woman from happening again.

   c. honored their good students far more than their athletes.

   d. were held to celebrate the individuality and diversity of all its students.

9. Which sentence provides support for this sentence (paragraph 5, line 1): "And why shouldn't they feel omnipotent?"

   a. "When you walked into the high school the first thing you saw were halls lined with trophy cases celebrating the exploits of the athletes."

   b. "The school held two-hour assemblies to honor the jocks."

   c. "But assemblies to honor the best students rarely lasted more than twenty minutes."

   d. both a and b

10. The author's claim that football players "openly boasted" about the rape is

    a. adequately supported with details.

    b. inadequately supported with details.

11. What is the topic of paragraph 7?

    a. how cliques are harmful

    b. cliques

    c. parents' tolerance of cliques

    d. educators' tolerance of cliques

12. Lefkowitz says that the kind of student schools tend to value most is

    a. aggressive, arrogant, and intensely competitive.

    b. studious, obedient, and well-organized.

    c. imaginative, creative, and artistic.

    d. well-rounded, friendly, and diligent.

13. Identify the relationship between the following sentences from paragraph 7.

    "After my book was published, I received hundreds of letters from people, some in their 70s and 80s, who recalled how excluded they felt when their schools anointed one group of guys as leaders." (lines 1–3)

    a. process

    b. time order

    c. addition

    d. statement and clarification

14. For paragraph 8, the author organizes the information by using

    a. process.

    b. examples.

    c. spatial order.

    d. comparisons.

15. "Often, educators are quick to venerate kids who are superficially attractive—who are handsome, who are athletic, who come from wealthy families." (paragraph 9, lines 4–6)

    The above sentence is a statement of

    a. fact.

    b. opinion.

    c. fact and opinion.

16. The word "venerate" in paragraph 9, line 4, most nearly means

    a. despise.

    b. spare.

    c. benefit from.

    d. honor.

17. Identify the relationship between the following sentences (paragraph 10, lines 1–4): "Kids with supportive families and friends may ultimately succeed in life although they were treated like outcasts in school. But even they will not easily recover from the wounds they suffered as adolescents."

    a. definition and example

    b. statement and clarification

    c. comparison

    d. contrast

18. One of Lefkowitz' suggestions for making other students—those not in the favored cliques—feel more valued by schools would be to

a. help underachieving students succeed by improving tutoring and counseling services.

b. get all students involved in intellectual and artistic endeavors as well as athletic activities.

c. honor achievements that are intellectual and artistic as well as athletic.

d. develop classes for improving peer social interactions.

19. The author shows a bias

a. against students who are honored needlessly.

b. toward students who are honored needlessly.

c. against students who excel academically.

d. toward students who do not excel academically.

20. Lefkowitz says that highly valued athletes at a school like Glen Ridge get away with behaviors that others would have been punished for. The most likely of these behaviors would be

a. hitting a teacher.

b. selling drugs on school grounds.

c. bringing a gun to school

d. cheating on a test.

READERS WRITE

1. When Lefkowitz interviewed people in the New Jersey suburb, what did many of them say about why the young men boasted at school about raping the young mentally challenged woman?

(Answers will vary.)

2. What kind of attention did Glen Ridge High School give to its athletes? How did this attention compare with that given to other types of students?

(Answers will vary.)

3. How does Lefkowitz define the type of student schools tend to value most? What kind of message does he say this preference sends to the student body of a school?

(Answers will vary.)

4. What are some suggestions Lefkowitz gives that would help to make other students—those not in the favored cliques—feel valued?

(Answers will vary.)

5. What are some ways "kids with supportive families and friends" can do all right in life even if they feel isolated at school? Why will "youngsters who already feel abandoned" (paragraph 10) be affected so much more?

(Answers will vary.)

1. Discuss with other students the types of behavior you think the athletes at Glen Ridge might have gotten away with. Would students who weren't athletes have been punished? Why?

   (Answers will vary.)

   _____

   _____

   _____

2. Discuss with other students what Lefkowitz seems to think Columbine High School was like at the time of the 1999 massacre. Why do you think that?

   (Answers will vary.)

   _____

   _____

   _____

Summary

MAKE AN EVALUATION

1 | Think objectively.

2 | Think subjectively.

CHAPTER 14

HOW DOES STRATEGY 14 HELP YOU BECOME AN ENGAGED READER?

Strategy 14 gives you a chance to put together all that you've learned about reading throughout this book. From the beginning, you've learned that reading begins with you. You've also learned strategies that increase your comprehension and enjoyment of what you read. Now, *Make an Evaluation* asks you to use everything you've learned in order to decide what you think about a reading, based on your objective as well as your subjective consideration of the writer's ideas.

HOW DOES THE MAKE AN EVALUATION STRATEGY WORK?

"Make an Evaluation" shows you how to put together what you've already learned in order to respond as fully as possible to a reading.

Strategy 14 reminds you to think objectively. Look for the overall point, the main ideas, and the details that support those points. Consider what the writer's point of view is, the writer's purpose, and the style. While thinking objectively, remember to keep your opinion to yourself.

Strategy 14 teaches you to think subjectively. Take into account what you feel about the reading before and after you read. In addition, consider your likes and your dislikes, your reactions and responses, and your opinions about what you read. Note any problems you may have had with the reading.

Key Terms

objective: neutral, free from emotional attachment to one side or the other

subjective: having emotional involvement or bias (leaning) to one side or the other

summary: a brief—usually one paragraph—restatement of main ideas

Think **AGAIN** ❯

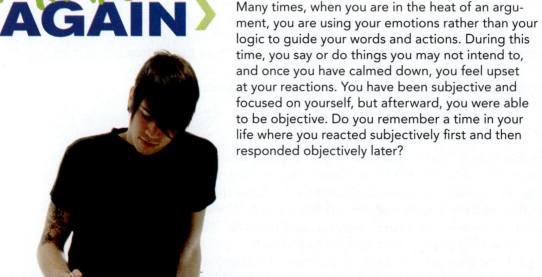

Many times, when you are in the heat of an argument, you are using your emotions rather than your logic to guide your words and actions. During this time, you say or do things you may not intend to, and once you have calmed down, you feel upset at your reactions. You have been subjective and focused on yourself, but afterward, you were able to be objective. Do you remember a time in your life where you reacted subjectively first and then responded objectively later?

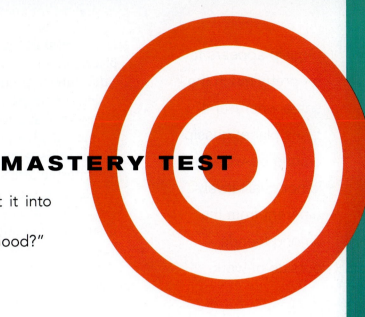

MASTERY TEST

Now that you understand Strategy 14, put it into

practice with Reading 28, "Can Gossip Be Good?"

Can Gossip Be Good?

FRANK T. MCANDREW

READING 28

Frank T. McAndrew is a professor of psychology at Knox College, in Galesburg, Illinois. A social psychologist, he is interested in environmental and evolutionary psychology. He is also a fellow of the Association for Psychological Science. This article is from a 2008 *Scientific American;* it reflects his curiosity about gossip and discusses some of the studies on gossip he and his colleagues have completed.

1   In the past few years I have heard more people than ever before puzzling over the 24/7 coverage of people such as Paris Hilton who are "celebrities" for no apparent reason other than we know who they are. And yet we can't look away. The press about these individuals' lives continues because people are obviously tuning in. Although many social critics have bemoaned this explosion of popular culture as if it reflects some kind of collective character flaw, it is in fact nothing more than the inevitable outcome of the collision between 21st century media and Stone Age minds.

2   When you cut away its many layers, our fixation on popular culture reflects an intense interest in the doings of other people; this <u>preoccupation</u> with the lives of others is a by-product of the psychology that evolved in prehistoric times to make our ancestors socially successful. Thus, it appears that we are hardwired to be fascinated with gossip.

3   Only in the past decade or so have psychologists turned their attention toward the study of gossip, partially because it is difficult to define exactly what gossip is. Most researchers agree that the practice involves talk about people who are not present and that this talk is relaxed, informal and entertaining. Typically the topic of conversation also concerns information that we can make moral judgments

> Gossip appears to be pretty much the same wherever it takes place; gossip among co-workers is not qualitatively different from that among friends outside of work.

about. Gossip appears to be pretty much the same wherever it takes place; gossip among co-workers is not qualitatively different from that among friends outside of work. Although everyone seems to detest a person who is known as a "gossip" and few people would use that label to describe themselves, it is an exceedingly unusual individual who can walk away from a juicy story about one of his or her acquaintances, and all of us have firsthand experience with the difficulty of keeping spectacular news about someone else a secret.

Why does private information about other people represent 4 such an irresistible temptation for us? In his book *Grooming, Gossip, and the Evolution of Language* (Harvard University Press, 1996), psychologist Robin Dunbar of the University of Liverpool in England suggested that gossip is a mechanism for bonding social groups together, analogous to the grooming that is found in primate groups. Sarah R. Wert, now at the University of Colorado at Boulder, and Peter Salovey of Yale University have proposed that gossip is one of the best tools that we have for comparing ourselves socially with others. The ultimate question, however, is, How did gossip come to serve these functions in the first place?

An Evolutionary Adaptation?

When evolutionary psychologists detect something that is shared by 5 people of all ages, times and cultures, they usually suspect that they have stumbled on a vital aspect of human nature, something that became a part of who we are in our long-forgotten prehistoric past. Evolutionary adaptations that enabled us not only to survive but to thrive in our prehistoric environment include our appreciation of landscapes containing freshwater and vegetation, our never-ending battle with our sweet tooth and our infatuation with people who look a certain way.

It is obvious to most people that being drawn to locations that offer re- 6 sources, food that provides energy, and romantic partners who appear able to help you bear and raise healthy children might well be something that evolution has selected for because of its advantages. It may not be so clear at first glance, however, how an interest in gossip could possibly be in the same league as these other preoccupations. If we think in terms of what it would have taken to be successful in our ancestral social environment, the idea may no longer seem quite so far-fetched.

As far as scientists can tell, our prehistoric forebears lived in relatively 7 small groups where they knew everyone else in a face-to-face, long-term kind of way. Strangers were probably an infrequent and temporary phenomenon. Our caveman ancestors had to cooperate with so-called in-group members for success against out-groups, but they also had to recognize that these same in-group members were their main competitors when it came to dividing limited resources. Living under such conditions, our ancestors faced a number of consistent adaptive problems such as remembering who was a reliable exchange partner and who was a cheater, knowing who would be a reproductively valuable mate, and figuring out how to successfully manage friendships, alliances and family relationships.

THE READER'S EDGE: BOOK TWO

8   The social intelligence needed for success in this environment required an ability to predict and influence the behavior of others, and an intense interest in the private dealings of other people would have been handy indeed and would have been strongly favored by natural selection. In short, people who were fascinated with the lives of others were simply more successful than those who were not, and it is the genes of those individuals that have come down to us through the ages. Like it or not, our inability to forsake gossip and information about other individuals is as much a part of who we are as is our inability to resist doughnuts or sex—and for the same reasons.

9   A related social skill that would have had a big payoff is the ability to remember details about the temperament, predictability and past behavior of individuals who are personally known to you; there would have been little use for a mind that was designed to engage in abstract statistical thinking about large numbers of unknown outsiders. In today's world, it is advantageous to be able to think in terms of probabilities and percentages when it comes to people, because predicting the behavior of the strangers with whom we deal in everyday life requires that we do so. This task is difficult for many of us because the early wiring of the brain was guided by different needs. Thus, natural selection shaped a thirst for, and a memory to store information about, specific people; it is even well established that we have a brain area specifically dedicated to the identification of human faces.

10   For better or worse, this is the mental equipment we must rely on to navigate our way through a modern world filled with technology and strangers. I suppose I should not be surprised when the very same psychology students who get glassy-eyed at any mention of statistical data about human beings in general become riveted by case studies of individuals experiencing psychological problems. Successful politicians take advantage of this pervasive "power of the particular" (as cognitive psychologists call it) when they use anecdotes and personal narratives to make political points. Even Russian dictator Joseph Stalin noted that "one death is a tragedy; a million deaths is a statistic." The prevalence of reality TV shows and nightly news programs focusing on stories about a missing child or the personal gaffes of politicians is a beast of our own creation.

Is Gossip Always Bad?

11   The aspect of gossip that is most troubling is that in its rawest form it is a strategy used by individuals to further their own reputations and selfish interests at the expense of others. This nasty side of gossip usually overshadows the more benign ways in which it functions in society. After all, sharing gossip with another person is a sign of deep trust because you are clearly signaling that you believe that this person will not use this sensitive information in a way that will have negative consequences for you; shared secrets also have a way of bonding people together. An individual who is not included in the office gossip network is obviously an outsider who is not trusted or accepted by the group.

Like it or not, our inability to forsake gossip and information about other individuals is as much a part of who we are as is our inability to resist doughnuts or sex—and for the same reasons.

There is ample evidence that when it is controlled, gossip can indeed be **12** a positive force in the life of a group. In a review of the literature published in 2004, Roy F. Baumeister of Florida State University and his colleagues concluded that gossip can be a way of learning the unwritten rules of social groups and cultures by resolving ambiguity about group norms. Gossip is also an efficient way of reminding group members about the importance of the group's norms and values; it can be a deterrent to deviance and a tool for punishing those who transgress. Rutgers University evolutionary biologist Robert Trivers has discussed the evolutionary importance of detecting "gross cheaters" (those who fail to reciprocate altruistic acts) and "subtle cheaters" (those who reciprocate but give much less than they get). . . .

Gossip can be an effective means of uncovering such information about **13** others and an especially useful way of controlling these "free riders" who may be tempted to violate group norms of reciprocity by taking more from the group than they give in return. Studies in real-life groups such as California cattle ranchers, Maine lobster fishers and college rowing teams confirm that gossip is used in these quite different settings to enforce group norms when an individual fails to live up to the group's expectations. In all these groups, individuals who violated expectations about sharing resources and meeting responsibilities became frequent targets of gossip and ostracism, which applied pressure on them to become better citizens. Anthropological studies of hunter-gatherer groups have typically revealed a similar social control function for gossip in these societies.

Anthropologist Christopher Boehm of the University of Southern California has proposed in his book *Hierarchy in the Forest: The Evolution of Egalitarian Behavior* (Harvard University Press, 1999) that gossip evolved as a "leveling mechanism" for neutralizing the dominance tendencies of others. Boehm believes that small-scale foraging societies such as those typical during human prehistory emphasized an egalitarianism that suppressed internal competition and promoted consensus seeking in a way that made the success of one's group extremely important to one's own fitness. These social pressures discouraged free riders and cheaters and encouraged altruists. In such societies, the manipulation of public opinion through gossip, ridicule and ostracism became a key way of keeping potentially dominant-group members in check.

Favored Types of Gossip

According to one of the pioneers of gossip research, anthropologist Jerome Barkow of Dalhousie University, we should be especially interested in information about people who matter most in our lives: rivals, mates, relatives, partners in social exchange, and high-ranking figures whose behavior can affect us. Given the proposition that our interest in gossip evolved as a way of acquiring fitness-enhancing information, Barkow also suggests that the type of knowledge that we seek should be information that can affect our social standing relative to others. Hence, we would expect to find higher interest in negative news (such as misfortunes and scandals) about high-status people and potential rivals because we could exploit it. Negative information about those lower than us in status would not be as useful. There should also be less interest in passing along negative information about our friends and relatives than about people who are not allies. Conversely, positive information (good fortune and sudden elevation of status, for example) about allies should be likely to be spread around, whereas positive information about nonallies should be less enticing because it is not useful in advancing one's own interests.

16   For a variety of reasons, our interest in the doings of same-sex others ought to be especially strong. Because same-sex members of one's own species who are close to our own age are our principal evolutionary competitors, we ought to pay special attention to them. The 18-year-old male caveman would have done much better by attending to the business of other 18-year-old males rather than the business of 50-year-old males or females of any age. Interest about members of the other sex should be strong only when their age and situational circumstances would make them appropriate as mates.

17   The gossip studies that my students and I have worked on at Knox College over the past decade have focused on uncovering what we are most interested in finding out about other people and what we are most likely to spread around. We have had people of all ages rank their interest in tabloid stories about celebrities, and we have asked college students to read gossip scenarios about unidentified individuals and tell us about which types of people they would most like to hear such information, about whom they would gossip and with whom they would share gossip.

18   In keeping with the evolutionary hypotheses suggested earlier, we have consistently found that people are most interested in gossip about individuals of the same sex as themselves who happen to be around their own age. We have also found that information that is socially useful is always of greatest interest to us: we like to know about the scandals and misfortunes of our rivals and of high-status people because this information might be valuable in social competition. Positive information about such people tends to be uninteresting to us. Finding out that someone already higher in status than ourselves has just acquired something that puts that person even further ahead of us does not supply us with ammunition that we can use to gain ground on him. Conversely, positive information about our friends and relatives is very interesting and likely to be used to our advantage whenever possible. For example, in studies that my colleagues and I published in 2002 and in 2007 in the *Journal of Applied Social Psychology,* we consistently found that college students were not much interested in hearing about academic awards or a large inheritance if it involved one of their professors and that they were also not very interested in passing that news along to others. Yet the same information about their friends or romantic partners was rated as being quite interesting and likely to be spread around.

19   We have also found that an interest in the affairs of same-sex others is especially strong among females and that women have somewhat different patterns of sharing gossip than men do. For example, our studies reveal that males report being far more likely to share gossip with their romantic partners than with anyone else, but females report that they would be just as likely to share gossip with their same-sex friends as with their romantic partners. And although males are usually more interested in news about other males, females are virtually obsessed with news about other females.

This fact can be demonstrated by looking at the actual frequency with which males and females selected a same-sex person as the most interesting subject of the gossip scenarios we presented them with in one of our studies published in 2002. On hearing about someone having a date with a famous person, 43 out of 44 women selected a female as the most interesting person to know this about, as compared with 24 out of 36 males who selected a male as most interesting. Similarly, 40 out of 42 females (versus 22 out of 37 males) were most interested in same-sex academic cheaters, and 39 out of 43 were most interested in a same-sex leukemia sufferer (as opposed to only 18 out of 37 males). In fact, the only two scenarios among the 13 we studied in which males expressed more same-sex interest than females did involved hearing about an individual heavily in debt because of gambling or an individual who was having difficulty performing sexually.

20

Why Such Interest in Celebrities?

Even if we can explain the intense interest that we have in other people who are socially important to us, how can we possibly explain the seemingly useless interest that we have in the lives of reality-show contestants, movie stars and public figures of all kinds? One possible explanation may be found in the fact that celebrities are a recent occurrence, evolutionarily speaking. In our ancestral environment, any person about whom we knew intimate details of his or her private life was, by definition, a socially important member of the in-group. Barkow has pointed out that evolution did not prepare us to distinguish among members of our community who have genuine effects on our life and the images and voices that we are bombarded with by the entertainment industry. This, the intense familiarity with celebrities provided by the modern media trips the same gossip mechanisms that have evolved to keep up with the affairs of in-group members. After all, anyone whom we see *that* often and know *that* much about *must* be socially important to us. News anchors and television actors we see every day in soap operas become familiar friends.

21

In our modern world, celebrities may also serve another important social function. In a highly mobile, industrial society, celebrities may be the only "friends" we have in common with our new neighbors and co-workers. They provide a common interest and topic of conversation between people who otherwise might not have much to say to one another, and they facilitate the types of informal interaction that help people become comfortable in new surroundings. Hence, keeping up on the lives of actors, politicians and athletes can make a person more socially adept during interactions with strangers and even provide segues into social relationships with new friends in the virtual world of the Internet. Research published in 2007 by Charlotte J.S. De Backer, a Belgian psychologist now at the University of Leicester in England, finds that young people even look to celebrities and popular culture for learning life strategies that would have been learned from role models within one's tribe in the old days. Teenagers in particular seem to be prone to learning how to dress, how to manage relationships and how to be socially successful in general by tuning in to popular culture.

22

THE READER'S EDGE: BOOK TWO

23   Thus, gossip is a more complicated and socially important phenomenon than we think. When gossip is discussed seriously, the goal usually is to suppress the frequency with which it occurs in an attempt to avoid the undeniably harmful effects it often has in work groups and other social networks. This tendency, however, overlooks that gossip is part of who we are and an essential part of what makes groups function as well as they do. Perhaps it may become more productive to think of gossip as a social skill rather than as a character flaw, because it is only when we do not do it well that we get into trouble. Adopting the role of the self-righteous soul who refuses to participate in gossip at work or in other areas of your social life ultimately will be self-defeating. It will turn out to be nothing more than a ticket to social isolation. On the other hand, becoming that person who indiscriminately blabs everything you hear to anyone who will listen will quickly get you a reputation as an untrustworthy busybody. Successful gossiping is about being a good team player and sharing key information with others in a way that will not be perceived as self-serving and about understanding when to keep your mouth shut.

24   In short, I believe we will continue to struggle with managing the gossip networks in our daily lives and to shake our heads at what we are constantly being subjected to by the mass media, rationally dismissing it as irrelevant to anything that matters in our own lives. But in case you find yourself becoming just a *tiny* bit intrigued by some inane story about a celebrity, let yourself off the hook and enjoy the guilty pleasure. After all, it is only human nature.

ACTIVE READERS RESPOND

After you've finished reading, use these questions to respond to "Can Gossip Be Good?" You may write your answers in the spaces provided or on a separate sheet of paper.

VITAL VOCABULARY

Some words in this reading may be unfamiliar to you. Use the methods of Strategy 3 to explain what the listed words mean.

USE CONTEXT CLUES

a. mechanism (paragraph 4)

_____

b. infatuation (paragraph 5)

_____

c. norms (paragraph 12)

_____

USE WORD PARTS

a. preoccupation (paragraph 2)

_____

b. qualitatively (paragraph 3)

_____

c. deterrent (paragraph 12)

_____

USE THE DICTIONARY

Choose the correct definition of each word as it is used in the context of this reading.

a. detest (paragraph 3) _____

_____

b. alliances (paragraph 7) _____

_____

c. temperament (paragraph 9) _____

_____

d. gaffes (paragraph 10) _____

_____

SKILLS TEST: ANALYSIS AND EVALUATION

A. Write an analysis of the reading. (Create a cluster map if that helps you.)
   (Answers will vary.)

_____

_____

_____

_____

B. Write an evaluation of the reading. Remember to include your opinions, parts that you like, and parts that you dislike in your evaluation. You may also wish to mention new information or ideas you learned from the reading.
   (Answers will vary.)

_____

_____

_____

_____

_____

OBJECTIVE OPERATIONS

1. Who is the writer's intended audience?
   a. Americans
   b. general audience
   c. quidnuncs
   d. scientists

2. What is the author's purpose?
   a. to inform
   b. to persuade
   c. to entertain

3. What is the tone of the passage?
   a. condescending
   b. probing
   c. curious
   d. apathetic

4. Many reasons exist for why we share gossip, but we are most likely to share

    a. information about which we can make a moral judgment.

    b. information about people who are present in our conversations.

    c. information about people who gossip.

    d. information that is strictly useful and harmless.

5. The word "anecdotes" in paragraph 10, line 8, most nearly means

    a. poisons.

    b. cures.

    c. lies.

    d. short stories.

6. Which of the following sentences is the stated overall point of the passage?

    a. "Although many social critics have bemoaned this explosion of popular culture as if it reflects some kind of collective character flaw, it is in fact nothing more than the inevitable outcome of the collision between 21st century media and Stone Age minds."

    b. "When you cut away its many layers, our fixation on popular culture reflects an intense interest in the doings of other people; this preoccupation with the lives of others is a by-product of the psychology that evolved in prehistoric times to make our ancestors socially successful."

    c. "I believe we will continue to struggle with managing the gossip networks in our daily lives and to shake our heads at what we are constantly being subjected to by the mass media, rationally dismissing it as irrelevant to anything that matters in our own lives."

    d. "But in case you find yourself becoming just a *tiny* bit intrigued by some inane story about a celebrity, let yourself off the hook and enjoy the guilty pleasure."

7. What is the stated main idea of paragraph 23?

    a. "Thus, gossip is a more complicated and socially important phenomenon than we think."

    b. "When gossip is discussed seriously, the goal usually is to suppress the frequency with which it occurs in an attempt to avoid the undeniably harmful effects it often has in work groups and other social networks."

    c. "This tendency, however, overlooks that gossip is part of who we are and an essential part

of what makes groups function as well as they do."

    d. "Perhaps it may become more productive to think of gossip as a social skill rather than as a character flaw, because it is only when we do not do it well that we get into trouble."

8. According to the passage, gossip is tempting to us because

    a. it is sinful.

    b. it is something everyone does.

    c. it helps our social groups bond.

    d. it means we are a more advanced species.

9. Which sentence provides support for this sentence (paragraph 11, lines 3–4): "This nasty side of gossip usually overshadows the more benign ways in which it functions in society."

    a. "The aspect of gossip that is most troubling is that in its rawest form it is a strategy used by individuals to further their own reputations and selfish interests at the expense of others."

    b. "After all, sharing gossip with another person is a sign of deep trust because you are clearly signaling that you believe that this person will not use this sensitive information in a way that will have negative consequences for you; shared secrets also have a way of bonding people together."

    c. "An individual who is not included in the office gossip network is obviously an outsider who is not trusted or accepted by the group."

    d. none of the above

10. The author's claim that celebrity gossip does serve certain social functions is

    a. adequately supported with details.

    b. inadequately supported with details.

11. What is the topic of paragraph 19?

    a. males' lack of obsession with gossip

    b. females' obsession with same-sex gossip

    c. females and gossip

    d. sharing gossip

12. The social intelligence needed for survival during prehistoric times required us to be able to

    a. deal privately with others.

    b. predict and influence the behavior of others.

    c. accept and tolerate others.

    d. accept and tolerate the behavior of others.

13. Identify the relationship between the parts of the following sentence from paragraph 8.

"The social intelligence needed for success in this environment required an ability to predict and influence the behavior of others, and an intense interest in the private dealings of other people would have been handy indeed and would have been strongly favored by natural selection." (lines 1–5)

a. addition
b. comparison
c. clarification
d. summary

14. For paragraph 16, the author organizes the information using

a. comparisons.
b. examples.
c. cause and effect.
d. clarification.

15. "There should also be less interest in passing along negative information about our friends and relatives than about people who are not allies." (paragraph 15, lines 12–13) This sentence is a statement of

a. fact.
b. opinion.
c. fact and opinion.

16. The word "irrelevant" in paragraph 24, line 4, most nearly means

a. important.
b. disrespectful.
c. unimportant.
d. pertinent.

17. Identify the relationship between the following sentences (paragraph 19, lines 7–8): "And although males are usually more interested in news about other males, females are virtually obsessed with news about other females."

a. contrast
b. comparison
c. definition and example
d. statement and clarification

18. According to Roy F. Baumeister from Florida State University, gossip is a tool that

a. resolves problems among social groups.
b. gets people involved with each other.
c. is used for punishing those who do not conform to the social group.
d. teaches us the written rules of social groups and cultures.

19. The author shows a bias

a. against people who gossip.
b. toward people who gossip.
c. against the benefits of gossip in social groups.
d. toward the benefits of gossip in social groups.

20. According to research by Charlotte J.S. De Backer, young people look to celebrities to

a. mimic them completely.
b. be reminded of their elders.
c. learn life strategies.
d. learn what not to do.

READERS WRITE

1. Why do psychologists believe that gossip is an evolutionary adaptation to society? Why do they think gossip was as important as food, shelter, and sexual partners?

(Answers will vary.)

2. Why would knowing who was "a reliable exchange partner and who was a cheater" be important in a social group?

(Answers will vary.)

3. Why is predicting the behavior of strangers difficult for us in the modern world?

(Answers will vary.)

_____

_____

4. How do politicians take advantage of the fact that we tend to be apathetic about statistics but enthusiastic about anecdotes? How do news programs contribute to the problem?

(Answers will vary.)

_____

_____

5. What are the reasons that women tend to care more about gossip about the same-sex? In comparison to women, how do men react to gossip?

(Answers will vary.)

_____

_____

READERS DISCUSS

1. Discuss with other students the types of gossip you believe are acceptable. When is it all right to share information with others? When should you keep your mouth shut?

(Answers will vary.)

_____

_____

2. Discuss with other students what it feels like to be a victim of "bad" gossip. What did you learn yourself from this situation? What did you learn about others? Was your behavior influenced by the gossip?

(Answers will vary.)

_____

_____

MAKE AN EVALUATION

1 | Think objectively.

2 | Think subjectively.

PRACTICE PAGES

Chapter 14

For practice thinking objectively, do this exercise.

PRACTICE EXERCISE 1

A. Read the following passage. Then, complete the exercise.

The History of Capital Punishment

Capital punishment is the legal execution of a person by the government after he or she has been convicted of a crime. The death penalty is rooted in the ancient practice of retribution, the resolution of any injury or wrong by the inflicting of the same injury on the wrongdoer. The crimes for which death is considered appropriate punishment, however, vary widely throughout history and in different cultures. 　　　1

The death penalty appears in the legal code written for Hammurabi, the ruler of Mesopotamia almost 4,000 years ago. The Code of Hammurabi was a list of 282 decisions made by judges on a variety of matters, both civil and criminal. About one-tenth of the acts described, including theft and false accusation, carried the death penalty. To the modern mind, some of these punishments may seem excessive and unfair. If, for example, the carelessness of a builder caused the death of the owner's son through the collapse of a building, the builder's son would be executed in return. 　　　2

In ancient Greece, murder and treason were two of the crimes punished by death. Accidental death was more often punished by banishment and a loss of property. 　　　3

As Rome began its rise to world dominance, it created a written code of law that would provide guidance for the nation's leaders and protection for its citizens. These laws, known as the "twelve tables," were published in 450 B.C. Although the original tables specified death as punishment for a number of acts, they also strictly forbade the execution of any man who had not formally been convicted of a capital offense. After the fall of the Roman Empire in the fifth century A.D., Roman law became the basis for many legal systems developed in Europe. 　　　4

> Although the original tables specified death as punishment for a number of acts, they also strictly forbade the execution of any man who had not formally been convicted of a capital offense.

5   Throughout the Middle Ages and beyond, the death penalty was widely used. Punishment was often horrific and slow. Public executions were a popular spectacle, a kind of entertainment. By the eighteenth century, however, critics of the death penalty became increasingly numerous and vocal, questioning its justness. By the year 2001, 75 countries around the world had banned the death penalty altogether. Several others retained it only for the worst crimes, including treason and war crimes. Although capital punishment for common crimes still exists in countries in the Caribbean, Africa, and Asia, it is believed that the United States and China are the countries that most frequently carry out the death penalty.

B. *Complete the cluster map for "The History of Capital Punishment."*

Cluster Map
"History of Capital Punishment"

- "Code of Hammurabi": theft and false accusation can equal death penalty. (2)
- The crimes for which capital punishment is considered appropriate, however, vary widely throughout history and in different cultures.
- Greece and Rome (3–4)
- death penalty— murder or treason; otherwise banishment
- Middle Ages and after: wide world use (5)
- used almost for entertainment
- "twelve tables"— written Roman laws specifying punishment for crime.
- banned by 2002 in nearly every country

C. *Based on your cluster map, write an analysis.*
    (Answers will vary.)
    _____
    _____
    _____
    _____
    _____

For practice thinking subjectively, do this exercise.

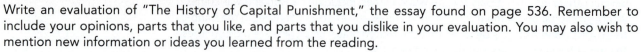

PRACTICE EXERCISE 2

Write an evaluation of "The History of Capital Punishment," the essay found on page 536. Remember to include your opinions, parts that you like, and parts that you dislike in your evaluation. You may also wish to mention new information or ideas you learned from the reading.

(Answers will vary.)

_____

_____

_____

_____

_____

PRACTICE READING

To get practice with reading, read the passage, and then answer the questions that follow. You may write your answers in the spaces provided or on a separate sheet of paper.

The Formation of Modern American Mass Culture

JAMES KIRBY MARTIN, RANDY ROBERTS, STEVEN MINTZ, LINDA O. MCMURRY, JAMES H. JONES

James Martin and the four other writers of the history textbook *America and Its Peoples: A Mosaic in the Making* (2001) are all university professors of history. Each of these authors has special interests in a certain area of history, such as the history of the family and the history of sports and films in America. This reading is an excerpt from the chapter "Modern Times: 1920–1929." It tells about how much of our current popular culture was born in the 1920s.

1   Many of the defining features of modern American culture emerged during the 1920s. The best-seller, the book club, the record chart, the radio, the talking picture, and spectator sports all became popular forms of mass entertainment. But the primary reason the 1920s stand out as one of the most important periods in American cultural history is that the decade produced a generation of artists, musicians, and writers who were among the most <u>innovative</u> and creative in the country's history.

Mass Entertainment

2   Of all the new appliances to enter the nation's homes during the 1920s, none had a more revolutionary impact than radio. Sales soared from $60 million in 1922 to $426 million in 1929. The first commercial radio station began broadcasting in 1919, and during the 1920s, the nation's airwaves were filled with musical variety shows and comedies.

3   Radio drew the nation together by bringing news, entertainment, and advertisements to more than ten million households. Radio blunted regional differences and imposed similar tastes and lifestyles. No other media had the power to create heroes and villains so quickly; when Charles Lindbergh became the first person to fly nonstop across the Atlantic from New York to Paris in 1928, the radio brought his incredible feat into American homes, transforming him into a celebrity overnight.

> Radio blunted regional differences and imposed similar tastes and lifestyles.

4   Radio also brought the nation decidedly unheroic images. The nation's most popular radio show, "Amos 'n Andy," which first aired in 1926 on Chicago's WMAO, spread vicious racial stereotypes into homes whose white occupants knew little about African Americans. Other minorities fared no better. The Italian gangster and the tightfisted Jew became stock characters in radio programming.

5   The phonograph was not far behind the radio in importance. The 1920s saw the record player enter American life in full force. Piano sales sagged as phonograph production rose from just 190,000 in 1923 to 5 million in 1929.

6   The popularity of jazz, blues, and "hillbilly" music fueled the phonograph boom. Novelist F. Scott Fitzgerald called the 1920s the "Jazz Age"— and the decade was truly jazz's golden age. Duke Ellington wrote the first extended jazz compositions; Louis Armstrong popularized "scat" (singing of nonsense syllables); Fletcher Henderson pioneered big band jazz; and trumpeter Jimmy McPartland and clarinetist Benny Goodman popularized the Chicago school of improvisation.

7   The blues craze erupted in 1920, when a black singer named Mamie Smith released a recording called "Crazy Blues." The record became a sensation, selling 75,000 copies in a month and a million copies in seven months. Recordings by Ma Rainey, the "Mother of the Blues," and Bessie Smith, the "Empress of the Blues," brought the blues, with its <u>poignant</u> and defiant reaction to life's sorrows, to a vast audience.

8   "Hillbilly" music broke into mass culture in 1923, when a Georgia singer named "Fiddlin' John" Carson sold 500,000 copies of his recordings. "Country" music's appeal was not limited to the rural South or West; city people, too, listened to country songs, reflecting a deep <u>nostalgia</u> for a simpler past.

> Americans spent 83 cents of every entertainment dollar going to the movies—and three-fourths of the population went to a movie theater every week.

The single most significant new instrument of mass entertainment **9** was the movies. Movie attendance soared, from 50 million patrons a week in 1920 to 90 million weekly in 1929. Americans spent 83 cents of every entertainment dollar going to the movies—and three-fourths of the population went to a movie theater every week.

During the late teens and 1920s, the film industry took on **10** its modern form. In cinema's earliest days, the film industry was based in the nation's theatrical center—New York. By the 1920s, the industry had relocated to Hollywood, drawn by cheap land and labor, the ready accessibility of varied scenery, and a climate ideal for year-round filming. Each year, Hollywood released nearly 700 movies, dominating worldwide film production. By 1926, Hollywood had captured 95 percent of the British and 70 percent of the French markets.

A small group of companies consolidated their control over the film **11** industry and created the "studio system" that would dominate film production for the next thirty years. Paramount, 20th-century Fox, MGM, and other studios owned their own production facilities, ran their own worldwide distribution networks, and controlled theater chains committed to showing their companies' products. In addition, they kept certain actors, directors, and screenwriters under contract.

The popularity of the movies soared as films increasingly featured glamour, sophistication, and sex appeal. New kinds of movie stars appeared: **12** the mysterious sex goddess, personified by Greta Garbo; the passionate hot-blooded lover, epitomized by Rudolph Valentino; and the flapper, with her bobbed hair and skimpy skirts. New film genres also debuted, including swashbuckling adventures, sophisticated comedies, and tales of flaming youth and the new sexual freedom. Americans flocked to see Hollywood spectacles such as Cecil B. DeMille's *Ten Commandments* (1923) with its "cast of thousands" and dazzling special effects.

Like radio, movies created a new popular culture, with common speech, **13** dress, behavior, and heroes. And like radio, Hollywood did its share to reinforce racial stereotypes by denigrating minority groups. The radio, the electric phonograph, and the silver screen all molded and mirrored mass culture.

Spectator Sports

Spectator sports attracted vast audiences in the 1920s. The country **14** yearned for heroes in an increasingly impersonal, bureaucratic society, and sports, as well as the film industry, provided them. Prize fighters like Jack Dempsey became national idols. Team sports flourished, but Americans focused on individual superstars, people whose talents or personalities made them appear larger than life. Knute Rockne and his "Four Horsemen" at Notre Dame spurred interest in college football, and professional football began during the 1920s. In 1925, Harold "Red" Grange, the "Galloping Ghost" halfback for the University of Illinois, attracted 68,000 fans to a professional football game at Brooklyn's Polo Grounds.

15　　Baseball drew even bigger crowds than football. The decade began with the sport mired in scandal. In 1920, three members of the Chicago White Sox told a grand jury that they and five other players had thrown the 1919 World Series. As a result of the "Black Sox" scandal, eight players were banished from the sport. But baseball soon regained its popularity, thanks to George Herman ("Babe") Ruth, the sport's undisputed superstar. Up until the 1920s Ty Cobb's defensive brand of baseball, with its emphasis on base hits and stolen bases, had dominated the sport. Ruth transformed baseball into the game of the home-run hitter. In 1921, the New York Yankee slugger hit 59 home runs—more than any other team combined. In 1927, the "Sultan of Swat" hit 60.

Low-Brow and Middle-Brow Culture

16　　"It was a characteristic of the Jazz Age," novelist F. Scott Fitzgerald wrote, "that it had no interest in politics at all." What, then, were Americans interested in? Entertainment was Fitzgerald's answer. Parlor games like Mah Jong and crossword puzzles became enormously popular during the 1920s. Americans hit golf balls, played tennis, and bowled. Dance crazes like the fox trot, the Charleston, and the jitterbug swept the country.

17　　New kinds of "pulp fiction" found a wide audience. Edgar Rice Burroughs' *Tarzan of the Apes* became a runaway best-seller. For readers who felt concerned about urbanization and industrialization, the adventures of the lone white man in "dark Africa" revived the spirit of frontier individualism. Zane Grey's novels, such as *Riders of the Purple Sage,* enjoyed even greater popularity, with their tried but true formula of romance, action, and a moralistic struggle between good and evil, all in a western setting.

18　　Other readers wanted to be titillated, as evidenced by the boom in "confession magazines." Urban values, liberated women, and Hollywood films had all relaxed Victorian standards. Confession magazines rushed to fill the vacuum, <u>purveying</u> stories of romantic success and failure, divorce, fantasy, and adultery. Writers survived the censors' cut by placing moral tags at the end of their stories, in which readers were advised to avoid similar mistakes in their own lives.

19　　Readers too embarrassed to pick up a copy of *True Romance* could read more <u>urbane</u> magazines such as *The New Yorker or Vanity Fair,* which offered entertainment, amusement, and gossip to those with more sophisticated tastes. They could also join the Book-of-the-Month Club or the Literary Guild, both of which were founded during the decade.

The Avant-Garde

20　　Few decades have produced as many great works of art, music, or literature as the 1920s. At the decade's beginning, American culture stood in Europe's shadow. By the decade's end, Americans were leaders in the struggle to liberate the arts from older canons of taste, form, and style. It was during the twenties that Eugene O'Neill, the country's most talented dramatist, wrote his greatest plays, and that William Faulkner, Ernest Hemingway, F. Scott Fitzgerald, and Thomas Wolfe published their first novels.

> Writers survived the censors' cut by placing moral tags at the end of their stories, in which readers were advised to avoid similar mistakes in their own lives.

American poets of the 1920s—such as Hart Crane, e.e. cummings, **21** Countee Cullen, Langston Hughes, Edna St. Vincent Millay, and Wallace Stevens—experimented with new styles of punctuation, rhyming, and form. Likewise, artists like Charles Demuth, Georgia O'Keeffe, and Joseph Stella challenged the dominant realist tradition in American art and pioneered nonrepresentational and expressionist art forms.

The 1920s marked America's entry into the world of serious music. It **22** witnessed the founding of fifty symphony orchestras and three of the country's most prominent music conservatories—Julliard, Eastman, and Curtis. The decade also produced America's first great classical composers—including Aaron Copland and Charles Ives—and witnessed George Gershwin create a new musical form by integrating jazz into symphonic and orchestral music.

World War I had left many American intellectuals and artists disillu- **23** sioned and alienated. Neither Wilsonian idealism nor Progressive reformism appealed to America's postwar writers and thinkers, who believed that the crusade to end war and to make the world safe for democracy had been a senseless mistake.

During the 1920s, many of the nation's leading writers exposed the shal- **24** lowness and narrowmindedness of American life. The United States was a nation awash in materialism and devoid of spiritual vitality, a "wasteland," wrote the poet T. S. Eliot, inhabited by "hollow men." No author offered a more scathing attack on middle-class boorishness and smugness than Sinclair Lewis, who in 1930 became the first American to win the Nobel Prize for Literature. In *Main Street* (1920) and *Babbitt* (1922) he satirized the narrow-minded complacency and dullness of small-town America, while in *Elmer Gantry (1922)* he exposed religious hypocrisy and bigotry.

As editor of Mercury magazine, H. L. Mencken wrote hundreds of essays **25** mocking practically every aspect of American life. Calling the South a "gargantuan paradise of the fourth rate," and the middle class the "booboisie," Mencken directed his choicest barbs at reformers, whom he blamed for the bloodshed of World War I and the gangsters of the 1920s. "If I am convinced of anything," he snarled, "it is that Doing Good is in bad taste."

The writer Gertrude Stein defined an important group of American in- **26** tellectuals when she told Ernest Hemingway in 1921, "You are all a lost generation." Stein was referring to the expatriate novelists and artists who had participated in the Great War only to emerge from the conflict convinced that it was an exercise in futility. In their novels, F. Scott Fitzgerald and Hemingway foreshadowed a philosophy now known as "existentialism"—which maintains that life has no transcendent purpose and that each individual must salvage personal meaning from the void. Hemingway's fiction lionized toughness and "manly virtues" as a counterpoint to the softness of American life. In *The Sun Also Rises* (1926) and *A Farewell to Arms* (1929) he emphasized meaningless death and the importance of facing stoically the absurdities of the universe. In the conclusion of *The Great Gatsby (1925)*, Fitzgerald gave pointed expression to an existentialist outlook: "so we beat on, boats against the current, borne back ceaselessly into the past."

Wilsonian idealism: refers to Woodrow Wilson, U.S. president during World War I

Progressive reformism: political movement emphasizing social progress for the poor, underprivileged

The Sex Debate

27   "If all girls at the Yale prom were laid end to end, I wouldn't be surprised," sighed Dorothy Parker, the official wit of New York's smart set. Parker's quip captured the public's perception that America's morals had taken a nosedive. Practically every newspaper featured articles on prostitution, venereal disease, sex education, birth control, and the rising divorce rate.

28   City life nurtured new sexual attitudes. With its crowded anonymity, urban culture eroded sexual inhibitions by relaxing community restraints on individual behavior. Cities also promoted secular, consumer values, and city people seemed to tolerate, if not welcome, many forms of diversity.

29   While cities provided the ideal environment for liberalized sexual values, Sigmund Freud provided the ideal psychology. A Vienna physician, Freud revolutionized academic and popular thinking about human behavior by arguing that unconscious sexual anxieties cause much of human behavior. Freud also explained that sexual desires and fears develop in infancy and stay with people throughout their lives. During the 1920s, Freud's theories about the sexual unconscious were widely debated by physicians, academics, advice columnists, women's magazine writers, and preachers.

30   The image of the "flapper"—the liberated woman who bobbed her hair, painted her lips, raised her hemline, and danced the Charleston—personified the public's anxiety about the decline of traditional morality. In the 1950s Alfred C. Kinsey, a sex researcher at Indiana University, found that women born after 1900 were twice as likely to have had premarital sex as their mothers, with the most pronounced changes occurring in the generation reaching maturity in the early 1920s.

31   Sexual permissiveness had eroded Victorian values, but the "new woman" posed less of a challenge to traditional morality than her critics feared. Far from being promiscuous, her sexual experience before marriage was generally limited to one or two partners, one of whom she married. In practice, this narrowed the gap between men and women and moved society toward a single standard of morality. Instead of turning to prostitutes, men made love with their sweethearts, who in many instances became their wives.

ACTIVE READERS RESPOND

After you've finished reading, use these questions to respond to "The Formation of Modern American Mass Culture." You may write your answers in the spaces provided or on a separate sheet of paper.

VITAL VOCABULARY

Some words in this reading may be unfamiliar to you. Use the methods of Strategy 3 to explain what the listed words mean.

USE CONTEXT CLUES

a.   nostalgia (paragraph 8) _____

b. epitomized (paragraph 12) _____

c. purveying (paragraph 18) _____

d. transcendent (paragraph 26)

_____

USE WORD PARTS

a. denigrating (paragraph 13) _____

b. urbane (paragraph 19) (Use the context to see how "urbane" relates to the word "urban.")

_____

c. alienated (paragraph 23) _____

d. expatriate (paragraph 26) _____

e. lionized (paragraph 26) _____

USE THE DICTIONARY

Choose the correct definition of each word as it is used in the context of this reading.

a. innovative (paragraph 1) _____

b. poignant (paragraph 7) _____

c. complacency (paragraph 24) _____

d. bigotry (paragraph 24) _____

e. stoically (paragraph 26) _____

OBJECTIVE OPERATIONS

1. Who is the writer's intended audience?

    a. professors

    b. history students

    c. general audience

    d. historians

2. What is the author's purpose?

    a. to inform

    b. to persuade

    c. to entertain

3. What is the tone of the passage?

    a. subjective

    b. objective

    c. nostalgic

    d. apathetic

4. Three features of modern American life were introduced in the 1920s. They were:

    a. the phonograph, the vacuum cleaner, and the washing machine.

    b. radio, the phonograph, and the movies.

    c. radio, television, and the telephone.

    d. the movies, television, and computers.

5. The word "urbane" in paragraph 19, line 2, most nearly means

    a. crude.

    b. well-designed.

    c. sophisticated.

    d. tasteful

6. Which of the following sentences is the stated main idea?

    a. "Many of the defining features of modern American culture emerged during the 1920s."

    b. "The best-seller, the book club, the record chart, the radio, the talking picture, and spectator sports all became popular forms of mass entertainment."

    c. "But the primary reason the 1920s stand out as one of the most important periods in American cultural history is that the decade produced a generation of artists, musicians, and writers who were among the most innovative and creative in the country's history."

d. "Of all the new appliances to enter the nation's homes during the 1920s, none had a more revolutionary impact than radio."

7. What is the implied main idea of paragraph 7?

   a. The blues were important in the 1920s.

   b. The blues became popular during the 1920s when a few recordings brought the music to a wider audience.

   c. The 1920s introduced blues to a wider audience but its popularity as a music genre did not increase.

   d. Louis Armstrong sang the blues.

8. America longed for heroes during this decade because

   a. families had lost so many of their young men during World War I.

   b. the society had grown more impersonal and bureaucratic.

   c. the country was at war.

   d. they needed inspiration to carry on with the hard work most Americans did.

9. Which sentence provides support for this sentence (paragraph 4, line 1): "Radio also brought the nation decidedly unheroic images."

   a. "The nation's most popular radio show, "Amos 'n Andy," which first aired in 1926 on Chicago's WMAO, spread vicious racial stereotypes into homes whose white occupants knew little about African Americans."

   b. "Other minorities fared no better."

   c. "The Italian gangster and the tightfisted Jew became stock characters in radio programming."

   d. all of the above

10. The author's claim that the 1920s helped to create modern culture is

    a. adequately supported with details.

    b. inadequately supported with details.

11. What is the topic of paragraph 10?

    a. modern film industry

    b. 1920s film industry

    c. markets of the film industry

    d. cheap labor

12. The reading that appealed to a 1920s mass audience—the low-brow audience—included

    a. new styles of poetry.

    b. early forms of science fiction.

    c. self-help books.

    d. confession magazines.

13. Identify the relationship between the parts of the following sentence from paragraph 12.

    "The popularity of the movies soared as films increasingly featured glamour, sophistication, and sex appeal." (lines 1–2)

    a. statement and clarification

    b. addition

    c. cause and effect

    d. illustration

14. For paragraphs 17 and 18, the author organizes the information by

    a. giving examples.

    b. contrasting.

    c. comparing.

    d. describing.

15. "Few decades have produced as many great works of art, music, or literature as the 1920s." (paragraph 20, lines 1–2)

    The above sentence is a statement of

    a. fact.

    b. opinion.

    c. fact and opinion.

16. The word "transcendent" in paragraph 26, line 7, most nearly means

    a. tender.

    b. apparent.

    c. expressive.

    d. uplifting

17. Identify the relationship between the following sentences (paragraph 23, lines 1–5): "World War I had left many American intellectuals and artists disillusioned and alienated. Neither Wilsonian idealism nor Progressive reformism appealed to America's postwar writers and thinkers, who believed that the crusade to end war and to make the world safe for democracy had been a senseless mistake."

    a. statement and clarification

    b. time order

    c. definition and example

    d. process

18. The emergence of the "flapper" of the 1920s reflected the decade's

    (a.) changed attitudes about sex.

    b. return to the traditional role for women.

    c. oppression of women at home and in the workplace.

    d. experimentation with legalized prostitution.

19. From the passage, you can conclude that

    a. the authors enjoy the 1920s history.

    b. the 1920s had little influence on modern culture.

    (c.) modern culture is greatly influenced by the 1920s.

    d. film stars were very popular.

20. Radio programs, such as "Amos 'n Andy" promoted racial or ethnic stereotypes because

    a. prejudiced white and non-ethnic actors played all the roles on these programs.

    b. people who owned radios tended to be more prejudiced than those in the general population.

    (c.) they portrayed caricatures of people from these groups rather than real people.

    d. the programs were intended as propaganda that would support both real and de facto segregation.

QUICK QUESTIONS

1. Baseball drew even smaller crowds than football. True or (False)

2. Readers loved confessions magazines. (True) or False

3. The country "yearned for heroes" in the 1920s because society was becoming more __impersonal__ and __bureaucratic__.

4. The 1920s changed several types of entertainment such as __movies__, __books__, and __sports__. (Answers will vary.)

5. What kind of reading appealed to a 1920s mass audience—the low-brow audience? What types of magazines appealed to more sophisticated readers—the high-brow audience?

    (Answers will vary.) _____

    _____

    _____

6. Why had American culture "stood in Europe's shadow" at the beginning of the decade?

    (Answers will vary.) _____

    _____

    _____

TEXT CREDITS

p. 5 Jan Harold Brunvand. 2001. *Encyclopedia of Urban Legends.* NY: Norton and Company, 2001, pp. xxix-xxx. Jerome Beatty. 1970. Excerpt from *Esquire* magazine, November 1970.

p. 9 Thomas Lux. 1997. "The Voice You Hear When You Read Silently," *New and Selected Poems.* New York: Houghton Mifflin; also appeared *The New Yorker,* July 14, 1997, p. 14.

p. 14 Rebecca Grabiner. 1997. "I Do Not Like Reading, Sam-I-Am." First appeared in the February 1997 University of Chicago Magazine.

p. 20 "The One-Room Schoolhouse of the Nineteenth Century." *Timed Readings Plus in Social Studies. Book 1,* 2003. Jamestown Education. Columbus: Glencoe McGraw-Hill. © 2003 by The McGraw-Hill Companies.

p. 27 Charles Perry. 1995. "The Deadhead Phenomenon," from *Rolling Stone's Garcia,* 1995. © Rolling Stone LLC 1995. All Rights Reserved. Reprinted by permission.

p. 33 Alberto Manguel. 1996. "Forbidden Reading" from *A History of Reading.* Copyright © 1996 by Alberto Manguel. Used by permission of Viking Penguin, a division of Penguin Group (USA) Inc., and the author c/o Guillermo Schavelzon & Asociados, SL, Agencia Literaria, info@schavelzon.com.

p. 38 Ellen Tashie Frisina. 1998. "See Spot Run: Teaching My Grandmother to Read." The author is a professor at Hofstra University, NY.

p. 45 Dr. Benjamin Carson, M.D.; Cecil Murphey. 1992. Taken from *Think Big!* Copyright © 1992 by Benjamin Carson, M.D. Used by permission of Zondervan.

p. 57 Nancy Friedman. 2005. "Watch That Tone of Voice." *My Article Archive.com.* Reprinted by permission of the author.

p. 65 Definition of "assimilate." Copyright © 2010 by Houghton Mifflin Harcourt Publishing Company. Reproduced by permission from *The American Heritage Dictionary of the English Language, Fourth Edition.*

p. 70 Deborah Silvey. 2003. "Where English Words Come From," © 2003 by Deborah Silvey from *Reading From the Inside Out.* NY: Longman/Pearson, 2003. Reprinted by permission of the author.

p. 77 Jess Blumberg. 2007. "Point. Shoot. See" Originally appeared in *Smithsonian,* November 2007.

p. 89 Madeline Levine. 1998. "Does Media Violence Desensitize Children to Violence?" in *See No Evil: A Guide to Protecting Our Children from Media Violence.* San Francisco: Jossey-Bass, 1998.

p. 104 Thomas Kida. 2006. *Don't Believe Everything You Think: The 6 Basic Mistakes We Make in Thinking,* (Amherst, NY: Prometheus Books, 2006), pp. 134–135, 257. Copyright © 2006 by Thomas Kida. All rights reserved. Reprinted with permission of the publisher.

p. 107 James M. Henslin. 2000. "What Deprived Children Tell Us about Human Nature." *Essentials of Sociology: A Down-to Earth Approach,* 3e, pp. 57–58, 60–61. © 2000 Pearson Education, Inc. Reproduced by permission of Pearson Education, Inc.

p. 110 Maya Pines. 1981. "The Civilizing of Genie." *Psychology Today,* 15, September 1981, 28–34. Reproduced with permission from Psychology Today. Copyright © 2009 www.psychologytoday.com.

p. 118 Robert Coles. 1997. *The Moral Intelligence of Children,* copyright © 1997 by Robert Coles. Used by permission of Random House, Inc., and by Bloomsbury Publishing Ltd.

p. 126 Ronald J. Ebert and Ricky W. Griffin. 2000. "Managing Workforce Diversity," *Business Essentials,* 3rd ed., © 2000, pp. 220–222. Reprinted by permission of Pearson Education, Inc., Upper Saddle River, NJ.

p. 136 Thomas Kida. 2006. *Don't Believe Everything You Think: The 6 Basic Mistakes We Make in Thinking,* (Amherst, NY: Prometheus Books, 2006), pp. 61–64. Copyright © 2006 by Thomas Kida. All rights reserved. Reprinted with permission of the publisher.

p. 139 Laura E. Berk. 2000. "How Babies Use Patterns to See," *Child Development,* 5e, pp. 155, 157. © 2000 Pearson Education, Inc. Reproduced by permission of Pearson Education, Inc.

p. 140 Figure 5.1 Adapted from M. S. Banks & p. Salapatek, 1983, "Infant Visual Perception," in M. M. Haith and J. J. Campos [Eds.], *Handbook of Child Psychology: Vol. 2. Infancy and Developmental Psychobiology* 4th ed., New York: Wiley. p. 504. Copyright 1983 by John Wiley & Sons.

p. 149 bell hooks. 1989. Excerpt from *talking back: thinking feminist, thinking black,* pp. 5–9. Reprinted by permission of South End Press.

p. 159 Tobias Wolff. 1996. "Powder," *Night in Question.* Copyright © 1996 by Tobias Wolff. Used by permission of Alfred A. Knopf, a division of Random House, Inc., and by permission of International Creative Management, Inc.

p. 170 F. John Reh. 2009. "Getting Your Point Across." about.com: management. © 2009 by F. John Reh, http://management.about .com/cs/communication/a/GetPointOver702.htm. Used with permission of About, Inc. which can be found online at www .about.com. All rights reserved.

p. 184 Steven A. Beebe, Susan J. Beebe, and Diana K. Ivy. 2001. *Communication: Principles for a Lifetime.,* pp. 39–42, © 2001. Reproduced by permission of Pearson Education, Inc.

p. 197 John Holt. 1969. "School Is Bad for Children." *The Saturday Evening Post* Magazine, © 1969. Saturday Evening Post Society.

p. 226 Karen L. Hudson. 2009. "You'd Better (Not!) Shop Around: Why Tattoos and Piercings Shouldn't be Bargains." About.com. July 7, 2009. © 2009 by Karen L. Hudson, http://tattoo.about.com/ cs/articles/a/nobargain.htm. Used with permission of About, Inc., which can be found online at www.about.com. All rights reserved.

p. 230 Michael Giltz. 2008. "Celebrity Book Club," *Daily News,* January 11, 2008.

p. 235 Daniel Goleman. 1995. "Optimism; The Great Motivator," *Emotional Intelligence.* Copyright © 1995 by Daniel Goleman. Used by permission of Bantam Books, a division of Random House, Inc., and by Bloomsbury Publishing Ltd.

p. 244 Carole Wade and Carol Tavris. 2000. "How Conscious Is Thought?" *Psychology,* 6th ed. © 2000. Reprinted by permission of Pearson Education, Inc., Upper Saddle River, NJ.

p. 255 Grace Paley. 1997. "Traveling." Originally published in *The New Yorker,* September 8, 1997. Grace Paley c/o Markson Thoma Literary Agency.

p. 266 Jeremy Oduber. 2009. "The Importance of Getting Your Ideas Down on Paper." *Superluminal* website. February 3, 2009.

p. 275 John M. Darley and Bibb Latané. 1968. "Why People Don't Help in a Crisis." *Psychology Today,* December 1968, 2, 54–57, 70–71. Reproduced with permission from *Psychology Today.* Copyright © 2009 www.psychologytoday.com.

p. 287 Amy Tan. 1989. "Mother Tongue," *The Threepenny Review.* Copyright © 1989 by Amy Tan. First appeared in *Threepenny Review.* Reprinted by permission of the author and the Sandra Dijkstra Literary Agency.

p. 301 Robert A. Wallace. 1997. *Biology: The World of Life,* 7th ed. pp. 467–468. Copyright © 1997 by Addison-Wesley Educational Publishers, Inc. Reprinted by permission of Addison Wesley Longman Publishers, Inc.

p. 309 © The New Yorker Collection 1997 Arnie Levin from cartoonbank.com. All rights reserved.

p. 310 © The New Yorker Collection 1996 Mike Twohy from cartoonbank.com. All rights reserved.

p. 312 Rick Brenner. 2004. "Hot and Cold Running People," *Point Lookout.* ChacoCanyon.com, 12 May 2004.

p. 316 Kate Boyes. 2000. "Letter to My Teacher," in *Fortitude: True Stories of True Grit,* edited by Malinda Teel. Red Rock Press, 2000. Used by permission of the publisher.

p. 326 Natalie Angier. 1999. "Why Men Don't Last." *The New York Times,* February 17, 1999. © 1999 The New York Times. All rights reserved. Used by permission and protected by the Copyright Laws of the United States. The printing, copying, redistribution, or retransmission of the Material without express written permission is prohibited.

p. 337 Barbara Smuts. 1999. "The Gorilla's Embrace." First appeared in *Whole Earth Review,* Summer 1999, 10–13. Reprinted by permission of the author.

p. 350 Sarah Rice. 2006. "Using Adoption Metaphors to Increase Customer Acceptance." Boxes and Arrows.com, June 5, 2006, This story first appeared in Boxes and Arrows, www .boxesandarrows.com. Used by permission of the author.

p. 356 Tim Cahill. 1999. "Terror Unlimited." *Outside* Magazine, August 1999. Used by permission of the publisher.

p. 367 William Ecenbarger. "Buckle Up. And Behave." 2009. Originally appeared in *Smithsonian,* April 2009.

p. 378 Julia Alvarez. 1998. "Victor" from *Off the Beaten Path: Stories of Place,* edited by Joseph Barbato and Lisa Weinerman Horak of The Nature Conservancy. Copyright © 1998 by The Nature Conservancy. Reprinted by permission of North Point Press, a division of Farrar, Straus, and Giroux, LLC.

CREDITS

p. 390 Lindsay Roberts. 2009. "Peer Pressure: How College Life Can Change You." *The Quinnipiac Chronicle.* April 15, 2009. Reprinted by permission of the author.

p. 401 Mark Hertsgaard. 2000. "A Global Green Deal." *Time,* Special Edition, Earth Day, April 26, 2000. Copyright TIME INC. Reprinted by permission. TIME is a registered trademark of Time. Inc. All rights reserved.

p. 410 Barbara Kingsolver. 1995. Excerpt from "Infernal Paradise" (pp. 196–200), *High Tide in Tucson: Essays from Now or Never.* Copyright © 1995 by Barbara Kingsolver. Reprinted by permission of HarperCollins Publishers, and by The Frances Goldin Literary Agency.

p. 423 John Vivian. 2002. "Pitching Messages." *The Media of Mass Communication,* 6th ed., pp. 310–313. © 2002. Reproduced by permission of Pearson Education, Inc.

p. 435 Josey Vogels. 2009. "Communication Breakdown." *The J Spot.* MetroNews.ca. July 28, 2009.

p. 441 George F. Cole and Christopher E. Smith. 1999. "Police and the Community" in *Criminal Justice in America,* 2e. © 1999 Wadsworth, a part of Cengage Learning. Reproduced by permission. www.cengage.com/permissions.

p. 451 Robert L Heilbroner. 1961. "Don't Let Stereotypes Warp Your Judgments." Copyright © 1961 by International Business Machines Corp., transferred to Robert L. Heilbroner. Reprinted by permission of William Morris Endeavor Entertainment, LLC on behalf of the author.

p. 464 Deborah Tannen. 1998. "How to Turn Debate into Dialogue: Why It's So Important to End Americans' War of Words and Start Listening to One Another," *USA Today Weekend,* Feb. 27–Mar. 1, 1998, copyright Deborah Tannen. This article is taken from *The Argument Culture: Stopping America's War of Words.* Reprinted by permission of the author.

p. 476 Matthew Glotzbach. 2007. "Don't Believe Everything You Read." www.googleenterprise.com, 24 July 2007. http://googleenterprise.blogspot.com/2007/07/dont-believe-everything-you-read.html. Data accurate as of July 2007; Google's Enterprise Search has continued to search for ways to grow and improve. Copyright © 2009 Google Inc. All rights reserved.

p. 483 Kenneth R. Fletcher. 2008. "Four for a Quarter." Originally appeared in *Smithsonian Magazine,* (September 2008).

p. 491 Jean Kilbourne. 1999. "Buy This 24-Year-Old and Get All His Friends Absolutely Free." Reprinted and edited with the permission of The Free Press, a Division of Simon & Schuster, Inc., from *Can't Buy My Love: How Advertising Changes the Way We Think and Feel* by Jean Kilbourne, Firestone/Touchstone, 1999. Originally published as Deadly Persuasion by Jean Kilbourne. Copyright © 1999 by Jean Kilbourne. All rights reserved.

p. 502 Christopher Buckley. 1998. "Memo from Coach." Copyright Christopher T. Buckley. Originally published in The New Yorker, January 1998.

p. 512 ApartmentReviews.net. 2009. "How To Find the Right Roommate." ApartmentReviews.net. 17 August 2009. www.apartmentreviews.net/find-right-roommate.htm.

p. 516 Bernard Lefkowitz. 1999. "Don't Further Empower Cliques." *The Los Angeles Times,* May 2, 1999. Copyright © 1999 by Bernard Lefkowitz.

p. 515 Frank T. McAndrew. 2008. "Can Gossip Be Good?" *Scientific American Magazine.* Vol. 19, Issue 5. October/November 2008.

p. 539 James Kirby Martin, Randy Roberts, Steven Mintz, Linda O. McMurry, and James H. Jones. 2004. *America and its Peoples: A Mosaic in the Making,* Volume II (Chapters 16–32), 5th ed., © 2004, pp. 649–653. Reprinted by permission of Pearson Education, Inc., Upper Saddle River, NJ.

PHOTO CREDITS

Back cover: © 2009 Masterfile Corporation; page i: Stockdisc/Getty Images; iii: iStock/Kelleth Chinna; xxx: Anne Ackermann/Getty Images; 3T: Courtesy of Zondervan; 3M: Axel Koester/Corbis; 3B: Getty Images/Rubberball; 4TL: FilmMagic/Getty Images; 4TR: Stockbyte/PunchStock; 4B: Michael Newman/PhotoEdit Inc.; 5T: Comstock Images/Alamy; 5B: Spencer Grant/PhotoEdit Inc.; 7: Corbis; 8: Digital Vision Ltd/Getty Images; 19: Photodisc/Getty Images; 21: Royalty-Free/Corbis; 24: The Image Bank/Getty Images; 26T: Peter Finger/Corbis; 27: Stockbyte/Getty Images; 28T: Courtesy of A-Men Project; 28B: FilmMagic/Getty Images; 30: Ingram Publishing/SuperStock; 32: Anderson Ross/Getty Images; 44: Jupiterimages/Thinkstock/Getty Images; 49: Ian Miles-Flashpoint Pictures/Alamy; 49: Siede Preis/Getty Images; 50: Dr. Parvinder Sethi; 54: Niels Poulsen DK/Alamy; 58: SW Production/Monsoon/Photolibrary/Corbis; 59: C Squared Studios/Getty Images; 61T: Courtesy of Hyperion, an imprint of Buena Vista Books; 61M: FilmMagic/Getty Images; 61B: Courtesy of Emergency Medical Products, Inc./School Kids Healthcare, Inc.; 63T: The McGraw-Hill Companies, Inc/ Jack Holtel photographer; 63B: Stockdisc (Stockbyte)/Getty Images; 67: Siede Pries/Getty Images; 68: Jeff Greenberg/PhotoEdit; 78T: Burke/Triolo/Brand X Pictures.Jupiterimages; 78B: Ingram Publishing/Alamy; 91: Digital Archive Japan/Alamy; 98: Scott Halleran/Getty Images; 101: BananaStock/PunchStock; 102T: © 2000 by Armistead Maupin. Reprinted by permission of HarperCollins Publishers; 102B: Axel Koester/Corbis; 105L: Ingram Publishing/Fotosearch; 105M: Ingram Publishing/Fotosearch; 105R: Ingram Publishing/Fotosearch; 106: Peter Frank/Corbis; 111: Photo Researchers, Inc.; 119: Kevin Taylor/Alamy; 124: California History Collection, Cal. State Library/Getty Images; 132: © ONOKY - Photononstop/Alamy; 135T: C Squared Studios/Getty Images; 135B: Gideon Mendel/Corbis; 136: Punchstock/Image Source; 137: Joshua Ets-Hokin/Getty Images; 138T: © 2006 by Jeff Pearlman. Reprinted by permission of HarperCollins Publishers; 138M: Jason Mitchell/BuzzFoto/FilmMagic/Getty Images; 138B: Rubberball/Getty Images; 149: Barron Claiborne/Corbis; 159: Image Source/PunchStock; 166: Getty Images/PhotoAlto; 169: Brand X Pictures/PunchStock; 170: Ingram Publishing/Fotosearch; 172: Corbis Premium RF/Alamy; 173: Corbis; 174: Neal Preston/Corbis; 176: USDA, photo by Bill Tarpening; 178: Tom Grill/Corbis; 179: Silverstock/Getty Images; 180: Mark Andersen/Getty Images; 181T: Penguin Group; 181B: Rune Hellestad/Corbis; 183: Topham/ The Image Works; 198: Michael Newman/PhotoEdit Inc.; 210: Getty Images/Photodisc; 215: Library of Congress, Prints and Photographs Division, [LC-USZ62-5513]; 216: Library of Congress, Prints and Photographs Division, [LC-USZC2-2523]; 222: Michael Newman/PhotoEdit Inc.; 226: Brand X Pictures; 230: WireImage/Getty Images; 236: Bob Thomas/Getty Images; 245T: Brand X Pictures/PunchStock; 245B: ballyscanlon/Getty Images; 253: Bananastock/PictureQuest; 256: Hank Walker/Time & Life Pictures/Getty Images; 262: Westend61/Getty Images; 265: Reuters; 266: Stockbyte/PunchStock; 267: AFP/Getty Images; 268: Bernard Bisson/Sygma/Corbis; 269: Dennis Cook/AP Images; 271: JupiterImages; 276: Newyorker1987/Creative Commons; 287: Amy Sussman/Getty Images; 291: Photodisc/Getty Images; 300: Royalty-Free/Corbis; 301: Nina Leen/Time Life Pictures/Getty Images; 306: Image Source/Getty Images; 308: Comstock/Punchstock; 309: The McGraw-Hill Companies, Inc./Andrew Resek, photographer; 311: Mark Andersen/Getty Images; 312: Ken Karp for MMH; 313T: Getty Images; 313B: C Squared Studios/Getty Images; 315: Photodisc/Getty Images; 328: PhotoAlto/PunchStock; 339: 1996 PhotoDisc, Inc./Getty Images; 345: Creatas/PunchStock; 346: Jim Reed/Corbis; 348: Imagestate Media (John Foxx); 349: Ausloeser/Corbis; 351T: Stockbyte/PunchStock; 351BL: Photodisc/Getty Images; 351BR: Photodisc/Getty Images; 353T: Eric Ryan/Getty Images; 353B: Royalty-Free/Corbis; 355: Dennie Cody/Getty Images; 358: Jeremy Woodhouse/Getty Images; 368: Digital Vision/Alamy; 379: Iconotec/Alamy; 384: Iconotec/Alamy; 386: Joe McBride/Getty Images; 389T: Corbis; 389B: Alden/PhotoLink/Getty Images; 390: Image Club; 391: Library of Congress, Prints & Photographs Division, Civil War Photographs, [LC-USZ62-67819]; 392: Jupiterimages Corporation; 393T: FilmMagic/Getty Images; 393B: Richard Broadwell / Alamy; 395T: Comstock/Alamy; 395B: The McGraw-Hill Companies, Inc./ Rick Brady, photographer; 396: Rubberball Productions/Getty Images; 397: Ingram Publishing/Alamy; 421T: Scott & Zoe/Getty Images; 421B: The McGraw-Hill Companies, Inc/ Jack Holtel photographer; 423: Colin Underhill/Alamy; 430: Tim Pannell/Corbis; 432: BananaStock/PictureQuest; 433: RubberBall Productions; 434: Library of Congress, Prints and Photographs Division [LC-B201-5202-13]; 435: Royalty Free/Corbis; 437: Margaret Bourke-White/Time & Life Pictures/Getty Images; 438T: Houghton Mifflin Harcourt; 438B: WireImage/Getty Images; 439: S. Meltzer/PhotoLink/Getty Images; 452L: Stockdisc; 452R: Image Source/Getty Images; 472: Blue Syndicate/Corbis; 475T: Stockbyte/Getty Images; 475B: ABC/Photofest; 476T: The McGraw-Hill Companies, Inc./John Flournoy, photographer; 476B: Digital Vision/Getty Images; 478: Siri Stafford/Getty Images; 479: G.K. & Vikki Hart/Getty Images; 480: Siri Stafford/Getty Images; 481T: Courtesy of Hachette Book Group, Inc.; 481M: Getty Images; 481B: Peter Arnold, Inc./Alamy; 502: Photodisc/Getty Images; 508: Marty Melville/Getty Images; 511T: Arrow Books Ltd.; 511B: Getty Images; 512T: Ingram Publishing/SuperStock; 512B: Getty Images; 514: Bernard Hoffman/Time & Life Pictures/Getty Images; 515: Vincent Besnault/Getty Images; 518: Image Source/Punchstock; 524: David Aguilera/BuzzFoto/FilmMagic/Getty Images; 529: Getty Images/Blend Images; 530: The McGraw-Hill Companies Inc./John Flournoy, photographer; 539: Classic PIO/Fotosearch; 541: C Squared Studios/Getty Images